Chile
& Easter Island

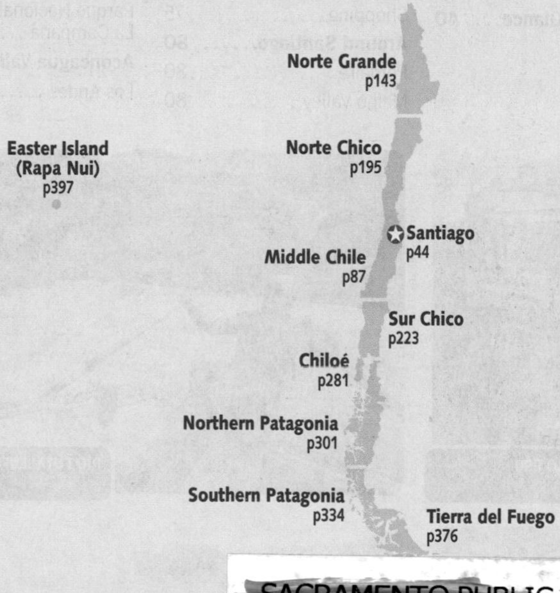

Norte Grande
p143

**Easter Island
(Rapa Nui)**
p397

Norte Chico
p195

⭐Santiago
p44

Middle Chile
p87

Sur Chico
p223

Chiloé
p281

Northern Patagonia
p301

Southern Patagonia
p334

Tierra del Fuego
p376

THIS EDITION WRITTEN AND RESEARCHED BY
Carolyn McCarthy,
Greg Benchwick, Jean-Bernard Carillet, Kevin Raub, Lucas Vidgen

PLAN YOUR TRIP

ON THE ROAD

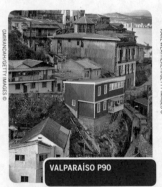
VALPARAÍSO P90

RÍO FUTALEUFÚ P310

COQUIMBO REGION P202

EL TATIO GEYSERS P162

Contents

DANITA DELIMONT/GETTY IMAGES ©

PARQUE NACIONAL
TORRES DEL PAINE P353

PORTILLO P110

Contents

ENCRIER/GETTY IMAGES ©

ISLA MAGDALENA P316

PHOTON-PHOTOS/GETTY IMAGES ©

EASTER ISLAND P397

Welcome to Chile

Chile is nature on a colossal scale, but travel here is surprisingly easy if you don't rush it.

Meet a Land of Extremes

Preposterously thin and unreasonably long, Chile stretches from the belly of South America to its foot, reaching from the driest desert on earth to vast southern glacial fields. Diverse landscapes unfurl over a 4300km stretch: parched dunes, fertile valleys, volcanoes, ancient forests, massive glaciers and fjords. There's wonder in every detail and nature on a symphonic scale. For the traveler, it's boggling how so much has stayed intact for so long. The very human quest for development could imperil these treasures sooner than we think. Yet for now, Chile guards some of the most pristine parts of our planet, and they shouldn't be missed.

Wine Culture

Before wine became an export commodity for the luxury set, humble casks had their place on every Chilean table. Grandparents tended backyard orchards. Now, Chile has become a worldwide producer catering to ever more sophisticated palates. Rich reds, crisp whites and floral rosés, there is a varietal that speaks to every mood and occasion. But at home, it's something different. Chileans embrace *'la buena mesa'*. It's not about fancy. Beyond a good meal, it's great company, the leisure of overlapping conversations with uncorkings, and the gaze that's met at the clink of two glasses. *Salud!*

Slow Adventure

In Chile, adventure is what happens on the way to having an adventure. Pedal the chunky gravel of the Carretera Austral and end up sharing ferries with SUVs and oxcarts, taking a wrong turn and finding heaven in an anonymous orchard. Serendipity takes over. Plans may be made, but try being just as open to experience. Locals never rush, so maybe you shouldn't either. 'Those who hurry waste their time,' is the Patagonian saying that would serve well as a traveler's mantra.

La Buena Onda

In Chile, close borders foster backyard intimacy. Bookended by the Andes and the Pacific, the country averages just 175km wide. No wonder you start greeting the same faces. Pause and it starts to feel like home. Perhaps it's because you've landed at the end of the continent, but one thing that stands out is hospitality. *Buena onda* (good vibes) means putting forth a welcoming attitude. Patagonians share round upon round of *maté* tea. The ritual of relating and relaxing is so integral to the fabric of local life, it's hardly even noticed. But they do say one thing: stay and let your guard down.

Why I Love Chile

By Carolyn McCarthy, Author

I've worked in Chile as a hiking guide and returned to spend part of each year in the Lakes District. For me, Chile has always meant nature as it should be, in so many places a tangled and vast wilderness not yet marred by human intervention. The more I travel, the more I realize that precious few of these places remain on the planet and yet we need them desperately. It's a practical matter, beyond the dollar value of guarding our resources, about seeking out the wild places that feed the soul.

For more about our authors, see page 480.

Above: Parque Nacional Torres del Paine (p353)

Chile & Easter Island

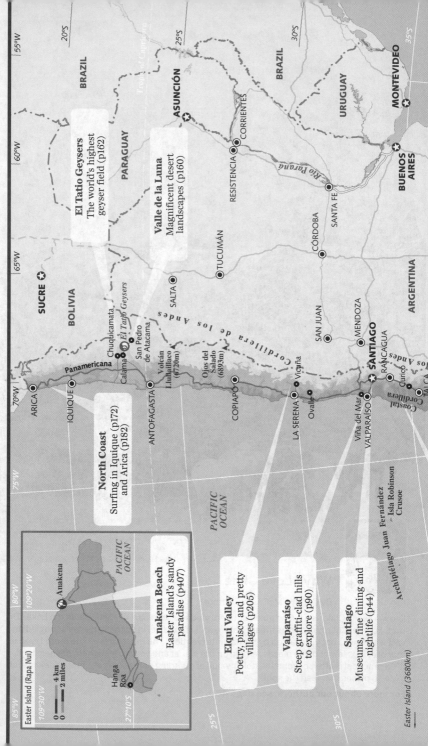

El Tatio Geysers
The world's highest geyser field (p162)

Valle de la Luna
Magnificent desert landscapes (p160)

North Coast
Surfing in Iquique (p172) and Arica (p182)

Anakena Beach
Easter Island's sandy paradise (p407)

Elqui Valley
Poetry, pisco and pretty villages (p205)

Valparaíso
Steep graffiti-clad hills to explore (p90)

Santiago
Museums, fine dining and nightlife (p44)

500 km
300 miles

Easter Island (Rapa Nui)
0   4 km
0   2 miles

Anakena

PACIFIC
OCEAN

Hanga
Roa

Easter Island (3680km)

BRAZIL

PARAGUAY

ASUNCIÓN

SUCRE

BOLIVIA

ARGENTINA

BRAZIL

URUGUAY

MONTEVIDEO

BUENOS
AIRES

CORRIENTES

RESISTENCIA

SANTA FE

CÓRDOBA

TUCUMÁN

SALTA

SAN JUAN

MENDOZA

SANTIAGO

RANCAGUA

Los Andes

Curicó

TALCA

Coastal
Cordillera

VALPARAÍSO

Viña del Mar

Vicuña

Ovalle

LA SERENA

COPIAPÓ

Ojos del
Salado
(6893m)

Volcán
Llullaillaco
(6726m)

San Pedro
de Atacama

El Tatio Geysers

Chuquicamata

Calama

ANTOFAGASTA

Panamericana

IQUIQUE

ARICA

Cordillera de los Andes

PACIFIC
OCEAN

Archipiélago Juan Fernández
~ Isla Robinson
Crusoe

Río Paraná

Rio

Itaipú (Argentina)

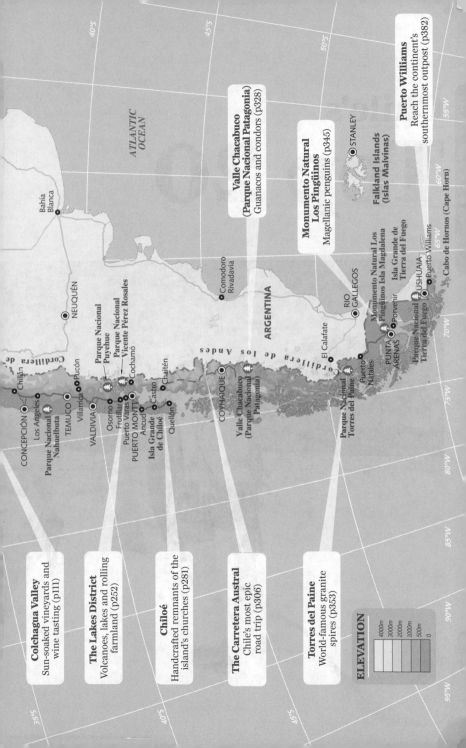

Colchagua Valley
Sun-soaked vineyards and wine tasting (p111)

The Lakes District
Volcanoes, lakes and rolling farmland (p252)

Chiloé
Handcrafted remnants of the island's churches (p281)

The Carretera Austral
Chile's most epic road trip (p306)

Torres del Paine
World-famous granite spires (p353)

Valle Chacabuco (Parque Nacional Patagonia)
Guanacos and condors (p328)

Monumento Natural Los Pingüinos
Magellanic penguins (p345)

Puerto Williams
Reach the continent's southernmost outpost (p382)

ELEVATION

| 4000m |
| 3000m |
| 2000m |
| 1000m |
| 500m |
| 0 |

ATLANTIC OCEAN

ARGENTINA

Cordillera de los Andes

Bahía Blanca

NEUQUÉN

Comodoro Rivadavia

RÍO GALLEGOS

STANLEY

Falkland Islands (Islas Malvinas)

CONCEPCIÓN
Chillán
Los Angeles
Parque Nacional Nahuelbuta
TEMUCO
Villarrica
Pucón
VALDIVIA
Osorno
Parque Nacional Puyehue
Frutillar
Parque Nacional Vicente Pérez Rosales
Puerto Varas
Cochamó
PUERTO MONTT
Ancud
Isla Grande de Chiloé
Castro
Chaitén
Quellón
COYHAIQUE
Valle Chacabuco (Parque Nacional Patagonia)
El Calafate
Puerto Natales
Parque Nacional Torres del Paine
Monumento Natural Los Pingüinos Isla Magdalena
PUNTA ARENAS
Porvenir
Isla Grande de Tierra del Fuego
Parque Nacional Tierra del Fuego
USHUAIA
Puerto Williams
Cabo de Hornos (Cape Horn)

Chile's
Top 20

Parque Nacional Torres del Paine

1 Some rites of passage never lose their appeal, so strap on that heavy pack and hike through howling steppe and winding forests to behold these holiest-of-holy granite mountain spires. Las Torres may be the main attraction of its namesake park (p353), but this vast wilderness has much more to offer. Ice trek the sculpted surface of Glacier Grey, explore the quiet backside of the circuit, kayak the calm Río Serrano or ascend Paso John Gardner for gaping views of the southern ice field.

Big City Culture Chaser

2 Santiago (p44) is the center of the nation's cultural and intellectual universe. Dig the poetry of Pablo Neruda's home, La Chascona, a tribute to the surrealist's affection for the wild-haired lover that would become his third wife. Mainstream museums such as the Museo Nacional de Bellas Artes and the Museo de Arte Contemporáneo are worth popping into, before you widen your optics to discover the hard-charging underground arts scenes in Barrios Brasil, Lastarria and Bellas Artes. Below: La Chascona (p55)

ALBERTOLOYO/GETTY IMAGES ©

Moai

3 The strikingly enigmatic *moai* (statues)
are the most pervasive
image of Easter Island
(Rapa Nui; p397). Dotted
all around the island, these
massive carved figures
stand on stone platforms,
like colossal puppets on a
supernatural stage. They
emanate mystical vibes
and it is thought that they
represent clan ancestors.
The biggest question
remains: how were these
giant statues moved from
where they were carved
to their platforms? It's
a never-ending debate
among specialists. Above
left: Ahu Tongariki (p407)

North Coast Surfing

4 Hit the potent tubes in
northern Chile's duo
of surf capitals, Iquique
and Arica (p179). Surf
dudes come in droves
year-round for the consistent swell and a string of
perfect gnarly reef breaks
that break close to the
desert shore. We're talking
huge, hollow and nearly
all left waves of board-
breaking variety, especially
in July and August when
hardcore surfers storm the
coast. But do bring booties
and wetsuits – the shallow
reefs are full of urchins and
the water is cold, courtesy
of the Humboldt Current.
Above right: Surf break at
Iquique (p168)

The Churches of Chiloé

5 No matter how many
European cathedrals,
Buddhist monasteries or
Islamic mosques you've
seen, the sixteen 17th- and
18th-century wooden
churches that make up
Chiloé's Unesco World
Heritage site (p289)
will be unlike any previ-
ously encountered. Each
an architectural marvel
marrying European and
indigenous design, boast-
ing unorthodox colors and
construction, these cathedrals were built by Jesuit
missionaries working to
convert pagans to the
papacy. Their survival mirrors the Chilote people's
own uncanny resilience.

Wine Tasting

6 Big round Cabernets and Carmeneres are the signature varietals of the Colchagua Valley (p111), a scorched parcel of earth that has become Chile's premier wine-tasting region. Oenophiles and gastronomes will be entranced by the epicurean delights of the valley's tony wineries, bistros and posh lodgings. For floral whites and mass-production reds, head just outside Santiago to visit the broad-faced wineries of the Casablanca and Maipo Valleys, before traveling your senses further south with a few heady but unpretentious reds in the Maule Valley. Right: Viña Las Niñas (p112)

Swoon over Valle de la Luna

7 See the desert don its surrealist cloak as you stand atop a giant sand dune, with the sun slipping below the horizon and multicolored hues bathing the sands, all with a backdrop of distant volcanoes and the rippling Cordillera de la Sal. In Valle de la Luna (p160), the moment the color show kicks in – intense purples, golds, pinks and yellows stretch as far as your eye can see – you'll forget the crowds around you, all squeezing in to catch sundown in the valley.

Elqui Valley

8 Spend a few languid days in the lush Elqui Valley (p205) and you'll start to wax lyrical, or even channel the late Nobel Prize–winning poet Gabriela Mistral who grew up in these parts. Infused by poetry, pisco, pretty villages and star-sprinkled night skies, this is a wholesome land of spiritual retreats, ecofriendly inns, hilltop observatories and artisanal distilleries of the potent little grape. Sample food cooked solely by sun rays, get your aura cleaned, feast on herb-infused Andean fusion fare and ride the valley's mystic wave. Right: Montegrande (p209)

7

IGNACIO PALACIOS/GETTY IMAGES ©

Skiing the Andes

9 The Chilean Andes are home to some of the best southern hemisphere skiing found throughout this powder-dusted planet. For steep slopes, expansive vistas, hot tub parties and plenty of après-ski revelry, head to top resorts (p85) such as the all-in-one Portillo, budget-friendly El Colorado and the ritzy La Parva. Valle Nevado has expanded terrain with more than 7000 skiable acres. At Termas de Chillán you can take an after-ski dip in a hot springs pool. Top right: La Parva ski resort (p85)

La Araucanía's National Park Trifecta

10 Sur Chico (p223) boasts seven national parks, none more otherworldly than Reserva Nacional Malalcahuello-Nalcas and Parque Nacional Conguillío, whose charred desertscapes were born from volcanic eruptions, Lonquimay and Llaima among them. Along with Parque Nacional Tolhuaca, flush with araucarias and intensely hued lagoons, this stunning trifecta – easily accessed via a base along the road to Lonquimay – is a microcosm of all that's beautiful about Sur Chico. Bottom right: Reserva Nacional Malalcahuello-Nalcas (p232)

Santiago Dining & Nightlife

11 Santiago's avant-garde restaurants (p67) are taking South American fusion to new levels by combining old-school sensibilities with new-school flavors. Explore the bistros of Bellavista, the sidewalk charmers in Lastarria and the high-falutin' eateries of Las Condes. Come night-time, Santiago knows how to rage against the dying of the light, and you'll find raucous beer halls, decibel-piercing *discotecas*, candlelit poetry houses and just about anything else your inner Bacchus desires along the alleyways of party districts such as Bellavista, Bellas Artes and Lastarria.

Road-Tripping the Carretera Austral

12 Find out what adventures await on this 1240km romp through Andean back-country dotted with parks and pioneer homesteads. The Carretera Austral (p306) is every wanderer's dream. The dusty washboard road to no-where was created in the 1980s under the Pinochet regime, in an attempt to link the country's most isolated residents to the rest of Chile. Now the connection is tenuous. If you have the time, offshoot roads to glaciers, seaside villages and mountain hamlets are worthy detours.

Puerto Williams, the Southernmost Spot

13 At the Americas' southernmost outpost, colts roam Main St, yachties trade round-the-world tales and the wilderness looms larger than life. Part of the appeal is getting there, which means crossing the Beagle Channel. As villages go, Puerto Williams (p382) is the kind of place where people know your name within days of your arrival. For adventure, you can trek right out of town onto the Dientes de Navarino circuit, a five-day walk through wild high country fringed by razor-faced peaks.

Valle Chacabuco (Parque Nacional Patagonia)

14 Dubbed the Serengeti of the Southern Cone, this new park (p328) is the best place to spot amazing Patagonian wildlife, such as guanacos, condors and flamingos. Once a down-and-out cattle and sheep ranch, its meticulous restoration is making it a model park worthy of worldwide recognition. Put aside a few days to take the trails to turquoise lagoons, undulating steppe and ridgetops, or just watch wildlife along the main road that climbs to the border of Argentina near Ruta 40.

El Tatio Geysers

15 Dress warmly and catch daybreak on a frigid walk through the gurgling geysers, gnarly craters and gassy fumaroles of El Tatio (p162), the world's highest geyser field ringed by pointy volcanoes and mighty mountains at 4300m above sea level. Hear this giant steam bath hiss, groan, spit and grumble as it shoots up white-vapor jets of steam, while the sun rises over the surrounding cordillera and bathes it in a sudden and surreal splash of red, violet, green, chartreuse and blue.

Anakena Beach

16 Fantasizing about idyllic white sands? Look no further than Anakena (p407). Easter Island's biggest and most popular beach is a wide curve of white sand and sparkling turquoise sea backed by a lovely coconut grove on the north coast. It has food kiosks, picnic shelters and a few facilities. What makes Anakena beach so special, though, are the two major archaeological sites that form the backdrop. A stunning beach with grandiose *moai* – it's hard to think of a more compelling sight.

The Lakes District

17 Don't judge a district by its name. The Lakes District (p252), Los Lagos in Spanish, only tells part of the story. While turquoise, blue and green glacial lakes dominate the landscape, they're hardly the only attraction. Play on towering, perfectly conal, snowcapped volcanoes. Visit charming lakeside hamlets such as Frutillar. Admire the green umbrella of national parks such as Parque Nacional Huerquehue. A long list of outdoor adventures and a unique, German-influenced Latin culture make for a cinematic region that appeals to all. Bottom: Frutillar (p262)

The Hills of Valparaíso

18 Generations of poets, artists, philosophers and shanty-singing dockworkers have been inspired by the steep technicolor *cerros* (hills) of Valparaíso (p90). A maze of winding paths leads you to some of the nation's best street art, remarkable views and a patchwork of dilapidated tin homes that whisper inspiration at every turn. A renaissance is bringing revived architecture, ultra-chic boutique hotels with million-dollar views and amazing restaurants to a port town whose soul is encapsulated by its syncopated cityscape, arching views, never-ceasing breeze and rumble-tumble docks.

Monumento Natural Los Pingüinos

19 Every year, 60,000 Magellanic penguin couples convene just off the coast of Punta Arenas on Isla Magdalena (p316). Watching them waddle around, guard their nests, feed their fluffy, oversized offspring and turn a curious eye toward visitors makes for a great outing. There's also a historic lighthouse-turned-visitor center worth exploring. The penguins reside on the island between the months of October and March.

Caleta Condor

20 Sometimes it's about the journey rather than the destination; other times the opposite. Caleta Condor (p256), an isolated piece of postcard paradise along a protected stretch of hard-to-reach indigenous coastline, is without question both. Be it by boat, foot or 4WD, preserved Valdivian forest eventually gives way to an impossibly gorgeous bay at the mouth of Río Chol-cuaco. The beach, the river and the nearly uninhabited landscape all conspire to be one of Chile's most surprising, inspiring and out-of-place tropical-style nirvanas.

Need to Know

For more information, see Survival Guide (p443)

Currency
Chilean peso (CH$)

Language
Spanish

Money
ATMs widely available, except along parts of the Carretera Austral. Credit cards accepted at higher-end hotels, some restaurants and shops. Traveler's checks not widely accepted.

Visas
Generally not required for stays of up to 90 days. Citizens of Australia and Canada must pay a 'reciprocity fee' when arriving by air.

Cell Phones
Local SIM cards are cheap and widely available, for use with unlocked GSM 850/1900 phones. 3G access in urban centers.

Time
Four hours behind GMT except for summer (usually mid-December to late March) when it is three hours behind GMT for daylight savings.

When to Go

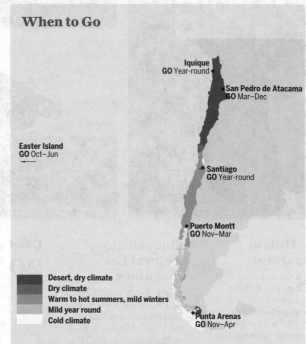

Iquique
GO Year-round

San Pedro de Atacama
GO Mar–Dec

Easter Island
GO Oct–Jun

Santiago
GO Year-round

Puerto Montt
GO Nov–Mar

Desert, dry climate
Dry climate
Warm to hot summers, mild winters
Mild year round
Cold climate

Punta Arenas
GO Nov–Apr

High Season (Nov–Feb)
➡ Patagonia is best (and most expensive) December to February

➡ Beaches throng with crowds from late December through January

Shoulder (Sep–Nov & Mar–May)
➡ Temperature-wise, these are the best times to visit Santiago

➡ The Lakes District is pleasant September to November; April brings fall foliage in the south

➡ Wine country has grape harvests and wine festivals in March

Low Season (Jun–Aug)
➡ Best time for ski resorts is June to August

➡ A good time to visit the north

➡ Few services on the Carretera Austral; mountain passes can be blocked by snow

➡ Transportation and accommodations are busy in July

Websites

Lonely Planet (www.lonely planet.com/chile) Travel news and tips.

Sernatur (www.chile.travel/ en.html) The national tourism organization, in English, Spanish and French.

Santiago Times (www.santiago times.cl) Online newspaper in English with national coverage.

Go Chile (www.gochile.cl) General tourist information.

Interpatagonia (www.inter patagonia.com) All things touristy in Patagonia.

Important Numbers

Chile Country Code	☎56
International Access Code	three-digit carrier + ☎0
Directory Assistance	☎103
National Tourist Information (in Santiago)	☎562-731-8310
Police	☎133

Exchange Rates

Australia	A$1	CH$490
Canada	C$1	CH$514
Euro zone	€1	CH$712
Japan	¥100	CH$513
New Zealand	NZ$1	CH$443
UK	UK£1	CH$985
US	US$1	CH$634

For current exchange rates see www.xe.com

Daily Costs

Budget:
Less than CH$65,000

➡ Inexpensive *hospedaje* room/dorm bed: CH$10,000

➡ Budget-restaurant dinner main: CH$5000

➡ Set lunches are good value; supermarkets have takeout

➡ Some free sights and parks

Midrange:
CH$65,000–80,000

➡ Double room in midrange hotel or B&B: CH$50,000

➡ Midrange-restaurant dinner main: CH$8000

➡ Car rentals start at CH$20,000 per day

Top End:
More than CH$80,000

➡ Double room in top-end hotel: CH$80,000

➡ Fine-restaurant dinner main: CH$14,000

➡ Hire an outfitter for outdoor adventures

Opening Hours

We list high-season hours in the book. In many provincial cities and towns, restaurants and services are closed on Sunday and tourist offices close in low season.

Banks 9am-2pm weekdays, sometimes 10am-1pm Sat

Government offices & businesses 9am-6pm on weekdays

Museums often closed on Mon

Restaurants noon-11pm, many close 4-7pm

Shops 10am-8pm, some close 1-3pm

Arriving in Chile

Aeropuerto Internacional Arturo Merino Benítez (Santiago; p454)

Minibus Shuttle Frequent connections to downtown Santiago hotels in 40 minutes; CH$6400

Local Bus One hour to downtown, then transfer to the metro or Transantiago bus; for pennypinchers only, CH$1600

Taxi CH$16,000

Getting Around

Chile is an easy country to get around, with frequent bus and air connections, but those going off the beaten path will need a car. Drivers are generally courteous and orderly. Toll highways are common.

Air A worthwhile time saver for long distances, with economical regional deals sold in-country.

Bus The best way to get around Chile: frequent, comfortable and reasonably priced, with service to towns throughout the country. Less useful for parks access.

Car Renting your own wheels help to better explore remote regions like Patagonia.

Train Limited. A few lines can be useful for travelers in central Chile.

For much more on **getting around**, see p457.

If You Like...

Urban Exploration

Life spills into the streets as pop-up graffiti murals, sprawling food markets, narrow winding staircases and leafy museum neighborhoods in the vibrant Chilean cities of Santiago and Valparaíso.

La Vega Central Vendors hawk a feast of ripe figs, avocados and chirimoyas. Nearby Mercado Central dishes up seafood lunches. (p64)

Santiago Museums Classic Museo Chileno de Arte Precolombino contrasts with funky Museo de Arte Contemporáneo and fashion-forward Museo de la Moda. (p45)

Graffiti Art Compelling graffiti murals flank the alleys and steep staircases of Valparaíso, making any stroll an exploration. (p91)

Night Cycling At sunset the air cools, traffic eases and Santiago lights up – the witching hour for touring. (p61)

Centro Gabriela Mistral Grab the cultural pulse at Santiago's new cutting-edge performing arts center. (p52)

Barrio Recoleta Get off the beaten path and sample an authentic neighborhood with great ethnic eats. (p64)

Hiking

Chile has 4000km of mountains bumping down its spine. From desert to temperate rainforest, trails are everywhere, so expand your itinerary to include a lesser-known route. You won't regret it.

Putre Ideal base camp for high altitude desert treks, less crowded than San Pedro de Atacama. (p189)

Siete Tazas Near wine country, a clear river drops through seven pools carved of black basalt. (p118)

Cochamó Valley A pristine valley of waterfalls, granite panoramas and well-marked trails, though the mud is infamous. (p271)

Cerro Castillo In the heart of Patagonia, trekking around this cathedral peak provides a top-notch four-day adventure. (p323)

Reserva Nacional Jeinimeini Stunning contrasts, from tough backpacking over mountain passes to short hikes to rock art. (p325)

Animal Encounters

Andean condors soar the peaks and the cold Humboldt Current means abundant marine life, from sea lions to migrating blue whales. Chile hosts a variety of camelids, diverse bird species and the huemul, an endangered national symbol.

Lago Chungará Teeming with birdlife, including the flamboyant Chilean flamingo, this surreal mirror lake sits high in the altiplano. (p192)

Reserva Nacional Las Vicuñas Over 20,000 of the park's namesake camelids roam this high desert reserve surrounded by sky-hugging volcanoes. (p193)

Chiloé Both Magellanic and Humboldt penguins nest near Ancud; pudú and avian life inhabit Parque Tantauco. (p299)

Valle Chacabuco From guanaco, fox and condor to elusive puma and huemul, a treasure of Patagonian wildlife. (p328)

Food & Nightlife

In agricultural Chile, food is all about freshness, from amazing seafood to local wines and California-style produce. Nightlife ranges from rustic to sophisticated, hitting its apogee in the capital.

Norte Chico With firewood scarce, women in the desert village of Villaseca power up solar ovens to rave reviews. (p208)

San Pedro de Atacama Take a tour of the night sky in one of the world's best spots for stargazing. (p146)

Santiago Contempo stylings and bold South American fusions ignite the restaurant scene at places like Peumayen and Étniko. (p67)

Lakes District Beyond German staples, *asados* (barbecues) feature natural local beef, berry pies and organic summer salad. (p252)

Santiago neighborhoods Revelers light up the night in the party-til-you-drop dancehalls of Bellavista and Lastarria's upscale sidewalk cafes. (p71)

Patagonia *Cocinas custombristas* are rudimentary restaurants banked on the talents of grandmas stirring fresh seafood concoctions.

Memorable Landscapes

Potent scenery is not hard to find in Chile, where the climate ranges from parched desert to glacial peaks.

Atacama Desert Red rock canyons, cactus scrub and copper mountains give contrast to the piercing blue sky. (p146)

Archipelago of Chiloé From western cliffs to eastern inlets pocked with stilt houses, these green isles feed the imagination. (p281)

Lakes District Rolling, rainsoaked countryside marked by dozens of deep-blue lakes and snowcapped volcanoes that stand sentinel. (p252)

Patagonian Andes The Andes range reaches its dramatic crescendo in the deepest south. (p353)

Rano Kau Among the South Pacific's most striking landscapes,

Top: Painted steps, Valparaíso (p90)
Bottom: Atacama Desert (p146)

this crater lake overlooks the vast cobalt ocean. (p406)

Tierra del Fuego Both rugged and mystical, a last frontier destination of remote isles and wind-sculpted landscapes. (p376)

Remote Getaways

Over 90% of Chile's population is concentrated in its middle. Escape in any direction, from the Atacama to remote Carretera Austral and barren Tierra del Fuego. Or visit Easter Island, the remotest Pacific isle.

Belén Precordillera Off the beaten path, visit ancient pictographs, old colonial churches and lovely landscapes. (p190)

North Coast of Easter Island This eerie stretch north of Ahu Tahai passes towering *moai* and climbs grassy hills to the Pacific. (p406)

Raúl Marín Balmaceda With overgrown ferns and streets of sand, this lost village is flanked by otters, dolphins and sea lions. (p314)

Caleta Condor An isolated, postcard-worthy paradise along a protected stretch of hard-to-reach indigenous coastline near Osorno. (p256)

Wine Country

Flanked by colonial bodegas, a Pacific breeze and the dazzling backdrop of the Andes, wine never tasted so good.

Ruta del Vino Link up with local experts touring the powerhouse wine region responsible for Chile's best reds. (p119)

Lapostolle Winery A posh and lovely setting to acquaint yourself with Chile's richest terroir. (p112)

Casablanca Valley A hub of excellent cool-climate winemaking and a quick getaway from Santiago. (p105)

Museo de Colchagua Don't miss 'El Gran Rescate,' an exhibit on the daring rescue of the 33 miners. (p113)

Emiliana Winery Make tasting dessert with the chocolate and wine pairings at this organic winemaker. (p107)

Living History

Take a break from museums. Out of doors, you can explore history that persists in coastal battleships, on pioneer trails and in Chilote villages still using their ancestral inventions.

Humberstone This whole nitrate boomtown gone ghost city whets the traveler's imagination. (p176)

Ascensor Concepción Relive Valparaíso's glory days climbing above the city on its oldest cable-car elevator. (p91)

Orongo Ceremonial Village This ancient village places you in the geographical heart of Easter Island's strange bird cult culture. (p406)

Lago Llanquihue Historic German villages confound Latin

sensibilities with unique architecture and German sweets. (p262)

Iquique Docks old naval vessel *Esmeralda*, a famous warship with a dark role in the dictatorship. (p169)

Northern Patagonia Ride the well-worn trails first forged by Patagonian pioneers around Palena and Futaleufú. (p310)

Pure Adrenaline

With high-quality outfitters, wild geography and pristine settings, Chile is a natural playground for adventure sports. Mountaineers, kite surfers and backcountry skiers should bring their own equipment.

Skiing & Snowboarding Chile's top ski resorts include Valle Nevado, Portillo and hot-springs mecca Nevados de Chillán. (p35)

Glacier Treks Scramble up Torres del Paine's Glacier Grey, Glaciar San Rafael or remote glaciers on the Carretera Austral. (p353)

Surfing Ride famous waves at Pichilemu or Iquique, or discover the quiet surf-shack style of Buchupureo. (p37)

Rafting & Kayaking Paddle Cajón de Maipo near Santiago, Puerto Varas' Río Petrohué or the world-class Futaleufú. (p36)

Sand-boarding Sample this relatively new sport in San Pedro Atacama and Iquique. (p150)

Month by Month

January

It's summer peak season and Chileans start flocking to beaches. Annual celebrations break out in every Chilean town and city with live music, special feasts and fireworks. It's also high season in Patagonia.

☆ Santiago a Mil

Latin America's biggest theater festival (www.stgoamil.cl) brings acts to the streets of Santiago, as well as international works, emerging theater and acrobats.

Muestra Cultural Mapuche

Six days of all things Mapuche in Villarrica: artisans, indigenous music, foods and ritual dance.

☆ Semanas Musicales

All month, prestigious international acts ranging from classical to hip-hop come south to perform in Frutillar's stunning Teatro de Frutillar (www.semanas-musicales.cl) with sublime lake and volcano views.

Brotes de Chile

One of Chile's biggest folk festivals takes place in the second week of January and includes traditional dances, food and crafts in Angol.

Ruta del Huemul

Held the last week in January, this two-day, hundred-person community hike traverses Reserva Nacional Tamango near Cochrane. Reserve ahead to participate.

February

February is Chileans' favorite month to vacation. With unrelenting heat from the north to Santiago, people flock south. Beaches fill and Santiago nightlife transplants to Viña del Mar and Valparaíso.

Fiesta de la Candelaria

A religious festival in early February, most fervently celebrated in Copiapó, where thousands of pilgrims and dancers converge.

☆ Festival Internacional de la Canción

This fancy star-studded concert series held in Viña del Mar showcases top names in Latin American pop.

Festival Costumbrista

Castro struts Chiloé's distinctive folk music and dance, plying revelers with heaps of traditional foods in mid-February.

Carnaval

Putre puts out highland merriment and flour bombs, ending with the burning of the *momo* – a figure symbolizing the frivolity of Carnaval.

Tapati Rapa Nui

The premier festival on Easter Island is an incredibly colorful event that keeps the party going for two weeks, with a series of dance, music and cultural contests.

Carnaval Ginga

Held in Arica in mid-February, this festival features the musical skills of regional *comparsas* (traditional dancing groups).

March

A great month to travel Chile. As fall ushers in, summer crowds disperse. Though all of Chile cools a bit, usually southern Patagonia is still dry and less windy, with great hiking weather. The Central Valley's grape harvest begins.

☆ Lollapalooza Chile

Chile rocks this international edition (www.lollapaloozacl.com) mid-month, with 60 bands playing Santiago's Parque O'Higgins; kids get their hair punked at the adjoining Kidsapalooza.

☆ Campeonato Nacional de Rodeo

In Rancagua in late March, the National Rodeo Championship features feasting, *cueca* (a playful, handkerchief-waving dance that imitates the courtship of a rooster and hen) and, most importantly, Chilean cowboys showing off their fancy horse skills.

🍷 Fiesta de la Vendimia

Santa Cruz celebrates the grape harvest with stands from local wineries in the plaza, a crowned harvest queen, and folk dancing.

April

Bright reds and yellows highlight the forests of Northern Patagonia, though rain will come any day now. The south is clearing out, but you might get lucky with decent hiking weather. Santiago and the Central

Top: Dancers, Tapati Rapa Nui (p25)
Bottom: Campeonato Nacional de Rodeo

Valley enjoy still-pleasant temperatures.

June

Winter begins. With days at their shortest, nightlife and cultural events pick up. The world-class ski resorts around Santiago start gearing up and it's a good time to visit the desert.

★☆ Festival de la Lluvia

Why not celebrate what's most plentiful in a Lakes District winter – rain? In early June, this week of free events in Puerto Varas includes a parade of decorated umbrellas and live music.

★☆ Fiesta de San Pedro y San Pablo

In San Pedro de Atacama, folk-dancing groups, a rodeo and solemn processions mark this animated religious festival held on June 29.

July

Chilean winter vacation means family travel is in full swing. Ski resorts are up and running and those who brave Patagonia will find lovely winter landscapes without the infamous wind of summer.

★☆ Festival de la Virgen del Carmen

Some 40,000 pilgrims pay homage to Chile's virgin with lots of street dancing, curly-horned devil masks with flashing eyes and spangly cloaks. Held in La Tirana in mid-July.

★☆ Carnaval de Invierno

Punta Arenas gets through the longest nights with fireworks, music and parades in late July.

August

A fine time to visit, August represents the tail end of the ski season and cheaper lodgings in holiday destinations, now that school vacation is over. In the south, winter rains begin to taper off.

☆ Festival de Jazz de Ñuñoa

Held in late August, this free winter jazz fest brings together Chile's best jazz acts for a weekend of music.

★☆ Fiesta de Santa Rosa de Lima

A huge Catholic celebration of the criollo saint with a colorful street procession, held August 30.

September

Spring comes to Santiago, with mild, sunny days. Though low season throughout Chile, it's not a bad time to travel. Everything closes and people get boisterous the week of the national holiday.

★☆ Fiestas Patrias

Chilean Independence is feted during Fiestas Patrias (week of September 18), with a week of big barbecues, *terremotos* (potent wine punch) and merrymaking all over Chile.

October

A fine time to travel with spring flowers in northern and central Chile.

🍷 Oktoberfest

Join the swillers and oompah bands in Puerto Varas and Valdivia for live music and beer festivals.

November

Chile's south is in full bloom though the weather is still crisp. It's a good time to visit the beach resorts and Patagonia; the crowds and high prices are still a month or so away.

★☆ Feria Internacional de Artesanía

Artisans show off Chile's best traditional crafts at a huge fair in Providencia's Parque Bustamante.

★☆ Puerto de Ideas

In Valparaíso, this 'conference on everything' attracts intellectuals and big thinkers from across Latin America to share in an open formula akin to the TED conferences.

December

Summer begins and services return to the Carretera Austral. It's still quiet but ideal for outdoor activities in the Lakes District and Patagonia.

★☆ New Year's Eve

The year's biggest bash in Valparaíso, where revelers fill open balconies and streets to dance, drink and watch fireworks on the bay.

Itineraries

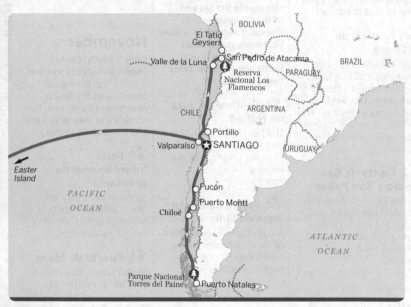

BOLIVIA

El Tatio
Geysers

Valle de la Luna · · · · · · San Pedro de Atacama

BRAZIL

Reserva
Nacional Los
Flamencos

PARAGUAY

CHILE

ARGENTINA

Portillo

Valparaíso ★ SANTIAGO

URUGUAY

Easter
Island

PACIFIC
OCEAN

Pucón

Puerto Montt

Chiloé

ATLANTIC
OCEAN

Parque Nacional
Torres del Paine · · · Puerto Natales

Best of Chile

Skate through Chile's amazing diversity in one month. From **Santiago**, feed your imagination exploring boho **Valparaíso**. In winter, hit nearby powder stashes at top Andean resorts like **Portillo**.

Then turn up the dial with desert heat. Fly or bus to the highland village of **San Pedro de Atacama**. Absorb altiplano ambience visiting the moon-like **Valle de la Luna**, the steaming and strange **El Tatio geysers** and the stark **Reserva Nacional Los Flamencos**. Wind up days of hiking, horseback riding or volcano climbing with mellow evening bonfires and star-stocked skies.

Return south to delve into temperate rainforest in **Pucón**, where rafting, hiking and hot springs fill up your Lakes District dance card. From **Puerto Montt**, detour to folklore capital **Chiloé**, or cruise on a four-day ferry ride through glacier-laced fjords to **Puerto Natales**. By now you are probably in top shape for **Parque Nacional Torres del Paine**. Take three days to a week at this world-famous hiking destination. Or skip southern Patagonia to hop a plane to **Easter Island (Rapa Nui)** and puzzle over its archaeological treasures for five days.

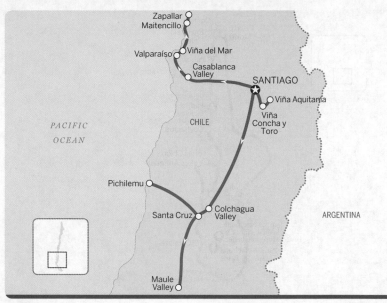

La Capital & Wine Country

It's hard to beat central Chile when it comes to wining and dining in the finest South American traditions. From urban vinotecas to vineyards that sit in the shadows of the Andes, the scene ranges from vibrant and dynamic to deliciously chilled out.

Start with a few nights in the happening capital, **Santiago**. Stroll around the historic center, break for a lively seafood lunch in the clamoring Mercado Central and tour La Chascona, Pablo Neruda's Bellavista home. Sip champagne at Boca Naríz or catch experimental dance at the Centro Gabriela Mistral.

Big-bodied reds are crafted in Santiago's outskirts; sample from commercial heavy hitters **Viña Concha y Toro** and boutique winemakers **Viña Aquitania**. Sample the whites of **Casablanca Valley**, where aspiring pickers can join Viña Casas del Bosque's March harvest. In summer, the Santa Cruz Tren Sabores del Valle offers train service from Santiago and on-board wine tastings.

On to funky **Valparaíso** to walk its famously steep hills and ride antique elevators, like Cerro Concepción, the city's oldest. Wander the graffitied passageways, step into Neruda's La Sebastiana getaway and feast on freshly caught fish. Exhausted from the urban hiking? Unwind at nearby resort cities **Viña del Mar**, **Zapallar** or **Maitencillo** for a quick beach getaway.

Finish in Chile's best-known wine region, **Colchagua Valley**. Overnight in **Santa Cruz** with a morning visit to the Museo de Colchagua before a carriage ride at Viu Manent, or a world-class prix-fixe lunch at Lapostolle. Go surfing at relaxed party town **Pichilemu** or visit the lesser-known wineries of **Maule Valley**.

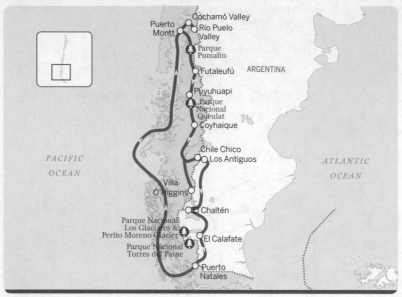

4 WEEKS **Pioneer Patagonia**

If you wish to travel only back roads, if you desire getting dirty, almost lost and awe-inspired, look no further than this four-week plan. Following the Carretera Austral, this route crisscrosses its little-known offshoots and gives you plenty of time on the hoof. Summer, with better connections and warm weather, is the best time to go.

Leave **Puerto Montt** or Puerto Varas for the **Cochamó** or **Río Puelo** valleys, where you can hike or horseback ride, camp or stay at remote lodgings. From Puerto Montt, ferry to **Parque Pumalín** and explore ancient forests and climb to the steaming crater of Volcán Chaitén. Ramble the Carretera Austral to **Futaleufú**, for stunning rural vistas and heart-pumping whitewater. Check out the hot-springs options near **Puyuhuapi** or camp under the hanging glacier at **Parque Nacional Queulat**.

Coyhaique is the next major hub. After making connections to **Chile Chico** on the enormous Lago General Carrera, hop the border to **Los Antiguos** and travel Argentina's classic Ruta 40 to **El Chaltén** for hiking around the gnarled tooth of Cerro Fitz Roy. Take two days to visit **El Calafate**, spending one under the spell of the magnificent glacier **Perito Moreno** in the **Parque Nacional Los Glaciares**. While you're there, feast on giant steaks and bottles of peppery Malbec.

From El Calafate it's an easy bus connection to **Parque Nacional Torres del Paine** via **Puerto Natales**. Hike the 'W' route or go for the full week-long circuit. By now you're in prime hiking shape – enjoy passing others on the trail. Return to Natales for post-trek pampering, namely handcrafted beer, hot tubs and thin-crust pizza. If you have time, return to Puerto Montt via the Navimag ferry.

An alternative route would be to skip Chile Chico and follow the Carretera Austral to its southern terminus – **Villa O'Higgins**. Relax, go fishing and hike. From here, a rugged boat-hike combination can get you across the border to El Chaltén, where you can rejoin the itinerary a week behind schedule.

Above: Laguna
Miscanti (p161),
Reserva Nacional Los
Flamencos

Right: Cochamó
Valley (p271)

FLOOU/GETTY IMAGES ©

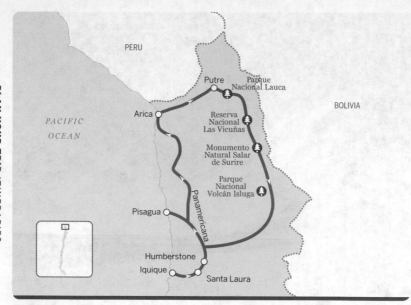

1 WEEK Desert Solitaire

How about a few days sleeping under star-crazy skies and following condor shadows along desert mountaintops? You'll need a 4WD and plenty of food, water and extra gas. Start with a surfboard in **Iquique** to sample the swells of Playa Cavancha and Playa Huaiquique, then jump off a cliff on a tandem paragliding jaunt. With the adrenaline rush in place, slow things down with a contemplative wander around nitrate ghost towns **Santa Laura** and **Humberstone**, where you can poke around the creepy abandoned buildings of these once flourishing spots and explore their crumbling grandeur.

Head north, with an optional stop in the isolated coastal town of **Pisagua**, once a bustling nitrate-era port, then a penal colony and today a nearly abandoned and strangely lyrical place where algae gatherers work alongside the ruins of busted mansions; don't miss the windswept old cemetery sloping forlorn on a nearby hill.

Cheer up in sunny **Arica**, where plenty of surf awaits below the dramatic headland of El Morro and remarkably preserved Chinchorro mummies lie in situ at the small museum just below the hill. From the coast, head inland via Hwy 11, passing geoglyphs, colonial chapels and misty mountain hamlets, to the pretty Andean village of **Putre**. Take a day or two here to catch your breath, literally, as Putre sits at a dizzying altitude of 3530m.

Once you've adjusted to the height, head to nearby **Parque Nacional Lauca**, where you can take in the perfect cone of Volcán Parinacota, wander through the tiny Aymara village with the same name and walk around the lovely Lago Chungará, all paired with awesome wildlife sightings in this Unesco Biosphere Reserve.

Further south, the remote **Reserva Nacional Las Vicuñas** shelters thousands of these flighty creatures and few interlopers to spook them, so go easy. Heading south on tough terrain past dazzling landscapes and through the isolated salt flat of **Monumento Natural Salar de Surire** with its three flamingo species (best seen between December and April), your reward for an adventurous ride is reaching the ultra-removed **Parque Nacional Volcán Isluga**, before looping back to Iquique.

Parque Nacional Torres del Paine (p353)

Plan Your Trip
Chile Outdoors

From the parched Atacama Desert to temperate rainforest and the glacier-studded south, Chile's dazzling geography is seemingly made for active vacations. The possibilities are only limited by the time at hand. Plan carefully for seasonal changes, equipment needs and expert advice and this world is your oyster.

Chile's Biggest Thrills

Hiking Valle Francés
In Torres del Paine, this valley rimmed by steep summits inspires awe.

Climbing a Volcano
Chile's Ojos del Salado is the highest volcano in the world, but dozens more are well-equipped for exploration.

Exploring the Atacama
Scale massive dunes, admire petroglyphs and question the shimmering visions of oases.

Surfing Pichilemu
Punta de Lobos is considered a perfect left break.

Powder Day at Portillo
Steep and deep terrain is the delight of boarders and skiers.

Diving off Easter Island
The water around stunning sea stack Motu Kao Kao boasts 60m visibility.

Cycling the Carretera Austral
Every summer, more cyclists take up the challenge of this epic journey.

Hiking & Trekking

The sublime Torres del Paine is one of the continent's most beloved hiking destinations, graced by glaciers, gemstone lakes and the world-famous granite spires. The park has good public access, *refugios* (huts) and campsites that allow for multi-day treks. However, its popularity has led to overcrowding. For awe-inspiring isolation, Tierra del Fuego's Dientes de Navarino hiking circuit is also stunning but harder to access.

The Lakes District abounds with trails and tantalizing terrain. Within the northern corner of Patagonia, Parque Pumalín also has great day hikes; a highlight is hiking to the crater overlook of steaming Volcán Chaitén.

Santiago's worthwhile city escapes include nearby Monumento Natural El Morado or Parque Nacional La Campana. Altos de Lircay, in Chile's middle, has a great backcountry circuit. In the north, desert oasis San Pedro de Atacama has a number of intriguing hikes, as does Parque Nacional Lauca. Fly to the Pacific to hike Parque Nacional Juan Fernández or Easter Island.

Opportunities are not limited to the national parks: check out the Sendero de Chile and opportunities for rural community tourism in the south. Horse-packing is offered in many rural areas. Private reserves, such as Chiloé's Parque Tantauco and El Mirador de Chepú, as well as future Parque Nacional Patagonia near Cochrane and others, are preserving top-notch destinations.

Some regional Conaf offices have reasonable trail maps; the JLM maps also have trail indicators on the more specific tourist-oriented maps.

Mountaineering & Climbing

Prime mountaineering and ice-climbing territory, Chile has hundreds of peaks to choose from, including 50 active volcanoes. They range from the picture-perfect cone of dormant Parinacota in the northern altiplano to the challenging trek up Ojos del Salado.

A charm bracelet of lower volcanic cones rises through La Araucanía and the Lakes District and Torres del Paine. Popular climbs here include Volcán Osorno, which has summit ice caves. Ice-climbers can look into the Loma Larga and Plomo massifs, just a few hours from Santiago.

Climbers intending to scale border peaks like the Pallachatas or Ojos del Salado must have permission from Chile's Dirección de Fronteras y Límites (p358). Climbers can request permission prior to arriving in Chile via a request form on the agency's website.

For more information, contact the **Federación de Andinismo** (☎02-222-9140; www.feach.cl; Almirante Simpson 77, Providencia, Santiago).

For detailed stats, route descriptions as well as inspirational photos, visit www.escalando.cl.

Skiing & Snowboarding

Powder junkies rejoice. World-class resorts in the Chilean Andes offer myriad possibilities for skiing, snowboarding and even heliskiing. Don't expect too many bargains; resorts are priced to match their quality. 'First descents' of Chilean Patagonia's numerous mountains is a growing (but limited) trend.

Most resorts are within an hour's drive of Santiago, including a wide variety of runs at family-oriented La Parva, all-levels El Colorado and Valle Nevado, with a lot of terrain and renowned heliskiing. Legendary Portillo, the site of several downhill speed records and the summer training base for many of the northern hemisphere's top skiers, is northeast of Santiago near the Argentine border crossing to Mendoza.

Termas de Chillán, just east of Chillán, is a more laid-back spot with several beginners' slopes, while Parque Nacional Villarrica, near the resort town of Pucón, has the added thrill of skiing on a smoking volcano (the resort may still be temporarily closed due to an eruption in 2015). On Volcán Lonquimay, Corralco has great novice and expert terrain, as well as excellent backcountry access. Volcanoes Osorno and Antillanca, east of Osorno, have open terrain with incredible views and a family atmosphere. These southern resorts are often close to hot springs, a godsend after a hard day of descents. Coyhaique has its own small resort, while Punta Arenas offers an ocean view, if little challenge.

Ski season runs from June to October, though snowfall in the south is less consistent. Santiago has some rental shops; otherwise resorts rent full packages.

NATIONAL GEOGRAPHIC IMAGE COLLECTION/ALAMY ©

Divers, Easter Island (p397)

A good website to gather general information is www.andesweb.com, with photo essays, reviews and trail maps.

Cycling & Mountain Biking

From a leisurely ride around the lakes to bombing down still-smoking volcanoes, Chile's two-wheel options keep growing.

RESPONSIBLE TREKKING

➡ Exercise caution with campfires on the windy Patagonian steppe.

➡ Cook on a camp stove (not open fires) and dispose of butane cartridges responsibly.

➡ Carry out all rubbish.

➡ Where there is no toilet, bury human waste. Dig a small hole 15cm deep and at least 100m from any watercourse. Cover the waste with soil and a rock. Pack out toilet paper.

➡ Wash with biodegradable soap at least 50m away from any watercourses.

➡ Do not feed the wildlife.

➡ Trails can pass through private property. Ask permission before entering and leave all livestock gates as you found them.

Kitesurfing, with the Andes as a backdrop

A favorite mountain-biking destination in the north is San Pedro de Atacama. Fabulous trips in the Lakes District access pristine areas with limited public transportation. The new bike lane around Lago Llanquihue is very popular, as is the Ojos de Caburgua loop near Pucón. The long, challenging, but extremely rewarding Carretera Austral has become an iconic route for international cyclists.

More and more bikers are taking on the ultimate challenge: to cycle Chile's entire length. Most large towns have bike-repair shops and sell basic parts, but packing a comprehensive repair kit is essential.

Horseback Riding

Saddling up and following in the path of Chile's *huasos* (cowboys) is a fun and easy way to experience the wilderness. Chilean horses are compact and sturdy, with amazing skill for fording rivers and climbing Andean steeps. Now more than ever, multiday horseback-riding trips explore cool circuits, sometimes crossing the Andes to Argentina, on terrain that would be inaccessible otherwise. Except in the far north, opportunities can be found just about everywhere.

With strong initiatives for community-based rural tourism in the south, guided horseback riding and trekking with packhorses is a great way to discover remote areas. Rural guides charge affordable rates, provide family lodging in their own homes and offer invaluable cultural insight. Check out offerings in Río Cochamó, Palena and Coyhaique.

Adventure outfitters offer multilingual guides and a more elaborate range of services. Most places offer first-time riders preliminary lessons before taking to the trails. Favorites for single- or multiday horse treks are: Pucón, Puelo Valley, Elqui Valley, Hurtado, San Pedro de Atacama and around Torres del Paine. The island of Chiloé is also popular.

Rafting & Kayaking

The wealth of scenic rivers, lakes, fjords and inlets in southern Chile make it a dream destination. Chile's rivers, raging

BUT WAIT, THERE'S MORE...

Canyoning Navigate stream canyons by jumping into clear pools and rappelling alongside gushing waterfalls. Hot spots are near Puerto Varas and Pucón.

Canopy Go with well-recommended tour operators. Minimal gear is a secure harness with two straps that attach to the cable (one is a safety strap), a hard hat and gloves.

Paragliding & Land-sailing With its steep coastal escarpment, rising air currents and soft, extensive dunes, Iquique ranks among the continent's top spots for paragliding, desert land-sailing and kite-buggying.

Fly-fishing Reel in monster trout (brown and rainbow) and Atlantic salmon (a non-native species) in the Lakes District and Patagonia. The season generally runs from November to May.

Sand-boarding Be prepared to get sand in places you never imagined possible. Try it in San Pedro de Atacama or Iquique.

Diving Exciting dive sites can be found on the Juan Fernández archipelago and around Easter Island. On the mainland, check out the coast of Norte Chico.

Swimming Chile's almost endless coastline has sandy beaches, but the Humboldt Current makes waters cold, except in the far north around Arica.

---

through narrow canyons from the Andes, are world class. Northern Patagonia's Río Futaleufú offers memorable Class IV and V runs. Less technical runs include those outside Pucón and the beautiful Petrohué, near Puerto Varas, as well as Aisén's Río Simpson and Río Baker.

Near Santiago, the Cajón del Maipo offers a gentle but enjoyable run. For detailed kayaking information, see rivers ofchile.com.

Agencies in Santiago, Pucón, Puerto Varas and elsewhere offer trips for different levels. Since there is no certifying body for guides, check to see if the company has specialized river safety and first-aid training and verify that equipment is of high quality. Wetsuits may be necessary.

The southern fjords are a sea-kayaker's paradise. Popular trips go around Parque Pumalín and the sheltered bays of Chiloé. Lake kayaking and stand-up paddling (SUP) is catching on throughout the Lakes District.

Surfing & Kitesurfing

With breaks lining the long Pacific coast, Chile nurtures some serious surf culture, most active in middle and northern Chile. With big breaks and long left-handers, surf capital Pichilemu hosts the national surfing championship. Pilgrims crowd the perfect left break at Pichilemu's Punta de Lobos, but beginners can also have a go nearby at La Puntilla. Iquique has a shallow reef break; bring booties for sea urchins. The coastal Ruta 1 is lined with waves.

Only at Arica is the water comfortably warm, so wetsuits are imperative. The biggest breaks are seen in July. Rough surf and rip currents also make some areas inadvisable, and it's best not to surf alone. You can buy or hire boards and track down lessons in any surfing hot spot.

Chile also has opportunities for kitesurfing, although equipment and lessons are harder to come by: try Pichilemu and Puclaro (near Vicuña). Spanish-speakers can find more information on www.kitesurf.cl.

Plan Your Trip

Travel with Children

Chile is a top family destination where bringing children offers up some distinct advantages. Little ones are welcomed and treasured and empathy for parents is usually keen. Even strangers will offer help and hotels and services tend to accommodate. There's lots of active adventures and family-oriented resorts and lodgings.

Highlights for Kids

Adventure

➡ Rafting the Petrohué River

➡ Horseback riding in the Andean foothills

➡ Ski resort Valle Nevado's terrain park and family barbecues

Entertainment

➡ Rodeos in *medialuna* (half moon) stadiums in summer

➡ The kids' area at Lollapalooza

➡ Santiago's free tours and Parque Bicentenario

Dining

➡ *Asados* (barbecues) with oversized grills and backyard ambience

➡ Burgers eaten on the shiny stools of a *fuente de soda* (soda fountain)

➡ Fresh berry *küchen* (sweet German-style cakes) served in teahouses in the Lakes District

Rainy-Day Refuges

➡ Museo Interactivo Mirador in Santiago

➡ Kids' workshops at Teatro del Lago in Frutillar

➡ Making masterpieces in the kids' studio of Museo Artequín in Santiago

Practicalities

Chile is as kid-friendly as a destination gets, though it's best to take all the same travel precautions you would at home. Free or reduced admission rates are often given at events and performances. In Chile, people are helpful on public transportation; often someone will give up a seat for parent and child. Expecting mothers enjoy a boon of designated parking spaces and grocery store checkout lines.

Though upper-middle-class families usually employ a *nana* (live-in or daily childcare), finding last-minute help is not easy. Babysitting services or children's activity clubs tend to be limited to upmarket hotels and ski resorts. If you're comfortable with an informal approach, trusted acquaintances can recommend sitters.

Formula, baby food and disposable diapers are easy to find. In general, public toilets are poorly maintained; always carry toilet paper, which tends to run out in bathrooms, and hand sanitizer, as there's rarely soap and towels. While a woman may take a young boy into the ladies' room, it is socially unacceptable for a man to take a girl into the men's room.

There are no special food and health concerns, but bottled water is a good idea for delicate stomachs.

Adventure

Children love plenty of sports, such as hiking or cycling, as long as they can go at their own pace. Scale activities down, bring snacks, and have a plan B for when bad weather or exhaustion hits. Routine travel, like crossing fjords on a ferry or riding the subway, can amount to adventure. Activities like guided horse rides (usually for ages eight and up), rafting and canyoning usually have age limits but are invariably fine for teenagers.

In rural areas, agritourism can be a great option, which can involve farm chores or just hiking with pack horses taking all the load. Some rivers may be suitable for children to float or raft; make sure outfitters have life vests and wetsuits in appropriate sizes.

Dining

While restaurants don't offer special kids' meals, most offer a variety of dishes suitable for children; none are spicy. It is perfectly acceptable to order a meal to split between two children or an adult and a child; most portions are abundant. High chairs are rarely available. The only challenge to dining families is the Latin hours. Restaurants open for dinner no earlier than 7pm, sometimes 8pm, and service can be quite slow.

Best Regions for Kids

Santiago

Brimming with children's museums, parks and winter resorts with easy terrain, fun events and kids' classes. Eco-adventure parks, horseback riding and ziplines offer excitement in nearby Cajón del Maipo.

Sur Chico

For horseback riding, lake dips, farm visits, water sports and volcano thrills. Lake towns Pucón or Puerto Varas provide the best bases to explore the region, with kid-centered events in summer.

Norte Chico

Seaside resorts provide beach fun, swimming and surf lessons. Kids love playing in the tide pools of La Piscina in Bahía Inglesa. The gentle, sunny climate here helps keep your plans on target.

PLANNING

If renting a car, communicate ahead if you will need a child's seat; you might have to bring one. If you don't want to be tied town to a schedule while traveling, plenty of activities can be booked last minute.

When to Go
➡ Summer (December to February) for good weather and outdoor fun.
➡ The desert north can be visited year-round.
➡ Avoid the south during the rainiest months (May to July).
➡ Winter (June to August) is fun as kids can try out skis.

Accommodations
➡ Hotels often give discounts for families and some can provide cribs.
➡ Aparthotels in cities are convenient and offer good value.
➡ Cabins are widely available in summer and often have self-catering options.
➡ Campgrounds in the south may have *quinchos* (barbecue huts) for some shelter from the rain.

What to Pack
➡ Bathing suit, sunhat and warm clothing
➡ Non-toxic bug spray
➡ Baby backpack – strollers aren't always convenient

Regions at a Glance

Skinny Chile unfurls toward Cape Horn, cartwheeling from the stargazing center of the Atacama, the world's driest desert, to patchwork vineyards and farms, the deep green of temperate rainforest and the cool blue of glacial fields. Throughout, there's the constant blue of the roiling Pacific to the west and the ragged bulwark of the Andes to the east. With the country's population cinched in the middle, Santiago keeps humming unto the wee hours. Yet Valparaíso is a close challenger for urban cool, with its narrow, graffiti-cloaked passages. Roam in any direction for vibrant country life, visiting villages where time seems to tick a little slower and reaching out to wilderness that begs to be explored.

Santiago

History
Arts
Nightlife

Political Past

From the early independence to Salvador Allende's deposition in 1973 and the years of military government, Chile's fascinating past is laid bare in the museums of Santiago.

Path of Beauty

Santiago has the best of old and new. Pre-Columbian objects and Chilean masterpieces abound at traditional museums, while up and coming artists, photographers and filmmakers show at contemporary centers and galleries.

Nighttime Revelry

Chile's lively capital pulls all-nighters. Find *carrete* (nightlife) in the down-to-earth bars of Bellavista and Barrio Brasil, the posh cocktail lounges of Vitacura and rocking live-music venues about town.

p44

Middle Chile

Wine
Beaches
Outdoors

Wine Country

¿Tinto o blanco? These welcoming wineries literally overflow with both reds and whites. The Colchagua Valley specializes in Cabernet Sauvignon, while the Casablanca Valley produces delectable Chardonnay and Sauvignon Blanc.

Along the Coast

There are waves to be pioneered up and down this coast. Grab a board in Pichilemu or Buchupureo, or head to lower-key Maitencillo to learn how to catch a wave.

Hiking & Skiing

Dare to brave South America's longest ski slope, a 14km run. In summer, travelers bolt for Chile's star outdoor attractions – Torres del Paine and the Atacama – leaving central Chile's national parks crowd-free.

p87

Norte Grande

Landscapes
Activities
History

Natural Beauty

Take in the diversity and drama of Norte Grande's landscapes – from the heights of the altiplano to the desert sunsets and star-studded night skies.

Active Adventures

Norte Grande offers up a healthy dose of adrenaline, from hitting Arica's waves and paragliding off Iquique's cliff to sand-boarding near San Pedro de Atacama and horseback riding through the world's driest desert.

Ghosts of the Past

Wander around the nitrate-era ghost towns of Humberstone and Santa Laura, tour the storied *Esmeralda* ship in Iquique's harbor and take in creepy Chinchorro mummies in situ at an Arica museum.

p143

Norte Chico

Beaches
Activities
Architecture

Sunny Shores

A string of pretty beaches lines the coast of Norte Chico, including activity hubs like buzzy La Serena and virtually virgin strips of sand and hip beach hideaways like the tiny Bahía Inglesa.

Volcanoes to the Sea

You can climb the world's highest active volcano, Ojos del Salado, sail the coast around Bahía Inglesa, hop on a boat to see Humboldt penguins and windsurf off the coast of La Serena.

Colonial Charms

From the colonial charms of leafy La Serena to Caldera's neoclassical mansions of the early mining era, Norte Chico showcases a hodgepodge of eye-candy for architecture buffs.

p195

Sur Chico

Parks
Outdoors
Lakes

Nature Reserves

Sur Chico parks offer a wealth of landscapes. Explore the verdant nature around Pucón. Parks showcase alpine lakes, araucaria forests and ski slopes.

Adrenaline Rush

While trekkers relish the laundry list of trails, rafting, kayaking, mountain biking and volcano climbing are other great options here. Pucón is Chile's high-adrenaline epicenter, while Puerto Varas is a close cousin.

Watery Diversions

Deep-blue and jade-green lakes pepper the region, but there are also hot springs, none more enticing than Termas Geométricas. Rivers are rich with trout and waterfalls.

p223

Chiloé

Churches
Culture
Nature

Jesuit Legacy

These Unesco-registered churches will have you worshipping architecture. Each village centerpiece was built at the call of Jesuit missionaries in the 17th and 18th centuries.

Local Flavors

Chiloé's distinctive flavor, notable in mythology and folklore, lives in the architecture of churches and *palafitos* (stilt houses). Cuisine dates to pre-Hispanic cultures and features seafood and potatoes, famously in *curanto* (meat, potato and seafood stew).

Native Rainforests

Parque Nacional Chiloé and Parque Tantauco protect rainforest with native wildlife. To meet Magellanic and Humboldt penguins, visit Monumento Natural Islotes de Puñihuil.

p281

Northern Patagonia

Culture
Outdoors
Nature

Cowboy Culture

Long the most isolated part of Chile, Patagonia's northern region is a cowboy stronghold. Visit rural settlers off the grid who live in harmony with a wicked and whimsical mother nature.

Nature Unbound

Land the big one fly-fishing, raft wild rivers or mosey into the backcountry on a fleece-mounted saddle. Scenery and real adventure abound on the Carretera Austral, Chile's unpaved southern road.

Wildlife Watching

Patagonia can get pretty wild. The best wildlife watching is in the Valle Chacabuco, home to guanaco and flamingos. Near Raúl Marín Balmaceda, observe dolphins and sea lions at play from your kayak.

p301

Southern Patagonia

Seafaring
Trekking
Parks

Isles & Inlets

Sailors of yore mythologized these channels rife with craggy isles, whales and dolphins. Today ferry trips go to Puerto Montt and Puerto Williams. Kayakers can paddle still sounds and glacier-strewn bays.

Andean Highs

Between Torres del Paine and Argentina's Fitz Roy range, the trekking doesn't get any better. Snug *refugios* (rustic shelters) make the day's work a little easier. Or go off the beaten path to Pali Aike or historic Cabo Froward.

Cinematic Landscapes

Glaciers, rock spires and rolling steppe. Patagonia is a feast for the eye, and Torres del Paine and Argentina's Parque Nacional Los Glaciares rate among the finest parks on the continent.

p334

Tierra del Fuego

Wilderness
History
Landscapes

Wild Outdoors

Whether you are backpacking the rugged Dientes de Navarino circuit, observing penguins or boating among glaciers and sea lions, this special spot on the planet connects you to your wild side.

Local Heritage

The past is ever present on this far-flung isle. Coastal shell middens remain from native inhabitants. Trace its history in Puerto Williams' Museo Martín Gusinde and Ushuaia's former jail Museo del Presidio.

Unfettered Vistas

From steep snow-bound peaks and tawny plains to labyrinthine channels scattered with rugged isles, the scenery of the land of fire is breathtaking. Take it in on a trek, coastal stroll or long boat ride.

p376

Easter Island

History
Landscapes
Outdoors

Ancient Past

Easter Island (Rapa Nui) is an open-air museum, with archaeological remains dating from pre-European times. Think *moai* (anthropomorphic statues), *ahu* (ceremonial platforms) and burial cairns.

Perfect Panoramas

Ready your wide-angle lens for some shutter-blowing landscapes. For the most dramatic, stand on the edge of Rano Kau, a lake-filled crater, or walk across the beautiful Península Poike.

Hiking & Diving

Outdoorsy types will be in seventh heaven. Hike up Mt Terevaka for extraordinary views. Learn to surf, then snorkel or dive in crystal-clear waters. Clip clop around Península Poike and bike your way around the island.

p397

On the
Road

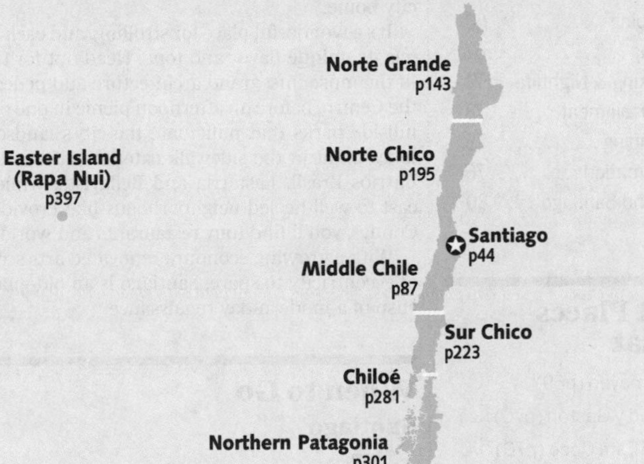

Norte Grande
p143

Norte Chico
p195

Easter Island
(Rapa Nui)
p397

★ Santiago
p44

Middle Chile
p87

Sur Chico
p223

Chiloé
p281

Northern Patagonia
p301

Southern Patagonia
p334

Tierra del Fuego
p376

Santiago

⏺ 02 / POP 6,034,000

Best Places to Eat

➜ Peumayen (p69)
➜ Astrid y Gastón (p70)
➜ Aquí Está Coco (p70)
➜ Etniko (p69)
➜ Mercado Central (p67)

Best Places to Stay

➜ W Santiago (p67)
➜ Aubrey Hotel (p66)
➜ Hotel Boutique Tremo (p65)
➜ Happy House Hostel (p66)
➜ La Chimba (p65)

Why Go?

Surprising, cosmopolitan, energetic, sophisticated and worldly, Santiago is a city of syncopated cultural currents, madhouse parties, expansive museums and top-flight restaurants. No wonder 40% of Chileans call the leafy capital city home.

It's a wonderful place for strolling, and each neighborhood has its unique flavor and tone. Head out for the day to take in the museums, grand architecture and pedestrian malls of the Centro, before an afternoon picnic in one of the gorgeous hillside parks that punctuate the city's landscape. Nightlife takes flight in the sidewalk eateries, cafes and beer halls of Barrios Brasil, Lastarria and Bellavista, while as you head east to well-heeled neighborhoods like Providencia and Las Condes, you'll find tony restaurants and world-class hotels.

With a growing economy, renovated arts scene and plenty of eccentricity to spare, Santiago is an old-guard city on the cusp of a modern-day renaissance.

When to Go
Santiago

Mar–Aug The wine harvest kicks off, while May brings snow to nearby ski areas.

Sep–Nov Comfortable temperatures make the shoulder season an ideal time for sightseeing.

Dec–Feb Summer brings street festivals and excellent quick adventures in the countryside.

History

Nomadic hunter-gatherers wandered here as early as 10,000 BC, but only in 800 BC did Mapuche settlers begin to permanently populate the area. Not long after the Inka made the area a major hub on their road network, Spanish soldier Pedro de Valdivia arrived and founded the city of Santiago de la Nueva Extremadura on February 12, 1541, marching on to attack the Mapuche to the south. The Mapuche living nearby weren't happy and kicked off a counter-insurgency. Valdivia's girlfriend, Inés de Suárez, turned out to be as bloodthirsty as he was, and led the defense of the city, personally decapitating at least one Mapuche chief. Despite ongoing attacks, floods and earthquakes, the conquistadores didn't budge, and eventually Santiago began to grow.

Santiago was the backdrop for Chile's declaration of independence from Spain in 1810 and the final battle that overthrew the colonial powers in 1818. As the population grew, public-works projects transformed the city, which became the hub of Chile's growing rail network before displacing Valparaíso as Chile's financial capital in the early 20th century. Not everyone prospered, however. Impoverished farmers flocked to the city and the upper classes migrated to the eastern suburbs. Rapid post-WWII industrialization created urban jobs, but never enough to satisfy demand, resulting in scores of squatter settlements known as *callampas* ('mushrooms,' so-called because they sprang up virtually overnight).

Santiago was at the center of the 1973 coup that deposed Salvador Allende. During the dark years that followed, thousands of political prisoners were executed, and torture centers and clandestine prisons were scattered throughout Santiago. Despite this, military commander-in-chief General Augusto Pinochet was Chile's president until 1990. The nation's democratic government was restored in 1990 when Patricio Aylwin was elected president, with Pinochet continuing on as head of the nation's military.

The gap between rich and poor widened during the '90s, and social inequality – though less pronounced than in other Latin American cities – looks set to linger for some time at least. Occasional student and worker strikes continue to ripple through the city, and over the past decade there have been an estimated 200 small-scale bombings in the capital. Many attribute the bombings – most of which take place at night and target banks and government buildings using basic pipe bomb technology – to anarchist groups. Only one person has been killed in the bombings – a would-be bomber in 2009. Nevertheless, most indicators still point to Santiago as one of the safest large cities in Latin America, and relative economic prosperity has sparked something of a renaissance, particularly in the period leading up to Chile's bicentennial celebration in 2010.

Recent years have seen brand-new parks and museums popping up around town, a cleaned-up riverfront, construction of super-modern apartment buildings and large-scale projects like new metro lines and the Costanera Center (which, when finished, will be the tallest skyscraper in South America).

◎ Sights

Thanks to the recent wave of construction surrounding Chile's bicentennial, Santiago is alive with ultra-modern cultural centers, sleek museums and vast green parks dotted with colorful sculptures and locals basking in the sunshine. The city's food markets, leafy residential streets, outdoor cafes and bustling shopping strips are often the best places to witness the particular mix of distinctly Latin American hustle-and-bustle and more Old World reticence that defines Santiago.

◉ Centro

The wedge-shaped Centro is the oldest part of Santiago, and the busiest. It is hemmed in by three fiendishly hard-to-cross borders: the Río Mapocho, the Autopista Central expressway (which have only occasional bridges over them) and the Alameda, where the central railing puts your vaulting skills to the test. Architecturally, the Centro is exuberant rather than elegant: haphazardly maintained 19th-century buildings sit alongside the odd glittering high-rise, and its crowded *paseos* (pedestrian precincts) are lined with inexpensive clothing stores, fast-food joints and cafes staffed with scantily clad waitresses. Government offices, the presidential palace and the banking district are also here, making it the center of civic life. You'll find some interesting museums, but it pays to head to other neighborhoods for your lunch and dinner.

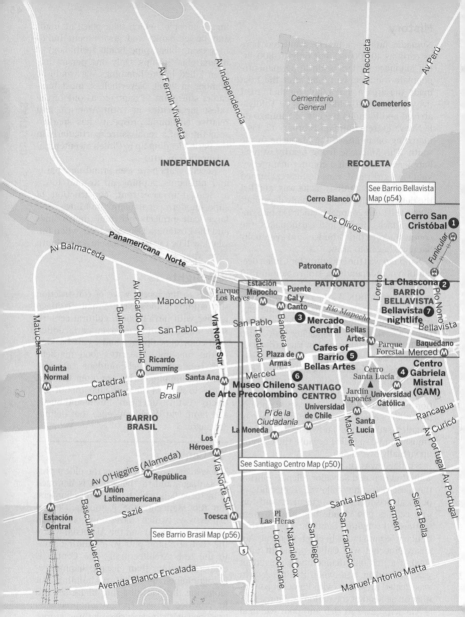

Santiago Highlights

1 Gaze out over Santiago from the breathtaking summit of **Cerro San Cristóbal** (p55).

2 Walk in Pablo Neruda's footsteps at **La Chascona**

(p55), the one-time home of Chile's legendary poet.

3 Sample *paila marina* (seafood stew) and watch locals bargain for fresh fish

at the clamoring **Mercado Central** (p67).

4 Catch experimental dance performances at the incendiary **Centro Gabriela**

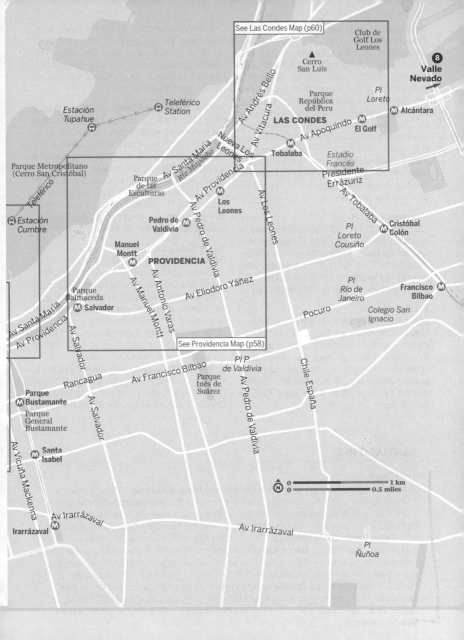

Mistral (p52) performing arts complex.

5 People-watch from a spirited sidewalk cafe in **Barrio Bellas Artes** (p52).

6 Trace the roots of Chilean culture and art at the **Museo Chileno de Arte Precolombino** (p48).

7 Dine, drink and dance till dawn at party central **Bellavista** (p72).

8 Tear up the slopes at Chile's top ski resort, **Valle Nevado** (p85).

9 Raft, hike or bike through the magical countryside in the **Cajón del Maipo** (p81).

★ **Museo Chileno de Arte Precolombino**   MUSEUM
(Chilean Museum of Pre-Columbian Art; Map p50; 📱02-928-1500; www.precolombino.cl; Bandera 361; entrance CH$3500; ⊙10am-6pm Tue-Sun; Ⓜ Plaza de Armas) Exquisite pottery from most major pre-Columbian cultures is the backbone of Santiago's best museum, the Museo Chileno de Arte Precolombino. As well as dozens of intricately molded anthropomorphic vessels, star exhibits include hefty Maya stone stele and a fascinating Andean textile display. More unusual are the wooden vomit spatulas used by Amazonian shamans before taking psychoactive powders.

Mercado Central   MARKET
(Central Market; Map p50; www.mercadocentral. cl; cnr 21 de Mayo & San Pablo; ⊙7am-5pm Mon-Sat, 7am-3pm Sun; Ⓜ Puente Cal y Canto) Gleaming piles of fresh fish and crustaceans atop mounds of sparkling ice thrill foodies and photographers alike at the Mercado Central.

Plaza de Armas   PLAZA
(Map p50; cnr Monjitas & 21 de Mayo; Ⓜ Plaza de Armas) Since the city's founding in 1541, the Plaza de Armas has been its symbolic heart. In colonial times a gallows was the square's grisly centerpiece; today it's a fountain celebrating *libertador* (liberator) Simón Bolívar, shaded by more than a hundred Chilean palm trees.

Parallel pedestrian precincts Paseo Ahumada and Paseo Estado disgorge scores of strolling Santiaguinos onto the square on weekends and sunny weekday afternoons: clowns, helium-balloon sellers and snack stands keep them entertained.

Catedral Metropolitana   CHURCH
(Map p50; Plaza de Armas; ⊙9am-7pm Mon-Sat, 9am-noon Sun; Ⓜ Plaza de Armas) Overlooking the Plaza de Armas is the neoclassical Catedral Metropolitana, built between 1748 and 1800. Bishops celebrating mass on the lavish main altar may feel uneasy: beneath them is the crypt where their predecessors are buried. The church's exterior was undergoing renovations as of press time. They expect to pull back the curtains in June 2015.

Cerro Santa Lucía   PARK
(Map p50; entrances cnr O'Higgins & Santa Lucía, cnr Santa Lucía & Subercaseaux; ⊙9am-6pm Mar-Sep, to 8pm Oct-Feb; Ⓜ Santa Lucía) FREE Take a break from the chaos of the Centro with an afternoon stroll through this lovingly manicured park. It was just a rocky hill until 19th-century mayor Benjamín Vicuña Mackenna had it transformed into one of the city's most memorable parks.

A web of trails and steep stone stairs leads you up through terraces to the Torre Mirador at the top, and there are a scattering of churches and other interesting buildings in

SANTIAGO IN...

Two Days

Start your day in the heart of town, at the bustling **Plaza de Armas**, setting aside the morning for tours of the art and cultural exhibits at central **museums** like the Museo Chileno de Arte Precolombino, Centro Cultural Palacio La Moneda or Museo Nacional de Bellas Artes. Dive into a savory seafood lunch at the **Mercado Central**, then hotfoot it up **Cerro Santa Lucía** to revel in the city from above. Take a break for afternoon tea and people-watching at a **Barrio Lastarria cafe**, then head to **Bellavista** for a one-of-a-kind dining experience at Peumayen, as you warm up for a night of *carrete* (partying) in the beer halls and discoteques of Bellavista. Get inspiration for your second day at Pablo Neruda's house, **La Chascona**, then take in more great views atop **Cerro San Cristóbal**. After a ceviche lunch at Azul Profundo, consider taking a guided walking or bike **tour**. Later, have a pisco sour at the **W Santiago** before a show at the **Centro Gabriela Mistral**.

Four Days

On your third day cruise out to the countryside with a visit to the **Cajón del Maipo** or tour of nearby **wineries**. In winter, head for the snow at **Tres Valles**. Spend your fourth day admiring street art in **Barrio Brasil**, stopping for lunch at antique Peluquería Francesa. Toast your stay in Santiago with a wine flight at Lastarria's lauded Boca Naríz.

between. There's a free elevator to the top if you want to save your legs.

Centro Cultural
Palacio La Moneda   ARTS CENTER
(Map p50; ☑02-355-6500; www.ccplm.cl; Plaza de la Ciudadanía 26; exhibitions from CH$5000; ☺9am-9pm, exhibitions to 7:30pm; 🛜♿; Ⓜ La Moneda) Underground art takes on a new meaning in one of Santiago's newer cultural spaces: the Centro Cultural Palacio La Moneda beneath Plaza de la Ciudadanía. A glass-slab roof floods the vault-like space with natural light, and ramps wind down through the central atrium past the Cineteca Nacional, a state-run art-house movie theater, to two large temporary exhibition spaces. The uppermost level contains a fairtrade crafts shop, a few cafes and a gallery space.

Palacio de la Moneda   HISTORIC BUILDING
(Map p50; Morandé 130; ☺10am-6pm Mon-Fri; Ⓜ La Moneda) **FREE** Chile's presidential offices are in the Palacio de la Moneda. The ornate neoclassical building was designed by Italian architect Joaquín Toesca in the late 18th century and was originally the official mint. The inner courtyards are generally open to the public; schedule a guided tour with a week's notice by emailing visitas@presidencia.cl.

The north facade was badly damaged by air-force missile attacks during the 1973 military coup when President Salvador Allende – who refused to leave – was overthrown here. A monument honoring Allende now stands opposite in Plaza de la Constitución.

Barrio París-Londres   NEIGHBORHOOD
(Map p50; cnr París & Londres; Ⓜ Universidad de Chile) This pocket-sized neighborhood developed on the grounds of the Franciscan convent of Iglesia de San Francisco and is made up of two intersecting cobblestone streets, París and Londres, which are lined by graceful European-style townhouses built in the 1920s. Look for the memorial at Londres 38, a building that served as a torture center during Pinochet's government.

Iglesia de San Francisco   CHURCH
(Map p50; O'Higgins 834; ☺11am-6pm Mon-Sat, 10am-1pm Sun; Ⓜ Universidad de Chile) The first stone of the austere Iglesia de San Francisco was laid in 1586, making it Santiago's oldest surviving colonial building. Its sturdy walls have weathered some powerful earthquakes, although the current clock tower, finished in

1857, is the fourth. There is an attached colonial art museum. On the main altar look for the carving of the Virgen del Socorro (Our Lady of Perpetual Help), which Santiago's founder Pedro de Valdivia brought to Chile on his 1540 conquistador mission.

Londres 38   HISTORIC SITE
(Map p50; www.londres38.cl; Londres 38; ☺10am-1pm & 3-6pm Tue-Fri, 10am-2pm Sat; Ⓜ Universidad de Chile) **FREE** Explore the dark history of the early days of the Pinochet regime at this former detention center. There are both guided and unguided tours.

Museo Histórico Nacional   MUSEUM
(National History Museum; Map p50; ☑02-411-7010; www.museohistoriconacional.cl; Plaza de Armas 951; adult/child CH$600/300; ☺10am-5:30pm Tue-Sun; Ⓜ Plaza de Armas) Colonial furniture, weapons, paintings, historical objects and models chart Chile's colonial and republican history at the Museo Histórico Nacional. After a perfunctory nod to pre-Columbian culture, the ground floor covers the conquest and colony. Upstairs goes from independence through Chile's industrial revolution right up to the 1973 military coup – Allende's broken glasses are the chilling final exhibit.

Casa Colorada   HISTORIC BUILDING
(Map p50; www.santiagocultura.cl/casa-colorada; Merced 860; Ⓜ Plaza de Armas) Few colonial houses are still standing in Santiago, but the

Santiago Centro

Parque Los Reyes

⊕9

Caly Canto Bridge

Av La Paz

Av Santa María

Av Recoleta

Manzano

Bellavista

Av Santa María

✪58

Puente Cal y Canto

Ⓜ

Parque Venezuela

Valdés Vergara

General Mackenna

11
⊕

43 ⊗
⊗46

Esmeralda

Diagonal Cervantes

San Pablo

Bandera

Morandé

Rosas

Teatinos

Amunátegui

Santo Domingo

Paseo Puente

21 de Mayo

Santo Domingo

Maciver

Sa

See Barrio Brasil Map (p56)

Santo Domingo

Plaza de Armas

📮
24 ⊞
ℹ️ 14

Monjitas

Merced

Catedral

🏛

Ⓜ 5
19

⊕18

Manzur Expediciones

Museo Chileno de Arte Precolombino

Portal Fernández Concha

🏛 4

63
🔒

Compañía de Jesús

🏛2

⊗45
31 ⊞

Tribunales de Justicia

⊗40

⊗39

⊗42

BARRIO CÍVICO

Departamento ℹ️ *de Extranjería*

Agustinas

Matías Cousiño

Paseo Estado

San Antonio

Moneda

Tenderini

Maciver

✪59

Biblioteca Nacional

Huérfanos

🏛27

Agustinas

Moneda

Pl de la Constitución

Teatinos

Morandé

Bandera

La Bolsa

Nueva York

Paseo Ahumada

🏛33

16
🏛

Amunátegui

Almirante Gotuzzo

6 ⊙

Pl de la Ciudadanía

🔒60

22

La Moneda Ⓜ

Ⓜ

Universidad de Chile

25

Av O'Higgins (Alameda)

35 🏛
3 ⊙
ℹ️8

34 🏛
36 🏛

⊕10

París

Londres

San Francisco

54

San Martín

Lord Cochrane

Natanael Cox

Paseo Buines

Zenteno

Universidad de Chile

BARRIO PARÍS LONDRES

San Diego

Arturo Prat

Paseo Serrano

Ovalle

Londres

Ovalle

Tarapacá

Concaf (200m) ↓

↓ *Teatro Caupolicán (1km)*

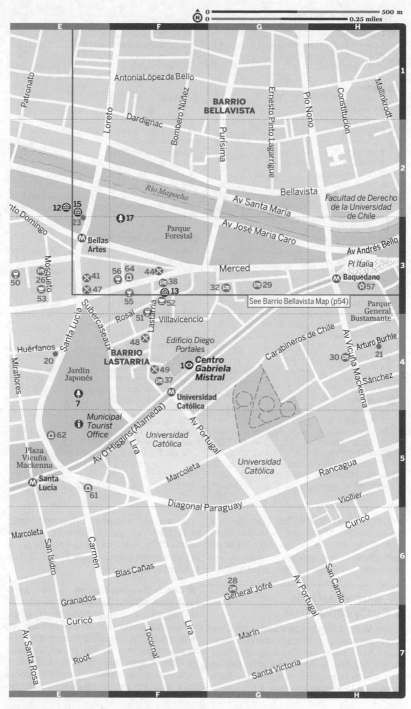

Santiago Centro

simple, oxblood-colored Casa Colorada is a happy exception, although only the front half of the original 18th-century building has survived. The building was set to reopen after renovations in November 2015.

◉ Barrio Lastarria & Barrio Bellas Artes

Home to three of the city's best museums, these postcard-pretty neighborhoods near Cerro Santa Lucía are also Santiago's twin hubs of hip. East of the Cerro, Barrio Lastarria takes its name from its narrow cobbled main drag JV Lastarria, which is lined with arty bars and restaurants. The real center of Santiago cafe culture, however, is over at Barrio Bellas Artes, as the few blocks north of Cerro Santa Lucía are now known. JM de la Barra is the main axis.

★ **Centro Gabriela Mistral**   ARTS CENTER
(GAM;   Map p50;   ☑ 02-566-5500;   www.gam.cl; Av O'Higgins 227;   ⊙ plazas 8am-midnight, exhibition spaces 10am-8pm Tue-Sat, from 11am Sun; ☜; Ⓜ Universidad Católica) **FREE** This striking cultural and performing arts center – named for Chilean poet Gabriela Mistral, the first Latin American woman to win the Nobel Prize in Literature – is an exciting addition

to Santiago's art scene. There are concerts and performances most days.

No matter what, you should drop by just to check out the large exhibition spaces and rotating art exhibits on the bottom floor, the iconic architecture that vaults and cantelevers on the inside and looks like a giant rusty cheese grater from the street, the little plazas, murals, cafes and more. Free tours of the center leave every hour; inquire at the information desk.

Museo Nacional de Bellas Artes   MUSEUM
(National Museum of Fine Art; Map p50; www. mnba.cl; Parque Forestal s/n; adult/child CH$600/ free; M Bellas Artes) This fine art museum is housed in the stately neoclassical Palacio de Bellas Artes, which was built as part of Chile's centenary celebrations in 1910. The museum features an excellent permanent collection of Chilean art. There are free guided tours Saturday and Sunday starting at 10:30am.

Look out for works by Luis Vargas Rosas, member of the Abstraction Creation group, along with fellow Chilean Roberto Matta, whose work is also well represented.

Museo de Arte Contemporáneo   MUSEUM
(MAC, Contemporary Art Museum; Map p50; www.mac.uchile.cl; Parque Forestal s/n; admission CH$600; ⊙11am-7pm Tue-Sat, 11am-6pm Sun; M Bellas Artes) Temporary exhibitions showcasing contemporary photography, design, sculpture, installations and web art are often held at the Museo de Arte Contemporáneo, located inside the Palacio de Bellas Artes. Its pristine galleries are the result of extensive restoration work to reverse fire and earthquake damage. Twentieth-century Chilean painting forms the bulk of the permanent collection.

Museo de Artes Visuales   MUSEUM
(MAVI, Visual Arts Museum; Map p50; ✐02-664-9337; www.mavi.cl; Lastarria 307, Plaza Mulato Gil de Castro; admission CH$1000, free Sun; ⊙10:30am-6:30pm Tue-Sun; M Bellas Artes) Exposed concrete, stripped wood and glass are the materials local architect Cristián Undurraga chose for the stunningly simple Museo de Artes Visuales. The contents of the four open-plan galleries are as winsome as the building: top-notch modern engravings, sculptures, paintings and

---

SANTIAGO FOR CHILDREN

Santiaguinos are family-oriented and usually welcome travelers with children. Kids stay up late and often accompany their parents to parties or restaurants, where they order from the regular menu rather than a separate one for children. That said, most kiddy-oriented activities here are helpful distractions rather than standout sights. In a pinch, children also love creamy Chilean ice cream, which is available everywhere, and the clowns and acrobats that put on performances in the Plaza de Armas and Parque Forestal on weekends. Trips to the Cajón del Maipo or ski areas make great quick getaways.

Fantasilandia (✐02-476-8600; www.fantasilandia.cl; Av Beaucheff 938; adult/child from CH$10,900/5490, children under 90cm free; ⊙noon-9pm daily; M Parque O'Higgins) Give your children their dose of adrenaline and cotton candy at this colorful amusement park. Check the Fantasilandia website for further information, updates, frequent promotions and discounts.

Cerro San Cristóbal (p55) Your one-stop shop for good clean fun is the Cerro San Cristóbal, which combines a modest zoo, two great outdoor swimming pools and a well-maintained playground with interesting transport – a creaky funicular. Toffee-apple vendors and fee-charging, photogenic llamas crowd the Bellavista entrance on weekends.

Museo Interactivo Mirador (MIM; Mirador Interactive Museum; ✐02-828-8000; www. mim.cl; Punta Arenas 6711, La Granja; adult/child CH$3900/2700, tickets half-price Wed; ⊙9:30am-6:30pm Tue-Sun; ♿; M Mirador) The stimulus is more intellectual (but still fun) at the Museo Interactivo Mirador. Forget 'do not touch': you can handle, push, lie on and even get inside most of the exhibits. Ages four and up.

Museo Artequín (✐02-681-8656; www.artequin.cl; Av Portales 3530; adult/child CH$1000/500; ⊙9am-5pm Tue-Fri, 11am-6pm Sat & Sun, closed Feb; ♿; M Quinta Normal) Education and entertainment come together at the Museo Artequín, a museum that showcases copies of famous artworks, hung at children's height in a striking cast-iron and glass structure that was once used as Chile's pavilion in the 1889 Paris Exhibition.

photography form the regularly changing temporary exhibitions.

Admission includes the **Museo Arqueológico de Santiago** (MAS; Santiago Archeological Museum), tucked away on the top floor. The low-lighted room with dark stone walls and floors makes an atmospheric backdrop for a small but quality collection of Diaguita, San Pedro and Molle ceramics, Mapuche jewelry and Easter Island carvings.

Parque Forestal   PARK
(Map p50; ⊕; Ⓜ Bellas Artes) On weekend afternoons, the temperature rises in Parque Forestal, a narrow green space wedged be-

tween Río Mapocho and Merced. The rest of the week it's filled with joggers and power walkers.

⊙ Bellavista

Tourists associate Bellavista with Pablo Neruda's house and the Virgin Mary statue looming over the city from the soaring hilltop park on Cerro San Cristóbal. For locals, Bellavista equals *carrete* (nightlife). Partying to the wee hours makes Bellavista's colorful streets and cobbled squares deliciously sleepy by day. Toss your map aside: the leafy residential streets east of Constitución are

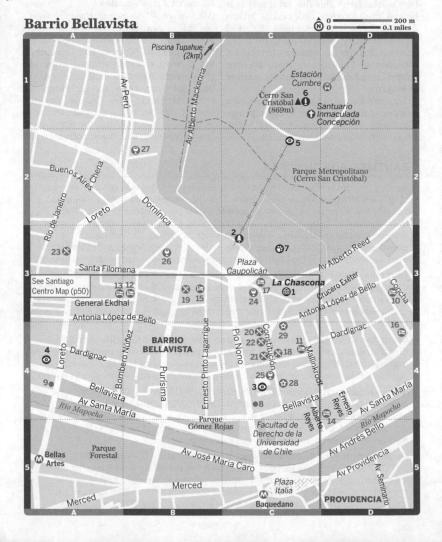

Barrio Bellavista

perfect for aimless wandering, while the graffitied blocks west of it are a photographer's paradise.

★La Chascona   HISTORIC BUILDING
(Map p54; ☑02-777-8741; www.fundacionneruda.org; Fernando Márquez de La Plata 0192; adult/student CH$5000/1500; ⊙10am-7pm Tue-Sun Jan & Feb, to 6pm Tue-Sun Mar-Dec; ⋈Baquedano) When poet Pablo Neruda needed a secret hideaway to spend time with his mistress Matilde Urrutia, he built La Chascona (loosely translated as 'messy hair'), the name inspired by her unruly curls. Neruda, of course, was a great lover of the sea, so the dining room is modeled on a ship's cabin and the living room on a lighthouse.

Audio tours (available in English, French, German, Portuguese and Spanish) take you through the history of the building and the collection of colored glass, shells, furniture and artwork by famous friends – sadly much more was lost when the house was ransacked during the dictatorship. The Fundación Neruda, which maintains Neruda's houses, has its headquarters here and runs a lovely cafe and gift shop. Book at least one day ahead using the online form or by calling directly.

Cerro San Cristóbal   PARK
(Map p54; www.parquemet.cl; Pío Nono 450; funicular train round-trip CH$2000; ⊙funicular train 10am-7pm Tue-Sun, 2-7pm Mon; ⊕; ⋈Baquedano)

The best sweeping views over Santiago are from the peaks and viewpoints of the Parque Metropolitano, better known as Cerro San Cristóbal. At 722 hectares, the park is Santiago's largest green space, but it's still decidedly urban: a funicular carries you between different landscaped sections, and roads through it are aimed at cars rather than hikers.

A snowy white 14m-high statue of the Virgen de la Inmaculada Concepción (Map p54) towers atop the *cumbre* (summit) at the Bellavista end of the park. The benches at its feet are the outdoor church where Pope John Paul II said mass in 1984. To get here, take a steep switchbacked dirt trail or the funicular train from Plaza Caupolicán (where you'll also find a tourist info kiosk).

Other attractions on the hillside include the National Zoo (p56); the Jardín Botánico Mapulemu, a botanical garden; the child-oriented Plaza de Juegos Infantiles Gabriela Mistral featuring attractive wooden playground equipment and an interactive water fountain; and two huge public swimming pools, the Piscina Tupahue and Piscina Antilén. The small but perfectly landscaped Jardín Japonés (Japanese Garden) is 400m east.

Near the top of the funicular is the Terraza Bellavista (Map p54) where there are a few snack stands and extraordinary views across the city. The park lies north of Bellavista and Providencia and has entrances in both neighborhoods.

Barrio Bellavista

Zoológico Nacional
ZOO

(National Zoo; Map p54; ☎02-730-1334; www.
parquemet.cl/zoologico-nacional; Parque Metropolitano; adult/child CH$3000/1500; ⊙10am-6pm
Tue-Sun; Ⓜ Baquedano) The dinky Zoológico
Nacional houses an aging bunch of neglected animals. It is, however, probably the
only place in Chile where you are assured
a glimpse of the pudú deer, Chile's national
animal. Note that the funicular stops at the
zoo on the way up, but not on the way down.

Patio Bellavista
BUILDING

(Map p54; www.patiobellavista.cl; Constitución
30-70, Bellavista; ⊙ 11am-2am Sun-Wed, 10am-4am
Thu-Sat; Ⓜ Baquedano) Upmarket eateries and
posh souvenir shops ranged around a huge
courtyard make up Patio Bellavista, a clear
attempt by developers to spruce up the Barrio Bellavista. Check the online schedule for
full listings and the schedule of live music
and theater performances.

◎ Barrio Brasil & Barrio Yungay

Toss aside the map, but don't forget your
camera – wandering through these slightly sleepy barrios west of the center is like
stepping back in time. Characterized by
vibrant street art, socialist students, crumbling old-fashioned houses, down-to-earth
outdoor markets and a range of hole-in-
the-wall ethnic eateries, these *barrios
históricos* (historic neighborhoods) offer a
charming counterpoint to the high-rise glitz
of Santiago's business sector. True, the area
is short on tourist sights and has a dodgy
reputation after dark – but a stroll through
the neighborhood offers a glimpse of faded
grandeur you're unlikely to find elsewhere
in the Chilean capital.

A spindly monkey-puzzle tree shades
Plaza Brasil, the green heart of the 'hood.
A wave of urban renovation is slowly
sweeping the surrounding streets, where
more and more bars and hip hostels are

Barrio Brasil

popping up. Incongruous among the car-parts shops between here and the Alameda is pint-sized **Barrio Concha y Toro**, featuring a gorgeous little square fed by cobblestone streets and overlooked by art deco and beaux arts mansions.

Museo de la Memoria y los Derechos Humanos   MUSEUM
(Museum of Memory & Human Rights; Map p56; ✆02-597-9600; www.museodelamemoria.cl; Matucana 501; ⊙10am-6pm Tue-Sun; ⓂQuinta Normal) **FREE** Opened in 2010, this museum isn't for the faint of heart: the exhibits expose the terrifying human rights violations and large-scale 'disappearances' that took place under Chile's military government between the years of 1973 and 1990.

There's no way around it – learning about the 40,000 victims subjected to torture and execution is positively chilling – but a visit to this carefully curated museum helps to contextualize Chile's tumultuous recent history.

Parque Quinta Normal   PARK
(Map p56; ⓂQuinta Normal) Strolls, picnics, pedal-boating, soccer kickabouts and soapbox rants are all popular activities at the 40-hectare Parque Quinta Normal, just west

Barrio Brasil

⊙ Sights

of Barrio Brasil. Several museums are also located here, though they're not up to the standard of the offerings elsewhere in the city.

Museo de Arte Contemporáneo Espacio Quinta Normal   MUSEUM
(Museum of Contemporary Art, Quinta Normal Branch; Map p56; ✆02-977-1741; www.mac.uchile.cl; Matucana 464; admission CH$600; ⊙11am-7pm Tue-Sat, 11am-6pm Sun; ⓂRicardo Cumming) This branch of the downtown Museo de Arte Contemporáneo specializes in offbeat and experimental exhibitions. It's housed in the **Palacio Versailles**, declared a national monument in 2004.

⊙ Barrio Estación Central

Museo de la Solidaridad Salvador Allende   MUSEUM
(Map p56; ✆02-689-8761; www.mssa.cl; Av República 475; admission CH$1000; ⊙10am-6pm Tue-Sun; ⓂRepública) Picasso, Miró, Tàpies and Matta are some of the artistic heavyweights who gave works to the Museo de la Solidaridad Salvador Allende. Begun as a populist art initiative during Allende's presidency – and named in his honor – the incredible collection was taken abroad during the dictatorship, where it became a symbol of Chilean resistance.

The 2000 works finally found a home in 2006, when the Fundación Allende bought and remodeled this grand old townhouse. The permanent collection sometimes goes on tour and is replaced by temporary exhibitions, and there's a darkened room with an eerie display of Allende's personal effects. Guided tours (email ahead) visit the basement, where you can see tangled telephone wires and torture instruments left over from when the house was used by the dictatorship's notorious DINA as a listening station.

Palacio Cousiño   PALACE
(✆02-698-5063; www.palaciocousino.co.cl; Dieciocho 438; admission on guided tour only; ⊙9:30am-1:30pm & 2:30-5pm Tue-Fri, 9:30am-1:30pm Sat & Sun, last tours leave an hour before closing; ⓂToesca) 'Flaunt it' seems to have been the main idea behind the shockingly lavish Palacio Cousiño. It was built between 1870 and 1878 by the prominent Cousiño-Goyenechea family after they'd amassed a huge fortune from winemaking and coal and silver mining, and it's a fascinating glimpse of how Chile's 19th-century elite lived. Carrara marble

columns, a half-tonne Bohemian crystal chandelier, Chinese cherrywood furniture, solid gold cutlery, and the first electrical fittings in Chile are just some of the ways they found to fritter away their fortune. Currently, only the grounds are open as the interior has been closed for restorations since the 2010 earthquake.

◉ Providencia

Head east from the Centro, and Santiago's neighborhoods slowly get swisher. First up: Providencia, a traditionally upper-middle-class area that's short on sights but very long indeed on drinking and dining possibilities. The '70s and '80s tower blocks along the area's main artery, Av Providencia, aren't aesthetically interesting, but the more residential side streets contain some lovely early-20th-century buildings.

Parque de las Esculturas Exhibition Hall
PARK

(Sculpture Park; Map p58; Av Santa María 2205; ◷ 10am-7:30pm; Ⓜ Pedro de Valdivia) FREE On the north side of the Río Mapocho lies a rare triumph in urban landscaping: the Parque de las Esculturas, a green stretch along the river decorated with 20 unique sculptures by noted Chilean artists.

Casa Museo Eduardo Frei Montalva
HISTORIC BUILDING

(☎ 02-881-8674; www.casamuseoeduardofrei.cl; Hindenburg 683; adult/child & senior CH$1300/700, free last Sun of every month; ◷ 10am-6pm Tue-Sun, closed Feb; Ⓜ Pedro de Valdivia) This historic former home of Chilean president Eduardo Frei Montalva (elected in 1964) holds a collection of his original furniture, textiles, paintings, glassware and cutlery alongside family photographs and mementos from his official travels.

Providencia

Las Condes, Barrio El Golf & Vitacura

Glittering skyscrapers, security-heavy apartment blocks and spanking-new malls: Las Condes is determined to be the international face of Chile's phenomenal economic growth. In addition to posh eateries and American chain restaurants, these ritzy neighborhoods also contain Santiago's most exclusive shopping street, Av Alonso de Córdova – not to mention a steady stream of business travelers who take up temporary residence in the area's gleaming high-rise hotels. The tongue-in-cheek nickname 'Sanhattan' is sometimes used to describe the financial district around the Costanera Center, about to be the tallest building in South America. As you'd expect, it lacks the soul of other Santiago neighborhoods, but delivers on fashion, shopping and good eats.

★ **Museo de la Moda** MUSEUM
(Museum of Fashion; ☑02-219-3632; www.museodelamoda.cl; Av Vitacura 4562; adult/student & senior/child CH$3500/2000/free, CH$1800 for all visitors on Wed & Sun; ⊙10am-6pm Tue-Fri, 11am-7pm Sat & Sun; Ⓜ Escuela Militar) This slick, privately operated fashion museum comprises a vast and exquisite permanent collection of

Western clothing – 20th-century designers are particularly well-represented.

Star attractions include John Lennon's jacket from 1966, the 'cone bra' Jean Paul Gaultier designed for Madonna and an evening gown donned by Lady Diana in 1981. Note, however, that only a fraction of items from the 10,000-piece collection are on display at any given time. Lighthearted temporary exhibits have ranged from a Michael Jackson tribute and a 'Back to the 80s' show to a *fútbol*-themed exhibit featuring athletic wear from the World Cup held in Chile in 1962. The airy on-site cafe is a fashionable spot for coffee or lunch.

From Escuela Militar metro, grab a taxi or take bus 305 from the west side of Américo Vespucio (you need a Bip! card) and get off at the intersection with Av Vitacura.

Parque Bicentenario PARK
(Bicentennial Park; Andrés Bello 2461; Ⓜ Tobalaba) This gorgeous urban oasis was created, as the name suggests, in celebration of the Chilean bicentennial. In addition to more than 4000 trees, a peaceful location alongside the Río Mapocho and access to city bike paths, the park features inviting chaise lounges and sun umbrellas, plus state-of-the-art playground equipment for kids.

It's a quick taxi ride from the Tobalaba metro station, or hop on bus 405 and get off at Alonso de Córdova. Keep walking in the direction of the bus until you turn onto Av Bicentenario, a few blocks from the park.

Costanera Center BUILDING
(Map p60; www.costaneracenter.cl; Andrés Bello 2461; Ⓜ Tobalaba) Financial woes have halted construction several times on this ambitious ongoing project slated to be fully operational in 2015. The four skyscrapers that make up the Costanera Center include **Gran Torre Santiago**, the tallest building in South America (300m). The towers contain luxury apartments, a high-end hotel, a shopping mall and a food court with panoramic views.

🏃 Activities

Swimming

There are fabulous views from the two huge, open-air pools atop Cerro San Cristóbal, **Piscina Tupahue** (☑02-732-0998; Cerro San Cristóbal s/n; adult/child CH$6000/3500; ⊙10am-7:30pm Tue-Sun Nov-Mar; Ⓜ Baquedano) and **Piscina Antilén** (Map p60; ☑02-732-0998; Cerro San Cristóbal s/n; adult/child CH$7500/4000;

SANTIAGO ACTIVITIES

Las Condes

See Providencia Map (p58)

Las Condes

⊙ Sights
1 Costanera Center A3

✪ Activities, Courses & Tours
2 Piscina Antilén.................................. A1

🛏 Sleeping
3 Ritz-Carlton C3
4 W Santiago...C3

✪ Eating
5 Café Melba..B3
6 Dominó..B3

🍷 Drinking & Nightlife
7 Flannery's B3

🛍 Shopping
8 Andesgear...B3
El Mundo del Vino ....(see 4)

⊙10am-7:30pm Tue-Sun Nov-Mar; MBaquedano). Both are more for splashing about than serious training.

Centro Deportivo Providencia SWIMMING
(☎02-341-4790; www.cdprovidencia.cl; Santa Isabel 0830; day pass CH$5000-7000; ⊙6:30am-10pm Mon-Fri, 9am-6pm Sat & Sun) You can do your lengths year-round at this 25m indoor pool in Providencia.

Walking, Running & Cycling
Locals run, walk and cycle along the Río Mapocho (especially through the Parque Forestal), in Parque Quinta Normal and along the steep roads of Cerro San Cristóbal. In town on the first Tuesday of the month? Join the crowds of cyclists who cruise through the city on two wheels, part of the **Movimiento Furiosos Ciclistas** (Furious Bikers Movement; www.furiosos.cl). Check in with La Bicicleta Verde for more information.

★ **La Bicicleta Verde** GUIDED TOUR
(Map p54; ☎02-570-9338; www.labicicletaverde.
cl; Loreto 6; bike tours from CH$18,000, rentals per
hr/full-day CH$2000/15,000; ⓂBellas Artes) You
can rent bikes and helmets here or choose
from highly recommended guided tours like
Bike at Night (CH$30,000).

🥢 Courses

Although Santiago isn't the cheapest place
to kick-start your Spanish, these language
schools have excellent reputations. Consider a homestay with a Chilean family to
really supercharge your learning. Check at
the Universidad de Chile for language ex-
changes and potential guerrilla learning
opportunities.

Universidad de Chile LANGUAGE COURSE
(Map p50; www.uchile.cl; O'Higgins 1058; Ⓜ Universidad de Chile) Check at the Universidad de
Chile Santiago campuses for language ex-
changes and potential guerrilla learning opportunities. The main campus on O'Higgins
houses the International Relations program.

**Escuela de Idiomas Violeta
Parra/Tandem Santiago** LANGUAGE COURSE
(Map p58; ☎ 02-236-4241; www.tandemsantiago.
cl; Triana 863, Providencia; enrollment fee US$55,
hour-long course US$22, 20-hour course US$180;
ⓂSalvador) Combines an outstanding aca-
demic record with a friendly vibe and cultural activities. Accommodations (optional)
are in shared or private apartments. Check
the website for special courses like 'Spanish
for Lawyers' or 'Medical Spanish.'

Natalislang LANGUAGE COURSE
(Map p50; ☎ 02-222-8685; www.natalislang.com;
Arturo Bürhle 047, Centro; intensive 3-day traveler
crash course from CH$135,000; ⓂBaquedano)
Great for quick, intense courses. The website
has an extensive list of options.

**Instituto Británico
de Cultura** LANGUAGE COURSE
(Map p50; ☎800-387-900; www.britanico.cl;
Huérfanos 554, Centro; ⓂSanta Lucía) Quali-
fied English teachers may find work at this
language school.

🕵 Tours

A few companies offer free walking tours in
English that take in the city's central tourist
sights. Guides work for tips only, so travelers
are encouraged to offer them some gratuity
for the service. For excellent tours on two

PARQUE POR LA PAZ

During Chile's last dictatorship some
4500 political prisoners were tortured
and 266 were executed at Villa Grimaldi
by the now-disbanded DINA (National
Intelligence Directorate). The com-
pound was razed to conceal evidence
in the last days of Pinochet's dictatorship – no doubt to conceal evidence of
torture – but since the return of democracy it has been turned into a powerful
memorial park known as **Parque por
la Paz** (☎02-292-5229; www.villagrimal-
di.cl; Av José Arrieta 8401, Peñalolén;
⊙10am-6pm).

Each element of the park symbolizes
one aspect of the atrocities that went on
there and visits here are fascinating but
harrowing – be sensitive about taking
pictures as other visitors may be former
detainees or family members. Check
the website ahead of time to arrange a
guided tour. Take Transantiago bus D09
(you need a Bip! card) from right outside the Av Vespucio exit of Plaza Egaña
metro station; it drops you opposite.

wheels, try the cycling tours offered by La
Bicicleta Verde.

Tours 4 Tips TOUR
(Map p50; www.tours4tips.com; Parque Forestal
s/n; ⊙departs 10am & 3pm; ⓂBellas Artes) Following the free tour model (tip just what you
think they deserve), this operation has tours
departing from in front of the Museo de Bellas Artes daily at 10am and 3pm – the guides
wear red-and-white-striped Where's Waldo
(Wally) gear. The morning tour focuses on
off-beat Santiago, while in the afternoon you
just get the highlights.

Free Tour Santiago WALKING TOUR
(Map p50; ☎ cell 9236-8789; www.freetoursan-
tiago.cl; Catedral Metropolitana, Plaza de Armas;
⊙departs 10am & 3pm; ⓂPlaza de Armas) A free
four-hour walking tour of downtown Santiago: guides work for tips only, so be prepared
to offer gratuity. No booking necessary, just
look for the guides wearing red shirts in
front of Catedral Metropolitana (p48).

Spicy Chile WALKING TOUR
(Map p50; ☎ cell 9821-3026; www.spicychile.cl;
⊙departs 10am & 2pm Mon-Sat; ⓂLa Moneda)
The main tour leaves from a meeting spot

outside Palacio de la Moneda. The guides wear green shirts. Check online for alternative tours that depart from the Patronato and República metro stations.

Enotour TOUR
(Map p54; ☑02-481-4081; www.enotourchile.com; Patio Bellavista, Constitución 30-70; CH$20,000-39,000; Ⓜ Baquedano) Head out for intoxicating group tastings at the nearby Maipo, Casablanca and Colchagua Valleys on one- or two-day excursions. The guides all specialize in wine and gastronomy.

Santiago Adventures TOUR
(☑022-244-2750; www.santiagoadventures.com) Savvy English-speaking tour guides lead personalized tours covering Santiago's food and wine, day trips to the coast and throughout Chile.

Turistik BUS TOUR
(Map p50; ☑02-820-1000; www.viajesturistik.com; Plaza de Armas s/n, Municipal Tourist Office; day pass from CH$20,000; ⊘9:30am-6pm; Ⓜ Plaza de Armas) Hop-on, hop-off double-decker bus tours run to 12 stops between the Centro district and Parque Arauco mall. Check the online map for further information.

✺ Festivals & Events

Summer brings free concerts and plenty of events to the city's parks. Check out **El Mercurio** (www.elmercurio.cl), **Estoy** (www.estoy.cl)

WORTH A TRIP

CEMENTERIO GENERAL

More than just a graveyard, Santiago's **Cementerio General** (www.cementeriogeneral.cl; Av Profesor Alberto Zañartu 951; ⊘8:30am-6pm; Ⓜ Cementerios) is a veritable city of tombs, many adorned with works by famous local sculptors. The names above the crypts read like a who's who of Chilean history: its most tumultuous moments are attested to by Salvador Allende's tomb and the **Memorial del Detenido Desaparecido y del Ejecutado Político**, a memorial to the 'disappeared' of Pinochet's dictatorship.

To reach the memorial from the main entrance, walk down Av Lima, turning right into Horvitz for another 200m; it's over the bridge to the right.

---

and **The Santiago Times** (www.santiagotimes.cl) for events.

Santiago a Mil THEATER
(www.fundacionteatroamil.cl/santiago-a-mil) This major theater festival draws experimental companies from all over the world to the stages of Santiago each January.

Festival Nacional del Folklore MUSIC
(www.sanbernardo.cl) In the southern suburb of San Bernardo, this five-day festival in late January celebrates traditional Chilean music, culture, dance and food.

Fiesta del Vino WINE
(www.fiestadelvinodepirque.cl) This early April wine festival in Pirque, one of many taking place around Santiago during harvest time, also features traditional cuisine and folkloric music.

Rodeo Season RODEO
(www.rodeochileno.cl) In Chile, March is all about *huasos* (cowboys) and bucking broncos. The focus of the action is Rancagua (p112), 145km south of Santiago, but events also take place in Santiago.

Lollapalooza Chile MUSIC
(www.lollapaloozacl.com) The famous music festival now has a Chilean edition; national and international acts roll into Santiago, generally sometime in March.

Santiago Festival Internacional de Cine FILM
(SANFIC; www.sanfic.com) Each August, Santiago's weeklong film festival showcases choice independent cinema throughout several movie theaters.

Festival de Jazz de Ñuñoa MUSIC
(www.ccn.cl) Free concerts that showcase jazz and blues from some of Chile's top musicians take place at the Teatro Municipal de Ñuñoa over a weekend in August. The theater's summer festival takes place in January, featuring music, dance and more (for free).

Feria Internacional de Artesanía ART
Talented craftspeople show off their creations each November in Parque Bustamente, Providencia.

Feria Internacional del Libro BOOKS
(www.camlibro.cl) Scores of publishing houses and authors from throughout the Spanish-speaking world move into the Estación Mapocho and set up in the last week of November.

ART GALLERY HOP

Ground zero for the exhibition of contemporary Chilean art – and a choice spot to observe a fashionable crowd of Santiaguinos in their natural habitat – is the gallery circuit around Alonso de Córdova. Drop by one of these art spaces for an opening to see the champagne-fueled scene at its most happening. Check the galleries' websites for upcoming events and times.

Galería Animal (☎02-371-9090; www.galeriaanimal.com; Nueva Costanera 3731) Edgy contemporary works in a stunning multilevel space.

La Sala Galería de Arte (www.galerialasala.cl; Alonso de Córdova 2700) Featuring the photography, sculpture and painting of rising Chilean artists.

Galería Isabel Aninat (☎02-481-9870; www.galeriaisabelaninat.cl; Espoz 3100) Since 1983, this well-known gallery has exhibited the works of major Chilean and international artists, including Joan Miró and Antoni Gaudí.

🛏 Sleeping

Santiago's unique neighborhoods provide the backdrop for your stay. For easy access to museums and restaurants, consider the Centro, budget-friendly Barrio Brasil or nightlife districts like classy Barrios Lastarria and raucous Bellavista. For fancier digs and sophisticated dining – but limited access to most major sights – head to leafy Providencia or high-lofting Las Condes. For longer stays, consider renting a furnished apartment. **Contact Chile** (☎02-264-1719; www.contactchile.cl) is a reliable rental service, while **Augustina Suites** (Map p50; ☎02-710-7422; www.augustinasuite.cl; Huérfanos 1400 Oficina 106B, Centro; apt from US$59; 🛜🖥; Ⓜ Santa Ana) provides furnished mini-apartments that are well situated in the Centro.

🛏 Centro

Hostel Plaza de Armas   HOSTEL $
(Map p50; ☎02-671-4436; www.plazadearmashostel.com; Compañía de Jesus 960, Apt 607, Plaza de Armas; dm CH$6000-10,000, d CH$24,000, d without bathroom CH$20,000; @🛜; Ⓜ Plaza de Armas) You'll think you're in the wrong place when you show up to this busy apartment building on Santiago's main square. Take the elevator to the 6th floor to reach the suprisingly cheery hostel that sports tiny dorms, a well-equipped communal kitchen, and great balconies with views over the Plaza de Armas. All in all, it's a solid budgeteers' buy.

Ecohostel   HOSTEL $
(Map p50; ☎02-222-6833; www.ecohostel.cl; General Jofré 349B, Barrio Estación Central; dm/ s/d without bathroom CH$8000/15,000/21,000;

@🛜; Ⓜ Universidad Católica) 🖊 Backpackers and families looking to chill love this hostel's personalized service, cozy couches and sunny patio (complete with hammock). Six- and eight-bed dorms in the converted old house can be dark, but bunks and lockers are both big and there are plenty of well-divided bathrooms. There's a women's-only dorm.

Located on a quiet street in the Barrio Estación Central, it's a bit of a jaunt to the nightlife.

Hotel Plaza Londres   HOTEL $
(Map p50; ☎02-633-3320; Londres 35; s/d/tr CH$25,000/35,000/40,000; ❄🛜; Ⓜ Universidad de Chile) At the end of quiet cobblestoned Calle Londres, this simple hotel has modernish '70s-style rooms with non-sequitur pictures of private jets and other odds-and-ends. The worn, slightly raggedy colonial building is not without its charms, and there's some decent modern art scattered through the hallways.

Hostal Río Amazonas   GUESTHOUSE $$
(Map p50; ☎02-635-1631; www.hostalrioamazonas.cl; Av Vicuña Mackenna 47; s/d CH$25,000/ 40,000; @🛜; Ⓜ Baquedano) A great choice for those looking for the social life of a hostel without having to share a room. This long-running guesthouse in a mock-Tudor mansion has bright rooms, a big terrace and modern shared kitchen.

Hotel Vegas   HOTEL $$
(Map p50; ☎02-632-2498; www.hotelvegas.net; Londres 49; s/d CH$44,500/54,400; 🅿❄@🛜; Ⓜ Universidad de Chile) There's a vintage twist to the grand old rooms at the Hotel Vegas: think a collision of the ages with wood paneling, beige bathrooms and lime green

BARRIO RECOLETA

Bustling Korean eateries and Middle Eastern takeaway counters, a happening marketplace overflowing with ripe fruit, a colorful jumble of street vendors, an achingly hip cocktail lounge – this burgeoning barrio just west of Bellavista is a slight detour off the beaten path. Here are a few spots you shouldn't miss.

Patronato (Map p54; bordered by Recoleta, Loreto, Bellavista & Dominica ; Ⓜ Patronato) This barrio within a barrio, roughly bordered by Recoleta, Loreto, Bellavista and Dominica streets, is the heart of Santiago's immigrant communities, particularly Koreans, Chinese and Arabs. The colorful, slightly run-down blocks are lined with antique buildings and illuminated by neon signs; a soundtrack of cumbia always seems to keep the beat in the background. Come to poke around the bare-bones ethnic supermarkets, feast on street food, or wander through the clothing market to watch the locals haggling over *quinceañera* (15th birthday) dresses and Chinese slippers.

La Vega Central (Map p50; www.lavega.cl; cnr Nueva Rengifo & López de Bello; ⊙6am-6pm Mon-Sat, 6am-3pm Sun; Ⓜ Patronato) Raspberries, quinces, figs, peaches, persimmons, custard apples…if it grows in Chile you'll find it at La Vega Central, which is bordered by Dávila Baeza, Nueva Rengifo, López de Bello and Salas. Go early to see the hollering vendors in full swing.

Vietnam Discovery (Map p54; ☎02-737-2037; www.vietnamdiscovery.cl; Loreto 324; mains CH$4800-7600; ⊙lunch & dinner Sun-Fri, lunch Sat; ☏; Ⓜ Patronato) Hip Santiaguinos were already lined up around the block when a French-Thai couple opened this intimate eatery. It's a young, stylish twist on the barrio's traditional ethnic restaurant, serving inspired Thai and Vietnamese dishes. Book ahead, using the online form, or you'll never see the inside.

Restobar KY (Map p54; www.restobarky.cl; Av Perú 631; ⊙Tue-Sun; Ⓜ Cerro Blanco) Taking inspiration from the barrio's Southeast Asian flavor is this stunning cocktail bar. The photographer owner has done wonders with a rambling old house – the interior is otherworldly, glowing with Chinese lanterns and the soft light of antique chandeliers, and filled with a fascinating mix of vintage chairs, exotic plants, carved wooden furnishings and vibrant artwork.

accents, all within the confines of a colonial-inspired building. The rooms are clean and large – some even sport sitting areas – though the beds can be spongy and bowed.

Hotel Galerías HOTEL **$$$**
(Map p50; ☎02-470-7400; www.hotelgalerias.cl; San Antonio 65; s/d CH$78,000/88,000; ❄@ 🔊🏊🛗; Ⓜ Santa Lucía) This hotel is certainly proud to be Chilean: mock *moai* (Easter Island statues) guard the entrance, the restaurant specializes in regional cuisine and the simple but well-appointed rooms are accented with traditional weavings and hardwood furniture. Thanks to the outdoor swimming pool and the fact that kids under 10 stay free with their parents, it's also a solid family pick.

Hotel Plaza San Francisco LUXURY HOTEL **$$$**
(Map p50; ☎02-639-3832; www.plazasanfrancisco.cl; O'Higgins 816; d CH$91,500; ❄@🔊🏊; Ⓜ Universidad de Chile) With an oak-paneled reception, hunting prints and sober maroon and mustard furnishings in the rooms, this hotel is angling for the English drawing-room look. The impeccably mannered staff are a match for any butler, the fitness center is convenient and the buffet breakfast and on-site restaurant are excellent, but overall the place feels overdue for some updates.

🏨 Barrio Lastarria & Barrio Bellas Artes

Andes Hostel & Apartments HOSTEL **$**
(Map p50; ☎02-632-9990; www.andeshostel.com; Monjitas 506; dm CH$15,100-16,400, d with/without bathroom CH$55,700/39,000, apt CH$72,200; @🔊🏊; Ⓜ Bellas Artes) Pistachio-colored walls, a zebra-print rug, mismatched retro sofas and a mosaic-tiled bar are some of the pop-art charms of this centrally located hostel. The four- and six-bed dorms can get a bit hot on summer nights. It's worth splashing out more for an Andes apartment on the next block if you've got a group.

Hostal Forestal HOSTEL $
(Map p50; ☑ 02-638-1347; www.hostalforestal.cl; Coronel Santiago Bueras 120; dm CH$6500-8000, s without bathroom $18,000, d with/without bathroom CH$27,000/22,000; @🛜; Ⓜ Baquedano) This hostel wins big on location, but feels just a little worn, with dorms that are dark and slightly run-down. You do get a shared kitchen, a pool table and a great central locale.

Lastarria 43 APARTMENT $$
(Map p50; ☑ 02-638-3230; www.apartmentsantiago.cl; Lastarria 43; studio CH$38,000-45,000, 3-6 person apt CH$75,000-92,000; 🛜🛁; Ⓜ Universidad Católica) On a quiet street at the entrance to the Lastarria neighborhood, these studios and apartments are a great value for families. You'll miss the common areas of most hotels, but the furnished apartments with upscale amenities offer a chance at high-flying Santiago condo living. Unlike other apartment rentals, they offer a daily cleaning service.

The Singular BOUTIQUE HOTEL $$$
(Map p50; ☑ 02-306-8810; www.thesingular.com; Merced 294, Lastarria; r from US$250; 🅿❄🛜🏊; Ⓜ Universidad Católica) Setting new standards for boutique luxury, this standout in the heart of the Lastarria neighborhood is sharp, refined, thoughtful and, well, singular. The large rooms feature eclectic furniture and artwork, and will appeal to even the most discerning fashionista. The pool and spa bookend the hotel top to bottom.

Hotel Boutique Lastarria BOUTIQUE HOTEL $$$
(Map p50; ☑ 02-840-3700; www.lastarriahotel.com; Coronel Santiago Bueras 188; r US$279-339, ste US$369-399; ❄🛜🏊; Ⓜ Bellas Artes) Even though it sets a pretty high mark, we still feel this 14-room boutique hotel is a bit overpriced. Reasons to stay here: a ridiculously lush pool in the back garden, vaulted-ceiling rooms with travertine tiles, modern-classic furnishings and plenty of space to move around, plus a small gym and about the most ideal location you could imagine.

🛏 Bellavista

La Chimba HOSTEL $
(Map p54; ☑ 02-735-8978; www.lachimba.com; Ernesto Pinto Lagarrigue 262; dm CH$11,000, s/d CH$24,000/36,000, without bathroom CH$18,000/30,000; @🛜; Ⓜ Baquedano) A massive mural announces your arrival at this Bellavista party hostel. There's a cooled-

out '50s-style throwback lounge perfectly mismatched with a glowing chandelier and other odds and ends that span the decades. The rooms feel punk-rock beat – it's a bit grungy, but quite flavorful. And you'll love swapping stories at the rambling back plaza.

Nomades Hostel HOSTEL $
(Map p54; ☑ 02-789-7600; Bellavista 0318; dm/s CH$10,000/18,000, d with/without bathroom CH$36,000/27,000; Ⓜ Baquedano) Mod-deco design meets old-time architectural elegance in this Bellavista hostel. There's excellent art throughout, a cool outside patio and a gorgeous shared kitchen that plays center stage. The dorms sleep five.

Bellavista Hostel HOSTEL $
(Map p54; ☑ 02-899-7145; www.bellavistahostel.com; Dardignac 0184; dm CH$12,000, s/d without bathroom CH$18,000/30,000; @🛜; Ⓜ Baquedano) This highly social hostel is a Bellavista classic. Brightly painted walls crammed with colorful paintings and graffiti announce the relaxed, arty vibe. There's a super cool terrace and two kitchens. We only wish it was a bit cleaner. The city's best bars and clubs are on your doorstep and so, sometimes, are their clients. If you aren't staying out late, sleep in the annex or look elsewhere.

Hostal Caracol HOSTEL $
(Map p54; ☑ 02-732-4644; www.caracolsantiago.cl; General Ekdhal 151; dm CH$9000-10,000, d from CH$30,000; @🛜; Ⓜ Patronato) Clean and modern (but empty and uncaring), this hostel has darned decent dorm rooms rambling over three stories. There's a shared kitchen and a terrace for guests to hang.

Hostal del Barrio Bellavista HOSTEL $
(Map p54; ☑ 02-732-0598; hostal.del.barrio@gmail.com; General Ekdhal 159; dm/d CH$10,000/25,000; 🛜; Ⓜ Patronato) We like that the shared rooms sleep just three or four people, but the lack of good common areas (and any real traveler scene) may make this a second-tier option for most.

★ Hotel Boutique Tremo BOUTIQUE HOTEL $$
(Map p54; ☑ 02-732-4882; www.tremohotel.cl; Alberto Reyes 32; r CH$67,000; 🛜; Ⓜ Baquedano) For those looking for a boutique experience on a realistic budget, this is your best bet. The lovely converted mansion on a quiet Bellavista street has a terrific patio lounge, fresh art deco stylings, top-tier service and a cooled-out air.

A spiraling stairway takes you to the high-ceilinged rooms, which are bathed in white, and feature minimalist Scandanavian design sensibilities, some funky art and modern bathrooms.

Bellavista Home B&B $$

(Map p54; 📞02-247-3598; www.bellavista-home.cl; Capellán Abarzúa 143; s/d CH$35,000/45,000, s/d/tr without bathroom CH$25,000/40,000/55,000; @🛜🚍🛗; Ⓜ️Baquedano) This four-room B&B, housed inside an antique building that once contained artists' workshops, is a tranquil and family-friendly respite from the *carrete* and crowds of Bellavista. Breezy rooms are outfitted with pristine white linens, colorful throw rugs and brightly painted wooden doors. Make your reservations well in advance.

All guests have kitchen access; an adorable breakfast and round-the-clock coffee and tea can be enjoyed on the pretty garden patio.

The Aubrey Hotel LUXURY HOTEL $$$

(Map p54; 📞02-940-2800; www.theaubrey.com; Constitución 299-317; d from US$250, ste US$450-550; ❄️@🛜🚍; Ⓜ️Baquedano) Redefining sophistication, this transformed Spanish-style patrician mansion dating from 1926 is the best luxury boutique in Santiago. True standout features include the lovely (and well-heated) outdoor swimming pool, tech-forward lighting throughout, romantic alfresco dining at the on-site Italian restaurant and the stunning location at the foot of Cerro San Cristóbal.

The fusion between art deco, contempo and classic design will entrance as you pass through the common areas to the well-appointed rooms. Customize your experience with a quick chat with the on-call concierge.

Barrio Brasil & Barrio Yungay

Happy House Hostel HOSTEL $

(Map p56; 📞02-688-4849; www.happyhousehostel.com; Moneda 1829; dm/s/d without bathroom CH$10,000/23,000/30,000, s/d CH$36,000/40,000; @🛜🚍; Ⓜ️Los Héroes) The best hostel in Barrio Brasil is happy news for weary travelers. This 1910 mansion has a fabulous molded ceiling, funky modern touches and non-sequitur art deco stylings. There's a pool, bar and patio out back, a few stories of dorm rooms and definitely worthwhile private rooms.

La Casa Roja HOSTEL $

(Map p56; 📞02-696-4241; www.lacasaroja.cl; Agustinas 2113; dm CH$8000-10,000, d with/without bathroom CH$32,000/28,000; @🛜🚍; Ⓜ️Ricardo Cumming) With its swimming pool, airy patios, outdoor bar, garden and a huge, well-designed kitchen, it's easy to see why this Aussie-owned outfit is backpacker central. Serious socializing isn't the only appeal: the sweeping staircases and sky-high molded ceilings of this lovingly restored 19th-century mansion ooze character.

Especially great value are the doubles, fitted with stylish retro furniture and bijoux bathrooms.

Providencia

Castillo Surfista Hostel HOSTEL $

(📞02-893-3350; www.castillosurfista.com; Maria Luisa Santander 0329; dm CH$8500, d without bathroom CH$21,400-25,400; @🛜; Ⓜ️Baquedano) Off the beaten path and run by a California surfer, this renovated house features homey dorms and doubles, tidy communal areas and laid-back hosts who can help you access the surf scene – the owner even runs daylong surf trips to lesser-known breaks and arranges Wicked camper rentals if you want to venture to the beaches alone.

Intiwasi Hotel BOUTIQUE HOTEL $$

(Map p58; 📞02-985-5285; www.intiwasihotel.com; Josue Smith Solar 380, Providencia; r US$85-90; ❄️@🛜; Ⓜ️Los Leones) This cozy, centrally located hotel is more like a boutique hostel for grown-ups. The proud owners are eager to help you plan your travels, and the look is native Chilean – Intiwasi means 'house of the sun' in Quechua – with indigenous textiles, dark wood and bright hues of red and orange throughout. Rooms have private bathrooms and LCD televisions.

Hotel Orly LUXURY HOTEL $$$

(Map p58; 📞02-630-3000; www.orlyhotel.com; Av Pedro de Valdivia 027, Providencia; s/d US$145/165, apt US$145; 🅿️❄️@🛜; Ⓜ️Pedro de Valdivia) This stately (and rather staid) hotel has a lovely glassed-in terrace. The look is classic, with dark wood furnishings, crisp white linens and heavy maroon drapes. There's coffee, tea and cake available all day in the breakfast room. Families might consider the Orly's 12 apartments down the block; service includes breakfast at the hotel.

Las Condes, Barrio El Golf & Vitacura

W Santiago
LUXURY HOTEL $$$
(Map p60; ☑02-770-0000; www.starwoodhotels. com; Isidora Goyenechea 3000, Las Condes; r from US$269; P❈@🛜🏊; MEl Golf) Fashion forward, high energy, decadent and sexy, the W Santiago offers everything you would expect from this international chain – parties, drop-in fashion shows, outrageously good restaurants, bumping nightclubs, celebs and plenty of beautiful people. The sleek guest rooms and suites feature floor-to-ceiling views, and all the modern tech-friendly amenities you could imagine.

Nonguests should consider dining or partying here. Choose from several bars and the raucous discoteque, or dine on French, Japanese fusion or Chilean at the terrace bistro. Guests love the rooftop pool and 3rd-floor spa.

Ritz-Carlton
LUXURY HOTEL $$$
(Map p60; ☑02-470-8500; www.ritzcarlton.com/santiago; El Alcalde 15; r from US$398; ❈@🛜🏊; MEl Golf) A glittering symbol of Chile's soaring economy, the Ritz is the luxury choice in Santiago. Detail is what it does best: the king-sized beds have Egyptian cotton sheets and deliciously comfortable mattresses, and there's even a menu of bath treatments.

The jewel in the crown is the top-floor health club and pool, with a vaulted glass roof that means you can swim beneath the stars. If you prefer liquid treats that come in a glass, the bar's novelty pisco sours are legendary.

Eating

More than ever before, Santiago is a foodie wonderland. In recent years, the arrival of creative restaurateurs from Peru, Argentina and Europe has added extra flair to the city's already excellent restaurant scene, and while traditional Chilean seafood still reigns supreme, modern Peruvian and Japanese are also having a moment, as is sophisticated cafe fare.

The best high-end restaurants are concentrated in Lastarria, Bellavista and Providencia – you can sample many of them for less by going for midweek set lunch menus. More classic Chilean food experiences include cheap and cheerful seafood lunches at the central fish market, empanadas from takeaway counters around the city and *completos* (hot dogs piled high with avocado) at downtown diners.

Centro

A good bet for a midday meal is one of the Centro's vintage *fuente de sodas* (soda fountains), atmospheric diner-style eateries where businessmen feast on sandwiches and Chilean comfort food. At night, you'll find better cuisine elsewhere in the city.

★ Mercado Central
SEAFOOD $
(Central Market; Map p50; www.mercadocentral.cl; cnr 21 de Mayo & San Pablo; ⊙food stands & restaurants 9am-5pm Mon-Fri, 7am-3:30pm Sat & Sun; MPuente Cal y Canto) Santiago's wrought-iron fish market is a classic for seafood lunches (and hangover-curing fish stews like the tomato- and potato-based *caldillo de congrio,* Pablo Neruda's favorite). Skip the touristy restaurants in the middle and head for one of the tiny low-key stalls around the market's periphery.

Bar Nacional
CHILEAN $
(Map p50; Huérfanos 1151; mains CH$3400-5500; ⊙9am-11pm Mon-Sat; MPlaza de Armas) From the chrome counter to the waitstaff of old-timers, this *fuente de soda* is as vintage as they come. It has been churning out Chilean specialties like *lomo a lo pobre* (steak and fries topped with fried egg) for years. To save a buck (or a few hundred pesos) ask for the sandwich menu.

El Naturista
VEGETARIAN $
(Map p50; www.elnaturista.cl; Huérfanos 1046; mains CH$3400-5000; ⊙9am-10pm Mon-Sat; 🖋; MPlaza de Armas) A downtown vegetarian classic, El Naturista does simple but filling soups, sandwiches, salads, tarts and fresh-squeezed juices, plus light breakfasts and fruit-infused ice cream. There's another location nearby at Moneda 846.

Empanadas Zunino
BAKERY $
(Map p50; www.empanadaszunino.cl; Puente 801; empanadas CH$650-800; ⊙9am-5pm Mon-Sun; MPuente Cal y Canto) Founded in the 1930s, this classic bakery makes fantastic empanadas – Chilean food journalists recently awarded it second place in a contest for the best empanadas in Santiago.

Bar Nacional 2
CHILEAN $
(Map p50; Bandera s/n; mains CH$3400-5500; ⊙9am-11pm Mon-Sat; MPlaza de Armas) The

Bar Nacional is so popular it has two nearby downtown locations for Chilean food and traditional fare.

Fast-Food Stands   CHILEAN $
(Map p50; Portal Fernández Concha; items CH$500-2000; ⊙ 9am-9pm Mon-Sat; Ⓜ Plaza de Armas) Some of the cheapest meals in town come from the string of food stands that line the Portal Fernández Concha, the arcade along the north side of Plaza de Armas. Supersized empanadas, *completos* and pizza slices are the staples here, day and night.

Barrio Lastarria & Barrio Bellas Artes

These stylish neighborhoods boast some of the city's culinary hot spots, not to mention a range of contemporary cafes, several ethnic eateries and a wealth of lovely sidewalk tables for dining alfresco.

Sur Patagónico   CHILEAN $
(Map p50; Lastarria 92; mains CH$6900-7700; ⊙ noon-11pm Mon-Sat; Ⓜ Universidad Católica) Service is notoriously slow here, but if you can score one of the pretty sidewalk tables on this well-traveled corner, you might not mind – the people-watching is fantastic, especially if you have a cold Chilean microbrew in hand.

The steamed mussels are ideal for sharing; more substantial Patagonian-inspired options range from mushroom risotto to steak and lamb seared on the *parrilla* (grill). Indoors, you'll find a pleasantly rustic dining room resembling an antique general store.

Tambo   PERUVIAN $
(Map p50; www.tambochile.cl; Lastarria 65; mains CH$5500-7700; ⊙ noon-11pm Mon-Sat; Ⓜ Universidad Católica) Occupying a prime spot along one of Lastarria's most scenic passages, this contemporary Peruvian eatery offers spicy twists on dishes and drinks that Chileans have since adopted – go ahead, taste-test the fantastic ceviche. Kick off your sampling from the other side of the border with a delicious *maracuyá* (passion fruit) pisco sour.

Café Bistro de la Barra   CAFE $
(Map p50; JM de la Barra 455; sandwiches CH$3500-7000; ⊙ 9am-9:30pm Mon-Fri, 10am-9:30pm Sat & Sun; 🖉; Ⓜ Bellas Artes) Worn old floor tiles, a velvet sofa, 1940s swing and light fittings made from cups and teapots make a quirky-but-pretty backdrop for some of the best brunches and *onces* (afternoon tea) in town. The rich sandwiches include salmon-filled croissants or Parma ham and arugula on flaky green-olive bread, but make sure you save room for the berry-drenched cheesecake.

Emporio La Rosa   ICE CREAM $
(Map p50; www.emporiolarosa.com; Merced 291; ice cream CH$900-1800, salads & sandwiches CH$2500-3900; ⊙ 9am-11pm Mon-Sat; 🖉; Ⓜ Bellas Artes) Choco-chili, rose petal and strawberry and black pepper are some of the fabulous flavors of this extra-creamy handmade ice cream, which has been known to cause addiction. Flaky *pains au chocolat* and squishy focaccia sandwiches are two more reasons to plonk yourself at the chrome tables.

Opera   FRENCH $$
(Map p50; 🖉 02-664-3048; www.operacatedral. cl; Merced 395; mains CH$9200-12,000; ⊙ 1-3:30pm & 8-11pm Mon-Fri, 8pm-midnight Sat; Ⓜ Bellas Artes) From the first mouthful of foie gras to the last smear of crème brûlée, the food at Opera bears the mark of classic French cooking, but it's made with the best Chilean ingredients. Hefty mains include lamb shank in a Cabernet reduction or the perfectly pink veal ribchop in a buttery béarnaise sauce. The upstairs sister bar, Catedral, does simpler but equally excellent food. The stunning antique corner building is a national historic landmark.

Bellavista

Bellavista is a hot spot for eating and drinking around the clock. Restaurants fit into a few categories: family-run classics that have been popular with locals for years, posh new eateries that come and go along Constitución and Dardignac, and finally, on Pío Nono, the rough-and-ready staples that sustain young people through nights of drinking with inexpensive empanadas, pizza slices, *completos* and sandwiches.

Galindo   CHILEAN $
(Map p54; www.galindo.cl; Dardignac 098; mains CH$2800-5800; ⊙ noon-11pm Mon-Sat; Ⓜ Baquedano) Retro neon signs adorn the wood-backed bar at this long-running local favorite, usually packed with noisy but appreciative crowds. It's easy to see why: unlike the precious restaurants around it, Galindo's all about sizzling *parrilladas* (mixed grills)

and hearty Chilean staples like *chorrillana* (french fries topped with grilled onions and meat). All washed down with freshly pulled pints or carafes of house wine.

El Caramaño
CHILEAN $

(Map p54; http://caramano.tripod.com; Purísima 257; mains CH$3200-7500; ☺noon-11pm Mon-Sat; Ⓜ Baquedano) An extensive menu of well-prepared Chilean classics like *machas a la parmesana* (gratinée razor clams), *merluza a la trauca* (hake baked in chorizo and tomato sauce) and *oreganato* (melted oregano-dusted goat cheese) keep local families coming back here year after year. It's a reliable choice for a classy but affordable dinner.

★ Peumayen
CHILEAN $$

(Map p54; www.peumayenchile.cl; Constitución 136; tasting menu CH$10,500; ☺7-11pm Tue-Sat, 1-3pm Sun; Ⓜ Baquedano) Without a doubt one of the most unique culinary experiences in Chile, this Bellavista upstart is innovating Chilean cuisine by looking back to the culinary roots of the Mapuche, Easter Islanders and Quechua.

Don't even bother ordering à la carte, unless you are in a big group. Instead, ask for the tasting menu served on a stone slab and featuring modern takes on traditional indigenous fare like llama, lamb tongue, sweet breads, horse and salmon. The dramatically lit patio and low-ceilinged interior provide the perfect backdrop for your technicolor trip through Chile's gastronomic roots.

Azul Profundo
SEAFOOD $$

(Map p54; www.azulprofundo.cl; Constitución 111; mains CH$7500-13,000; ☺noon-11pm Mon-Sat; Ⓜ Baquedano) Step into the deep blue for fabulously fresh and inventive seafood. If you're up for sharing, order the delicious ceviche sampler and a round of pisco sours; the colorful (and oversized) platter might be one of the most memorable meals on your Chilean adventure.

Etniko
FUSION $$

(Map p54; ☎02-732-0119; www.etniko.cl; Constitución 172; mains CH$5900-11,000; ☺noon-3am Mon-Sat; Ⓜ Baquedano) With an airy transcendental energy, gigantic sushi platters and a sprinkling of other culinary offerings from Japan, Thailand and Chile, this hipped-out eatery is fashionable and friendly. It stretches a long way back with a mix of stone, metal, bamboo, light and sound.

✗ Barrio Brasil & Barrio Yungay

Platipus
ASIAN $

(Map p56; www.platipus.cl; Agustinas 2099; sushi CH$2900-5900; ☺dinner Mon-Sat; ✐; Ⓜ Ricardo Cumming) Candles cast a warm glow on the exposed brick walls of this laid-back sushi spot. Don't come here in a hurry, but both the sushi and the *tablas* (boards of finger food) are worth the wait. Vegetarians will find plenty to dine on here, too.

Las Vacas Gordas
STEAK $

(Map p56; Cienfuegos 280; mains CH$4000-7000; ☺noon-11pm Mon-Sat; Ⓜ Ricardo Cumming) Steak, pork, chicken and vegetables sizzle on the giant grill at the front of the clattering main dining area, then dead-pan old-school waiters cart it over to your table. This popular steakhouse is often packed, so reserve or get there early.

Plaza Garibaldi
MEXICAN $

(Map p56; www.plazagaribaldi.cl; Moneda 2319; mains CH$3800-6200; ☺noon-4pm & 7pm-midnight Mon-Sat; Ⓜ Ricardo Cumming) From the bright walls and saloon-style doors to the tacos, quesadillas and *chimichangas* (fried burritos), Plaza Garibaldi turns out classic Mexican dishes. The food's not spicy enough to be truly authentic – this is Mexican with a Chilean touch – but it's fresh and filling, and service is friendly.

★ Peluquería Francesa
FRENCH $

(Boulevard Lavaud; Map p56; ☎02-682-5243; www.boulevardlavaud.cl; Compañía de Jesús 2789; mains CH$3300-7000; ☺noon-11pm Mon-Sat; Ⓜ Ricardo Cumming) This is one of Santiago's more innovative dining experiences. The name means 'French barbershop,' and that's exactly what this elegant corner building, dating from 1868, originally was. Decorated with quirky antiques (all available for purchase), it still has turn-of-the-century charm; it gets crowded on weekend evenings with hip Santiaguinos who come for the excellent French-inflected seafood dishes.

Squella Restaurant
SEAFOOD $$

(Map p56; www.squellarestaurant.cl; Ricardo Cumming 94; mains CH$7200-9500; ☺7pm-midnight Mon-Sat; Ⓜ Ricardo Cumming) When you enter this minimal white eatery, your dinner may still be swimming (or crouching) in the bubbling pools that line one side of the dining room. The fresh oysters, shrimp, clams and ceviche have kept locals loyal to this seafood institution for decades.

Providencia

El Huerto
CAFE $

(Map p58; www.elhuerto.cl; Orrego Luco 054; mains CH$5700-6100; ⊘ noon-midnight Mon-Sat; ⚡; Ⓜ Pedro de Valdivia) This earthy restaurant's healthy, vegetarian-focused fare is a big hit with both hip young things and ladies who lunch. Come for egg-white omelets, strawberry smoothies, quinoa salads and wonderfully rich desserts with *café au lait*.

Voraz Pizza
PIZZA $

(Map p58; www.vorazpizza.cl; Av Providencia 1321; pizzas CH$3300-4000; ⊘ noon-11pm Mon-Sat; ⚡; Ⓜ Manuel Montt) This hole-in-the-wall spot serves great-value thin-crust pizzas and craft beers at sidewalk tables; it will happily deliver too. An added bonus for non-meat eaters: the pizzeria has a few tasty vegetarian options and will also cater to vegans.

Aquí Está Coco
CHILEAN $$

(Map p58; ☎02-410-6200; www.aquiestacoco. cl; La Concepción 236; mains CH$9100-13,000; ⊘ noon-11pm Mon-Sat; ⚡; Ⓜ Pedro de Valdivia) ⚡ This beautifully restored mini-mansion – reconstructed with sustainable building materials – houses one of Providencia's hippest dining venues. The name, translating to 'Here's Coco,' refers to the imaginative owner who uses the space to showcase art and artifacts from his world travels (not to mention his considerable culinary talent and zeal for fine wine).

The centolla (king crab sourced from Patagonia) is a hit every time. Highlights of Coco's self-proclaimed 'simple and honest cooking' also include scallops with coconut sauce and seared tuna from Easter Island.

Liguria
MEDITERRANEAN $$

(Map p58; ☎02-334-4346; www.liguria.cl; Av Pedro de Valdivia 47; mains CH$5300-9800; ⊘ noon-11pm Mon-Sat; Ⓜ Pedro de Valdivia) A mainstay on the Santiago restaurant circuit, Liguria mixes equal measures of bar and bistro perfectly. Stewed rabbit and other specials are chalked up on a blackboard, then dapper old-school waiters place them on the red-checked tablecloths with aplomb.

Vintage adverts, Chilean memorabilia and old bottles decorate the wood-paneled inside, but it's the sidewalk tables that diners really fight over – even on weeknights you should book ahead. There are two other locations in the city.

Astrid y Gastón
PERUVIAN $$$

(Map p58; ☎02-650-9125; www.astridygaston. com; Antonio Bellet 201; prix-fixe menu CH$40,000; ⊘ lunch Mon-Fri, dinner Mon-Sat; Ⓜ Pedro de Valdivia) The seasonally changing menu of Peruvian haute cuisine has made this restaurant (a spin-off of the Peruvian-based juggernaut) one of Santiago's most critically acclaimed eateries. The warm but expert waitstaff happily talk you through the chef's subtle, modern take on traditional ceviches, *chupes* (fish stews) and *cochinillo* (suckling pig), all beautifully presented.

Las Condes, Barrio El Golf & Vitacura

Santiago's plushest neighborhoods are home to the über-rich – and the seriously expensive restaurants and bars they frequent. You'll also see countless Starbucks locations and American-born chain restaurants.

Café Melba
CAFE $

(Map p60; Don Carlos 2898; sandwiches CH$2900, mains CH$4000-7500; ⊘ 7am-3pm daily; ⚡; Ⓜ Tobalaba) Eggs and bacon, muffins, bagels and gigantic cups of coffee are some of the all-day breakfast offerings at this cozy cafe run by a New Zealand expat. Well-stuffed sandwiches and heartier dishes like green fish curry or pork medallions are popular with lunching local finance workers, but the specialty here is the leisurely brunch.

Dominó
SANDWICHES $

(Map p60; Isidora Goyenechea 2930, Las Condes; sandwiches CH$1800-4000; ⊘ 8am-10pm Mon-Wed, to 11pm Thu & Fri, noon-11pm Sat; Ⓜ Tobalaba) This location of Dominó – a contemporary take on the traditional *fuente de soda* – is hopping at lunchtime with good-looking young office workers. The cool all-white and chrome interior, plus budget-friendly sandwiches and *completos* equal stylish fast food, Chilean-style. You'll see other locations throughout the city.

Ñuñoa

A low-profile but happening food and bar scene makes Ñuñoa a favorite night out for urbane Santiaguinos. East of Centro but well south of Providencia, it's far from the metro, but don't let that put you off: bus 505 runs along Merced and Salvador to Plaza Ñuñoa, the heart of all the action. A taxi here from Centro will cost around CH$5000.

Fuente Suiza   DINER $
(www.fuentesuiza.cl; Av Irarrázaval 3361; sandwiches CH$2400-3600; ⊙11am-midnight Mon-Thu, to 2am Fri, to 1am Sat) Dripping *lomo* (pork) sandwiches and flaky deep-fried empanadas make this simple family-run restaurant the perfect place to prepare for (or recover from) a long night of drinking.

🍷 Drinking & Nightlife

Traditional nightlife starts with afternoon coffee or tea, accompanied by a little cake, in the still-beloved tradition of the *once,* generally taken from 5pm to 8pm.

You can always replace your coffee with beer and join the raucous revelry at the pubs and lounges that start to pack in by 8pm. It would seem that Santiaguinos only take Sunday off from drinking, and you can always find a good party. Bellavista is the biggest party district, but you can find plenty of good times in chic Lastarria, working-class Brasil and in the upscale Las Condes and Providencia neighborhoods.

If you want to go clubbing, you'll need to stay up late. Most clubs don't start until midnight, staying open until 4am or 5am. The after-after hours continue until dawn.

🍸 Centro

★ Café Mosqueto   CAFE
(Map p50; ✆02-664-0273; Mosqueto 440; ⊙8:30am-10pm Mon-Fri, 10am-9:30pm Sat, 11am-9pm Sun; Ⓜ Bellas Artes) This adorable cafe offers a cozy spot on a rainy day, while the sidewalk tables, facing a pedestrian street, provide fantastic people-watching when the sun shines. The pedestrian mall that runs along Mosqueto between Monjitas and Santo Domingo is lined with several similar cafes.

Confitería Torres   BAR
(Map p50; www.confiteriatorres.cl; O'Higgins 1570; ⊙10:30am-midnight Mon-Sat; Ⓜ Los Héroes) Even after restorations that added contemporary elegance to its appearance, Confitería Torres – one of Santiago's oldest cafes – still wears its history on its sleeve. Aging waiters attend with aplomb, chandeliers glow and the green-and-white floor tiles are worn from use.

Former president Barros Luco always ordered a steak and melted cheese sandwich here; other famous figures who downed coffee or pisco sours on the premises include illustrious figures from Plácido Domingo to Rubén Darío.

🍷 Barrio Lastarria & Barrio Bellas Artes

★ Bar The Clinic   COCKTAIL BAR
(Map p50; www.bartheclinic.cl; Monjitas 578; Ⓜ Bellas Artes) This cool, quirky bar and eatery has an intellectual edge – it's the official watering hole of Chilean political magazine *The Clinic.* You'll be downing classic cocktails and gourmet pub food alongside hipster journalists in dark-rimmed glasses.

Boca Naríz   WINE BAR
(Map p50; ✆02-638-9893; www.bocanariz.cl; Lastarria 276; mains CH$5000-9000; ⊙noon-midnight Mon-Sat, 7-11pm Sun; Ⓜ Bellas Artes) You might get better ceviche in the market, but you won't get a better wine list nearly anywhere in Chile. We love the intimate atmosphere, wine flights and oeno-tastic energy. Reservations recommended.

Café del Museo   CAFE
(Map p50; Lastarria 305, Plaza Mulato Gil; ⊙11am-8:30pm Mon-Fri, 10am-9:30pm Sat & Sun; Ⓜ Bellas Artes) Adjacent to a small visual arts museum (hence the name) on one of Lastarria's quaint cobblestoned passageways, this colorful courtyard cafe does lovely cappuccinos, loose-leaf teas, pastries, gourmet sandwiches and salads.

Catedral   COCKTAIL BAR
(Map p50; www.operacatedral.cl; cnr JM de la Barra & Merced; Ⓜ Bellas Artes) Classy Catedral has a menu that goes way beyond bar snacks – anyone for a glass of champagne with violet crème brûlée? A poised crew of professionals in their 20s and 30s love this cocktail bar's minimal two-tone couches, smooth wood paneling and mellow music.

It's just one of the stylish offerings of the restaurateurs behind the Opera restaurant; both are located in the same gorgeously restored corner building.

El Diablito   BAR
(Map p50; Merced 336; Ⓜ Bellas Artes) Old photos and vintage household items clutter the already dark walls of this smoky den. After dark, the tiny candlelit tables seem to invite you to huddle conspiratorially into the small hours; great value *schop* (draft beer) and pisco sours are two more reasons to stay.

Mamboleta   BAR
(Map p50; Merced 337; ⊙9am-2am Tue-Sat; 🔊; Ⓜ Bellas Artes) With eclectic music that spans the continents and the decades, as

well as a pretty decent patio, this is a good spot to begin your *noche de carrete* pub crawl.

Bellavista

In Santiago, the life and soul of the *carrete* (nightlife) is Barrio Bellavista. By 10pm tables inside and outside of its many bars are filled with rowdy groups of Santiaguinos giving their all to the *previa* (preclub drinking). Many of the restaurants and clubs in Bellavista also double as drinking spots.

The identical watering holes along Pío Nono are basic and ultracheap – pitchers of beer are the standard order. Both the drinks and the crowds are a bit more sophisticated along Constitución and Antonia López de Bello, peppered with arty cocktail bars. Further west, Bombero Núñez is home to a handful of more underground bars and clubs, including some of Santiago's best gay nightlife.

Although the bars and cafes inside **Patio Bellavista** (Map p54; ☑ 02-777-4582; www.patiobellavista.cl; Pío Nono 73; Ⓜ Baquedano) are a bit bland, they're just about the only places open on Sunday nights.

Dublin
PUB

(Map p54; ☑ 02-732-0526; www.dublin.cl; Constitución 58; ⊘ noon-midnight Sun-Thu, noon-4am Fri & Sat; 🛜; Ⓜ Baquedano) This lively Irish pub may not offer much in the way of local flavor – well, except for the Chilean-inspired bar food – but there is a great selection of whiskey and a happy-go-lucky crowd of young Santiaguinos and expats kicking their heels up here nearly every night of the week. Alas, the front patio is reserved for diners.

Club La Feria
CLUB

(Map p54; www.clublaferia.cl; Constitución 275; cover CH$3000-5000; ⊘ from 11pm Thu-Sat; Ⓜ Baquedano) Euphoric house and techno, an up-for-it crowd and banging DJs mean this is still the place to go for a fix of electronic music.

El Clan
CLUB

(Map p54; www.elclan.cl; Bombero Núñez 363; cover CH$2000-5000; ⊘ from 11pm Tue-Sat; Ⓜ Baquedano) The name's short for 'El Clandestino,' a throwback to this small club's undercover days. A small crew of resident DJs keep the 20-something crowds going – expect anything from '80s to house, R&B, funk or techno.

Barrio Brasil & Barrio Yungay

This left-of-center barrio is becoming increasingly happening at night, but be aware that the quiet side streets can be sketchy after hours. Taking a taxi is advised.

Baires
BAR

(Map p56; Brasil 255; Ⓜ Ricardo Cumming) Technically it's a 'sushi club,' but the nightlife at Baires is what brings in the crowds. The terrace tables fill up quickly, even on weeknights; there's an encyclopedia-sized drink list, and DJs get going upstairs on weekends.

Blondie
CLUB

(Map p56; ☑ 02-681-7793; www.blondie.cl; O'Higgins 2879; cover CH$3000-5000; ⊘ from 11pm Thu-Sat; Ⓜ Union Latinoamericano) The '80s still rule at least one floor of Blondie, while the other could have anything from goth rock and techno to Britpop or Chilean indie. A favorite with both Santiago's student and gay communities, it's usually packed.

Providencia

California Cantina
SPORTS BAR

(Map p58; ☑ 02-361-1056; www.californiacantina.cl; Las Urbinas 56; ⊘ 5:30pm-2am Mon-Tue, from 12:30pm Wed-Fri, from 3:30pm Sat & Sun; Ⓜ Los Leones) A popular stop on the Providencia happy hour circuit is this spacious California-inspired bar with something for (almost) everyone – a dozen beers on tap, Mexican pub grub like tacos and quesadillas, terrace seating, everyday cocktail specials and *fútbol* matches on the big screen.

Santo Remedio
COCKTAIL BAR

(Map p58; www.santoremedio.cl; Román Díaz 152; ⊘ 1-3:30pm & 6:30pm-4am Mon-Fri, 1-3:30pm & 8:30pm-4am Sat & Sun; Ⓜ Manuel Montt) Strictly speaking, this low-lighted, high-ceilinged old house is a restaurant, and an aphrodisiacal one at that. But it's the bar action people really come for: powerful, well-mixed cocktails and regular live DJs keep the 20- and 30-something crowds happy.

Mito Urbano
CLUB

(Map p58; www.mitourbano.cl; Manuel Montt 350; cover CH$4000-6000; Ⓜ Manuel Montt) At this fun-loving nightclub, disco balls cast lights on the good-looking 20-, 30- and 40-somethings dancing to vintage hits and Chilean pop. Check the schedule for salsa classes, karaoke, live jazz and other promotions that aim to bring people in before midnight.

Las Condes, Barrio El Golf & Vitacura

Flannery's   IRISH PUB
(Map p60; www.flannerys.cl; Encomenderos 83; ⊙12:30pm-2:30am Mon-Sat, 5:30pm-12:30am Sun; M Tobalaba) This spot is popular with gringos and well-toned and well-lubricated locals alike. The three stories contain plenty of nooks and crannies. A rooftop terrace and excellent beer list round out the offerings.

Ñuñoa

HBH Brewery   BREWPUB
(www.cervezahbh.cl; Av Irarrázaval 3176; ⊙5pm-2am Mon-Fri, from 7:30pm Sat) Beer buffs and students rave about this laid-back microbrewery. As well as pouring out icy glass mugs of its own house-brewed stout and lager, HBH stocks a fantastic selection of craft beers from all over the world.

☆ Entertainment

Whether you get your kicks on the dance floor or at the soccer stadium, whether you'd rather clap in time to strumming folksingers or at the end of three-hour operas, Santiago has plenty to keep you entertained. National dailies *El Mercurio* (p62) and *La Tercera* (www.latercera.cl) carry cinema, theater and classical music listings. Information and tickets for many major performances and sporting events are available through **Ticketek** (www.ticketek.cl). For the latest on clubbing, live music and nightlife check out the searchable listings on **Saborizante** (www.saborizante.com) or go straight to the source by visiting the websites or blogs of the clubs and bars themselves.

Live Music

Chile doesn't have the musical reputation of other Latin American countries. But there are some seriously good bands here – top indie acts are featured at Santiago's edition of Lollapalooza. Music-oriented bars are usually the best places to catch them. Save the salsa and tango for the countries that do them best: instead, your best bets in Santiago will be folksy singer-songwriters, Chilean or Argentinean indie groups, *rock nacional* (Chilean rock) upstarts, and purveyors of the most Latin of local beats, *cumbia chilombiana*. International greats also visit Chile regularly, and tickets are usually much cheaper than at home.

Bar Constitución   LIVE MUSIC
(Map p54; Constitución 62, Bellavista; ⊙8pm-4am; M Baquedano) Bellavista's coolest nightspot hosts live bands and DJs nightly – the bar's eclectic (but infallible) tastes include electroclash, garage, nu-folk, house and more, so check the website to see if the night's program suits.

La Casa en el Aire   PERFORMING ARTS
(Map p54; ☑02-735-6680; www.lacasaenelaire.cl; Antonia López de Bello 0125, Bellavista; ⊙8pm-late Mon-Sun; M Baquedano) Latin-American folk music, storytelling gatherings, film cycles and poetry readings are some of the arty events that take place nightly in this low-key boho bar.

Club de Jazz   JAZZ
(☑02-830-6208; www.clubdejazz.cl; Av Ossa 123; ⊙10:30pm-3am Thu-Sat) One of Latin America's most established jazz venues – Louis Armstrong and Herbie Hancock are just two of the greats to have played here – this venerable club hosts local and international jazz, blues and big band performers. It also plays a hand in promoting jazz acts at other venues.

La Batuta   LIVE MUSIC
(www.batuta.cl; Jorge Washington 52, Ñuñoa; M Plaza Egaña) Enthusiastic crowds jump to ska, *patchanka* (think: Manu Chao) and *cumbia chilombiana;* rockabilly and surf; tribute bands and goth rock...at La Batuta, just about anything alternative goes.

Galpón Víctor Jara   LIVE MUSIC
(Map p56; Huérfanos 2146, Barrio Brasil; ⊙8pm-2am; M Ricardo Cumming) Named in memory of 'disappeared' folk singer-songwriter and activist Víctor Jara (a Chilean revolutionary who was assumed to have been executed by the military government after publicly expressing his liberal views), this warehouse-like space hosts gigs from up-and-coming local acts.

Teatro Caupolicán   LIVE MUSIC
(☑02-699-1556; www.teatrocaupolican.cl; San Diego 850; ⊙8pm-1am; M Parque O'Higgins) Latin American rockers who've played this stage include far-out Mexicans Café Tacuba, Argentinean electro-tango band Bajofondo and Oscar-winning Uruguayan Jorge Drexler; international acts like Garbage and Snow Patrol also play concert dates at Teatro Caupolicán.

Theater, Dance & Classical Music

Although much of Chilean theater revolves around the sequined, tassel-toting showgirls that star in so-called *comedias musicales*, Santiago is also home to some excellent stage and ballet companies, orchestras and choirs. The Centro Gabriela Mistral (p52) hosts nightly music, dance and theater performances.

Teatro Municipal   THEATER
(Map p50; ☑02-463-1000; www.municipal.cl; Agustinas 794, Centro; tickets from CH$3000; ☺box office 10am-7pm Mon-Fri, 10am-2pm Sat & Sun; Ⓜ Santa Lucía) This exquisite neoclassical building is the city's most prestigious performing-arts venue. It's home to the Ballet de Santiago, and also hosts world-class opera, tango and classical music performances.

Estación Mapocho   CULTURAL CENTER
(Mapocho Station; Map p50; www.estacionmapocho.cl; ☺ event times vary, check website; Ⓜ Puente Cal y Canto) Rail services heading north once left from Estación Mapocho. Earthquake damage and the decay of the rail system led to its closure, but it's been reincarnated as a cultural center which hosts art exhibitions, major concerts and trade expos.

It's worth a walk-by, just to check out the soaring cast-iron structure of the main hall, which was built in France then assembled in Santiago behind its golden beaux arts–style stone facade.

Centro Cultural Matucana 100   ARTS CENTER
(Map p56; ☑02-946-9240; www.m100.cl; Matucana 100; ticket prices vary; ☺11am-1pm & 2-9pm; Ⓜ Quinta Normal) FREE One of Santiago's hippest alternative arts venues, the huge red-brick Centro Cultural Matucana 100 gets its gritty industrial look from its previous in-carnation as government warehouses. Renovated as part of Chile's bicentennial project, it now contains a hangar-like gallery and a theater for art-house film cycles, concerts and fringe productions.

Centro de Extensión
Artística y Cultural   THEATER
(Map p50; ☑02-978-2480; www.ceacuchile. com; Providencia 043, Centro; Ⓜ Baquedano) The Orquesta Sinfónica de Chile and Ballet Nacional de Chile are two high-profile companies based at this excellent theater run under the auspices of the University of Chile. There is a fall season of ballet, choral, orchestral and chamber music, as well as the occasional rock gig.

Cineteca Nacional   CINEMA
(Map p50; www.ccplm.cl/sitio/category/cineteca-nacional; Centro Cultural La Moneda; adult/student CH$3000/1500; Ⓜ La Moneda) Located in the Centro Cultural La Moneda, this underground cinema plays art-house favorites (mostly in Spanish).

Spectator Sports

Estadio Nacional   SOCCER
(National Stadium; ☑02-238-8102; Av Grecia 2001, Ñuñoa; Ⓜ Irrarrázaval) On the whole, Chileans are a pretty calm lot – until they step foot in a soccer stadium. The most dramatic matches are against local rivals like Peru or Argentina, when 'Chi-Chi-Chi-Lay-Lay-Lay' reverberates through the Estadio Nacional.

Tickets can be bought at the stadium or from the Feria del Disco. Equally impassioned are the *hinchas* (fans) of Santiago's first-division soccer teams like Colo Colo, Universidad de Chile and Universidad Católica.

Club Hípico de Santiago   HORSE RACING
(☑02-693-9600; www.clubhipico.cl; Av Blanco Encalada 2540; Ⓜ Parque O'Higgins) The main

---

DON'T MISS

EL HUASO ENRIQUE

To see Chileans performing their national dance, *la cueca* – a playful, handkerchief-waving ritual that imitates the courtship of a rooster and hen – you usually have to make your way to a folk festival, an Independence Day celebration or a dusty country town. But at **El Huaso Enrique** (Map p56; ☑02-681-5257; www.elhuasoenrique.cl; Maipú 462, Barrio Yungay; cover CH$2500-3000; Ⓜ Quinta Normal), a traditional restaurant and *cueca* venue that's been in business in Barrio Yungay for almost 60 years, you can watch proud locals hit the dance floor while you feast on hearty regional dishes like *pastel de choclo* (a casserole-like dish consisting of baked corn, meat and cheese). The place comes alive on weekends with live music. If you really want to get into the spirit, El Huaso Enrique also offers *cueca* lessons; check out the website for details.

racetrack is the grand Club Hípico de Santiago, where views of the Andes compete for your attention with the action on the turf.

Shopping

Santiago may not be a world-class shopping destination, but you can still pick up interesting craft pieces and unusual clothing or housewares by young local designers. The Centro's busiest shopping streets, pedestrianized Ahumada and Huérfanos, are lined with cheap clothing, shoe and department stores. For seriously cheap clothes, head to the Korean and Palestinian immigrant area of Patronato, west of Bellavista between Patronato and Manzano. Secondhand clothes stores abound in the city (often marked by signs reading 'Ropa Europea/Americana'), especially around Providencia's Manuel Montt metro station.

The top-quality Chilean crafts you can find in Santiago include hand-woven alpaca shawls, Mapuche silver jewelry, lapis lazuli, wood, leatherwork and, occasionally, copperware. Near the entrance to Cerro Santa Lucía, look for outdoor vendors at the indigenous-focused **Centro de Exposición de Arte Indígena** (Map p50; O'Higgins 499, Centro; ⏰10am-6pm Mon-Sat; MSanta Lucía) and the more commercial **Centro Artesanal Santa Lucía** (Map p50; cnr Carmen & Diagonal Paraguay, Centro; ⏰10am-7pm; MSanta Lucía).

★**Artesanías de Chile** ARTS & CRAFTS
(Map p50; 📞02-235-2014; www.artesaniasde chile.cl; Plaza de la Ciudadanía 26; ⏰10am-6pm Mon-Sat; MLa Moneda) 🖋 Not only do this foundation's jewelry, carvings, ceramics and woolen goods sell at reasonable prices, most of what you pay goes to the artisan that made them. Look for other locations in Santiago and throughout Chile.

Patio Bellavista SHOPPING CENTER
(Map p54; www.patiobellavista.cl; Pío Nono 73, Bellavista; ⏰11am-10pm; MBaquedano) Posh contemporary crafts, leather goods, weavings and jewelry sell at premium prices at this courtyard shopping center.

Galería Drugstore FASHION
(Map p58; www.drugstore.cl; Av Providencia 2124, Providencia; ⏰10:30am-8pm Mon-Sat; MLos Leones) Head to this cool four-story independent shopping center for clothes no one back home will have – it's home to the tiny boutiques of several up-and-coming designers, arty bookstores and cafes.

WORTH A TRIP

PERSA BÍO BÍO

Antiques, collectibles and fascinating old junk fill the cluttered stalls at this famous **flea market** (Franklin Market; ⏰9am-7pm Sat & Sun; MFranklin) between Bío Bío and Franklin. Sifting through the jumble of vintage sunglasses, antique brandy snifters, cowboy spurs, old-fashioned swimsuits and discarded books is an experience.

It's also a choice spot to try some Chilean street food, from fried empanadas, tacos and grilled pork sandwiches to fresh-squeezed juices and the classic *mote con huesillo* (a sweet local snack made with dried peaches and husked wheat). Just be sure to keep one hand on your valuables while stuffing food into your mouth; pickpockets have been known to prey on unsuspecting shoppers.

Kind of Blue MUSIC
(Map p50; Merced 323; ⏰10am-10pm Sun-Thu, 10am-11pm Fri & Sat; MBellas Artes) At the best music shop in town, savvy multilingual staff happily talk you through local sounds and artists, and can get hard-to-find imports in a matter of days.

El Mundo del Vino WINE
(Mundo del Vino; Map p60; 📞02-584-1173; www.emdv.cl; Isidora Goyenechea 3000, Las Condes; ⏰10am-9pm; MTobalaba) This revamped location of the high-end wine chain (look for other branches throughout Santiago and Chile) features 6000 bottles from around the world – or from just a short drive away in the Colchagua Valley – at the hip W Hotel.

Alto Las Condes MALL
(www.altolascondes.cl; Av Kennedy 9001, Las Condes; ⏰10am-10pm) As well as top-end Chilean and Argentine clothing brands, this mall has a branch of department store Falabella and a cinema complex. The best way to get here is to catch a bus marked 'Alto Las Condes' outside the Escuela Militar metro station.

Parque Arauco MALL
(www.parquearauco.cl; Av Kennedy 5413; ⏰10am-9pm; MManquehue) A huge range of local and international clothing stores make this the fashionista mall of choice. From Manquehue

metro station, it's about a mile-long walk (or a quick taxi ride) northwest along Alonso de Córdova.

Contrapunto   BOOKS
(Map p50; www.contrapunto.cl; Huérfanos 665; ◎10:30am-8pm Mon-Fri, 10:30am-2pm Sat; Ⓜ Santa Lucía) This chain bookstore has a broad selection, though the English titles are limited.

Andesgear   OUTDOOR EQUIPMENT
(Map p60; ☑02-592-0540; www.andesgear.cl; Helvecia 210, Las Condes; ◎10am-8pm Mon-Fri, 10:30am-2pm Sat; Ⓜ Tobalaba) Imported climbing and high-altitude camping gear for your journey to Chilean Patagonia, with several locations throughout the city.

ⓘ Information

DANGERS & ANNOYANCES
Violent crime is relatively rare in Santiago, a city that is regularly ranked as the safest big city in Latin America. Pickpocketing and bag-snatching, however, are on the rise, and tourists are often targets. Keep your eyes open and your bags close to you around the Plaza de Armas, Mercado Central, Cerro Santa Lucía and Cerro San Cristóbal in particular. Look around you before whipping out a digital camera, be aware that organized groups of pickpockets sometimes target drinkers along Pío Nono in Bellavista. Barrio Brasil's smaller streets can be dodgy after dark.

Political strife has taken the form of protests (which occasionally turn violent) and anarchist bombings in recent years. It's advisable to avoid political protests unless you are really part of the movement.

If you are robbed, head to the police department to fill out a report (and hopefully) have the goods covered by your travel insurance. Your consulate can also help, but rarely steps in when drugs are involved.

EMERGENCY
Ambulance (☑131)
Fire Department (Bomberos; ☑132)
Police (Carabineros; ☑133)
Prefectura de Carabineros (Main police station; ☑02-922-3660; O'Higgins 280, Centro)

INTERNET ACCESS & TELEPHONES
Cybercafes are a dying breed, but you can still find a few in the Centro and around the universities: prices range from CH$400 to CH$1000 per hour. Many are part of a *centro de llamados* (public telephone center) where you can also make local and long-distance calls. Many cafes and most hotels now have free wi-fi for their clients.

Centro de Llamados (Moneda 1118, Centro; per hr CH$600; ◎9:30am-10:30pm Mon-Fri, 10am-8pm Sat & Sun; Ⓜ Universidad de Chile)

Cyber Station (Av Brasil 167, Barrio Brasil; per hr CH$700; ◎1-11pm Mon-Sat, from 4pm Sun; Ⓜ Ricardo Cumming)

LAUNDRY
Nearly all hotels and hostels offer laundry service; you can also drop off your clothes anywhere called *lavandería* (expect to pay about CH$6000 per load). Note that self-service launderettes are uncommon in Chile.

Laundromat (Monjitas 504, Centro; $5900 per load; ◎8am-8pm; ☎; Ⓜ Plaza de Armas)

MAPS
Tourist offices distribute an ever-changing collection of free (ie sponsored) maps of Centro and Providencia, but many lack entire streets or sights. The searchable maps at **Map City** (www.mapcity.com) and **EMOL** (www.mapas.emol.com) are reliable online resources.

For trekking and mountaineering information, as well as inexpensive maps and other national park publications (mostly in Spanish), visit **Conaf** (Corporación Nacional Forestal; ☑02-663-0000; www.conaf.cl; Bulnes 285, Centro; ◎9:30am-5:30pm Mon-Thu, 9:30am-4:30pm Fri; Ⓜ Toesca).

MEDICAL SERVICES
Consultations are cheap at Santiago's public hospitals but long waits are common and English may not be spoken. For immediate medical or dental assistance, go to a *clínica* (private clinic), but expect hefty fees – insurance is practically a must.

Clínica Alemana (☑02-210-1111; www.alemana.cl; Av Vitacura 5951, Vitacura; Ⓜ Escuela Militar) One of the best – and most expensive – private hospitals in town.

Clínica Las Condes (☑022-210-4000; www.clinicalascondes.cl; Lo Fontecilla 441, Las Condes) Las Condes clinic.

Clínica Universidad Católica (☎ 02-676-7000; www.clinicauc.cl; Lira 40; Ⓜ Universidad Católica) University hospital.

Farmacia Ahumada (☎ 600-222-4000; www.farmaciasahumada.cl; Av Portugal 155, Centro; Ⓜ Universidad Católica) A 24-hour pharmacy.

Hospital de Urgencia Asistencia Pública (☎ 02-568-1100; www.huap.cl; Av Portugal 125; ⊙ 24hr; Ⓜ Universidad Católica) Santiago's main emergency room.

Hospital San Juan de Dios (☎ 600-360-7777; www.hsjd.cl; Huérfanos 3255, Barrio Brasil; Ⓜ Quinta Normal) Major public hospital.

MONEY

You're never far from an ATM in Santiago. Supermarkets, pharmacies, gas stations and plain old street corners are all likely locations: look for the burgundy-and-white 'Redbanc' sign. Counterfeit currency does circulate in town; be especially wary of non-licensed money changers.

Cambios Afex (☎ 02-636-9090; www.afex.cl; Agustinas 1050, Centro; ⊙ 9am-6pm Mon-Fri, 10am-2pm Sat; Ⓜ Universidad de Chile) Reliable exchange office with branches around town.

POST

FedEx (Map p58; ☎ 02-361-6000; www.fedex.com/cl_english/contact; Av Providencia 1951; ⊙ 9am-1:30pm & 2:30-7pm; Ⓜ Pedro de Valdivia) International shipping.

Post Office (Map p50; ☎ 800-267-736; www.correos.cl; Catedral 987, Plaza de Armas; ⊙ 8am-10pm Mon-Fri, to 6pm Sat; Ⓜ Plaza de Armas) With offices around town.

TOURIST INFORMATION

Sernatur (Map p58; ☎ 02-731-8336; www.chile.travel; Av Providencia 1550; ⊙ 9am-6pm Mon-Fri, 9am-2pm Sat; Ⓜ Manuel Montt) Gives out maps, brochures and advice; reserves winery visits.

TRAVEL AGENCIES

Navimag (☎ 022-442-3120; www.navimag.cl; Av El Bosque Norte 0440, Piso 11; ⊙ 9am-6:30pm Mon-Fri; Ⓜ Tobalaba) Book ahead for ferry tickets in Chilean Patagonia.

ⓘ Getting There & Away

AIR

Chile's main air hub for both national and domestic flights is Aeropuerto Internacional Arturo Merino Benítez (p454). It's 26km west of central Santiago.

Lan (☎ 600-526-2000; www.lan.com), **Aerolíneas Argentinas** (☎ 800-610-200; www.aerolineas.com.ar) and low-cost airline **Gol** (www.voegol.com.br) run regular domestic and regional services from here. Major international

airlines that fly to Chile have offices or representatives in Santiago.

BUS

A bewildering number of bus companies connect Santiago to the rest of Chile, Argentina and Peru. To add to the confusion, services leave from four different terminals and ticket prices fluctuate wildly at busy times of year, and often double for *cama* (sleeper) services. The following sample of *clásico* or *semi-cama* (standard) fares (approximate only) and journey times are for major destinations that are served by a variety of companies – discounts often apply so shop around. For fares to smaller destinations, see the listings under each terminal.

DESTINATION	COST (CH$)	DURATION (HR)
Antofagasta	30,000	19
Arica	45,900	30
Buenos Aires (Argentina)	81,000	22
Chillán	7900	5
Concepción	8000	6½
Copiapó	20,000	12
Iquique	37,400	25
La Serena	10,000	7
Los Andes	2900	1½
Mendoza (Argentina)	25,400	8
Osorno	21,800	12
Pichilemu	5000	4
Pucón	16,800	11
Puerto Montt	21,800	12
San Pedro de Atacama	40,600	23
Santa Cruz	4000	4
Talca	5000	3½
Temuco	14,900	9½
Valdivia	16,900	10-11
Valparaíso	1900	2
Viña del Mar	1900	2¼

Terminal de Buses Alameda

Tur Bus (☎ 600-660-6600; www.turbus.cl) and **Pullman Bus** (☎ 600-320-3200; www.pullman.cl) operate from this **terminal** (cnr O'Higgins & Jotabeche; Ⓜ Universidad de Santiago), next door to Terminal de Buses Santiago. The two companies run comfortable, punctual services to destinations all over Chile, including every 15 minutes to Valparaíso and Viña del Mar.

Terminal de Buses Santiago

Santiago's largest **terminal** (O'Higgins 3850; Ⓜ Universidad de Santiago) is also known as Terminal Sur, and is usually manically busy. The companies operating from the large, semicovered ticket area mainly serve destinations south of Santiago, including the central coast, the Lakes District and Chiloé. A few companies also operate northbound buses and international service.

Bus Norte (Ⓓ 600-401-5151; www.bus-nortechile.cl) runs excellent-value services to Puerto Montt and Valparaíso. The modern, well-appointed buses operated by **Línea Azul** (www.buseslineaazul.cl) connect Santiago with southern destinations, as do **JAC** (Ⓓ 02-680-6927; www.jac.cl) and **Andimar** (Ⓓ 02-779-3810; www.andimar.cl).

Nilahué (Ⓓ 02-776-1139; www.busesnilahue.cl) goes to Cobquecura (CH$11,000, seven hours, once daily), Termas de Chillán ski resort (CH$14,000, seven hours, twice daily), Santa Cruz (CH$7000, four hours, two hourly) and Pichilemu (CH$5500, four hours, hourly). **Pullman del Sur** (Ⓓ 02-776-2424; www.pdelsur.cl) has similar services to Santa Cruz and Pichilemu, but is slightly more comfortable. **Condor** (Ⓓ 600-660-6600; www.condorbus.cl) goes to Concón and Quintero (CH$5000, 2½ hours, three hourly) and to major southern cities.

International tickets are sold from booths inside the terminal. **Cata Internacional** (Ⓓ 800-122-2282; www.catainternacional.com) has four daily services to Mendoza and Buenos Aires. **El Rápido** (www.elrapidoint.com.ar) has similar but slightly cheaper services, as does **Tas Choapa** (Ⓓ 02-490-7561; www.taschoapa.cl).

Terminal Los Héroes

Also known as Terrapuerto, this small but central **terminal** (Map p56; Ⓓ 02-420-0099; Tucapel Jiménez 21; Ⓜ Los Héroes) is the base for a handful of companies, mostly servicing northern routes. **Libac** (Ⓓ 02-646-8940; www.buseslibac.cl) runs two daily northbound services while **Cruz del Sur** (Ⓓ 065-436-410; www.busescruzdelsur.cl) has several services going south, and also sells connecting tickets to Bariloche in Argentina via Osorno (CH$28,000, 24 hours). **Ahumada** (Ⓓ 02-784-2512; www.busesahumada.cl) goes three times daily to Mendoza; some services continue to Buenos Aires.

Terminal San Borja

Services to the area around Santiago depart from this renovated **terminal** (Map p56; O'Higgins 3250, San Borja 184; Ⓜ Estación Central). Ticket booths are on the 2nd floor, divided by region. The most useful services from here are **Ahumada** (www.busesahumada.cl) and **Pullman Bus** (Ⓓ 600-320-3200; www.pullman.cl). Bus services to Pomaire also leave from here.

Terminal Pajaritos

Buses from Santiago to the airport and Valparaíso and Viña call in at this small **terminal** (General Bonilla 5600; Ⓜ Pajaritos). It's on Metro Línea 1, so by getting on buses here you avoid downtown traffic.

CAR

Intense rush-hour traffic and high parking fees mean there's little point hiring a car to use in Santiago. However, having your own wheels is invaluable for visiting the Casablanca Valley and places of natural beauty like Cerro la Campana and the Cajón del Maipo.

Chilean rental-car companies tend to be cheaper than big international ones, but note that they often have sky-high deductibles. Most rental companies have their own roadside assistance; alternatively, the **Automóvil Club de Chile** (Acchi; Ⓓ 600-464-4040; www.automovilclub.cl; Andrés Bello 1863, Santiago) provides reciprocal assistance to members of the American Automobile Association and some other associations, but you need to stop by the office to register. Some of the companies listed here also have airport offices at Pudahuel.

Budget (Ⓓ 600-441-0000; www.budget.cl; Av Francisco Bilbao 1439, Providencia) Incredibly helpful staff and no deductible.

Chilean (Ⓓ 02-963-8760; www.chileanrenta-car.cl; Bellavista 0183, Bellavista) High deductibles and add-ons.

First Rent a Car (Ⓓ 02-225-6328; www.firstrentacar.cl; Rancagua 0514, Providencia) National rent a car.

Hertz (Ⓓ 800-360-8666; www.hertz.cl; Av Andrés Bello 1469) International rental agency.

Piamonte (Ⓓ 02-751-0230; www.piamonte.cl; Irarrázaval 4290, Ñuñoa) Rock-bottom rates.

United (Ⓓ 02-737-9650; www.united-chile.com; Curicó 360, Centro) Reasonable rates and low deductibles.

TRAIN

Chile's slick interurban train system, **Trenes Metropolitanas** (Ⓓ 600-585-5000; www.tmsa.cl), operates out of **Estación Central** (O'Higgins 3170; Ⓜ Estación Central). Train travel is generally slightly slower and more expensive than going by bus, but wagons are well maintained and services are generally punctual.

The TerraSur rail service connects Santiago three to five times daily with Rancagua (CH$5600, one hour), Curicó (CH$5600 to CH$19,000, 2¼ hours), Talca (CH$8000 to CH$19,000, three hours) and Chillán (CH$8000, 5½ hours), from where there's a connecting bus to Concepción. There's a 10% discount if you book online; 1st-class tickets cost about 20% more.

🛈 Getting Around

TO/FROM THE AIRPORT

Two cheap, efficient bus services connect the airport with the city center: **Buses Centropuerto** (Map p56; ☑ 02-601-9883; www.centropuerto.cl; Manuel Rodríguez 846; one way/round trip CH$1500/2900; ⊘ 5:55am-11:30pm, every 10-15min) and **TurBus Aeropuerto** (☑ 600-660-6600; www.turbus.cl; CH$1550). Both leave from right outside the arrivals hall, and you can buy tickets on board or from the ticket desks inside the terminal. All but the earliest buses stop at metro station Pajaritos on Line 1 – you avoid downtown traffic by transferring to the metro here. The total trip takes about 40 minutes.

A pushy mafia of 'official' taxi drivers tout their services in the arrivals hall. Although the ride to the city center should cost around CH$16,000, drivers may well try to charge much more. A safer bet for private transfers is to approach the desk of **Transvip** (☑ 02-677-3000; www.transvip.cl) which offers fixed-price taxis (from CH$18,000) and eight-seat minibuses (from CH$6400) to the Centro. Trips to Providencia and Las Condes cost slightly more. TurBus Aeropuerto offers similar services.

BICYCLE

Santiago is flat and compact enough to get around by bike and the climate is ideal for it. Although the city isn't particularly bike-friendly, it does have a small network of ciclovías (bike lanes), and more and more Santiaguinos are cycling to work. Check out the interactive map of bike paths and cyclist-friendly facilities at **Recicleta** (www.recicleta.cl/mapa-de-santiago-en-bicicleta), a group that promotes urban biking. Another linchpin of the local cyclist movement is Movimiento Furiosos Ciclistas (p60), which organizes a Critical Mass–style bike rally the first Tuesday of each month. You can rent bikes and helmets from tour operator La Bicicleta Verde (p61).

Bike Santiago (☑ 600-750-5600; www.bikesantiago.cl) You have to pay a monthly registration fee to use this bike share program (CH$4990). The first 30 minutes are free, after that it's CH$500 per half hour.

BUS

Transantiago buses are a cheap and convenient way of getting around town, especially when the metro shuts down at night. Green-and-white buses operate in central Santiago or connect two areas of town. Each suburb has its own color-coded local buses and an identifying letter that precedes route numbers (eg routes in Las Condes and Vitacura start with a C and vehicles are painted orange). Buses generally follow major roads or avenues; stops are spaced far apart and tend to coincide with metro stations. There are route maps at many stops and consulting them (or asking bus drivers) is usually more reliable than asking locals, who are still confused by new routes.

On Sundays and holidays, take advantage of the new **Circuito Cultural Santiago** (www.transantiago.cl; ⊘ 10am-6:30pm Sun & holidays), a bus loop tour that passes by the city's main attractions (museums, cultural centers) starting at Estación Central. You use your Bip! card to pay one regular bus fare, and the driver will give you a bracelet that allows you to board the circuit's buses as many times as you like. The buses are clearly marked 'Circuito Cultural.'

CAR & MOTORCYCLE

To drive on any of the expressways within Santiago proper, your car must have an electronic sensor known as a TAG in the windshield – all rental cars have them. On-street parking is banned in some parts of central Santiago and metered (often by a person) in others – costs range from CH$1000 to CH$3000 per hour, depending on the area. If you're not paying a meter, you're expected to pay a similar fee to the 'parking attendant.' For more detailed information on driving and parking in Santiago, check out the helpful English-language section at **Car Rental in Chile** (www.mietwagen-in-chile.de); it will also rent you a vehicle.

METRO

Now part of Transantiago, the city's ever-expanding **metro** (www.metrosantiago.cl; ⊘ 6:30am-11pm Mon-Sat, 8am-11pm Sun) is a clean and efficient way of getting about. Services on its five interlinking lines are frequent, but often painfully crowded. A new line is slated to open in 2016. To get on the trains, head underground. You can use your Bip! card or purchase a one-way fare. Pass through the turnstiles and head for your line. It's a fine way to get around during the day, but during the morning and evening rush, you may prefer to walk.

TAXI

Santiago has abundant metered taxis, all black with yellow roofs. Flagfall costs CH$250, then it's CH$120 per 200m (or minute of waiting time). For longer rides – from the city center out to the airport, for example – you can sometimes negotiate flat fares. It's generally safe to hail cabs in the street, though hotels and restaurants will happily call you one, too. Most Santiago taxi drivers are honest, courteous and helpful, but a few will take roundabout routes, so try to know where you're going. Taxis Colectivos are black with roof signs indicating routes (you'll share the ride, which generally costs CH$1000 to CH$1500).

TRANSANTIAGO

In 2006, sleek extra-long buses replaced the city's many competing private services when the bus and metro were united as **Transantiago** (⎘ 800-730-073; www.transantiago.cl), a government-run public transportation system that's quick, cheap and efficient for getting around central Santiago. The Transantiago website has downloadable route maps and a point-to-point journey planner.

You'll need a *tarjeta* Bip! (a contact-free card you wave over sensors). You pay a nonrefundable CH$2700 for a card, and then 'charge' it with as much money as you want. Two people can share a card, and they also work on the metro. Transantiago charges CH$720 during rush hour (7am to 9am and 6pm to 8pm) and CH$640 the rest of the time. One fare allows you two hours in the system, including multiple transfers.

AROUND SANTIAGO

National parks, sleepy villages and wine-producing valleys, plus snowy slopes (in winter) and high-altitude hiking trails (in summer) all make easy escapes from the city.

Pomaire

In this small, rustic country village 68km southwest of Santiago, skilled potters make beautifully simple brown and black earthenware ceramics and sell them for incredibly cheap prices (a homemade coffee mug goes for CH$1000). A trip here makes a pleasant half-day out, especially as the town is also celebrated for its traditional Chilean food.

Note that while Pomaire is packed with day-trippers on weekends, the town is practically deserted on Monday, when the potters have a day off.

✖ Eating

In Pomaire you'll see delicious baked empanadas, *humitas* (corn tamales), steak sandwiches and homemade pastries for sale at casual food stands set among the ceramics shops; there are also several traditional eateries along the main drag where you can have a relaxed and authentic meal.

La Greda   CHILEAN
(⎘ 02-832-3955; Manuel Rodríguez 251; mains CH$3000-5800; ⊗10am-midnight) Grilled meats make up most of the menu at the ever-popular La Greda. The name means 'clay,' and indeed, the hearty casseroles are cooked

in locally made dishes. La Greda's claim to fame is that it was listed in Guinness World Records for the largest empanada in the world in 1995.

ⓘ Getting There & Away

Several lines run buses between Santiago and the Pomaire area from Santiago's San Borja terminal (CH$1200, one hour). A direct bus usually leaves at 9:30am; otherwise, take one of the regular services to Melipilla (CH$1300, 30 minutes, four hourly) and get off at the Pomaire cruce (crossroads), where *colectivos* and *liebres* (minibuses) take you into town (CH$500). **Buses Jiménez** (⎘ 02-776-5786) runs several buses to Melipilla each hour.

Maipo Valley

When you've had your fill of museums and plazas, head south of the city center to check out the gorgeous vineyards and mass production wine operations of the Maipo Valley. Big-bodied reds, featuring varietals such as Cabernet Sauvignon, Merlot, Carmenere and Syrah – many that have notes of eucalyptus or mint – are what the valley is all about.

You can go it alone as many wineries are within 1½ hours of the city center on public transportation. But if you'd like to hit the wine circuit with a knowledgeable guide, try the specialized tours at **Uncorked Wine Tours** (⎘ 02-981-6242; www.uncorked.cl; half-/full-day tour US$135/195): an English-speaking guide will take you to three wineries, and a lovely lunch is included. Also recommended is the winery bike tour with La Bicicleta Verde (p61). Enotour (p62) is another curated wine-tour outfit. Most wine tours require advance reservations.

◎ Sights

Reserva Nacional Río Clarillo   PARK
(www.conaf.cl/parques/reserva-nacional-rio-clarillo; adult/child CH$3000/1000; ⊗8:30am-6pm) A mix of Andean forest and scrubland make up this hilly, 100-sq-km nature reserve in a scenic tributary canyon of the Cajón del Maipo, 18km southeast of Pirque. It's home to abundant bird species, foxes and rodents, and the endangered Chilean iguana.

Two short, clearly labeled trails start near the Conaf rangers office, 300m after the entrance: Quebrada Jorquera takes about half an hour; Aliwen Mahuida takes 1½ hours. The rangers give advice on longer hikes along the river, but plan on starting early as camping is not allowed here. There are several picnic areas with tables and barbecue pits for your midday break.

Viña Aquitania
WINERY

(📞02-791-4500; www.aquitania.cl; Av Consistorial 5090; tour & tasting CH$8000-15,000; ⊙by appointment only 9am-5pm Mon-Fri) Set at the foot of the Andes is Santiago's most interesting winery. Aquitania works with tiny quantities and sky-high quality.

From Grecia metro station (Línea 4), take bus D07 south from bus stop 6 and get off at the intersection of Av Los Presidentes and Consistorial (you need a Bip! card). Aquitania is 150m south. Note that Viña Cousiño Macul is located only 2km away.

Viña Cousiño Macul
WINERY

(📞02-351-4100; www.cousinomacul.com; Av Quilín 7100, Peñalolen; tours CH$9000-18,000; ⊙tours 11am, noon, 3pm & 4pm Mon-Fri in English, 11am & noon Sat; Ⓜ Quilín) A pretty winery set in Santiago's urban sprawl. Most of the vineyards are now at Buin, but tours take in the production process and underground bodega, built in 1872. It's a 2.25km walk or a quick taxi ride from the metro.

Viña Almaviva
WINERY

(📞02-270-4200; www.almavivawinery.com; Av Santa Rosa 821, Paradero 45, Puente Alto; tours incl 1 pour US$80; ⊙by appointment only 9am-5pm Mon-Fri) This boutique vineyard runs in partnership with Baron Philippe de Rothschild and Concha y Torro. High-end tastings are available by reservation only.

Bus 207 from Estación Mapocho runs past the entrance, about 1km from the winery building. It's the more sophisticated sister of Viña Concha y Toro where you can see winemaking on a vast scale on one of the winery's mass-market tours.

Viña Santa Rita
WINERY

(📞02-362-2000; www.santarita.com; Camino Padre Hurtado 0695, Alto Jahuel; tours CH$10,000-30,000) Famous for the premium Casa Real Cabernet, Santa Rita offers bike and wine tours as well as picnics. To get here, take the metro to Buin station, then take bus 5064 to the entrance of the winery.

Viña de Martino
WINERY

(📞02-819-2959; www.demartino.cl; Manuel Rodríguez 229, Isla de Maipo; tours from CH$20,000) 🍃 The first carbon neutral winery in South America offers tastings in a Tuscan-style manor.

Viña Undurraga
WINERY

(📞02-372-2900; www.undurraga.cl; Camino a Melipilla, Km 34, Talagante; tours from CH$34,000) The subterranean bodegas at Undurraga date from 1885.

Viña Concha y Toro
WINERY

(📞02-476-5269; www.conchaytoro.com; Virginia Subercaseaux 210, Pirque; standard tour & tasting CH$8000; ⊙10am-5pm) To see winemaking on a vast scale, do one of the mass-market tours at Viña Concha y Toro in Pirque.

🍴 Eating

La Vaquita Echá
CHILEAN $$

(www.lavaquitaecha.cl; Ramón Subercaseaux 3355; mains CH$5200-8500) The long-running local favorite, La Vaquita Echá is rightly famed for its grill – steaks, ribs, fish and even wild boar all sizzle over the coals. It's located in the town of Pirque.

ℹ Getting There & Away

The town of Pirque is a central kick-off point to explore the Maipo Valley, though most wineries are pretty spread out, and you're best off with your own wheels. To get to Pirque, take the Santiago metro to Plaza de Puente Alto, the end of line 4. Then catch a blue minibus (labeled 'Pirque' in the window) and tell the driver you want to go to Plaza Pirque or Viña Concha y Toro. Departures are frequent and the fare is CH$500. Plaza Pirque is about 4km before the entrance to Reserva Natural Río Clarillo – some services continue to the park entrance.

Cajón del Maipo

Rich greenery lines the steep, rocky walls of this stunning gorge of the Río Maipo. Starting only 25km southeast of Santiago, it's popular on weekends with Santiaguinos, who come here to camp, hike, climb, cycle, raft and ski. Lots of traditional restaurants and teahouses, and a big winery, mean that overindulgence is also on the menu. Recently, a few new offerings in the Cajón del Maipo – including motorcycle tours and a venue for 'glamping' (ie glamorous camping) – have brought some buzz to the otherwise quiet region.

Plans for a hydroelectric station here could have serious consequences on the region's ecosystem. So take advantage of this pristine natural playground; it's an easy getaway from the capital city by car or public transportation.

Around Santiago

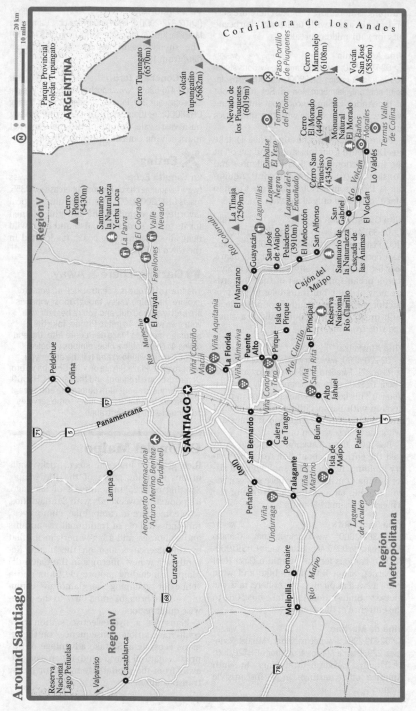

Cordillera de los Andes

ARGENTINA

Parque Provincial
Volcán Tupungato

Cerro Tupungato
(6570m)

Volcán
Tupungatito
(5682m)

Paso Portillo
de Piuquenes

Cerro
Marmolejo
(6108m)

Volcán
San José
(5856m)

Nevado de
los Piuquenes
(6019m)

Termas
del Plomo

Cerro
El Morado
(4490m)

Monumento
Natural
El Morado

Cerro
Plomo
(5430m)

Santuario de
la Naturaleza
Yerba Loca

La Parva

El Colorado

Valle
Nevado

Farellones

El Arrayán

Embalse
El Yeso

Laguna
Negra

Laguna del
Encañado

Cerro San
Francisco
(4345m)

Baños
Morales

Termas Valle
de Colina

Lo Valdés

El Volcán

San
Gabriel

Santuario de
la Naturaleza
Cascada de
las Ánimas

Lagunillas

La Tinaja
(2509m)

Guayacán

San José
de Maipo

Peladeros
(3910m)

El Melocotón

San Alfonso

Cajón del
Maipo

Río Volcán

Río Colorado

El Manzano

Isla de
Pirque

El Principal

Reserva
Nacional
Río Clarillo

Río Clarillo

Viña Aquitania

Viña Cousiño
Macul

Viña Almaviva

La Florida

Viña Concha
y Toro

Puente
Alto

Pirque

Viña
Santa Rita

Alto
Jahuel

Peldehue

Colina

Río Mapocho

57

Panamericana

71

5

SANTIAGO

Aeropuerto Internacional
Arturo Merino Benítez
(Pudahuel)

San Bernardo

Calera
de Tango

Buin

Paine

5

Región V

Lampa

Peñaflor

Viña
Undurraga

Talagante

Viña De
Martino

Isla de
Maipo

Río Maipo

Laguna
de Aculeo

Región
Metropolitana

Curacaví

68

Pomaire

Melipilla

78

Reserva
Nacional
Lago Peñuelas

Casablanca

Valparaíso

N

0   20 km
0   10 miles

Two roads wind up the Cajón on either side of the river and join at El Melocotón, 7km before San Alfonso. The numberless road on the southern side goes through Pirque, while the G-25 runs along the north side past San José de Maipo and San Alfonso to Baños Morales and the Monumento Natural el Morado.

November to March is rafting season; ski bums and bunnies flock here June to September; and walking, horseback riding and lunching are popular year-round. Make sure you take your documents with you if you are going beyond San Gabriel (the end of the paved road and the turnoff to Baños Morales): the closeness of the Argentine border means the police run regular checks here.

San Alfonso & Cascada de las Animas

Halfway up the Cajón del Maipo, a cluster of houses and tearooms make up San Alfonso. It's home to the beautiful private nature reserve Santuario de la Naturaleza Cascada de las Animas, which is set up like a natural, outdoorsy theme park.

◉ Sights & Activities

Unfortunately, most of the good hiking here is in the private reserve. Ask locals about free hill hikes nearby.

Cascada de las Animas   OUTDOORS
(☑02-861-1303; www.cascada.net; Camino al Volcán 31087, Casilla 57, San Alfonso; rafting trips CH$21,000) Organized activities are the only way to visit this nature reserve, which takes its name from a stunning waterfall reached by the shortest walk offered (CH$4000); there are also guided half-day hikes into the hills (CH$10,000). Horseback riding is the real specialty, however – indeed, the reserve is also a working ranch.

Weather permitting, it offers two-hour rides (CH$20,000) and all-day trips (CH$45,000 including *asado* lunch) and overnighters (CH$160,000). Book in advance.

Río Maipo Rafting   RAFTING
(www.cajondelmaipo.com; trips CH$16,000-23,000) Three-hour rafting trips descend Class III or IV rapids, taking in some lovely gorges before ending up in San José de Maipo. Cascada Animas runs guided tours, as do several other operations. All tours are led by experienced guides; helmets, wetsuits and life jackets are provided.

The river itself is made up of a series of mostly Class III rapids with very few calm areas – indeed, rafters are often tossed into the water. Still, it's less hazardous than when the first kayakers descended in the 1970s and found themselves facing automatic weapons as they passed the grounds of General Pinochet's estate at El Melocotón (the narrow bedrock chute here, one of the river's more entertaining rapids, is now known as 'El Pinocho,' the ex-dictator's nickname).

Geoaventura   ADVENTURE SPORTS
(☑02-871-2110; www.geoaventura.cl; Camino a San José del Maipo s/n; bungee CH$15,000, parapent CH$70,000; ⊙10am-6pm Sat & Sun) Just before you enter the Cajón del Maipo, this adventure center has bungee jumps, parapenting, a rock wall, paintball and more.

🛏 Sleeping & Eating

Cascada Lodge   LODGE $$
(d with/without bathroom CH$40,000/25,000, cabins for 3/6/8 people CH$60,000/95,000/120,000, campsite per person CH$10,000) If you're into the peace and quiet, spend the night here in one of the bungalow suites at the Cascada Lodge. The rustic-chic design features organic wood and stone fixtures, skylights, mosaic tilework and king-sized beds imported from Italy.

You can also choose to stay in one of the wood cabins with log fires and well-equipped kitchens, or smaller guest rooms. Alternatively, pitch your tent in the shady campsite.

Santuario del Río   LODGE $$$
(☑02-790-6900; www.santuariodelrio.cl; Camino al Volcán, San Alfonso; d/q CH$92,000/162,000; P🕸🛜⛲) Just outside San Alfonso, this tranquil lodge specializes in corporate retreats, but has a very nice selection of wood and adobe rooms and cabins that feature relaxing views over the river, hardwood bed frames and vaulted wood ceilings. There's a canopy and zipline course here, and the onsite restaurant is excellent.

Los Baqueanos   CAMPING $$$
(☑cell 9618-7066; www.losbaqueanos.cl; package incl meals from CH$80,000; 🛜) New on the scene in 2011 was the 'glamping' experience offered by Los Baqueanos. Overnighting in the great outdoors no longer means roughing it: guests sleep in luxurious dome-shaped tents heated by solar power and comfortably furnished with cozy cots, ergonomic chairs and wi-fi access.

Gourmet breakfasts and meals are prepared by the chef, while beautiful Chilean horses wait on the sidelines to take travelers on day excursions into the Cajón del Maipo.

❶ Getting There & Away

The reserve runs private van transportation to and from Santiago and Valparaíso (for one/two people round-trip CH$70,000/170,000). If you'd rather save the money and use public transportation, take metro line 4 to the Las Mercedes terminal, then hop onto bus 72 (CH$550) – or any bus that says 'San Alfonso' on the window. Note that some bus services only go as far as San José de Maipo (CH$450, 1½ hours, four hourly) – but that will be marked clearly on the bus. These buses may also be boarded outside Bellavista La Florida metro station (Línea 5), but the journey will be shorter if you take the Santiago metro as far as Las Mercedes.

Baños Morales & Monumento Natural El Morado

The G-25 continues uphill from San Alfonso; there's about 10km of tarmac, then 20km of rutted, unpaved dirt before you reach the small thermal springs of Baños Morales. There's excellent hiking here as well as hot springs pools. Serious trekkers can continue on for high-Andean adventures, mountain climbing and more.

◉ Sights & Activities

The owners of Refugio Lo Valdés run a number of excursions: excellent journeys on horseback (CH$14,000 to CH$30,000) can be combined with a barbecue in the mountains (from CH$30,000, including ride). They'll also arrange guides, trekking and trips to the hot springs at Termas Valle de Colina; in winter, you can rent snowshoes (CH$10,000 per day).

Monumento Natural El Morado PARK
(www.conaf.cl/parques/monumento-natural-el-morado; adult/child CH$2000/1000; ◷8:30am-2:30pm Oct-Apr) At Baños Morales is the entrance to Monumento Natural El Morado, a small national park. From the banks of sparkling Laguna El Morado are fabulous views of the San Francisco glacier and the 5000m summit of Cerro El Morado. It takes about two hours to reach the lake on the well-marked 8km trail from the Conaf post.

In summer, motivated hikers can continue to the base of Glaciar El Morado (six

hours one way from the trailhead), on the lower slopes of the mountain; there are free campsites around the lake.

**Balneario Termal
Baños Morales** HOT SPRINGS
(Baños Morales; CH$2500; ◷9am-6pm Tue-Sun, 9am-3:45pm Mon) These murky hot springs offer a curative dip after a day of hiking.

🛏 Sleeping & Eating

Refugio Lo Valdés GUESTHOUSE $
(✆cell 9230-5930; www.refugiolovaldes.com; Refugio Alemán, Ruta G-25 Km 77; dm CH$15,000, d incl breakfast from CH$48,000) Across the Río Volcán from Baños Morales, this chalet offers simple wood-clad rooms. Popular on weekends, the hotel boasts a stunning view over the Cajón. The on-site restaurant is renowned for its hearty meals and *onces*. Note that the dorm-style 'attic' accommodations do not include sheets or towels; they're designed for campers traveling with their own equipment.

❶ Getting There & Away

Some lines from San Alfonso continue to Baños Morales from September to March; there's one service a day from April to October at 7am on weekends, returning at 5pm.

Termas Valle de Colina

About 16km after the turnoff to Baños Morales, the G-25 reaches the thermal springs of **Termas Valle de Colina** (✆02-985-2609; www.termasvalledecolina.com; entrance incl camping adult/child CH$8000/4000, d without bathroom CH$30,000; ◷Oct-Feb), where hot natural pools overlook the valley. There's a well-organized campground and a basic but clean hostel; be sure to bring plenty of food supplies. The administration also offers guided hikes and one- to three-day horseback-riding expeditions.

For a real adventure, join a guided motorcycle tour of the region through **Enduro Trip** (✆cell 8764-2774; www.endurotrip.com; tours per person CH$100,000). Leaving from Santiago at 9am, these energetic guides run four standard circuits, including one that goes to Baños Morales, Termas Valle de Colina and Glaciar El Morado. In addition to the ride itself and some excellent wildlife viewing, you'll be stopping along the way to try regional treats from empanadas to homemade bread.

ℹ️ Getting There & Away

There is no public transportation to Termas Valle de Colina. However, private vans run by **Manzur Expediciones** (Map p50; ✉ cell 9335-7800; round-trip from CH$15,000) go to the baths from Santiago's Plaza Italia, usually on Wednesday, Saturday and Sunday.

The 93km drive from central Santiago to Baños Morales takes about two hours and is usually doable in a regular car. Count on another 20 minutes to reach Termas Valle de Colina; depending on the state of the last stretch of road, you may need a 4WD.

Ski Centers

Several of Chile's best ski resorts are within day-tripping (or two-day tripping) distance from Santiago. Aim to go midweek, if you can: snow-happy Santiaguinos crowd both the pistes and the roads up to the resorts on weekends.

Lagunillas

The cheapest skiing to be had near Santiago is at **Lagunillas** (www.skilagunillas.cl; day ski pass adult/child CH$25,000/20,000), a small resort 67km southeast of Santiago via San José de Maipo. Run by the Club Andino de Chile, it has four lifts and 13 runs; note that though the scenery is stunning, the snow here is generally not as good as at Santiago's more exclusive resorts. Club Andino runs a few small cabins here, but it's an easy day trip from Santiago.

Cajón de Mapocho – Tres Valles

Santiago's four most popular ski centers – Farellones/El Colorado, La Parva and Valle Nevado – are clustered in three valleys in the Mapocho river canyon, hence their collective name, Tres Valles. Although they're only 30km to 40km northeast of Santiago, the traffic-clogged road up can be slow going. All prices given here are for weekends and high season (usually early July to mid-August). Outside that time, there are hefty midweek discounts on both ski passes and hotels. Well-marked off-piste runs connect the three valleys. The predominance of drag lifts means that lines get long during the winter holidays, but otherwise crowds here are bearable. Ask about combination tickets if you're planning on skiing at multiple resorts.

🏃 Activities

Farellones & El Colorado   SKIING

(✉ 02-889-9210) Just 32km from Santiago, these two resorts are close enough together to be considered a single destination. The eating and after-ski scenes are scanty here, so locals tend just to come up for the day.

The cheaper of the two is the village of **Farellones** (www.farellones-centroski.com; day pass CH$15,000), Chile's first ski resort. At about 2500m, it's lower than **El Colorado** (www.elcolorado.cl; Nevería 4680, Las Condes) and its handful of runs tend to attract mainly beginner skiers, as well as tubing fans. There's more choice further up the mountain at El Colorado. The 22 runs range from beginner to expert and the highest of its 18 lifts takes you 3333m above sea level.

La Parva   SKIING

(✉ 02-964-2100; www.laparva.cl; office Av El Bosque Norte 0177, 2nd fl, Las Condes, Santiago; day pass adult/child CH$40,000/27,500) The most exclusive of Santiago's ski resorts, La Parva is definitely oriented toward posh families rather than the powder-and-party pack. Private cottages and condos make up ski base Villa La Parva, from where 14 lifts take you to its 30 runs, the highest of which starts at 3630m above sea level.

Snow permitting, there's plenty of off-piste skiing here too. The ski between La Parva and Valle Nevado or Farellones is also a favorite among more experienced skiers.

Valle Nevado   SKIING

(✉ 02-477-7700; www.vallenevado.com; Av Vitacura 5250, Oficina 304, Santiago; day pass adult/child CH$43,000/31,000) Modeled on European setups, Valle Nevado boasts almost 7000 acres of skiable terrain – the largest in South America. It's also the best-maintained of Santiago's resorts and has the most challenging runs. A variety of beginner runs make it good for kids too.

Thirteen chairlifts, a kick-ass eight-person gondola and surface lifts take you to high-altitude start points, which range from 2860m to 3670m. Adrenaline levels also run high here: there's a snow park, good off-piste action and heli-skiing.

In summer, the **Mirador chairlift** (round-trip ticket CH$10,000), transporting hikers and picnic-toting families to a 3300m peak, is open daily. Check the website for more on horseback-riding excursions, rock climbing, guided trekking, children's activities and lunch with panoramic views at the mountaintop restaurant. The resort is 12km from Farellones.

🛏 Sleeping

Valle Nevado's three hotels are expensive, yet the quality of both accommodations and service can be hit or miss. Rates at all include a ski pass and half-board. During July, only weeklong stays are available; for more flexibility, come in June, August or September.

Alternatively, the resort offers pleasant condo-style apartments; lift tickets and meals are not included in the room price (apt for two/three/six people from US$427/586/1137 per night).

Hotel Tres Puntas   HOTEL $$$
(Camino Farellones s/n; dm/d incl breakfast & dinner US$219/412) The 'budget' option skimps on luxury but not on prices: at Hotel Tres Puntas there's a mix of regular and dorm-style rooms, all of which are cramped but functional. Alternatively, the resort offers pleasant condo-style apartments; lift tickets and meals are not included in the room price.

Hotel Valle Nevado   LUXURY HOTEL $$$
(Camino Farellones s/n; d incl breakfast & dinner from US$724; @🖳) You can ski right onto your balcony at Hotel Valle Nevado. The best-appointed option, it has a heated outdoor pool, spa, and piano bar with a huge open fire. Dinner at the hotel's Fourchette D'or restaurant goes some way to offsetting the rates.

Eating

For a quick sandwich or snack, try the fast-food joint adjacent to the ski area at Hotel Puerta del Sol. Note that the resorts don't have supermarkets – you'll want to stock up on groceries and supplies before leaving Santiago.

La Fourchette d'Or   CHILEAN $$$
(Hotel Valle Nevado; mains CH$15,000-22,000; ⊙8-11pm Mon-Fri, 12:30-3:30pm & 8-11pm Sat & Sun) The most distinguished of Valle Nevado's six restaurants.

ℹ Getting There & Away

There is no public transportation to Santiago's ski resorts. Several private companies run regular shuttle services to the Tres Valles and Lagunillas during ski season. You can also reach Lagunillas by taking a bus to San José de Maipo and getting a taxi for the remaining 20km.

KL Adventure (☑02-217-9101; www.kladventure.com; Augusto Mira Fernández 14248, Las Condes, Santiago; round trip to Tres Valles CH$26,500, with hotel pick-up CH$37,000) The shuttle leaves at 8am and returns at 5pm.

SkiTotal (☑02-246-0156; www.skitotal.cl; Av Apoquindo 4900, Local 39-42, Las Condes, Santiago; one way CH$13,000-15,000) The shuttle leaves at 8am and returns at 5pm, running from Santiago to Lagunillas and Tres Valles.

Middle Chile

Best Places to Eat

➡ Café Vinilo (p98)

➡ Vino Bello (p114)

➡ Lapostolle (p112)

➡ Restaurante Miguel Torres (p117)

➡ Emiliana (p107)

Best Places to Sleep

➡ La Joya del Mar (p127)

➡ Zerohotel (p98)

➡ Hostal Casa Chueca (p120)

➡ Hotel Casa Pando (p113)

➡ Ecobox Andino (p126)

Why Go?

If you love wine, fine dining, never-ending springs, street art, skiing, hiking, mountain biking, surfing or just lazing for days on lost coasts, there's a spot in Middle Chile that was created just for you. This is Chile's most important wine-producing region, and the wineries and cozy bed and breakfasts of the sun-kissed Colchagua, Maule and Casablanca Valleys will tickle your palate and travel your senses. For board riders, there are killer breaks up and down the coast, with surf culture exploding in towns like Pichilemu and Buchupureo. Hikers and skiers will love the lost lagoons and steep pistes found eastward in the Andes, while cultural explorers won't want to miss the murals and tumble-fumble alleyways of Valparaíso and the hard-rocking musical exploits of Concepción. The 2010 earthquake hit this region especially hard, but the recovery continues, and most businesses are back up and running.

When to Go
Valparaiso

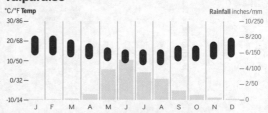

Jun–Sep Frequent snowfall brings skiers and snowboarders to the slopes in full force.

Oct–Dec Before the summertime rush, the beach towns are calm and hotel rates are cheaper.

Jan–May Wine lovers migrate to the vineyards for the grape harvest and the festivals surrounding it.

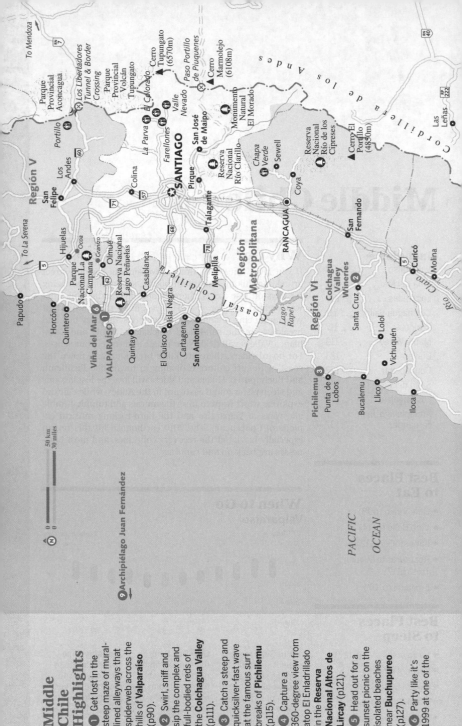

Middle Chile Highlights

1 Get lost in the steep maze of mural-lined alleyways that spiderweb across the hills of **Valparaíso** (p90).

2 Swirl, sniff and sip the complex and full-bodied reds of the **Colchagua Valley** (p111).

3 Catch a steep and quicksilver-fast wave at the famous surf breaks of **Pichilemu** (p115).

4 Capture a 360-degree view from atop El Enladrillado in the **Reserva Nacional Altos de Lircay** (p121).

5 Head out for a sunset picnic on the isolated beaches near **Buchupureo** (p127).

6 Party like it's 1999 at one of the

light-up-the-night discos of **Viña del Mar** (p105).

7 Ski through the trees on the longest ski slope in South America at **Nevados de Chillán** (p125).

8 Tickle your senses with wine, spa treatments and fine dining in the **Maule Valley** (p119).

9 Relive a castaway's Robinson Crusoe–style adventure in the **Archipiélago Juan Fernández** (p137).

ℹ Getting There & Away

Santiago sits in the middle of the region, providing easy international access, while to the south, Concepción also has a large airport. The excellent long-distance bus services that travel up and down the Panamericana highway are the quickest and cheapest way to arrive, whether you're coming from the Lakes District to the south, from Santiago or the north, or internationally via Mendoza in Argentina.

ℹ Getting Around

Frequent local and long-distance buses connect all the major towns in Middle Chile to each other and to Santiago. Trains are also an option for travel between cities on the Panamericana between Santiago and Chillán – journeys take as long as on a bus, and are markedly more expensive, so train travel is probably only worth doing for the novelty value.

Getting to national parks and smaller towns can be trickier: snow closes some areas in winter, in others public transportation reduces to a trickle outside summer, and a few have no public transportation at all.

Having a car is invaluable for quick trips to far-flung parks and for touring wineries in the Colchagua, Maule and Casablanca Valleys.

VALPARAÍSO & THE CENTRAL COAST

This distinctive coastline is dominated by the twin maritime cities of Valparaíso and Viña del Mar. Tanned-and-tawny beach destinations stretch to the north and south and are hugely popular with vacationing Santiaguinos. Inland, you can explore Chile's best white wines in the Casablanca vineyards or head off track to Parque Nacional La Campana.

ℹ HOP ON THE BUS

Sure, you can take the creaky antique elevators or huff it uphill on foot – but there's another unforgettable way to experience some of Valparaíso's magic. The route of local bus O (labeled *micro O* or sometimes *micro 612*) carries a mix of weary locals and camera-toting tourists through the narrow alleyways and across several of the city's steep hillsides; you can board in front of Congreso Nacional, atop Cerro Alegre or at various other points throughout town.

Valparaíso

☎ 032 / POP 263,500

Syncopated, dilapidated, colorful and poetic, Valparaíso is a wonderful mess. Pablo Neruda, who drew much inspiration from this hard-working port town, said it best: 'Valparaíso, how absurd you are...you haven't combed your hair, you've never had time to get dressed, life has always surprised you.'

But Neruda wasn't the only artist to fall for Valparaíso's unexpected charms. Poets, painters and would-be philosophers have long been drawn to Chile's most unusual city. Along with the ever-shifting port population of sailors, dockworkers and prostitutes, they've endowed gritty and gloriously spontaneous Valparaíso with an edgy air of 'anything goes.' Add to this the spectacular faded beauty of its chaotic *cerros* (hills), some of the best street art in Latin America, a maze of steep, sinuous streets, alleys and *escaleras* (stairways) piled high with crumbling mansions, and it's clear why some visitors are spending more time here than in Santiago. Concerted efforts have been made to bring top-tier restaurants and hotels to the city – and to keep at least the major tourist zones safe in a notoriously unsafe port city – making Valpo's midnight lights shine brighter than ever.

History

The sea has always defined Valparaíso and the region surrounding it. Fishing sustained the area's first inhabitants, the Chango, and no sooner had the Spanish conquistadores arrived than Valparaíso became a stop-off point for boats taking gold and other Latin American products to Spain. More seafaring looters soon followed: English and Dutch pirates, including Sir Francis Drake, who repeatedly sacked Valparaíso for gold.

The port city grew slowly at first, but boomed with the huge demand for Chilean wheat prompted by the California gold rush. The first major port of call for ships coming round Cape Horn, Valparaíso became a commercial center for the entire Pacific coast and the hub of Chile's nascent banking industry.

After Valparaíso's initial glory days, the port saw hard times in the 20th century. The 1906 earthquake destroyed most of the city's buildings, then the opening of the Panama Canal had an equally cataclysmic effect on the port's economy. Only the Chilean navy remained a constant presence.

Today Valparaíso is back on the nautical charts as a cruise-ship stop-off, and Chile's growing fruit exports have also boosted the port. More significantly, the city has been Chile's legislative capital since 1990 and was voted the cultural capital in 2003. Unesco sealed the deal by giving it World Heritage status, prompting tourism to soar.

◉ Sights & Activities

Your best activity is wandering through the city streets as you check out the murals and teetering architecture. Don't miss a trip or two on one of the 15 rattling *ascensores* (funiculars) built between 1883 and 1916 that crank you up into the hills and meandering back alleys. Beach lovers should head north to Viña and Zapallar. Just west of town, a good walk can be had at the beaches of San Mateo, Carvallo and Torpederas.

◉ Cerros Concepción & Alegre

These steep cobbled streets are lined by traditional 19th-century houses with painted corrugated-iron facades that form a vivid patchwork of colors. Some of the city's best cafes and restaurants are here (though not clubs, as late-night music is banned).

Museo de Bellas Artes MUSEUM
(Paseo Yugoslavo 166; admission CH$2000) The rambling art-nouveau building at the western end of Cerro Alegre is called Palacio Baburizza; it houses the Museo de Bellas Artes (Fine Arts Museum), which has a decent permanent collection plus plenty of details on the original palace owners. **Ascensor El Peral** (Plaza de Justicia (El Plan) & Paseo Yugoslavo (Cerro Alegre); admission CH$100; ◷10:30am-5:30pm Tue-Sun) runs here from just off Plaza Sotomayor. A quick way up to the eastern side of Cerro Alegre is the **Ascensor Reina Victoria** (admission CH$250; ◷7am-11pm), which connects Av Elias to Paseo Dimalow.

Ascensor Concepción HISTORIC SITE
(Prat (El Plan) & Paseo Gervasoni (Cerro Concepción); admission CH$300; ◷7am-10pm) The city's oldest elevator, Ascensor Concepción takes you to Paseo Gervasoni, at the lower end of Cerro Concepción. Built in 1883, it originally ran on steam power.

Museo Lukas MUSEUM
(☏032-222-1344; www.lukas.cl; Paseo Gervasoni 448, Cerro Concepción; adult/child & senior CH$1000/500; ◷10:30am-2pm & 3-6pm Tue-Sun) Local cartoonist Lukas had a sharp eye for

VALPARAÍSO'S MURALS

Wandering up and down the winding hills of Valparaíso, you'll see colorful public art everywhere, from dreamlike wall paintings of glamorous women to political graffiti-style murals splashed across garage doors. Top spots to view street art are Cerros Concepción, Alegre and Bellavista. Cerro Polanco was 'bombed' by grafitti artists from across Latin America at the First Latin American Graffiti-Mural Festival, with 80-plus murals going up in just a few days. The neighborhood is great for wandering by day, but avoid it at night.

As you cruise the streets, keep your eyes peeled for Chilean artist Inti. His large-scale mural, painted across the surface of several neighboring buildings and visible from Cerro Concepción, was unveiled in early 2012. The vibrant sideways image shows a mysterious, partially fragmented figure draped with exotic jewelry.

the idiosyncrasies of Valparaíso. You need to speak Spanish to understand his sardonic political strips in the Museo Lukas, but the ink drawings of iconic Valpo buildings speak for themselves.

◉ Cerro Cárcel

Parque Cultural de Valparaíso ARTS CENTRE
(www.pcdv.cl; Castro s/n, Cerro Cárcel) FREE This cultural center built from the bones of a prison has a little bit of everything the mind-traveler could ask for. There are excellent murals in the old exercise yards (with practically no chance of getting shanked), rotating arts exhibits, live theater and dance, and occasional classes, courses, round tables and other intellectually stimulating events.

Reach it by walking up Subida Cumming.

◉ Cerro Panteón

Cementerios 1 & 2 CEMETERY
(Dinamarca s/n; ◷8am-dusk) The city's most illustrious, influential and infamous residents rest in peace in Cementerio 1, where the tombs look like ornate mini palaces. Adjoining it is Cementerio 2, including the **Cementerio de Disidentes** ('dissident cemetery') where English and European immigrants were buried.

Valparaíso

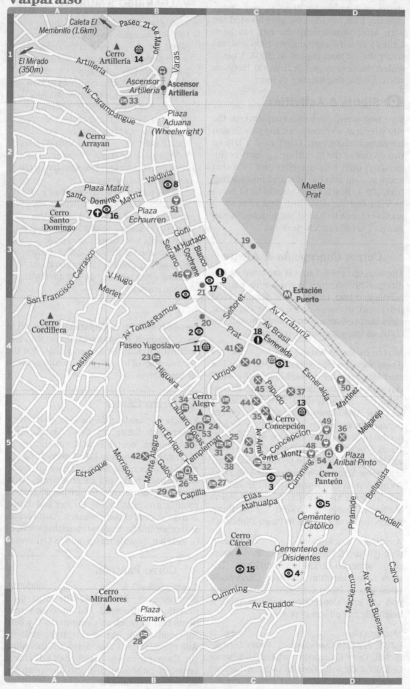

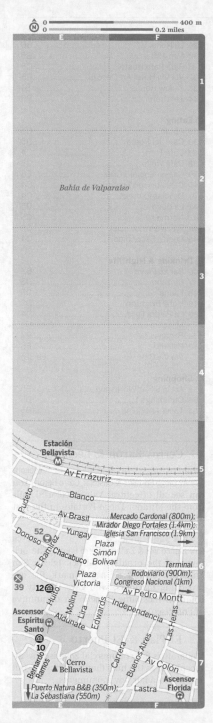

Despite the name, these departed souls weren't rabble-rousers; they were simply Protestants, and therefore not accepted at the traditional cemeteries. The views from here are worthwhile in themselves. If you're up for the walk, you can also get here by hiking up Av Ecuador.

⊙ Cerro Bellavista

Artists and writers have long favored this quiet residential hill. And there's a few good restaurants and cafes worth checking out.

★**La Sebastiana**   HISTORIC BUILDING
(☎032-225-6606; www.fundacionneruda.org; Ferrari 692; adult/child & senior CH$5000/1500; ⊙10:30am-6:50pm Tue-Sun Jan & Feb, 10:10am-6pm Tue-Sun Mar-Dec) Bellavista's most famous resident artist was Pablo Neruda, who made a point of watching Valparaíso's annual New Year's fireworks from his house at the top of the hill, La Sebastiana. Because it's first-come, first-served, it's recommended that you get here in the morning.

Getting here involves a hefty uphill hike, and the climbing continues inside the house – but you're rewarded on each floor with ever more heart-stopping views over the harbor. Unlike Neruda's other houses, you can wander around La Sebastiana at will, lingering over the chaotic collection of ships' figureheads, glass, 1950s furniture and artworks by his famous friends. Alongside the house, the Fundación Neruda has built the Centro Cultural La Sebastiana, containing a small exhibition space, cafe and souvenir shop. To get here, walk 800m uphill along Héctor Calvo from Ascensor Espíritu Santo. Alternatively, take green bus O on Serrano near Plaza Sotomayor in El Plan, or from the plaza at the top of Templeman on Cerro Alegre and get off at the 6900 block of Av Alemania.

Museo a Cielo Abierto   MUSEUM
(Open-Air Museum; cnr Rudolph & Ramos; ⊙24hr) **FREE** Twenty classic, colorful murals are dotted through this *cerro's* lower streets, forming the Museo a Cielo Abierto, created between 1969 and 1973 by students from the Universidad Católica's Instituto de Arte. The Ascensor Espíritu Santo takes you from behind Plaza Victoria to the heart of this art.

⊙ Cerro Artillería

Clear views out over the sea made this southwestern hill a strategic defense spot, hence the name. It lacks the great murals

Valparaíso

of other *cerros*, but has a nice grouping of crafts shops on top, making this more of a journey for your second or third day.

Museo Naval y Marítimo　MUSEUM
(Naval & Maritime Museum; ☏032-243-7651; www.museonaval.cl; Paseo 21 de Mayo 45, Cerro Artillería; adult/child CH$1000/300; ◎10am-6pm Tue-Sun) Cannons still stand ready outside this naval museum. Much space is devoted to Chile's victory in the 19th-century War of the Pacific.

Other exhibits include historical paintings, uniforms, ships' furniture, swords, navigating instruments and medals, all neatly displayed in exhibition rooms along one side of a large courtyard. Rattling **Ascensor Artillería** (which is closed for restoration) brings you here from Plaza Aduana.

◎ Cerros Barón & Lecheros

Mirador Diego Portales　LOOKOUT
(cnr Av Diego Portales & Castelar, Cerro Barón) You can see all of central Valpo's colorful hills from the Mirador Diego Portales in the east of town.

Iglesia San Francisco　CHURCH
(cnr Blanco Viel & Zañartu, Cerro Barón) The bell tower of the ornate, red-brick Iglesia San Francisco served as a landmark for approaching mariners, who gave the city its common nickname 'Pancho' (a diminutive of Francisco).

◎ El Plan & El Puerto

Valparaíso's flat commercial zone isn't as atmospheric as the hills that rise above it, but it contains a fair few monuments.

Plaza Matriz　　　　　　　　PLAZA

The historic heart of the city is Plaza Matriz, which is watched over by **Iglesia La Matriz.** Begun in 1837, it's the fifth church to occupy this site since the construction of the original chapel in 1559.

In nearby streets, luridly lit 'cabarets' (read: brothels) and liquor stores testify that port life in Valpo is still very much alive.

Reloj Turri　　　　　　　　MONUMENT

(cnr Esmeralda & Gómez Carreño) Where Prat and Cochrane converge to become Esmeralda, the Edificio Turri narrows to the width of its namesake clock tower, the Reloj Turri.

Plaza Sotomayor　　　　　　PLAZA

The Plaza Sotomayor is dominated by the impressive blue-colored palatial **Edificio de la Comandancia Naval** (Naval Command Building). In the middle of the square lies the **Monumento a los Héroes de Iquique,** a subterranean mausoleum paying tribute to Chile's naval martyrs.

The **Aduana Nacional** (Customs House) and Estación Puerto, the terminal for Merval commuter trains, are also nearby. The plaza has a helpful tourist kiosk and a tacky handicrafts market, the Feria de Artesanía. **Muelle Prat,** the pier at the foot of Plaza Sotomayor, is a lively place on weekends, and is the prime point for spotting cranes and containers.

Museo de Historia Natural　　MUSEUM

(www.mhnv.cl; Condell 1546, El Plan) FREE Explore the natural history of central Chile in nine rooms that focus on biology and ecosystems. Signage is in Spanish only.

Congreso Nacional　　HISTORIC BUILDING

(cnr Av Pedro Montt & Rawson) One of Valpo's only modern landmarks is the controversial Congreso Nacional, located in the east section of El Plan. Its roots lie in Pinochet's presidency both literally and legislatively: it was built on one of his boyhood homes and mandated by his 1980 constitution (which moved the legislature away from Santiago).

Mercado Cardonal　　　　　　MARKET

(⊙ 6am-5pm) As colorful as Valparaíso's trademark houses – and built almost as high – are the fruit and vegetable displays in the Mercado Cardonal, bordered by Yungay, Brasil, Uruguay and Rawson.

Barrio El Puerto　　　　　　AREA

In the west of El Plan, Barrio El Puerto (the port neighborhood) has the twin honors of being the oldest part of Valparaíso, the most run-down. Crumbling stone facades hint of times gone by – such as the **Mercado Puerto** (cnr Cochrane & San Martín, Puerto), a defunct food market now home to a pack of street cats.

Courses

Chilean Cuisine　　　　COOKING COURSE

(☑ cell 6621-4626; www.cookingclasseschile.cl; location varies; course per person from CH$37,000) An energetic chef takes you to shop for ingredients at the local market, then teaches you to make pisco sours, taste local wines and cook – then eat – a menu of Chilean classics.

Gonzalo Lara　　　　　COOKING COURSE

(☑ 032-223-0665; gonzalolarachef@yahoo.es) The madcap chef of Café Vinilo runs a culinary course that has won rave reviews from travelers; email him directly for prices and availability.

Natalis Language Center　LANGUAGE COURSE

(☑ 032-225-4849; www.natalislang.com; Plaza Justicia 45, 6th fl, Oficina 602, El Plan; courses per week from CH$90,000, 3-day crash courses CH$135,000) Has a good reputation for quick results.

TOP FIVE VALPO VIEWS

➡ **Paseo 21 de Mayo on Cerro Artillería** to survey the cranes and containers of the port.

➡ **Plaza Bismark on Cerro Cárcel** for a panoramic take of the bay.

➡ Mirador Diego Portales (p94) **on Cerro Barón** for a sweeping perspective of Valpo's colorful house-cluttered central views.

➡ The viewpoint at the end of **Calle Merlet on Cerro Cordillera** to see the rusting roofs of Barrio El Puerto (p95) and the civic buildings of Plaza Sotomayor from above.

➡ **Paseo Atkinson on Cerro Concepción** for views of typical Valpo houses during the day, and a twinkling sea of lights on the hills at night.

> ## SENDERO BICENTENARIO
>
> If you only do one thing in Valparaíso, this is it. Get to the bottom – or rather, the top – of the city by exploring part of the **Sendero Bicentenario**, a 30km cultural and historical route designed by local not-for-profit organization **Fundación Valparaíso**. The trail is divided into 15 themed sections and takes in parts of the port, El Plan and many of the city's lesser-known hills. Check at hotels and tourist offices for a map.

👉 Tours

Santiago Adventures (📞 02-2244-2750; www.santiagoadventures.com; Guardia Vieja 255, Oficina 403, Providencia, Santiago) offers a complete full-day tour from the capital.

⭐ Tours 4 Tips WALKING TOUR
(www.tours4tips.com; Plaza Sotomayor, El Plan; ⏰ 10am & 3pm) Just show up at Plaza Sotomayor, look for the guides with the red-and-white shirts in the middle of the plaza, and head off for a friendly introduction to the city that focuses on street art, cultural history and politics. You only tip if you like the tour. We think CH$5000 to CH$10,000 is a good tip if you enjoy yourself.

Harbor Boat Tours BOAT TOUR
(Muelle Prat; 30min tour CH$3000; ⏰ 9:30am-6:30pm) Pass alongside giant cruise vessels or naval battleships, or spot sea lions frolicking in the harbor. Several companies operate boats – ask around for the best price and group up for savings.

🎉 Festivals & Events

Puerto de Ideas CULTURAL
(www.puertodeideas.cl; ⏰ Nov) Held every November, this intellectual conference is Chile's equivalent to TED. If you speak Spanish, it can be fascinating.

Año Nuevo NEW YEAR
(⏰ Dec 31) Fantastic fireworks displays over the harbor draw hundreds of thousands of spectators to the city each December 31. Book accommodations well in advance.

🛏 Sleeping

Yellow House B&B $
(📞 032-233-9435; www.theyellowhouse.cl; Capitán Muñoz Gamero 91, Cerro Artillería; r incl breakfast with/without bathroom CH$38,000/25,000; @ 🐕 🛜) Oh-my-god views over the old port set this quiet B&B apart, as does the friendly care lavished on guests by the Chilean owner. The cozy, pastel-painted rooms come with thick white comforters. The Oceano by far has the best views. The only drawback: you're quite removed from the action, dining and nightlife of the more popular *cerros*.

Use caution arriving late at night.

La Nona B&B $
(📞 cell 6618-6186; www.bblanona.com; Galos 660, Cerro Alegre; s/d/tr incl breakfast CH$25,000/36,000/46,000; 🛜) The English-speaking owners of this B&B are mad about Valpo, and love sharing insider tips with their guests. The rooms are simple but highly passable. Stained glass and skylights add an open air, and the central location on Cerro Alegre is also a serious selling point. Ask for a room with a view.

Hostal Jacaranda HOSTEL $
(📞 032-327-7567; www.hostaljacaranda.blogspot .com; Urriola 636, Cerro Alegre; dm/d from CH$7000/20,000; 🛜) 🌿 Small but very welcoming – and perfectly located in a lively section of Cerro Alegre – this cheerful, sustainably run hostel (note the recycling efforts) features a terrace that's romantically illuminated at night. The owners have a wealth of knowledge; if you ask nicely, they might even show you how to make Chilean specialties like pisco sours and empanadas.

Pata Pata Hostel HOSTEL $
(📞 032-317-3153; www.patapatahostel.com; Templeman 657, Cerro Alegre; dm CH$7500-10,000, d without bathroom CH$28,000; 🛜) The most youth-forward of Valparaíso's hostels, this spot up a picturesque flower-dotted stairway has a positive energy, plenty of hangout places and pumped-in music. It's a bit unkempt (but so is the city) and the dorm mattresses are blandish.

Mm 450 HOSTEL $
(📞 032-222-9919; www.mm450.cl; Lautaro Rosas 450, Cerro Alegre; dm CH$14,080-17,850, r with/without bathroom incl breakfast CH$71,400/53,500; 🛜) This 'boutique hostel' has a streamlined modern look, and super-comfy dorm rooms with new mattresses and gleaming white comforters. It's attached to a hip restaurant and lounge, so there's always somebody around, but despite a gorgeous interior patio, it doesn't seem like there's much of a

traveler's scene... at least not yet. There's no shared kitchen.

Hostal Luna Sonrisa
HOSTEL $

(☑032-273-4117; www.lunasonrisa.cl; Templeman 833, Cerro Alegre; dm/s/d without bathroom CH$9000/14,000/25,000, d/apt CH$32,000/52,000; ☜) Small, quiet and close to Cerro Alegre's restaurants and bars, this hostel is a decent value, though it doesn't seem as lively as other spots, and the smiles from staff are hard won.

Hostal Cerro Alegre
B&B $

(☑032-327-0374; www.hostalcerroalegre.cl; Urriola 562, Cerro Alegre; dm CH$12,000, r with/without bathroom CH$39,000/25,000; ☜) Funky antiques, original oil paintings by the former owner and an eclectic mix of colors, styles and design sensibilities make this a good bet for the BoHo crowd. There's a shared kitchen and smallish living area, and the dorm sleeps just three.

Casa Aventura
HOSTEL $

(☑032-275-5963; www.casaventura.cl; Pasaje Gálvez 11, Cerro Concepción; dm/s/d without bathroom CH$9000/17,000/25,000; ☜) One of Valpo's oldest hostels, this ramshackle old house has airy, pastel-painted dorms, while doubles feature sky-high ceilings and original wooden floors. There's a shared kitchen, but it's missing a cool terrace or large common areas.

El Mirador
B&B $

(☑032-234-5937; www.elmiradordevalparaiso.cl; Levarte 251, Cerro Playa Ancha; s/d/tr incl breakfast CH$15,500/36,200/51,700, apt for 2 people CH$62,000; ☻) Budget-minded couples and solo travelers rave about this lovely B&B. Though slightly out of the way, the beautifully tended property – a restored house

with comfortable doubles, apartments with kitchenettes, accommodating hosts and a spacious terrace – is tremendous value. To get here, from the Museo Naval y Maritimo, walk uphill along Playa Ancha and turn left on Levarte.

Vía Vía Hotel Art Deco
BOUTIQUE HOTEL $$

(☑032-319-2134; www.viaviacafe.cl; Almirante Montt 217, Cerro Alegre; r CH$39,000-58,000; ☜) Run by a friendly Ecuadorian-Belgian couple, this round-walled art-deco boutique is a favorite for the arts-poetry-and-chunky-glasses set. With just five rooms, it's a cozy affair. The rooms are sparse but quite airy, and the bathrooms have solar showers and elegant stone accents. There is an outrageously fun cafe on the main floor, making this a good spot for midnight-candle burners.

Puerto Natura B&B
B&B $$

(☑032-222-4405; www.puertonatura.cl; Héctor Calvo 850, Cerro Bellavista; d with/without bathroom incl breakfast CH$67,000/44,000; ☜☒) The fluffy beds and spotless, individually decorated rooms in this 1935 castle make it a good midrange bet. The owners are actually natural therapists: reiki, massages, yoga and Turkish baths are available on-site. A terraced garden filled with fruit trees is tucked away behind the house and Pablo Neruda's house, La Sebastiana, is a stone's throw away.

Hostal Morgan
B&B $$

(☑032-211-4931; www.hostalmorgan.cl; Capilla 784, Cerro Alegre; d with/without bathroom CH$54,000/48,000; @☜) Old-fashioned iron and wooden bedsteads, springy mattresses and crisp white sheets at this deliciously homey old house make this cheery yellow B&B a perennial travelers' favorite.

MIDDLE CHILE VALPARAÍSO

---

❶ NAVIGATING VALPARAÍSO

Valparaíso is a city of two parts: El Plan, the congested, flat commercial district closest to the sea; and the 42 *cerros* (hills) that rise up steeply behind it.

Valparaíso's hills defy even determined cartographers. Av Almirante Montt and Urriola lead from El Plan to Cerros Concepción and Alegre. From Plaza Aníbal Pinto, Cummings takes you to Cerro Cárcel; from nearby Av Ecuador, Yerbas Buenas winds up Cerro Bellavista, accessible from the other side by Ferrari. Av Alemania winds along the top of the more central *cerros*.

Valparaíso Map (www.valparaisomap.cl) is by far the best map of this notoriously hard-to-navigate city, while Ascensores de Valparaíso (www.ascensoresvalparaiso.org) has an interactive map of the city's old lifts. Also check out the cool online maps of the city's barrios at Ciudad de Valparaíso (www.ciudaddevalparaiso.cl). Look for print maps at hotels and tourist information kiosks.

Zerohotel　　　　　　BOUTIQUE HOTEL **$$$**
(☎032-211-3113; www.zerohotel.com; Lautaro Rosas 343, Cerro Alegre; d incl breakfast CH\$166,000-238,000; ❇🏩🛜🏊) This boutique has one of the best patios around. And sprawling out poolside, taking in the Valparaíso sunshine, is a decadant treat that will last a lifetime. There are just nine rooms, all with high ceilings, minimalist design and plenty of creature comforts – like an honor bar that gives you access to some of Chile's best wines.

The contempo digs match surprisingly well with the lofty architecture that dates back to 1880.

Casa Higueras　　　　BOUTIQUE HOTEL **$$$**
(☎032-249-7900; www.casahigueras.cl; Higuera 133, Cerro Alegre; r CH\$190,000-324,000; 🛜🏊) Rich Santiaguinos always preferred weekending in Viña to Valpo but they've been won over by this hotel's slick rooms with dark-wood furniture and huge beds, mosaic-tiled bathrooms with big bowl sinks and the quiet living room filled with Asian sculptures and low beige sofas.

It has views out over the bay, plus a lovely swimming pool, Jacuzzi and terrace, ideal for cocktails at sunset.

Hotel Ultramar　　　　BOUTIQUE HOTEL **$$$**
(☎032-221-0000; www.hotelultramar.com; Pérez 173, Cerro Cárcel; d incl breakfast CH\$83,000; 🛜) Unparalleled views over the bay justify the trek to sleek Ultramar, high on Cerro Cárcel. Behind the brown-brick front it's very mod, with soaring red-and-white walls, black banisters and checkered floor tiles.

Just make sure you understand which room you're booking ahead of time – there's a big difference between a spacious double with a view and a smaller room that doesn't face the ocean.

✕ Eating

✕ Cerro Concepción

Puerto Escondido　　　　CHILEAN **$**
(www.puertoescondido.cl; Papudo 424; mains CH\$3500-6200) Situated in one of Valparaíso's quaint antique houses, this family-run eatery offers a short menu of well-made Chilean classics like *pastel de papas* (a potato casserole similar to shepherd's pie) and other homey dishes you won't find in contemporary restaurants. Come for the down-to-earth ambience as well as the food.

Café Turri　　　　　　SEAFOOD **$**
(www.cafeturri.cl; Templeman 146; mains CH\$4500-8200) Though service can be hit or miss and prices steep for what you get, Café Turri boasts unforgettable views over the harbor and ocean. Especially if you're not in a hurry, you can't go wrong by grabbing a seat on the terrace and ordering a pisco sour with steamed mussels or *palta cardenal* (avocado stuffed with shrimp).

Abtao　　　　　　　　SEAFOOD **$$**
(☎032-222-3442; www.restauranteabtao.cl; Abtao 550, Cerro Concepción; mains CH\$8500-10,900) If it's warm out, sit in the glassed-in patio; if not, head toward the art-deco-inspired dining room for warmth, intimacy and elegance. The food is playful and inventive, matching fruit with fish, sweet with tart and spiced flavors from across the globe.

✕ Cerro Alegre

⭐**Café Vinilo**　　　　　CHILEAN **$**
(Almirante Montt 448, Cerro Alegre; mains CH\$5800-8500) Vying for Valparaíso's top spot, this eclectic resto-bar is studied, quirky, esoteric and sublime. The dinner plates feature fresh salmon, albacore and other local catches with inventive presentations and delicious flavor combinations.

The retro-chic atmosphere matches (and perfectly mis-matches) the colors and rhythms of the city. As the last plates are licked, the vinyl gets turned up and things slip into bar mode.

Delicias Express　　　　CHILEAN **$**
(Urriola 358, Cerro Alegre; empanadas CH\$1000-1300; ⊙8am-6pm) Boasting 60 varieties of empanadas, friendly service and a crispy crust you'll love, this is one of the best empanada joints on the coast.

Delicatessen Emporio　　　CHILEAN **$**
(Urriola 383, Cerro Alegre; set lunch CH\$3900-5900; ⊙11am-3pm Mon-Thu, 11am-11pm Fri & Sat; 🛜) This small dining room has a high-quality fixed-menu lunch with your choice of soup or salad, main plates like fresh-caught salmon or homemade gnocchi in Tuscan sauce, followed by a sumptious dessert. There's a semi-open kitchen – so you know it's clean!

La Cocó　　　　　　　SANDWICHES **$**
(www.lacoco-sangucheriaartesanal.blogspot. com; Monte Alegre 546, Cerro Alegre; sandwiches CH\$3800-5000; ⊙closed Mon & Tue, lunch only

Sun; 🍴) Popular with hip *porteños* and savvy travelers, this *sanguchería artesanal* (artisan sandwich-maker) is a true delight. Gourmet sandwiches come piled high with fresh seafood (smoked salmon with spicy chorizo is a current hit) or vegetarian-friendly toppings. A line-up of live-music performances and poetry readings enliven the space in the evening.

Norma's
CHILEAN $

(Almirante Montt 391, Cerro Alegre; set lunch $4900-6900; ⊙closed Mon) Don't let the name (or the nondescript entryway) throw you off: just climb the tall stairway into this cheerful, casually elegant restaurant for a surprisingly well-prepared set lunch that's friendlier on your wallet than most others in the area. The restored house still has the grand dimensions, polished wood and charming antique window frames of the original structure.

Pasta e Vino
ITALIAN $$

(☎ 032-249-6187; www.pastaevinoristorante.cl; Templeman 352; mains CH$6900-9900) If you want to compete with local foodies, you'll probably have to reserve ahead (you can simply fill out the online form on the website); you'll be dining on inventive pastas of the day in a sleek, intimate atmosphere with only a dozen tables.

🍴 El Plan & El Puerto

Casino Social J Cruz
CHILEAN $

(Condell 1466, El Plan; mains CH$4500-6000) Liquid-paper graffiti covers the tabletops and windows at this tiny cafe, tucked away down a narrow passageway in El Plan. Forget about menus, there's one essential dish to try: it's said that *chorrillana* (a mountain of french fries under a blanket of fried pork, onions and egg) was invented here. Folk singers serenade you into the wee hours.

Café del Poeta
CAFE $

(Plaza Aníbal Pinto 1181, El Plan; mains CH$3500-7800; ⊙8:30am-midnight Mon-Fri, from 11am Sat & Sun; 🛜) This sweet cafe and eatery brings some sophistication to a busy central plaza in El Plan. On the menu are savory crepes, pasta and seafood; there's also sidewalk seating, a relaxing afternoon tea, wines by the glass and a collection of books about Valparaíso that guests are invited to linger over.

Mercado Cardonal
MARKET $

(Mercado Cardonal, 2nd fl, El Plan; mains CH$3500-5000; ⊙9am-10pm) There's a good selection of seafood stands at Valparaíso's main food market. El Rincón de Pancho and Desayunador Paloma are top local recommendations.

Caleta El Membrillo
SEAFOOD $

(Av Altamirano 1569, El Puerto; mains CH$2800-5200; ⊙noon-6pm Mon-Thu, open later Fri & Sat) This casual, family-friendly seafood marketplace on the waterfront is a laid-back lunch spot where you can sit outside and watch the commercial fishermen coming and going while feasting on fresh, simply prepared shrimp, fried fish and Chilean specialties.

🍷 Drinking & Entertainment

★ Viá Viá Café
CAFE

(☎ 032-319-2134; www.viaviacafe.cl; Almirante Montt 217, Cerro Alegre; ⊙noon-2am; 🛜) 🍴 Set below a precipitous stairway and looming three-story mural, this garden cafe brims with creativity and serendipitous energy. There's occasional live music, simple dining options, and a good mix of Belgian beers and Chilean wines on tap. It's a must-stop on any mural or pub crawl.

Fauna
BAR

(www.faunahotel.cl; Pasaje Dimalow 166, Cerro Alegre; ⊙1-11pm) One of the best decks in town is found at this hip lounge and resto-bar (with a sophisticated attached hotel). It is a top spot for locals to suck down craft beers, cocktails and wine.

Hotel Brighton
BAR

(www.brighton.cl; Paseo Atkinson 151, Cerro Concepción; ⊙10am-midnight Sun-Thu, to 3am Fri & Sat) Teetering over the edge of Cerro Concepción, this funked-out house has a terrific terrace restaurant that overlooks the port and city. Come around sunset for cocktails and stay for decent food and live music on weekends.

Pajarito
BAR

(www.pajaritobar.blogspot.com; Donoso 1433, El Plan; ⊙closed Sun) Artsy *porteños* in their 20s and 30s cram the formica tables at this laid-back, old-school bar to talk poetry and politics over beer and piscola.

Cinzano
BAR

(www.barcinzano.cl; Plaza Aníbal Pinto 1182, El Plan; ⊙closed Sun) Drinkers, sailors and crooners have been propping themselves up on the cluttered bar here since 1896. It's now a favorite with tourists, too, who come to see tuneful old-timers knocking out tangos and boleros like there's no tomorrow.

La Piedra Feliz
BAR, CLUB

(www.lapiedrafeliz.cl; Av Errázuriz 1054, El Plan; admission from CH$3000; ☺ from 9pm Tue-Sun) Jazz, blues, tango, son, salsa, rock, drinking, dining, cinema: is there anything this massive house along the waterfront doesn't do? In the basement, DJs spin till 4am at the nightclub **La Sala**.

Bar La Playa
BAR

(Serrano 567, El Puerto) Valparaíso's longest-running bar shows no signs of slowing down. On weekend nights, cheap pitchers of beer, powerful pisco and a friendly but rowdy atmosphere draw crowds of local students and young bohemian types to the wood-paneled bar upstairs and the cellar-level disco.

Máscara
CLUB

(www.mascara.cl; Plaza Aníbal Pinto 1178, El Plan; cover CH$2500-3500) Music-savvy clubbers in their 20s and 30s love this gay-friendly club: the beer's cheap, there's plenty of room to move and hardly any teenyboppers. Happy hours run from 6pm to 10pm Tuesday to Friday.

Pagano
CLUB

(☏ 032-223-1118; www.paganoindustry.cl; Blanco 236; cover varies) Die-hard clubbers both gay and straight can dance all week on Pagano's packed, sweaty floor.

🛍 Shopping

Most of the galleries and crafts shops are concentrated on Cerros Concepción and Alegre.

Taller Antiquina
ACCESSORIES

(San Enrique 510, Cerro Alegre; ☺ 11am-8pm) Beautifully worked leather bags, belts and wallets are lovingly made on-site here.

Art in Silver Workshop
JEWELRY

(Lautaro Rosas 449A, Cerro Alegre) Silver and lapis lazuli come together in unusual designs at this small jewelry store, where you can sometimes see their creator, silversmith Victor Hugo, at work.

Cummings 1
BOOKS

(www.cummings1.cl; Subida Cummings 1, Plaza Aníbal Pinto, El Plan; ☺ noon-9pm Mon, 11:30am-2pm & 4:30-9pm Tue-Sat) Latin American literature in Spanish, English, French and German. ´

ℹ Information

DANGERS & ANNOYANCES

Petty street crime and muggings are often reported in the old port area of Valparaíso, so keep a close watch on your belongings, especially cameras and other electronics. The rest of Valparaíso is fairly safe, but stick to main streets at night and avoid sketchy stairways and alleyways.

INTERNET ACCESS & TELEPHONE

Many lodgings and restaurants have free internet or wi-fi.

LAUNDRY

Lavanda Café (Av Almirante Montt 454, Cerro Alegre; per load CH$7500; ☺ 9:30am-7pm Mon-Fri, 10am-2pm Sat) This is the place to do laundry; you can also get coffee and food here.

MEDIA

Ciudad de Valparaíso (www.ciudaddevalparaiso.cl) Helpful, comprehensive listings of services in the city.

El Mercurio de Valparaíso (www.mercuriovalpo.cl) The city's main newspaper.

Valparaíso Times (www.valparaisotimes.cl) Online English-language newspaper run by the same people as the *Santiago Times*.

MEDICAL SERVICES

Hospital Carlos Van Buren (☏ 032-220-4000; Av Colón 2454, El Plan) Public hospital.

MONEY

Banco Santander (☏ 032-220-7940; Prat 882, El Plan) One of many banks with ATMs along Prat.

Inter Cambio (Plaza Sotomayor 11, El Plan; ☺ 9am-6pm Mon-Fri, 10am-1pm Sat) An exchange house.

POST

Post Office (Prat 856, El Plan; ☺ 9am-6pm Mon-Fri, 10am-1pm Sat)

TOURIST INFORMATION

Tourist Information Kiosks (☏ 032-293-9262; www.ciudaddevalparaiso.cl; ☺ 10am-2pm & 3-6pm Mon-Sat) At these small information stands on Muelle Prat (www.ciudaddevalparaiso.cl; opposite Plaza Sotomayor, El Plan) and Plaza Aníbal Pinto (www.ciudaddevalparaiso.cl; cnr O'Higgins & Plaza Aníbal Pinto, El Plan) you can pick up maps and battle with other tourists for a chance to talk to the experts.

ℹ Getting There & Away

BUS

All major intercity services arrive and depart from the **Terminal Rodoviario** (Av Pedro Montt 2800, El Plan), about 20 blocks east of the town center. Be aware, especially if you're arriving at night, that taxis often aren't waiting around the terminal; if you need a ride to your hotel or hostel, you might have to call one or arrange a pick-up ahead of time.

Services to Santiago leave every 15 to 20 minutes with **Tur Bus** (☑ 600-660-6600; www.turbus.cl) and **Condor Bus** (☑ 02-2822-7528; www.condorbus.cl), which both also go south to Puerto Montt (three each daily), Osorno (three each daily) and Temuco (three each daily). In addition, Tur Bus goes to Pucón (three daily), Concepción (three daily) and Chillán (three daily).

Tur Bus also operates to the northern cities of Iquique (twice daily), Calama (three daily) and Antofagasta (three daily). **Romani** (☑ 032-222-0662; www.busesromani.cl) has less-frequent services on the same routes.

You can reach Mendoza in Argentina with Tur Bus, **Cata Internacional** (☑ 800-122-2282; www.catainternacional.com), **El Rápido** (☑ 810-333-6285; www.elrapidoint.com.ar), **Ahumada** (☑ 02-696-9798; www.busesahumada.cl) and **Andesmar** (www.andesmar.com). Some buses continue to Buenos Aires. **Buses JM** (☑ 034-344-4373; www.busesjm.cl) offers hourly services to Los Andes.

Pullman Bus Lago Peñuela (☑ 032-222-4025) leaves to Isla Negra every 15 minutes. From 12 de Febrero, just outside the terminal, **Transportes Quintay** (☑ 032-236-2669) runs *taxi colectivos* (shared taxis) every 15 minutes to Quintay.

The city transport network, **Transporte Metropolitano Valparaíso** (TMV; www.tmv.cl), has services to the beach towns north of Valparaíso and Viña del Mar. For Reñaca, take the orange 607, 601 or 605. The 601 and 605 continue to Concón. All run along Condell then Yungay.

Note that fares may increase considerably during school holidays or long weekends, and you'll pay more for the *cama* class (with fully reclining seats) on long-haul rides.

DESTINATION	COST (CH$)	DURATION (HR)
Antofagasta	31,000	15
Calama	34,700	23
Chillán	8200	8
Concepción	8400	9
Iquique	38,400	20
Isla Negra	2600	1½
Los Andes	4500	7
Mendoza	29,800	8
Osorno	22,000	14
Pucón	19,500	12
Puerto Montt	25,000	16
Santiago	2100	1½
Temuco	16,900	11

CAR

The closest car-rental agencies to Valparaíso are in Viña del Mar – if you book in advance, some will bring cars to your hotel.

❶ Getting Around

Walking is the best way to get about central Valparaíso and explore its *cerros* – you can cheat on the way up by taking an *ascensor* or a *taxi colectivo* (CH$500). *Colectivos* to Cerros Concepción and Alegre line up at the bottom of Almirante Montt, while those to Cerros La Cárcel and Bellavista leave from Av Ecuador.

Countless local buses run by **TMV** (one way within El Plan CH$310, El Plan to Cerro CH$370) run along Condell and Av Pedro Montt, Av Brasil and Yungay, connecting one end of El Plan with the other. A few climb different *cerros* and continue to Viña or along the northern coast; destinations are displayed in the windshield. The city's most famous line is the 801, which uses the oldest working trolleybuses in the world. The curvy cars date to 1947 and have been declared a national monument.

The **Metro Regional de Valparaíso** (Merval; ☑ 032-252-7633; www.merval.cl) operates commuter trains every six to 12 minutes from Valparaíso's **Estación Puerto** (cnr Errázuriz & Urriola) and **Estación Bellavista** (cnr Errázuriz & Bellavista) to Viña del Mar (CH$410 to CH$456, depending on hour of departure).

Taxis are much more expensive in Valparaíso than other Chilean cities.

If you're willing to brave the hills on a bike, you'll see several outfitters around town renting bicycles (CH$5000 per half-day). For an extra CH$1000, they'll deliver to your hostel.

Viña del Mar

☑ 032 / POP 286,931

Clean and orderly Viña del Mar is a sharp contrast to the charming jumble of neighboring Valparaíso. Manicured boulevards lined with palm trees, a sprawling public beach and beautiful expansive parks have earned it the nickname of Ciudad Jardín (Garden City). Its official name, which means 'vineyard by the sea,' stems from the area's colonial origins as the hacienda of the Carrera family.

Not many foreign travelers stay here, opting instead for a day trip from Valparaíso. Nevertheless, Viña remains a popular weekend and summer destination for well-to-do Santiaguinos – and the *carrete* (partying) here is first rate.

MIDDLE CHILE VIÑA DEL MAR

Viña del Mar

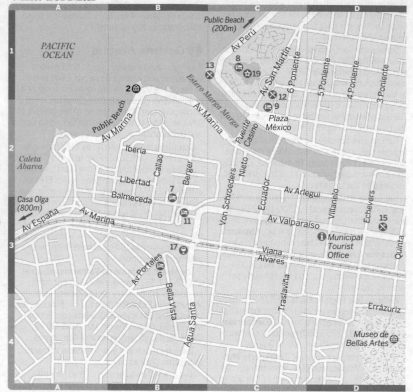

◉ Sights & Activities

Most streets are identified by a number and direction, either Norte (north), Oriente (east) or Poniente (west). Av Libertad separates Ponientes from Orientes. The city was pretty hard hit by the 2010 earthquake, and the Plaza Sucre was being renovated when we passed through.

Viña's white-sand beaches stretch northward from the northern bank of the Estero Marga Marga to the suburbs of Reñaca and Concón.

Parque Quinta Vergara   PARK
(Errázuriz 563; ⊙7am-6pm) Nowhere is Viña's nickname of the Garden City better justified than at the magnificently landscaped Parque Quinta Vergara, which you enter from Errázuriz at the south end of Libertad. It once belonged to one of the city's most illustrious families, the Alvares-Vergaras.

Their residence was the Venetian neo-Gothic-style **Palacio Vergara**, which later housed an interesting collection of 17th- to 19th-century European and Chilean art at the **Museo Municipal de Bellas Artes**.

Unfortunately, the museum was badly damaged in the 2010 earthquake and was closed indefinitely at the time of writing.

**Museo de Arqueología
e Historia Francisco Fonck**   MUSEUM
(☎032-268-6753; www.museofonck.cl; 4 Norte 784; adult/child CH$2500/500; ⊙10am-2pm & 3-6pm Mon, 10am-6pm Tue-Sat, 10am-2pm Sun) The original *moai* (Easter Island statues) standing guard outside the Museo de Arqueología e Historia Francisco Fonck are just a teaser for the beautifully displayed archaeological finds from Easter Island within, along with Mapuche silverwork and anthropomorphic Moche ceramics. Upstairs are old-school insect cases and a lively explana-

tion of how head shrinking works (finished examples are included).

Artequin MUSEUM
(☎032-294-3637; www.artequinvina.cl; Parque Portrenillos 500; adult/child CH$1000/500; ⊙9am-5:30pm Tue-Fri, 11am-6pm Sat & Sun; ⊕) This children's museum has plenty of play areas and a big workshop. There are a few reproductions of masterpieces from the 15th to 20th centuries.

**Parroquia Nuestra
Señora de Dolores** CHURCH
(Alvares s/n) Check out the cool iconography at Viña's oldest church, built and rebuilt between 1882 and 1912.

Castillo Wulff HISTORIC BUILDING
(Av Marina s/n; ⊙10am-1:30pm & 3-5:30pm Tue-Sun) **FREE** Pretty Castillo Wulff, built by a prominent Valparaíso businessman in the early 20th century, hangs out over the sea:

pass through the art exhibitions to the tower at the back, where you can peer through the thick glass floor at the rocks and waves below.

Jardín Botánico Nacional PARK
(National Botanical Garden; ☎032-267-2566; www.jardin-botanico.cl; Camino El Olivar s/n; adult/child CH$2000/1000; ⊙10am-6pm May-Aug, 10am-7pm Sep-Apr) There are over 3000 plant species in the 61 hectares of parkland that comprise Chile's Jardín Botánico Nacional. It's 8km southeast of the city center; take a taxi or catch bus 203 from Viña along Calle Alvarez to Puente El Olivar, then cross the bridge and walk about 500m north to the park's entrance signs.

✿ Festivals & Events

**Festival Internacional
de la Canción** SONG
(International Song Festival; www.festivaldevina.cl) At Chile's biggest music festival, usually held in February or March, Latin American pop, rock and folk stars have been drawing huge crowds since 1960.

🛌 Sleeping

Expect price jumps in the summer and on weekends.

Vista Hermosa 26 HOTEL $

(☎ 032-266-0309; www.vistahermosa26.cl; Vista Hermosa 26; s/d/tr incl breakfast CH$24,000/ 38,000/42,000; 🛜) Polished wooden floors and a big fireplace lend stately charm to the lounge of this quiet but friendly hotel on the edge of Cerro Castillo (a must-see *cerro* with some of the city's prettiest architecture). You get plenty of space in the simple rooms, making this a solid bet for midrange comfort.

Delirio Hostel HOSTEL $

(☎ 032-262-5759; www.deliriohostel.com; Portales 131; dm CH$6000-10,000; 🖥🛜) The huge long garden in front of Viña's best hostel means you don't have to limit your open-air lounging to the beach. The right-on vibe stops at the door. While there's a shared kitchen, you'll miss a big indoor hangout area. Good news is that the young owners help organize activities from tours to pub crawls.

Kalagen Hostel HOSTEL $

(☎ 032-299-1669; www.kalagenhostel.com; Av Valparaíso 618; dm CH$7500-11,200, d with/without bathroom incl breakfast CH$37,000/24,900; 🛜) This fun urban hostel contains stylish dorms and doubles with colorful linens, hard-wood floors and Asian-style paper lanterns. It's a bit dirty, but the central location is great and there's a communal kitchen, a girls-only dorm and a chill room with TV set. The private rooms are actually pretty passable.

Eco-Hostal Offenbacher-hof B&B $$

(☎ 032-262-1483; www.offenbacher-hof.cl; Balmaceda 102; s/d incl breakfast CH$35,000/44,000; 🛜) 🏃 There are fabulous views over the sea and the city from this commanding chestnut-and-yellow mansion atop quiet Cerro Castillo. Sea views, newly renovated bathrooms and antique furnishings make this your best buy in the city. It's spotless, the owner is charming, and there's an amazing patio for afternoon tea.

Casa Olga B&B $$

(☎ 032-318-2972; www.casa-olga.com; 18 de Septiembre 31; d/apt incl breakfast CH$55,000/65,000; 🛜) This gorgeous boutique-style B&B, outfitted with breezy all-white decor, brand-new LCD TVs and cozy doubles with renovated private bathrooms, is practically right on the beach. It's just outside of Viña – an advantage or disadvantage depending on your travel plans.

Hotel del Mar LUXURY HOTEL $$$

(☎ 032-250-0800; www.enjoy.cl; cnr Av Perú & Los Héroes; r incl breakfast CH$158,000-214,200; ❄🛜🏊) The view from the sleek, glass-fronted lobby of Viña's top luxury hotel is a preview of what awaits upstairs – on many floors you can see the sea from your bed and even the indoor pool seems to merge with the waves beyond the window. The glamorous service and style evokes the roaring '20s.

Hotel Monterilla HOTEL $$$

(☎ 032-297-6950; www.monterilla.cl; 2 Norte 65; s/d CH$86,600/108,350; 🛜) The dead-plain facade is deceiving: bright artworks and engravings offset the white walls and boxy sofas in this hotel's lobby and restaurant. The tiled floors and sparse furnishings look refreshing in hot weather, but might leave you longing for some color in winter – it's best for those looking for American-style amenities over Chilean charm.

🍴 Eating

Most of Viña's cheap eats are clustered on and around busy Av Valparaíso in the town center. These include the string of *schopperias* (beer-and-sandwich joints) that fill the open-fronted 2nd floor of **Portal Álamos** (Av Valparaíso 553).

Panzoni ITALIAN $

(Paseo Cousiño 12-B; mains CH$3000-4800) One of the best-value eateries in central Viña, Panzoni's well-prepared Italian pastas and friendly service reel in the lunchtime diners. The location is slightly hidden on an out-of-the-way passageway.

Samoiedo SANDWICHES $

(☎ 032-268-1382; Valparaíso 637; sandwiches CH$2500-4500, set lunch CH$5000-7000) For half a century the old boys have been meeting at this traditional *confitería* (tearoom) for lunchtime feasts of steak and fries or well-stuffed sandwiches. The outdoor seating is greatly preferable to the interior, which is open to a busy shopping mall.

Divino Pecado ITALIAN $$

(www.divinopecado.cl; Av San Martín 180; mains CH$6500-9900) The short but surprising menu at this intimate, candlelit Italian restaurant includes scallops au gratin, tuna carpaccio and fantastic fettuccini with lamb ragu – a divine sin indeed.

Mercado del Mar CHILEAN $$
(Av Perú s/n; CH$5500-9500;) A sunset drink here should be on everyone's Viña to-do list – there are panoramic views of the Pacific from its glassed-in terrace above the mouth of the Marga Marga.

Drinking & Entertainment

From the beach, head up 5 Norte for the best clubs and lounges in town.

La Flor de Chile BAR
(www.laflordechile.cl; 8 Norte 601; mains CH$3000-6500) For nearly a century, Viñamarinos young and old have downed their *schops* (draft beer) over the closely packed tables of this gloriously old-school bar.

Café Journal CLUB
(cnr Agua Santa & Alvares; cover free-CH$3000; ⊗10pm-late Wed-Sat) Electronic music is the order of the evening at this boomingly popular club, which has three heaving dance floors.

Scratch CLUB
(www.scratch.cl; Quillota 898; cover CH$2000-5000) This superclub is immensely popular with the university set and 20-something locals who dance to reggaeton and DJ-spun tunes until 5am.

Casino Municipal CASINO
(⊅032-250-0700; www.enjoy.cl/enjoy-vina-del-mar; Av San Martín 199) Overlooking the beach on the north side of the Marga Marga, this elegant local landmark is the place to squander your savings on slot machines, bingo, roulette and card games. Formal attire is encouraged.

Anfiteatro Quinta Vergara PERFORMING ARTS
(Parque Quinta Vergara) This giant amphitheater in the Parque Quinta Vergara has concerts and more.

Information

Banco Santander (⊅032-226-6917; Plaza Vergara 108) One of several banks with ATMs on the main square.
Conaf (⊅032-232-0210; www.conaf.cl; 3 Norte 541; ⊗8:30am-5:30pm Mon-Fri) Provides information on nearby parks, including Parque Nacional La Campana.
Hospital Gustavo Fricke (⊅032-265-2200; Alvares 1532) Viña's main public hospital, located east of downtown.
Lavarápido (⊅032-290-6263; Av Arlegui 440; per load CH$4200; ⊗10am-9pm Mon-Sat) Offers an express service.

Municipal Tourist Office (www.visitevinadelmar.cl) Check online for a city map and cultural happenings.
Post Office (Plaza Vergara s/n; ⊗9am-7pm Mon-Fri, 10am-1pm Sat)

Getting There & Away

All long-distance services operate from the **Rodoviario Viña del Mar** (⊅032-275-2000; www.rodoviario.cl; Valparaíso 1055). There's tourist information here and luggage storage downstairs (CH$1000).

Several local bus lines through the **Transporte Metropolitano Valparaíso** (TMV; www.tmv.cl; one way CH$440), plus privately run line **Sol del Pacífico** (⊅032-275-2030; www.soldelpacifico.cl), make frequent departures for northern coastal towns from Reñaca to Concón. To catch one, go to Plaza Vergara and the area around Viña del Mar's metro station; expect to pay between CH$1200 and CH$2200 one way, depending on your final destination. For Reñaca, take the orange 607, 601 or 605. The 601 and 605 continue to Concón.

Getting Around

Frequent local buses run by Transporte Metropolitano Valparaíso connect Viña and Valparaíso. Some routes run along the waterfront following Av Marina and Av San Martín; others run through the town center along Av España and Av Libertad. Destinations are usually displayed in the windshield. The commuter train **Metro Regional de Valparaíso** (Merval; ⊅032-252-7633; www.merval.cl) also runs between Viña and Valpo.

In summer Viña is congested and very tricky to park in. However, a car can be very useful for touring the northern coast or the Casablanca Valley wineries. **Budget** (⊅032-268-3420; www.budget.cl; Marina 15) is your best bet for a rental.

Casablanca Valley

A cool climate and temperatures that vary greatly from day to night have made this valley halfway between Santiago and Valparaíso one of Chile's best regions for fruity Chardonnays, Sauvignon Blancs and Pinots. Its well-organized wineries take food and wine tourism seriously, and many have on-site restaurants. There's no public transportation to any of the wineries, but in a rental car you can easily blitz four or five of them in a day – most are on or around Ruta 68. Alternatively, contact the **Ruta del Vino de Casablanca** (⊅032-274-3755; www.casablancavalley.cl; Punta Arenas 46, Casablanca) or Enotour (p62) for curated wine tours.

IF YOU LIKE... BEACH TOWNS

North of Viña del Mar, a beautiful road snakes along the coast, passing through a string of beach towns that hum with holidaying Chileans December through February. The beaches range from small, rocky coves to wide open sands. Towering condos overlook some, while others are scattered with rustic cottages and the huge summer houses of Chile's rich and famous.

Reñaca & Concón

Viña's high-rises merge into the multitiered apartments of Reñaca, a northern suburb with a wide, pleasant beach. Come to local landmark **Roca Oceánica**, a rocky hill looking out over the Pacific, for a sunset hike with incredible views (it's on your left, on the ocean side, as you head north from the town.)

Concón, just north of Reñaca, is known for its casual and wonderfully authentic seafood restaurants. Top on the list are the crab-stuffed empanadas at **Las Deliciosas** (Av Borgoño 25370; empanadas CH$900) and evening cocktails and *machas* (razor clams) at local legend **La Gatita** (Av Borgoño 21550; mains CH$6000-8500).

Horcón

Chile's hippie movement began at the small fishing town of Horcón, on a small curving peninsula that juts out into the Pacific 28km north of Concón. Brightly painted, ramshackle buildings clutter the steep main road down to its small, rocky beach where fishing boats come and go. These days there's still a hint of peace, love and communal living – note the happy-go-lucky folks gathering on the beach with dogs, guitars and bottles of liquor in paper bags at sunset.

Maitencillo

About 21km north of Horcón, Maitencillo's long, sandy beaches stretch for several kilometers along the coast and attract many visitors. **Escuela de Surf Maitencillo** (cell 9238-4682; www.escueladesurfmaitencillo.cl; Av del Mar 1250; group class CH$16,000 per person) is a relaxed place to learn how to surf.

Although the town's packed with holiday homes, it retains a pleasant low-key vibe. A favorite restaurant, bar and cabin complex is **La Canasta** (www.hermansen.cl; Av del Mar 592; mains CH$5900-8800, cabin CH$77,000) for wood-baked pizzas and – of course – fresh fish.

Cachagua

This small, chillaxed town 13km north of Maitencillo sits on the northern tip of a long crescent beach. Just across the water is the **Monumento Nacional Isla de Cachagua** (www.conaf.cl/parques/monumento-natural-isla-cachagua/), a guano-stained rocky outcrop that's home to more than 2000 Humboldt penguins, as well as a colony of sea lions. You can ask local fishermen to take you closer to the island, but you're not allowed to get off the boat.

Zapallar

Santiago's elite wouldn't dream of taking their beach holidays anywhere but here, the most exclusive of Chile's coastal resorts, 2km north of Cachagua. Instead of high-rises, multimillion-dollar mansions cover the wooded hillsides leading up from the beach, which is an unspoiled arc of yellow sand in a sheltered cove.

Everyone who's anyone in Zapallar makes a point of lunch at **El Chiringuito** (Caleta de Pescadores; mains CH$8200-12,400), where terrace tables look out over the rocks and pelicans fishing for their dinner.

Getting There & Away

To arrive at the northernmost beaches from Viña del Mar or Valparaíso, a rental car is your best bet. You can also catch a ride on a local bus or come directly to Concón from Santiago on **Pullman del Sur** (02-776-2424; www.pdelsur.cl).

Drivers should note that Chile has a zero tolerance (zero alcohol) driving under the influence policy. Make sure you have a designated driver. Some of the larger wineries offer drop-in visits, but it's recommended to reserve in advance.

🏃 Activities

★ Emiliana
WINERY

(📋 02-353-9130; www.emiliana.cl; Ruta 68, Km61.5; tastings from CH$9000; ⊙10am-5pm) 🍃 Tastings take place in a gorgeous slate-and-wood building looking out over the vines that are grown organically using biodynamic principles. Reserve ahead for chocolate-pairings, bike tours, premium tastings or picnics.

Viña Indómita
WINERY

(📋 032-215-3900; www.indomita.cl; Ruta 68, Km6; tour incl 3 pours CH$9000; ⊙11am-5pm) There's no beating the views from these vineyards – the Hollywood-style sign on the hillside is easily spotted from afar. Indómita's top-shelf Carmenere scored an honorable mention at the recent edition of the International Wine Competition.

Viña Matetic
WINERY

(📋 02-595-2661; www.matetic.com; Fundo Rosario, Lagunillas; tasting with 2 pours & tour CH$10,000; ⊙11am-3:30pm Tue-Sun) A real show-stopper of a winery: the glass, wood and steel gravity-flow winery has attracted almost as much attention as the wines. Reservations several days in advance are usually necessary; you can stay the night at La Casona, the boutique hotel on-site.

House of Morandé
WINERY

(📋 032-275-4701; www.morande.cl) Featuring a fantastic gourmet restaurant.

Viña Casas del Bosque
WINERY

(📋 02-480-6940; www.casasdelbosque.cl; Hijuelas 2 Ex Fundo Santa Rosa; tastings from CH$9000) With a stunning mirador over the Casablanca Valley, this winery also offers bike trips.

William Cole Vineyards
WINERY

(📋 032-215-7777; www.williamcolevineyards.cl) With architecture that is inspired by old-fashioned Chilean missions, this contemporary winery is visitor-friendly.

Catrala
WINERY

(📋 02-243-2861; www.catrala.cl) Wine tastings include a hike through the vineyard at Catrala, which is named after an enigmatic Chilean woman from the 17th century.

Viña Mar
WINERY

(📋 032-275-4301; www.vinamar.cl; ⊙10am-4pm Tue-Sun) The striking manor at the heart of this carefully landscaped property houses the gourmet Ristorante San Marco.

Viña Veramonte
WINERY

(📋 032-232-9999; www.veramonte.cl; tastings from CH$11,000) Veramonte's Cabernets and Chardonnays win frequent 'top value' awards from Wine Spectator.

ℹ Getting There & Around

You'll need a car to visit these wineries. Drive over from Valparaíso, or rent a car from Santiago.

Quintay

As the sun sets over the Pacific, the craggy rocks protecting the tiny fishing cove of **Caleta Quintay** are stained a rich pink. Several of the colorful houses clustered here are seafood restaurants. One of the best places for sundowners and garlic prawns or centolla (king crab) is the terrace of **Restaurant Miramar** (Costanera s/n; mains CH$5900-8500). You can see your future dinner up close on the guided scuba dives run by **Austral Divers** (📋 02-492-7975; www.australdivers.cl), a PADI-certified dive company with an outpost here.

A signposted turnoff about 1.2km back down the road toward Valparaíso takes you down a 1.5km dirt road to the long, sweeping **Playa de Quintay**, one of the prettiest, most natural beaches in the region.

ℹ Getting There & Away

Quintay is an easy half-day trip from Valparaíso. **Transportes Quintay** (📋 032-236-2669) operates *taxi colectivos* between just outside Valparaíso's bus terminal and Quintay's main street (from CH$1800, one hour), 500m from Caleta Quintay and 2.5km from Playa de Quintay.

If you're coming by car, take Ruta 68 from Valparaíso or Viña toward Santiago; the turnoff is 18km south of Valpo, then it's another 23km to Quintay.

Isla Negra

The spectacular setting on a windswept ocean headland makes it easy to understand why **Casa de Isla Negra** (Pablo Neruda's House; 📋 035-461-284; www.fundacionneruda.org; Poeta Neruda s/n; admission by guided tour only

Around Valparaíso & Viña del Mar

Getting There & Away

Isla Negra is an easy half-day trip from Valparaíso. **Pullman Bus Lago Peñuela** (☑032-222-4025) leaves from Valparaíso's bus terminal every 30 minutes (CH$3200, 1½ hours). **Pullman Bus** (☑600-320-3200; www.pullman.cl) comes here direct from Santiago's Terminal de Buses Alameda (CH$7500, 1½ hours, every 30 minutes).

Parque Nacional La Campana

Within this **national park** (☑033-244-1342; www.conaf.cl/parques/parque-nacional-la-campana; adult/child CH$2500/1500; ⊙9am-5:30pm Sat-Thu, 9am-4:30pm Fri) are two of the highest mountains in the coastal range, **Cerro El Roble** (2200m) and **Cerro La Campana** (1880m), which Charles Darwin climbed in 1834. Visitor numbers have risen since then, but La Campana remains relatively uncrowded despite its proximity to Santiago. It's subdivided into two main sectors: Conaf's main administration station is at **Granizo**, near Olmué, 1.5km before the southwest entrance side of the park; and there are sometimes rangers at **Ocoa**, in the north of the park.

Most of the park's 80 sq km resemble the dry, jagged scrubland of the mountains of Southern California. The park protects around 100 animal species, and several endemic plant species. There's excellent hiking to be had here. Paved access roads lead to the two entrances, but there are no roads within the park. Spring is the best time to visit. Bring your own water (or filter).

Activities

Sendero Andinista   HIKING
Most people come to make like Darwin and ascend Cerro La Campana: on clear days its summit affords spectacular views stretching from the Pacific to the Andean summit of Aconcagua. From the Granizo park entrance (373m above sea level), the Sendero Andinista climbs 1455m in only 7km.

Mercifully, most of the hike is in shade, and there are three water sources en route. Prior to the final vertiginous ascent you pass a granite wall with a plaque commemorating Darwin's climb. Figure at least four hours to the top and three hours back down.

Sendero Los Peumos   HIKING
The 5.5km Sendero Los Peumos connects the Granizo entrance to the Sendero Amasijo, which winds for another 7km through a

CH$5000; ⊙10am-6pm Tue-Sun, to 8pm Sat & Sun Jan-Feb) was Pablo Neruda's favorite house. Built by the poet when he became rich in the 1950s, it was stormed by soldiers just days after the 1973 military coup when Neruda was dying of cancer.

Overenthusiastic commercialization gives a definite Disney-Neruda vibe to visits here: indifferent guides quick-march you through the house, and they'd rather you lingered in the gift shop than over the extraordinary collections of shells, ships in bottles, nautical instruments, colored glass and books. Despite this, the seemingly endless house (Neruda kept adding to it) and its contents are still awe-inspiring. There's no one to stop you taking your time on the terrace outside, however, where Neruda's tomb and that of his third wife, Matilde, overlook the sea.

Note that reservations are essential in high season.

palm-studded canyon to Ocoa. The whole hike takes five hours one way. The southern part of Sendero Amasijo plunges down into Cajón Grande, a canyon with deciduous forests of southern beech.

Sendero La Cascada
HIKING

From Ocoa, Sendero La Cascada leads 6km to Salto de la Cortadera, an attractive 30m waterfall that is best during the spring runoff.

🛏 Sleeping

Conaf Camping
CAMPING $

(campsite CH$7000) Conaf runs two basic 23-tent campsites with toilets, barbecue areas and cold-water showers at Granizo and Cajón Grande, further south. Backcountry camping is not permitted. You need to bring all food – and, depending on the weather, drinking water – with you.

❶ Getting There & Away

Ranger presence is sporadic at Ocoa, so it makes more sense to go through the Granizo entrance. Buses go regularly from Errázuriz in Valparaíso to Limache (CH$1000); from here local buses and *colectivos* continue to Olmué, and some to Granizo. Talca-based **Casa Chueca/Trekking Chile** (☑ 071-197-0096; www.trekkingchile.com) operates guided hiking trips (CH$30,000) to the park.

The park is accessible by car from Santiago (160km) and Viña del Mar/Valparaíso (60km). Head north from Santiago on the Panamericana (CH-5), take the turnoff to Tiltil and continue to Olmué, 4km from Granizo. From Viña and Valparaíso take the Autopista Troncal Sur (CH-62) past Quilpué and Villa Alemana to Limache, where you head east to Olmué.

ACONCAGUA VALLEY

If you arrive in Chile overland from Mendoza, the fertile Aconcagua Valley is the first scenery you see. It's watered by the Río Aconcagua, which flows west from the highest mountain in the Americas, Cerro Aconcagua (6962m), just over the Argentine border. Scenic highway CH-60 runs the length of the valley and across the Andes to Mendoza.

Los Andes

☑ 034 / POP 61,000

A stopover on your way to the Portillo ski area or over to Argentina, this dusty agricultural town has great views of the neighboring foothills, a few quiet museums and little else. Ask at your hotel for local hiking options. They might even point out that Nobel Prize–winner Gabriela Mistral taught school here. Another remarkable Chilean woman, nun Santa Teresa de los Andes, worked her miracles here.

◉ Sights & Activities

Museo Arqueológico
MUSEUM

(☑ 034-242-0115; Av Santa Teresa 398; admission CH$1000; ◷ 10am-6pm Tue-Sat) The small Museo Arqueológico contains some interesting pre-Columbian pottery displayed in dusty exhibit cases.

Museo Antiguo
Monasterio del Espíritu Santo
MUSEUM

(☑ 034-242-1765; Av Santa Teresa 389; adult/child CH$500/300; ◷ 9am-1pm & 3-6pm Mon-Fri, 10am-6pm Sat & Sun) The award for the most unintentionally bizarre museum displays in Middle Chile goes to the Museo Antiguo Monasterio del Espíritu Santo. Mannequins in nuns' habits re-create scenes from Santa Teresa's life: she took her vows in this ex-convent then died of typhus, aged 19.

Also celebrated is folk saint and preteen rebel Laura Vicuña, who willed herself to die because her widowed mother took a married lover.

Góndola Carril
TOURIST TRAIN

(www.chiletren.cl; tickets CH$35,000) This infrequent tourist train leaves the FEPASA Los Andes station at 10:30am, chugging up the valley in a throwback passanger-engine combo across the old Trans-Andean route to Río Blanco, where you stop for lunch. You arrive back in Los Andes at 6:30pm. Check online to see if it has a trip headed out.

🛏 Sleeping & Eating

Family-friendly restaurants line Av Santa Teresa.

Hotel Manuel Rodríguez
HOTEL $

(☑ 034-229-6217; tresmerce@hotmail.com; Rodríguez 234; s/d CH$12,000/18,000; ☜) Barebones, clean, cell-like and cheap. It's not the best spot in the world, but it will do. There's even a nice little patio.

Hotel Plaza
HOTEL $$

(☑ 034-259-2400; www.hotelplazalosandes.cl; Rodríguez 368; s/d incl breakfast CH$49,000/55,000; ⛃☜⛺) With its beige bedspreads and varnished wood furnishings, there's something very 1970s about Los Andes' upmarket option.

ACONCAGUA MOUNTAIN

So you're dying to get closer to the highest peak in the Americas – but you don't have time to travel? Santiago-based outfitter **Andes Wind** (☎ cell 9710-7959; www.andeswind.cl; day trip CH$60,000) runs day-long journeys that take you into Argentina and closer to the mountain. After stopping in Portillo on the way back, you'll be back in the capital city around 7:30pm.

Rooms look out onto the car park but they're big, airy and light-filled, and have heating and cable TV.

Fuente de Soda Primavera   CHILEAN $
(cnr Santa Rosa & O'Higgins; mains CH$2850-5200) The house special at this popular *fuente de soda* (soda fountain) is the delicious *completo* (hot dog) piled high with fresh toppings.

La Table de France   FRENCH $$
(Camino Internacional Km3, El Sauce; mains CH$4500-12,900) Rolling countryside is the only thing between the Andes and the sweeping terrace of this French-run restaurant on a hill 3km out of town. Duck, rabbit, wild boar and even ostrich satisfy creative carnivores, while dishes such as goat's-cheese gnocchi or kingklip in Carmenere cater to vegetarians.

From the center of town, take Av Esmeralda east to General del Canto; it's a quick three-minute drive.

ℹ Information

The highway to the Argentine border (CH-60, the Carretera Internacional) runs across the north of Los Andes, where it's called Av Argentina. The bus station lies north of it, eight blocks from the town center. Esmeralda, the main commercial street, runs along the south side of the Plaza de Armas where you'll find most travelers' services.

ℹ Getting There & Away

Los Andes is the last (or first) Chilean town on the route between Santiago and Mendoza in Argentina – buses pass through its **Rodoviario Internacional** (Av Carlos Díaz 111), eight blocks northwest of the Plaza de Armas on the northern extension of Av Santa Teresa.

Ahumada (☎ 034-421-227; www.busesahumada.cl) and **Pullman Bus** (☎ 034-425-973; www.pullman.cl) have regular services to Santiago's terminal San Borja (CH$1500 to CH$2900, 1½ hours, hourly). **El Rápido** (☎ 810-333-6285; www.elrapidoint.com.ar) goes to Mendoza (CH$25,200, six hours, five daily).

Portillo

Set around the spectacular alpine lake of Laguna del Inca on the Argentine border, **Portillo** (☎ 02-263-0606; www.skiportillo.cl; daily ski pass adult/child CH$39,000/26,000) is one of Chile's favorite ski resorts. There's not much to do here in the summer but hike to the other side of the lake (two hours one way), and the resort is basically shuttered outside the ski season. But when the snow comes, so does the fun. It's not just amateurs who love its ultrasteep slopes: the US, Austrian and Italian national teams use it as a base for their summer training and the 200km/h speed barrier was first broken here. Some of its terrain is apt for novices but it's hard-core powder junkies that really thrive. Altitudes range from 2590m to 3310m on its 19 runs, the longest of which measures 3.2km. Aside from the hotel and attached lodges, there are no other businesses here.

🛏 Sleeping & Eating

Accommodations in Portillo are geared around weeklong all-inclusive stays. (If you're looking for something a lot cheaper, consider sleeping 70km west in Los Andes.) All hotels are booked through the resort's website. Regardless of where you stay, you can use the gym, yoga facilities, skating rink, games room, small cinema and babysitting services for free. Shops, an internet cafe and a bar and disco are also on-site. But far and away the most stand-out amenity is the spectacular heated outdoor swimming pool.

Inca Lodge   LODGE $
(☎ 02-263-0606; www.skiportillo.com; r per person per week full board US$990; P🛜❄) The Inca Lodge has a bit of a dirt-bag, ski-bum vibe to it. Share a four-bed dorm room to save big.

Octagon Lodge   LODGE $$
(☎ 02-236-0606; www.skiportillo.com; r per person per week incl meals & lift pass US$1800) The Octagon Lodge has four-bunk rooms with bathrooms and draws a slightly older crowd.

Hotel Portillo   HOTEL $$$
(☎ 02-263-0606; www.skiportillo.com; r per person per week incl meals & lift pass US$3100-6800; P🛜❄) Portillo's most luxurious option is

the Hotel Portillo, which has smallish doubles with views of the lake or valley. The hotel and all its facilities except for the restaurant are closed during the summer.

Chalets CABIN $$$

(☑02-263-0606; www.skiportillo.com; s/d CH$88,000/114,000; P🐕🛜🐾) The chalets are the only summer option. They sleep six to eight people in a '70s-style ship-cabin-feeling space. The views are amazing.

ⓘ Getting There & Away

Driving to Portillo takes two to four hours from Santiago, depending on road conditions.

The ski resort (www.skiportillo.cl) runs shuttle buses (US$70 one way) to and from Santiago airport, but only on Saturdays. **Portillo Tours & Travel** (☑02-2263-0606; ptours@skiportillo. com) can arrange shuttle transportation for a slightly higher price other days of the week.

An alternative is provided by private ski transfers that run affordable Wednesday and Saturday shuttles from Santiago to the slopes; we like **Ski Total** (☑02-2246-0156; www.skitotal. cl; Apoquindo 4900, locales 37-46, Las Condes, Santiago; one way CH$23,000). It will also rent equipment, which will save you time once you reach Portillo.

The Santiago–Mendoza services run by **Buses Tas Choapa** (www.taschoapa.cl) stop at Portillo – if there are seats you can catch them to Los Andes, Santiago or Mendoza.

SOUTHERN HEARTLAND

South of Santiago, squeezed between the Andes and the coastal cordillera, the central valley is Chile's fruit bowl. With a Mediterranean climate and endless orchards and vineyards, this region produces most of Chile's wine. The Andes in this sector are spectacular, with deciduous beech forests climbing their slopes and broad gravel-bedded rivers descending into the valley. Along the coast, you have laid-back surf towns, broad vistas and never-ending beaches.

The 8.8-magnitude earthquake that rocked Chile in February 2010 was particularly devastating to this region. In addition to the countless houses and offices that were destroyed in Curicó, Concepción and Chillán, historic landmarks like Talca's central market were so badly damaged that they may never reopen. While you'll see a fair few cracks in the historic buildings, businesses are by and large back up and running.

History

After 7000 relatively undisturbed years, central Chile's Mapuche communities were invaded twice in quick succession, first by the Inka and then by the Spanish. Earthquakes and constant Mapuche sieges meant that early Spanish colonial cities floundered almost as often as they were founded. Eventually the Mapuche retreated south of the Río Biobío, and colonial central Chile grew, becoming a linchpin in the struggle for independence. Political change gave way to economic growth: massive irrigation projects transformed the central valleys into fertile agricultural land, and major natural resources were discovered and exploited – coal mines near Concepción, copper at Rancagua. The area was a focus of repression during the dictatorship, and since the return to democracy it has been the backdrop for vociferous strikes by students and workers.

ⓘ Getting There & Away

The comfortable and easily accessible TerraSur (p78) train line connects Santiago to Chillán, stopping at all major towns and cities along the way. The prices are cheaper, and departures more frequent, through the various bus lines that serve the region.

ⓘ Getting Around

From a practical point of view, a rental car is a must for visiting wineries and far-flung national parks. It's possible to take public transportation to some destinations, though service is rarely direct – travelers should be prepared to walk a few kilometers from where the bus drops off. Outside major cities, you may be able to catch a ride by hitchhiking.

Colchagua Valley

Protected by mountains on all sides, this sun-scorched parcel of vines and orchards produces Chile's best red wines. The town of Santa Cruz has a few good hotels and a picturesque plaza, and serves as your central departure point. But the real *encanto* here is heading to the countryside to learn about wine, visit with eccentric vintners and experience the lyrical pull of wine country.

Colchagua Valley Wineries

Wine production started here shortly after the conquest in the mid-16th century with the introduction of vineyards by Jesuit

MIDDLE CHILE COLCHAGUA VALLEY

RANCAGUA'S RODEO

Buckin' broncos in a dusty arena, real-life cowboys in leather chaps – it's the **Campeonato Nacional de Rodeo** (National Rodeo Championship; www.caballoyrodeo.cl; Medialuna de Rancagua, cnr Av España & Germán Ibarra; admission CH$7500-12,000). Held from late March to early April in Rancagua, the championship is the culmination of Rancagua's rip-roaring annual rodeo season. At night, the Plaza de los Héroes comes alive with traditional Chilean *cueca* dancing (a playful, handkerchief-waving dance that imitates the courtship of a rooster and hen) and a colorful market of regional foods and crafts.

Rancagua is an easy day trip from Santiago. From the EFE train station there are five to seven daily Terrasur (p78) trains north to Santiago (CH$5600, one hour). From terminals in the west of town, **Tur Bus** (☏ 600-660-6600; www.turbus.cl; O'Carroll 1175) and **Pullman** (☏ 600-320-3200; www.pullman.cl; cnr Av Brasil & Lastarria) have hourly services to and from Santiago (CH$1700 to CH$2200, 1½ hours).

missionaries. The mining boom of the late 19th century brought wealth and noble grapes of French origin. An extremely helpful resource, with a friendly office on Santa Cruz's main square, is **Ruta del Vino** (☏032-823-199; www.rutadelvino.cl; Plaza de Armas 298; ⊙9am-6pm Mon-Fri, 10am-6pm Sat & Sun). In addition to providing tourists with information and recommendations about the region's wineries, it offers tasting tours (CH$10,000 to CH$20,000; reservations required 48 hours before tour). Small-batch producers have gotten together to form the **Red Del Vino** (☏072-282-3422; www.reddelvino.com; tours from CH$30,000), which does interesting tours of the smaller operations in the valley. Visiting the wineries in the area is best done in a rental car or on a tour. Do not drink and drive. There's a zero-tolerance policy.

🏃 Activities

Reservations are required at most wineries. Note that some wineries close in August.

Lapostolle WINERY
(☏ 072-295-5330; www.lapostolle.com; Apalta Valley; tour CH$20,000, prixe-fixe lunch CH$40,000-60,000; r US$1500; ⊙10:30am-5:30pm) 🍷 This iconic winery has an excellent tasting tour at its six-story complex set on a hill above the Apalta Valley. The reds here are excellent, and the tour includes a taste of the signature Clos de Apalta wine. Set aside some more time for an outstanding lunch.

Viña Las Niñas WINERY
(www.vinalasninas.cl; Apalta Valley) This winery, with its all-ladies leadership team, is making a new visitor center just outside it's pine-box vinting facility. They are looking to including mountain-bike tours and hikes into the surrounding mountains, along with tastings.

Emiliana WINERY
(☏ cell 9225-5679; www.emiliana.cl; Camino Lo Moscoso s/n, Placilla; biodynamic tours incl 4 pours CH$10,000; ⊙tours 10:30am, 11:30am, 12:30pm, 2:30pm & 4:30pm) 🍷 Biodynamic growing techniques are explained at this ecofriendly vineyard through the 'organic & biodynamic' tour (CH$10,000). To make a day of it, add on the gourmet organic picnic (CH$28,000 for two people, including organic tour).

Viu Manent WINERY
(☏ 02-840-3181; www.viumanent.cl; Carretera del Vino, Km37; tasting CH$10,000; ⊙tours 10:30am, noon, 3pm & 4:30pm) At this third-generation family-owned vineyard tours involve a carriage ride through 80-year-old vineyards and an insightful visit to the winery. It's located close to Santa Cruz, and offers up an unexpected malbec (better known as an Argentinean wine).

MontGras WINERY
(☏ 072-282-3242; www.montgras.cl; Camino Isla de Yáquil s/n, Palmilla; 2/4/6 reservas tastings CH$6000/9000/12,000; ⊙tastings 10:30am-6pm Mon-Fri, 10:30am-4:30pm Sat) In addition to tastings and 'make your own wine' workshops, this friendly, award-winning winery offers horseback riding, hiking, ziplining and mountain biking, all on the vineyard.

Estampa WINERY
(☏ 02-202-7000; www.estampa.com) Have a picnic under a huge fig tree after a hands-on tasting.

Montes WINERY
(☏ cell 9969-1017; www.monteswines.com; Apalta Valley; tours from CH$12,000) Ecofriendly, high-tech winemaking and vineyards covering picturesque hillsides. The tours start with a

visit through the vineyards and end with a four-wine tasting.

Viña Bisquertt   WINERY
(☑ 02-756-2500; www.bisquertt.cl) Famous for its La Joya Cabernet. You can stay overnight at the winery's charming Las Majadas guesthouse.

Viña Casa Silva   WINERY
(☑ 072-291-3117; www.casasilva.cl) One of Chile's oldest wineries, Casa Silva features carriage rides and a polo pitch.

Tren Sabores del Valle   TRAIN TOUR
(☑ 600-585-5000; www.tmsa.cl/link.cgi/servicios/tren-valle-colchagua; tickets CH$39,900-49,900) Departing Santiago's Alameda Terminal at 9:50am, this eight-hour round-trip train excursion takes you through the Colchagua Valley stopping at the San Fernando Terminal, where you disembark and head out by bus to a popular area winery for a tasting.

The tourist-oriented trip includes food and one tasting on board. It doesn't work year-round, but seems to depart at least once a month in the summer. The website has up-to-date schedules.

Santa Cruz

Your jumping-off point for journeys into wine country is a rather sleepy place with a pretty main square, an excellent private museum, a smattering of fine restaurants, and, of course, a casino. Other than a cruise around the plaza and an afternoon in the museum, there's not much else to be seen or done here. But it makes for a pleasant base as you head into the countryside for picnics and tastings.

◉ Sights & Activities

Museo de Colchagua   MUSEUM
(☑ 072-821-050; www.museocolchagua.cl; Errázuriz 145; adult/child CH$7000/3000; ⊙ 10am-7pm) Exhibiting the impressive private collection of controversial entrepreneur and alleged arms dealer Carlos Cardoen, this is the largest private museum in Chile. The collection includes pre-Columbian anthropomorphic ceramics from all over Latin America; weapons, religious artifacts and Mapuche silver; and a whole room of *huasos* (cowboy) gear.

The headlining exhibit here is El Gran Rescate (The Big Rescue), showing objects, photos and films related to the August 2010 rescue of the 33 miners trapped 700m underground in San José. Perhaps as interesting as the museum is the story of its founder, Carlos Cardoen, who allegedly sold armaments to Iraq during the time of Saddam Hussein's regime, and was instrumental in bringing tourism to the Colchagua Valley by supporting the creation of museums and other wine-centric attractions.

✷ Festivals & Events

Fiesta de la Vendimia   WINE
Santa Cruz celebrates the grape harvest each March with the lively Fiesta de la Vendimia. Local wineries set up stands in the Plaza de Armas, a harvest queen is crowned, and there is singing and folk dancing all round.

🛏 Sleeping & Eating

Wine country is filled with beautiful B&Bs and wine lodges, many located at the wineries themselves; they're mostly high-end and geared to travelers who are getting around in their own cars.

★ Hotel Casa Pando   B&B $$
(☑ 072-282-1734; www.casapando.cl; Cabello 421, 6 blocks north of Plaza de Armas; r CH$75,000; P🖥🎧🐕) Food and wine lovers José María and Mariela run this remarkably friendly bed-and-breakfast just on the edge of town. The converted house has large rooms (that could be a bit brighter, but are nevertheless highly serviceable) surrounded by gorgeous gardens. There's a large pool, and the owners know everything you'll need to know to savor your experience in wine country.

Hotel Plaza Santa Cruz   RESORT $$$
(☑ 072-220-9600; www.hscp.cl; Plaza de Armas 286; r/ste incl breakfast from US$335/456; P🎧🐕🏨) 🍃 Pass through the archway off the main square to enter this striking Spanish colonial-inspired resort. Lush landscaping, a lagoon-style swimming pool, classy *vinoteca,* a pair of gourmet restaurants (recommended and open to the public), a spa and, of course, the gleaming Casino Colchagua round out the offerings.

Guest rooms are large and impeccable, furnished with wooden beds from Peru and glowing lamps made by local artisans.

Casa Silva   HISTORIC HOTEL $$$
(☑ 072-716-519; www.casasilva.cl; Hijuela Norte s/n, San Fernando; d incl breakfast from CH$120,000) Maple trees shade the stone-tiled courtyard, complete with fountain, at the heart of this 100-year-old house on the edge of a vineyard, near Ruta 5 Km132. The sumptuous

WORTH A TRIP

LOLOL

Sleepy Lolol, 23km southeast of Santa Cruz, makes a picture-perfect side trip from Santa Cruz. Walk past beautifully preserved colonial houses with wooden columns and terracotta roofs before stepping into a few excellent museums and wineries.

Museo Artesanía Chilena (www.museocolchagua.cl; Los Aromos 95; adult/child CH$3000/1500; ⊗noon-7pm Tue-Sun) This smart folk-art museum shows thousands of pieces of Chilean rural artwork, from ceramics to textiles to cowboy spurs; many were collecting dust in the Universidad Católica de Chile's storage for decades.

Viña Santa Cruz (☑072-235-4920; www.vinasantacruz.cl; Lolol; adult/child CH$17,000/500; ☑) This 900-hectare winery caters specifically to tourists, and is the only winery in the area that's suitable for kids. The three-pour winery tour takes you up a gondola to a small observatory (inquire about night star tours) and a grouping of replica indigenous villages.

Museo del Automóvil (☑072-235-4838; www.museodelcolchagua.cl; Viña Santa Cruz; adult/child CH$5000/2000) At the entrance to Viña Santa Cruz, this car museum showcases older models in a big showroom.

rooms ooze old-world style with their padded fabric wall-coverings, old prints, and antique wardrobes and bedsteads (many are four-posters).

Residencia Histórica de Marchihue
HISTORIC HOTEL **$$$**
(☑cell 9307-4183; www.residenciahistorica.com; 5km north of Marchihue; r incl breakfast CH$115,000; ☑☑☑) This sprawling hotel was originally built in 1736 and used as an administrative building for Jesuits. It's quite far out from everything, but has all you will need, including a pool, a wine cellar, mountain bikes, horses to rent and plenty of opportunities for exploration on the 50-hectare *fundo* (estate).

The historic rooms are massive, though less elegant than we'd like. Ask for a room with a chimney.

179 Sandwich Bar
SANDWICHES **$**
(www.bar179.cl; Besoain 179; sandwiches CH$3400-5900) Gourmet sandwiches and excellent wines by the glass bring in a small lunch crowd to this stylish space just above Plaza de Armas. At night, the bar comes alive with glowing blue lights, DJ lineups and creative, potent cocktails.

Vino Bello
ITALIAN **$**
(www.vinobello.cl; Barreales s/n; mains CH$4600-7800) It's just 1km out of town, but this warm Italian restaurant really makes you feel like you're in the heart of wine country – especially when you're sipping a glass of Carmenere on the gorgeous patio at sunset or dining by candlelight on homemade gnocchi, thin-crust pizzas and baked Brie with pears.

From Plaza de Armas, take Nicolas Palacios, passing the Laura Hartwig vineyards; you'll see the entrance to Vino Bello on the left.

Viña La Posada
CONTEMPORARY **$$**
(Barreales s/n; mains CH$5600-8500) About 10 blocks west of the Plaza de Armas, this colonial-style winery has an excellent grouping of international restaurants. **La Casita de Barreales** features lip-smacking Peruvian fare. You can get your red-meat fix at the Argentinean *parrillada* joint **La Cava de Fuasto**.

El Cazador features unique takes on wild game typical of the region, while **Retinto** serves Spanish tapas and gets things moving.

ℹ️ Information

BancoEstado (Besoain 24; ⊗9am-2pm Mon-Fri) Has an ATM and changes dollars.

Post Office (☑800-267-736; Besoain 96; ⊗9am-2pm & 3-6pm Mon-Fri, 10am-1pm Sat)

ℹ️ Getting There & Away

Long-distance buses operate from the open-air **Terminal de Buses Santa Cruz** (Rafael Casanova 478), about four blocks west of the Plaza de Armas. **Buses Nilahué** (www.busesnilahue.cl) and other lines offer two hourly departures from Santa Cruz to Pichilemu (CH$4000, 3½ hours), San Fernando (CH$1000, 30 minutes) and Santiago (CH$7000, four hours).

To get to Lolol or Curicó (CH$800 to CH$1200), look for the fleet of local minibuses; they're usually waiting to fill up with passengers at the parking lot that is adjacent from the main terminal.

Pichilemu

072 / POP POP 12,500

Wave gods and goddesses brave the icy waters of Chile's unofficial surf capital year-round, while mere beach-going mortals fill its long black sands December through March. Just outside the town center, the streets are still unpaved, lending an atavistic air to this peaced-out surfer village. Further south, you'll find a string of small villages that have amazing surf, small lodges and plenty of good-times vibes that harken back to the golden days of surfing.

Sights & Activities

Centro Cultural Agustín Ross MUSEUM
(072-297-6595; Ross s/n; 9am-10pm) FREE
This three-story cultural center is housed in a gorgeous building that used to be the town's casino. Rotating art exhibits make for a welcome break from beach life and bonfires.

Surf Shop Puesta del Sol BIKING
(Ortúzar 262; bike rental hour/day CH$1000/3500) Rents bikes in bad repair.

Surfing

The westernmost part of Pichi juts out into the sea, forming **La Puntilla**, the closest surfing spot to town, where you'll find a long and slow point break. Fronting the town center to the northeast is calm **Playa Principal** (main beach), while south is the longer and rougher **Infiernillo**, known for its more dangerous lefts, fast tow and fun beachfront leftovers. The best surfing in the area is at **Punta de Lobos**, 6km south of Pichi proper, where you'll find a steep left. Waves break year-round, but get better in September through May. You definitely want a wetsuit. Inquire at Pichilemu Surf Hostal for kite boards and boat trips to remote beaches (from CH$50,000).

Lobos del Pacífico SURFING
(www.lobosdelpacifico.cl; Av Costanera 720; full-day board hire CH$8000, 2hr classes CH$12,000) You can hire boards, wetsuits (a must) and take classes with internationally certified instructors at Lobos del Pacífico at Infiernillo. It's also said to be the best board-repair shop in Pichi.

Escuela de Surf Manzana 54 SURFING
(cell 9574-5984; www.manzana54.cl; Av Costanera s/n; full-day board & gear hire CH$7000-8000, 2hr classes CH$10,000) A reliable surf school, on La Puntilla beach, where conditions are good for beginners.

Horseback Riding

Always fantasized about galloping along the beach on horseback? You're in luck. When the weather's not too hot in Pichilemu, you'll see a small group of beautiful horses – saddled up and ready to ride – on the northern end of the main beach, near the lake. It's easy to negotiate a lovely guided hour-long ride (CH$4000 to CH$6000) that goes past the lake, through the forest and returns along the oceanfront.

Courses

Pichilemu

Language School LANGUAGE COURSE
(www.studyspanishchile.com; Aníbal Pinto 21, Piso 3, Oficina 3; per hour CH$9000) Take a break from surf sessions at this language school that can arrange homestays.

Sleeping

Reserve well ahead during summer, and inquire about discounts during winter and fall.

Pichilemu Surf Hostal HOSTEL $
(cell 9270-9555; www.surfhostal.com; Eugenio Díaz Lira 167; dm/s/d incl breakfast CH$13,000/30,000/45,000;) Attic-style lookouts with incredible sea views top most of the rooms at this unusually designed clapboard hostel opposite Infiernillo beach. Each has firm beds, pale linens and huge framed photos of the nearby waves. You get expert wave advice from the windsurfing Dutch owner, Marcel. It has free bikes and can set you up with a saltwater bath overlooking the beach.

Cabañas Waitara CABIN $
(072-284-3026; www.waitara.cl; Costanera 1039; d/tr/q CH$35,000/40,000/45,000;) Looking above the town's main beach, these cabins have pitched roofs, sunny porches, beat down bathrooms and small living rooms with kitchenettes, making them a good bet for groups. The cabins range in size, accommodating two to 12 people.

Hotel Chile España HOTEL $
(072-841-270; www.chileespana.cl; Av Ortúzar 255; s/d/tr incl breakfast CH$20,000/35,000/50,000;) Once a popular surfer hangout, this budget hotel, located at the entrance to town, caters largely to older travelers. If you're

MIDDLE CHILE PICHILEMU

FINDING LOST BEACHES & BUNGALOWS FURTHER SOUTH

South of Pichilemu following the Costanera, there are several little villages and a few offbeat surf spots worth checking out. Here are our favorites.

La Loica (☑cell 7897-8190; www.loicachile.cl; Punta de Lobos; d/q CH$75,000/80,000; ☏) These Punta de Lobos cabins have pine walls, gorgeous picture windows that just catch the sea and chilled-out terraces. It's the perfect spot for families and surfers. The cabins all come with kitchens, wood-burning stoves and modern amenities. We totally heart Numero 3.

Cahuil This little village has good ocean views and a few restaurants and cabins. Head to the bridge for a half-hour boat tour of the Laguna de Cahuil (CH$5000 per boat up to five people), and to purchase locally crafted ceramics.

Surf Farm (☑cell 9539-8693; www.surffarm.cl; 1km south of Cahuil Bridge; dm/d CH$10,000/25,000, horseback ride CH$12,000, surf class CH$15,000) To really get away from it all, head to this old workers' camp that young upstart Nico has converted to a rustic hostel and surf lodge. You get a pretty decent break right outside your door. The dorm rooms are quite rustic, while the doubles are quite a bit nicer with pine walls, firm beds and private bathrooms. You'll need to bring your own food. To get here, call ahead and Nico will pick you up.

not looking to join the party with other surfers at a youth hostel, score a room here.

The Spanish-style building, with its leafy central patio, wooden shutters and antique interior, is utterly charming, though the rooms can be a bit cell-like.

Camping La Caletilla CAMPGROUND $
(☑cell 8171-2725; www.campingpichilemu.cl; Eugenio Suarez 905, 1km south of town; camping per person CH$4000-5000) Enjoy hot showers, an outside kitchen area, and sheltered campsites out of the wind at this groovy campground. Most of the structures are made from repurposed materials.

Cabañas Guzmán Lyon BUNGALOW $$
(☑072-284-1068; www.cabanasguzmanlyon.cl; San Antonio 48; d/tr/q incl breakfast CH$40,000/45,000/55,000; ☏▨) This rambling cliff-top resort just north of the town's main intersection is comprised of a series of brightly painted clapboard cottages. The privileged views over the ocean and lake are stunning from the private patio off the front of each bungalow, where your breakfast will be served each morning.

✖ Eating & Drinking

Many restaurants are closed June through August.

Pulpo PIZZERIA $
(Ortúzar 275; mains CH$6900-7900, set lunch CH$2000-4000; ☺noon-1am Tue-Sun; ☏▨) This central pizza joint has a pleasant patio and

airy inside. It serves up crispy stone-fired pies with plenty of veggie offerings such as artichoke hearts and sun-dried tomato. The crust is just right, but you'll need to hit the condiments for pitch-perfect flavor.

La Casa de las Empanadas CHILEAN $
(Aníbal Pinto 268; empanadas CH$1200-1900) Just look for all the surfers eating out of brown paper bags at the wooden benches outside this cheerful takeaway counter that does killer gourmet empanadas. The seafood versions, like *machas y queso* (razor clams and cheese), are to die for.

Restaurant Los Colchaguinos CHILEAN $
(Aníbal Pinto 298; empanadas & pailas CH$900-2500; ☺noon-3pm & 7:30-11pm Mon-Sat, noon-3pm Sun) Big, dripping empanadas are the star attraction at this small, family-run hole-in-the-wall, which also makes rich, homey *paila marina* (seafood stew).

El Puente Holandés SEAFOOD $
(☑cell 9270-0955; Eugenio Díaz Lira 167; mains CH$3500-6900; ☺9am-11pm, closed Jun-Aug) An arching wooden bridge leads from the Costanera into this high-ceilinged bar and restaurant overlooking Infiernillo beach, run by the same owners as Pichilemu Surf Hostal. It does simple seafood dishes well – grilled sea bass or clam and prawn ravioli, for example – or you can nurse a beer and some empanadas on the terrace.

Disco 127   CLUB
(Av Angel Gaete 217; ☺10pm-late Thu-Sat Mar-Dec, 10pm-late daily Jan & Feb) Most travelers' stories of derring-do in Pichilemu feature at least one 'and then I collapsed on the dance floor' moment at this rowdy club.

❶ Information

BancoEstado (Errázuriz 397; ☺9am-2pm Mon-Fri) ATM and currency exchange.
Oficina de Información Turística (www. pichilemu.cl; Av Angel Gaete 365, Municipalidad; ☺9am-6pm) Basic information about accommodations and events is available from this office within the main municipal building.
Post Office (Av Ortúzar 568; ☺9:30am-4pm Mon-Fri, 9:30am-noon Sat)

❶ Getting There & Away

The **Terminal de Buses** (☎072-841-709; cnr Av Millaco & Los Alerces) is in the southwestern section of Pichilemu – the closest stop to the town center is the corner of Santa María and Ortúzar. From the terminal there are frequent services to Santa Cruz (CH$3000, three hours), San Fernando (CH$4000, 3½ hours) and Santiago (CH$5500, four hours) with **Buses Nilahué** (☎02-7676-1139; www.busesnilahue.cl; Aníbal Pinto 301) and **Pullman del Sur** (☎02-2776-2424; www.pdelsur.cl; Aníbal Pinto 213, Local A) – you can buy tickets at the downtown offices. Change at San Fernando for buses or trains south.

If you're going to Santiago, make sure to ask for a bus that goes through Melipilla; though it bumps along country roads for miles, it's a newer, more direct service that gets you into Santiago in less than four hours.

Curicó

☑075 / POP 244,053
'Nice plaza' is about as much as most locals have to say about Curicó. They're right: some 60 towering palm trees ring the square, while the inside is decorated with cedars, monkey puzzles, a striking early-20th-century wrought-iron bandstand and a wooden statue of the Mapuche chief Toqui Lautaro. (Fun fact: Curicó means 'black water' in Mapuche.) Luckily, the postcard-pretty plaza was mostly untouched by the 2010 earthquake. The rest of the town didn't fare as well: up to 90% of the older buildings in Curicó's historic center fell.

Despite the recent hardship, Curicó still bursts into life for the **Festival de la Ven-** dimia (Wine Harvest Festival), which lasts three days in early fall.

Most travelers use Curicó as a base for exploring the stunning Reserva Nacional Radal Siete Tazas, or the nearby wineries in the Curicó and Maule Valleys.

🏃 Activities

Ruta del Vino Curicó   TOUR
(☎075-232-8977; www.rutadelvinocurico.cl; Carmen 727, Hotel Raíces) Arrange a guided tour to the best Curicó Valley vineyards, including Miguel Torres, San Pedro, Echeverria and Millamar.

🛏 Sleeping & Eating

Hotel Prat   HOSTEL $
(☎075-231-1069; www.hotelpratcurico.cl; Peña 427; s/d with shared bathroom incl breakfast CH$15,000/25,000, s/d with bathroom CH$25,000/35,000; ☏) A rambling old building painted in acid colors houses Curicó's cheapest digs. The kitchen and in-room cable TV make it popular with exchange students. It's a super-friendly joint and the common areas are a great way to meet other travelers. The bathrooms could use a good scrub.

Hostal Viñedos   B&B $$
(☎075-326-785; www.hostalvinedos.cl; Chacabuco 645; s/d/tr incl breakfast CH$30,000/40,000/45,000; ☏🖳♿) Rooms at this modern, wine-themed B&B are named after different grapes – the ones at the front are lighter. Whether you've been drinking or not, the huge bouncy beds are a godsend.

Hotel Raíces   BUSINESS HOTEL $$
(☎075-543-440; www.hotelraices.cl; Carmen 727; s/d incl breakfast CH$66,400/73,500; ☏) This contemporary hotel has slate floors, a sleek wine bar and a glass-encased cafe that is drenched with sunlight. Guest rooms, though somewhat generic, feature large plasma TVs and comfortable beds where you can relax after drinking Cabernet all day. Ask for a garden-view room.

El Rincón Che   SANDWICHES $
(Carmen 485; mains CH$3500-5200) A laid-back spot near Plaza Talca for sandwiches and microbrews.

Restaurante Miguel Torres   CHILEAN $$
(☎075-242-9360; www.migueltorres.cl; Panamericana Sur, Km195; mains CH$8100-13,400) Set amid rolling vineyards, this high-end eatery does gourmet versions of Chilean classics –

and every dish is listed with a recommended wine pairing (olive ravioli stuffed with smoked salmon and blue cheese, paired with Santa Digna rosé? *Si, por favor.*) It's just south of town off Hwy 5.

ℹ Information

Banco Santander (Estado 356; ⊙ 9am-2pm Mon-Fri) One of many banks with ATMs around the Plaza de Armas.

ℹ Getting There & Away

BUS

Most Curicó buses arrive at and leave from the **Terminal de Buses** (cnr Prat & Maipú), near the train station five blocks west of the Plaza de Armas. From here **Andimar** (☑ 075-312-000; www.andimar.cl) and **Pullman del Sur** (☑ 02-2776-2424; www.pdelsur.cl) have frequent services to Santiago (CH$2000 to CH$3200, 2½ hours, every 30 minutes).

To get to Reserva Nacional Radal Siete Tazas, catch a bus to Molina (CH$500, 35 minutes, every five minutes) with **Aquelarre** (☑ 075-314-307) from the Terminal de Buses Rurales, opposite the main bus terminal. From Molina there are frequent services to the park in January and February, and one daily service to Radal, 9km before the park proper, the rest of the year.

Tur Bus (☑ 600-660-6600; www.turbus.cl; Av Manso de Velasco 0106) has its own terminal southeast of town. From here, services leave to Santiago (CH$3900, 2½ hours, three daily) and Valparaíso (CH$6900, 4½ hours, one daily), and also south to Osorno (CH$16,600, 10 hours, four daily), Puerto Montt (CH$17,500, 12 hours, two daily) and Valdivia (CH$14,400, 11 hours, two daily).

TRAIN

Trenes Metropolitanos (p78) passenger trains between Santiago and Chillán stop at Curicó's **train station** (Maipú 657), five blocks west along Prat from the Plaza de Armas, near the bus station. There are seven trains a day to Santiago (CH$5600 to CH$19,000, 2¼ hours) and Chillán (CH$8000 to CH$19,000, 2½ hours), with connections from there to Concepción.

Reserva Nacional Radal Siete Tazas

The upper basin of the Río Claro marks the beginning of the ecological transition between the drought-tolerant Mediterranean vegetation to the north and the moist evergreen forests to the south. Here, 78km southeast of Curicó along a narrow gravel road, lies the **Reserva Nacional Radal Siete Tazas** (☑ 071-222-4461; www.conaf.cl; adult/child CH$4000/600; ⊙ 8:30am-8pm Dec-Feb, to 5:30pm Mar-Nov).

Conaf's main post is at the **Parque Inglés** sector, 9km beyond the park entrance at Radal, but there are two interesting stop-offs between the two points. **Velo de la Novia** (literally, 'The Bridal Veil') is a 40m waterfall which you can see from a small roadside viewing point 2.6km from Radal. Another 4.4km on is the car park and Conaf ranger hut (usually only used in summer) that mark the access point for the 400m trail to the **Siete Tazas** (seven cups), a breathtaking series of seven waterfalls and pools carved out of black basalt rock by the Río Claro. From here, another short trail leads to a viewpoint for the **Salto la Leona**, a waterfall that drops more than 50m from a narrow gorge to the main channel of the Río Claro.

Two well-marked hiking trails loop from Camping Los Robles at Parque Inglés: the 1km **Sendero el Coigüe** and 7km **Sendero Los Chiquillanes**, which has great views of the Valle del Indio (plan on about four hours in total). The first segment of this trail is part of the **Sendero de Chile** (www.senderodechile.cl), which continues to El Bolsón, where there is a refuge, and Valle del Indio. From here you can trek across the drainage of the Río Claro to Reserva Nacional Altos de Lircay, taking about two days: the route is unsigned and crosses private land, so either do it with a guide or get detailed information from Conaf and carry a topographical map, compass and adequate supplies. **Casa Chueca** (☑ 071-197-0097; www.trekkingchile.com) can take you on guided trips.

🛏 Sleeping & Eating

Conaf runs two cold-water **campsites** (☑ 075-228-029; campsites per person CH$1500) at the Parque Inglés: Camping Rocas Basálticas and Camping Parque Inglés. Both get very busy during summer.

Camping Los Robles   CAMPGROUND $
(☑ 075-228-029; 6-person campsites CH$8000) There's hot water and barbecue areas at this privately run campsite. Bring food supplies with you – there's a big supermarket opposite the bus station in Molina.

Valle de las Catas   CAMPGROUND $$
(☑ cell 9168-7820; www.sietetazas.cl; Camino Privado s/n; campsites per person CH$6000, cabins

CH$45,000) This well-organized camping and cabin complex will help you organize kayaking and mountain-biking excursions.

🛈 Getting There & Away

During January and February Buses Hernández operates frequent services from Molina (Maipú CH$1735) to the Parque Inglés sector of the park (CH$1800, 2½ hours, eight daily). From March to December there is one daily bus to Radal (CH$2000, two hours, daily at 4pm), 10km down the hill from Parque Inglés.

To drive to Radal Siete Tazas, take the Panamericana south of Curicó then turn off to Molina. Leave Molina to the south on paved road K-25 toward Cumpeo, 25km further on, where the road turns to gravel. From here, it's a bumpy 39km more to Radal, and another 10km to Parque Inglés.

Maule Valley

The Maule Valley, a hugely significant wine-producing region for Chile, is responsible for much of the country's export wine; the specialty here is full-bodied Cabernet Sauvignon. The area was at the epicenter of the February 2010 earthquake – one winery reported losing its 80,000-bottle collection, and countless vineyard workers were left homeless, while the nearby city of Talca lost its historic marketplace, hospital and museum. Needless to say, tourist activity has been down, but the wine industry has largely recovered, thanks in part to some inspired community efforts.

Many visitors use Talca as a base for exploring the wineries and the nearby Reserva Nacional Altos de Lircay. Ask for the free *Región del Maule* booklet for great information (in English) on recommended treks, local tips and a guide to flora and fauna of the region.

Maule Valley Wineries

You can visit many of the vineyards independently or through one of the tours run by the **Ruta del Vino** (📞08-157-9951; www.valledelmaule.cl; Av Circunvalación Oriente 1055, Casino Talca Hotel Lobby, Talca; ⊙9am-6:30pm Mon-Fri). More than a dozen wineries are associated with the tour operator.

🏃 Activities

Viña Balduzzi   WINERY
(📞073-232-2138; www.balduzziwines.cl; Av Balmaceda 1189, San Javier; tour incl 4 pours from

CH$3600; ⊙9am-6pm Mon-Sat) A visitor-friendly fourth-generation winery surrounded by spacious gardens and well-kept colonial buildings. Unlike at many other wineries, no reservation is required.

Balduzzi is also one of the few wineries that's easy to reach by public transportation. From the bus terminal in Talca, look for a bus labeled 'San Javier Directo' (CH$750), which drops passengers off near the winery.

Via Wines   WINERY
(📞02-2355-9900; www.viawines.com; Fundo Las Chilcas s/n; tour incl 3 pours CH$10,000; ⊙9am-5pm Mon-Sat, reservations required) 🍷 One of Chile's first certifiably sustainable wineries, Via Wines turns out delicious Sauvignon Blanc and Syrah. Visitor-friendly programs include the organic winery tour and the 'Vino, Arte y Sabores' tour (CH$60,000 to CH$94,500 per person including lunch) that takes guests to meet local artisans before serving four Reserva selections.

Viña Gillmore   WINERY
(📞073-197-5539; www.gillmore.cl; Camino Constitución, Km20; tour incl 2 pours CH$5000; ⊙9am-5pm Mon-Sat) 🍷 There's more to do at this boutique winery than sip and swirl (though its Cabernet Franc is indeed fantastic). The winery, which is converting to an organic system, also features beautiful hiking trails and a spa offering various wine-based therapies.

Viña J Bouchon   WINERY
(📞073-197-2708; www.jbouchon.cl; Evaristo Lillo 178, oficina 21, Las Condes; ⊙9am-6pm Mon-Sat) 🍷 Located 30km from Constitución, this sustainable winery offers horseback riding and other outdoor activities, plus a beautiful inn for overnight stays.

Casa Donoso   WINERY
(📞071-234-1400; www.casadonoso.cl; Camino a Palmira, Fundo La Oriental, Km3.5; ⊙8am-6pm Mon-Fri) A traditionally run vineyard set around a colonial homestead, this winery is located 30km from Constitución.

Talca

📞071 / POP 189,500

Founded in 1690, Talca was once considered one of the country's principal cities; Chile's 1818 declaration of independence was signed here. These days it's mainly known as a convenient base for exploring the gorgeous

Around Curicó & Talca

0 ——— 10 km
0 ——— 5 miles

Reserva Nacional Altos de Lircay and the Maule Valley wineries. Parts of Talca were badly damaged in the 2010 earthquake, and there are several blocks of abandoned buildings in the city center.

You'll find a decent range of traveler's services, including dining and lodging options, plus lovely views of the Andes when you're strolling down the sun-baked pedestrian thoroughfare at midday.

🛏 Sleeping & Eating

Cabañas Stella Bordestero　BUNGALOW $
(☑071-235-545; www.turismostella.cl; 4 Poniente 1 Norte 1183; s/d without bathroom incl breakfast CH$16,000/24,000, s/d/cabin CH$22,000/30,000/48,000; ✸🕾✿) Four blocks from the Plaza de Armas but a world apart, these clapboard cabins are surrounded by a leafy garden with a swimming pool, deck chairs and swings. The owners have been just as

thorough inside: these pretty bungalows have firm beds, cable TV and small decks where you can relax with a glass of wine in the evening.

Hostal Maea　GUESTHOUSE $
(☑071-221-0910; www.hostalmaea.cl; 1377 Calle 3 Norte; d with/without bathroom from CH$30,000/20,000; 🕾) This basic but welcoming guesthouse has 1950s-style decor. The breezy twin rooms are halfway servicable. But all in all, the place feels just a little run-down.

Hostal Casa Chueca　HOTEL $$
(☑071-197-0096; www.trekkingchile.com/casa-chueca; Viña Andrea s/n, Sector Alto Lircay; dm CH$12,500, d CH$44,000-75,000; 🕾✿🐾) Gardens looking over the Río Lircay surround the rustic cabins at the German-run Casa Chueca. It's in the countryside outside Talca, but the hostel has become a destination in its own right for fans of the great outdoors – the knowledgeable owners can help you plan trekking and horseback-riding adventures in the nearby Parque Nacional Altos de Lircay.

They'll also arrange wine tastings, Spanish lessons, even a kid-friendly treasure hunt. Call first from Talca terminal (or contact the hostel ahead of time with your arrival time), then take the Taxutal 'A' micro toward San Valentín to the last stop, where you'll be picked up.

La Buena Carne　CHILEAN $
(cnr 6 Oriente & 1 Norte; mains CH$3000-5500) This cozy, contemporary steakhouse offers friendly service, a fantastic central location, and a menu of gigantic steak sandwiches, wine by the glass, classic Chilean platters and even well-prepared Peruvian ceviche. In the evenings, locals come to drink beer and watch *fútbol*.

Las Viejas Cochinas　CHILEAN $
(☑071-221-749; www.lasviejascochinas.cl; Rivera Poniente; mains CH$4200-10,000; ⊙noon-midnight) One of Talca's most popular restaurants is a huge, clattering, low-roofed canteen out of town alongside the Río Claro. Dour waiters take forever to bring out the house specialty, *pollo mariscal* (chicken in a brandy and seafood sauce), but it's worth the wait and big enough to share.

To get there, leave town heading west along Av Bernardo O'Higgins, cross the Río Claro bridge, keep right, then stay right at the fork in the road.

Rossini   CAFE $

(cnr 1 Norte & 3 Oriente; set lunch CH$3300; 🛜)
This central, contemporary cafe is a great
place to catch up on emails over coffee or
grab a quick lunch.

ℹ Information

BancoEstado (🖉 071-345-201; 1 Sur 971;
☉9am-2pm) One of many ATMs along 1 Sur.

Hospital Regional (🖉 071-242-406; www.
hospitaldetalca.cl) Busy public hospital
on the corner of 13 Oriente.

Post Office (🖉 800-267-736; 1 Oriente 1150;
☉9am-6pm Mon-Fri, 9am-noon Sat) Inside a
large building off Plaza de Armas.

Sernatur (www.chile.travel; 1 Oriente 1150;
☉8:30am-5:30pm Mon-Fri) Exceptionally
helpful, English-speaking staff offer travelers
advice on accommodations and activities as
well as money-saving tips in Talca.

ℹ Getting There & Away

BUS

Most companies use the **Terminal de Buses de
Talca** (2 Sur 1920, cnr 12 Oriente), 11 blocks east
of the Plaza de Armas. **Talca, París y Londres**
(🖉 071-221-1010; www.busestalcaparisylondres.
cl) has hourly buses to Santiago. So does **Buses
Linatal** (🖉 071-242-759; www.linatal.cl), which
also has 11 southbound buses daily. **Buses Línea
Azul** (www.buseslineaazul.cl) has hourly buses
south to Chillán. Buses Vilches has five daily
buses to Vilches Alto, gateway to the Reserva
Nacional Altos de Lircay. To get to Villa Cultural
Huilquilemu, take a bus to San Clemente and
ask to be let off at Ruta del Vino (CH$500, 10
minutes).

Tur Bus (🖉 600-660-6600; www.turbus.
cl; 3 Sur 1960) has hourly buses to Santiago
and six buses south to Puerto Montt, stopping
at Chillán, Los Angeles, Temuco, Osorno and
other cities on the Panamericana. Other companies operating with similar services include
Pullman del Sur (🖉 02-2776-2424; www.
pdelsur.cl) and **Pullman Bus** (🖉 600-320-
3200; www.pullman.cl).

DESTINATION	COST (CH$)	DURATION (HR)
Chillán	4800	3
Osorno	16,700	11
Puerto Montt	14,000	12
Santiago	4500	3
Temuco	10,500	6
Valparaíso/ Viña del Mar	6900	6
Vilches	1400	1½

TRAIN

From the **train station** (11 Oriente 1000) there
are eight trains a day to Santiago (CH$8000
to CH$19,000, 2¾ hours) and south to Chillán
(CH$8000, two hours) on the Trenes Metropoli-
tanos (p78) Terra Sur Line.

Reserva Nacional Altos de Lircay

The range of challenging hikes at this well-
organized and easily accessible **national park**
(www.conaf.cl/parques/reserva-nacional-altos-de
-lircay; adult/child CH$4000/600; ☉8am-1pm &
2-5:30pm) will leave you as short of breath as
the fabulous views. Its 121 sq km are made
up of a mix of high-Andean steppes, lagoons
and deciduous forest that turns a glorious
gold and red in the fall. Pudú deer, Patagonian foxes and Pampas cats also live here,
though sightings are uncommon.

About 2km before the park entrance,
Conaf runs the **Centro de Información
Ambiental**, which has displays on local natural and cultural history (the area has seen
four sequential indigenous occupations).
You pay admission and register for camping
and trekking at the **Administración**, about
500m after the entrance.

🥾 Activities

The helpful team of Conaf rangers who run
the park give detailed advice about hiking
and camping within it, and distribute pho-
tocopied maps of the area.

If you want a taste of the wilderness
without getting chafed feet, you could always let a beast of burden take the strain.
Several Vilches residents rent horses from
near the park entrance (horse/guide per day
CH$12,000/15,000).

Sendero Enladrillado   HIKING

Arguably the best hike in the whole of Middle Chile, the Sendero Enladrillado takes
you to the top of a 2300m basalt plateau.

The trail starts with a two-hour stretch
east along the Sendero de Chile, then a
signposted right-hand fork climbs steeply through dense forest for about an hour
before leveling off. You eventually emerge
onto the dead-flat platform of El Enladrillado – many people think it's a UFO-landing
ground. To the west you can see the flat-
topped crater of the Volcán Descabezado
(literally, 'Headless Volcano') and next to it
the sharp peak of Cerro Azul. The 10km trek

WORTH A TRIP

VILLA CULTURAL HUILQUILEMU

Once an important *fundo* (farm), this complex of restored 19th-century buildings is a cultural landmark and a wonderful example of colonial architecture. It was damaged in the 2010 earthquake and the museum (containing folk art, religious tableaux, and the basin where local hero Bernardo O'Higgins was baptized) was forced to close.

At the time of writing, the space had opened for special events and festivals, and it's worth a trip to check out the building's old adobe walls and the surrounding gardens filled with sequoias, araucarias, magnolias, palms and oaks. Ask at Talca's Ruta del Vino office for more information. It's located 7km east of Talca; all buses to San Clemente from Talca's bus station pass Huilquilemu.

takes about four hours up and three down. There are two or three potable springs before the trail emerges above the tree line, but carry as much water as possible.

Sendero Laguna
HIKING

The Sendero Laguna follows the Sendero de Chile for an hour before forking right into a steep, three-hour uphill stretch to the gorgeous Laguna del Alto, a mountain-ringed lake at 2000m above sea level. Plan on three hours there and back, or you can continue for two hours on a trail leading northwest to El Enladrillado. The round-trip takes eight hours.

Mirador del Valle Venado
HIKING

A gentle three-hour hike along the Sendero de Chile takes you from the Administración to the Mirador del Valle Venado, which has views over the Volcán Descabezado and the Río Claro Valley.

A trail continues southeast from here (still along the Sendero de Chile) through a long gorge, before arriving at Río Claro, 15km (six hours) from the Administración, where there's a small refuge. Another 5km (three hours) further on is Valle del Venado, where camping is permitted. It's a two-day trip.

Circuito de los Cóndores
HIKING

Longer hikes in and around the park include the seven-day Circuito de los Cóndores, for

which it's advisable to carry topographic maps or hire a guide. Another such offering is the loop across the drainage of the Río Claro to exit at Reserva Nacional Radal Siete Tazas.

☞ Tours

Casa Chueca/Trekking Chile   GUIDED TOUR
(☎071-197-0096; www.trekkingchile.com) Excellent tours run by an expert German hiker based out of Casa Chueca. Expect about CH$15,000 per day for guided tours.

Costa y Cumbre Tours   GUIDED TOUR
(☎cell 9943-5766; www.costaycumbretours.cl) Runs horseback riding and trekking excursions; provides camping equipment.

🛌 Sleeping

Camping Antahuara   CAMPGROUND $
(campsites CH$10,000) Conaf runs the excellent Camping Antahuara about 500m beyond the Adminstración, next to Río Lircay. It's accessible by car and has electricity, hot water, flush toilets and garbage collection. There are two *campings primitivos* (designated camping areas with no facilities), which are respectively a one-hour and a 2½-hour hike east from the Administración along the Sendero de Chile.

Hostería de Vilches   CABIN
(☎cell 9826-7046; www.hosteriadevilches.cl; Camino Vilches Alto, Km22, San Clemente; 2-person cabin from CH$50,000; ☒) ✿ You can stay just outside the park but keep the back-to-nature vibe at Hostería de Vilches, where adorable private cabins overlook well-tended gardens and a pair of swimming pools. The hearty homemade cuisine (dinner CH$7500), laid-back atmosphere and inviting hot tub and mud baths are a godsend after a day of trekking.

ⓘ Getting There & Away

Buses Vilches goes from the **Terminal de Buses de Talca** (2 Sur 1920, Talca) to Vilches Alto (CH$1400, two hours), a scattering of houses about 2km below the Centro de Información Ambiental and 5km from the Administración of the Reserva Nacional Altos de Lircay. Buses leave Talca daily at 7:15am, 10am, noon, 1pm and 4:55pm from March to December, and there are 10 services daily in January and February.

It takes about 1½ hours to drive to the reserve from Talca. Take road 115 through San Clemente; 38km from Talca is the left-hand turnoff to Vilches, another 25km further on.

Chillán

📞 042 / POP 180,197

Earthquakes have battered Chillán throughout its turbulent history; the 2010 earthquake was yet another hit. While this perpetually rebuilding city isn't especially interesting, it is a gateway to some of the loveliest landscapes in Middle Chile, not to mention amazing skiing and summer trekking in the nearby mountains.

⊙ Sights

Catedral de Chillán   CHURCH
(cnr Av Libertad & Arauco; ⊙10am-6pm Mon-Sat, 10am-2pm Sun) FREE On the northeast corner of Chillán's main square stands the stark, modernist Catedral de Chillán. Built in 1941, its soaring semi-oval form is made of a series of earthquake-resistant giant arches. The 36m-high cross next to it commemorates the thousands of Chillán residents who died in the 1939 earthquake.

Escuela México   MONUMENT
(Av O'Higgins 250; donations welcome; ⊙10am-1:30pm & 2-6pm Mon-Fri, 10am-6pm Sat & Sun) In response to the devastation that the 1939 quake caused, the Mexican government donated the Escuela México to Chillán. At Pablo Neruda's request, Mexican muralists David Alfaro Siqueiros and Xavier Guerrero decorated the school's library and stairwell, respectively, with fiercely symbolic murals, now set within an otherwise normal working school.

Mercado de Chillán   MARKET
(set lunches CH$1500-3200; ⊙9am-6pm) The city's main market is split into two sections on either side of Maipón between Isabel Riquelme and 5 de Abril. It is currently closed for renovations, with a possible reopening in 2015.

🛏 Sleeping

Chillán's hotels fill up very rapidly during the ski season so try to book ahead.

Hotel Bavaria   GUESTHOUSE $
(📞042-221-7235; www.hotelbavaria.cl; 18 de Septiembre 648; s/d incl breakfast CH$30,000/35,000; P🐾) Exit the concrete jungle of Chillán and find yourself in a non-sequitor Bavarian countryside villa. It's a quiet setting and the rooms are cozy though dated.

Hostal Canadá   GUESTHOUSE $
(📞042-234-515; Av Libertad 269; s/d CH$8000/16,000; 🐾) Spending a night in this no-nonsense mother-and-daughter setup is like staying in their apartment – fraying floral sheets, worn carpets, lumpy pillows and all. Get one in the back to avoid the street noise.

Hotel Las Terrazas Express   HOTEL $$
(📞042-243-7000; www.lasterrazas.cl; Constitución 663; s/d incl breakfast CH$53,000/60,000; @🐾) The rooms are a bit cramped, but for those seeking a few creature comforts in the city proper, this business hotel is just the ticket. The downstairs lobby and cafe are open and airy, and there are a few lounge areas throughout.

🍴 Eating & Drinking

Arcoiris Vegetariano   VEGETARIAN $
(El Roble 525; buffet CH$5900, mains CH$4000; ⊙9am-6:30pm Mon-Sat; 🐾) A good vegetarian restaurant in provincial Chile? We'll take it. Filling lentil-and-bulgur-style buffet lunches are served at the back, while a cafe upfront does sandwiches and cakes, all to the tune of wind-chime and whale music.

Fuego Divino   STEAK $
(📞042-243-0900; www.fuegodivino.cl; Gamero 980; mains CH$5500-7800) Stylish restaurants are thin on the ground in Chillán – perhaps that's why the gleaming black tables here are always booked up on weekends. Or maybe it's because the expertly barbecued prime cuts of Temuco beef taste so delicious.

Santos Pecadores   COCKTAIL BAR
(www.santospecadores.cl; Av Vicente Méndez 275; ⊙8:30pm-late Tue-Sat; 🐾) Divine sinners with plenty of dash and cash pour into this chichi red-walled bar northeast of the city center for sushi, ceviche and lots and lots of cocktails.

ℹ Information

Look for internet cafes, call centers, laundromats and other travelers' services along pedestrianized Arauco.

BancoEstado (Constitución 500; ⊙9am-2pm Mon-Fri) One of many ATMs on this street.

Hospital Herminda Martín (📞042-208-221; Francisco Ramírez 10) Public hospital on the corner of Av Argentina.

Post Office (📞800-267-736; Av Libertad 501; ⊙8:30am-6:30pm Mon-Fri, 9am-12:45pm Sat)

Sernatur (www.chile.travel; 18 de Septiembre 455; ⊙8:30am-1:30pm & 3-6pm Mon-Fri)

Chillán

Chillán

◉ Sights
1 Catedral de Chillán C3
2 Escuela México B1
3 Mercado de Chillán............................C4

🛏 Sleeping
4 Hostal Canadá......................................B2
5 Hotel Bavaria C3
6 Hotel Las Terrazas Express C3

⊗ Eating
7 Arcoiris Vegetariano...........................C3

Friendly staff provide city maps and information on accommodations and transport.

🛈 Getting There & Away

BUS

Chillán has two long-distance bus stations. The most central is **Terminal de Buses Interregion-**
al (Constitución 01), five blocks west of the Plaza de Armas on the corner of Rosas. From here, **Tur Bus** (☎ 600-660-6600; www.turbus.cl) has services to Santiago (hourly), some of which stop in Talca and other cities along the Panamericana. Tur Bus also goes direct to Valparaíso and south to Temuco, Osorno, Valdivia and Puerto Montt (seven daily). There are similar services to Santiago with **Línea Azul** (www.buseslineaazul.cl), which also goes to Los Angeles (10 daily), Angol (two daily) and Concepción (every 15 minutes).

Other long-distance carriers use the **Terminal María Teresa** (O'Higgins 010), north of Av Ecuador. These include Buses Jota Be, which makes daily journeys to Salto del Laja and has direct services to Los Angeles (hourly). **Pullman Bus** (☎ 600-320-3200; www.pullmanbus.cl) runs north to Calama, Antofagasta and Arica (five daily), and south to Puerto Montt (five daily).

Sol del Pacífico (www.soldelpacifico.cl) also goes to Santiago, Viña and Valparaíso.

Local and regional services leave from the **Terminal de Buses Rurales** (Maipón 890). **Rembus**

(📞 042-222-9377; www.busesrembus.cl) takes you to Valle Las Trancas (six to seven daily); the 7:50am and 1:20pm buses continue to Valle Hermoso on Fridays, Saturdays and Sundays. **Vía Itata** (www.busesviaitata.cl) operates routes to Ninhué (10 daily) and Cobquecura (four daily), while Tur Bus goes to Quirihue (three daily) with connections to surf hangout Buchupureo.

DESTINATION	COST (CH$)	DURATION (HR)
Angol	4100	2¼
Cobquecura	1800	2¾
Concepción	2500	1½
Los Angeles	2600	1½
Osorno	10,100	8
Puerto Montt	11,200	9
Quirihue	2000	1
Santiago	7000	6
Talca	4000	3
Temuco	9000	5
Termas de Chillán	3000	1½
Valdivia	10,700	6
Valparaíso	9000	8
Valle Los Trancas	1500	1¼

CAR
Driving makes it possible to cram in lots of national park action or quick day trips up the mountain to Termas de Chillán. Try **Rent-a-car** (📞042-221-2243; www.rentacares.com; 18 de Septiembre 380) at the train station. Rates start at about CH$23,000 a day. Note that if the mountain roads are slippery you may need to hire wheel chains, too.

TRAIN
The Trenes Metropolitanos (p78) TerraSur line runs from the **train station** (cnr Avs Brasil & Libertad) to Santiago (CH$8000, 4½ hours, three daily), stopping along the way at Talca (CH$8000, 1¾ hours) and Curicó (CH$8000, 3¼ hours), among other places.

Termas de Chillán & Valle Las Trancas

A winding road leads from Chillán 80km up into the mountains to Valle Las Trancas and the Termas de Chillán. Chilean powder fiends flock to these slopes in winter, when bumper-to-bumper traffic is common at the top. The pace is less manic the rest of the year, when the valleys turn a luscious green and are perfect for hiking, climbing and horseback riding, or just lazing around and drinking in the views. Despite the hikers that come out on summer weekends, the place is almost dead on a weekday in summer – bring your own picnic and don't count on hotels being open. Note that there aren't ATMs around most of these accommodations; you'll want to bring cash from Chillán.

⊙ Sights & Activities

Cueva de los Pincheira   CAVE
(Ruta 55, Camino Termas de Chillán; adult/child CH$2000/1000; 🚗) On your way to the resort, stop at this roadside attraction, where you can visit a shallow cave and waterfall and learn about the escapades of the Outlaw Pincheira Brothers that hid out here. In high season, there's reenactments.

Observatorio   OBSERVATORY
(www.milodge.com; M I Lodge; CH$10,000; 🚗) In the summer, the M I Lodge brings an astronomer up to its observatory to do nightly star talks (in English).

Nevados de Chillán Ski Center   SKIING
(📞042-220-6100; www.nevadosdechillan.com; day ski pass adult/child CH$35,000/23,000) The southern slopes of the 3122m Volcán Chillán are the stunning setting of this ski mecca. Unusually for Chile's ski resorts, many of its 30 runs track through forest, and there's a good mix of options for beginner and more experienced skiers.

Superlatives abound here: they've got the longest piste in South America (13km Las Tres Marías), the longest chairlift and some of the biggest and best off-piste offerings. Since 2008 a snow park and summertime bike park have been added, too. The season can start as early as mid-May and usually runs to mid-October – locals swear that great snow, empty slopes and discounted ski passes make the beginning of October one of the best times to come. In summer, there's hiking, horseback riding, climbing, canyoning and bike rental; check the website for full offerings. If money's no object, stay onsite at the **Hotel Nevados de Chillán** (d incl breakfast CH$87,900-96,300; 🏊) , where warm thermal waters fill an outdoor pool surrounded by snow.

Valle Hermoso   OUTDOORS
(www.nevadosdechillan.com; adult/child CH$8000/6000, campsite per tent CH$21,000; ⊙thermal springs 9am-5pm) A turnoff halfway between

Valle Las Trancas and the ski center takes you to this leafy recreational area. Most people come here for the **thermal springs** – sheltered inside a wooden house, they're open year-round. Ziplines, climbing walls and horseback riding provide extra action in summer, when you can stay at the small **campsite**.

Eco Parque Shangri-Lá ZIPLINING
(☑cell 9321-7567; www.milodge.com; Camino Shangri-Lá, Km3; adult/child CH$15,000/12,000; ⊙Jan-Mar; ⛺) Adults enjoy 25 zipline platforms at this well-done hour-long canopy tour. The kids' route is just 15ft off the ground.

Marula Spa SPA
(☑cell 9321-7567; www.milodge.com; M I Lodge; CH$10,000) This spa is open to nonguests. It offers a pool, massage and yoga classes.

🛏 Sleeping & Eating

Accommodations on the mountain divide into two camps. The posh hotels in Termas de Chillán at the top of the road get you closest to the slopes. Prices are much lower, however, if you stay in the cabins, hostels and lodges downhill at Valle Las Trancas. Note that most places have huge low-season discounts.

Chil'in Hostería & Restaurante HOSTEL $
(☑042-224-7075; www.chil-in.com; Ruta 55, Camino Termas de Chillán, Km72; dm/d without bathroom CH$9000/22,000; @🔋) At this awesome ski lodge–style hostel, you get a cozy living room and bar and lots of camaraderie. The rooms are simple but clean. Some come with lofts to stack more skiers.

★ Ecobox Andino BOUTIQUE HOTEL $$
(☑042-242-3134; www.ecoboxandino.cl; Camino a Shangri-Lá, Km0.2; cabins 2-5 people from CH$120,000, d incl breakfast CH$65,000; 🔋🖥) 🍃 Some of the hippest, most unique lodgings in Middle Chile, these impeccably decorated cabins were once shipping containers. They interlocked them (lego style) to create remarkable cabins with modern art deco exteriors and contemporary interiors (some won't love the low-slung beds).

Wooden decks overlook the tree-filled garden through which paths wind to the pool. A new *refugio* has six rooms with private bathrooms that look onto a common shared kitchen and living room.

M I Lodge LODGE $$$
(☑cell 9321-7567; www.milodge.com; Camino a Shangri-Lá; r per person incl breakfast & dinner CH$62,000; @🖥) 🍃 This ecofriendly lodge has plenty to offer: rustic-chic furnishings and a fire crackling in the middle of a beautifully designed glass-and-wood-walled French restaurant (specializing in crepes and open to the public). The rooms are a bit dark, but you have plenty of room and thick mattresses. Ask for a room with a view.

Restaurante El Tren CHILEAN $
(Camino Termas de Chillán, Km73; mains CH$4500-6800) The snug dining room of the classy El Tren is, in fact, an antique English train car. There's a good wine list, Chilean staples and a wooden terrace with lovely views of the snowcapped mountains.

Snow Pub PUB FOOD $
(Camino Termas de Chillán, Ruta 55, Km71; mains CH$3200-5000; ⊙1pm-late) For years the après-ski in Valle Las Trancas has centered on this feel-good bar, which gets packed with revelers in high season.

❶ Getting There & Away

From Chillán's Terminal de Buses Rurales, Rembus (p124) has buses to Valle Las Trancas (CH$2000, 1¼ hours) at approximately 7:50am, 8:50am, 10:15am, 11:15am, 12:40pm, 1:20pm, 3:10pm, 5pm, 5:50pm and 7:20pm Monday to Saturday (times may vary slightly with the season). All but the last departure also run on Sundays. On Fridays and weekends, some services continue to Valle Hermoso (CH$3000, 1½ hours) – if that's your final destination from Chillán, ask ahead of time which buses will take you all the way. From Santiago's Terminal Sur there are two direct services to Valle Las Trancas (CH$14,000, seven hours, 6:50am and 2:55pm) with **Buses Nilahué** (☑02-776-1139; www.busesnilahue.cl). In winter there are shuttle buses from Valle Las Trancas up to the ski center. Hitchhiking up is also possible.

Coastal Towns

Quiet beaches come with rural surroundings in the remote coastal towns northwest of Chillán. The area's perfect for long lazy walks along the sand, and there's good, low-key surfing for those who want the waves without the parties.

Cobquecura

A quiet little town with picturesque houses and dry walls made from local slate – a few too many that crumbled to pieces in the 2010 earthquake – Cobquecura has a long, wide beach with wild surf. The sands fill up in early February when Cobquecura hosts the **Campeonato Nacional de Surf y Body Board**. A deep baying sound resonates from a rock formation 50m offshore: known as the **Piedra de la Lobería**, it's home to a large colony of sunbathing sea lions. Follow the coast road 5km north and back to the beach and you reach the exquisite **Iglesia de Piedra** (Church of Stone), a massive mono-lith containing huge caves that open to the sea. The light inside the caves is mysterious – Cobquecura's pre-Hispanic inhabitants held ritual gatherings inside the stone, and it now contains an image of the Virgin Mary.

From Chillán's Terminal de Buses Ru-rales, **Via Itata** (☑042-211-196; www.busesviaitata.cl) has buses to Cobquecura (CH\$2200, 2½ hours) continuing on to Buchupureo (CH\$2500). Note that there are several daily departures during summer, but in the off-season there's only one bus, leaving at 7:30am from Chillán. **Nilahué** (☑02-776-1139; www.busesnilahue.cl) operates a direct bus from Santiago's Terminal Sur to Cobquecura (CH\$11,000, seven hours, once daily).

Buchupureo

Magic is alive in this tranquil farming vil-lage 13km north of Cobquecura. Steep slopes covered with lush greenery sur-round the settlement, lending it a tropical air. Despite growing interest from tourists and surfers, the pace of life is slow here: oxen-pulled carts are still a common sight. It's also a famous fishing spot – *corvina* (sea bass) apparently jump onto any hook dangled off the beach.

Dunes and scrubland separate the deso-late brown-sand beach from the main road, which runs parallel to the shore before loop-ing through the small town center to the beach. A couple of wooden walkways also connect the road and the sand.

🛏 Sleeping & Eating

Ayekán Aldea Turística CABIN **$**
(☑cell 9988-5986; www.turismoayekan.cl; camp-sites CH\$20,000, 2-/4-person cabins CH\$35,000/80,000; 🖣) In summer you can pitch your tent at one of 20 campsites in a pretty clear-ing at the bottom of a eucalypt-lined drive, close to the beach. A circular restaurant serves cheap homemade food, and the cab-ins come with kitchens and log furniture. You can just hear the beach from your porch.

La Joya del Mar B&B **$$$**
(☑042-197-1733; www.lajoyadelmar.com; 2-/5-per-son villas incl breakfast CH\$78,000/137,000; 🖥🖨) Rich tropical plants overhang the terraces, and the pool seems to merge with the view of the sea at this romantic spot run by a Cali-fornia family. The vibe spills over into the airy, glass-fronted farm-to-table restaurant (mains CH\$7900 to CH\$9600, open noon to 10pm). The three villas can sleep two to five people.

The rooms are pretty shwanky, but it's the views from the picture windows that make this spot a winner.

ℹ️ Getting There & Away

From Chillán's Terminal de Buses Rurales, **Via Itata** (☑042-211-196; www.busesviaitata.cl) has a few daily buses to Buchupureo (CH\$2500, three hours) during high season. It's your best bet for making a connection to other destinations.

Concepción
☑ 041 / POP 229,000

Concepción is an important and hard-working port city that is best known for its universi-ties and music scene (many of Chile's best rock acts got their start here). There are a few plazas and museums worth checking out, and Spanish speakers will be reward-ed with the energetic, youthful arts, music and culture scene. The city sits on the north bank of the Río Biobío, Chile's only signifi-cant navigable waterway, about 10km from the river's mouth. The metropolis seems to go on forever, with an estimated 900,000 liv-ing in the greater area. 'Conce,' as it's known locally, was yet another city terribly damaged in the February 2010 earthquake. It was also ravaged by looting and lawlessness during the aftershocks, but because of its economic importance it is being quickly rebuilt.

History

In 1551 Pedro de Valdivia founded the orig-inal city of Concepción north of where it is today, near Penco (indeed, Conce's inhabit-ants are still known as Penquistas). Over the next few centuries the city was repeatedly besieged during the Spanish-Mapuche war, attacked by British and Dutch pirates and devastated by earthquakes in 1730 and 1751. But the colonizing residents stuck to their guns, and Concepción eventually became one of the Spanish empire's southernmost fortified outposts.

LOTA MINE TOUR

Concepción's exponential industrial and economic growth owes much to the huge off-shore coal deposits discovered south of the city along the so-called Costa del Carbón (Coal Coast). The hilly coastal town of Lota spiraled into poverty when the mines closed in 1997, resulting in some of the most deprived shantytowns in the country. However, it has now reinvented itself as a tourist destination and makes an interesting half-day out from Concepción.

The star attraction is the **Mina Chiflón del Diablo** (Devil's Whistle Mine; ☑041-287-1565; www.lotasorprendente.cl; tours CH$5000, museum CH$800, park CH$2000, village CH$800; ☺9am-6:30pm), a naturally ventilated undersea mine that operated between 1884 and 1976. Ex-coal miners now work as guides on well-organized 45-minute tours that take you through a series of galleries and tunnels to a coal face some 50m under the sea. Before clambering into the rattling metal cage-elevator that takes you down, you're kitted out with safety gear. You can also visit the **Pueblito Minero**, painstaking re-creations of typical miners' houses built for the Chilean movie *Sub Terra* (Underground), which was filmed here. The stunning 14-hectare **Parque Botánico Isidora Cousiño** is just down the road. Paths wind through the mix of manicured flower beds, small ponds and wilder woodland to a lighthouse on a tip of land jutting out into the sea.

To reach Lota from Concepción, catch a bus labeled 'Coronel-Lota' (CH$800, 30 minutes, every 15 minutes). Ask the driver to drop you at the Iglesia Parroquial, then follow the signs downhill to the mine.

After independence, Concepción's isolation from Santiago, coupled with the presence of lignite (brown coal) near Lota, a coastal town south of Concepción, fomented an autonomous industrial tradition. The export of wheat for the California gold-rush market further spurred the area's economic growth.

During the early 1970s the city was a bulwark of support for Marxist President Salvador Allende and his Unidad Popular party, and it suffered more than other regions under the military dictatorship of 1973 to 1990.

◉ Sights

La Casa del Arte
MUSEUM

(☑041-224-2567; cnr Chacabuco & Paicaví, Barrio Universitario; ☺10am-6pm Tue-Fri, 10am-5pm Sat, 10am-2pm Sun) FREE The massive, fiercely political mural *La Presencia de América Latina* is the highlight of the university art museum La Casa del Arte. It's by Mexican artist Jorge González Camarena, a protégé of the legendary muralist José Clemente Orozco, and celebrates Latin America's indigenous peoples and independence from colonial and imperial powers.

For more socially minded artwork, take a stroll around the campus and check out the vibrant public murals covering nearly every wall.

Parque Ecuador
PARK

(Av Lamas) Parque Ecuador is a narrow stretch of well-maintained urban parkland that runs along the foot of **Cerro Caracol** – walk up one of the two access roads (continuations of Caupolicán and Tucapel) to a viewpoint with great views of Concepción.

⌨ Sleeping

There is a grouping of high-end business chain hotels by the airport. These are best reserved using online aggregators. To stay nearer to the city center, try the following.

Hotel Alborada
BOUTIQUE HOTEL $

(☑041-291-1121; www.hotelalborada.cl; Barros Arana 457; d incl breakfast from CH$37,000; ☞) A surprisingly stylish addition to Concepción's hotel scene is this centrally located, coolly minimalist hotel. The public spaces – outfitted with all-white furnishings, glass and mirrors – are sleeker than the guest rooms themselves, which are spacious and comfortable, but standard.

Hotel Boutique Antiyal
MOTEL $

(☑041-221-8623; Caupolicán 1067; s/d incl breakfast CH$25,000/35,000; ℗☞) These friendly lodgings – think of the place as a 'boutique motel' – contain a long line of comfortable guest rooms with down comforters, wood paneling and cable TV. It's a short walk to the city center and several large supermarkets.

Hostal Bianca
HOSTEL $

(☎041-225-2103; www.hostalbianca.cl; Salas 643-C; s/d incl breakfast CH$22,500/29,900, without bathroom CH$15,900/26,500; ☎) Conce's best-value bargain-basement hotel has bright, newly renovated – if rather small – rooms with firm beds and cable TV.

✕ Eating & Drinking

For inexpensive ethnic food (Japanese, piz-za, gyros, tacos, you name it) and free-flowing beer and pisco, head down to the university area around Plaza Perú. There are more late-night eats and nightlife around Plaza España, in the neighborhood known as Bar-rio Estación.

★ Deli House
CHILEAN $

(www.delihouse.cl; Av Diagonal Pedro Aguirre Cerda 12-34; mains CH$3500-4800; ☎) These leafy sidewalk tables are a relaxed place to kick back for coffee, sandwiches, gourmet pizza or happy hour while watching the bohemian university set pass by.

Café Rometsch
CAFE $

(☎041-274-7040; Barros Arana 685; ☺8:30am-8:30pm) Delicious cakes and gelato, classy sidewalk tables on the plaza – need we say more?

Fina Estampa
PERUVIAN $

(Angol 298; mains CH$4900-7500) Starched tablecloths, fiercely folded napkins and deferential bow-tied waiters bring old-time elegance to this Peruvian restaurant. Ce-viches, *ají de gallina* (chicken in a spicy yellow-pepper sauce) and other classics are perfectly executed, as is grilled seasonal fish.

❶ Information

BancoEstado (O'Higgins 486; ☺9am-2pm Mon-Fri) One of many banks with ATMs near Plaza Independencia.

Conaf (☎041-262-4000; www.conaf.cl; Barros Arana 215; ☺8:30am-1pm & 2:30-5:30pm Mon-Fri) Limited information on nearby national parks and reserves.

Hospital Regional (☎041-220-8500; cnr San Martín & Av Roosevelt) Public hospital.

Post Office (cnr O'Higgins & Colo Colo; ☺8:30am-7pm Mon-Fri, 8:30am-1pm Sat)

Sernatur (☎02-741-4145; www.chile.travel; Pinto 460; ☺8:30am-8pm Jan & Feb, 8:30am-1pm & 3-6pm Mon-Fri Mar-Dec) Provides brochures, but little else.

❶ Getting There & Away

BUS

Concepción has two long-distance bus terminals. Most companies use the **Terminal de Buses Col-lao** (Tegualda 860), 3km east of central Concep-ción. From outside the terminal, grab a taxi into town. Some companies also use the separate **Terminal Chillancito** (Camilo Henríquez 2565), northeast along the extension of Bulnes.

There are dozens of daily services to Santiago with companies including **Eme Bus** (☎041-232-0094; www.emebus.cl), **Pullman Bus** (☎600-320-3200; www.pullmanbus.cl), **Nilahué** (☎02-776-1139; www.busesnilahue.cl) and **Tur Bus** (☎600-660-6600; www.turbus.cl; Tucapel 530), which also goes to Valparaíso and south to Temuco, Valdivia and Puerto Montt.

Línea Azul (☎042-203-800; www.buseslin-eaazul.cl) goes to Chillán (half-hourly). Buses Jota Be connects Conce with Los Angeles (25 daily); some stop at the Salto del Laja. **Buses Bio Bio** (www.busesbiobio.cl) has similar services and also goes to Angol (10 daily). For services south along the coast, try **Jota Ewert** (☎041-285-5587; downtown ticket office Lincoyán 557).

DESTINATION	COST (CH$)	DURATION
Angol	4000	2½hr
Chillán	2500	2hr
Los Angeles	3300	2hr
Lota	800	30min
Puerto Montt	9000	7hr
Santiago	7000	6½hr
Talcahuano	500	30min
Temuco	7200	4hr
Valdivia	8100	6hr
Valparaíso/ Viña del Mar	9500	8hr

CAR

A car can be useful for exploring the national parks south of Concepción. **Hertz** (☎041-279-7461; www.autorentas.cl; Av Arturo Prat 248) has an office downtown.

Salto del Laja

Halfway between Los Angeles and Chillán, the Río Laja plunges nearly 50m over a steep escarpment to form a horseshoe-shaped waterfall. Some have dubbed the sight a miniature Iguazú Falls when it's full, but the comparison is far-fetched. Still, there are great views from where the road bridges the

(Continued on p134)

Wine

Picture a delirious blue sky, neat rows of grapes robust on the vine, tall poplars and shimmering peaks in the distance. The languorous landscape says California or northern Italy. Guess again. Chile's wine country spans from the grand estates of family dynasties to upstart garage wines. Uncork it and savor.

2

HOBERMAN COLLECTION/UIG/GETTY IMAGES ©

4

STEVEN MORRIS PHOTOGRAPHY/GETTY IMAGES ©

1. Chilean grape varietals (p430)

The Maipo and Colchagua Valleys are two of the best areas for Cabernet Sauvignon production.

2. Colchagua Valley (p111)

With mountains on all sides, this scenic valley makes for a perfect picnic spot.

3. Cellar at Viña Indómita (p107)

This Casablanca Valley winery is noted for its top-shelf Carmenere.

4. Maipo Valley (p80)

Huasos (cowboys) survey the vineyards.

3

DANITA DELIMONT/GETTY IMAGES ©

1. Casablanca Valley (p105)
Enjoy alfresco dining in this valley, best known for its fruity Chardonnays, Sauvignon Blancs and Pinots.

2. Grape harvest
March is the month for grape harvests and related festivals across Chile's wine regions.

3. Maipo Valley (p80)
Gorgeous wineries and mass-production operations characterize the Maipo Valley, just south of Santiago.

4. Colchagua Valley (p111)
Jesuit missionaries introduced vineyards to this part of Chile in the mid-16th century.

(Continued from p129)

Río Laja. This road is the old Panamericana, but a new Ruta 5 bypass to the west means that only a few buses between Chillán and Los Angeles detour through here. A cluster of tacky souvenir stands and competing restaurants are evidence of the Salto del Laja's popularity with Chileans on road trips or outings from nearby cities.

🛏 Sleeping & Eating

Los Manantiales   RESORT $
(☎043-314-275; www.losmanantiales.saltosdella-ja.com; Variante Salto del Laja, Km480; campsite CH$21,000-26,000, s/d CH$24,000/35,000; 🏊) To linger longer at Salto del Laja, check into Los Manantiales, a popular budget hotel whose large restaurant has spectacular views over the falls. The wood-paneled rooms are spacious and clean, and the decor of the whole complex seems gloriously unchanged since the 1970s.

There's also camping if you happen to be traveling with a tent. Regardless of what the signs at the entrance say, it's a good 15-minute walk along the winding access road.

Residencial El Rincón   LODGE $$
(☎cell 9082-3168; www.elrinconchile.cl; s/d CH$40,000/45,000, without bathroom CH$28,000/35,000) With its gorgeous rural setting, 15km south of Salto del Laja, the German-run Residencial El Rincón is a relaxing place to take time out from traveling. The lodge has cozy, all-wood rooms and does fabulous homemade breakfasts and dinners (three-course dinner CH$16,000).

The owners also lead hiking and horseback-riding excursions. Get off southbound buses at the Perales/Los Olivos exit of the Panamericana (Km494), also known as Cruce La Mona (tell the driver and he'll stop for you). Signs point the 2km to the lodge; if you call or email ahead of time, the owners will pick you up here for free.

ℹ Getting There & Away

Many of the services run by **Buses Jota Be** (☎041-286-1533) between Los Angeles and Concepción or Chillán stop at Salto del Laja. Timetables change frequently, so always confirm the time of the next bus through to make sure you don't get stranded – and be sure to tell the driver that you want to be dropped off at Salta del Laja, or he might barrel right by your stop.

Los Angeles
📞 043 / POP 169,929

A useful base for visiting Parque Nacional Laguna del Laja, Los Angeles is an otherwise unprepossessing agricultural and industrial service center 110km south of Chillán.

🛏 Sleeping & Eating

Hotel del Centro   HOTEL $$
(☎043-236-961; www.hoteldelcentro.cl; Lautaro 539; s/d incl breakfast CH$31,500/40,000) Though this hotel underwent extensive renovations in 2010, it's still more traditional than stylish – but with colorful paintings on the walls, flat-screen TVs in the rooms and a convenient continental breakfast, it's fine for an overnight stop.

Four Points Sheraton   BUSINESS HOTEL $$
(☎043-240-6400; www.starwoodhotels.com; Colo Colo 565; r incl breakfast from CH$58,000; 🌐🏊) This spiffy new business hotel is the place to be if you need to recharge your batteries with North American–style amenities: there's a beautiful swimming pool, a fitness center and a spa, plus a cocktail bar in the lobby that's open to the public. Los Angeles' casino is housed in the same building.

Se Llama Perú   PERUVIAN $$
(☎043-223-0391; San Martín 357; mains CH$5900-8900; ⏱11am-midnight) It's a bit of a trek to get here, but this is one of Los Angeles' most sophisticated eateries. Skip the beef and head straight for the seafood and ceviche. The dining room has a pine roof and cozy air, with a few traces of Peru.

ℹ Getting There & Away

BUS

Long-distance buses leave from two adjacent bus terminals on Av Sor Vicenta, the continuation of Villagrán, on the northeast outskirts of town.

Pullman Bus (☎600-320-3200; www.pullman.cl) and **Tur Bus** (☎600-660-6600; www.turbus.cl) leave from the **Tur Bus terminal** (Av Sor Vicenta 2061). Both have numerous daily departures to Santiago (CH$6900, 6½ hours), most of which stop at Talca, Curicó and Rancagua. Over 20 daily services head south to Temuco (CH$4900, two hours), Osorno (CH$8500, 5½ hours) and Puerto Montt (CH$9000, seven hours).

All other services use the next-door **Terminal Santa María** (Av Sor Vicenta 2051). From here **Buses Jota Be** (www.busesjotabe.cl) runs buses to Concepción (CH$3300, two hours, every 30 minutes) and Angol (CH$2800, 1½ hours, hourly), the gateway to Parque Nacional Nahuelbuta. Some buses to Chillán (CH$2900, 1¾ hours, hourly) pass by Salto del Laja (CH$2000, 45 minutes). **Buses Bío Bío** (www.busesbiobio.cl) operates along the same routes slightly less frequently.

Local bus routes operate out of the **Terminal de Buses Rurales** (Terminal Santa Rita; Villagrán 501), on the corner of Rengo.

CAR

As there's no public transportation right up to the entrance of Parque Nacional Laguna del Laja, a rental car can be useful, especially for one- or two-day visits. **Interbruna** (☎043-231-3812; www.interbruna.com; Almagro 191) is one of a few agencies that rents cars.

Parque Nacional Laguna del Laja

Some 93km east of Los Angeles lies the 116-sq-km **Parque Nacional Laguna del Laja** (☎043-232-1086; http://www.conaf.cl/parques/parque-nacional-laguna-del-laja; adult/child CH$1200/600; ☉8:30am-8pm Dec-Apr, to 6:30pm May-Nov). Within the park is the symmetrical cone of Volcán Antuco (2985m). Lava from this volcano dammed the Río Laja, creating the lake that gives the park its name. The lava fields immediately around the lake form an eerie lunar landscape. Although the volcano may seem quiet, it is not extinct: volcanic activity was last recorded about 70 years ago.

The park protects the mountain cypress (*Austrocedrus chilensis*) and the monkey-puzzle tree, as well as other uncommon tree species. Mammals are rare, though puma, fox and viscacha have been sighted. Nearly 50 bird species inhabit the area, including the Andean condor.

There's a small Conaf post at **Los Pangües**, the park entrance, where you sign in. From here, a winding road takes you to the park headquarters at **Chacay**, 3km on.

🏃 Activities

As well as hiking, you can drive through parts of the park: there's 6km of uphill hairpin bends between Chacay and the start of the lava-edged Laguna del Laja. The road then winds alongside the lake for 28km until it reaches the red army hut at Los Barros, from where 4WD vehicles can continue to the Argentine border (closed April through September).

Chacay   HIKING

Chacay is the starting point for several well-marked hiking trails. On the left-hand side of the road is the easy 1½-hour trail to two small but stunning waterfalls, the **Salto de Las Chilcas** (the point where the underground Río Laja emerges) and the **Salto del Torbellino**.

A 10km section of the **Sendero de Chile** leaves from the right-hand side of the road and goes to **Laguna del Laja**. Nearby is the starting point for **Sendero Los Coigües**, a 2.5km hike to a spot with fabulous views of Volcán Antuco.

Sendero Sierra Velluda   HIKING

The park's star trek is the three-day Sendero Sierra Velluda circuit, named for the hanging glacier you pass along the way. It winds around Volcán Antuco, passing waterfalls and lava fields; condors are also a common sight.

Club de Esquí de los Ángeles   SKIING

(☎043-232-2651; www.skiantuco.cl; lift ticket CH$20,000) In winter, the Club de Esquí de los Ángeles operates three drag-lifts and a small restaurant (mains CH$3000 to CH$4500), on the slopes near Chacay, known as the Cancha de Ski Antuco.

🛏 Sleeping

Lagunillas   CAMPGROUND $

(☎043-232-1086; campsites CH$10,000, 6-person cabins CH$30,000) You can camp inside the park at Lagunillas, 2km from the park entrance, where there are 22 sites with electricity, showers and toilets. Basic cabins with hot water and electricity are also for rent.

ℹ Getting There & Away

Departing from Los Angeles' Terminal de Buses Rurales, local buses go through Antuco to the village of El Abanico, 11km from the entrance to Parque Nacional Laguna del Laja (CH$1600, 1½ hours, seven daily). The last bus back to Los Angeles leaves Abanico at 5:30pm, except on Sundays, when the last bus leaves at 7:15pm. Note that there's no public transportation between Abanico and the park. It takes about 1½ hours to walk this stretch, and another half-hour to reach the Lagunillas campsite. Hitchhiking is technically possible, but vehicles are a rare sight. If you're driving, you'll need a 4WD and chains to negotiate this road between May and September.

Angol

📱 045 / POP 56,204

Despite a turbulent and interesting history – the village was razed on six separate occasions during the conflict between the Mapuche and the conquistadores – Angol's only real appeal is its easy access into mountainous Parque Nacional Nahuelbuta.

The town straddles the Río Vergara, an upper tributary of the Biobío formed by the confluence of the Ríos Picoiquén and Rehue. The city's older core lies west of the river and centers on the attractive Plaza de Armas with a fountain adorned by four gloriously poised marble statues that represent Europe, Asia, the Americas and Africa; and huge, shady trees and well-kept flower beds.

✵ Festivals & Events

Brotes de Chile MUSIC
(www.brotesdechile.com; ⊙ Jan) One of Chile's biggest folk festivals takes place in the second week of January and includes traditional dances, food and crafts.

🛏 Sleeping & Eating

Hotel Angol HOTEL $
(📱 045-719-036; Lautaro 176; d incl breakfast CH$28,000; � 🛜) These 15 simple, centrally located rooms come with private bathrooms and cable TV. Breakfast is served downstairs at the Café de la Rueda, which is open to the public.

Duhatao BOUTIQUE HOTEL $$
(📱 045-714-320; www.hotelduhatao.cl; Arturo Prat 420; s/d incl breakfast CH$36,00/45,000; 🛜) Here's a surprise: there's a design hotel in Angol. The Duhatao blends clean modern lines with local crafts and colors – the springy beds have headboards made from old gate posts and hand-woven throws, and bathrooms have big bowl sinks. A slick restaurant and bar are on-site.

Sparlatto Pizza PIZZA $
(Lautaro 418; mains CH$3500-5200) This bustling little restaurant on the plaza serves steak sandwiches, salads, Chilean comfort food and pizza; in the evening it fills up with a younger, beer-drinking crowd.

ⓘ Getting There & Away

Most long-distance bus services leave from Angol's **Terminal Rodoviario** (Bonilla 428), a 10-minute walk from the Plaza de Armas. To get to the center of town, turn left from the main exit and walk four blocks along José Luis Osorio to Bulevar O'Higgins, the main road, where you turn right and cross the bridge.

Several companies run multiple daily services north to Santiago (CH$9300 to CH$11,200, eight hours), including Pullman JC, **Línea Azul** (www.buseslineaazul.cl) and **Tur Bus** (📱 600-660-6600; www.turbus.cl) also stopping at Chillán (CH$5100, 3¼ hours, two daily), Talca (CH$7500, five hours, two daily), and Los Angeles (CH$2800, one hour, 22 daily).

Leaving from its own terminal, **Buses Bio Bio** (www.busesbiobio.cl; Caupolicán 98) serves Los Angeles (CH$1600, one hour, 11 daily) and Concepción (CH$4700, 2½ hours, 25 daily).

Local and regional services leave from the **Terminal de Buses Rurales** (Ilabaca 422), including buses to Parque Nacional Nahuelbuta.

Parque Nacional Nahuelbuta

Between Angol and the Pacific, the coast range rises to 1550m within the 68-sq-km **Parque Nacional Nahuelbuta** (www.parquenahuelbuta.cl; adult/child CH$4000/2000; ⊙ 8:30am-8pm), one of the last non-Andean refuges of araucaria, or monkey-puzzle trees. In summer, other interesting plant life includes 16 varieties of orchids and two carnivorous plant species. Various species of *Nothofagus* (southern beech) are common here, and the Magellanic woodpeckers that typically inhabit them make for great birdwatching. Rare mammals such as pumas, Darwin's fox and the miniature Chilean deer known as the pudú also live in the park. According to some, it's a prime location for UFO spotting, too.

The dirt road between Angol and Canete runs through the park. Conaf maintains the park headquarters and information center at Pehuenco, roughly halfway between the two park entrances, which are sometimes staffed by rangers, too. There are no shops or restaurants within Nahuelbuta, so bring your own supplies. The park enjoys warm, dry summers, but is usually snow-covered during winter. November to April is the best time to visit.

🏃 Activities

Some 30km of roads and 15km of footpaths crisscross the park, so you can tour by car and on foot. Several marked hiking trails start at Pehuenco.

Cerro Piedra del Águila HIKING

The most popular hike is an easy 4.5km walk through *pehuén* forests to the 1379m granite outcrop of Cerro Piedra del Águila (literally, 'Eagle Rock'), which has fabulous views from the Andes to the Pacific.

To the southeast you can see the entire string of Andean volcanoes – from Antuco, east of Chillán, to Villarrica and Lanín, east of Pucón. You can loop back to Pehuenco via the valley of the Estero Cabrería to the south: the trail starts beneath the west side of the outcrop and the whole hike takes about three hours. Alternatively, you can reach Piedra del Águila by walking 800m from the end of a shorter approach accessible by car.

Cerro Anay HIKING

This trail leads 5km north from Pehuenco to Cerro Anay, a 1450m hill with great views. It's an easy three-hour walk past wildflower beds and huge stands of araucarias.

🛏 Sleeping

Camping Pehuenco CAMPGROUND $

(www.parquenahuelbuta.cl; 6-person campsites CH$12,000) Next to the park headquarters, 5.5km from the entrance on the Angol side of the park. There are 11 campsites in shady forest clearings with picnic tables, and basic bathrooms with flush toilets and cold showers.

ℹ Getting There & Away

Several local bus lines, including **Buses Carrasco** (☏045-715-287), **Buses Nahuelbuta** (☏045-715-611) and **Buses Moncada** (☏045-714-090), depart Angol at 6:45am and 4pm for Vegas Blancas (CH$1700, 1½ hours), 7km from the eastern park entrance and 12.5km from the park headquarters at Pehuenco. Some lines go on Monday, Wednesday and Friday, others on alternate days. All leave from Angol's **Terminal de Buses Rurales** (cnr Ilabaca & Lautaro) and return from Vegas Blancas at 9am and 6pm (confirm these times so you don't get stranded). In January and February the morning service usually continues to the park entrance. Motorists with low-clearance vehicles may find the steep and dusty road difficult in spots, and you need a 4WD and chains June through August.

Mountain bikers generally need to dismount and walk at least part of the way up; note that water is hard to find along the way. However, local buses to Vegas Blancas are generally happy to carry bikes, so cycling from there is an alternative.

ARCHIPIÉLAGO JUAN FERNÁNDEZ

Although these remote islands are 667km west of Valparaíso, they are considered part of Valparaíso region; the archipelago was originally discovered by a sailor making his way from Peru to Valparaíso. This chain of small volcanic islands is also the place where castaway Alexander Selkirk (inspiration for Daniel Defoe's *Robinson Crusoe*) whittled away lost years scampering after goats and scanning the horizon for ships. Once an anonymous waypoint for pirates, sealers and war ships, the archipelago was later declared both a national park and a Unesco Biosphere Reserve.

There are three main volcanic islands in the chain. Robinson Crusoe, previously known as Más A Tierra, is the main tourist hub, while Alejandro Selkirk and Santa Clara islands are seldom visited.

This Pacific outpost has made headlines in recent times for two major tragedies: first, the islands' infrastructure was badly damaged in the tsunami following the 2010 earthquake, prompting action from a charity foundation, Desafío Levantemos Chile (Together We Pick Up Chile), intent on rebuilding after the disaster. And in September 2011, a group of prominent Chilean TV journalists and crew from the morning program *Buenos Días a Todos* boarded a plane to the islands to film a segment on the reconstruction efforts. The plane crashed near Robinson Crusoe Island, killing all 21 passengers, shocking the Chilean public and sending the islands into a further tailspin. At the time of writing, the islands were still recovering. Though the area may well emerge as a world-class diving destination in years to come, travel to the archipelago is still considered a sensitive issue. Check out www.comunajuanfernandez.cl (in Spanish) for the latest.

History

In November 1574, Portuguese mariner Juan Fernández veered off course between Peru and Valparaíso and discovered these islands that now bear his name. Unlike Easter Island, there is no historical records of visits to the islands by either Polynesians or Native Americans. In following centuries the islands proved a popular stop-off for ships skirting around the Humboldt Current. Pirates sought refuge in the few bays – hunting

Isla Robinson Crusoe

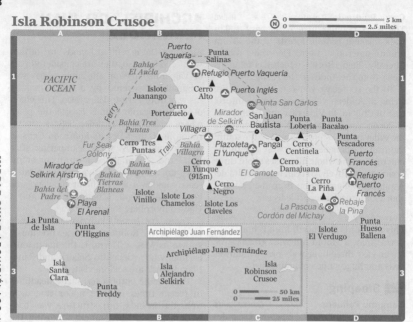

feral goats and planting gardens to stock future visits – and traffic increased with sealers.

After the turn of the 18th century, one island played a notorious role in Chile's independence struggle, as Spanish authorities exiled 42 criollo patriots to damp caves above San Juan Bautista after the disastrous Battle of Rancagua in 1814. The patriots in exile included Juan Egaña and Manuel de Salas, figures from the Chilean elite who would not quickly forget their cave-dwelling days.

Chile established a permanent settlement in 1877. For many years the island remained an escape-proof political prison for the newly independent country. During WWI it again played a memorable historic role, as the British naval vessels *Glasgow* and *Orama* confronted the German cruiser *Dresden* at Bahía Cumberland.

Geography & Climate

The islands' land areas are very small, but their topography is extraordinarily rugged; geologically, the entire archipelago is a group of emergent peaks of the submarine mountain range known as the Juan Fernández Ridge, which goes east–west for more than 400km at the southern end of the Chile Basin.

The archipelago is far enough from the continent for subtropical water masses to moderate the chilly sub-Antarctic waters of the Humboldt Current, which flows northward along the Chilean coast. The climate is distinctly Mediterranean, with clearly defined warm, dry summers and cooler, wet winters.

Wildlife

Animals

The Juan Fernández fur seal is the only native mammal of the archipelago: it inhabits the seas and shores of Isla Robinson Crusoe and Isla Santa Clara. Of 11 endemic bird species, the most eye-catching is the Juan Fernández hummingbird (*Sephanoides fernandensis*). Only about 700 hummingbirds survive, feeding off the striking Juan Fernández cabbage that grows in many parts of San Juan Bautista, but the birds do best in native forest.

Plants

The archipelago is considered a unique eco-region with plants that slowly evolved in isolation, adapting to local environmental niches. Today, the greatest concentration of native flora survives in sectors where goats can neither penetrate nor completely dominate.

Vegetation spans an extraordinary range of geographic affinities, from the Andes and sub-Antarctic Magallanes to Hawaii and New Zealand. Of 87 genera of plants on the islands, 16 are endemic, found nowhere else on earth; of 140 native plant species, 101 are endemic. These plants survive in three major communities: the evergreen rainforest, the evergreen heath and the herbaceous steppe.

Perhaps the most striking vegetation, however, is the dense understory of climbing vines and the towering endemic tree ferns *Dicksonia berteroana* and *Thyrsopteris elegans*.

❶ Getting There & Away

From Santiago, two airlines operate flights to Juan Fernández. There are usually several daily flights between September and April, with fewer departures the rest of the year. The 2¼-hour flight takes 10 to 20 passengers;

note that climate is a major factor with flight schedules – foul weather on the island can provoke last-minute departure changes and cancellations.

Flights depart from Santiago's International Airport. Upon arrival to the island, passengers take a one-hour boat taxi (usually included in the airfare) to the pier of San Juan Bautista. Return flights require a minimum number of passengers to depart, so keep travel arrangements flexible enough to allow for a few extra days on the island. Consult the airlines for prices, but count on paying upwards of CH$550,000 round-trip.

ATA (☎ 02-2611-3670; www.aerolineasata.cl; Larraín Alcalde s/n) ATA flies out of Aeródromo Tobalaba, but has few low-season departures and small planes.

Lassa (☎ 02-273-5209; www.aerolassa.cl; Larraín Alcalde s/n) Lassa has a 19-seat Twin Otter that usually departs at 9:30am. Flight payments can be made directly at Aeródromo Tobalaba upon departure.

MIDDLE CHILE ARCHIPIÉLAGO JUAN FERNÁNDEZ

SELKIRK: THE QUINTESSENTIAL CASTAWAY

Más a Tierra, today known as Robinson Crusoe Island, was the longtime home of one of the world's most famous castaways (no not Tom Hanks or his volleyball Wilson). After ongoing disputes with his captain over the seaworthiness of the privateer *Cinque Ports*, Scotsman Alexander Selkirk requested to be put ashore on the island in 1704. He would spend four years and four months marooned here before his rescue. Abandonment was tantamount to a death sentence for most castaways in his day, who soon starved or shot themselves, but Selkirk adapted to his new home and endured, despite his desperate isolation.

Although the Spaniards vigorously opposed privateers in their domains, their foresight made Selkirk's survival possible. Thanks to them, unlike many small islands, Más a Tierra had abundant water and goats. Disdaining fish, Selkirk tracked these feral animals, devoured their meat and dressed himself in their skins. He crippled and tamed some of the goats for easier hunting. Sea lions, feral cats and rats – the latter two European introductions – were among his other companions. Selkirk would often climb to a lookout above Bahía Cumberland (Cumberland Bay) in hope of spotting a vessel on the horizon, but not until 1708 did his savior, Commander Woodes Rogers of the British privateers *Duke* and *Duchess*, arrive with famed privateer William Dampier as his pilot. Rogers recalled his first meeting with Selkirk when the ship's men returned from shore. He called him 'a man Cloth'd in Goat-Skins, who look'd wilder than the first Owners of them.'

After signing on with Rogers and returning to Scotland, Selkirk became a celebrity and the inspiration for a rag-tag army of reality shows, theme-park rides and great literature alike. Daniel Defoe's classic *Robinson Crusoe* is thought to have been inspired by Selkirk. Other worthy reads include Captain Woodes Rogers' *A Cruising Voyage Round the World*, by Selkirk's rescuer; *Robinson Crusoe's Island* (1969) by Ralph Lee Woodward; and Nobel Prize winner JM Coetzee's revisionist novel *Foe* (1986).

Traditional biography was cast away when British writer Diane Souhami made a portrait of the man through the place. Her take, *Selkirk's Island*, won the 2001 Whitbread Biography Award. While in the archipelago researching, Souhami became intrigued with the way the island pared down modern life, leaving what was essential. Souhami noted how Selkirk's relationship to the island he once cursed changed post-rescue. 'He started calling it "my beautiful island,"' said Souhami. 'It became the major relationship in his life.'

🛈 Getting Around

With only a few kilometers of roads in San Juan Bautista and steep peaks that bookend the valleys, boating is the best way to get around. To arrange a water taxi, ask around at the Municipalidad across from the plaza.

San Juan Bautista

 032 / POP 600

The sole inhabited town on Isla Robinson Crusoe, San Juan Bautista (St John the Baptist) is the proverbial sleepy fishing village, down to the lobster catchers in knitted caps, and dusty stores that run out of cheese and beer before the provision ship arrives. The village's steep hills are strewn with lush gardens and modest cottages with paths leading into horse pastures and wooded hiking trails. Sadly, the town's landmark lighthouse and cemetery were destroyed in the earthquake.

◉ Sights

San Juan is the organizational and departure point for all of the islands' main activities, including fishing, hiking, boat tours of the islands, diving and tours of the local sights.

Fuerte Santa Bárbara   MONUMENT

Built in 1749 to discourage incursions by pirates, these Spanish fortifications were reconstructed in 1974. To get there, follow the path from Cuevas de los Patriotas, or climb directly from the plaza via Subida El Castillo. The track continues to Mirador de Selkirk.

Cuevas de los Patriotas   CAVE

Up a short footpath from Larraín Alcalde and illuminated at night, these damp caverns sheltered Juan Egaña, Manuel de Salas and 40 other patriots exiled for several years during Chile's independence movement after their defeat in the Battle of Rancagua in 1814.

🏃 Activities

Getting into the water around Robinson Crusoe is like slipping into a great abyss: this idiosyncratic ecosystem hosts world-class scuba diving. Moray eel, flounder, lobster and enormous schools of yellowtail troll the clear waters. But the biggest attraction is the playful Juan Fernández fur seal (*Arctocephalus philippii*). There is excellent hiking in the Parque Nacional Archipiélago Juan Fernández that encompasses the entire island.

☞ Tours

The Conaf kiosk on the plaza has a list of registered guides and tour schedules. Refugío Náutico has a PADI-certified dive operation.

✮✮ Festivals & Events

Rodeo de Villagra   RODEO

(☉ Jan-Feb) Held at the end of January or early February, this is an island-wide rodeo festival with more cattle than you can possibly imagine live out here.

Fiesta de San Pedro   RELIGIOUS

(☉ Jun) The patron saint of fishermen is honored on June 29 with decorated boats making a procession at sea.

Fiesta de Aniversario   HISTORICAL

(☉ Nov) On Día de la Isla, held on November 22, a celebration commemorates the day Portuguese sailor Juan Fernández discovered the archipelago in 1574. Festivities include a regatta and a 13km foot race from Punta de Isla to Bahía Cumberland.

🛏 Sleeping & Eating

Local businesses have been in flux since the tsunami. The municipal website (comunajuanfernandez.cl, in Spanish) lists a dozen basic lodging options that are open and receiving visitors. Since restaurants are few,

---

OFF THE BEATEN TRACK

ISLA ALEJANDRO SELKIRK

If Robinson Crusoe falls short of castaway ambience, search out Isla Alejandro Selkirk. Hard to reach and rarely visited by foreigners, the island lies 181km west of Robinson Crusoe. It's a seasonal lobstering base for 25 families from Crusoe who, when not fishing, can be found playing soccer, fixing boats or going on Crusoe-esque hunts for feral goats. More mountainous than Crusoe, Selkirk's highest point in the archipelago is 1650m Cerro Los Inocentes. Islanders are welcoming to respectful visitors, but you should plan to camp and bring provisions. Make sure to settle your return trip in advance, or you may be putting in some time as an island exile.

most guests take half-board (dinner and breakfast); lodging rates quoted include half-board. Full board is usually available on request. Reserve ahead when dining out, especially for groups or when requesting a specific dish.

Hostería Petit Breulh GUESTHOUSE $
(☎032-275-1107; Vicente González 80; r per person CH$22,500; @) Bedside minibars, dark leather, massage showers and cable TV nurture a haven for would-be playboys that relish a few pelts on the wall (think 1980s). Yet, meals (CH$6000) are showstoppers – think ceviche with capers and zucchini stuffed with fresh fish and baked under bubbling cheese. Nonguests should make reservations.

Residencial Mirador de Selkirk GUESTHOUSE $$
(☎032-275-1028; mfernandeziana@hotmail.com; Pasaje del Castillo 251; r per person incl breakfast CH$30,000; @) High on the hillside, this family home has three snug rooms and a sprawling deck overlooking the bay (where you recover your breath from the hike up). Señora Julia serves up fantastic meals (CH$5000). Foodies shouldn't miss her lobster empanadas or seafood *parol* (stew).

Refugio Náutico BOUTIQUE HOTEL $$$
(☎cell 7483-5014; www.islarobinsoncrusoe.cl; Carrera Pinto 280; s/d full board CH$78,000/144,000) This waterfront refuge is stylin' with kitchen competence and all the comforts of home. Its bright terraced rooms are plenty private but the real treat is the living area brimming with books, DVDs and music – perfect for that rainy day, or for your post-meal coma. The restaurant here is recommended.

Kayak rentals, hiking and dive trips are available through the on-site PADI-certified dive center. Credit cards are accepted.

Crusoe Island Lodge LUXURY HOTEL $$$
(☎cell 9078-1301; www.crusoeislandlodge.com; s/d incl breakfast from $US280/370; 🛜👶) 🐾 This stylish ecolodge has 15 rustic-chic rooms and suites overlooking Pangal Bay. In addition to a small spa and a gourmet restaurant specializing in fresh lobster and golden crab, the lodge arranges birdwatching, trekking, historical tours and fishing excursions.

ⓘ Information

There are no banks or money changers on the island, so bring all the pesos you need, preferably in small bills. Credit cards are rarely accepted,

San Juan Bautista

though some tour operators or hotels will take US dollars or euros, at poor rates.

Several kiosks have public telephones, although international rates are prohibitively expensive.

Conaf (Larraín Alcalde; ⊘8am-6pm Mon-Fri, 9am-6pm Sat & Sun) This small kiosk near the plaza collects park admission and distributes leaflets with decent maps. For information on visiting any part of the park outside the immediate environs of San Juan Bautista, it's advisable to contact Conaf in advance.

Post Office (⊙9am-6pm Mon-Fri, 9am-noon Sat) On the south side of the plaza.

Posta de Salud (Vicente González) A government medical clinic, just below the entrance to Conaf's grounds.

Parque Nacional Archipiélago Juan Fernández

This **national park** (www.www.conaf.cl/parques/parque-nacional-archipielago-de-juan-fernandezl; adult/child CH$3000/800) covers the entire archipelago, a total of 93 sq km, though the township of San Juan Bautista and the airstrip are de facto exclusions. In an effort to control access to the most fragile areas of the park, Conaf requires many of the hikes to be organized and led by local registered guides. A list of the guides with pricing information is posted at the kiosk near the plaza, where you should register before taking any self-guided hike. Day hikes for a group of six people cost CH$15,000 to CH$30,000. Still, a number of areas are accessible without guides.

Another way to see the park is by boat. Local tour operators can arrange trips to see fur seal colonies at different points around the island. Camping is possible only in organized campsites, each with a one-night limit.

🏃 Activities

Mirador de Selkirk   HIKING

Perhaps the most rewarding and stunning hike on the island is to Selkirk's mirador above San Juan Bautista, where he would look for ships appearing on the horizon. The 3km walk, gaining 565m in elevation, takes about 1½ hours of steady walking but rewards the climber with views of both sides of the island.

Villagra to La Punta de Isla   HIKING

Beyond Selkirk's overlook, the trail continues on the south side, taking one hour to reach Villagra (4.8km), where there are campsites. From here the wide trail skirts the southern cliffs to La Punta de Isla (13km; approximately four hours) and the airstrip, where there is also camping available.

En route is Bahía Tierras Blancas, the island's main breeding colony of Juan Fernández fur seals. This scenic and reasonably challenging hike takes in a significant part of the island and is an excellent way to enjoy its serenity. From Villagra guided hikes go to the base of Cerro El Yunque and Cerro Negro (3.5km).

Plazoleta El Yunque   HIKING

Plazoleta El Yunque is a tranquil forest clearing with bathrooms, water and picnic areas at the base of the 915m-high Cerro El Yunque (The Anvil). You will pass the crumbled foundation of the home of a German survivor of the *Dresden* who once homesteaded here. He was known as the 'German Robinson.'

Centinela   HIKING

Cerro Centinela (362m) holds the ruins of the first radio station on the island, which was established in 1909. The 3km hike is accessed from Pangal.

Salsipuedes   HIKING

At the top of La Pólvora, a trail zigzags through eucalyptus groves, then endemic ferns, then thickets of murtilla to reach the ridge Salsipuedes, which translates to 'Leave if you can.' To arrange a guided hike, contact any of the island's travel agencies.

Puerto Inglés   HIKING

The 2.3km trail to Puerto Inglés starts at Salsipuedes and continues down a very precarious ridge to the beach area, where there is a reconstruction of Selkirk's shelter.

Puerto Francés   HIKING

Located on the eastern shore of the island, Puerto Francés was a haven for French privateers, whose presence motivated Spain to erect a series of fortifications in 1779, the ruins of which are all but gone. From Cerro Centinela, a 6.4km trail reaches the port where there are five campsites, a *refugio*, running water and a bathroom.

Norte Grande

Best Places to Eat

➡ El Wagón (p174)

➡ La Casona (p153)

➡ Los Aleros de 21 (p184)

➡ Cafe del Sol (p167)

Best Places to Sleep

➡ Hotel Aruma (p184)

➡ Terrace Lodge & Cafe (p191)

➡ Casa Baquedano (p173)

➡ Hostal Quinta Adela (p151)

Why Go?

Devil dusters zoom wantonly through sun-scorched Norte Grande with its undulating curves of rock and stone, Andean lagoons, snow-capped volcanoes, salt flats and sensuously perforated coastline. Famous as much for its hilltop observatories as its massive copper mines, those vast, uninhabited spaces touch the soul and the imagination. Norte Grande's star attraction is the tiny adobe village of San Pedro de Atacama, just a day trip away from the world's highest geyser field and some astounding desert formations.

But there's more to Norte Grande than San Pedro. Go for lung-bursting, jaw-dropping adventure near the mountain village of Putre in the high-altitude reserve of Parque Nacional Lauca or further afield to Salar de Surire. Spend a week perfecting your tan on the beaches outlying Iquique and Arica, or make your own adventure in the lost ghost towns and hard-sprung mining centers that make this region unique.

When to Go
Iquique

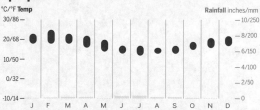

Jan–Feb Vacationers hit the coast and some highland spots become impossible to reach.

Sep–Oct The altiplano has solid weather and European summer visitors have gone home.

Jul–Aug Best for highland destinations (though it gets bitterly cold at night) and for hard-core surfing.

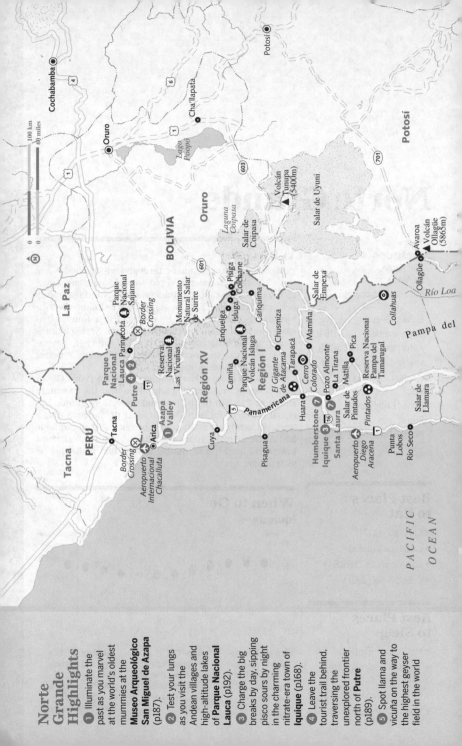

Norte Grande Highlights

1 Illuminate the past as you marvel at the world's oldest mummies at the **Museo Arqueológico San Miguel de Azapa** (p187).

2 Test your lungs as you visit the Andean villages and high-altitude lakes of **Parque Nacional Lauca** (p192).

3 Charge the big breaks by day, sipping pisco sours by night in the charming nitrate-era town of **Iquique** (p168).

4 Leave the tourist trail behind, traversing the unexplored frontier north of **Putre** (p189).

5 Spot llama and vicuña on the way to the highest geyser field in the world

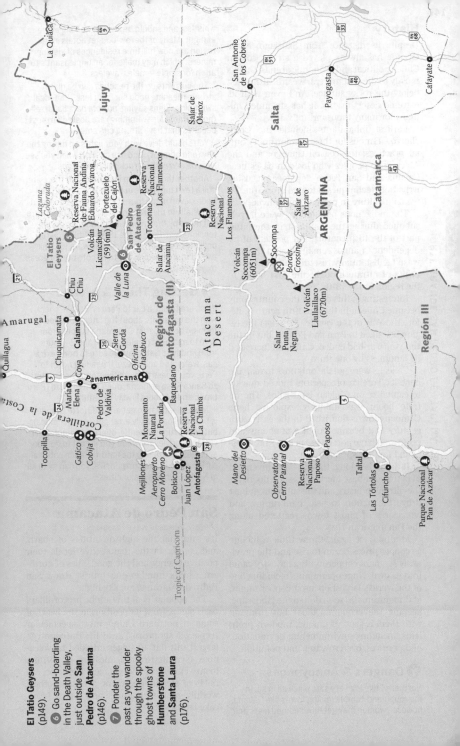

El Tatio Geysers
(p149).

6 Go sand-boarding in the Death Valley, just outside **San Pedro de Atacama** (p146).

7 Ponder the past as you wander through the spooky ghost towns of **Humberstone** and **Santa Laura** (p176).

History

Despite its distance from Santiago, Norte Grande has always played a strong role in Chile's political and economic arenas, thanks mostly to the vast mineral wealth sitting just below the rocky surface. And even with its extreme desert aridity, it has sustained humans for many thousands of years.

Earliest inhabitants include the Chinchorro – famous for their extraordinary burial practices; the coastal Chango; and the Atacameño peoples who lived in oases near Calama and San Pedro de Atacama, using irrigation techniques adopted from the Tiwanaku culture in present-day Bolivia.

The indigenous populations were largely subdued during the conquest in the latter part of the 16th century, but pockets of independent Changos remained, and the area wasn't substantially resettled until large deposits of nitrate brought the first boom to the region in the 1810s.

Interestingly, this part of the country only became Chilean in the late 19th century. Before the War of the Pacific (1879–84) the region belonged to Peru and Bolivia, but by the time the war had ended, Chile had increased its landmass by one-third

Chileans were not the only ones to reap the benefits. Foreign prospectors moved quickly to capitalize on Chilean land gains. The nitrate boom was uniquely explosive here. Company towns flourished in the early 20th century and became bubbles of energy and profit, and large port cities such as Antofagasta and Iquique sprang to life.

It didn't last long, though – the invention of petroleum-based fertilizers spelt doom for the nitrate industry and the subsequent bust drove the nation to near bankruptcy, and left scores of ghost towns scattered along the Panamerican Hwy.

Mining once again threw Chile a lifeline as copper prices began to rise and the previously stagnant copper-mining industry came into its own. Huge operations (including one of the world's largest open-pit copper mines, at Chuquicamata) soon dotted the landscape, keeping the economy afloat but bringing with them a slew of unique, modern problems, including environmental degradation, higher prices, overcrowding and pollution.

🛈 Dangers & Annoyances

Northern Chile is a very safe place all in all. In the rough-and-tumble mining towns like Calama, however, women may get unwelcomed leers and whistles, and should be careful walking alone at night. Many of the low-budget hotels in the region are now full-time residences of visiting miners, which may make for an unpleasant situation for single female travelers.

The currents on the beaches can be quite strong, meaning good surf, but less-than-ideal swimming. Signs saying 'no apta para bañarse' (not suitable for swimming) are posted on most beaches that have strong currents.

You should drive with your lights on during the day (and at night), and use caution when you see zona de derrumbes (rock-fall zone) signs.

Another thing to keep in mind is that there are still a few land mines in the desert around San Pedro, even in the touristy Valle de la Luna, and especially in the areas close to Peru. These were put down by the Pinochet dictatorship during tensions with Peru in the 1970s. While you're unlikely to step on one, you may want to think twice before heading out to remote border areas by yourself.

🛈 Getting There & Around

If you are taking a car to Peru or Bolivia, check with the consulate about the latest required forms. The border at Chacalluta is open from 8am to midnight (Chilean time) and 24 hours from Friday to Saturday. Be sure to bring extra gas, water and antifreeze. If heading north to Peru, you'll pass through the Complejo Fronterizo Santa Rosa at Tacna, open 7am to 11pm (Peru time), and 24 hours Friday to Saturday.

The easiest way to get around Norte Grande is by rental car (easily arranged in major cities), but buses run frequently, offering top-notch service to nearly everywhere you'll want to go. Tour agencies run trips to the hard-to-reach national parks. While it's very expensive, you can fly to all of Norte Grande's major cities.

San Pedro de Atacama

📞 055 / POP 3899 / ELEV 2438M

It's said that the high quantities of quartz and copper in the region give locals their positive energy, and the good vibes of northern Chile's number-one tourist draw, San Pedro de Atacama, are sky high.

The popularity of this adobe precordillera oasis stems from its position in the heart of some of northern Chile's most spectacular scenery. A short drive away lies the country's largest salt flat, its edges crinkled by volcanoes (symmetrical Licancábur, at 5916m, looms closest to the village). Here too are fields of steaming geysers, a host of otherworldly rock formations and weird layer-cake landscapes.

San Pedro itself, 106km southeast of Calama via paved Chile 23, seems hardly big enough to absorb the hordes of travelers that arrive; it's little more than a handful of picturesque adobe streets clustering around a pretty tree-lined plaza and postcard-perfect church. However, the last decade has seen a proliferation of guesthouses, upscale resorts, restaurants, internet cafes and tour agencies wedging their way into its dusty streets, and turning the town into a kind of highland adobe-Disneyland.

And sure enough, San Pedro suffers from the classic drawbacks of any tourist honey pot: high costs, irritating restaurant touts and lackadaisical tour agencies. However, the town has an addictively relaxed atmosphere and an enormous array of tours that can hook travelers for weeks. And at the end of every trip, there's the comfort of a creamy cappuccino, a posh meal and a soft bed waiting in San Pedro.

History

San Pedro was a pre-Columbian pit stop on the trading route from the highlands to the coast. It was visited by Pedro de Valdivia in 1540, and the town later became a major stop on early-20th-century cattle drives from Argentina to the nitrate *oficinas* of the desert.

Locals, the Atacameño people, still practice irrigated farming in the *ayllus* (a-*ee*-oos; small indigenous communities). Many still farm on terraces over a thousand years old.

⊙ Sights

The village itself is small and compact, with almost everything of interest within easy strolling distance of the plaza. Many buildings now have street numbers, although many still do without.

★**Museo Gustavo Le Paige**　　MUSEUM
(Le Paige 380; adult/student CH$2500/1000; ⊙9am-6pm Mon-Fri, 10am-6pm Sat & Sun) Even if museums aren't your thing, make an exception for San Pedro's superb Museo Gustavo Le Paige. The Atacama is nirvana for archaeologists because of its nearly rainless environment, which preserves artifacts for millennia. And so this octagonal museum is packed with such fascinating finds as well-preserved ceramics and textiles, and an extraordinary collection of shamanic paraphernalia for preparing, ingesting and smoking hallucinogenic plants.

Detailed English and Spanish explanations follow the region's evolution through the earliest cultures to the Inka conquest and the Spanish invasion. No opportunity is lost to link information with surrounding archaeological sites, including Pukará de Quitor and Aldea de Tulor.

The credit for this excellent museum goes principally to the Belgian priest and amateur archaeologist after whom it is named. Father Gustavo Le Paige arrived as a priest in San Pedro in 1955, and dedicated the next 35 years of his life to collecting ancient artifacts from the area. His statue now stands outside and a small exhibit is dedicated to him within. There are 45-minute guided tours a few times daily Tuesday to Sunday (CH$1800), in various languages. Temporary exhibits in the back section change every few months.

Iglesia San Pedro　　CHURCH
(Le Paige s/n) FREE The sugar-white Iglesia San Pedro is a delightful little colonial church built with indigenous or artisanal materials – chunky adobe walls and roof, a ceiling made from *cardón* (cactus wood) resembling shriveled tire tracks and, in lieu of nails, hefty leather straps. The church dates from the 17th century, though its present walls were built in 1745, and the bell tower was added in 1890.

☞ Tours

A bewildering array of tours is on offer. Unfortunately, the quality of some tours has become somewhat lax, and travelers complain of operators who cancel abruptly or run unsafe vehicles. Tour leaders are often merely drivers rather than trained guides. Agencies

NORTE GRANDE SAN PEDRO DE ATACAMA

San Pedro de Atacama

N 0 —————————————— 100 m

Tur Bus
Andesmar
Buses Atacama 2000
Buses Frontera del Norte

Licancábur

33

26

30

25

15

Le Paige

Museo Gustavo Le Paige
1

Oficina de Información Turística
4

Géminis

Atienza

Calama

9
19

Tocopilla

Plaza de Armas

Vilama

Toconao

20

2

31 27

14

5 7

3

8

10

16

Caracoles

29
24

18 23

6

34 32 11

28

22

Bus Terminal (700m)

Atienza

17

Palpana

Hostal Quinta Adela (250m)

12 13

San Pedro de Atacama

◎ Top Sights
1 Museo Gustavo Le Paige D2

◎ Sights
2 Iglesia San Pedro C2

✦ Activities, Courses & Tours
3 Ahlarkapin.. C3
4 Atacama Inca Tour D2
5 Cordillera Traveler C3
6 CosmoAndino Expediciones C3
7 Desert Adventure C3
8 Km 0 .... C3
9 Rancho La Herradura C2
10 Terra Extreme D3
11 Vulcano Expediciones C3

🛏 Sleeping
12 Hostal Edén Atacameño D4
13 Hostal La Ruca D4
14 Hostal Lickana.. A3
15 Hostal Sonchek...................................... B2

16 Hostelling International..........................D3
17 Hotel Don Sebastián..............................A4
18 Hotel Lomas Sanchez............................B3
19 Hotel Terrantai.......................................C2
20 Katarpe Hostal..A3
21 Residencial Vilacoyo...............................C2
22 Takha Takha Hotel &
     Camping...A3

🍽 Eating
23 Adobe...B3
24 Blanco...B3
25 Cafe Peregrino.......................................D2
26 Ckunna...C2
27 El Churruá...C3
28 El Toconar...D3
29 La Casona...B3
30 Las Delicias de Carmen........................B2
31 Paatcha...B3
32 Salon de Te O2.......................................C3
33 Tahira B1
34 Todo Natural..C3

often contract out to independent drivers, many of whom work for different companies, so the quality of your driver – or guide, for that matter – can depend on the luck of the draw. That said, don't unfairly dismiss local Spanish-speaking drivers. Many are very courteous and knowledgeable, and can provide a valuable insider's viewpoint.

You may find that the agency you paid is not the same agency that picks you up. Some agencies offer tours in English, German or Dutch, but these tours may require advance notice or extra payment. Competition keeps prices down, and operators come and go.

The tourist information office has a helpful, entertaining and occasionally terrifying book of complaints on various tour agencies; the problem is that nearly every agency is featured and, by the time you read about unlicensed or drunken drivers over the passes to Bolivia, you may decide to do nothing but write postcards from the safety of your hostel, which would be a tragic mistake in such a beautiful area. Nevertheless, when choosing an operator, ask lots of questions, talk to other travelers, trust your judgment and try to be flexible. Don't sign up for tours on the street – any decent tour operator will have an office, and smooth-talking scammers have been known to prey on unwary travelers. At last count, there were over 50 tour agencies in town, so shopping around is an option you may wish to explore.

Standard Tours

The following are the standard bestselling tours offered by most agencies in San Pedro. Note that entrance fees are not included in the tour prices.

Desert Adventure GUIDED TOUR
(☑ 055-285-1067; www.desertadventure.cl; cnr Caracoles & Tocopilla; ☺ 9am-1pm & 3-7pm Mon-Sat, 9am-1pm Sun) Has bilingual guides.

Terra Extreme GUIDED TOUR
(☑ 055-285-1274; www.terraextreme.cl; Toconao s/n; ☺ 9am-1pm & 3-6pm) ✿ Offers the full range of standard tours using a well-maintained fleet of its own vehicles.

Altiplano Lakes GUIDED TOUR
(tour CH$15,000-30,000, entrance fee CH$5000) Leaves San Pedro between 7am and 8am to see flamingos at Laguna Chaxa in the Salar de Atacama, then moves on to the town of Socaire, Lagunas Miñiques and Miscanti, Toconao and the Quebrada de Jere, returning between 4pm and 7pm.

El Tatio Geysers GUIDED TOUR
(tour CH$18,000-20,000, entrance fee CH$5000) This hugely popular tour leaves San Pedro at 4am in order to see the surreal sight of the geysers at sunrise, returning between noon and 1pm. Most tours include thermal baths and breakfast.

Valle de la Luna GUIDED TOUR
(tour CH$8000-10,000, entrance fee CH$2000) Leaves San Pedro mid-afternoon to catch the sunset over the valley, returning early evening. Includes visits to Valle de la Luna, Valle de la Muerte and Tres Marías.

Tulor & Pukará de Quitor GUIDED TOUR
(tour around CH$15,000, entrance fee CH$10,000) Half-day archaeological tours take in this pair of pre-Columbian ruins (departures between 8am and 9am, returning between 1pm and 3pm).

Less Standard Tours

Other available tours include a full-day excursion that takes in the Tatio geysers in the morning and continues on to the pueblos of **Caspana** and **Chiu Chiu**, then the **Pukará de Lasana**, finishing in Calama (a good tour to do before your flight the next day), or returning to San Pedro.

A few other tours are becoming increasingly popular, such as jaunts to **Laguna Cejar** and **Ojos de Salar** (you can swim in both, and in Cejar you can float just like in the Dead Sea), to **Valle del Arcoiris** with its rainbowlike multicolored rock formations and **Salar de Tara**. The last is one of the most spectacular, if back-breaking, trips from San Pedro, which involves a round-trip journey of 200km, to altitudes of 4300m.

Note that these tours don't leave as regularly and have a higher price tag than the bestsellers.

Trekking & Biking

Around San Pedro rise immense volcanoes, a few of them active, and begging to be climbed. If climbing isn't your cup of tea, consider a trekking or biking trip to the usual suspects in the area, such as Valle de la Luna. Bikes are available for rent at several agencies and hotels around town, for about CH$6000 per day; try **Km O** (Caracoles 282B; half-/full day CH$3500/6000).

Vulcano Expediciones ADVENTURE SPORTS
(☑ cell 5363-6648; www.vulcanochile.com; Caracoles 317) Runs treks to volcanoes and mountains, including day climbs to Sairecabur (5971m;

DESERT STARGAZING

The flats of Chajnantor plateau, at 5000m altitude and 40km east of San Pedro de Atacama, host the most ambitious radio telescope that the world has ever seen. The Atacama Large Millimeter/submillimeter Array (ALMA; meaning 'soul' in Spanish) consists of 66 enormous antennae, most of them with a diameter of around 12m. This field of interstellar 'ears' simulates a telescope an astonishing 16km in diameter, making it possible to pick up objects in space as much as 100 times fainter than those previously detected. It is also slated to open a visitor center in the near future; for up-to-the-minute info, see www.almaobservatory.org.

This is just the latest of northern Chile's cutting-edge astronomical facilities. Climatic conditions in the Atacama Desert make it an ideal location for stargazing. This is not only thanks to cloudless desert nights, but also the predictable winds that blow steadily in from the Pacific Ocean, causing minimal turbulence – a crucial requirement for observatories to achieve optimal image quality.

Other major facilities in northern Chile include the European Southern Observatory (ESO) at Cerro Paranal. Norte Chico has Observatorio Interamericano Cerro Tololo and the nearby Cerro El Pachón. Another ESO site is at La Silla (which also has free visits open to the public each Saturday at 1:30pm, except in July and August; see www.eso.org/public/teles-instr/lasilla.html), while the Carnegie Institution's Observatorio Las Campanas is just north of La Silla.

If all that whets your appetite for astronomy, consider taking a Tour of the Night Sky from San Pedro. There's a range of astronomical tours available from San Pedro, but one standout is **Ahlarkapin** (☑ 099-579-7816; www.ahlarkapin.cl; Caracoles 151), which offers more personalized observation tours (12 people maximum) with a focus on Andean cosmology. The two-hour tours (in Spanish and English) run nightly at 9:30pm in summer (earlier in winter) and cost CH$15,000/10,000 for adults/children.

CH$110,000), Lascar (5592m; CH$100,000) and Tocco (5604m; CH$70,000). Longer climbs take in Licancábur and Llullaillaco. It also runs downhill bike rides (CH$20,000 to CH$35,000) and can hook you up with motorbike tours offered by **On Safari** (www.onsafariatacama.com).

CosmoAndino Expediciones   GUIDED TOUR
(☑ 055-285-1069; www.cosmoandino.cl; Caracoles 259) This well-established operation specializes in trekking excursions to nearby highlights; expect to pay more than for a standard tour but you'll also get more 'quality time in the Atacama,' as their motto claims.

Azimut 360   ADVENTURE SPORTS
(☑ in Santiago 056-2235-3085; www.azimut360.com) Although it doesn't have an office in town, Santiago-based Azimut 360 still has its experts on the ground and remains one of the top choices for climbing and trekking tours. For information and bookings, call the office in Santiago.

Horseback Riding

Rancho La Herradura   HORSEBACK RIDING
(☑ 055-285-1956; www.atacamahorseadventure.com; Tocopilla 406) Sightseeing from the saddle is available from several places, including Rancho La Herradura. Tours vary from two hours for CH$15,000 to epic 10-day treks with camping. English-, German- and French-speaking guides are available.

Sand-boarding

Jumping on a sand-board and sliding down enormous sand dunes is the most popular of the adrenaline-pumping activities around San Pedro. This happens in Valle de la Muerte, where 150m-high dunes make perfect terrain.

Once you've got the hang of it, you can hire boards directly from several agencies in town, including Vulcano; it costs CH$4000 for half a day.

Atacama Inca Tour   ADVENTURE SPORTS
(☑ 055-285-1062; www.sandboardsanpedro.com; Toconao 421-A) While several agencies offer sand-boarding, many actually sell tours by Atacama Inca Tour, our top pick for its pro boards and experienced instructors. Standard trips, for CH$10,000, depart either at 9am and return at noon or leave at 3pm, returning at 7pm. They involve a 20-minute class, plus you get a DVD with a video clip of your escapade.

Its latest offering is the night sand-board party (CH\$12,000; 9pm till midnight), with spotlights for the dune, massive speakers and a DJ.

✨ Festivals & Events

Fiesta de Nuestra
Señora de la Candelaria
RELIGIOUS

(☉ Feb) In early February, San Pedro celebrates with religious dances.

Carnaval
CARNIVAL

Takes place in February or March, depending on the date of Easter.

Fiesta de San Pedro
y San Pablo
RELIGIOUS

(☉ Jun) June 29 has the locals celebrating with folk dancing, Mass, a procession of statues, a rodeo and modern dancing that gets rowdy by midnight.

Fiesta de Santa Rosa de Lima
RELIGIOUS

(☉ Aug) This traditional religious festival takes place on August 30.

🛏 Sleeping

While San Pedro has a dizzying choice of places to stay, don't expect to find many rock-bottom options. Prices are inflated as a result of San Pedro's status as the tourist hub of the north. Note that some budget places request that solo travelers share a room in the busy summer period.

Exclusively midrange hotels are in short supply at this backpackers' haven, but many hostels in the budget category have midrange rooms at the ready. Top-range hotels have sprouted all around San Pedro, though many are outside the center.

Hostal Sonchek
HOSTEL \$

(☏ 055-285-1112; www.hostalsonchek.cl; cnr Paige & Calama; dm CH\$8500, d CH\$36,000, s/d without bathroom CH\$12,000/20,000; 🛜) Thatched roofs and adobe walls characterize the carpeted rooms at this lovely hostel. It's centered on a small courtyard, and there's a shared kitchen, luggage storage and a small garden out back with ping-pong and a few hammocks. The common bathrooms with solar-heated showers are some of the cleanest in town. English and French spoken.

Hostal Edén Atacameño
HOSTEL \$

(☏ 055-285-1154; hostaleden@gmail.com; Toconao 592; s/d CH\$25,000/40,000, without bathroom CH\$12,000/20,000; 🅿@🛜) This is a laid-back hostel with rooms around a couple of sociable, hammock-strung patios with plentiful seating. Guests can use the kitchen, and there's laundry service and luggage storage. The shared bathrooms are clean; breakfast is included for rooms with private bathrooms.

Residencial Vilacoyo
GUESTHOUSE \$

(☏ 055-285-1006; vilacoyo@sanpedroatacama.com; Tocopilla 387; per person CH\$10,000; 🅿) A no-frills but friendly *residencial* with a snug gravel patio hung with hammocks, a kitchen and luggage storage. The shared showers only have hot water between 7am and 10pm.

Hostelling International
HOSTEL \$

(☏ 055-256-4683; hostelsanpedro@hotmail.com; Caracoles 360; dm/s/d CH\$7000/33,000/36,000, s/d without bathroom CH\$20,000/23,000; 🛜) This convivial spot offers dorms – with some bunks nearly 3m up – and a few doubles around a small patio. Services include a shared kitchen, lockers, and they'll book tours. HI members get a CH\$2000 discount.

★ Hostal Quinta Adela
B&B \$\$

(☏ 055-285-1272; www.quintaadela.wix.com/quinta-adela; Toconao 624; r from CH\$70,000; @🛜) This friendly family-run place, just a quick walk from town, has seven character-filled rooms (each with its own individual style) and a shady terrace, and is situated alongside a sprawling orchard with hammocks. There's luggage storage and they're flexible with check-in and check-out.

Hotel Lomas Sanchez
HOTEL \$\$

(☏ 055-242-3649; www.lomassanchez.cl; Caracoles 259-A; s/d CH\$25,000/45,000; 🛜) Sitting right in the middle of the Caracoles strip, front rooms at this family-run place may be a bit noisy for some. They're definitely cute, though, with pleasing touches like wooden floorboards and local weavings for decorations. Breakfast is offered in the sunny patio or cozy dining area.

Hostal La Ruca
HOSTEL \$\$

(☏ 055-285-1568; www.larucahostal.cl; Toconao 513; s/d CH\$37,000/50,000; @🛜) A nice touch of rustic style – think colorful Andean bedspreads and tapestries – graces the rooms of this sweet hostel with tiny but clean bathrooms, a sunny patio with hammocks and a shared kitchen, all presided over by friendly staff who speak English and some German.

Katarpe Hostal
HOTEL \$\$

(☏ 055-285-1033; www.katarpe.cl; Domingo Atienza 441; s/d CH\$38,000/48,000, d without bathroom CH\$32,000; 🅿🛜) A great location just

WORTH A TRIP

EXCURSION TO UYUNI, BOLIVIA

Colorful altiplano lakes, weird rock playgrounds worthy of Salvador Dalí, flamingos, volcanoes and, most famously of all, the blindingly white salt flat of Uyuni: these are some of the rewards for taking an excursion into Bolivia northeast of San Pedro de Atacama. However, be warned that this is no cozy ride in the country, and for every five travelers that gush about Uyuni being the highlight of their trip, there is another declaring it a waking nightmare.

The standard trips take three days, crossing the Bolivian border at Hito Cajón, passing Laguna Colorada and continuing to the Salar de Uyuni before ending in the town of Uyuni. The going rate of CH$98,000 includes transportation in crowded 4WD jeeps, basic and often teeth-chatteringly cold accommodations, plus food; an extra CH$15,000 to CH$23,000 will get you back to San Pedro on the fourth day (some tour operators drive through the third night). Bring drinks and snacks, warm clothes and a sleeping bag. Travelers clear Chilean immigration at San Pedro and Bolivian immigration on arrival at Uyuni. Note that entrance fees to Bolivian parks are charged extra, and amount to approximately CH$17,000.

None of the agencies offering this trip get consistently glowing reports. **Cordillera Traveler** (☑ 055-285-1291; www.cordilleratraveller.com; Toconao 447-B & Tocopilla 429-B) gets the best feedback from travelers.

off Caracoles, a range of reasonable-sized rooms, crisp sheets and decent beds make this a good if unexciting choice. Rooms are arranged around a couple of patios, one featuring long wooden tables. There's a laundry service, too, and the staff are accommodating.

Takha Takha Hotel & Camping   HOTEL, CAMPGROUND $$

(☑ 055-285-1038; www.takhatakha.cl; Caracoles 101-A; campsite per person CH$10,000, s/d CH$38,400/50,000, without bathroom CH$14,400/30,000; 🛜🏊) A popular catch-all outfit with decent campsites, plain budget rooms and spotless midrange accommodations set around a sprawling flowery garden with a swimming pool.

Hotel Don Sebastián   HOTEL $$

(☑ 055-285-1972; www.donsebastian.cl; Domingo Atienza 140; s/d CH$50,000/70,000, cabins CH$80,000; 🅿️@🛜) Solid midrange option a hop and a skip from town, with well-appointed heated rooms and a handful of cabins with kitchenettes. There are nice shared areas, but it can get busy with tour groups.

Hostal Lickana   GUESTHOUSE $$

(☑ 055-285-1940; www.lickanahostal.cl; Caracoles 140; s/d CH$34,000/47,000; 🛜) Just off the main drag, this strip hotel has super-clean rooms with big closets, colorful bedspreads and straw-covered front patios. What it lacks is the common-area ambience of other hostels.

Atacama Awasi   HOTEL $$$

(☑ 055-285-1460; www.awasiatacama.com; Tocopilla 4; s/d all-inclusive 2 nights US$2475/3300) A kilometer or so south of town, the Awasi is one of the finer upscale choices in the area. Rooms are gorgeously decorated using mostly local materials (even the bath salts are locally sourced) in a rustic-chic design. There's a great on-site restaurant, a sweet little pool area and perks include a personal guide/driver for each guest.

Tierra Atacama Hotel & Spa   HOTEL $$$

(☑ 055-255-5976; www.tierraatacama.com; Séquitor s/n; s/d all-inclusive 2 nights US$1650/2700; 🅿️@🛜🏊) All the luxe perks paired with heaps of style await those who stay at this resort-style hideaway 20 minutes out of town. Stone-floored rooms showcase an organic minimalist look, outdoor showers and terraces that sport wow vistas of Licancábur. There's a spa as well as a restaurant. The all-inclusive rate includes food, drinks and tours.

Hotel Terrantai   HOTEL $$$

(☑ 055-285-1045; www.terrantai.com; Tocopilla 411; d CH$105,000-120,000; 🅿️🛜🏊) This is arguably the most intimate and central of San Pedro's upscale hotels. The key is in the architecture: high, narrow passageways made from smooth rocks from the Río Loa lead guests to the elegant rooms with Andean textiles and ceiling fans. Slightly pricier superior rooms have more space and light and nicer views.

There's a bamboo-shaded sculpture garden out back as well as a dip pool and a bar.

✖ Eating & Drinking

A word of warning: while San Pedro restaurants offer welcome variety, especially for vegetarians, it comes with an elevated price tag. Touristy places have touts offering 10% off or a free drink (make sure you eat it).

To best avoid San Pedro's skyrocketing prices, follow the locals out to the town periphery, such as the eateries along Licancábur, where a set lunch goes for around CH$4000. Your best bet for really cheap is the food stalls by the parking lot on the northern edge of town, which serve simple set lunches of *cazuela*, mains and dessert (for around CH$3000), and all-day empanadas for snacking.

Salon de Te O2
CAFE $
(Caracoles 295; breakfast from CH$2500, mains around CH$5000; ⊗7am-9pm; 🛜) Early-morning breakfasts (from 7am), great quiches, juicy meat sandwiches and lovely tarts are the highlights of this colorful cafe run by a French-Chilean couple. You can while away the afternoon on the shady back patio.

Cafe Peregrino
CAFETERIA $
(Gustavo Le Paige 348; breakfast from CH$3000, sandwiches around CH$4000; ⊗9am-8pm; 🛜) The loveliest cafe in town, overlooking the plaza with a few benches strategically placed for people-watching. Inside are only four tables. Food-wise, you'll find pizzas, salads, sandwiches and nice cakes and pastries. And, yes, real espressos and cappuccinos!

El Toconar
INTERNATIONAL $
(cnr Toconao & Caracoles; mains CH$4000-9000; ⊗noon-1am) The best garden setup in town (complete with bonfires for those chilly desert nights) is at this place. Also on offer is a wide menu, a superb selection of cocktails (including pisco sours infused with desert herbs), cheap beers and a happy hour.

El Churruá
PIZZERIA $
(Tocopillo 442; mains CH$5000-8000; ⊗12:30-11pm) The best thin-crust pizzas in town are at this unassuming little place just off the main drag. There's only a few tables, but it's worth the wait. There's no alcohol on the menu, but they're happy to run to the store for you.

Las Delicias de Carmen
CHILEAN $
(Calama 370; mains CH$5000-10,000; ⊗8am-10:30pm; 🛜🍴) Great breakfasts, delicious cakes and empanadas, brick-oven pizzas (choose your own toppings) and different dishes daily are churned out at this light-flooded restaurant with leafy views. It shares its terrace with Hostal Sonchek next door.

Tahira
CHILEAN $
(Tocopilla 372; CH$3000-7000; ⊗noon-11pm) A down-to-earth cafe where the locals outnumber the gringos, Tahira serves up no-frills mainstays that are satisfying, and barbecues on weekends.

★La Casona
CHILEAN $$
(www.lacasonadeatacama.cl; Caracoles 195; set lunch CH$6000-7000, mains CH$8000-10,000; ⊗noon-1am; 🛜) A high-ceilinged dining room with dark wood paneling and an adobe fireplace in the middle, the classic La Casona serves up sizzling *parrilladas* and Chilean staples such as *pastel de choclo*. There's a long list of Chilean wines and a small patio for alfresco lunches.

Adobe
INTERNATIONAL $$
(Caracoles 211; mains CH$7500-9500; ⊗noon-1am Thu-Tue, 7pm-1am Wed; 🛜) Popular with travelers for its studied rusticity, rock-art decor, benchlike seating and smoky fire in the alfresco dining room. Adobe serves tasty but pricey dishes such as mushroom quinoa risotto and is a good spot for a drink.

Blanco
INTERNATIONAL $$
(Caracoles 195b; mains CH$7500-9000; ⊗7am-midnight Wed-Mon; 🛜) The hippest eatery in town, this all-white adobe-clad restaurant has fishtank windows, a terrace with a fireplace out back, a good range of dishes and a buzzy vibe. Set menus are a good deal, for CH$6000 to CH$7000.

Todo Natural
INTERNATIONAL $$
(Caracoles 271; set meal CH$7000, mains CH$7000-11,000; ⊗noon-11pm; 🛜🍴) Local ingredients like quinoa, Asian influences, whole-wheat sandwiches, good salads and other healthy offerings fill out the lengthy menu here. The service is erratic but the food decent, and there's happy hour (6pm to 8pm).

Ckunna
INTERNATIONAL $$
(Tocopilla 359; mains CH$8000-12,000; ⊗noon-3pm & 7-11:30pm; 🛜) Come for the homemade pastas and the fusion of altiplano and Mediterranean fare served inside an old school

building a stroll from the main strip. There's a welcoming bar and a terrace with a bonfire out back.

Paatcha   STEAKHOUSE **$$**
(Caracoles 218; mains CH$6000-10,000; ⊘noon-3pm & 7:30-11:30pm) An intimate little eatery serving up good *parrillada* (meat platters) accompanied by a decent cocktail list and some smooth music selections.

☆ Entertainment

While San Pedro's small community welcomes tourism, it draws the line at late-night revelers. Establishments that sell only alcohol have been outlawed, no alcohol is sold after 1am, police have cracked down on public drinking *and* local lawmakers recently banned nocturnal dancing in downtown San Pedro. The night is also cut short by travelers with early tours: after all, waking up for a 4am jaunt to El Tatio is enough of a headache *without* a hangover!

All that said, all is not lost for lovers of nightlife; a very cozy bar-cum-restaurant scene predominates here, with travelers swapping stories around open fires and making the most of abundant happy hours. And there's a well-kept public secret: rave-like parties in the desert occur on a regular basis, although they aren't advertised due to police crackdowns. It's all word of mouth, so ask around town to see what's happening and where.

🛍 Shopping

The shaded Paseo Artesanal, a poker-straight alley squeezing north from the plaza, is the place to hunt down novel *cardón* carvings, llama and alpaca woolens and other curious trinkets. More artisanal outlets are strewn throughout town.

ℹ Information

There are three ATMs in town (two on Caracoles and the other opposite the museum) but they do not always have money, so bring a big wad of cash, just in case. Many establishments take plastic, but some prefer the real stuff. Several moneychangers are found around town, especially along Toconao, but don't expect good exchange rates.

Internet cafes (CH$800 per hour) dot Caracoles, and most accommodations offer access; there's also free wi-fi on the main plaza.

Oficina de Información Turística (✆055-285-1420; cnr Toconao & Le Paige; ⊘9am-9pm) Helpful tourist office offering advice and doling out town maps and brochures. Check out the annual book of comments for up-to-date traveler feedback on tour agencies, hostels, restaurants, transportation providers and more.

Post Office (Tocanao s/n) The location changes almost yearly, so ask locals if you can't find it here.

Posta Médica (✆055-285-1010; Toconao s/n) The local clinic, on the plaza.

ℹ Getting There & Away

San Pedro has a new **bus terminal** (Tumisa s/n) about a kilometer southeast of the plaza. All buses now depart and arrive here, but you can still book tickets at the bus companies' downtown offices, along Licancábur.

Buses Atacama 2000 (Licancábur s/n; ⊘8am-7pm) has regular departures to Calama (from CH$2700, three daily), where you can connect to its Uyuni bus. **Buses Frontera del Norte** (Licancábur s/n) goes to Calama (five daily) as well as Arica (from CH$16,100) and Iquique (CH$15,000), departing at 8pm every night.

Tur Bus (✆055-851-549; Licancábur 294) has hourly buses to Calama (CH$3000), from where you can connect to all major destinations in Chile.

Andesmar (✆055-259-2692; www.andesmar.com; Licancábur s/n) serves Salta and Jujuy, Argentina, leaving at 9:30am on Tuesday, Wednesday, Friday and Sunday (from CH$30,000, 12 hours with border time). **Géminis** (✆055-892-049; Toconao 428) also goes to Salta (CH$32,000, 12 hours) on Tuesday and Sunday at 9:30am and on Friday at 8:30am.

Several agencies in town offer transfer services to Calama airport, which cost around CH$16,500 per person; try **Desert Adventure** (✆055-285-1067; Caracoles s/n).

ℹ Getting Around

Mountain bikes are a terrific way to steam around San Pedro. However, to ensure that only calories are burned, be sure to carry water and sunblock. Several agencies and hostels rent mountain bikes, for the current going rate of CH$6000 per day. Some agencies will give out photocopied maps to guide your forays.

Around San Pedro de Atacama

Most attractions are beyond walking distance from town, and public transportation is limited. Options include renting a car (in Calama), hiring a bike or taking a tour. Luckily, vigorous competition among numerous operators keeps tours reasonably priced. Also, consider staying the night in the remote villages and attractions you visit. By spreading the tourist trail, you help create a more sustainable future for the people of the region.

Dominating a curvy promontory over the Río San Pedro, the crumbling 12th-century **Pukará de Quitor** (admission CH$3000; ☉9am-7:30pm Jun-Aug, to 6pm Sep-May) was one of the last bastions against Pedro de Valdivia and the Spanish in northern Chile. The indigenous forces fought bravely but were overcome and many were promptly beheaded. A hundred defensive enclosures hug the slopes here, like big stone birds' nests. The hilltop commands an impressive view of the entire oasis. The fort is just 3km northwest of San Pedro, and easily accessible on foot, by bike or by vehicle.

Circular adobe structures huddle together like muddy bubble-wrap in the ruins of **Aldea de Tulor** (admission CH$5000; ☉9am-7:30pm Jun-Aug, to 6pm Sep-May), the oldest excavated village in the region. It's an interesting diversion 11km southwest of San Pedro; however, you'll have to take a tour, drive along sandy tracks or mountain-bike it.

The idyllic **Termas de Puritama** (admission adult/child CH$15,000/7000; ☉9:15am-5:30pm) puddle together in a box canyon 34km north of San Pedro, en route to El Tatio. Maintained by the Explora company, it has changing rooms on site. Few tours stop here because of the hefty admission charged, but taxis will take you from San Pedro. The springs are a 20-minute walk from the parking lot. The temperature of the springs is about 33°C (91°F), and there are several falls and pools. Bring food, water and sunblock.

Reserva Nacional Los Flamencos

This sprawling **reserve** (admission adult/child up to 12 years CH$2500/free; ☉9am-6pm summer, to 5pm winter) encompasses seven geographically distinct sectors south, east and west of San Pedro de Atacama, and encloses many of the area's top attractions.

(Continued on p160)

WORTH A TRIP

THE UPPER LOA & ITS TRIBUTARIES

A string of typically Andean villages and ancient forts fleck the difficult terrain to the north of San Pedro de Atacama and east of Calama. A few tour operators from San Pedro visit these villages after the early-morning spectacle of watching the El Tatio geysers – taking passes as high as 4800m and jiggling along some tight switchbacks.

From the geysers it's 46km along some switchbacks to highland idyll **Caspana**, as delightful as it is surprising. Nestled in its namesake valley, the 'new' village is built into the rocky escarpment, while the 'old' town teeters on the edge of a high plateau above. It's exactly what an Andean village is supposed to look like – verdant terraces, thatched roofs, the colonial **Iglesia de San Lucas** and a small archaeological **museum**. Do not drink the tap water here.

At this point you could head north to **Ayquina**, an agricultural village, and the nearby thermal springs **Vegas de Turi**, and then east to tiny **Toconce**.

However, most tours now take the road west from Caspana, taking the turn-off northwest via **Laguna Inca Coya** (also known as Laguna Chiu Chiu), a perfectly round oasis, 80m deep according to an expedition led by Jacques Cousteau. A legend claims it was filled by the tears of the jilted lover of Inka Tupac Yupanqui.

From here the dirt road continues west to a junction, where you can turn north to Chiu Chiu and the 12th-century **Pukará de Lasana**, an extensive fortress built into the salmon-pink volcanic rock of the valley. Its husk is pockmarked with defensive nooks and occasional petroglyphs. A touristy restaurant sits alongside.

On the trip back to Chiu Chiu, take time to appreciate the enigmatic petroglyphs that smother the valley, some in plain view and some hiding behind hefty boulders.

Chiu Chiu itself is just 33km from Calama via paved Ruta 21. It's difficult to overestimate the significance of its chunky little **Iglesia de San Francisco** (a national monument and thought to be Chile's oldest church, built in 1540). Peek inside at the cactus-wood ceiling and take a stroll around the sandcastle-like whitewashed exterior.

Several companies in San Pedro de Atacama offer organized tours to this area.

The Natural World

Set out to find sweeping desert solitude, climb craggy Andean summits or wander the sacred forests of poet Pablo Neruda. Surf, paddle or sail the endless coast. Explore the mysteries of Easter Island, stargaze, soak in hot springs or watch glaciers calve. In Chile, all roads lead to nature.

1. Parque Nacional Torres del Paine (p353)
Granite pillars soar dramatically above the Patagonian steppe.

2. Valparaíso (p90)
Take the panoramic coastal road to this port town.

3. Easter Island (p397)
Enigmatic *moai* (statues) dot this isolated island.

4. Guanacos (p436)
These delicate camelids are most highly concentrated on the plains of Patagonia, including Parque Nacional Torres del Paine.

KAVRAM/GETTY IMAGES ©

1. Parque Nacional Torres del Paine (p353)
Dramatic peaks and Laguna Azul present a magnificent backdrop for grazing horses.

2. Valle de la Luna (p160)
Experience giant sand dunes and surreal, lunar-like landscapes.

3. Parque Nacional Bernardo O'Higgins (p353)
Explore glaciers and remote ice fields by boat.

4. El Tatio Geysers (p162)
Resembling a giant, gurgling steam bath, El Tatio is fed by 64 geysers and 100 fumaroles.

159

FILUPERRAZZO/GETTY IMAGES ©

KRISTIN PILJAY/GETTY IMAGES ©

AD_FOTO/GETTY IMAGES ©

3

Around Calama & San Pedro de Atacama

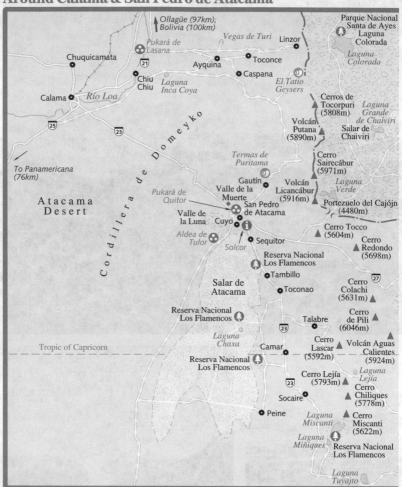

(Continued from p155)

Conaf maintains a **Centro de Información Ambiental** (☺usually 10am-1pm & 2:30-4:30pm) at the *ayllu* of Solcor, which is located 2km past San Pedro de Atacama's customs and immigration post on the road to Toconao.

Valle de la Luna

Watching the sun set from the exquisite **Valle de la Luna** (Valley of the Moon; adult/student CH$2000/1500; ☺dawn-dusk) is an unforgettable experience. As you sit atop a giant sand dune, panting from the exertion of climbing it, drinking in spectacular views and watching the sun slip below the horizon, a beautiful transformation occurs: the distant ring of volcanoes, rippling Cordillera de la Sal and surreal lunar landscapes of the valley are suddenly suffused with intense purples, pinks and golds.

The Valle de la Luna is named after its lunarlike landforms eroded by eons of flood and wind. It's found 15km west of San Pedro de Atacama at the northern end of the Cordillera de la Sal and forms part of Reserva Nacional Los Flamencos.

The valley is San Pedro's most popular and cheapest organized tour; trips typically depart about 4pm, leaving good time to explore before sunset. If you want to avoid dozens of tourist vans, all making the same stops, pick an alternative time. Some hardy souls come here at dawn to sidestep the sunset crowds.

Mountain biking is a great way to get here, but keep to the roads and trails, and make sure you take a flashlight if you're staying for the sunset. If driving, you can leave the highway to explore the dirt roads and box canyons to the north; take care not to get stuck in the sand. Park only on the shoulder or at other designated areas – do not tear up the fragile desert with tire tracks.

Note that camping is not permitted. The area is now being administrated by the Atacameño people, and these are their ancestral grounds and sacred space, so be considerate and clean up your trash.

Laguna Chaxa

The jagged crust of the **Salar de Atacama** looks for all the world like God went crazy with a stippling brush. But in the midst of these rough lifeless crystals is an oasis of activity: the pungent **Laguna Chaxa** (admission CH$5000), 65km from San Pedro, the reserve's most easily accessible flamingo breeding site. Three of the five known species (James, Chilean and Andean) can be spotted at this salt lake, as well as plovers, coots and ducks: bring zoom lenses and snappy reflexes. Sunrise is feeding time for the birds and is the best time to see them. The lagoon is also gorgeous at sunset.

Lagunas Miscanti & Miñiques

Shimmery high-altitude lakes dot the altiplano and make for long but worthwhile excursions from San Pedro. From a junction 3km south of the oasis town of **Toconao**, where some tours stop to take in the distinctive church made of volcanic rock and the nearby **Quebrada de Jere** (admission CH$2000), Ruta 23 heads 46km south toward the village of **Socaire**, which has a pretty colonial church with a cactus-wood ceiling, and a remarkable density of Inkan terraces.

The road then climbs 18km to an eastbound turn-off leading to the glittery-blue sweet-water lakes, **Miñiques** and **Miscanti** (admission CH$2500), watched over by snow-touched volcanoes. The smaller Laguna Miñiques is the largest breeding site for the horned coot on the western side of the Andes, and visitors are kept at bay when the birds are breeding. Conaf and the local community from Socaire maintain a lakeside **cabin** (per person CH$20,000) on Miscanti, where you can stay. Rejoining Ruta 23 about 15km south of the turn-off, the road heads eastward past more salt lakes, including **Laguna Tuyajto**, to the Argentine border at Paso de Lago Sico (4079m).

Socaire is 100km from San Pedro, and the *lagunas* are 110km distant at 4300m.

El Tatio Geysers

Visiting the world-famous El Tatio at dawn is like walking through a gigantic steam bath, ringed by volcanoes and fed by 64 gurgling geysers and a hundred gassy fumaroles. Swirling columns of steam envelop onlookers in a Dantesque vision, and the soundtrack of bubbling, spurting and hissing sounds like a field of merrily boiling kettles. The experience does not *feel* like bathtime, however: unless it's bathtime in the Arctic. Most visitors find themselves wishing the geysers would spread their heat more efficiently during the freezing dawn.

At 4300m above sea level, El Tatio is the world's highest geyser field. The sight of its steaming fumaroles in the azure clarity of the altiplano is unforgettable, and the mineral structures that form as the boiling water evaporates are strikingly beautiful. As dawn wears on, shafts of sunlight crown the surrounding volcanoes and illuminate the writhing steam. Plans have been in the works for several years to create a thermo-electric plant here, but at the time of writing the Tatio geysers were still free to shoot their steam skyward.

ℹ Information

The geysers are 95km north of San Pedro de Atacama. Administration of the geysers was handed over to indigenous Atacameño people in 2004. You'll need to stop to pay the entrance fee (CH$5000) at the site's administrative kiosk, about 2km before the geysers.

Tours, priced around CH$20,000, leave at the forbidding hour of 4am to reach the geysers by 6am, the best time to see them. Almost every tour agency in San Pedro offers this tour, so hundreds of sleepy-eyed tourists stumble from minibuses at the appointed hour. After about 8:30am, the winds disperse the steam, although most tours leave by that time so you can enjoy the large thermal pool in virtual privacy. Watch your step – in some places, visitors have fallen through the thin crust into underlying pools of scalding water and suffered severe burns. Dress in layers: it's toe-numbingly cold at sunbreak but you'll bake in the van on the way back down.

ℹ Getting There & Away

Tours from San Pedro include breakfast, sometimes with cartons of milk and fresh eggs boiled in geyser pools.

If driving, leave San Pedro no later than 4am to reach the geysers by sunrise. The route north is signed from San Pedro, but some drivers prefer to follow tour minibuses in the dark (the bus drivers do not appreciate this, however). Do not attempt this rough road, which has some difficult stream fords, without a high-clearance pickup or jeep, preferably one with 4WD.

If you rented a vehicle in Calama, consider returning via the picturesque villages of Caspana and Chiu Chiu rather than via San Pedro. Some tours from Calama and San Pedro take this route as well.

Calama

📞 055 / POP 138,588 / ELEV 2250M

It may appear drab and gritty but Calama happens to be the pride and joy of northern Chile, an economic powerhouse that pumps truckloads of copper money into the Chilean economy year on year. And while it holds little attraction for visitors – most people will only stop here for the night (if they have to) on their way to the la-la-land of San Pedro de Atacama – there is a visceral appeal to this mining town that definitely goes that extra mile in 'keeping it real.'

Everywhere are reminders of the precious metal: copper statues, copper wall-etchings and reliefs, and even a copper-plated spire on the cathedral. In 2004 the city also began to inherit a wave of copper refugees when the entire population of polluted mining town Chuquicamata relocated here, a process that was completed in 2007.

The city's short history is inextricably tied to that of Chuquicamata. It's a measure of Calama's relative youth that it did not acquire its cathedral until 1906 – until then, it was ecclesiastically subordinate to tiny Chiu Chiu.

Calama sits on the north bank of the Río Loa. Though the city has sprawled with the influx of laborers from Chuquicamata, its central core is still pedestrian-friendly. Calle Ramírez begins in an attractive pedestrian mall leading to the shady Plaza 23 de Marzo, which bristles with market stalls and pigeons.

🛏 Sleeping

Prices are grossly inflated in Calama, as most hotels cater to workers at the town's lucrative copper mines. Book ahead, especially if you want to stay on a weekday.

Hostal Abaroa HOTEL $
(📞 057-294-1025; Abaroa 2128; s/d CH$28,000/36,000, without bathroom CH$15,000/20,000; 🕸)

The best buy in its category, this friendly new hostel a couple of blocks from the plaza has bright clean rooms along a back patio, and a convenient location for bus departures. Meals are available.

Hotel Atenas HOTEL $
(☑ 055-234-2666; www.hotelatenas.cl; Ramírez 1961; s/d CH$16,000/21,000; 🛜) A dark warren of rooms right off the pedestrian mall, the Atenas is the best of Calama's rock-bottom choices, with spacious clean bathrooms and a good location.

Hotel Anpaymi HOTEL $$
(☑ 055-234-2325; www.hotelanpaymi.cl; Sotomayor 1980; s/d CH$33,000/42,000; 🛜) This is a surprisingly tranquil option in a busy downtown location. Doubles are good value, with wooden floors, spacious layouts and tiny bathrooms. Singles are cramped but adequate.

Hotel El Mirador HOTEL $$
(☑ 055-234-0329; www.hotelmirador.cl; Sotomayor 2064; s/d CH$44,000/55,000; P🛜) This historic hotel fronted by an octagonal tower has colonial-style rooms with a pleasant grandmotherly vibe and small bathrooms, all set around a sun-splashed patio. The sitting room comes complete with historic photos of Calama.

Hostería Calama HOTEL $$$
(☑ 055-234-1511; www.hosteriacalama.cl; Latorre 1521; s/d CH$81,000/91,000; P@🛜🏊) Calama's fanciest downtown hotel features spacious carpeted rooms decked out in a classic style, some with leafy views. It has all the conveniences of an upscale hotel, including a gym, a restaurant, a patio and a small swimming pool by the parking lot. Front rooms are noisy, but come with tree-shaded balconies.

✖ Eating

Boccado INTERNATIONAL $
(cnr Ramírez & Abaroa; mains CH$4500-8000; ⊙8am-10pm; 🛜) Right on the plaza, this is a great catch-all place, serving good set meals, healthy salads and excellent coffee. There's a fine selection of ice cream to top it all off.

Mercado Central MARKET $
(Latorre; set meals CH$2200-2500) For quick filling eats, take advantage of the *cocinerías* (greasy spoons) in this busy little market between Ramírez and Vargas.

Bavaria CHILEAN $$
(Latorre 1985 2nd fl; mains CH$7000-10,000; ⊙noon-11:30pm; 🛜) Part of a chain that covers pretty much all of northern Chile, this place still has some character and serves up a good variety of meat dishes and seafood. The attached cafeteria downstairs has cheaper fast-food options and set meals.

Barlovento CHILEAN $$
(Av Granaderos 2034; mains CH$7500-10,000; ⊙closed Sun) With *peña* (live folkloric performances) on Fridays and Saturdays (CH$5000 cover), this simple restaurant is a nice place to go for dancing or a meaty meal.

❶ Information

Several banks with ATMs are to be found in the city center, some of which also change currency.

There are pay phones and call centers all along Calama's pedestrian strip, and internet shops (about CH$500 per hour) throughout the pedestrian mall and the streets around it.

Hospital Carlos Cisternas (☑ 055-265-5700; Carlos Cisternas s/n) Five blocks north of Plaza 23 de Marzo.

Oficina Municipal de Información Turística (☑ 055-253-1707; www.calamacultural.cl; Latorre 1689; ⊙8:30am-1pm & 2-6pm Mon-Fri) The tourist office has cordial, helpful staff and can sign you up for a Chuqui tour.

❶ Getting There & Away

AIR

LAN (☑ 600-526-2000; www.lanchile.com; Latorre 1726; ⊙9am-1pm & 3-6:45pm Mon-Fri, 9:15am-1:15pm Sat.) flies to Santiago (CH$236,000) several times daily. **Sky** (☑ 600-600-2828; www.skyairline.cl; Latorre 1499) has flights to Santiago (from CH$102,500).

BUS

Bus companies are scattered throughout the town but mostly concentrated along Av Balmaceda and Antofagasta. Those with services northbound and southbound on the Panamericana include the following:

DESTINATION	COST (CH$)	DURATION (HR)
Antofagasta	5600	3
Arica	8900	6
Iquique	17,700	6½
La Serena	22,800	14
Santiago	27,600	22

Tur Bus provides regular services to San Pedro de Atacama (CH$2700, one hour). **Buses Frontera** (☑ 055-282-4269; Antofagasta 2046) also has buses to San Pedro (CH$2500, 1½ hours) as does **Buses Atacama 2000** (☑ 055-231-6664; Abaroa 2106) for a few cents less.

International buses are invariably full, so reserve as far in advance as possible. To get to Uyuni, Bolivia (CH$12,000, nine hours) via Ollagüe (CH$9000, three hours), ask at Frontera and Buses Atacama 2000; services go only several times per week so buy ahead.

Service to Salta and Jujuy, Argentina, is provided by Pullman on Monday, Wednesday and Friday mornings at 8am (CH$35,300, 12 hours), and by Géminis on Tuesday, Friday and Sunday at 8:30am (CH$34,000). Buy tickets in advance during the high summer season.

Condor Bus/Flota Barrios (☑ 055-234-5883; www.condorbus.cl; Av Balmaceda 1852)

Expreso Norte (☑ 055-234-7250; www.expresonorte.cl; Balmaceda 1902)

Géminis (☑ 055-289-2050; www.geminis.cl; Antofagasta 2239) To Salta and Arica only.

Pullman Bus (☑ 055-234-1282; www.pullmanbus.cl; Balmaceda 4155) Center (cnr Av Balmaceda & Sotomayor); Mall Calama (Balmaceda 3242, Local 130).

Tur Bus (☑ 055-268-8812; www.turbus.cl; Ramírez 1852) Buses depart from this office before swinging by the terminal at Granaderos 3048.

ⓘ Getting Around

Aeropuerto El Loa (☑ 055-234-2348; www.aeropuertocalama.com) is a short cab ride south of Calama (CH$3500). Minibus transfers cost CH$3000 per person to drop you at your hotel. Taxis (CH$28,000 to CH$40,000) will drive tourists to San Pedro de Atacama, but it's cheaper to arrange for a transfer ahead of time (CH$14,000 to CH$18,000); try **City Express** (☑ 099-816-2091) or **Transfer Lincancabur** (☑ 055-254-3426).

Car-rental agencies include **Hertz** (☑ 057-234-1380; Av Granaderos 1416) and **Avis** (☑ 055-256-3152; calama@avischile.cl; Aeropuerto El Loa); daily rates start at CH$26,500.

Fill up the tank in Calama, as the lone gas station in San Pedro charges a fortune. To visit the geysers at El Tatio, rent a 4WD or pickup truck; ordinary cars lack sufficient clearance for the area's rugged roads and river fords.

Chuquicamata

Slag heaps as big as mountains, a chasm deeper than the deepest lake in the USA, and trucks the size of houses: these are some of the mind-boggling dimensions that bring visitors to gawp into the mine of Chuquicamata (or just Chuqui). This awesome abyss, gouged from the desert earth 16km north of Calama, is one of the world's largest open-pit copper mines.

Chuqui was also, until quite recently, the world's largest single supplier of copper (a title just snatched by Mina Escondida, 170km southeast of Antofagasta), producing a startling 630,000 tonnes annually. It's largely thanks to Chuqui, then, that Chile is the world's greatest copper producer. In total, copper accounts for around one-third of Chilean exports. And with the price of copper shooting up in recent years (courtesy of huge demand in China and India) its importance to the Chilean economy is hard to overestimate.

The mine, which employs 20,000 workers, spews up a perpetual plume of dust visible for many miles in the cloudless desert, but then everything here dwarfs the human scale. The elliptical pit measures an incredible 8 million sq meters and has a depth of up to 1250m. Most of the 'tour' is spent simply gazing into its depths and clambering around an enormous mining truck with tires more than 3m high; information is minimal, although the bilingual guide answers questions.

Chuquicamata was once integrated with a well-ordered company town, but environmental problems and copper reserves beneath the town forced the entire population to relocate to Calama by 2007. The 'city of Chiquicamata' is not much more than a ghost town these days.

History

Prospectors first hit the jackpot at Chuquicamata in 1911. However, they were soon muscled out by the big boys, otherwise known as the US Anaconda Copper Mining Company, from Montana. In the blink of an eye, the company created a fully functioning mining town, with rudimentary housing, schools, cinemas, shops and a hospital, although labor unrest became rife and resentment toward the corporation snowballed. By the 1960s Chile's three largest mines (all run by Anaconda) accounted for more than 80% of Chile's copper production, 60% of total exports and 80% of tax revenues. Despite coughing up elevated taxes, Anaconda was a sitting duck for the champions of nationalization.

CHUQUI THROUGH THE EYES OF CHE

Over 50 years ago, when it was already a mine of monstrous proportions, Chuquicamata was visited by a youthful Ernesto 'Che' Guevara. The future revolutionary and his traveling buddy Alberto Granado were midway through their iconic trip across South America, immortalized in Che's *Motorcycle Diaries*.

An encounter with a communist during his journey to Chuqui is generally acknowledged as a turning point in Che's emergent politics. So it's especially interesting to read his subsequent memories of the mine itself (then in gringo hands). In one vivid paragraph, the wandering medical student writes of such mines: '...spiced as they would be with the inevitable human lives – the lives of the poor, unsung heroes of this battle, who die miserably in one of the thousand traps set by nature to defend its treasures, when all they want is to earn their daily bread.'

In a footnote to this much-analyzed encounter, the 'blond, efficient and arrogant managers' gruffly told the travelers that Chuquicamata 'isn't a tourist town.' Well, these days it receives around 40,000 visitors per year.

During the government of President Eduardo Frei Montalva in the late 1960s, Chile gained a majority shareholding in the Chilean assets of Anaconda and Kennecott. In 1971 Congress approved the full nationalization of the industry. After 1973 the military junta agreed to compensate companies for loss of assets, but retained ownership through the Corporación del Cobre de Chile (Codelco).

Tours

Codelco   GUIDED TOUR
(☑055-232-2122; visitas@codelco.cl; cnr Avs Granaderos & Central Sur, Calama; tour by donation; ☺bookings 9am-5pm Mon-Fri) Arrange visits through Codelco by phone or email, or through Calama's tourist office. Tours (minimum age eight) run on weekdays, in English and Spanish. Report to the Oficina on the corner of Avs Granaderos and Central Sur 15 minutes before your tour; bring identification.

The two-hour tour begins at 1pm. Wear sturdy footwear (no sandals), long pants and long sleeves.

Tours are limited to 40, but occasionally a second bus is added. Demand is high from January to March and in July and August, so book at least a week ahead.

❶ Getting There & Away

From Calama, Codelco has a free shuttle that picks people up at its Oficina. You must be there at 12:45pm. To get to the pickup point, take a *taxi colectivo* (CH\$600, 15 minutes) – look for 5, 65, 11 or 17 – from Latorre, or hop on the *micro* D (CH\$400).

Antofagasta

☑ 055 / POP 337,934

Chile's second-largest city is a rough-and-ready jumble of one-way streets, modern mall culture and work-wearied urbanites. As such, this sprawling port city tends not to tickle the fancy of passing travelers, who often choose to leapfrog over Antofagasta en route north to San Pedro de Atacama or south to Copiapó.

However, the city is not all high-rise concrete and gridlocked streets. The old-fashioned plaza is a pleasure to kick back in, and evidence of the golden nitrate era can be found in the wooden-fronted Victorian and Georgian buildings of the coastal Barrio Histórico. Ancient spindly *muelles* (piers) molder picturesquely along the grubby guano-stained port.

The port here handles most of the minerals from the Atacama, especially the copper from Chuquicamata, and is still a major import-export node for Bolivia, which lost the region to Chile during the War of the Pacific.

◎ Sights

Plaza Colón   PLAZA
The British community left a visible imprint on Antofagasta's beautiful 19th-century Plaza Colón, which sports rushing fountains amid its palms, mimosas and bougainvilleas. The cute Torre Reloj is a replica of London's Big Ben; its chimes even have a baby Big Ben ring to them, and tiled British and Chilean flags intertwine on its trunk.

Barrio Histórico AREA

British flavor prevails in the 19th-century Barrio Histórico, between the plaza and the old port, where handsome Victorian and Georgian buildings still stand. On Bolívar, the bottle-green-colored **train station** (1887) is the restored terminus of the Antofagasta–La Paz railway. It's closed to the public but you can see several old engines and British-style telephone boxes through the western railings.

Museo Regional MUSEUM

(Av Balmaceda & Bolívar; adult/child CH$600/300; ⏲9am-5pm Tue-Fri, 11am-2pm Sat & Sun) The former Aduana (customs house) now houses this two-floor museum, which contains well-presented displays on natural history, and prehistoric and cultural development. Artifacts include a deformed skull, early colonial tidbits and paraphernalia from the nitrate era, including toys fashioned from tin cans.

Resguardo Marítimo HISTORIC BUILDING

This handsome chocolate-colored building with wooden balustrades, built in 1910 as the coast guard, sits at the entrance to the decrepit **Muelle Salitrero** (Nitrate Pier), where locals defy danger signs and fish for crabs. A wrought-iron passageway links it to the former **Gobernación Marítima**.

Terminal Pesquero MARKET

A few blubbery male sea lions, snorting loudly and occasionally snapping at unwary pelicans, circle hopefully below Antofagasta's busy fish market, just north of the Port Authority.

Monumento Natural La Portada LOOKOUT

(⏲museum 10am-1pm & 2:30-5:30pm Tue-Sun) FREE While not in Antofagasta proper, but rather 25km north of the city, this enormous offshore arch – the centerpiece of a 31-hectare protected zone – is the most spectacular of the area's sights. Topped by marine sediments and supported by a sturdy volcanic base, the stack has been eroded into a natural arch by the stormy Pacific. It's situated on a short westbound lateral off the highway; there's a restaurant, a small Conaf-managed **museum** and cliff-top views over surrounding beaches. Take *micro* 129 from Antofagasta's Terminal Pesquero to the junction at La Portada, and then catch the connection (these run in the busy summer season only) or walk 3km west.

Sleeping

Antofagasta's lodging options are problematic. The budget hostels are no great shakes, many catering to visiting miners and to the surrounding red-light district that spreads around the city center. Midrange properties are mostly overpriced for what you get, and top-end options are mainly limited to chains. Note that weekdays tend to get busy with visiting miners; it's easier to nab a well-priced room on weekends.

Hotel San Marcos HOTEL $

(☎055-222-6303; www.hotelsanmarcos.cl; Latorre 2946; s/d CH$25,000/33,000; P wi-fi) A reasonable budget hotel on the edge of the city center, offering decent value for the price and very friendly service. The big breakfast takes a bit of the sting out of the inflated room price.

Hotel Costa Marfil HOTEL $

(☎055-228-3590; www.hotelcostamarfil.cl; Arturo Prat 950; s CH$28,000-33,000, d CH$35,000-38,500; P @ wi-fi) The blazing neon light might get to you, but the rooms in this large hotel block are acceptable. Don't go for the dark standard units that face the noisy inner hallway; upgrade to a bigger executive room, which comes with natural light.

Hotel Frontera HOTEL $

(☎055-228-1219; Bolívar 558; s/d CH$22,000/26,000, without bathroom CH$16,000/21,000; wi-fi) Behind the modern-looking front is a set of basic but decently clean rooms, each complete with a cable TV. No breakfast is included or available but at least there's wi-fi.

Hotel Paola HOTEL $$

(☎055-226-8989; www.hotelpaola.cl; Matta 2469; s/d CH$40,000/50,000; wi-fi) By far the most stylish choice in the center, the lovely Paola sports a white marble hallway, a contempo look, an inner patio on the 3rd floor and five floors of rooms featuring hardwood floors, fans, flat-screen TVs, fridges and ample closet space. Note that a single room is big enough to accommodate two, plus it runs great weekend discounts.

Hotel Ancla Inn HOTEL $$

(☎055-235-7400; www.anclainn.cl; Baquedano 516; s/d from CH$32,000/42,000; P wi-fi) Central location, friendly staff and well-equipped rooms make this a good choice, behind a funny chalet-like facade. The standard rooms are often booked up by miners Monday through Wednesday, when only executive units on the top three floors remain. These cost CH$60,000 but come with wi-fi, fridges and more space.

Hotel Rocomar
HOTEL $$

(☎ 055-226-1139; Baquedano 810; s/d CH$32,000/ 45,000; ☎) If you don't mind a bit of street noise, the bright, spacious rooms at this corner hotel are a good deal – decked out with modern fittings and set in a good downtown location.

Amaru Apart Hotel
APARTMENT $$

(☎ 055-254-2015; www.amaruaparthotel.cl; Av Argentina 2132; apt CH$54,000; ✳☎) Set uphill slightly out of the center, these super-modern apartments sleep two comfortably and three at a stretch. They've got small, functional kitchens, spacious modern bathrooms and comfy sitting areas. Snag one at the front and you'll be rewarded with sweeping views of the town and bay.

Hotel Antofagasta
HOTEL $$$

(☎ 055-222-8811; www.hotelantofagasta.cl; Balmaceda 2575; d CH$120,000-211,000; ☎@☎☎) Part of the Panamericana Hoteles chain, this five-star mammoth in the old harbor has great ocean views from the lobby, well-appointed rooms (those with ocean vistas are pricier) and all the luxe trimmings. It gets packed on weekdays but often runs great weekend promotions.

✗ Eating & Drinking

Perched on the north end of the old port, **Terminal Pesquero** is host to over 20 stalls that peddle tasty fresh shellfish; get there by early afternoon, before all the fish are sold. More fish, as well as meat, vegetables and fruity fare, is available at the attractive old **Mercado Central** (JS Ossa; set meals around CH$5000; ☺8am-6pm), which is located between Maipú and Uribe.

Bongo
DINER $

(Baquedano 743; set menu from CH$3000, mains CH$2900-5100; ☺9am-11pm Mon-Sat) Buzzy eatery with thick-cushioned booths, a tidy mezzanine above and a good 'n' greasy menu for those times when only a draft beer and burger will do. Place your order at the counter and pay before you sit down.

Don Pollo
FAST FOOD $

(JS Ossa 2594; chicken from CH$2000; ☺noon-1am) Cheap, cheerful and usually crowded, Don Pollo has plastic tables huddled around

a grass-hut patio. Locals come in droves for the succulent chicken.

★ Cafe del Sol
CHILEAN $$

(www.cafedelsolchile.com; Esmeralda 2013; set lunch CH$3500, mains CH$7000-8000; ☺closed Sun) On weekend nights, this ramshackle corner resto-bar comes alive with live Andean music and dancing (CH$3000 cover after 11pm). Other nights, it serves a good range of mains in the cozy wooden interior with dim lighting. Plus it does a good set lunch for CH$3500.

Cusco
PERUVIAN $$

(Matta 2660; mains CH$7000-12,000; ☺12:30-11pm) Nominally a Peruvian restaurant (evidenced mostly by the range of ceviches on offer), this is a good downtown spot, offering hearty meat and pasta dishes in a relaxed, slightly upmarket environment.

El Arriero
STEAKHOUSE $$

(Condell 2644; mains CH$4500-13,500; ☺noon-3:30pm & 8-11:30pm Mon-Sat) Meat is the specialty at this rustic dining room decked out with arches, dried hanging hams and a fountain in the middle. Full of old-fashioned charm, it serves huge portions of mainly meaty dishes. The *parrillada* for two (CH$17,000) is a feast.

ℹ Information

Numerous ATMs are located downtown. Internet cafes around the center offer access for around CH$450 per hour.

Conaf (☎055-238-3320; Av Argentina 2510; ☺8:30am-1:30pm & 3-5:30pm Mon-Thu, 8:30am-1:30pm & 3-4:15pm Fri) For information on the region's natural attractions.

Hospital Regional (☎055-265-6729; Av Argentina 1962) Medical services.

Sernatur (☎055-245-1818; Arturo Prat 384; ☺8:30am-7pm Mon-Fri, 10am-2pm Sat Jan-Mar, 8:30am-5:30pm Mon-Fri Apr-Dec) The city tourist office, conveniently located by the plaza, gives out a generous amount of brochures.

ℹ Getting There & Away

AIR

LAN (☎600-526-2000; www.lanchile.com; Arturo Prat 445; ☺9am-6:30pm Mon-Fri, 10am-1pm Sat) has several daily flights to Santiago (CH$233,800, two hours), as well as direct daily flights to Iquique (CH$19,300, one hour) and La Serena (CH$143,300, 1½ hours).

Sky (☑ 600-600-2828; www.skyairline.cl; General Velasquez 890, Local 3) also flies to Iquique (CH$30,500, Thursdays only), Arica (CH$64,000, one daily via Iquique), Copiapó (CH$94,000, one daily via La Serena) and Santiago (CH$101,700, six daily), with connections to the south.

BUS

The **Terminal de Buses Cardenal Carlos Oviedo** (☑ 055-248-4502; Av Pedro Aguirre Cerda 5750) serves most inter-city destinations. A few bus companies still operate also out of their own terminals near downtown, mainly along Latorre. Locally based companies use the **Terminal de Buses Evaristo Montt** (Riquelme 513), also known as the Terminal de Buses Rurales.

Nearly all northbound services now use coastal Ruta 1, via Tocopilla, en route to Iquique and Arica.

DESTINATION	COST (CH$)	DURATION (HR)
Arica	10,900	9
Calama	4000	3
Copiapó	7100	9
Iquique	7000	6
La Serena	11,200	12
Santiago	22,000	18

Condor/Flota Barrios (☑ 055-226-2899; www.flotabarrios.cl; Av Pedro Aguirre Cerda 5750)
Tur Bus (☑ 055-222-0240; www.turbus.cl; Bolívar 468)

❶ Getting Around

TO/FROM THE AIRPORT

Antofagasta's Aeropuerto Cerro Moreno is 25km north of the city. Private taxis cost CH$15,000; try calling **Gran Via** (☑ 055-224-0505).

CAR

Avis (☑ 055-256-3140; www.avis.cl; Baquedano 364; ⊗ 8:30am-6:30pm Mon-Sat)
First (☑ 055-222-5777; www.firstrentacar.cl; Bolívar 623)

South of Antofagasta

The Panamericana south of Antofagasta continues its trip through the dry Atacama Desert, where water, people and tourist attractions are scarce.

Mano del Desierto

A towering granite hand, its oddly tapering fingers outstretched in a mock salute, breaks through the desert crust about 45km south of the junction of the Panamericana and Ruta 28. This curious *mano del desierto* was built in 1992 by sculptor Mario Irarrázaval. Bus travelers should look to the west side of the highway.

Cerro Paranal Observatory

In the world of high-powered telescopes, where rival institutes jostle to claim the 'biggest,' 'most powerful' or 'most technologically advanced' specimens, **Cerro Paranal Observatory** (Observatorio Cerro Paranal; ☑055-271-6931; www.eso.org) is right up there with the big boys. This groundbreaking observatory has a Very Large Telescope (VLT) consisting of an array of four 8.2m telescopes – for a time at least, the most powerful optical array in the world.

The Cerro Paranal Observatory is run by the European Southern Observatory (ESO), and is so futuristic-looking that portions of the James Bond flick, *Quantum of Solace*, were filmed here. There's a hotel for scientists on site, which looks like it is built underground; you'll enter the foliage-filled lobby as part of the tour. The observatory complex is situated on Cerro Paranal at 2664m above sea level, 120km south of Antofagasta; a lateral leaves the Panamericana just north of the Mano del Desierto (assuming you're heading south). The drive from Antofagasta takes about two hours.

The fascinating free visits are allowed on Saturdays, at 10am and 2pm. You must show up half an hour early; tours last two hours. You'll need to schedule months in advance (reservations are only accepted through the website), and you'll also need your own vehicle to get there. Check the observatory's website for details and updates.

Iquique

☑ 057 / POP 180,601

Barefoot surfers, paragliding pros, casino snobs and frenzied merchants all cross paths in the rather disarming city of Iquique. Located in a golden crescent of coastline, this city is counted among Chile's premier beach resorts, with a glitzy casino, beachfront boardwalk and more activities (from paragliding to sandboarding) than any sane person can take on in a week. The big draw here is the swaths of pitch-perfect beach, which offer some of the best surfing around.

HALFWAY STOPS ALONG THE COAST

The distances between destinations in Norte Grande can be overwhelming and the drives dusty and boring. So if you're making your way up or down by car and need to break up the journey, here are two pit stops that will come in handy for refueling your car, filling your stomach and getting some rest.

Halfway between Antofagasta and Iquique, **Tocopilla** is an ugly port for the remaining nitrate *oficinas* of Pedro de Valdivia and María Elena, which offers a chance to break the long journey along a desolate stretch of coast. It sits off Ruta 1, the paved highway between Iquique and Tocopilla, which has largely superseded the older Panamericana for southbound travelers. The town has a handful of lodging options, although they are often booked up by miners; the best value is **Hotel Galvarino** (☎ 055-281-3585; www.hotelgalvarino.cl; 21 de Mayo 2182; s/d CH$30,000/34,000; ⓟ 🛜) with pleasant rooms on the northern end of the town's main drag. For a filling good-quality meal, try **El Trebol** (Bolívar 1345; mains around CH$5000; ⏰ 9am-10pm Mon-Sat), which serves up simple hearty meals in two cheerful dining rooms just up the main strip.

The only settlement of any size on the long thirsty haul from Chañaral to Antofagasta, the fishing port of **Taltal** is a surprisingly neat little town. For such a small place, it has a palpable pride in its heritage with elegantly manicured plazas and lovely period architecture from its nitrate export heyday when its population was 20,000. Still, there isn't much to see or do here, except have a stroll, a meal and a good night's sleep. You can fill up at **Club Social Taltal** (Torreblanca 162; mains CH$6500-10,000; ⏰ noon-11:30pm Mon-Sat), an old-school dining room just one block west of the plaza. Around since 1893, it's got high ceilings, grumpy service and good seafood. The town's most adorable place to stay is **Hotel Mi Tampi** (☎ 055-261-3605; www.hotelmitampi.cl; O'Higgins 138; s/d CH$24,000/29,000; ⓟ 🛜), where spacious rooms with firm beds and TVs come around a cheerful leafy patio.

Refurbished Georgian-style architecture from the 19th-century mining boom is well preserved, and the Baquedano pedestrian strip sports charming wooden sidewalks. Iquique's main claim, however, is its duty-free status, with a chaotic duty-free shopping zone (zona franca).

The city, 1853km north of Santiago and 315km south of Arica, is squeezed between the ocean and the desolate brown coastal range rising abruptly some 600m behind it.

History

The lifeless pampas around Iquique is peppered with the geoglyphs of ancient indigenous groups, and the shelf where the city now lies was frequented by the coastal Chango peoples. However, the Iquique area was first put on the map during the colonial era, when the Huantajaya silver mine was discovered.

During the 19th century, narrow-gauge railways shipped minerals and nitrates through Iquique. Mining barons built opulent mansions, piped in water from the distant cordillera and imported topsoil for lavish gardens. Downtown Iquique reflects this 19th-century nitrate boom, and the cor-roding shells of nearby ghost towns such as Humberstone and Santa Laura whisper of the source of this wealth.

After the nitrate bust, Iquique reinvented itself, primarily as a fishing port, shipping more fish meal than any other port in the world. However, it was the establishment of the zona franca in 1975 that made this one of Chile's most prosperous cities.

⊙ Sights

The good ol' nitrate days are evident throughout Iquique's center, focused on Plaza Prat and Av Baquedano, an attractive pedestrian mall that lies just to the south lined with Georgian-style balustraded buildings dating from 1880 to 1930.

Museo Corbeta Esmeralda   MUSEUM
(www.museoesmeralda.cl; Paseo Almirante Lynch; admission CH$3000; ⏰10am-1pm & 2-6pm Tue-Sun) This replica of sunken *Esmeralda*, a plucky little Chilean corvette that challenged ironclad Peruvian warships in the War of the Pacific, is Iquique's new pride and glory. The original ship was captained by Arturo Prat (1848–79), whose name now graces a hundred street maps, plazas and

Iquique

Iquique

Sights

1	Casino Español	B3
2	Centro Cultural Palacio Astoreca	B4
3	Museo Corbeta Esmeralda	B1
4	Museo Naval	B2
5	Museo Regional	B4
6	Plaza Prat	B3
7	Torre Reloj	B3

Activities, Courses & Tours

8	Academia de Idiomas del Norte	C5
9	Boat Rides	B2
10	Magical Tour Chile	B4
11	OC Travel	B2
12	Puro Vuelo	B5
13	Show Travel	B4
14	Vertical	C6

Sleeping

15	Casa Baquedano	B5
16	Hostal Catedral	B2
17	Hotel de La Plaza	B4
18	Hotel Esmeralda	B5
19	Hotel Pacifico Norte	C5
20	Hotel Velero	C3
21	Jham Hotel	B3
22	La Casona 1920	C6
23	Sunfish Hotel	C7

Eating

24	Antojos	C6
25	Cioccolata	B2
26	Club Croata	B3
27	El Tercer Ojito	B5
28	El Wagón	A3
29	La Mulata	C7
30	M.Koo	C3

Drinking & Nightlife

31	Lobby Resto Bar	B3
32	Mi Otra Casa	B5

institutions. Guided tours (reserve ahead for a tour in English) take you inside the staff quarters, past the orange-lit engine, and onto the ship's deck.

Book ahead or come on Sunday when it is first-come, first-served.

Plaza Prat PLAZA

The city's 19th-century swagger is hard to miss on Iquique's central square. Pride of place goes to the **Torre Reloj** (1877) clock tower, seemingly baked and sugar-frosted rather than built. Jumping fountains line the walkway south to the marble-stepped **Teatro Municipal**, a neoclassical building that has been hosting opera and theater since 1890. A handsomely restored **tram** sits outside and occasionally jerks its way down Av Baquedano in the high season.

Centro Cultural Palacio Astoreca HISTORIC BUILDING

(O'Higgins 350; 10am-6pm Tue-Sat, 11am-2pm Sun) FREE Originally built for a nitrate tycoon, this 1904 Georgian-style mansion is now a cultural center, which exhibits contemporary work produced by local artists. It has a fantastic interior of opulent rooms with elaborate woodwork and high ceilings, massive chandeliers, a gigantic billiard table and balconies.

Casino Español HISTORIC BUILDING

(Plaza Prat; 9am-9pm Mon-Sat) The prize for the showiest building in Iquique goes to this Moorish-style place from 1904, on the plaza's northeast corner. The gaudily tiled creation is now a club and restaurant, but staff are surprisingly tolerant of travelers taking a quick whirl around the fanciful interior, which features murals and paintings of Don Quixote.

Museo Regional MUSEUM

(Baquedano 951; admission CH$2000; 9am-5:30pm Tue-Fri, 9:30am-6pm Sat winter, plus 10am-2pm Sun summer) Iquique's former courthouse now hosts the catch-all regional museum, which earnestly recreates a traditional adobe altiplano village and also exhibits masked Chinchorro mummies and elongated skulls. Photographs explore Iquique's urban beginnings, and a fascinating display dissects the nitrate industry.

Museo Naval MUSEUM

(Esmeralda 250; 10am-1pm & 3-6pm Tue-Sat, 9:30am-6pm Sun) FREE Take in the artifacts salvaged from the sunken *Esmeralda* at this small museum inside the haughty colonial-style customs house, built in 1871 when Iquique was still Peruvian territory. Peru incarcerated prisoners here during the War of the Pacific, and the building would later see battle in the Chilean civil war of 1891.

Activities

Beaches

Iquique's main beaches are south of downtown, off which **Playa Cavancha**, from the corner of Avs Arturo Prat and Amunátegui, is the most popular. It's pleasant for swimming but sometimes gets crowded. There are also some decent surf breaks along its rocky northern parts, and a playground for children. In summer, the kiosk run by the municipal tourist office dishes out useful info.

Further south, crashing waves and rip currents at scenic **Playa Brava** make it dangerous for swimming, but there's plenty of space to sunbathe. Toward the hills, look for the massive dunes of Cerro Dragón, which looks like a set for a science-fiction movie.

Taxis colectivos (shared taxis) run to Playa Brava from downtown – look for the destination on the sign atop the cab. There are scores of sandy beaches further south, but you'll need to rent a car or bike, or take a taxi.

Surfing

An army of wetsuited warriors is always to be found dripping its way along Iquique's coastal road. Surfing and body-boarding are best in winter, when swells come from the north, but they're possible year-round. There's less competition for early-morning breaks at Playa Cavancha. **Playa Huaiquique**, on the southern outskirts of town, is also an exhilarating choice but the sea is warmer further north near Arica. One of Chile's biggest surf events takes place in Iquique on May 21, a championship called **Héroes de Mayo**.

Vertical   SURFING
(☑057-237-6031; www.verticalst.cl; Av Arturo Prat 580) This is Iquique's surfer central, which sells and rents equipment. Wetsuit and board will set you back CH$12,000 for two hours; one or the other only costs CH$7500. Private lessons start at CH$24,000 for 1½ hours, and it runs surf trips outside the city and **sand-boarding** trips to Cerro Dragón, which cost CH$25,000 for three hours.

Paragliding

Go jump off a cliff...and fly! That's the message you'll get from Iquique's many *parapente* (paragliding) fanatics. The city's unique geography, with its steep coastal escarpment, rising air currents and the soft, extensive dunes of Cerro Dragón, makes it one of the best places for paragliding in South America. It's theoretically possible to glide all the way to Tocopilla, 240km south – but that's not for novices. Bring along a windbreaker, sunblock and guts.

Altazor   ADVENTURE SPORTS
(☑057-238-0110; www.altazor.cl; Vía 6, Manzana A, Sitio 3, Flight Park, Bajo Molle) Located 500m south of Universidad del Mar (south of Iquique's center), Altazor offers paragliding courses (CH$42,500 per day, including equipment and transportation). An introductory tandem flight costs CH$40,000; two-week courses are also available, as is accommodations at its cozy **hostel**. Experienced paragliders can rent equipment or have their own repaired. Owners Philip and Marlene speak German, English, Portuguese and French.

Puro Vuelo   ADVENTURE SPORTS
(☑057-231-1127; www.purovuelo.cl; Baquedano 1440) Another well-run outfit that specializes in paragliding, it charges CH$40,000 for a tandem flight, with photos included. As with most paragliding jaunts in Iquique, this includes pickup at your hotel, brief instruction and about 20 minutes of flying time. Prices drop by about 10% in low season, between April and November.

Boat Rides

Boat Rides   BOATING
(adult/child CH$3000/2000, minimum 7 passengers; ☉10am-4pm) For nautical adventures, try the hour-long boat tours from Iquique's 1901 passenger pier just west of the Aduana, which pass by the commemorative buoy marking the spot where the *Esmeralda* sank and also approach a colony of sea lions.

Courses

Academia de Idiomas del Norte   LANGUAGE COURSE
(☑057-241-1827; www.languages.cl; Ramírez 1345) The Swiss-run Academia de Idiomas del Norte provides Spanish-language instruction. Classes are small (one to four students) and cost CH$305,000 to CH$383,600 per week, depending on intensity.

Tours

Public transportation to many surrounding attractions is tricky, so tours are worth considering. In summer, agencies set up streetside tables on Prat and along Baquedano, hawking their most popular offerings. Among these is a day trip, which runs daily in summer season, to the oasis towns of Pica, La Tirana and Matilla, taking in the nitrate ruins at Humberstone and Santa Laura en route (around CH$25,000). Other options, although running less regularly, include a history-themed day trip to the Gigante de Atacama and Pisagua (from CH$27,000) and four-hour city tours (from CH$12,000).

From March onwards, as the weather in the altiplano improves, more adventurous off-road tours become available, such as to stunning multicolored lagoons near Camiña (CH$85,000 per day, CH$120,000 for a two-day jaunt) and to Parque Nacional Volcán Isluga (CH$45,000). Note that these often require a five-person minimum.

If you have more time and cash, it's worth booking a three-day jaunt into the altiplano that takes in Isluga, Salar de Surire, Las Vicuñas and Lauca, finishing in Arica or returning late to Iquique.

OC Travel GUIDED TOUR
(☑ 057-257-3260; www.octravel.cl; Luis Uribe 445, Oficina 2H) Offers most of the major tours, including the popular day trip to Pica, which takes in Humberstone and Santa Laura. Also offers diving excursions (CH$38,000) at Playa Blanca and biking jaunts that take in the city and the beaches ($38,000 for six hours).

Magical Tour Chile GUIDED TOUR
(☑ 057-221-7290; www.magicaltour.cl; Baquedano 770; per person Ruta del Sol CH$23,000, Aventura Isluga CH$50,000; ⊘10:30am to 8pm) Sometimes runs creepy nocturnal tours of the *salitreras,* departing at 8pm and getting you back into town at around 2:30am. There's a 10-person minimum.

Llamatrekking CULTURAL TOUR
(☑cell 7898-6504; www.llamatrekking.cl) Soft treks to surrounding attractions focused on Aymara traditions of the altiplano, ranging from day trips to nearby villages to seven-day llama caravans.

Show Travel ADVENTURE TOUR
(☑ 057-234-2306; www.showtravel.cl; Baquedano 964) In addition to the usual roster of tours, this is a good bet for active trips to places off the beaten track, including the El Huarango eco-camp near La Tirana.

🛏 Sleeping

Taxi drivers earn commission from some *residenciales* (budget accommodations) and hotels; be firm in your decision or consider walking. The beachfront has a Holiday Inn Express and a Radisson, if you're craving a little dependable chain action.

La Casona 1920 HOSTEL $
(☑ 057-241-3000; www.casonahostel.com; Barros Arana 1585; dm CH$9000, s/d without bathroom CH$14,000/22,000; @🖥) Iquique's place to be, this cool and colorful hostel inside an old *casona* has four- to nine-bed dorms and a few doubles, some with balconies over the street, others overlooking the back patio. There's a shared kitchen, a pool table, lockers, multilingual staff, weekly sushi parties with live DJs, poker nights, salsa classes and movie nights.

Hotel Velero HOTEL $
(☑ 057-234-8067; www.hotelvelero.cl; Latorre 596; s/d CH$20,000/30,000, without bathroom CH$14,000/22,000) A very good looking hotel a short walk from the plaza. It doesn't quite live up to its 'boutique' claim, but rooms are spacious with modern fittings and there's a tranquil atmosphere throughout. Book ahead.

Hotel de La Plaza HOTEL $
(☑057-241-9339; Baquedano 1025; s/d CH$20,000/33,000; 🖥) One of the best deals in its category, this Georgian-style building fronts onto the pedestrian strip. There is a welcoming lobby with a big skylight and comfortable, medium-sized rooms arranged around a patio.

Hostal Catedral HOSTEL $
(☑057-242-6372; Obispo Labbé 253; s/d CH$18,000/30,000, without bathroom per person CH$12,500; 🖥) Homey place opposite the city's main church, handy for early or late Tur Bus connections. Has a range of rooms – some quite stuffy but others spacious. Have a look at a few if you can.

★ Casa Baquedano HOTEL $$
(☑ 057-234-7577; Baquedano 1470; s/d CH$35,000/40,000; 🖥) Right at the foot of the pedestrain mall, this older building has fantastically spacious rooms featuring king-sized beds, minifridges and modern bathrooms. Those on the ground floor also feature way-high ceilings. A leafy rear patio rounds out the picture.

Hotel Esmeralda HOTEL $$
(☑057-221-6996; www.esmeraldahotel.cl; Labbé 1386; s/d CH$42,000/51,000; 🖥) Spacious rooms and clean lines characterize this charming new hotel a few blocks from Paya Gaviota. It falls a bit short of its 'boutique' claim, but is a good deal for the price nonetheless.

Hotel Pacifico Norte HOTEL $$
(☑ 057-242-9396; hotelpacificonorte@chileagenda.cl; Ramirez 1941; s/d CH$30,000/40,000; ☜) Cozy, slightly cramped rooms in a pleasing older-style building. Get one at the front for their sweet little wooden balconies overlooking the street.

Jham Hotel HOTEL $$
(☑ 057-254-9134; www.hoteljham.cl; Latorre 426; s/d CH$42,000/51,000; P ☜) It is admittedly kitschy, with its dark-pink wall paint, but this well-appointed business hotel features spacious, bright and super-clean rooms (a few with Jacuzzis) and a small leafy patio in the back. It has another building across the street, if all is booked.

Sunfish Hotel HOTEL $$$
(☑ 057-254-1000; www.sunfish.cl; Amunátegui 1990; s/d CH$85,000/90,000; P ✳ @ ☜ ☵) This luxe option in a bright-blue high-rise just behind Playa Cavancha has a full spectrum of four-star facilities, including a business center, a sushi restaurant and a rooftop pool. Most rooms come with balconies. For best vistas, get one on the top two floors.

✖ Eating

For the cheapest and fastest place to fill out, head to Mercado Centenario, a boxy market on Barros Arana. Note that many restaurants close on Sundays.

Club Croata CHILEAN $
(Plaza Prat 310; set lunch CH$4500; ☺10am-6pm Mon-Sat; ☜) Plaza-side restaurant with arched windows, Croatian coats of arms and a clutch of tables outside. It has the best fixed-price lunch on the square – you get three courses plus a drink.

Cioccolata CAFE $
(Pinto 487; snacks CH$2000-4500; ☺8am-10pm Mon-Sat; ☜) Proof positive that Chileans do enjoy a decent espresso, this classy coffee shop is usually crammed with people. It offers filling breakfasts and lunches, plus sandwiches, scrumptious cakes and waffles.

M.Koo SWEETS $
(Latorre 600; snacks from CH$700; ☺8am-8pm Mon-Sat) Colorful corner shop famous for its crumbly *chumbeques* (sweet regional biscuits), the recipe for which is guarded zealously. It also sells snacks such as *humitas* (corn tamales) and empanadas.

Marrasquino ICE CREAM $
(Prat 3082; cones from CH$1700; ☺8am-9pm) If you're down south around Playa Brava, be sure to stop in at this little ice-cream store, which reputedly serves up the best scoops in town. The ocean views from the front deck aren't bad, either.

★ El Wagón CHILEAN $$
(Thompson 85; mains CH$8500-10,000; ☺noon-3pm & 7pm-midnight Mon-Sat) Almost single-handedly taking on the task of preserving the region's culinary traditions, this rustically decked-out dining hall serves up a fantastic collection of seafood plates, with inspiration for recipes coming from everywhere from grandma's classics to port workers and miners' staples. Pricey, but worth it.

La Mulata FUSION $$
(Prat 902; mains CH$8000-11,000; ☺12:30-4pm & 7:30-midnight Mon-Sat, 12:30-5pm Sun; ☜) Some of the most interesting dishes in town can be found on the menu of this Peruvian-Japanese restaurant. Service is snappy but personable, portions are well-sized without being over the top and there's a fine view of Playa Cavancha, too.

El Tercer Ojito INTERNATIONAL $$
(www.eltercerojito.cl; Lynch 1420; set weekday lunch CH$4500, mains CH$7500-9000; ☺noon-3pm Tue-Sun, 7-11:30pm Tue-Sat; ☜ ☑) Recognizable by the huge lump of quartz outside, this laid-back restaurant serves great vegetarian and carnivore-friendly dishes. Its globally inspired repertoire includes Peruvian dishes, Thai curries and occasional sushi. A pleasant bamboo-covered patio sports cacti and murals.

Antojos INTERNATIONAL $$
(Libertad 815; mains CH$7000-9500; ☺12:30pm-midnight Tue-Sat, to 5pm Sun & Mon) While there's a (limited) indoor seating, the place to be here is out in the shady garden, munching down on huge fresh salads, healthy juices and a selection of innovative seafood, meat and chicken dishes.

♼ Drinking & Nightlife

Iquique has a fun-filled nightlife, with a few boho resto-bars in the center and clubs and pubs lining the seafront south of town.

Lobby Resto Bar BAR
(Gorostiaga 142; ☺from 8pm Tue-Sat) Sweet resto-bar with a boho vibe, Lobby has four small rooms and a loungey back patio. Come

for great cocktails – try the *raspirinha,* with raspberry vodka and berries – the sushi bar, DJ-spun tunes on weekends, great-for-sharing *tablas* and happy hour nightly.

Mi Otra Casa   BAR
(Baquedano 1334; ☺3pm-2am Tue-Sat) Laid-back artsy bar at the far end of Baquedano, with an interior full of mismatched objects and a range of different events, from poetry readings to live music.

🛍 Shopping

Zona Franca   MALL
(Zofri; Av Salitrera Victoria; ☺11am-9pm Mon-Sat) Created in 1975, Iquique's zona franca is a massive monument to uncontrolled consumption – reputedly South America's largest. The entire region of Tarapacá is a duty-free zone, but its nucleus is this shopping center, housing over 400 stores selling imported electronics, clothing, automobiles and almost anything else.

If you want to shop, take any northbound *colectivo* from downtown. Don't walk – it's surrounded by some of the worst neighborhoods in town.

ℹ Information

There are many ATMs downtown and at the zona franca. Several *cambios* exchange foreign currency and traveler's checks.

Iquique's city center is jam-packed with internet cafes, which charge around CH$400 per hour.

Hospital Regional Dr Juan Noé (☎057-239-5555; Av Héroes de la Concepción 502) Ten blocks east of Plaza Condell.

Municipal Tourist Info Kiosks (☺10am-2pm & 3-7pm summer only) Superfriendly and knowledgeable staff dish out bilingual info and brochures at the two seasonal kiosks, one by the Museo Corbeta Esmeralda and another on Playa Cavancha.

Post Office (Bolívar 458)

Sernatur (☎057-241-9241; www.sernatur.cl; Pinto 436; ☺9am-8pm Mon-Sat & 10am-2pm Sun in summer, 9am-6pm Mon-Fri rest of year) This office has tourist information, free city maps and brochures.

ℹ Getting There & Away

AIR
The local airport, **Aeropuerto Diego Aracena** (☎057-242-6530; www.aeropuertodiegoaracena.cl), is located 41km south of downtown via Ruta 1.

LAN (☎600-526-2000; www.lan.cl; Pinto 699; ☺8:45am-2pm & 4-6;30pm Mon-Fri, 9:30am-1pm Sat) flies daily to Arica (CH$35,700, 50 minutes), Antofagasta (CH$19,500, 50 minutes) and Santiago (CH$233,000, 2½ hours). It also has four weekly flights to La Paz, Bolivia (around CH$42,600, 1½ hours). Prices are cheaper the further ahead you book.

Sky (☎600-600-2828; www.skyairline.cl; Tarapacá 530) also goes to Arica (CH$23,000, two daily), Antofagasta (CH$30,500, two daily), Santiago (CH$99,700, four daily) and other destinations in the south of Chile.

BUS
The main bus station, **Terminal Rodoviario** (☎057-242-7100; Lynch), is at the north end of Patricio Lynch. Most major bus companies, as well as a few local ones, also have offices clustered around the Mercado Centenario, mainly along Barros Arana. Services north and south are frequent, but most southbound services use Ruta 1, the coastal highway to Tocopilla (for connections to Calama) and Antofagasta (for Panamericana connections to Copiapó, La Serena and Santiago).

Several major bus companies travel north to Arica and south as far as Santiago:

Sample fares are as follows:

DESTINATION	COST (CH$)	DURATION (HR)
Antofagasta	16,000	6
Arica	7000	4
Calama	10,000	6
Copiapó	30,000	14
La Serena	35,000	18
Santiago	45,000	24

To get to Pica, try one of the agencies on Barros Arana, between Zegers and Latorre. **Chacón** (Barros Arana 957) has several departures daily to Pica (about CH$3000) as does **Agencia Barreda** (☎057-241-1425; Barros Arana 965) next door, which also goes to La Tirana (CH$2500) and Humberstone (CH$2500). **Santa Angela** (☎057-242-3751; Barros Arana 971) also travels to Pica for CH$2500.

Several bus companies travel to Bolivian destinations including La Paz, Cochabamba and Oruro. They're all clustered on one block of Esmeralda, between Amunategui and Martinez. It's not a great neighborhood – take a taxi for early or late departures.

For La Paz, Bolivia, **Busfer** (☎057-242-0632; Esmeralda 951) has 2pm departures daily (CH$7000, 17 hours) and **Lujan** (☎326-955; Esmeralda 999) has two daily departures (11am and 8:30pm) from Monday to Friday (CH$7000, 12 hours).

WORTH A TRIP

BEAT THE HEAT IN PICA

The friendly and laid-back desert oasis of Pica (population 4013) appears as a painter's splotch of green on a lifeless brown canvas. It boasts lush fruit groves and is justly famous for its limes, a key ingredient in any decent pisco sour. Visitors come here to cool off in the attractive but overcrowded freshwater pool and to slurp on the plethora of fresh fruit drinks.

Pica's main attraction is **Cocha Resbaladero** (admission CH$2000; ⊘9am-8pm; 🖀) at the upper end of General Ibáñez. Encircled by cool rock, hanging vegetation and a watery cave, it makes a terrific spot to beat the desert heat but gets crowded with vacationing families and screaming children in summer months.

We recommend visiting Pica on a day trip from Iquique but should you want to stay, a couple of lodging and eating options (all located on the road between the plaza and the resbaldero) are available.

Pica is served by buses and tours operating from Iquique.

The easiest way to get to Peru is by going first to Arica, then hooking up with an international bus there.

Many national bus companies have offices in the Mercado Centenario area – you can reserve tickets here (saving a trek out to the bus terminal), but buses depart from the terminal.

Expreso Norte (🖀057-257-3693; www.expresonorte.cl; Barros Arana 881)

Pullman (🖀057-242-9852; www.pullman.cl)

Ramos Cholele (🖀057-247-1628; www.ramoscholele.cl; Barros Arana 851)

Tur Bus (🖀057-242-0634; www.turbus.cl; Mercado Centenario)

❶ Getting Around

Colectivos are the easiest way to get around town. Destinations are clearly marked on an illuminated sign on top of the cab.

TO/FROM THE AIRPORT

Minibus transfer from Aeropuerto Diego Aracena to your hotel costs CH$6000; there are a few stands at the airport. Alternatively, shared taxis charge CH$7500 per person; private cabs cost CH$16,000. Try **Taxis Aeropuerto** (🖀057-241-3368; cnr Gorostiaga & Baquedano) just off the plaza.

BICYCLE

Magical Tour (p173) rents bikes for CH$5000 per day.

CAR

Cars cost from CH$25,000 per day. Local agencies often require an international driver's license. The following rental vehicles also have stands at the airport with longer weekend hours:

Alamo (🖀057-254-4889; O'Higgins 1590; ⊘8:30am-6:30pm Mon-Fri, 9am-1:30pm Sat)

Econorent Car Rental (🖀057-242-3723; Hernán Fuenzalida 1058; ⊘9am-7pm Mon-Fri, 9am-2pm Sat)

Procar (🖀057-247-0668; Serrano 796; ⊘8am-6pm Mon-Fri, to 2pm Sat)

East of Iquique
🖀057

Ghost towns punctuate the desert as you travel inland from Iquique; they're eerie remnants of once-flourishing mining colonies that gathered the Atacama's white gold – nitrate. Along the way you'll also pass pre-Hispanic geoglyphs, recalling the presence of humans centuries before. Further inland the barren landscape yields up several picturesque hot-spring villages, while the high altiplano is home to some knockout scenery and a unique pastoral culture.

Humberstone & Santa Laura

The influence and wealth of the nitrate boom whisper through the deserted ghost town of **Humberstone** (www.museodelsalitre.cl; adult/child CH$2000/500; ⊘9am-7pm). Established in 1872 as La Palma, this mining town once fizzed with an energy, culture and ingenuity that peaked in the 1940s. However, the development of synthetic nitrates forced the closure of the *oficina* by 1960; 3000 workers lost their jobs and the town dwindled to a forlorn shell of itself.

The grand theater (rumored to be haunted, like a lot of the town's other buildings) that once presented international starlets; the swimming pool made of cast iron scavenged from a shipwreck; the ballroom, where scores of young *pampinos* (those living or working in desert nitrate-mining towns) first caught the eye of their sweethearts; schools; tennis and basketball courts; a busy market; and a hotel frequented by industry big-shots: all now lie quiet and emptied of life.

Some buildings are restored, but others are crumbling; take care when exploring interiors. At the west end of town, the electrical power plant still stands, along with the remains of the narrow-gauge railway to the older Oficina Santa Laura.

Although designated a historical monument in 1970, Humberstone fell prey to vandalism and unauthorized salvage. However, the site's fortunes were boosted in 2002, when it was acquired by a nonprofit association of *pampinos* (Corporación Museo del Salitre) that set about patching up the decrepit structures. In July 2005 the site was designated a Unesco World Heritage site. Admission includes a free leaflet in English or Spanish.

The skeletal remains of **Oficina Santa Laura** `FREE`, 2km away, are a half-hour walk southwest across the highway. Even more atmospheric than Humberstone, it's worth the walk so that you can snoop around the haunting small museum with creaky floors and a series of rooms with old machinery, dusty dresses and heaps of old shoes. Like in Humberstone, ghost stories abound; visitors have heard children's crying and felt strange presences following them around.

❶ Getting There & Away

Humberstone is an easy day trip from Iquique. It sits less than 1km off the Panamericana, about 45km due east of the city. Any eastbound bus from Iquique will drop you off there, and it is easy to catch a return bus (CH$2000, 40 minutes). You can also catch any *colectivo* that goes to Pozo Almonte from the Iquique's Mercado Central area for CH$2000 to CH$2300; try **Taxi Pampa y Mar** (☏ 057-232-9832; cnr Barros Arana & Sargento Aldea) or **Taxi Chubasco** (☏ 057-275-1113; cnr Amunátegui & Sargento Aldea). Tours are available from Iquique.

Wear closed shoes and take food, sunblock, water and a camera, since it's easy to spend hours exploring the town. Early morning is best, although afternoon breezes often moderate the midday heat.

El Gigante de Atacama

It's the biggest archaeological representation of a human in the world – a gargantuan 86m high – and yet little is really known about the 'Giant of the Atacama.' Reclining on the isolated west slope of Cerro Unita 14km east of Huara, the geoglyph is thought to represent a powerful shaman. Experts estimate that the giant dates from around AD 900. Don't climb the slope, as it damages the site.

The Huara–Colchane road, the main Iquique–Bolivia route, is paved; only the very short stretch (about 1km) from the paved road to the hill itself crosses unpaved desert. The isolated site is 80km from Iquique; the best way to visit is to rent a car or taxi, or take a tour.

Parque Nacional Volcán Isluga

If you want to get off the beaten track, this isolated national park richly rewards the effort. Dominated by the malevolently smoking Volcán Isluga, the park is dotted with tiny pastoral villages that house just a few hardy families or, at times, nobody at all. The park's namesake village, **Isluga**, is itself uninhabited. It functions as a *pueblo ritual* (ceremonial village), where scattered migrational families converge for religious events that center on its picture-perfect 17th-century adobe church. Hot springs can be found 2km from the village of **Enquelga**.

Parque Nacional Volcán Isluga's 1750 sq km contain similar flora and fauna to those of Parque Nacional Lauca, but it is far less visited. The park is 250km from Iquique and 13km west of **Colchane**, a small village on the Bolivian border.

From Isluga it's a bouncy but beautiful off-road trip to the stunning **Monumento Natural Salar de Surire** and **Parque Nacional Lauca**, finishing up down in Arica. Inquire about the state of the roads first, especially in the summer rainy season, and do not attempt the trip without a high-clearance vehicle, extra petrol and antifreeze. Several tour agencies in Arica and Iquique offer this trip.

🛏 Sleeping

Chilly little Colchane, 3730m above sea level, is the easiest base for travelers.

Hotel Isluga   HOTEL **$**
(☏ 057-252-7668; www.hotelisluga.cl; Teniente González s/n, Colchane; s without bathroom CH$16,000, d $20,000-36,000) The nicest place to stay in the area, this little hotel has comfy rooms, although they tend to get cold

at night. It also organizes tours to nearby attractions.

Hostal Camino del Inca HOTEL $

(📱cell 8446-3586; hostal_caminodelinka@hotmail.com; Teniente González s/n, Colchane; r per person CH$13,500, without bathroom CH$10,500) Run by a local family, it has two floors of sparse but clean rooms, with hot showers. It gets bitterly cold, so bring a sleeping bag, and a flashlight, because electricity is cut at midnight. Rates include breakfast and dinner.

❶ Getting There & Away

The road to Colchane is paved, but the park itself is crisscrossed by myriad dirt tracks. Several daily buses (fewer on Sundays) that depart Iquique, 251km away, pass Colchane (CH$4000) on their way to Oruro (CH$6000, eight hours, plus more for border passing); try Busfer (p175), which has 2pm departures daily.

At Colchane it's also possible to cross the border and catch a truck or bus to the city of Oruro, in Bolivia.

La Tirana

Curly-horned devils prance, a sea of short skirts swirls, a galaxy of sequins twinkles, and scores of drum-and-brass bands thump out rousing rhythms during La Tirana's **Virgin of Carmen festival**. Chile's most spectacular religious event, the fiesta takes place in mid-July. For 10 days, as many as 230,000 pilgrims overrun the tiny village (permanent population 1300) to pay homage to the Virgin in a Carnaval-like atmosphere of costumed dancing.

The village, 72km from Iquique at the north end of the Salar de Pintados, is famed as the final resting place of a notorious Inka princess, and is home to an important religious shrine. The **Santuario de La Tirana** consists of a broad ceremonial plaza graced by one of the country's most unusual, even eccentric, churches.

Although several restaurants surround the plaza, there are no accommodations available.

Pintados

No less than 420 geoglyphs decorate the hills like giant pre-Columbian doodles at **Pintados** (adult/child CH$2000/free; ⊙10am-4pm), 45km south of Pozo Almonte. Geometrical designs include intriguing ladders, circles and arrows, and depictions of humans include vivid scenes of hunting in canoes and women giving birth. Animal and alienlike figures also roam the hillsides, which have a 2km trail skirting their base; walk or drive it to scan the figures.

These enigmatic geoglyphs are thought to have served as signposts to nomadic peoples: marking trade routes and meeting points, indicating the presence of water, identifying ethnic groups and expressing religious meaning. Most date from between AD 500 and AD 1450.

A derelict nitrate rail yard of ruined buildings and rusting rolling stock, Pintados lies 4.5km west of the Panamericana via a gravel road, nearly opposite the eastward turnoff to Pica.

THE TYRANT PRINCESS

The village of La Tirana is named after a bloodthirsty tale from the era of the conquistadores. It's said that an Inka princess was forced to accompany Diego de Almagro on his foray into Chile in 1535. The young miss gave him the slip at Pica, where she assembled a band of loyal Inka warriors eager for revenge. They promptly set about exterminating as many Spaniards as they could, as well as any indigenous people who had been baptized. Thus she earned the title La Tirana – The Tyrant.

However, her fearful image took a fatal blow in 1544, when her followers captured a Portuguese miner fighting for the Spanish. According to the legend, this pale-skinned soldier left the ferocious princess weak at the knees; and she provoked a major scandal by shielding him from execution. However, that was nothing compared to her followers' fury when she converted to her lover's Catholic faith: moments after her baptism, the pair was killed by a storm of arrows.

Ten years later, a traveling evangelist discovered a cross in the woods, supposedly marking the lovers' grave, and built a chapel. This structure was eventually replaced by a larger building, and the legend of La Tirana has flourished ever since.

Pisagua

📄 057 / POP 253

Another nitrate-era ghost town, Pisagua was once one of the largest ports in the region. It then served as a prison colony and later a prison camp, housing opponents to the Pinochet dictatorship. The town most likely would have continued slipping into obscurity, but the discovery of numerous unmarked mass graves in the cemetery provoked an international scandal that put little Pisagua back on the map.

These days it's a quiet little fishing village with an eerie atmosphere and several grand, crumbling reminders of its nitrate-fueled grandeur.

◎ Sights

Just beyond the police station, the abandoned train station recalls the time when Pisagua was the northern terminus of El Longino, the longitudinal railway that connected the nitrate mines with the ports of the Norte Grande.

Teatro Municipal   HISTORIC BUILDING
A once-lavish, now crumbling theater with a broad stage, opera-style boxes and peeling murals of cherubim on the ceiling. Ask for the key at the **library** (⊙10am-3pm & 4-7pm Mon to Fri) next door.

Cemetery   CEMETERY
(⊙daylight hours) Pisagua's most sobering site is its old cemetery 3km north of town, spread over a lonely hillside that slips suddenly into the ocean. Here, vultures guard over a gaping pit beneath the rock face, where a notorious mass grave of victims of the Pinochet dictatorship was discovered. A poignant memorial plaque quotes Pablo Neruda, 'Although the tracks may touch this site for a thousand years, they will not cover the blood of those who fell here.'

Beyond the cemetery, the road continues for 3.5km to Pisagua Vieja, with a handful of adobe ruins, a pre-Columbian cemetery and a broad sandy beach.

🛏 Sleeping & Eating

Hostal La Roca   HOTEL $
(📞057-273-1502; caterine.saldana@gmail.com; s/d CH$24,000/28,000; 🅿@🛜) This quirky little place is perched on a rocky rise overlooking the Pacific and run by a friendly historian and her husband. It offers four charming rooms, two of which have ocean views. The señora speaks French and some English, and will cook up seafood dinners upon request.

ℹ Getting There & Away

As the crow flies, Pisagua lies about 60km north of Iquique, but going by road doubles that. It's reached from a turn-off 85km south of the police checkpoint at Cuya, and 47km north of Huara. Leaving the Panamericana, travel 40km west by a paved but potholed road until you hit the coast. One bus a day leaves Iquique's terminal at 5pm (CH$2000, two hours), returning from Pisagua at 7am.

Arica

📄 058 / POP 210,216

The pace of Arica is simply delightful. It's warm and sunny year-round, there's a cool pedestrian mall to flip-flop around come sunset and decent brown-sugar beaches are just a short walk from the town center. Top this off with some kick-ass surf breaks and a cool cliff-top War of the Pacific battlefield at El Morro, and you may just stay another day or two before you head up to nearby Parque Nacional Lauca or take an afternoon off from 'beach duty' to visit the Azapa Valley, home to some of the world's oldest known mummies.

History

Pre-Hispanic peoples have roamed this area for millennia. Arica itself was the terminus of an important trade route where coastal peoples exchanged fish, cotton and maize for the potatoes, wool and charqui (jerky) from the people of the precordillera and altiplano.

With the arrival of the Spanish in the early 16th century, Arica became the port for the bonanza silver mine at Potosí, located in present-day Bolivia. As part of independent Peru, the city's 19th-century development lagged behind the frenzied activity in the nitrate mines further south. Following the dramatic battle over Arica's towering El Morro in the War of the Pacific, the city became de facto Chilean territory, an arrangement formalized in 1929.

◎ Sights

Lording over the city is the dramatic headland, El Morro de Arica, a major battle site during the War of the Pacific. At the foot of El Morro are the manicured gardens of Plaza Vicuña Mackenna.

Arica

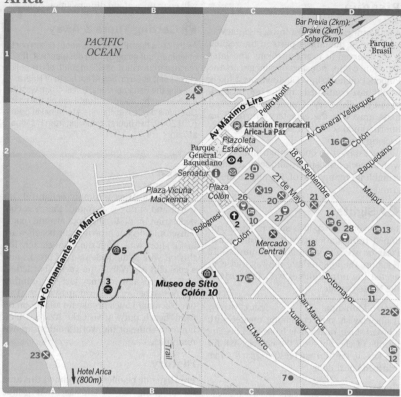

Arica

◎ Top Sights
1 Museo de Sitio Colón 10 .... C3

◎ Sights
2 Catedral de San Marcos C3
3 El Morro de Arica B3
4 Ex-Aduana de Arica C2
5 Museo Histórico y de Armas B3

◆ Activities, Courses & Tours
6 Academia de Artes y Lenguas D3
   Chinchorro
     Expediciones .... (see 24)
7 Raíces Andinas C4

◎ Sleeping
8 Apart Hotel Suma Warni E3
9 Arica Surfhouse E3
10 Casa Beltrán C3
11 Hostal Huanta-Jaya D3
12 Hostal Jardín del Sol D4
13 Hotel Aruma D3

14 Hotel Gavina Express D3
15 Hotel Inti-Jaya E4
16 Hotel Mar Azul D2
17 Hotel Savona C3
18 Hotel Sotomayor D3

◎ Eating
19 Boulevard Vereda Bolognesi C2
20 Cafe del Mar C2
21 El Arriero D3
22 Los Aleros de 21 .... D4
23 Maracuyá A4
24 Mata-Rangi B1
25 Salon de Te 890 .... E4

◎ Drinking & Nightlife
26 Así Sea Club C3
27 Naif C3
28 Vieja Habana D3

◎ Shopping
29 Solari Surf Shop C2

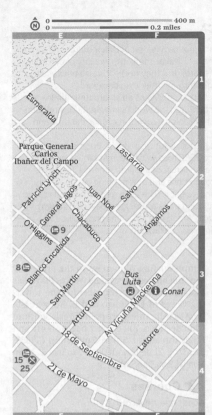

N 0 ————————— 400 m
0 ————————— 0.2 miles

★ **Museo de Sitio Colón 10**   MUSEUM
(Colón 10; adult/child CH$2000/1000; ⊘10am-7pm Tue-Sun Jan-Feb, to 6pm Tue-Sun Mar-Dec)
See the 32 excavated Chinchorro mummies in situ at this tiny museum below El Morro. They were discovered when an architect bought this former private home with the intention of converting it into a hotel. You can gape at the glass-protected bodies as they were found, in the sand below the floors, in different positions, complete with their funerary bundles, skins and feathers of marine fowl.

There are a few infants, with red-painted mud masks. Go up the wooden ramp for a better vantage point of the mummies and then check out the great view of the city from the covered terrace.

El Morro de Arica   LOOKOUT
This imposing coffee-colored shoulder of rock looms 110m over the city. It makes a great place to get your bearings, with vulture-eye views of the city, port and Pacific Ocean. This lofty headland was the site of a crucial battle in 1880, a year into the War of the Pacific, when the Chilean army assaulted and took El Morro from Peruvian forces in under an hour.

The hilltop is accessible by car or taxi (CH$4000 round trip with a 30-minute wait), or by a steep footpath from the south end of Calle Colón. The story of El Morro is told step by step in the flag-waving **Museo Histórico y de Armas** (adult/child CH$800/400; ⊘8am-6pm Tue-Fri, to 8pm Sat & Sun), which has information in Spanish and English.

Catedral de San Marcos   CHURCH
(San Marcos 260, Plaza Colón; ⊘8:30am-9pm Mon-Fri, 11am-1pm Sat, 9am-1pm & 7:30-9pm Sun)
This Gothic-style church has a threefold claim to fame. First, it was designed by celebrated Parisian engineer Alexandre Gustave Eiffel, before his success with the Eiffel Tower. Second, it was prefabricated in Eiffel's Paris shop in the 1870s (at the order of the Peruvian president) then shipped right around the world to be assembled on site. Still more curious is the construction itself: the entire church is made of stamped and molded cast iron, coated with paint.

Major renovations (taking a year or more) are planned for the cathedral, so it may be off-limits by the time you get there.

Ex-Aduana de Arica   CULTURAL BUILDING
(Casa de Cultura; ☎058-220-9501; Prat s/n; ⊘9am-5:30pm Mon-Thu, to 6:30pm Fri, 10:30am-2pm Sat) **FREE** Eiffel designed this former customs house. Prefabricated in Paris, it was assembled on site in 1874, with walls made of blocks and bricks stacked between metallic supports. Restored as the city's cultural center, it hosts a smattering of exhibitions and has an impressive 32-step wrought-iron spiral staircase.

🏃 **Activities**
Beaches
Surfers, swimmers and sunbathers can all find their niche along Arica's plentiful beaches. The Pacific is warm enough to bathe comfortably here, although there are strong ocean currents that make some beaches more dangerous for swimming than others. The mirror-like waters of sheltered Playa La Lisera are the safest place to take young children swimming.

THE DAKAR DOES SOUTH AMERICA

Traveling around northern Chile, you'll probably notice a fair bit of Dakar merchandise on offer, bumper stickers on display and even the odd 'Dakar route' trip available from travel agents. It's not just that Chileans love motor sports (but they do!) – it's also because the world's most famous off-road race passes right through their own backyard.

Originally called the Paris-Dakar, the race started in 1979 as an all-amateur affair – a three week ordeal from France to Senegal. It captured the world's imagination, stretched to include 27 countries and began to attract professional racers, more for the thrill and challenge than the modest prize money.

In 2008, terrorist threats in Mauritania put the rally's future in doubt, but the decision was made to move it to South America and the 2009 race was held in Argentina and Chile. In the few years since, the historic event has taken firm root in South America, traversing the continent annually from Buenos Aires through Chile and now popping into the Uyuni salt flats in Bolivia before returning to Argentina's capital. The 2015 route stretched around 9000km (distances vary for the car, motorcycle and truck routes) and passed through various towns in this book, with stops in Copiapó, Antofagasta, Calama and Iquique.

For more info, check out the official website: www.dakar.com.

The most frequented beaches are south of town, along Av Comandante San Martín, where there are several sheltered coves and seaside restaurants. The closest is **Playa El Laucho**, a 20-minute walk away, followed by decidedly prettier **Playa La Lisera**, 2km south of downtown, with change rooms and showers. Both have only gentle surf and are worthy spots for swimming and lounging alike. Nearby, rougher **Playa Brava** is suitable for sunbathing only.

About 9km south of town, past a pungent fish-meal processing plant, is **Playa Corazones**, with wild camping and a kiosk. Just past the beach a trail leads to caves, cormorant colonies, tunnels and a sea-lion colony. Hire a cab or bike it here.

Beaches are also strung along the Panamericana Norte for 19km to the Peruvian border; these beaches are longer and rougher, but cleaner. The enormous **Playa Chinchorro**, 2km north of downtown, is veritable playland: a long wide beach strung with overpriced restaurants, ice-cream shops and, in holiday seasons, jet-ski rentals. The sea is a bit on the rough side but fine for experienced swimmers. The water here turns somewhat silty in February.

Playa Las Machas, a few kilometers north, is a surfers' haunt. Take bus 12 or 14 from 18 de Septiembre; get off on the corner of Av Antarctica and Av España.

Surfing

The secret's out: Arica's reputation for terrific tubes has spread worldwide. It now hosts high-profile championships and tempts surfing film crews to the area. July sees the biggest breaks. As well as Playa Las Machas, expert surfers also hit the towering waves of El Gringo and El Buey at Isla de Alacrán, an expert point break south of Club de Yates. You can get board shorts and other threads at **Solari Surf Shop** (☑058-223-3773; 21 de Mayo 160; ⊘9am-1pm & 3-7pm Mon-Fri, 9am-1pm Sat).

 Courses

Academia de Artes y Lenguas   LANGUAGE COURSE
(☑058-225-8645; www.spanishinchile.blogspot.com; 21 de Mayo 483, 3rd fl) Offers Spanish courses (CH$8000 per hour or CH$216,000 for 30 hours) and occasional music lessons.

⌒ Tours

Several agencies in Arica offer anything from shopping day trips to Tacna to half-day visits to the Azapa Valley. The most popular tour takes in Parque Nacional Lauca (CH$25,000 for day trips, CH$80,000 to CH$110,000 for two days with lodging); note that many agencies don't go to Lauca on Mondays. While most people do it as a whirlwind day trip, it's better to devote at least two days to acclimatize properly. Other available tours take in less-known altiplano destinations and precordillera villages. Four-day circuits to Lauca, Surire and Isluga are also available, with a drop-off in Iquique at the end (from CH$190,000).

The agencies listed offer the usual roster of tours (except Chinchorro) but each has its specialty. Prices vary according to the number of participants.

Raíces Andinas
GUIDED TOUR

(☑ 058-223-3305; www.ecotourexpediciones.cl; Héroes del Morro 632; ☺ 9am-noon & 3-6pm Mon-Sat) A well-run outfit recommended for encouraging better understanding of the local people. It specializes in trips of two or more days, and offers expeditions to Sajama in Bolivia via Lauca as well as adventures into Salar de Uyuni. It has a few bikes for rent (CH$8000 per day).

Suma Inti
GUIDED TOUR

(☑058-222-5685; www.sumainti.cl; Gonzalo Cerda 1366; ☺9am-1pm & 3-7pm Mon-Fri, to 1pm Sat) A little Aymara-run outfit which focuses on ancestral traditions; tours often feature rituals involving coca leaves and chants. Can also arrange longer treks and climbing expeditions.

Chinchorro Expediciones
BOAT TOUR

(☑ 058-223-3404; chinchorroexpediciones@gmail.com; Muelle Pesquero; ☺ 8am-4pm) This specialist in marine expeditions offers three-hour sea safaris (with a picnic, swimming and kayaking) from the fishing jetty plus a two-day camping trip to Caleta de Camarones by 4WD, with hikes to virgin beaches, forgotten fishing hamlets and hidden archaeological sites.

✮✮ Festivals & Events

Carnaval Andino con
La Fuerza del Sol
CARNIVAL

Visitors in late January–early February witness blaring brass bands and dancing by traditional *comparsas* groups. The festival draws around 15,000 spectators during a three-day weekend, mostly happening on Av Comandante San Martín near El Morro.

Concurso Nacional de Cueca
DANCE

(☺Jun) A folkloric dance festival in the Azapa Valley held each June.

Semana Ariqueña
FESTIVAL

(☺ Jun) Arica week is held in early June.

🛏 Sleeping

Taxi drivers earn commission from some *residenciales* (budget accommodations) and hotels; avoid these. Free camping is possible in the north sector of Playa Las Machas and at dark-sand, no-shade Playa Corazones, 8km south at the end of Av Comandante San Martín, with dirty, crowded sites; bring water.

Arica Surfhouse
HOSTEL $

(☑ 058-231-2213; www.aricasurfhouse.cl; O'Higgins 661; dm CH$12,000, s/d CH$25,000/36,000, without bathroom CH$20,000/30,000; @🛜) Doubling as Arica's surfer central, this is one of Arica's top hostels, with a variety of clean rooms, a great open-air communal area, 24-hour hot water and laundry service. There's a shuttle service to the beaches in winter months, and they'll hook you up with surf classes and equipment rental.

Hotel Sotomayor
HOTEL $

(☑ 058-258-5761; www.hotelsotomayor.cl; Sotomayor 367; s/d CH$28,000/38,000; 🛜) Somewhat frayed around the edges, this four-story number just uphill from the plaza wins points for its spacious rooms and quiet location, set back from the street beside a small plaza.

Hostal Jardín del Sol
HOTEL $

(☑058-223-2795; www.hostaljardindelsol.cl; Sotomayor 848; s/d CH$15,000/$29,000; @🛜) It's been here for ages but still lives up to its reputation as one of Arica's best budget hotels, with small but spotless rooms, fans included. Guests mingle on the leafy patio, the upstairs terrace, in the shared kitchen and the lounge room. There's a book exchange and lots of tourist info.

Hotel Mar Azul
HOTEL $

(☑058-225-6272; www.hotelmarazul.cl; Colón 665; s/d CH$15,000/20,000; 🛜🏊) The flag-fronted Mar Azul at the heart of town has an all-white interior, an alluring little outdoor pool, cable TV, breakfast till 11am and massages on request.

Hostal Huanta-Jaya
HOTEL $

(☑ 058-231-4605; hostal.huanta.jaya@gmail.com; 21 de Mayo 660; s/d CH$20,000/30,000; 🛜) The pleasant, clean and spacious, if a bit dark, rooms are reached via a long hallway lined with African-themed artwork. There's a small shared lounge and dining room, where breakfast is served (CH$2000 extra).

Hotel Inti-Jaya
HOTEL $

(☑ 058-223-0536; www.hotelintijaya.cl; 21 de Mayo 850; s CH$25,000-35,000, d CH$39,000; P🅿🛜) Behind its glass-fronted facade, this over-the-top hotel hides intricate wood carvings, oversized mirrors, polished stone, statues and potted plants. Rooms are well equipped and the views from the 4th-floor terrace are worth the price of admission alone.

El Buey Hostal HOSTEL $$
(☎058-232-5530; www.elbueyhostal.com; Punta del Este 605, La Lisera; dm/s/d CH$14,000/20,000/45,000; @☎) The coolest beachside option, this whitewashed Med-style house sits on the residential hillside above La Lisera beach. It's for surfers with style, with hardwood floors, gorgeous terraces, sparkling kitchens, ocean views, and a communal rooftop terrace with hammocks. You can rent a whole floor (sleeps eight) for CH$131,000.

Casa Beltrán HOTEL $$
(☎058-225-7898; www.hotelcasabeltran.cl; Sotomayor 266; s/d CH$50,000/60,000; P@☎) This sleek city-center charmer inside an old *casona* comes with 17 well-designed rooms with dark hardwood floors and all the upscale trimmings. Some rooms have balconies. The gourmet restaurant (closed Sundays) serves *almuerzos* (set lunches) and afternoon tea overlooking a leafy patio. The 4th-floor terrace has great views of El Morro.

Hotel Gavina Express BUSINESS HOTEL $$
(☎058-258-3000; www.gavina.cl; 21 de Mayo 425; s CH$44,000-63,000, d CH$51,000-69,000; ✴☎) Right in the middle of the pedestrian strip, this business-class hotel offers all the expected comforts including king-size beds, spacious rooms and spotless modern bathrooms.

Apart Hotel Suma Warni APARTMENT $$
(☎058-225-8808; admhostalsummawarni660@gmail.com; Maipú 660; apt CH$49,000; ✴☎) If you're planning on being in town for a while (or even if you're not), you may want to check out the light and airy downtown apartments on offer here. They come fully equipped, with spacious rooms, big flatscreen TVs, wi-fi and full kitchens.

Hotel Savona HOTEL $$
(☎058-223-1000; www.hotelsavona.cl; Yungay 380; s/d CH$39,000/54,000; P@☎✲) This snowy-white hotel at the foot of El Morro has a concertina-style front and an attractive inner patio with bougainvillea blooms and a pill-shaped pool. The classic-style rooms are a bit clunky but well equipped. Those overlooking the pool can get noisy.

★**Hotel Aruma** BOUTIQUE HOTEL $$$
(☎058-225-0000; www.aruma.cl; Lynch 530; s/d standard CH$80,000/90,000, superior CH$110,000/120,000; ✴☎✲) Arica's best-looking hotel is a mixture of cool ambiance, modern stylings and friendly service. The spacious rooms have a contemporary, relaxed feel and the rooftop snack bar, lounge areas and dip pool further add to the appeal.

Hotel Arica HOTEL $$$
(☎058-225-4540; www.panamericanahoteles.cl; Av Comandante San Martín 599; s/d CH$99,000/116,000, cabin for 2 CH$136,000; P✴@☎✲) This large-scale oceanfront resort offers a range of rooms, including cabins overlooking the ocean, plus all four-star trappings. It's south of the center by Playa El Laucho. Request a room with an ocean view and check for web-only specials.

✖ Eating

Mata-Rangi SEAFOOD $
(Muelle Pesquero; set menu CH$4000-5000, mains CH$5000-6500; ☺noon-4pm Mon-Sat) Superb seafood is served at this adorable spot hanging over the harbor by the fishing jetty. A wooden shack-style place packed with wind chimes, it has a breezy dining room and a small terrace above the ocean. Get here early to grab a seat or be prepared to wait.

Boulevard Vereda Bolognesi INTERNATIONAL $
(Bolognesi 340; set meals around CH$4500; ☺9am-11pm Mon-Sat) Hip little shopping mall with a clutch of cool cafes, restaurants and bars. Choose between a salad bar, a Peruvian joint, an Italian trattoria or a sushi bar, and eat on the central patio.

Salon de Te 890 PIZZA $
(21 de Mayo 890; pizzas CH$3200-4500; ☺5pm-midnight Mon-Sat; ☎) Come to this cheerful teahouse for the great pizzas and cakes served in a pair of pastel-colored rooms with old-timey decoration. Don't miss the signature Siete Sabores cake.

Cafe del Mar CAFETERIA $
(21 de Mayo 260; mains CH$3000-5000; ☺9am-10pm Mon-Sat; ☎) A good range of burgers, sandwiches and salads paired with some of the best coffee in town. Pop next door for some of Arica's finest ice cream.

★**Los Aleros de 21** CHILEAN $$
(21 de Mayo 736; mains CH$7000-12,000; ☺noon-3:30pm & 7-11:30pm Mon-Sat; ☎) One of Arica's more highly esteemed restaurants, serving up a good selection of meats and seafood dishes with a few pasta and chicken dishes rounding out the picture. Good wine list, too.

El Arriero
STEAKHOUSE **$$**

(21 de Mayo 385; mains CH$5000-11,000; ⊘ noon-3pm & 7pm-midnight Mon-Sat) This old-school eatery is perfect for red-blooded carnivores who don't mind waiting for an old-fashioned *parrillada* (a mixture of grilled meats). Expect gracious service, a full English menu and an aging steakhouse atmosphere.

Maracuyá
SEAFOOD **$$**

(Av Comandante San Martín 0321; mains CH$7000-12,000; ⊘ noon-3pm & 7-11pm Mon-Sat; 🛜) To treat yourself to a superb seafood meal complete with bow-tie service and sea views, head to this villa-style restaurant next to Playa El Laucho.

🍷 Drinking & Nightlife

Take time out over a hot coffee or a chilled Escudo in one of a dozen streetside cafes strung along the 21 de Mayo pedestrian strip. At night, seek out the bars along Bolognesi between 21 de Mayo and Plaza Colón. Some of the hippest bars and discos are strung along Playa Chinchorro.

Así Sea Club
BAR

(San Marcos 251; ⊘ from 9pm Wed-Sat) This swank hideaway inside a rambling historic townhouse has a set of sleek rooms featuring original detail, and a back patio. It serves a menu of *tablas* (shared plates; CH$4200 to CH$9000), cocktails and all-Chilean wines, paired with loungey tunes.

Naif
BAR

(Colón 342; ⊘ 2-11pm Tue-Thu, 6pm-2am Fri & Sat) Food served by the kilo during the day and a smoky atmosphere with loud music and a young crowd keep this cavernous place going at all times. There's live music on weekends, and DJs on some weeknights.

Vieja Habana
BAR

(www.viejahabana.cl; 21 de Mayo 487; ⊘ midnight-4.55am Fri & Sat) Has salsa and bachata classes (CH$2000) Monday to Thursday at around 10pm, and functions as a lively *salsoteca* (salsa club) on weekends.

Soho
CLUB

(www.discosoho.com; cover with drink CH$6000-8000; ⊘ closed Sun) The city's most happening disco; gets a variety of DJs as well as live salsa and rock bands

Drake
PUB

(cover with drink CH$6000-8000; ⊘ closed Sun) Attached to the Soho disco, Drake is a laid-back pub where locals gather to start the night or take a breather from the hectic dancefloor action next door.

Bar Previa
BAR

(Av Buenos Aires 160) Has a large terrace with live music shows and karaoke nights and stays open seven days a week; if you spend more than CH$5000 in drinks, you get free entry to Soho.

Shopping

A part-kitsch, part-crafts artisans' market is strung along Pasaje Bolognesi, a narrow passageway running from Plaza Colón.

Poblado Artesanal
MARKET

(Hualles 2825; ⊘ 10:30am-1:30pm & 3:30-7pm Tue-Sun) On the outskirts of Arica, near the Panamericana Sur, is this full-on shopping experience: a mock altiplano village filled with serious craft shops and studios, selling everything from ceramic originals to finely tuned musical instruments. The village even has its own church, a replica of the one in Parinacota, complete with copies of its fascinating murals. *Taxis colectivos* (shared taxis) 7 and 8 pass near the entrance, as do buses 7, 8 and 9.

ℹ Information

DANGERS & ANNOYANCES

While Arica is a very safe city, it has a reputation for pickpockets. Be especially cautious at bus terminals and beaches.

INTERNET ACCESS

Several internet cafes can be found on and around 21 de Mayo and Bolognesi; most charge CH$600 per hour.

MEDICAL SERVICES

Hospital Dr Juan Noé (☑ 058-223-2242; 18 de Sepiembre 1000) A short distance east of downtown.

Pharmacy (cnr Colón & 18 de Sepiembre)

MONEY

There are numerous 24-hour ATMs as well as *casas de cambio*, which change US dollars, euros and Peruvian, Bolivian and Argentine currency, along the pedestrian mall (21 de Mayo).

TELEPHONE

The mall is lined with public payphones and phone centers are found throughout the city.

POST

Post Office (Prat 305) On a walkway between Pedro Montt and Prat.

TOURIST INFORMATION

Conaf (☑ 058-258-5704; tarapaca@conaf.cl; Av Vicuña Mackenna 820; ☻8:30am-5:35pm Mon-Thu, to 4pm Fri) This outlet carries some useful information about Región I (Tarapacá) national parks. To get there, take *micro* 9 or *colectivos* 7, 2 or 23 from downtown (*micro* CH$400, *colectivo* CH$600).

Sernatur (☑ 058-225-2054; infoarica@sernatur.cl; San Marcos 101; ☻9am-8pm Mon-Fri, 10am-2pm Sat Jan-Feb, 9am-6pm Mar-Dec) Friendly service with some brochures on Tarapacá and other Chilean regions.

ℹ️ Getting There & Away

From Arica, travelers can head north across the Peruvian border to Tacna and Lima, south toward Santiago or east to Bolivia.

AIR

Aeropuerto Internacional Chacalluta (☑ 058-221-1116) is 18km north of Arica, near the Peruvian border. Santiago-bound passengers should sit on the left side of the plane for awesome views of the Andes and the interminable brownness of the Atacama Desert.

LAN (☑ 600-526-2000; www.lan.com; Arturo Prat 391) has direct daily flights to Santiago (CH$286,000, 2½ hours) and to Iquique (CH$35,600, 50 minutes).

Sky (☑ 600-600-2828; www.skyairline.cl; 21 de Mayo 356) has less frequent flights to Santiago (around CH$101,000), Antofagasta (from CH$61,400) and Iquique (CH$23,000). It also flies to La Paz, Bolivia (CH$88,200 round trip).

BUS

Arica has two main bus terminals. **Terminal Rodoviario de Arica** (Terminal de Buses; ☑ 058-222-5202; Diego Portales 948) houses most companies traveling south to destinations in Chile. Next door, **Terminal Internacional de Buses** (☑ 058-224-8709; Diego Portales 1002) handles international and some regional destinations.

The area is notorious for petty thievery – keep an eye on your luggage at all times. To reach the terminals, take *colectivo* 8 from Maipú or San Marcos; a taxi costs around CH$3000.

More than a dozen companies have offices in Terminal Rodoviario de Arica, and ply destinations toward the south, from Iquique to Santiago.

A schedule board inside the terminal helps you find your bus (but it's not always accurate). Buses run less often on Sundays.

Some of the standard destinations and fares are shown here.

DESTINATION	COST (CH$)	DURATION (HR)
Antofagasta	18,000	10
Calama	15,000	9
Copiapó	24,000	18
Iquique	7000	4
La Paz, Bolivia	8000	9
La Serena	25,000	23
Santiago	30,000	27

Bus Lluta (cnr Chacabuco & Av Vicuña Mackenna) goes to Poconchile and Lluta four to five times daily (CH$1500, one hour).

Buses La Paloma (☑ 058-222-2710; Riesco 2071) travels to the Belén precordillera villages of Socoroma on Wednesday and Saturday (CH$4000), Belén on Tuesday and Friday (CH$4000), leaving Arica at 7am and returning at 1pm, and to Putre daily (CH$3500) at 7am, returning at 2pm. La Paloma also goes to Codpa on Monday, Wednesday and Friday at 8am (CH$3000, three hours), returning at 5pm. It's recommended you take a taxi to this area when leaving early in the morning.

For Parinacota (CH$4000) and Parque Nacional Lauca, look for **Trans Cali Internacional** (☑058-226-1068; Oficina 15) in the international terminal. Trips depart daily at 9:15am.

To get to Tacna, Peru, **Adsubliata** (☑ 058-226-2495) buses leave the international terminal every half-hour (CH$2000); *colectivos* charge CH$4000. No produce is allowed across the border.

To get to La Paz, Bolivia (around CH$8000, nine hours), the comfiest and fastest service is with **Chile Bus** (☑ 058-226-0505), but cheaper buses are available with Trans Cali Internacional and **Trans Salvador** (☑ 058-224-6064) in the international bus terminal. Buses on this route will drop passengers in Parque Nacional Lauca, but expect to pay full fare to La Paz.

Buses Géminis (☑ 058-351-465), in the main terminal, goes to Salta and Jujuy in Argentina via Calama and San Pedro de Atacama (CH$42,000) on Monday, Thursday and Saturday at 10pm.

TRAIN

Trains to Tacna may be running, depending on track maintenance. If they are, they depart from the **Estación Ferrocarril Arica-Tacna** (☑ 097-633-2896; Av Máximo Lira 791).

ℹ️ Getting Around

TO/FROM THE AIRPORT

Shared taxis charge CH$4000 to the airport. In town, call **Radio Taxi Aeropuerto Chacalluta** (☑ 058-225-4812; Patricio Lynch 371). **Arica Service** (☑ 058-231-4031) runs airport shuttles

(CH$3500 per person). **Radio Taxi service** (☑ 058-225-9000) – if you don't like sharing your cab – charges CH$8000.

BICYCLE
You can rent mountain bikes from several tour agencies and hostels in town for around CH$8000.

BUS & TAXI
Local buses *(micros)* and shared taxis *(colectivos)* connect downtown with the main bus terminal. *Taxis colectivos* are faster and more frequent, costing CH$600 per person. Destinations are clearly marked on an illuminated sign atop the cab.

Micros run to major destinations, and cost CH$400 per person. Radio Taxi service is between CH$1800 and CH$2500, depending on your destination.

CAR
Rental cars are available, starting at around CH$24,000 per day.

Cactus Rent a Car (☑ 058-225-7430; cactusrent@hotmail.com; General Lagos 666) Prices are cheaper than the chains.

Europcar (☑ 058-225-8911) At the airport.
Hertz (☑ 058-223-1487; Baquedano 999)
Klasse (☑ 058-225-4498; www.klasserentacar.cl; Av General Velásquez 762, Local 25) Cheaper than the chains.

Azapa Valley

Some of the world's oldest known mummies reside in the Azapa Valley's superb **Museo Arqueológico San Miguel de Azapa** (☑ 058-220-5551; Camino Azapa Km 12; adult/child CH$2000/1000; ⊙ 9am-8pm Jan & Feb, 10am-6pm Mar-Dec). Set in a lush garden dotted with tall palm trees, the museum has two sections. The original exhibition hall displays a large assemblage of exhibits from 7000 BC right up to the Spanish invasion, from dioramas, baskets and masks to pottery, pan flutes and an enormous 18th-century olive press. Well-written booklets in several languages are available to carry around this section.

Past the outdoor 'petroglyph park' is the new hall in a modern concrete building

NORTE GRANDE AZAPA VALLEY

---

10 STEPS TO A CHINCHORRO MUMMY

The Chinchorro mummies are the oldest known artificially preserved bodies in the world, predating their Egyptian counterparts by more than two millennia. They were created by small groups that fished and hunted along the coast of southern Peru and northern Chile from around 7000 BC. The mummification process was remarkably elaborate for such a simple culture.

While the order and methods evolved over the millennia, the earliest mummies were made more or less by doing the following:

➡ dismembering the corpse's head, limbs and skin

➡ removing the brain by splitting the skull or drawing it through the base

➡ taking out other internal organs

➡ drying the body with hot stones or flames

➡ repacking the body with sticks, reeds, clay and camelid fur

➡ reassembling parts, perhaps sewing them together with cactus spines

➡ slathering the body with thick paste made from ash

➡ replacing the skin, patched with sea-lion hide

➡ attaching a wig of human hair and clay mask

➡ painting the mummy with black manganese (or, in later years, red ochre)

Several hundred Chinchorro mummies have now been discovered; all ages are represented and there's no evidence to suggest that mummification was reserved for a special few. Interestingly, some mummies were repeatedly repainted, suggesting that the Chinchorro kept and possibly displayed them for long periods before eventual burial. Millennia later, the conquistadores were appalled by a similar Inka practice, in which mummified ancestors were dressed up and paraded in religious celebrations.

backed by mountains and olive groves. Inside is a swank permanent exhibit dedicated to Chinchorro mummies, with display cases featuring tools, clothing and adornments used in the process as well as infant mummies, a few skulls and life-size figures of Chinchorro peoples.

Once you've taken in the mummies, pop over to the cute **Machakuna Cafe** (☏098-684-7577; sandwiches CH$1200-3000; ⊗noon-4pm Mon-Sat) across the road, which serves *almuerzos* (set lunches) for CH$2300 as well as natural juices, coffee and sandwiches. The owner can arrange horseback rides into the valley and to the beach, from CH$17,000. Arrange at least a day ahead.

The museum is 12km east of Arica. From Parque General Carlos Ibáñez del Campo in Arica, at the corner of Chacabuco and Patricio Lynch, yellow *colectivos* charge CH$1000 (one way) to the front gate of the museum.

Chile 11 Highway

About 10km north of Arica, the Panamericana intersects paved Chile 11, which ushers traffic east up the valley of the Río Lluta to Poconchile and on to Putre and Parque Nacional Lauca. The road features a clutch of worthy stops, if you want to break up the journey. Note that this heavily trafficked winding route toward La Paz, Bolivia, gets about 500 trucks per day.

A short distance inland from the intersection of the Panamericana and Chile 11, you'll see the pre-Columbian **Lluta geoglyphs**, also known as the Gigantes de Lluta. These are sprinkled along an otherwise barren slope of the southern Lluta Valley; markers indicate when to pull over and squint toward the hillsides. The diverse figures include a frog, an eagle, llamas and the occasional human. These delightful geoglyphs recall the importance of pre-Columbian pack trains on the route to Tiwanaku.

Chile 11 & Parque Nacional Lauca

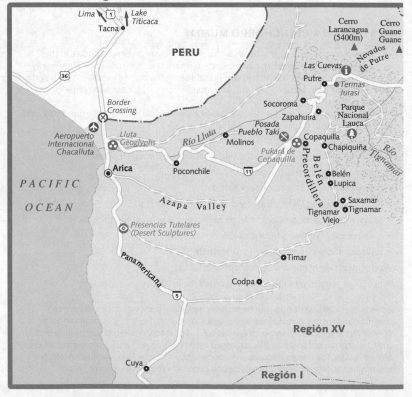

In the village of Poconchile, along a gravel road that runs for 1km along train tracks from the marked turnoff of Chile 11, is a slightly surreal Hare Krishna ashram called **Eco Truly** (📞096-875-0732; www.ecotrulyarica.cl; Sector Linderos, Km29; campsites per person CH$3000, r incl breakfast CH$8000). It's a nice spot to stop for vegetarian lunch (CH$4000, served 1pm to 3:30pm) or a sugar-free pie, or stay on for a few days of simplified relaxation. If you spend part of the day helping out with errands, you get free food and discounted lodging. Free yoga classes are held on Monday, Wednesday and Friday mornings; they do *temazcal* (sweat lodge) rituals the last weekend of the month. There's little proselytizing going on – though residents are happy to share their religious and spiritual views – and the funky conical 'truly' rooms are made with local and recycled materials.

To get to Poconchile, 35km from Arica, take Bus Lluta to the end of the line at the

police checkpoint. *Taxis colectivos* charge around CH$3000 from outside Arica's international bus terminal; you'll have to wait for it to fill up.

The road begins to climb steadily here so it's wise to stop by the roadside **Posada Pueblo Taki** (Km88; campsites per person with a loaf of homemade bread & coca tea CH$7000), where artsy owners Andrea and Alexis serve delicious herbal teas that will help you adjust to the altitude, and check your oxygen levels and heart pressure. They've raised and home-schooled their four children in their wind- and solar-powered home at 3166m, and now run a nonprofit that focuses on the Andean world and offbeat guided tours that highlight the area's hidden spots (CH$6000 per hour). Stop for delicious freshly baked bread, hot drinks and a chat with this fascinating couple.

Teetering on the brink of a spectacular chasm 1.5km beyond the *posada* (inn) is 12th-century fortress **Pukará de Copaquilla** (⊘daylight hours) FREE, built to protect pre-Columbian farmlands below and once home to 500 people. Peering over the canyon's edge will reward with views of the abandoned terraces and forbidding mountains all around. There's a great echo, too. At around 10am, you can sometimes see condors flying above the fortress.

Beyond Copaquilla, paved Chile 11 climbs steadily through the precordillera toward the altiplano proper. If you're driving, the Aymara farming village of **Socoroma** on the colonial pack route between Arica and Potosí is worth a quick detour. To see its cobbled streets, a 17th-century church that's currently being restored, bits of colonial remains and terraced hills of oregano, take the serpentine road that descends from Chile 11 for 4.5km.

Map scale: 40 km / 20 miles. Shows La Paz, Nevada Sajama (6520m), Caquena, Sajama (101), Volcán Pomerape (6240m), Parinacota, Volcán Parinacota (6350m), Chucuyo, Lago Chungará, Parque Nacional Sajama, Border Crossing, Tambo Quemado, Paso de Tambo Quemado (4660m), Volcán Guallatire (6060m), Guallatire, Reserva Nacional Las Vicuñas, BOLIVIA, Oruro, Chilcaya, Salar de Surire, Monumento Natural Salar de Surire, Polloquere, Parque Nacional Volcán Isluga.

Putre

📞058 / POP 1366

Pocket-sized Putre is an appealing Aymara village perched precariously on a hillside in the precordillera at a dizzying elevation of 3530m. Just 150km from Arica, it serves as an ideal acclimatization stop en route to the elevated Parque Nacional Lauca on the altiplano. As such, this languid mountain village now hosts a number of hostels and tour agencies.

Originally a 16th-century *reducción* (Spanish settlement to facilitate control of

WORTH A TRIP

THE NEW FRONTIER IN THE ANDEAN FOOTHILLS

There's a new frontier for adventurous travelers who want to get off the beaten path near Arica: a string of isolated villages that necklaces the Andean foothills. A series of rough gravel roads connects these pretty traditional hamlets in the precordillera, including **Belén**, **Saxamar**, **Tignamar** and **Codpa**. Highlights include colonial churches, ancient agricultural terraces and *pukarás* (pre-Hispanic fortifications).

There's been a recent effort to develop heritage tourism in this Andean region; the project is being promoted as the 'mission route.' This has been headed up by **Fundación Altiplano** (☑058-225-3616; www.fundacionaltiplano.cl; Andres Bello 1515), a foundation that is trying to promote sustainable development of these nearly forgotten Andean communities.

For travelers with vehicles (note that a 4WD is highly recommended, if not imperative) this spectacular route is a great way to get from Codpa to Putre, or vice versa. Make sure you get a good road map and don't attempt this journey during the rainy season (December through March), since rivers run amok due to heavy rains and often wash the roads away.

Accommodations and eating options in these villages are limited to a few simple *hospedajes* (budget accommodations); ask around when you arrive and you'll likely find someone willing to host you in their home. The fertile oasis of the Codpa Valley is home to the area's best place to overnight, **Codpa Valley Lodge** (☑cell 8449-1092; www.cod-pavalleylodge.cl; s/d CH$53,400/59,350; 🏊). This solar energy–powered hideaway (there's electricity only two hours nightly) has cozy rustic rooms with private patios set around a swimming pool, and a good restaurant. The lodge offers a variety of tours, including a scenic two-day overland to Putre through the precordillera, which includes a night in Putre, takes in Lauca and Surire the following day and returns to the lodge on the second night. Make sure you try the sweet dessert wine called *pintatani,* which is produced only in the Codpa Valley.

La Paloma in Arica has departures for Belen and Codpa several times per week. It's not possible, however, to make a loop through all of the villages on public transportation.

the native population), the village retains houses with late-colonial elements. In the surrounding hills local farmers raise alfalfa for llamas, sheep and cattle on extensive stone-faced agricultural terraces of even greater antiquity.

 Tours

Tours to Parque Nacional Lauca aren't necessarily cheaper than from Arica but will give you more time to acclimatize to the altitude.

Other destinations reachable from Putre include Salar de Surire, Parque Nacional Volcán Isluga and the little-explored northern wilderness toward the border with Peru. The latter, with spectacular areas such as the canyons of Quebrada de Allane and the multicolored mountains of Suriplaza, is becoming the new frontier for explorer types, so get there before everyone else discovers it.

Note that things seriously wind down in Putre from mid-December through February, which is the rainy season. Some areas become inaccessible, roads get washed away and many agencies work by request only. Before jumping on the bus from Arica during this time of year, call one of the agencies in Putre (they only check their email sporadically) to arrange things ahead of your arrival. Otherwise you may find yourself waiting a couple of days to find a tour.

Before booking a tour, ask what kind of vehicle they use, whether the guide speaks English (which is rare) and if they carry oxygen. These are all factors that can make or break your trip.

Terrace Lodge & Tours   GUIDED TOUR
(☑058-258-4275; www.terracelodge.com; Circunvalación 25) Flavio of Terrace Lodge is not only a fountain of info but runs a range of excellently guided tours, which take you away from the crowds and to some hidden spots, both in the immediate area around Putre as well as further up north.

Tour Andino
ADVENTURE TOUR
(cell 9011-0702; www.tourandino.com; Baquedano 340) A one-man show run by local guide Justino Jirón. While he does the usual roster of tours – which get mixed reviews – his specialty is treks into the surrounding mountains and volcano climbs.

✦ Festivals & Events

Carnaval
CARNIVAL
(☉Feb) Visitors get dragged into the fun during Putre's Carnaval in February. Scores of balloon-bombs filled with flour are pelted around, not to mention clouds of *chaya* (multicolored paper dots). Two noncompetitive groups, the older *banda* and younger *tarqueada,* provide the music. The event ends with the burning of the *momo,* a figure symbolizing the frivolity of Carnaval.

Feria Regional
FAIR
(☉Nov) Held in November; music and dancing are accompanied by dozens of stalls selling crafts, regional produce and tasty local dishes.

🛏 Sleeping

Book well in advance during Putre's high season (July through October).

★ Terrace Lodge & Cafe
LODGE $
(058-258-4275; www.terracelodge.com; Circunvalación 25; s/d CH$29,000/CH$34,000; @ 🕏) A friendly pair of multilingual Italian expats runs this hideaway with five rustic-chic rooms. Units are small but well-heated, with mountain views through tiny long windows, down duvets and all-day hot water. Look for the sign as you enter town. It's also the only place in town that accepts plastic. Book way ahead. The owner also runs tours.

Hotel Kukuli
HOTEL $
(cell 9161-4709; reservashotelkukuli@gmail.com; off Baquedano; s/d CH$20,000/30,000; P 🕏) Kukuli is a decent choice on the main strip, with spotless rooms sporting either a small terrace or a sunny alcove but, regrettably, no heating. If the hotel seems closed, inquire in the owner's store at Baquedano 301.

Residencial La Paloma
GUESTHOUSE $
(058-222-2710; lapalomaputre@hotmail.com; O'Higgins 353; r per person with/without bathroom CH$10,000/8000; P) Putre's most established *residencial* and restaurant slots nine rooms around two concrete courtyards. It has hot showers (morning and evening only) and noisy rooms which vary greatly – those at the front are a better bet. Enter from the back on Baquedano or through the restaurant.

Hotel Q'antati
HOTEL $$
(058-222-8916; www.hotelqantati.blogspot.com.ar; Hijuela 208; s/d CH$46,000/52,000; P) The favorite of tour groups, this Aymara-run hotel is Putre's most upscale and priciest option, with 24-hour hot showers, firm beds, heated doubles with unheated large bathrooms and a fancy living room with a fireplace. Get rooms 8, 9 or 10 for best views. It's behind the army barracks on the edge of town.

🍴 Eating

Residencial La Paloma has a decent restaurant, which serves simple breakfasts and lunches.

Kuchu Marka
CHILEAN $
(Baquedano 351; set lunch CH$4000, mains from CH$6000; ☉noon-10:30pm) Colorful and cozy Kuchu Marka dishes out tasty local staples such as alpaca steaks as well as a range of vegetarian options and drinks.

Cantaverdi
INTERNATIONAL $
(Arturo Perez Canto 339; set lunch CH$4500, mains CH$4500-6500; ☉noon-10pm) Two rustic rooms with contemporary artwork and a fireplace right off the main plaza. The menu features a few Andean staple dishes as well as crowd-pleasers such as sandwiches, pizzas, *tablas* and empanadas.

ⓘ Information

BancoEstado (Arturo Prat 301) Putre's only bank, off the main plaza, has a 24-hour ATM, but note that it doesn't accept some Visa cards. It changes US cash and euros but it's wise to bring sufficient cash with you from Arica.

Hospital (Baquedano 261) This 24-hour clinic will give you oxygen if the dizzying altitude gets to you.

Oficina de Información Turística (058-259-4897; impurte@entelchile.net; Latorre s/n; ☉10am-1pm & 2-5:45pm Mon, 8:30am-1pm & 2-5:45pm Tue-Fri) A handy resource on the plaza, although it has no town maps and opens only sporadically.

ⓘ Getting There & Away

Putre is 150km east of Arica via paved Chile 11, the international highway to Bolivia. **Buses La Paloma** (058-222-2710; Germán Riesco

2071) serves Putre daily, departing Arica at 7am, returning at 2pm (CH$3500). Buy return tickets at Hotel Kukuli.

Transportes Gutiérrez (☑058-222-9338; Esteban Ríos 2140) also runs from Arica to Putre on Monday, Wednesday and Friday at 6:45am and Sunday at 8pm (CH$3500, three hours). From Putre, buses leave from the plaza for Arica on Monday, Wednesday and Friday at 5pm.

Buses to Parinacota, in Parque Nacional Lauca, pass the turn-off to Putre, which is 5km from the main highway.

Parque Nacional Lauca

It's not just the exaggerated altitude (between 3000m and 6300m above sea level) that leaves visitors to this national park breathless. Lauca is home to some breathtaking altiplano scenery, snow-sprinkled volcanoes, sparkling lakes and isolated hot springs. It also shelters pretty highland villages and a huge variety of wildlife. The nimble-footed vicuña and the rabbit-like viscacha are the star attractions, but you're also likely to see other South American camelids and a variety of bird species (there are more than 150 species in the park, including the occasional condor and fast-footed rhea).

Lauca's most spectacular feature is the glistening Lago Chungará, one of the world's highest lakes and particularly abundant with bird life. Looming over it is the impossibly perfect cone of Volcán Parinacota, a dormant volcano with a twin brother, Volcán Pomerape, just across the border. These pristine white-capped volcanoes could almost be painted onto the landscape, but the ominous Volcán Guallatire puffs up dark fumes a short distance to the south.

Situated 160km northeast of Arica, near the Bolivian border, Parque Nacional Lauca, comprising 1380 sq km of altiplano, is a Unesco Biosphere Reserve rich in wildlife. It nuzzles close to two more protected areas, the Reserva Nacional Las Vicuñas and Monumento Natural Salar de Surire. Once part of the park, they now constitute technically separate units but are still managed by Conaf. A trip that combines these parks is well worth the extra time and energy.

Rainfall and vegetation increase with altitude and distance from the coast; it can snow in the park during the summer rainy season, known as *invierno boliviano* (Bolivian winter), when heavy fog often covers the precordillera approaches to the park.

❶ Dangers & Annoyances

Take it easy at first: the park's altitude is mostly well above 4000m and overexertion is a big no-no until you've had a few days to adapt. Eat and drink moderately; have mainly light food and no fizzy drinks or (little) alcohol. If you suffer anyway, try a cup of tea made from the common Aymara herbal remedy *chachacoma, rica rica* or *mate de coca*. Keep water at your side, as the throat desiccates rapidly in the arid climate and you lose lots of liquids, and definitely wear sunblock and a wide-brim hat – tropical rays are brutal at this elevation.

◉ Sights & Activities

Most agencies will cover the following highlights. Lauca's crown jewel, the glittering Lago Chungará (4517m above sea level), is a shallow body of water formed by lava flows damming the snowmelt stream from Volcán Parinacota (6350m), a beautiful snow-capped cone that rises immediately to the north. Now sadly shallow, but still picturesque (although crisscrossed by power lines, which spoil the photo ops), Laguna Cotacotani sparkles at the foot of sprawling lava flows and cinder cones.

The lake has been partially drained by the national electricity company, but you will still see diverse bird life along its shores and scattered groves of queñoa *(Polylepis tarapacana)*, one of the world's highest-elevation trees.

Tours include a wander around beautiful Parinacota, a tiny Aymara village of whitewashed adobe and stone streets. If you're lucky, the guide will procure the key for the town's undisputed gem, its 17th-century colonial church (donations welcome) reconstructed in 1789. Inside is a glorious display of surrealistic murals by artists from the Cuzco school: think Hieronymus Bosch in a hurry. Look for a small table tethered down like a dog; local legend tells how this little critter once escaped, walked through town and stopped in front of someone's house; the next day, that man died. At the park's western entrance, Las Cuevas has a viewing point, marked by a sculpture resembling *zampoña* (panpipes) balanced on a garish staircase.

Some (but not all) tours will include a quick dip in Termas Jurasi (adult/child CH$2000/1000; ☉daylight hours), a pretty cluster of thermal and mud baths huddled amid rocky scenery 11km northeast of Putre.

Tours

Some agencies offer one-day blitzes from sea-level Arica to 4517m Lago Chungará in Parque Nacional Lauca – a surefire method to get *soroche* (altitude sickness). These tours cost from CH$26,000 (including a late lunch in Putre) and leave around 7:30am, returning about 8:30pm.

Verify whether the operator carries oxygen on the bus, as many people become very sick at high altitudes. Avoid overeating, smoking and alcohol consumption the day before and while you are on your tour. Tours that include at least a night in Putre are a wiser option, allowing more time to acclimatize.

ⓘ Information

The park is administered from the *refugio* (rustic shelter) at Parinacota. Otherwise, rangers at the Las Cuevas entrance and at Lago Chungará are sometimes available for consultation; posts are, in theory, staffed from around 9am to 12:30pm then 1pm to 5:30pm.

If you prefer to visit the park independently, you'll need a car (with extra supplies of gas), lots of flexibility and a laid-back attitude. Inquire with Conaf about hikes and lodgings (the latter are mainly basic options for the hardcore).

ⓘ Getting There & Away

Parque Nacional Lauca straddles Chile 11, the paved Arica–La Paz highway; the trip from Arica takes just under three hours. There are several buses from Arica. Other bus companies with daily service to La Paz, Bolivia, will drop you off in the park, but you will probably have to pay the full fare.

Agencies in Arica and Putre offer tours. Renting a car will provide access to the park's remoter sites such as Guallatire, Caquena and beyond into the Salar de Surire (the latter only with a high-clearance vehicle, since you'll ford several watercourses, and not during the rainy season). Carry extra fuel in cans; most rental agencies will provide them. Do not forget warm clothing and sleeping gear, and take time to acclimatize.

South of Parque Nacional Lauca

More than 20,000 wild vicuña are thought to roam the sparsely inhabited 2100 sq km of the off-the-beaten-path **Reserva Nacional Las Vicuñas**, directly south of Lauca and surrounded by sky-hugging volcanoes. Formed to provide a protective zone for Lauca, the reserve is facing environmental degradation with the Vilacollo mining company winning approval in August 2007 to explore for mineral resources in the reserve. At the base of smoking Volcán Guallatire, 60km from Parinacota via a roundabout route, the

---

VICUÑA RESURGENCE: AN ENVIRONMENTAL SUCCESS STORY

Back in Inka times, vast herds of vicuña, numbering in the millions, roamed the altiplano from here all the way to southern Ecuador. But overpredation and habitat loss have sorely depleted the herds over the years, and in the 1970s barely a thousand vicuña were left in northern Chile. Today, there are more than 25,000 in the region and several hundred thousand throughout the Andes: an environmental success story that seems to only be getting better.

Unlike the alpaca or llama, the vicuña has never been domesticated. These shy fellows just don't seem to want to mate in captivity. So conservationists had to figure out a way to protect them, while still providing an economically viable trade for local Aymara who for centuries have relied on vicuña for their valuable meat and fur. Initially, species-protection measures were put in place, but even its endangered status could not save the vicuña, whose buttery wool is used to make shawls that cost hundreds (if not thousands) of US dollars.

In the 1990s the local Aymara started to catch the vicuña live, shear them on the spot, and then release them back in the wild. This innovative program has allowed for continued cultivation of vicuña wool, while providing a deterrent to poachers: a shorn vicuña is essentially worthless. These measures, combined with larger national parks and greater protection, mean that herds of these beautiful, elegant creatures may again trundle across the vast expanses of the high Andes.

NORTE GRANDE SOUTH OF PARQUE NACIONAL LAUCA

village of **Guallatire** features a 17th-century church and a couple of no-frills lodging options. Bring a warm sleeping bag.

Visiting nearby **Monumento Natural Salar de Surire** is a surefire way to see huge herds of roaming vicuña, pockets of cuddly viscacha, as well the occasional ungainly ñandú (the ostrich-like rhea). But the star attraction of this isolated 113-sq-km salt flat is the flamingo: three species, including the rare James flamingo, come to nest in the sprawling salt lake. The best time to see them is from December to April.

Situated 126km from Putre, the reserve was formed in 1983, when the government chopped up Parque Nacional Lauca. In 1989, the outgoing dictatorship gave 45.6 sq km to mining company Quiborax. There is no public transportation and lodging is possible only at a simple *refugio* (rustic shelter); reserve with Conaf in Arica. Camping is possible beside Polloquere's tempting thermal baths, but there are no toilet facilities and it's bitterly exposed to the elements.

Although most visitors return to Putre, it's possible to make a southerly circuit through Parque Nacional Volcán Isluga and back to Arica via Camiña or Huara. Always consult Conaf or the police first. This route is particularly iffy during the summer rainy season.

Most agencies in Arica and Putre offer two- to four-day circuits that take in these two reserves and drop you off either back in Arica or in Iquique.

Norte Chico

Includes ➡

Best Places to Eat

➡ Chaski (p208)

➡ Coral de Bahía (p220)

➡ Nativo (p214)

➡ Kardamomo (p201)

➡ Cafe Museo (p219)

Best Places to Stay

➡ Hotel La Casona (p216)

➡ Ckamur (p219)

➡ Hacienda Los Andes (p204)

➡ El Tesoro de Elqui (p210)

➡ Coral de Bahía (p220)

Why Go?

For such a small sliver of land, Chile's Norte Chico (Little North) offers up fantastic diversity. La Serena, a coastal colonial capital and the region's largest city, is a must-see for anybody visiting. From there, move on to the mystical Elqui Valley: the verdant home to Chile's pisco producers, new-age communes and cutting-edge observatories. Further north are some amazing national parks, a trendy little beach hideaway, and kilometers of uncharted coastline just waiting for you to set up camp or charge out for an afternoon surf.

Wildlife lovers won't want to miss the playful penguins of Reserva Nacional Pingüino de Humboldt and Parque Nacional Pan de Azúcar. And high in the Andes, the seldomvisited Parque Nacional Nevado Tres Cruces is a great place to spot vicuña and flamingos. Despite its diminutive moniker, the Little North is actually quite a bit bigger than most people expect.

When to Go
La Serena

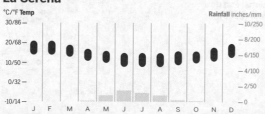

Jan–Feb Chileans on vacation storm the beaches, making hotel options scarcer and sights crowded.

Jul–Aug Temperatures drop dramatically at night but days are hot and blissfully free of crowds.

Sep–Nov Catch the storied sight of the flowering desert, best in Parque Nacional Llanos de Challe.

Norte Chico Highlights

1 Lounge around Norte Chico's coolest little beach town, the pretty **Bahía Inglesa** (p219).

2 Learn just how potent the little pisco grape can be as you hop through villages of the groovy **Elqui Valley** (p205).

3 Take in starry southern skies at one of many **observatories** (p206) dotting Norte Chico.

4 Get lost on your way to the high-Andean lagoons of **Parque Nacional Nevado Tres Cruces** (p217).

5 Hop on a boat to the penguin colonies at **Reserva Nacional Pingüino de Humboldt** (p211).

6 Bop through the colonial center of **La Serena** (p197), then head to the beach for surf, sun and sand.

7 Find your own way as you pioneer campsites and surf spots in the beachfront **Parque Nacional Pan de Azúcar** (p220).

ℹ️ Getting Around

The Panamericana wiggles its way along Norte Chico's coastline, making it easy to reach by car or bus. There are also busy domestic airports near La Serena and Copiapó. Turning off the Panamericana can quickly feel like venturing into the outback as gravel and dirt roads deteriorate rapidly and public transportation quickly dwindles. As a result, getting to many out-of-the-way national parks and attractions can be tricky without taking a tour or having your own wheels; in some cases only high-clearance pickup trucks or 4WDs will do.

La Serena

📞 051 / POP 198,160

Chile's second-oldest city and the thriving capital of Región IV, La Serena is doubly blessed with some beautiful architecture and a long golden shoreline, making it a kind of thinking-person's beach resort. The city absorbs hoards of Chilean holidaymakers in January and February, though it is fairly peaceful outside the summer rush. Saunter-ing through downtown La Serena reveals dig-nified stone churches, tree-shaded avenues and some pretty plazas. Some of the city's ar-chitecture is from the colonial era, but most of it is actually neocolonial – the product of Serena-born president Gabriel González Vi-dela's 'Plan Serena' of the late 1940s.

La Serena also has numerous attractions in the surrounding countryside, with pretty villages and pisco vineyards aplenty, as well as international astronomical observatories that take advantage of the region's exception-al atmospheric conditions and clear skies.

⊙ Sights

Plaza de Armas   PLAZA

La Serena has 29 churches to its credit, many beautiful stone creations in neoclassi-cal or eclectic styles. A bunch of the prettiest can be found on or near the Plaza de Armas. On the east side, the handsome neoclassical **Iglesia Catedral** (Plaza de Armas; ⊙10am-1pm & 4-8pm) dates from 1844; it has a small mu-seum of religious art. Just to its north are the bluff facades of the **Municipalidad** – pop your head inside to check out photos of the city's past – and **Tribunales** (Law Courts; cnr Prat & Los Carrera), built as a result of González Videla's Plan Serena.

Museo Histórico Casa Gabriel González Videla   MUSEUM

(Matta 495; adult/child CH$600/300; ⊙10am-6pm Mon-Fri, to 1pm Sat) Although richly stocked with general historical artifacts, this two-story museum in an 18th-century mansion concentrates on one of La Serena's best-known (and most controversial) sons. González Videla was Chile's president from 1946 to 1952. Ever the cunning politician, he took power with communist support but then promptly outlawed the party, driving poet Pablo Neruda out of the Senate and into exile. The reverent exhibits omit such episodes, but pop upstairs for the historical displays and changing modern-art exhibits.

Museo Arqueológico   MUSEUM

(cnr Cordovez & Cienfuegos; adult/child CH$600/300, Sun free; ⊙9:30am-5:50pm Tue-Fri, 10am-1pm & 4-7pm Sat, 10am-1pm Sun) Inside a crescent-shaped building with a leafy patio, this museum makes an ambitious attempt to corral Chile's pre-Columbian past. Its highlights include an Atacameña mummy, a hefty 2.5m-high *moai* (large anthropomor-phic statue) from Easter Island and interest-ing Diaguita artifacts that include a dinghy made from sea-lion hide.

The Museo Histórico Casa Gabriel González Videla and Museo Arqueológico share admission – entry to one is valid for the other.

Parque Japones Kokoro No Niwa   PARK

(Parque Pedro de Valdivia; adult/child 5-12yr CH$1000/300; ⊙10am-8pm summer, to 6pm rest of year) With its trickling brooks, drifting swans and neatly manicured rock gardens, this Japanese garden makes a good escape from the city bustle.

🏃 Activities

A bike path runs all the way to Coquimbo; **Vicamawi** (📞051-222-7939; Vicente Zorrilla 990; ⊙9am-6pm) rents bikes for CH$8000 per day.

Other popular activities include sailing, surfing and windsurfing (but keep an eye on swimmers within 200m of the beach or you'll run afoul of the Gobernación Maríti-ma). Playa Totoralillo, south of Coquimbo, is rated highly for its surf breaks and wind-surfing potential. **Poisson** (📞cell 9138-2383; Av del Mar 1001; ⊙8am-9pm) rents surfboards for CH$6000 per hour.

Beaches   BEACH

A swath of wide sandy beaches stretches from La Serena's nonfunctional lighthouse right to Coquimbo: there are so many that

NORTE CHICO LA SERENA

you could visit a different beach every day for a two-week vacation. Unfortunately, strong rip currents make some unsuitable for swimming – but good for surfing. Safe swimming beaches generally start south of Cuatro Esquinas.

Those between the west end of Av Francisco de Aguirre and Cuatro Esquinas (ie closer to town) are friskier and generally dangerous for bathers. Look for the signs 'Playa Apta' (meaning beach safe for swimming) and 'Playa No Apta' (meaning beach not safe for swimming).

For quick beach access, take either bus Liserco or *colectivos* running between La Serena and Coquimbo, and get off at Peñuelas and Cuatro Esquinas, a block from the beach. During January and February direct buses (CH$500) head down Av Francisco de Aguirre to Playa El Faro. During the remainder of the year, you'll have to take a *colectivo* (CH$600) or do the 3km walk to the lighthouse from town.

🍃 Courses

La Serena School LANGUAGE COURSE
(☎ 051-221-1487; www.laserenaschool.cl; Rodríguez 450) This institution offers Spanish courses (from CH$20,000 per hour).

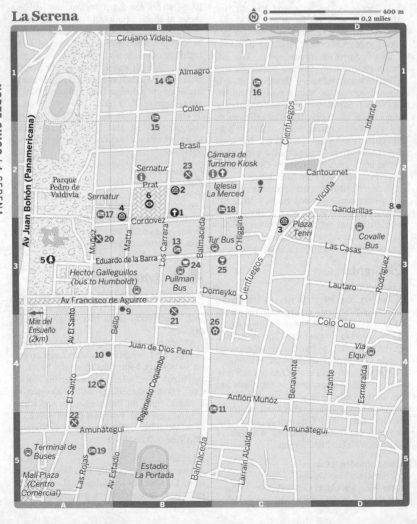

La Serena

☞ Tours

Agencies offer a wealth of excursions, ranging from national park visits to nighttime astronomical trips and pisco tasting tours to new-age jaunts in UFO central, Cochiguaz. Traditional excursions include half-day city tours (from CH$5000), full-day trips through the Elqui Valley (around CH$25,000), Parque Nacional Bosques de Fray Jorge and Valle del Encanto (from CH$35,000), and Parque Nacional Pingüino de Humboldt (CH$32,000 to $35,000). Agencies also provide excursions to the observatories, mainly going out to Mamalluca (CH$16,000 to CH$20,000). If there is a demand, they will also do trips to Andacollo as well as treks to mines (the so-called Ruta del Quarzo) that are located nearby. The minimum number of passengers ranges from two to six.

Tembeta Tours   CULTURAL TOUR
(☑051-221-5553; www.tembeta.cl; Andrés Bello 870) Sign up for a walking city tour; these cost CH$5000 per person and depart daily if at least two people sign up.

Elqui Valley Tour   GUIDED TOUR
(☑051-221-4846; www.goelqui.com; Prat 567; ⊙9am-6pm Mon-Sat) Daily departures to the Elqui Valley, with a discount if you take a day trip plus a night visit to Mamalluca.

**Talinay Adventure
Expeditions**   ADVENTURE TOUR
(☑051-221-8658; www.talinaychile.com; Av Francisco de Aguirre 301; ⊙8:30am-5:30pm Mon-Sat) Good choice for adventure tours, from kay-

aking, mountain biking and horseback riding to diving, trekking and rock climbing.

🎉 Festivals & Events

Jornadas Musicales de La Serena   MUSIC
Held in early January, this traditional festival sees a series of musical events.

**Feria Internacional
del Libro de La Serena**   BOOK FAIR
Brings prominent Chilean authors to the historical museum in early February.

🛏 Sleeping

La Serena gets booked up fast in January and February and some hotels won't accept one-night stays. Off-season, most midrange hotels offer discounts for longer stays.

★ Hostal El Punto   HOSTEL $
(☑051-222-8474; www.hostalelpunto.cl; Bello 979; dm/s/d without bathroom CH$8500/17,000/18,000, s CH$24,000-26,000, d CH$26,000-30,000; @🖥) This is La Serena's best hostel, with a wide range of rooms, a bunch of sunny terraces, bright mosaics and tree-trunk tables. The staff speak German and English, and provide travel tips, tours, bike rental, nice cakes, laundry, book exchange...you name it. You'll want to book months ahead, especially in high season.

Hostal Tierra Diaguita   HOSTEL $
(☑051-221-6608; www.fogoncasatamaya.cl; Eduardo de la Barra 440; s/d CH$34,000/40,000, without bathroom CH$28,000/32,000; 🖥) Inside a colonial house, this friendly place has well-kept

NORTE CHICO LA SERENA

La Serena

◉ Sights

rooms in the main building and add-ons in the back reached through the verdant garden. Guests can use the shared kitchen and the lovely patio. Free perks include breakfast and luggage storage. The sign out front says 'Casa Tamaya.'

Maria's Casa
GUESTHOUSE $

(☎051-222-9282; www.hostalmariacasa.cl; Las Rojas 18; dm/s/d without bathroom CH$9000/15,000/18,000; ☎) The cottage-style rooms at this family-run spot are simple and cozy. There's a garden in the back, where you can camp (CH$3500 per person). Other backpacker-friendly amenities include well-scrubbed shared bathrooms, a quaint country kitchen with free tea and coffee, laundry service and bike rental.

Hostal Balmaceda
HOTEL $

(☎051-221-8565; www.hostalbalmaceda.cl; Balmaceda 1032; s/d CH$24,000/30,000) Straddling the line between hotel and hostel, the Balmaceda sports a fine collection of rooms accessed from an unassuming door at the street front (the sign simply reads 'Hospedaje'). There's a cool little side-garden/patio area, a good kitchen for guest use and a range of rooms to choose from.

Hotel del Cid
HOTEL $$

(☎051-221-2692; www.hoteldelcid.cl; O'Higgins 138; s/d CH$50,000/60,000; P☎) A dependable midrange option, this pleasant hotel has rooms with classic flair around a colonial-style patio and a set of more modern units in the extension out back. It's all paired with very friendly service.

Hotel Cristobal Colón
HOTEL $$

(☎051-222-4656; www.hotelcristobalcolon.cl; Colón 371; s/d CH$36,000/48,000; P☎) An unexciting if dependable midrange option set in a colonial building. It comes with a series of snug rooms, an upstairs terrace with nice views and a restaurant on-site.

Hotel Londres
HOTEL $$

(☎051-221-9066; www.hotellondres.cl; Cordovez 550; s/d CH$32,000/42,000; P☎) Besides having a great location, this friendly family-run hotel features very beige rooms with a bit of chintz, but firm beds and spacious bathrooms. Rooms in the front are noisier but also brighter.

Hotel Bleu Blanc
HOTEL $$

(☎051-248-2802; www.bleublanchotel.com; Almagro 399; s/d CH$36,000/42,000, ste from CH$61,000) A fine little corner hotel with boutique pretensions, the Bleu Blanc features thoroughly modern rooms with modern stylings and fittings, friendly personalized service and a hushed, tranquil atmosphere.

Hotel Francisco de Aguirre
HOTEL $$$

(☎051-222-2991; www.dahoteles.com; Cordovez 210; s/d from CH$69,000/82,000; P@☎☎) This large hotel's imposing neocolonial frontage faces Iglesia Santo Domingo, the bells of which often wake late risers. Rooms range in size, but generally you'll have to upgrade to a superior (CH$15,000 extra) to get a large one. There's a gym and sauna.

Mar del Ensueño
HOTEL $$$

(☎051-222-2381; www.hotelmarensueno.com; Av del Mar 900; s/d CH$85,000/105,000; ☎☎☎☎) For instant beach access, it's hard to beat the Ensueño – it's right across the road. A family-friendly place (play equipment, games room etc), it's a reasonable deal for couples, too – the bright spacious rooms all face the ocean and there's a decent on-site restaurant.

✖ Eating

For those wanting to self-cater, there are several markets in town. Some have food stalls, others offer good options to make your own picnic lunch. The biggest is Mercado La Recova on the corner of Cienfuegos and Cantournet, which has a string of seafood restaurants upstairs. Supermarkets are ubiquitous.

Ayawasi
VEGETARIAN $

(Pedro Pablo Muñoz 566; mains CH$4000-6000; ☺9am-8pm Mon-Sat) A short walk from the plaza, this little vegetarian oasis serves some fantastic set lunches, delicious fresh juices and innovative sandwiches and salads in a shady garden setting or laid-back dining room.

Casona del 900
PARRILLA $$

(Av Francisco de Aguirre 431-443; mains CH$4500-9500; ☺noon-3pm & 7pm-midnight Mon-Sat) Inside an old beer factory, this high-ceilinged steakhouse with a glassed-in garden ambience and packs in meat-loving locals for its good-value barbecues (CH$18,900 for two, with wine).

Rapsodia
INTERNATIONAL $$

(Prat 470; mains CH$6000-9500; ☺9am-9pm Mon-Wed, to 11pm Thu & Fri, to 6pm Sat) With several side rooms looking onto the inner courtyard with a giant palm tree, this old *casona* serves up good-value meat and seafood dishes, a range of healthy sandwiches and live music on some nights.

★ Kardamomo
SEAFOOD $$

(Av del Mar 4000; mains CH$7000-11,000; ☺noon-11pm Mon-Sat, to 4pm Sun; ☏) An excellent beachfront location, art-covered walls and a smooth soundtrack are the foundations for this laid-back but elegant seafood restaurant. Good-value set lunches, a wide menu and carefully prepared sushi platters round out the picture.

El Santo
INTERNATIONAL $$

(cnr El Santo & Amunátegui; mains CH$6000-9000; ☺noon-12:30am Mon-Sat) Perched up on a hillside, this large indoor/outdoor setup serves up some tasty pizzas along with some of the best steak dishes in town. A range of craft beers and a small but well-selected wine list are also on offer.

🍷 Drinking & Entertainment

The happening part of town is the area around the corner of Eduardo de la Barra and O'Higgins, where you'll find boho student crowds. Nightclubs sparkle along the seafront, past the lighthouse and all the way to Barrio Inglés in Coquimbo; they're especially hot during summer.

Cafe W
CAFE, BAR

(Eduardo de la Barra 435; sandwiches CH$3000-6000; ☺9am-11pm Mon-Thu, to 1am Fri & Sat) With a large wooden deck overlooking a relatively quiet street, this is a great stop for coffee and to recharge the batteries. There are some yummy cakes on offer too, and a good range of sandwiches. Turns into a lively bar later at night.

La Rocca
BAR

(Eduardo de la Barra 569; ☺8pm-late Tue-Sat) Stay out late drinking on the interior patio at this popular student hangout with occasional live music.

Caseron
LIVE MUSIC

(Balmaceda 824; ☺7pm-2am Tue-Sat) This seedy-looking bar in a 130-year-old house hosts regular acts, including jazz on Thursdays and Latin rhythms on weekends.

ℹ Information

Banks with ATMs are readily available in the blocks around Plaza de Armas. There are several money exchange shops on Balmaceda, between Cordovez and Prat.

There are numerous internet joints around town, most charging around CH$600 per hour.

Hospital Juan de Dios (☑051-223-3312; Balmaceda 916; ☺24hr) The emergency entrance is at the corner of Larraín Alcalde and Anfión Muñóz.

Sernatur (☑051-222-5199; www.turismoregiondecoquimbo.cl; Matta 461; ☺9am-8pm summer, 9am-6pm Mon-Fri, 10am-2pm Sat winter) Excellent tourist info shelled out from this office by the Plaza de Armas. During the summer, the municipal tourist office runs an information kiosk by Iglesia La Merced and another in the lighthouse by the beach.

ℹ Getting There & Away

AIR

La Serena's **Aeropuerto La Florida** (☑051-227-1870; www.aeropuertolaserena.com) is 6km east of downtown along Ruta 41. **Lan** (☑600-526-2000; Balmaceda 406; ☺9am-2pm & 3-6pm Mon-Fri, 10:30am-1:30pm Sat) flies daily to Santiago (CH$123,800, one hour) and to Antofagasta (CH$143,200, 1½ hours). There's another Lan office with longer hours in Mall Plaza.

BUS

La Serena's **Terminal de Buses** (☑051-222-4573; cnr Amunátegui & Av El Santo), which lies just southwest of the center, has dozens of carriers plying the Panamericana from Santiago north to Arica, including **Tur Bus** (☑051-221-9828; www.turbus.cl; Balmaceda 437) and **Pullman Bus** (☑051-221-8879; www.pullman.cl; Eduardo de la Barra 435).

Typical destinations and fares:

DESTINATION	COST (CH$)	DURATION (HR)
Antofagasta	31,200	12
Arica	37,600	23
Calama	31,900	14
Copiapó	9000	5
Iquique	32,900	19
Santiago	10,800	6
Vallenar	7700	3

To get to Vicuña (CH$2500, 1½ hours), Ovalle (CH$2500, two hours), Montegrande (CH$3800, two hours) or Pisco Elqui (CH$3800, 2½ hours), try **Via Elqui** (☑051-231-2422; cnr Juan de Dios Pení & Esmeralda). You can even do Elqui Valley as a day trip; the first bus to Vicuña departs at 6:40am and the last returns at 9pm.

For Argentine destinations, **Covalle Bus** (☑051-221-3127; Infante 538) travels to Mendoza (CH$34,000, 12 hours) and San Juan (CH$34,000, 18 hours) via the Libertadores pass every Sunday, leaving at 11pm.

TAXI COLECTIVO

A large number of regional destinations are frequently and rapidly served by *taxi colectivo*. *Colectivos* to Coquimbo (CH$1000, 15 minutes) leave from Av Francisco de Aguirre between Balmaceda and Los Carrera.

❶ Getting Around

Private taxis to Aeropuerto La Florida, 5km east of downtown on Ruta 41, cost CH$6000; try **Turismo Nielsen** (☑ cell 7659-9341; www.turismonielsen.cl). Alternatively, **She Transfer** (☑ 051-229-5058) provides door-to-door minibus transfer for CH$2500.

Women traveling alone should be wary of taxi drivers in La Serena; sexual assaults have been reported. Only take company cabs.

For car hire, try **Avis** (☑ 051-254-5300; Av Francisco de Aguirre 063; ⊘ 8:30am-6:30pm Mon-Fri, 8:30am-2pm Sat), **Hertz** (☑ 051-222-6171; Av Francisco de Aguirre 0225; ⊘ 9am-7pm Mon-Fri, 8:30am-1pm Sat) or **Econorent** (☑ 051-222-0113; Av Francisco de Aguirre 0135; ⊘ 8:30am-6pm Mon-Fri, 9am-2pm Sat). They all have stands at the airport as well as their downtown offices.

South of La Serena

Coquimbo

☑ 051 / POP 200,117

The rough-and-tumble port of Coquimbo, next door to La Serena, has been undergoing something of a revolution in recent years. Clinging to the rocky hills of Península Coquimbo, the town was long written off as La Serena's ugly cousin, but it has blossomed into the area's up-and-coming spot for nightlife. Despite its slow and steady gentrification, Coquimbo remains a gritty working port.

The **Casa de la Cultura y Turismo** (☑ 051-231-3204; Av Costanera 701; ⊘ 8:30am-5:30pm Mon-Thu, 8:30am-4:30pm Fri) houses a small exhibition hall and the town library. You may be able to get some tourist information here.

◉ Sights & Activities

On top of its nighttime buzz, Coquimbo is worth a trip for a wander around its beautifully restored 19th-century Barrio Inglés (English Quarter) and a visit to the fishing jetty for some fresh seafood.

Cruz del Tercer Milenio　　NOTABLE BUILDING

(Cross of the Third Millennium; www.cruzdeltercermilenio.cl; Cerro El Vigía; adult/child CH$2000/1000;

⊘ 9:30am-6pm; 🅿) A cross between a holy pilgrimage site and theme park, this whopping 93m-high concrete cross can be clearly seen from La Serena's beaches and makes for an outstanding lookout. The cross contains a museum (largely devoted to the late Pope John Paul II), prayer rooms and an elevator ride to the top. Mass is held every Sunday. The first level is free.

Boat Tours　　BOAT TOUR

(CH$3000; ⊘ 11am-8pm) Hour-long boat tours of the harbor depart regularly from Av Costanera in January and February, weekends only in winter.

🛏 Sleeping & Eating

You'll find a much wider variety of options in nearby La Serena, but Coquimbo does offer a few decent choices. For cheap seafood, hit the little restaurants around the market on Melgarejo.

Hostal Nomade　　HOSTEL $

(☑ 051-231-5665; www.hostalnomade.cl; Regimiento Coquimbo 5; dm CH$9000, s/d CH$10,000/20,000; 🅿🛜) Built in 1850 and once the French Consulate, Nomades houses several living rooms complete with odds and ends from the 19th century, a full kitchen, on-site bar, ping-pong table, large garden area and, of course, dorm rooms. It earns bonus points for only putting four people in each dorm.

Hotel Liverpool　　HOTEL $$

(☑ 051-232-6103; www.liverpoolhotel.blogspot.com; Las Heras 403; s/d CH$30,000/40,000; 🛜) Coquimbo's best hotel is nothing fancy, but the location in the Barrio Inglés just off the plaza is fantastic. Rooms are decent sized and comfortable enough – the best feature plaza or sea views.

Puerto Brasas　　INTERNATIONAL $

(Aldunate 865; mains CH$5000-8000; ⊘ noon-midnight Mon-Sat; 🛜) Some excellent fish dishes, good *parrilla* (barbecued meat) and live music on weekends make this a solid choice, tucked among the bars of the Barrio Inglés. The cafeteria also serves up the best coffee in town.

🍷 Drinking & Nightlife

Most of the nightlife action is along Aldunate, heading northwest from the plaza in Barrio Inglés, and below on Costanera. This entire area, stretching for several blocks, is chock-full with bars and clubs, which get going on weekends. Weeknights in Coquimbo can be pretty quiet, although the small strip between Aldunate and Costanera, called Ramón Freire, is likely to have a couple of bars open. Places in Coquimbo seem to come and go so we won't recommend any in particular. Wander around the area and you're bound to find plenty of action.

ℹ Getting There & Away

Coquimbo's bus terminal is between Borgoño and Alcalde. Many local buses and *colectivos* link Coquimbo with La Serena (bus CH$600, *colectivo* CH$1000, private taxi CH$7000 to CH$12,000).

Guanaqueros

📞 051

Petite Guanaqueros' long white beach makes it one of the area's most popular bucket-and-spade destinations. Situated 30km south of Coquimbo and 5km west of the Panamericana, it's suitable for a day trip, although cabin complexes dot the entrance road.

In town, the budget standout is **Hotel La Bahia** (📞 051-239-5380; Prat 58; s/d CH$20,000/25,000, r without bathroom CH$15,000), featuring great views and basic but acceptable rooms. A far better deal if you have a few extra pesos is **El Guanaquito** (📞 051-239-5218; www.elguanaquito.com; Av del Ocaso 2920; d/apt CH$40,000/50,000), offering spacious apartments with private balconies overlooking the bay. Doubles aren't so great, being located next to a noisy restaurant.

For eats, the local's choice is the **Centro Gastrononico El Suizo** (Av Guanaqueros 2427; mains CH$5000-10,000; ⊙9am-11pm), a semi-enclosed food court ringed by small bars and restaurants. Cheap seafood eats are also on offer around the fishing wharf.

To get here, catch any of the frequent buses leaving from the bus terminals in La Serena and Coquimbo (45 minutes, CH$1500).

Tongoy

📞 051

Just 18km beyond Guanaqueros, Tongoy is another lively little beach resort – the perfect place to savor fresh seafood, sink a few chilled *copas* (glasses) and be serenaded by full-throated buskers; you'll find the *marisquerías* (seafood restaurants) alongside Playa Grande. Playa Socos, on the north side of the peninsula, is a much more sheltered spot for a dip.

Hotel Aqua Marina (📞051-239-1870; Fundación Sur 93; s/d CH$28,000/35,000), right off the plaza on the main road in Tongoy, is the best budget hotel in town. It's just a few blocks to the beach, and the clean rooms, with their key-lime color scheme, are bright and cheery. Once it reopens after renovations, the **Hotel Yachting Club Tongoy** (📞051-239-1259; Costanera Norte 20) promises to offer fine upscale accommodations overlooking Playa Socos.

Frequent buses leave from the bus terminals in La Serena and Coquimbo, passing Guanaqueros en route to Tongoy (CH$1500, 80 minutes).

Parque Nacional Bosques de Fray Jorge

The last thing you'd expect to stumble across in a cactus-riddled semidesert would be lush cloud forest of the type found around Valdivia, 1205km south. But that's exactly what you'll find at **Parque Nacional Bosques de Fray Jorge** (Parque Nacional Fray Jorge; adult/child CH$2500/1000; ⊙9am-5:30pm), a smear of green squeezed between the ocean and the desert.

The puzzle of how this pocket of verdant Valdivian cloud forest came to exist in such a parched environment is answered by the daily blanket of moist *camanchaca* (thick fog) that rolls in from the Pacific Ocean. Come around noon and you'll witness this white cushion of clouds cloaking the sea and progressively swallowing the forest's base, giving the impression that you could be on top of the world – when you're only really 600m above the sea. That said, the best time to appreciate the forest's ecology is early morning, when condensation from the fog leaves the plants dripping with moisture.

Patches of green inland suggest that the forest was once far more extensive. Of Fray Jorge's 100 sq km, there remain only 400 hectares of its truly unique vegetation – enough, though, to make it a Unesco World Biosphere Reserve.

Scant mammals include skunks and sea otters, as well as two species of fox. There are also some 80 bird species; small hawks sit atop the cacti while eagles wheel high above in search of prey.

🏃 Activities

In the late afternoon the rising *camanchaca* moistens the dense vegetation at **Sendero El Bosque**, a 1km trail that runs along the ridge above the ocean. The trail is at the end of the 27km-long road from the Panamericana. The last segment of the road is very steep, rough and dusty.

❶ Information

Fray Jorge's gated road may be locked outside opening hours. The Centro de Información has piecemeal displays about 1km past the entrance; admission is paid here. The park is only open for day use; no camping is allowed.

❶ Getting There & Away

Take a westward lateral off the Panamericana, at Km387, about 20km north of the Ovalle junction. There's no public transportation but several agencies in La Serena offer tours. The park is a six-hour drive from Santiago.

Río Hurtado Valley

📞 053

The least explored of Norte Chico's valleys, this verdant region is crisscrossed with curvy roads, hillside hamlets and endless vineyards, all enveloped by barren mountains rising on all sides. It's the type of place where you won't see anyone for kilometers on end, and then a man on horseback will trot along its dusty roads.

By far the nicest place to stay is **Hacienda Los Andes** (📞 053-269-1822; www.hacienda-losandes.com; campsites per person CH$4500, s/d incl breakfast from CH$34,000/49,000; ⓟ), overlooking the lush banks of Río Hurtado. This gorgeously rambling hideaway offers skinny dipping in a cool highland river, dozy afternoons spent in a hammock and other ways to disconnect. It also has horseback trips (from CH$51,000 for three hours) during the day and even at night, as well as 4WD jaunts to nearby attractions. Free activities include scenic walks on the marked trails that dot the property. The latest addition is a small observatory, where you can observe the night skies for CH$10,000.

To get here, take one of the buses from Ovalle to Hurtado (CH$2100, roughly between noon and 7pm but check the website for details). The hacienda is 6km before Hurtado, just before the bridge. It can provide a pick-up service from Ovalle, La Serena and Vicuña. The hacienda is 46km from Vicuña via a gravel mountain road (best tackled with a 4WD but passable in a normal car), and 75km from Ovalle (the road is paved as far as Pichasca).

In nearby Hurtado, if budget is a concern, try **Tambo del Limarí** (📞 053-269-1854; Caupolicán 027; r per person CH$10,000) on the main drag, which has three immaculate rooms (one of which has a private bathroom) decorated with iron bedstands and light comforters above the *dueña's* (female owner's) home. She'll also prepare simple meals upon request for CH$4000 per pop, which is a boon since the only restaurant in town is mostly closed.

Limarí Valley

If you have your own transportation you can make a loop from La Serena to Vicuña, Hurtado and Ovalle. The 43km gravel road from Vicuña to Hurtado is usually manageable in a regular car, but a 4WD or high-clearance vehicle would be less hair-raising. The drive is through beautiful, sometimes steep, desert scenery with cacti, multicolored rocks and views of hilltop observatories. Public transportation from Ovalle goes as far as Hurtado, but there is no direct connection to Vicuña.

OVALLE

📞 053 / POP 103,700

The unassuming market town of Ovalle on the north bank of the Río Limarí is the capital of the prosperous agricultural province of Limarí. This workaday place is more famous for its surrounding attractions than its own modest charms, but it can be a useful base for exploring the area.

❖ Sights

Museo de Limarí   MUSEUM
(cnr Covarrubias & Antofagasta; adult/child CH$600/300; ⊙9am-6pm Tue-Fri, 10am-1pm Sat & Sun) Housed in the right flank of the grand old train station building, this sparsely labeled museum houses a beautiful selection of ceramics, the majority of which are Diaguita, dating from around AD 1000 to AD 1500, and changing modern art exhibits. There are also pieces from the earlier Huentelauquén and El Molle cultures.

🛏 Sleeping & Eating

Hotel Roxi   HOTEL $
(📞053-262-0080; www.hotelroxi.cl; Libertad 155; s/d CH$19,000/27,000, without bathroom CH$16,000/20,000) The best of the budget picks offers decent-sized rooms with blasting hot showers a couple of blocks from the plaza.

Hotel PlazaTurismo   HOTEL $$
(📞053-266-2500; www.plazaturismo.cl; Victoria 295; s/d CH$42,000/64,000; ⓟ❀📶) Ovalle's

grandest hotel has surprisingly average rooms (some with microscopic bathrooms – have a look at a few if you can). The plaza-side location and good on-site restaurant make up for them, though.

ⓘ Getting There & Away

Although Ovalle is 30km east of the Panamericana, many north–south buses pass through here. There are two major stations in town. The biggest is the **Terminal Media Luna** (Ariztia Oriente s/n), with service to most northern destinations and Santiago (CH$9000, five hours). **Terminal Norte Grande** (Maestranza 443) services northern destinations, including La Serena (CH$6700, two hours), Arica (CH$44,000, 25 hours), Iquique (CH$40,000, 22 hours) and Antofagasta (from CH$16,000, 14 hours). Regional companies provide service to more out-of-the-way places. For details on buses to Hurtado, check the Hacienda Los Andes website.

VALLE DEL ENCANTO

An intriguing gallery of pre-Columbian rock art can be found at **Monumento Arqueológico Valle del Encanto** (adult/child CH$500/300; ☺8:15am-8:30pm summer, to 7pm winter), a rocky tributary canyon of the Río Limarí 19km west of Ovalle. An array of petroglyphs and pictographs depict dancing stick-men, alien-like figures with antennae and characters sporting spectacular headdresses. The valley rocks are also riddled with holes called *tacitas,* which were used as mortars to grind ceremonial plants and food.

The figures mostly date to the El Molle culture, which inhabited the area from the 2nd to the 7th century AD. The rock art is best viewed around noon when shadows are fewer, but it can be very hot at that time of day.

To get here, take any westbound bus out of Ovalle and disembark at the highway marker; Valle del Encanto is an easy 5km walk along a gravel road, but with luck someone will offer you a lift.

TERMAS DE SOCOS

After a grueling day in the desert it's blissful to sink into the steamy thermal baths or a refreshingly cool swimming pool at Termas de Socos, a tiny spring hidden 1.5km off the Panamericana at Km370. Here you can indulge in saunas (CH$8000), Jacuzzis (CH$6500) and massages (CH$17,000). Private tubs cost CH$4500 for a half-hour soak; access to the public swimming pool also costs CH$4500 for nonguests. Spring water is bottled on-site.

The **Hotel Termas Socos** (☑053-198-2505; www.termasocos.cl; s/d CH$45,000/78,000; Ⓟ☒) is an unexpected delight. It is guarded by tall eucalyptus, surrounded by lush foliage and isolated amid arid hills. Its room rates include a piping-hot private bath and access to the pool. Slightly pricier rooms on the lower level have patios and TVs. All-inclusive rates are available.

Camping Termas de Socos (☑053-263-1490; www.campingtermassocos.cl; campsites per person CH$6000; ☒▥) is a pleasant gravel-and-sand campsite with its own pool and baths, though they are less swanky than those in the neighboring hotel. There's only partial shade but it has a good game room and playground. Nonguests can use the pool and picnic area for CH$3500, have a dip in the thermal waters for CH$3700 and rent bikes for CH$1500 per hour.

Elqui Valley

The heart of Chilean pisco production, the Elqui Valley is carpeted with a broad cover of striated green. Famous for its futuristic observatories, seekers of cosmic energies, frequent UFO sightings, poet Gabriela Mistral and quaint villages, this is a truly enchanting – and enchanted – area, and one of the must-visit places in Norte Chico.

Vicuña

☑051 / POP 25,085

The spirit of Gabriela Mistral's somnambulist poetry seeps from every pore of snoozy little Vicuña. Just 62km east of La Serena, this is the easiest base from which to delve deeper into the Elqui Valley. The town itself, with its low-key plaza, lyrical air and compact dwellings, is worth a visit for a day or two before you head out into the countryside to indulge in the nearby solar kitchens (where the sun cooks the food), and the fresh avocados, papayas and other fruits grown in the region – not to mention the famous grapes that are distilled into Chile's potent grape-brandy pisco.

◉ Sights

Vicuña itself offers a clutch of sights. All of the out-of-town attractions listed here are easily reached on bike and appear on the map available from Elki Magic.

THE BEST OF STARGAZING IN NORTE CHICO

Observatorio Cerro Mamalluca (☎ 051-267-0330; adult/child CH$4500/2000) The star of the stargazing show, the purpose-built Observatorio Cerro Mamalluca, 9km northeast of Vicuña, is Elqui Valley's biggest attraction. So big, in fact, that you're likely to share the tour with hordes of other tourists, all looking for their chance to goggle at distant galaxies, star clusters and nebulae through a 30cm telescope.

Bilingual guided two-hour tours take place nightly every two hours between 8:30pm and 2:30am in summer and between 7:30pm and 1:30am in winter. The cheesy Cosmo Visión Andina tour (in Spanish only) includes presentations and music but no access to the telescopes – so you're better off booking the basic astronomy tour.

Make reservations through the office at Av Gabriela Mistral 260 in Vicuña; advance booking is recommended. There is no public transportation, but a minivan takes visitors from the Vicuña office (reserve in advance; per person CH$1500). Some La Serena tour agencies arrange trips, or you can hire a taxi in Vicuña.

Observatorio Collowara (☎ 051-243-1419; www.collowara.cl; adult/child & senior CH$3500/2500) Like Mamalluca, the shiny hilltop Observatorio Collowara in Andacollo is built for tourists; no serious interstellar research is conducted here. Two-hour tours run in summer at 9pm, 10:30pm and midnight; in winter they run at 7pm, 8:30pm and 10:30pm. The facility boasts three viewing platforms and a 40cm telescope – slightly larger than that at Mamalluca. There are also three smaller telescopes available, so you won't have to wait for long.

There are plenty of accommodations in Andacollo, 54km from La Serena and connected by bus (CH$2000, 1½ hours) and *colectivo* (CH$2500, one hour).

Observatorio del Pangue (☎ 051-241-2584; www.observatoriodelpangue.blogspot.com; with transportation CH$21,000) The latest on the observatory front is Observatorio del Pangue, 17km south of Vicuña, run by three enthusiastic French and Chilean astronomers. The two-hour tours (in English, French and Spanish) leave nightly – unless there's a full moon – at 8:30pm (and on demand at 10:30pm) and offer pure observation, with a 10-person maximum.

Observatorio Interamericano Cerro Tololo (☎ 051-220-5200; www.ctio.noao.edu) Probing the mysteries of stars billions of miles into the past is all in a night's work at the futuristic Observatorio Interamericano Cerro Tololo, which sits at 2200m atop its hill. And while visitors can't stargaze through its monstrous telescopes (even the astronomers don't do that as the telescopes first feed data into computer monitors), a daytime tour of the facilities is still an enlightening experience.

Operated by the Tucson-based Association of Universities for Research in Astronomy (AURA; a group of about 25 institutions, including the Universidad de Chile), Tololo has an enormous 4m telescope. Free bilingual tours take place on Saturday only; make reservations at least one month ahead in high season. Two-hour tours are held at 9am and 1pm. There is no public transportation so rent a car or taxi, or arrange to come with a tour operator (you'll still need to make your own reservations with the observatory).

Alfa Aldea Astronomical Tours (☎ 051-241-2441; www.alfaaldea.cl; La Vinita; adult/child CH$10,000/5000) If you tire of getting herded around in the large observatories, you may be interested in the small, personalized astronomical tours (in English or Spanish) on offer at the Alfa Aldea. Held in the on-site amphitheater, tours start with a short video exploring the basics of astronomy, then get you up close and personal with the celestial bodies via scientific-grade telescopes. It's an open-air event – the whole thing takes place under the star-filled sky and small group sizes mean plenty of telescope time for everybody – but it can get frosty. Dress warmly (although the blankets, wine and chicken soup that come with the tour help cut the chill).

Astronomy Adventures (www.astronomyadventures.cl) For professionally guided astronomy tours, contact Astronomy Adventures, a La Serena–based outfit that arranges customized stargazing experiences all around Chile.

Museo Gabriela Mistral
MUSEUM

(Av Gabriela Mistral 759; adult/child & senior CH$600/300; ⊙10am-5:45pm Tue-Fri, 10:30am-6pm Sat, 10am-1pm Sun) The town's landmark Museo Gabriela Mistral, between Riquelme and Baquedano, is a tangible eulogy to one of Chile's most famous literary figures. Gabriela Mistral was born Lucila Godoy Alcayaga in 1889 in Vicuña. The museum charts her life (in Spanish only), from a replica of her adobe birthplace to her Nobel Prize, and has a clutch of busts making her seem a particularly strict schoolmarm.

Inti Runa
OBSERVATORY

(☑cell 9968-8577; www.observatorios.cl; Chacabuco 240; tours CH$8000; ⊙closed Jun-Aug) The German owner of this sun observatory claims he has two of the world's biggest solar telescopes. He keeps them in his lovely *casona,* and offers one-hour 'tours.' Basically, he talks while you look at the sun through the telescope.

Pisquera Aba
PISQUERA

(☑051-241-1039; www.pisquera-aba.cl; Ruta 41, Km66; ⊙10am-5.30pm) **FREE** This family-run boutique *pisquera*, in operation since 1921, offers quite a different view of pisco production to the mass-production setup down the road at Capel. The 40-minute tours take you through all the aspects of production and end up in the tasting room, with samples of their full range of products, from the classics to some innovative fruit blends. It's located on the edge of town – an easy bike or hike or CH$3000 in a taxi from the plaza.

Cervecería Guayacan
BREWERY

(☑cell 8360-7002; Calle Principal 33, Diaguitas; ⊙11am-6pm daily) **FREE** You won't get far in the Elqui Valley without someone offering you a Guayacan, and if you're even vaguely interested in beer, you should accept. This little craft brewery's reputation is growing fast and brief tours of the facilities are accompanied by a generous sampling of its products. The brewery's located in the cute little village of Diaguitas, about 7km from downtown Vicuña, and there's a beer garden serving up tasty pizzas (CH$6000) on-site.

Planta Pisco Capel
PISQUERA

(admission CH$1500; ⊙10am-7:30pm Jan & Feb, to 6pm Mar-Dec) A 20-minute walk from town, here you can take a 45-minute bilingual tour of the facilities, which includes an on-site museum and a few skimpy samples (CH$10,000 gets you the premium tour,

with top-shelf tastings). Capel distills pisco at this facility and has its only bottling plant here. To get here, head southeast of town and across the bridge, then turn left.

🏃 Activities

Vicuña is a great base if you want to devote more time to exploring the Elqui Valley. Not only is it the gateway to some great observatories, but it also offers bike rides into the surrounding countryside, trips to remote mountains around Paso del Agua Negra (in summer only) and horseback jaunts. There is even kitesurfing on the Puclaro reservoir, 10km away along the road to La Serena; **KiteSurf Puclaro** (☑cell 8464-9906; www.kitesurfpuclaro.cl; Herrera 161, Gualliguaiaca) offers classes.

Elki Magic
ADVENTURE SPORTS

(☑cell 7459-8357; www.elkimagic.com; Av Gabriela Mistral 472) Run by an enthusiastic Chilean-French couple, this agency offers guided downhill bike jaunts (from CH$15,000), half-/one-day van tours to valley highlights (from CH$15,000/25,000, with lunch in the solar kitchens) and trips to the lagoons near Argentina. They also rent bikes (CH$7000 per day) and can supply you with a map of the 16km trail around the surrounding villages.

🎊 Festivals & Events

Carnaval Elquino
CARNAVAL

Vicuña holds its annual grape harvest festival, Carnaval Elquino, in mid-January. It ends February 22, the anniversary of the city's founding, with activities including live music and folkloric dancing.

🛏 Sleeping

Alfa Aldea
GUESTHOUSE $

(☑051-241-2441; www.alfaaldea.cl; La Vinita; s/d/5-person cabin CH$15,000/25,000/60,000; ℗) It's worth the CH$2000 taxi ride (or 15-minute walk) to the outskirts of town to stay in this fabulously low-key family-run *hostal*. Nestled in the vineyards and with a priceless valley and mountain views, the rooms here are simple but extremely comfortable. The stars (sorry) of the show, however, are the excellent astronomical tours (p206) held on-site.

Hostal Valle Hermoso
GUESTHOUSE $

(☑051-241-1206; www.hostalvallehermoso.com; Av Gabriela Mistral 706; s/d CH$19,000/30,000; ☎) Great lodging choice with eight airy and immaculately clean rooms around a sun-drenched patio inside an old adobe *casona* with Oregon pine beams and walnut floors. Staff is warm and friendly and the ambience is laid-back – as if staying with old friends.

Hostal Aldea del Elqui HOTEL $$
(☑ 051-254-3069; www.hostalaldeadelelqui.cl; Av Gabriela Mistral 197; s/d CH$25,000/40,000; ☎☒) Another of the *casonas* converted into accommodations, this friendly hotel has well-kept rooms with good beds and TVs, some on the 2nd floor of a newer adjacent building. There's a tranquil garden with a small pool, swings, sauna, hot tub and a gazebo. Off-season, prices drop considerably.

Hostería Vicuña HOTEL $$
(☑ 051-241-1301; Sargento Aldea 101; s/d/tr CH$40,000/54,000/69,000; P☎☒) Its floral rooms leave a bit to be desired for the price, but the gardens have warm vine-touched patios with gazebos, sentinel palm trees and swinging chairs, a big pool area (available to nonguests for CH$4000 per day) and a tennis court.

Hotel Halley HOTEL $$
(☑051-241-2070; www.turismohalley.cl; Av Gabriela Mistral 542; d/tr CH$39,000/45,000; P☎☒) This breezy old mansion with creaking wooden floors has rooms with chintzy decor (think lots of lace, old radios and crosses), some with nice views onto the street. There's a swimming pool and ping-pong table out back.

Eating & Drinking

Antawara CHILEAN $
(Mistral 109; mains CH$3000-7000; ☺noon-midnight Mon-Thu, to 5am Fri & Sat) This is your best bet for late-night eats – otherwise problematic in sleepy Vicuña. Service is warm, the wine list is impressive and there's a good range of hot and cold *tablas* (platters) along with sandwiches and a good-value set lunch for CH$3500.

★Chaski CHILEAN $
(O'Higgins 159; mains CH$6500-8000; ☺noon-10pm Mon-Thu, to 11pm Sat, to 8pm Sun) This tiny restaurant run by a Diaguita couple offers up Elqui Valley's most innovative dining. Local ingredients, like quinoa, goat and amaranth, are prepared with a twist, and doused in fragrant Andean herbs.

Donde Martita Solar Kitchen CHILEAN $
(Villaseca village; menu with wine CH$6000-8500; ☺noon-4pm daily, closed Mon low season) Don't miss lunch at this restaurant 5km out of town, where back in 2000 a group of women discovered a groundbreaking way to cook with sun rays instead of hard-to-find firewood. At this best of Villaseca's solar kitchen restaurants, service is slow, but the food is deliciously tasty and paired with lovely vineyard views.

Frida CAFE $
(cnr Baquedano & Mistral; sandwiches around CH$7000; ☺9am-11pm) Vicuña's coolest cafe is whimsically decorated with Mexican knickknacks (the owners lived there for a while) and serves up super-strong espresso, good sandwiches and hosts taco night on Fridays.

Paraiso del Elqui CHILEAN $$
(Chacabuco 237; mains CH$5000-9000; ☺noon-6pm Mon-Thu, to 11pm Fri & Sat; ☒) Opened by a professional chef, this cozy spot with a backyard, two small dining rooms and tables on the patio serves up regional specialties, no less than 319 kinds of empanadas and good-value *almuerzos* (set lunches). Vegetarian offerings are also good.

❶ Information

There is a bank on the main plaza, which changes US dollars. The city center also has three ATMs.

Hospital San Juan de Dios (☑ 051-233-3424; cnr Independencia & Prat; ☺24hr) Located a few blocks north of Plaza de Armas.

Oficina de Información Turística (☑ 051-267-0308; www.munivicuna.cl; San Martín 275; ☺8:30am-8pm Jan & Feb, 8:30am-5:30pm Mon-Fri, 9am-6pm Sat, 9am-2pm Sun Mar-Dec) Gather a bit of info on the town's past and present at the municipal tourist office.

❶ Getting There & Away

From Vicuña, eastbound Ruta 41 leads over the Andes to Argentina. A rugged, dusty and bumpy (though passable in a regular car) secondary road leads south to Hurtado and back down to Ovalle.

The **bus terminal** (cnr Prat & O'Higgins) has frequent buses that travel to La Serena (CH$2000, one hour), Coquimbo (CH$2000, 1¼ hours), Pisco Elqui (CH$1500, 50 minutes) and Montegrande (CH$1500, 40 minutes). Expresso Norte has a twice-daily service to Santiago (CH$12,000 to CH$17,000, seven hours). There's a wider choice of destinations in La Serena.

Located inside the bus terminal complex is the **Terminal de Taxis Colectivos** (cnr Prat & O'Higgins), which has fast *taxi colectivos* that run to La Serena (CH$2500, 50 minutes) as well as Pisco Elqui (CH$2500, 50 minutes) via Montegrande.

Montegrande

📖 051

This skinny roadside village is the former home of the internationally renowned poet Gabriela Mistral, who is a Nobel Prize winner and national icon. Her burial site, found on a nearby hillside, is the destination of many Chilean and literary pilgrims. Mistral received her primary schooling at the Casa Escuela y el Correo, where there is a humble **museum** (admission CH$500; ⊗10am-7pm Dec-Feb, 10am-1pm & 3-6pm Tue-Sun Mar-Nov) dedicated to the poet, with a reconstructed schoolroom and dorm.

The small **tourist office** (📞cell 6320-2075; ⊗8:30am-5:30pm Mon-Fri) opposite the church has maps of the area and the latest on the transport situation to Cochiguaz.

Stop by **Casa de la Cultura Gabriela Mistral** (admission free, guided tour CH$1000; ⊗9am-1pm & 2-7pm Mon-Fri). On the main road through town, it's a cultural center and women's cooperative that conducts textile and art workshops with underemployed women from the area. There's a library for children on-site, free internet (tip if you use it) and gorgeous handmade crafts on sale, made on-site by the women.

There's a short trail leading down to the river just north of the Hotel Las Pleyades. It makes for a nice afternoon excursion – be sure to bring a swimsuit.

Set in an old adobe *casona*, the gorgeously rustic **Hotel Las Pleyades** (📞cell 8520-6983; monica.baltra@gmail.com; Montegrande s/n;

d CH$55,000; 🅿️🌊) is a boutique five-room hotel hideaway that offers nice touches such as cane roofs, leafy views, a shared kitchen and an outdoor plunge swimming pool with mountain views.

Mesón del Fraile (mains CH$6000-10,000; ⊗noon-10pm, closed Mon & Tue in low season), opposite Casa Escuela y el Correo, is worth a stop for pizzas with local goat cheese, stewed *cabrito* (goat) and great pisco sours. For the town's best *mote con huesillos,* a traditional dessert, stop at Los Paltos on Montegrande's plaza.

Local buses provide regular service from Vicuña (CH$1500, 40 minutes).

Pisco Elqui

📖 051

Renamed to publicize the area's most famous product, the former village of La Unión is a laid-back hideaway in the upper drainage area of the Río Claro, a tributary of the Elqui. It has become the area's most popular backpacker draw in recent years, and while it can get overcrowded, it's well worth a couple of days' stay.

⊙ Sights

Distilería Pisco Mistral   PISQUERA
(📞051-245-1358; www.destileriapiscomistral.cl; O'Higgins 746; tours from CH$6000; ⊗noon-7pm Jan & Feb, 10:30am-6pm Tue-Sun Mar-Dec) The star attraction is the Distilería Pisco Mistral, which produces the premium Mistral brand of pisco. The hour-long 'museum' tour gives

NORTE CHICO ELQUI VALLEY

SOUR RELATIONS OVER PISCO

Chileans celebrate the ubiquitous pisco sour – a tangy cocktail made from a type of grape brandy called pisco – as their national tipple. But mention this to a Peruvian and you risk having your drink thrown in your face. The trouble is, the Peruvians also claim pisco as their national beverage, and the bitter row over the liquor's rightful origin has been intensifying for decades.

Local legend tells how back in the 1930s the former Chilean president Gabriel González Videla personally changed the village of La Unión's original name to Pisco Elqui to undermine Peruvian claims of having originated the beverage. Meanwhile, Peru points to its own colonial port named Pisco in a grape-growing valley of the same name. The Peruvians have a strong historical case for appellation, if only because it was there that the Spaniards first introduced vineyards, and historical records demonstrate that the drink was consumed in Peru as early as 1613.

But Chileans argue that pisco has also been produced in Chile for centuries and claim that its pisco is of superior quality. They also point out that Chile produces, imbibes and exports vastly more pisco than Peru, and thus claim to have popularized the drink.

After years of acrimony Peru scored a partial victory in 2005 when it received a favorable enactment by the World Intellectual Property Organization (WIPO). But the legal wrangling looks set to continue for some time yet.

you glimpses of the distillation process and includes a free tasting of two piscos and a drink at the adjacent restaurant, which hosts occasional live music.

🏃 Activities

Pisco Elqui may be small in size but it's big in terms of tours and activities you can do in and around the valley. These include guided treks (from CH$12,000 per half day), horseback riding trips (from CH$6000 per hour, and more for multiday trips into the mountains), mountain-bike excursions (from CH$14,000) and stargazing trips (CH$15,000 to CH$25,000).

Reputable agencies in town include **Paralelo 30 Aventura** (📞 051-245-1061; www.turismoparalelo30aventura.blogspot.com; Prat s/n) and **Turismo Migrantes** (📞 051-245-1917; www.turismomigrantes.cl; O'Higgins s/n; ⏰ 10am-2pm & 3-7pm).

Bikes can be rented in several places around town for around CH$1500 per hour or CH$7000 per day.

🛏 Sleeping

Cabañas Pisco Elqui　　　　CABIN $
(📞 cell 8331-2592; Prat s/n; cabins CH$25,000; 🅿) Basic, medium-sized wood-floored cabins with full kitchen and a sweet front deck. The property rambles down the hillside, with a burbling stream running through it.

Refugio del Angel　　CAMPGROUND $
(📞 051-245-1292; refugiodelangel@gmail.com; campsites per person CH$6000, day-use CH$3000) This idyllic spot by the river comes complete with swimming holes, bathrooms and a little shop. The turnoff is 200m south of the plaza on Manuel Rodríguez.

Hostal Triskel　　　　　HOSTEL $
(📞cell 9419-8680; www.hostaltriskel.cl; Baquedano s/n; r without bathroom per person CH$15,000; 🛜) Up the hill from town, this lovely adobe and wood house has seven stylish and clean rooms with four shared bathrooms and a shared kitchen. A giant fig tree provides shade for the patio and there's a fruit orchard with lots of nooks, crannies and hammocks, plus bikes for rent and laundry services.

★ El Tesoro de Elqui　　　HOTEL $$
(📞 051-245-1069; www.tesoro-elqui.cl; Prat s/n; dm CH$13,000, d CH$32,000-50,000; 🛜🅿) Up the hill from the center plaza, this tranquil oasis dotted with lemon trees, lush gardens and flowering vines has 10 wooden bungalows with terraces. There's a restaurant that serves great coffee and cake and you can even get a massage or have your aura cleaned in the cabin by the swimming pool's 'beach.'

Refugio Misterios de Elqui　　CABIN $$$
(📞 051-245-1126; www.misteriosdeelqui.cl; Prat s/n; cabins for 2 CH$85,000; 🅿🛜🐕) Pisco Elqui's most luxe choice, sitting on the edge of town on the road to Alcoguaz, with seven cabins set around lush gardens that slope down toward the swimming pool and the valley below. Cabins come with stylish decor, such as headboards made of recycled train tracks, wooden beams, cool tile floors and terraces.

🍴 Eating & Drinking

Most restaurants in Pisco Elqui double as bars, and stay open until 2am or 3am.

El Rumor　　　　　　　RESTO-BAR $
(O'Higgins s/n; mains around CH$5000; ⏰noonlate) This jazzy resto-bar on the main road into town serves up great lunches (CH$5000) and giant sandwiches (CH$4000 to CH$5000) and, come night, 15 varieties of pisco cocktails. There's a Moroccan vibe to this tiny colorful spot that buzzes late into the night to a loungey soundtrack and occasional strumming of guitars in the lovely garden with a firepit.

El Durmiente Elquino　　　RESTO-BAR $
(Carrera s/n; mains CH$5000-7000; ⏰9am-10pm) Sample the tasty tapas, pizzas and interesting mains, like quinoa risotto, in the all-natural interior of this resto-bar full of wood, bamboo, clay and pebbles. Sip an artisanal beer or a glass of organic wine on the small patio out back, with nice mountain views.

Rustika　　　　　　　RESTO-BAR $
(Carrera s/n; mains CH$6000-8000; ⏰from noon) Across the street from El Durmiente, Rustika's outdoor section by a gurgling brook serves natural juices, pizzas and artisanal chocolates during the day. The cozy restaurant-bar section opens for dinner and remains buzzing till 3am.

ℹ Information

Note that Pisco Elqui doesn't have an ATM or a bank so make sure to bring enough cash with you. It also has no gas station so fill up before leaving Vicuña.

ℹ️ Getting There & Away

Frequent buses travel between Pisco Elqui (CH$1500, 50 minutes) and Vicuña.

Cochiguaz

📞 051

New-age capital of northern Chile, the secluded valley of Cochiguaz is accredited with an extraordinary concentration of cosmic vibes, a vortex of powerful energies, much-publicized UFO sightings and formidable healing powers. But you needn't be a believer to enjoy the beautiful valley, which is also the jumping-off point for hiking and horseback rides in the backcountry. It sometimes snows here in the winter, so bring warm clothes.

The town's latest attraction is **Observatorio Cancana** (www.cancana.cl; adult/child CH$5000/2500), run by the owners of El Alma Zen, located right across the road. They shuttle people in for the nightly two-hour tours with observation (at 9:30pm and 11:30pm in summer, 30 minutes earlier in winter).

🛏️ Sleeping

Camping Cochiguaz   CAMPGROUND **$**
(📞 051-245-1154; www.campingcochiguaz.blogspot.com; campsites per person CH$6000) Camping Cochiguaz has some labyrinthine camping grounds down by the river. It's located 17km from Monte Grande at the end of a tortuous dirt track. They also offer horseback-riding trips.

Tambo Huara   CABIN **$**
(📞 cell 9220-7237; www.tambohuara.cl; campsites river/forest per person CH$5000/10,000, cabins without/with bathroom CH$25,000/32,000) An idyllic little spot nestled between the trees by the river, Tambo Huara offers medium-sized eco-cabins (those with bathroom have composting toilets and solar showers). The riverside campsites are fantastic and there's meditation, healing therapies and yoga available on-site.

El Alma Zen   HOTEL **$$**
(📞 cell 9047-3861; www.refugiocochiguaz.cl; Km11; s/d CH$35,000/40,000, domes without/with bathroom CH$25,000/30,000; 🏊) The village is presided over by the hippy-kitsch El Alma Zen, which serves up conveyor belt spirituality. While, paradoxically, it lacks soul and service, it does have a full-service spa (book an aura cleaning), a restaurant (which doesn't open until 10am and charges CH$2500 for breakfast and CH$6000 for lunch or dinner), a small shop, two swimming pools and six concrete domes in a eucalyptus forest down by the river.

ℹ️ Getting There & Away

At the time of writing one bus left Cochiguaz on Mondays, Wednesdays and Fridays at 7am for Montegrande, returning at 6pm the same day. You can call the Montegrande tourist office to confirm the schedule. Otherwise, you can contract a driver in Montegrande who will charge around CH$8000 per vehicle (up to four people), or do as the locals do and try to hitch a ride.

Paso del Agua Negra

A spectacular roller-coaster of a road crosses the mountains into Argentina, 185km east of Vicuña. At an ear-popping 4765m above sea level, it's one of the highest Andean passes between Chile and Argentina. It's also one of the best areas to see the frozen snow formations known as *penitentes*, so called because they resemble lines of monks garbed in tunics. There are also accessible glaciers on both the Chilean and Argentinean sides.

From Vicuña, Ruta 41 climbs along the Río Turbio to the Chilean customs and immigration post at Juntas del Toro. It continues south along the turquoise reservoir known as La Laguna before switchbacking steeply northeast to Agua Negra. The road leads to the hot-springs resort of Termas de Pismanta in Argentina, and to the provincial capital San Juan.

The route is usually open to vehicular traffic from mid-November to mid-March or April, and cyclists enjoy the challenge of this steep, difficult route. The road is passable for any passenger vehicle in good condition.

There is no public transportation, but agencies in Vicuña and Pisco Elqui offer trips during summer.

Reserva Nacional Pingüino de Humboldt

Pods of bottle-nosed dolphins play in the waters of this **national reserve** (adult/child 5-15yr CH$2500/1000), while slinky sea otters slide off boulders and penguins waddle along the rocky shoreline – keeping their distance from sprawling sea-lion colonies. The 888-hectare reserve embraces three islands on the border between Regiónes III

EXPLORING THE ELQUI VALLEY

The first point of interest on the drive from Vicuña, at Km14.5 just before Montegrande and at an altitude of 1080m, is the **Cavas del Valle winery** (☑ 051-245-1352; www. cavasdelvalle.cl; ⏱ 10am-8pm summer, to 7pm rest of year) **FREE**. Opened in 2004, this little boutique bucks the trend by serving actual wine, rather than pisco. The *cosecha otoñal* dessert wine, made of pink muscatel grapes, alone is worth the stop. A quick tour of the facilities, with a tasting of three wines, is free, although you are encouraged to purchase a bottle.

An artisanal *pisquera* established in 1868, located 3km south of Pisco Elqui, **Fundo Los Nichos** (☑ 051-245-1085; www.fundolosnichos.cl; tours CH$3000; ⏱ 10am-6pm) still produces pisco the old-fashioned way. Its four guided tours (CH$1000; in Spanish only; at 12:30pm, 1:30pm, 4:30pm and 5:30pm daily in summer) include a visit to the facilities and a tasting of three piscos. Or just stop by between 11am and 7pm for a free tasting; bottles start at CH$3200.

Drive on from here and you'll reach the **Horcón artisanal market** (☑ 051-245-1015; ⏱ noon-7:30pm in summer, 1-6:30pm Tue-Sun rest of year) in the valley of its namesake village, worth a browse for its wealth of gorgeous handmade arts and crafts, local all-natural food and cosmetic products, all sold out of bamboo stalls. It's a feast of colors, dream catchers, wind chimes, knit dresses and jewelry.

From here, the paved road turns into a dusty dirt track leading to the adorable village of **Alcoguaz**, 14km beyond Pisco Elqui. Note its yellow and red wooden church and, if you wish to stay, move on to **Casona Distante** (☑ cell 9226-5440; www.casonadistante.cl; s/d from CH$45,000/50,000; ⓟ ⌗), a big wooden 1930s farmhouse beautifully restored into a rustic eight-room ecolodge with a swimming pool, riverside trails, a small observatory and a split-level restaurant.

and IV, and makes one of the best excursions in Norte Chico. The reserve takes its name from the Humboldt penguin, which nests on rocky Isla Choros.

Humboldt penguins breed along the Peruvian and Chilean coasts. The International Union for the Conservation of Nature and Natural Resources lists them as a 'vulnerable species,' with an estimated population of around 12,000 breeding pairs. Overfishing and the exploitation of guano were the primary causes for the penguin's decline, and experts say that if new conservation measures are not put in place, the species could well become extinct in the next few decades.

While noise and pollution from boats visiting the area is affecting local marine life, it is really Isla Damas – the only place where boats can land – that is suffering the most. Local biologists are reporting that the number of birds that call the island home has significantly dropped in recent years. The island was originally supposed to have a maximum visitation of 60 people per day. But these days, it seems that hundreds of tourists are flocking to the island daily. If you do decide to visit the park, you may consider skipping an excursion to Isla Damas altogether. If you visit the island, you should definitely keep to the established paths.

◉ Sights

At Punta de Choros boats ply the route to Isla Damas for CH$11,000; it lies 5.6km away from the shore. This 60-hectare metamorphic outcrop capped by a low granite summit has two snowy-white beaches with crystal-clear water: **Playa La Poza**, where boats land, and the fine-sand **Playa Tijeras**, a 1km walk away. Visitors are required to pay the visitor fee at a Conaf stand located at the Isla Damas dock and are only allowed to stay on the island for one hour.

Hired boats also pass Isla Choros where you're likely to see pods of bottle-nosed dolphins that splash alongside the boat, a large sea-lion colony, groups of otters and Humboldt penguins, and massive rookeries of cormorants, gulls and boobies.

Isla Chañaral, the largest and most northerly of the three islands comprising the reserve, is less easily accessible but most protected and least crowded. Its access point is the scenic coastal village of Caleta Chañaral de Aceituno, where boats take people to the island for about CH$94,000 (based on 10 people) between 9am and 4pm. There are a couple of campgrounds and a simple eatery.

Bad weather and high waves can occasionally prevent boat trips: call the **Conaf station** (☑cell 9544-3052; www.conaf.cl; ☺8:30am-5:30pm) to check conditions before leaving. Note that tickets for boat trips are only sold till 2pm.

From a turnoff on the Panamericana, about 87km north of La Serena, a rough gravel road passes through Los Choros and continues to Punta de Choros (123km from La Serena; about two hours by car). Caleta Chañaral de Aceituno is another 25km to the north.

🏃 Activities

Explora Sub   DIVING
(☑cell 9279-6723; www.explorasub.cl; 1-tank dive with rental CH$60,000) Arranges diving trips near Isla Damas. You'll find it 200m south of the Punta de Choros dock.

🛏 Sleeping & Eating

There are numerous homes offering both camping (around CH$2500 per person) and *cabañas* (beginning at CH$25,000) along the main road and in Caleta San Agustín, which also has food stands serving fish sandwiches and seafood empanadas.

Explora Sub   CABIN $$
(www.explorasub.cl; for 6 people CH$65,000; P🤚🏠) This cute group of cabins, 200m south of the Punta de Choros dock, looks out onto the sea. Each has a double room, bunk-bed room and a kitchen and living area. It offers free kayaks for guests.

Eneyde   SEAFOOD $$
(Punta de Choros plaza; mains CH$5500-10,000; ☺9am-7pm) This requisite post-trip lunch spot has pleasant outdoor seating that looks onto the town's main 'plaza.' It has a changing menu of locally caught seafood.

ℹ Getting There & Away

The park is best reached from La Serena. **Hector Galleguilos** (☑051-225-3206; Aguirre s/n) offers bus service to and from La Serena (CH$4000, two hours). Buses from La Serena depart from in front of the Los Griegos *panadería* (bakery) near the corner of Aguirre and Matta at 8:30am, beside the Japanese Garden at 9am. Call first to reserve a spot. La Serena–based travel agencies also offer tours. Unfortunately, the one-way 123km distance means transit time is long.

Huasco Valley

A lush thumb of greenery snaking its way down from the Andes, the fertile valley of the Río Huasco, roughly midway between Copiapó and La Serena, is famous for its plump olives, pisco and a deliciously sweet wine known as *pajarete*. However, the region's other claim to fame – mining – is now threatening this agricultural oasis after Canadian mining conglomerate Barrick Gold began a controversial mining project here back in 2009. To learn more about this issue, and the indigenous Diaguita community's struggle to protect their ancestral land, see the *Cry of the Andes* documentary.

Vallenar

☑051 / POP 52,090
The valley's principal town, Vallenar, is a bucolic settlement that runs at a soothingly slow pace. Strange as it seems, its name is a corruption of Ballinagh – an Irish town and home to the region's colonial governor, Ambrosio O'Higgins. After serious earthquake damage in 1922, Vallenar was rebuilt with wood instead of adobe, but the city's buildings still rest on unconsolidated sediments.

Though there is little to do in town other than stroll around the central plaza, it's a good jumping-off point for visits to Parque Nacional Llanos de Challe and a place to break the journey if driving or heading up north.

Motorists often bypass Vallenar because Puente Huasco (Huasco Bridge), which spans the valley, does not drop into the town itself. At the bridge's southern end, the Vallenar–Huasco Hwy leads east then branches across the river.

🛏 Sleeping & Eating

Hostal Real Quillahue   HOTEL $
(☑051-261-9992; pedroprokurica@yahoo.com; Plaza 70; s/d CH$18,000/29,000, without bathroom CH$16,000/26,000; P🤚) Located right on the south side of the plaza, this freshly painted blue building has 11 rather boring and noisy rooms with decent beds and TVs. Rates include a modest breakfast.

Humucao B&B   B&B $$
(☑cell 9822-8581; www.humucaobyb.com; Marañon 740; s/d from CH$30,000/45,000; P🤚) A stylish little option set in the back streets a short walk from the plaza. Rooms are graciously

appointed and the sitting areas have a very home-like feel. The generous buffet breakfast is another draw.

Hotel Cecil　　　　　　　　　　　　　HOTEL $$
(☑051-261-4400; Prat 1059; s/d CH$30,000/ 38,000; ☑☑) A few blocks east of the plaza, Hotel Cecil offers more soul and value in the cabin-style rooms, a verdant patio and a pool that sometimes has water.

Damiana　　　　　　　　　　　INTERNATIONAL $
(Prat 1451; mains CH$4000-7000; ☉noon-4pm & 7:30-11pm Mon-Sat) A cute little restaurant/ cafe a few blocks east of the plaza. The set lunches are good value, but the star of the show is the belly-busting Cabeza del Rey hamburger, which comes stacked with fried mushrooms, onion, pickles and bacon among other goodies. There's live music some weekends.

★Nativo　　　　　　　　　　　　　CHILEAN $$
(Ramírez 1387; mains CH$5200-13,000; ☉noon-midnight Mon-Thu, till 2am Fri & Sat; ☑) On a leafy block 10 minutes from the plaza, this stylish bar and restaurant offers up earthy decor of wood and adobe, snacks, and pizzas with unusual toppings like river shrimp and charqui (jerky). Stays open late, has set lunch menus, a nice sunny patio and a dome lounge in the back.

❶ Information

Banks with ATMs, a post office, internet shops and long-distance telephone offices are all available around the plaza.

Municipal Tourism Office (☑051-261-1501; turismovallenar@gmail.com; cnr Prat & Colchagua, 2nd fl; ☉8am-6pm Mon-Fri) Tucked away upstairs and sharing space with the department of culture, this office is extremely helpful, but woefully under-resourced. Can scrounge together a decent selection of brochures and maps.

❶ Getting There & Away

Vallenar's **Terminal de Buses** (cnr Prat & Av Matta) is at the west end of town, some 500km west of Plaza de Armas. **Pullman** (☑051-261-9587; cnr Atacama & Prat) is right next door, while **Tur Bus** (☑051-261-1738) is opposite the main bus terminal; both have extensive north- and southbound routes. Destinations include Santiago (CH$21,100, nine hours), La Serena (CH$6900, three hours), Copiapó (CH$5000, two hours) and Antofagasta (CH$10,900, 10 hours).

Huasco

☑051 / POP 8970

The picturesque fishing port of Huasco, an hour west of Vallenar by paved highway, has a beautiful seafront studded with squat palms, sculpture, shady benches and a scarlet lighthouse. There's also a good beach that sprawls as far as the eye can see.

Oddly out of place overlooking a desert shoreline, the alpine-style **Hostal San Fernando** (☑051-253-1726; Valdivia 176; s/d CH$24,000/28,000) has great ocean views from every room. Ask for a new room. Closer to Huasco's center, **Hotel Solaris** (☑051-253-9001; www.hotelsolaris.cl; Cantera 207; r CH$60,000-80,000; ☑☑) is modern and slightly soulless, but is by far Huasco's best hotel.

Just below the lighthouse, **El Faro** (Av Costanera s/n, Playa Grande; mains CH$7000-10,000; ☉noon-11pm Tue-Sat, noon-4pm Sun) offers the best views in town and an eclectic menu featuring everything from tacos to ceviche.

Buses to Huasco depart from the Vallenar bus terminal, and cost CH$1000. To return to Vallenar just flag down a bus from Huasco's main plaza. They pass every 15 minutes or so.

Parque Nacional Llanos de Challe

This isolated **national park** (adult/child 6-12yr CH$4000/1500; ☉8:30am-8pm summer, 8:30am-5:30pm rest of year) hugs the desert coastline 40km north of Huasco. It generally sees little traffic, except in those years when the *desierto florido* bursts into bloom. There is also an interesting selection of cacti, flighty guanacos and canny foxes.

The park is accessible only by private vehicle. It consists of a coastal sector south of Carrizal Bajo around Punta Los Pozos, and an inland sector along the Quebrada Carrizal, 15km southeast of Carrizal Bajo. You can guerrilla (free) camp at Playa Blanca near the park's entrance. There are good beach breaks along the coast here: good news for surfers, bad news for swimmers.

From Huasco, take the decaying asphalt road along the coast north from the nearby farming village of Huasco Bajo. Alternatively, a reasonable dirt road leaves the Panamericana 40km north of Vallenar.

Copiapó

☑ 052 / POP 154,900

With its pleasing climate, a leafy main plaza and many historic buildings, you may find yourself oddly comfortable amid the milling miners and down-to-business pace of Copiapó. That said, it's not really worth stopping here for too long unless you want to make a foray into the remote mountains near the Argentine border, especially the breathtaking Parque Nacional Nevado Tres Cruces, Laguna Verde and Ojos del Salado, the highest active volcano in the world.

The town, nestling in the narrow valley floor on the north bank of Río Copiapó, does earn some kudos for being the site of several historical firsts: South America's first railroad (completed in 1852) ran from here to Caldera; here, too, appeared the nation's first telegraph and telephone lines, and Chile's first gas works. All came on the back of the 18th-century gold boom and the rush to cash in on silver discovered at neighboring Chañarcillo in 1832. Today it's mainly copper that keeps the miners and beer-hall gals in the green.

⊙ Sights

Copiapó's mining heyday is evident throughout its town center. Shaded by century-old pepper trees, Plaza Prat, which marks the city's historical center, is graced by several buildings from the early mining era, not least the elegant Iglesia Catedral, with its three-tiered bell tower and neoclassical design.

Museo Mineralógico MUSEUM
(cnr Colipí & Rodríguez; adult/child CH$500/200; ⊙10am-1pm & 3:30-7pm Mon-Fri, 10am-1pm Sat)
This must-see museum literally dazzles. A tribute to the raw materials to which the city owes its existence, it displays a kaleidoscopic collection of more than 2300 samples, some as delicate as coral, others bright as neon under fluorescent light.

Museo Minero de Tierra Amarilla MUSEUM
(www.museomINerodetierraamarilla.cl; ⊙8am-5pm Mon-Fri, 9am-1pm Sat & Sun) FREE To find out more about the region's geology, head 18km east of town to this private museum near the village of Tierra Amarilla. Surrounded by working mines, the restored 200-year-old *quincho* (traditional mudhouse) features eight rooms exhibiting fossils, volcanic rocks, meteorites, minerals and oxidated rare stones. Catch a yellow *colectivo* from the corner of Chacabuco and Chañarcillo (CH$1000).

☞ Tours

Copiapó is the gateway for trips to highland destinations, such as Parque Nacional Nevado Tres Cruces and Ojos del Salado, and the coastline highlights like Bahía Inglesa and Parque Nacional Pan de Azúcar. Sandduning with a 4WD in the desert just outside town is another thrilling option. Guided tours to the surrounding mines are just getting started in the area; ask at the Sernatur office.

Puna de Atacama GUIDED TOUR
(☑cell 9051-3202; www.punadeatacama.com; O'Higgins 21; ⊙9am-1pm & 3-6pm Mon-Fri, 9am-1pm Sat) Ercio Mettifogo Rendic offers fun customized tours to surrounding highlights as well as lots of secret spots in the desert and the mountains.

NORTE CHICO COPIAPÓ

THE FLOWERING DESERT

In some years a brief but astonishing transformation takes place in Norte Chico's barren desert. If there has been sufficiently heavy rainfall, the parched land erupts into a multicolored carpet of wildflowers – turning a would-be backdrop from *Lawrence of Arabia* into something better resembling a meadow scene from *Bambi*.

This exquisite but ephemeral phenomenon is appropriately dubbed the *desierto florido*, or 'flowering desert.' It occurs between late July and September in wetter years when dormant wildflower seeds can be coaxed into sprouting. Many of the flowers are endangered species, most notably the endemic *garra de león* (lion's claw, one of Chile's rarest and most beautiful flowers). Even driving along the Panamericana near Vallenar you may spot clumps of the delicate white or purple *suspiro de campo* (sigh of the field), mauve, purple or white *pata de Guanaco* (Guanaco's hoof) and yellow *corona de fraile* (monk's crown) coloring the roadside.

Llanos de Challe is one of the best places to see this phenomenon, although the region's erratic rainfall patterns make it difficult to predict the best sites in any given year.

Aventurismo Expediciones ADVENTURE TOUR
(☑ cell 9599-2184; www.aventurismo.cl; Atacama 240) This agency has the concession on Ojos del Salado climbs.

★ Festivals & Events

Copiapó celebrates its own creation on December 8. August 10 is Día del Minero (Miner's Day).

Fiesta de la Candelaria RELIGIOUS
The first Sunday of February sees this festival celebrated at the Iglesia de la Candelaria at Los Carrera and Figueroa, 2km east of Plaza Prat. The Virgin of the Candelaria is said to protect miners – hence her celebrity in the region.

🛏 Sleeping

Hotels and *residenciales* (budget accommodations) get booked up by visiting miners during the week and prices are generally inflated year-round.

Hotel El Sol HOTEL $
(☑ 052-221-5672; Rodríguez 550; s/d CH$22,000/28,000; ℗🐾🗘) Cheerful yellow-painted hotel with a string of simple but clean rooms at a good price. It's just a short walk from the plaza.

★ Hotel La Casona HOTEL $$
(☑ 052-221-7277; www.lacasonahotel.cl; O'Higgins 150; s/d from CH$48,000/54,000; @🗘) There's airiness and charm to this wonderfully homey 12-room hotel a 10-minute walk west of the plaza, boasting a series of leafy patios and bilingual owners. All room categories have a country-casual feel, hardwood floors and cable TVs. The restaurant serves delicious dinners.

Hotel Bordeaux HOTEL $$
(☑ 052-223-0080; www.hotelbordeaux.cl; O'Higgins 490; s/d CH$42,000/56,000; ℗❄🗘) A good-value if somewhat bland business hotel boasting bright and spacious rooms with modern fittings. They're nice and quiet despite the downtown location.

Hotel Chagall HOTEL $$$
(☑ 052-235-2900; www.chagall.cl; O'Higgins 760; d CH$79,000-89,000; ℗@🗘☒) This four-star business property just off Plaza Prat has a swanky spotlit lobby, a full set of facilities and plush rooms; the more expensive ones are equipped with air-conditioning (and the cheaper ones with dinky little fans).

✗ Eating & Drinking

Restaurants in Copiapó may be pricier than you expect. There's a restaurant and bar scene popping up on Atacama, a few blocks west of Chacabuco – a good place to go for a wander to see if something catches your eye.

Café Colombia CAFE $
(Colipí 484; snacks CH$1800; ⊙9am-9pm) Right on the main plaza by Mall Plaza Real, this is a good choice for real coffee and snacks. Great people-watching from the sidewalk tables.

Six Fusion FUSION $$
(Atacama 181; mains CH$7000-10,000; ⊙noon-3pm & 8pm-1am; 🗘) Specializing in home-made pasta and doing a great sideline in sushi, this laid-back restaurant is one of Copiapó's new wave of innovative, stylish eateries. The shady backyard is the place to be on a sunny day.

Tololo Pampa BAR
(Atacama 291; ⊙from 8pm Tue-Sat) A happening boho joint with a series of artsy colorful rooms and an open-air back patio with rough-hewn furniture and an outdoor fireplace. Come for drinks and late-night snacks (CH$4000 to CH$5500).

ℹ Information

Numerous ATMs are located at banks around the plaza. There's a *cambio* (money exchange) on the 1st floor of Mall Plaza Real.

Internet cafes charge around CH$500 and can be found all over the center.

Hospital San José (☑ 052-246-5600; Los Carrera 1320; ⊙24hr) Medical care, eight blocks east of Plaza Prat.

Sernatur (☑ 052-221-2838; Los Carrera 691; ⊙8:30am-7:30pm Mon-Fri, 9am-3pm Sat & Sun summer, 9am-7pm Mon-Fri, 9am-3pm Sat rest of year) The well-run tourist office on the main plaza gives out a wealth of materials and information in English.

ℹ Getting There & Away

AIR

The Aeropuerto Desierto de Atacama is about 50km west of Copiapó.

LAN (☑ 600-526-2000; Colipí 484, Mall Plaza Real, Local A-102; ⊙9am-2pm & 3-6pm Mon-Fri, 10:30am-1:30pm Sat) Flies to Santiago daily (CH$178,800, 1½ hours).

Sky Airline (☑ 600-600-2828; www.skyairline.cl; O'Higgins 460) Flies to Santiago daily (CH$67,800, 1½ hours).

BUS & TAXI COLECTIVO

Bus companies are scattered through Copiapó's southern quarter. Virtually all north–south buses stop here, as do many bound for the interior. **Pullman Bus** (☑ 052-221-2629; Colibrí 109) has a large terminal and a central **ticket office** (cnr Chacabuco & Chañarcillo). **Tur Bus** (☑ 052-223-8612; Chañarcillo 650) also has a terminal and a **ticket office** (Colipí 510) downtown. Other companies include **Expreso Norte** (☑ 052-223-1176; Chañarcillo 655), **Buses Libac** (☑ 052-221-2237; Chañarcillo 655) and **Flota Barrios** (☑ 052-221-3645; Chañarcillo 631), all located in a common terminal on Chañarcillo. Note that many buses to northern desert destinations leave at night.

Standard destinations and common fares are shown in the following table:

DESTINATION	COST (CH$)	DURATION (HR)
Antofagasta	10,800	8
Arica	21,900	16
Calama	12,900	10
Iquique	21,100	15
La Serena	10,000	5
Santiago	26,900	11
Vallenar	7000	2

Colectivos take passengers to Caldera (CH$3500, one hour) from the terminal on Chacabuco. **Buses Casther** (☑ 052-221-8889; Buena Esperanza 557) also go to Caldera for CH$2500.

ⓘ Getting Around

TO/FROM THE AIRPORT

Private taxis to the Aeropuerto Desierto de Atacama cost CH$28,000; try **Radio Taxi San Francisco** (☑ 052-221-8788). There's also **Transfer Casther** (☑ 052-223-5891) which ferries new arrivals to town (CH$7200, 40 minutes). Buses and *taxi colectivos* plowing between Copiapó and Caldera may agree to drop you at the junction, from where it's a straightforward 300m walk to the airport.

CAR

Copiapó's car-hire agencies include **Hertz** (☑ 052-221-3522; Av Copayapu 173; ☺ 9am-6pm Mon-Fri, 9am-2pm Sat), **Avis** (☑ 052-252-4591; Rómulo Peña 102; ☺ 8:30am-6:30pm Mon-Fri, 8:30am-1:30pm Sat) and **Budget** (☑ 052-221-6272; Ramón Freire 050; ☺ 8am-6pm Mon-Fri, 8:30am-1:30pm Sat); all three can also be found at the airport. Another Chilean option is **Rodaggio** (☑ 052-221-2153; www.rodaggio.cl; Colipí 127) which has slightly cheaper rates and occasional multiday deals.

Parque Nacional Nevado Tres Cruces

Hard-to-reach **Parque Nacional Nevado Tres Cruces** (adult/child 6-12yr CH$4000/1500; ☺8:30am-6pm) has all the rugged beauty and a fraction of the tourists of more famous high-altitude parks further north. Apart from pristine peaks and first-rate climbing challenges, the park shields some wonderful wildlife: flamingos spend the summer here; large herds of vicuñas and guanacos roam the slopes; the lakes are home to giant and horned coots, Andean geese and gulls; and even the occasional condor and puma are spotted.

The 591-sq-km park is separated into two sectors of the high Andes along the international highway to Argentina via Paso de San Francisco. The larger **Sector Laguna Santa Rosa** comprises 470 sq km surrounding its namesake lake at 3700m, and includes the dirty-white salt-flat Salar de Maricunga to the north. There's a basic shelter on the south side of the lake.

The considerably smaller **Sector Laguna del Negro Francisco** surrounds a lake of the same name. The shallow waters are ideal for the 8000 birds that summer here, including Andean flamingos, Chilean flamingos and a few rare James flamingos. The highest quantity of birds is present from December through February. Conaf runs the **Refugio Laguna del Negro Francisco** (per person per night CH$12,500) here, cozy with beds, cooking facilities, electricity, flush toilets and hot showers. Bring your own bed linen, drinking water and cooking gas.

ⓘ Getting There & Away

It's easy to get lost on your way to the national park and there is no public transportation, so we recommend taking a tour from Copiapó. If you do decide to attempt it by car, a high-clearance 4WD is highly recommended, as well as a satellite phone and a really good map.

Sector Laguna Santa Rosa is 146km east of Copiapó via Ruta 31 and another (nameless) road up the scenic Quebrada de Paipote. Sector Laguna del Negro Francisco is another 81km south via a rambling road that drops into the Río Astaburuaga valley.

Ojos del Salado

Located just outside the Nevado Tres Cruces park boundaries, 6893m-high Ojos del Salado is Chile's highest peak (69m below

South America's highest peak, Aconcagua in Argentina) and the highest active volcano in the world; its most recent activity (steam and gas expulsion) was in 1993.

The mountain can be climbed between November and March. While some people try to climb it in eight days, this is not advisable. Only 25% of people attempting to reach the peak actually get there, and that's not because it's a technical climb – only the last 50m or so requires skill. It's because people don't take time to acclimatize slowly, so be wiser and allow 12 days for the climb.

Expeditions typically spend nights in two shelters en route to the peak. They start at the spectacular turquoise lake **Laguna Verde** (elevation 4342m), about 65km beyond Laguna Santa Rosa, which glows like liquid kryptonite – brighter even than the intense blue of the sky. There's a frigid campsite beside the lake, as well as shallow thermal baths in which to heat frozen toes.

Further up, at 4540m, climbers stay at Refugio Claudio Lucero. The next one up, at 5100m, is the Universidad de Atacama, managed by Refugio Atacama. Determined climbers then reach Refugio Tejos (5700m), from where only the peak remains.

Aventurismo Expediciones is the only agency allowed to take people up (US$200 to US$260 for the expedition). Because Ojos del Salado straddles the border, foreign climbers must get authorization from Chile's Dirección de Fronteras y Límites (Difrol), which oversees border-area activities. Permission can be granted on its **website** (www.difrol.cl) – it's free and should take less than 24 hours.

For more information on the park, stop by the Conaf or Sernatur offices in Copiapó.

Caldera

📱 052 / POP 16,150

Year-round sun, some great beaches and abundant seafood make Caldera – once the second-biggest port during the 19th-century mining boom – and its sister resort at nearby Bahía Inglesa the most popular seaside retreats in Región III. While Caldera is hugely popular with vacationing Chileans, most foreign visitors fall in love with neighboring Bahía Inglesa for its crop of great little hotels and restaurants and its laid-back vibe. If you're on a budget, it's cheaper to stay in Caldera by night and spend your days on Bahía's beach.

 Sights

Casa Tornini   MUSEUM
(www.casatornini.cl; Paseo Gana 210; admission CH$2000; ⏱6 tours daily during summer, at 11am rest of year) This red neoclassical mansion from the early 1890s, once owned by a family of Italian immigrants, is the town's newest attraction. The six guided tours daily in Spanish, English or German during summer take in six period rooms, with historical items and original furniture, plus two spaces that host temporary photo and art exhibits.

Centro Cultural Estación Caldera   HISTORIC BUILDING
(Wheelwright s/n; paleontology museum CH$1000; ⏱10am-2pm & 4-7pm Tue-Sun) **FREE** Built in 1850, this distinctive building on the north side of the jetty was the terminus for South America's first railroad. Today it houses a gorgeously airy exhibition space with wooden beams, sometimes used for festivals and various events, and a paleontology museum.

Muelle Pesquero   HISTORIC BUILDING
Down by the seafront, Caldera's colorful fishing jetty teems with hungry pelicans, colorful little boats and knife-wielding *señoras* busily gutting and frying the day's catch.

☞ **Tours**

The town's beach is slightly contaminated with gasoline from the nearby dock. You are better off taking a short day trip to Bahía Inglesa or further afield to Playa La Virgen. There's a 7km bike trail from Caldera to Bahía Inglesa.

Trimaran Ecotour   BOAT TOUR
(adult/child CH$3000/2000) You can take a one-hour boat tour to the lighthouse, spotting penguins and sea lions en route. Trimaran Ecotour has a kiosk on the jetty; it runs four tours daily (12:30pm, 2pm, 3:30pm and 5:30pm) during the summer, and on weekends only out of season.

🛏 **Sleeping**

El Aji Rojo   HOSTEL $
(www.elajirojo.cl; Tocornal 453; s/d CH$12,000/ 25,000; 🖥) Don't let the prices fool you – these are some of the best rooms in town. Beds are new, bathrooms are spacious and there's a fully equipped kitchen for guest use and a sweet little backyard sitting area. Bike hire is available for CH$5000 per day. No telephone.

Hotel Costa Fosil
HOTEL **$$**

(☑ 052-231-6451; www.jandy.cl; Gallo 560; s/d CH$33,200/43,600; **P**☎) This ship look-alike is the town's best-value hotel as well as its most central, just half a block from the plaza. Its 23 pleasant rooms are set around a breezy patio and there's a small sun-drenched terrace upstairs.

★Ckamur
HOTEL **$$$**

(☑cell 9220-9544; www.ckamur.cl; Camino al Faro 1018; r CH$87,200; ☎) ✗ Set up on the head-land 2km out of town, these are by far the most charming rooms around, built using traditional techniques and decorated with local handicrafts. Bonuses include fullly functional kitchens, killer bay views and a shady terrace area with communal barbecue.

✗ Eating

For the cheapest seafood, head to the Terminal Pesquero behind the old train station. The food stands here serve up simple fish dishes with sides from CH$3500, which you can enjoy on a wraparound seaside terrace. Outside the markct are several stands serving seafood empanadas and fried fish sandwiches.

For more interesting restaurants, head over to Bahía Inglesa.

★Cafe Museo
CAFE **$**

(Edwards 479a; cakes CH$1000-2200, sandwiches CH$2000; ☺8am-2pm & 5-10pm) Head to this cute little cafe with old posters and news-paper clips, adjacent to Casa Tornini, for its delicious cakes, sandwiches and real espressos on six wooden tables inside and a couple more on the sidewalk.

Miramar
SEAFOOD **$$**

(Gana 090; mains CH$6500-11,000; ☺noon-3pm & 7:30-11:30pm Mon-Sat) A posh pink restaurant on the seafront, with lots of windows offer-ing beach and harbor views, dependable sea-food mainstays and a decent wine list.

❶ Information

Oficina de Turismo (☑ 052-231-6076; Plaza Condell; ☺9am-9pm summer, 9am-2pm & 4-7pm Mon-Sat rest of year) The friendly tourist kiosk, on the western side of the plaza, offers a wealth of brochures although staff speak limited English.

❶ Getting There & Around

Private taxis to **Aeropuerto Desierto de Ata-cama** (☑ 052-252-3600; Ruta 5 Norte, Km863, Caldera), 20km to the south, cost CH$6000.

The **Pullman** (☑ 052-231-5227; cnr Gallo & Cousiño) and **Tur Bus** (☑ 052-231-7399; Gana 241) terminal is about five blocks southeast of the plaza, but you can buy tickets at their offices on the plaza. Buses run to Copiapó (CH$2500, one hour), Antofagasta (CH$12,600 to CH$22,700, six hours) and Santiago (around CH$28,000, 12 hours). Buses and *taxi colectivos* run between Caldera and Bahía Inglesa for CH$500 and CH$1000 respectively.

Bahía Inglesa
☑052

A short distance south of Caldera is the sweet little seaside resort of Bahía Inglesa. With rocky outcrops scudding out of the crystal waters, this is the place to come for a spot of beachside fun. It has become one of the north's most popular vacation spots, with a trendy vibe and a long white-sand beach. Most tourist businesses are on or around the beachfront Av El Morro, includ-ing the Domo Bahía Inglesa hotel, at the south end, which many locals use as a point of reference

Bahía Inglesa takcs its name from the British pirates who took refuge here in the 17th century; there are legends of their treasure still being hidden somewhere in these parts.

✗ Activities

Morro Ballena
WATER SPORTS

(☑cell 9886-3673; www.morroballena.cl; ☺9am-6pm summer, hours vary rest of year) Has a kiosk at the far end of the beach, below Coral de Bahía. It offers two-hour boat trips to El Morro island across the way (CH$60,000 for six people), one-hour kayaking jaunts (CH$18,000 for two) and one-hour snor-keling trips (from CH$18,000). It rents kay-aks (from CH$3000 for 30 minutes) and snorkeling equipment (CH$14,000 for two hours) as well.

Caldera Tour Atacama
GUIDED TOUR

(www.calderatouratacama.cl; Av El Morro 610b) Next to Domo Bahía Inglesa hotel. Arrang-es excursions and day trips (CH$17,000 to CH$34,000, with a six-person minimum) to nearby beaches such as Playa La Virgen, as well as to Pan de Azúcar and the San José mine near Copiapó.

Nautica La Rada
SAILING

(☑cell 6846-4032; www.morroballena.cl) For a worthwhile splurge, book a sailing trip with Nautica La Rada, run by seawolf Antonio and his sons. The shortest one (from CH$15,000 per person, with a two-person minimum, raw food snacks and drinks included) takes you to El Morro; you'll see humpback whales if luck strikes.

To rent the sailboat for a day costs CH$300,000 and overnight and multiday trips to Playa La Virgen are also available.

🛏 Sleeping & Eating

Cabañas Villa Alegre APARTMENT $
(☎052-231-5074; El Morro 578; apt with/without kitchen CH$50,000/35,000) The town cheapie offers decent little apartments with full kitchen just behind the Coral de Bahía hotel. The location is great. Rooms are a bit faded, but it's the best bet in town for budget watchers.

★ Coral de Bahía HOTEL $$
(☎052-231-9160; www.coraldebahia.cl; Av El Morro 564; d CH$55,000-75,000, ste CH$90,000, restaurant mains CH$7000-12,000; P 🛜) Eleven lovely rooms upstairs, some with balconies and sweeping ocean views at the far end of the beach. This hotel gets booked up in summer, when it accepts either seven-night advance reservations or walk-ins. The beachfront restaurant downstairs has a nice terrace, and dishes up delectable seafood with a twist. Asian, African and Mediterranean influences inspire the menu.

Nautel GUESTHOUSE $$
(☎cell 7849-9030; www.nautel.cl; Copiapó 549; d/tr CH$70,000/85,000, cabin CH$125,000; P 🛜) Stylish boutiquey guesthouse on a street just up from the Domo hotel. The modern building has six earth-toned doubles (four with ocean views) and there's an adorable four-person wooden cabin on the beachfront. The open-air kitchen and living space are a boon if you want to mingle, and there's direct access to the beach.

Hotel Rocas de Bahía HOTEL $$$
(☎052-231-6032; www.rocasdebahia.cl; El Morro 888; r CH$95,400; P @ 🛜 ≋) The town's swankiest hotel is this sparkling-white five-floor maze that shoots up the cliff overlooking the bay. All the rooms have balconies and lots of natural light; about half come with ocean views. The small pool on the 4th floor has stretching vistas.

Naturalia PIZZA $
(Miramar s/n; pizzas CH$3500-4800; ⊙10am-4pm & 7-11pm) Next door to Punto de Referencia and sharing the same terrace, this simple eatery churns out pizzas, empanadas and freshly squeezed juices.

Punto de Referencia FUSION $$
(Miramar 182; mains CH$8000-10,000; ⊙noon-1am) Chic choice tucked inside a side street right next to the Domo, this place specializes in sushi and sashimi. It has a good range of pastas too, served on light-colored wooden tables inside and a small terrace up front.

ℹ Information

There is no money exchange or ATM in Bahía Inglesa. The nearest ATM is in Caldera, so stock up before you arrive.

The small **oficina de turismo** (⊙10am-9pm Mon-Fri, 11am-9pm Sat & Sun summer, 10am-6pm daily rest of year), right on the seafront, is staffed with young enthusiastic Chileans who happily shell out useful phone numbers as well as info about secret beaches and spots in the area.

ℹ Getting There & Away

Most transit is out of neighboring Caldera. You can get there by *colectivo* for CH$1000 or arrange a transfer by minivan for a little less; the tourist office has phone numbers. In summer months *colectivos* get packed at the end of the day so you may have to wait a while. Minivans charge about CH$12,000 per person to get to Playa La Virgen, with a three- or four-person minimum.

Parque Nacional Pan de Azúcar

An abundance of white sandy beaches, sheltered coves and stony headlands line the desert coastline 30km north of Chañaral. Chañaral itself is a cheerless mining and fishing port set among the rugged headlands of the Sierra de las Animas and offers little appeal to the traveler; it's best used only as the gateway for the park.

It's the wildlife that brings most international travelers to Pan de Azúcar, which straddles the border between Regiónes II and III. That's because the cool Humboldt Current supports a variety of marine life. Star of the show is the endangered Humboldt penguin, which nests on an offshore island. Here you'll also spot slippery marine otters and rowdy sea lions, as well as scores of pelicans and cormorants.

The 437-sq-km park's altitude ranges from sea level to 900m. There are great coastal campsites, which get busy in summer.

⊙ Sights & Activities

Isla Pan de Azúcar ISLAND

The subtriangular-shaped Sugarloaf Island, or Isla Pan de Azúcar, lies a tantalizingly short distance offshore, its base often shrouded by *camanchaca* (thick fog) at twilight. It is home to about 2000 Humboldt penguins, as well as other birds, otters and sea lions. The island is a restricted area, but local fishers approach the 100-hectare island by boat for up-close-and-personal views.

Launches charge CH$5000 to 10,000 per person (depending on number of passengers, with a 10-person minimum) from Caleta Pan de Azúcar; in the low season, you could end up forking out as much as CH$50,000. Round trips take 1½ hours, and run from 10am to 6pm in summer, and to 4pm in winter. You'll have to sign up at the bay kiosk and wait for the next tour. Note that it is more difficult to round up enough people during the week; prepare to wait longer or pay more.

Trails HIKING

There are five trails in the park. The most popular is the 2.5km **El Mirador**; en route you will see sea cacti, guanaco and chilla fox. Next up is **Las Lomitas**, an easy 4km trail with minimal slope; look out for the black-hooded sierra finch. You can also walk the 1.5km coastal path that goes from Pan de Azúcar harbor to Playa Piqueros.

☞ Tours

Etty Tour GUIDED TOUR

(☏052-248-1733; www.pandeazucarettytour.cl; Gaspar Cabrales 3, Barquito; ⊙9am-6pm Mon-Sat) Guided tours (in Spanish) to Isla Pan de Azúcar from Chañaral for about CH$45,000 (up to five people) for half a day or CH$24,000 if the guide joins you in your own car. The owner can also hook you up with taxi transfers. In the high season these cost around CH$5000 per person.

🛏 Sleeping & Eating

Camping is available at Playa Piqueros, Playa El Soldado and Caleta Pan de Azúcar. The most basic facilities start at CH$2000 per person. Caleta also has two privately owned campsites. The closest town to the park is Chañaral, which is quite down-at-heel. Most people prefer to stay in Caldera, an hour further south.

There are three restaurants in Caleta Pan de Azúcar, which all charge about CH$5000 for a dish of fish with sides.

Pan de Azúcar Lodge CAMPGROUND, CABINS $$

(☏cell 9444-5416; www.pandeazucarlodge.cl; campsite per person CH$7000, cabins for 2/6/8 people CH$60,000/80,000/100,000) The best camp is run by the ecological Pan de Azúcar Lodge. It has two sites, one on Playa Piqueros and another on El Soldado, both with bathrooms, hot water, solar energy and activities (in summer) like yoga, treks and

NORTE CHICO PARQUE NACIONAL PAN DE AZÚCAR

WORTH A TRIP

VIRGIN SLICE OF BEACH PARADISE

Until just a couple of years ago, the stunning **Playa La Virgen** (☏cell 6393-5233; www.playalavirgen.cl), 46km south of Bahía Inglesa along a lovely coastal road, was a well-guarded treasure of just a few in-the-know Chileans. While the secret is now out, it's worth a day trip or a couple of days' stay at this little sliver of sandy paradise. In January the parasol-dotted beach gets packed with a young party crowd; in February it's families who move in.

You can head there with one of the tour agencies in Caldera or Bahía Inglesa or arrange your own minivan transport. If you have your own wheels, note that the road is rough (but doable with a regular car) and that it costs CH$6000 to park by the reception, unless you're renting one of the cabins. To avoid the fee, park at the top and walk downhill for 10 minutes to the crescent-shaped beach.

Kayaks are for rent on the beach (CH$3500 for a single, CH$7000 for a double).

For accommodations, two-person cabins start at CH$65,000 in high season; it's CH$95,000 for one with a kitchen. A campsite (no electricity) for six people costs CH$42,000. The pricey restaurant-bar, earthy **Turqueza** (mains CH$8500-12,000; ⊙8am-11pm), has sandy floors, a thatched roof, straw chairs and a terrace with panoramic ocean views.

various workshops. The lodge also has five beach cabins and an outdoor spa.

ⓘ Information

One kilometer south of Caleta Pan de Azúcar, Conaf's **Environmental Information Center** (Playa Piqueros; ⊙8:30am-12:30pm & 2-6pm) has exhibits on the park's flora and fauna, and a cactarium. It also has a brochure in English, with explanations and a trails map. There is a Conaf checkpoint at Km15 on the southern entrance road from Chañaral, where you pay the CH$3000 fee. Make sure you hold on to your ticket, as you'll be asked to present it at different trailheads.

ⓘ Getting There & Away

Pan de Azúcar is 30km north of Chañaral by a well-maintained paved road. Most people reach it by tour or transfer from Caldera/Bahía Inglesa or Copiapó.

Taxis from Chañaral charge around CH$25,000 to drop you off in the morning and return to pick you up in the afternoon.

If you are driving from the north, there are two minor park entrances off the Panamericana – one at Km1014 (connecting to Route C-112) and another at Km968 (connecting to Route C-110).

Sur Chico

Best Places to Eat

➡ Cotelé (p275)

➡ La Fleur de Sel (p242)

➡ Chile Picante (p275)

➡ Cocina Mapuche Mapu Lyagl (p247)

➡ Cervecería Artesenal Armin Schmid (p258)

Best Places to Stay

➡ Refugio Tinquilco (p247)

➡ Refugio Cochamó (p272)

➡ La Montaña Magica (p253)

➡ Los Caiquenes (p264)

➡ Hotel Antumalal (p241)

Why Go?

Hence begins the Chilean south. The regions of La Araucanía, Los Ríos and the Lakes District jar travelers with menacing ice-topped volcanoes, glacial lakes overflowing with what looks like melted jade, roaring rivers running through old growth forests and coastal enclaves inhabited by the indomitable Mapuche people. Sur Chico is home to eight spectacular national parks, many harboring exquisitely conical volcanoes, and is a magnetic draw for outdoor adventure enthusiasts and devil-may-care thrillseekers.

Peppered about sprawling workhorse travel hubs, you'll find well-developed lakeside hamlets, most notably Pucón and Puerto Varas, dripping in charm and draped by stunning national parks and nature reserves, each one like an Ansel Adams photograph leaping from the frame. But the region – call it Patagonia Lite – isn't all so perfectly packaged. Off-the-beaten-path destinations like the Cochamó Valley and Caleta Condor reward the intrepid spectacularly, their isolation fodder for that ever-elusive travel nirvana.

When to Go
Puerto Montt

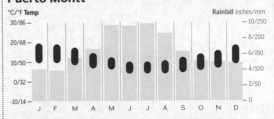

Jan–Feb Summer in this weathered region brings less rain, but you'll still need a raincoat.

Nov–Mar Navimag ferry high season: spectacular Patagonian sunsets and glaciers.

Jan One of the most crowded months for visiting Volcán Villarrica but also the sunniest skies.

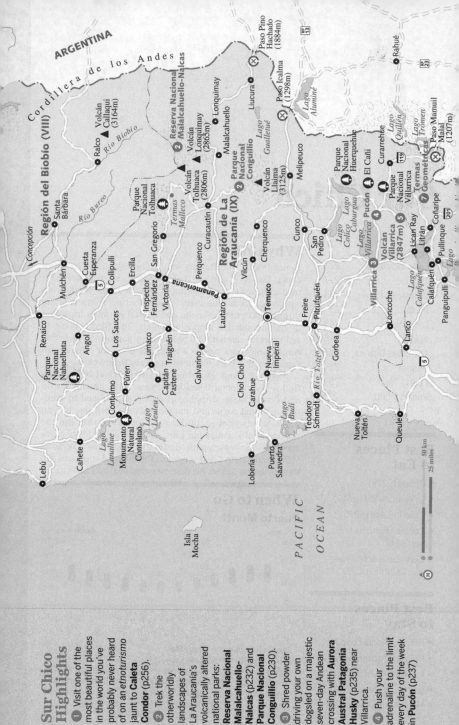

Sur Chico Highlights

1 Visit one of the most beautiful places in the world you've probably never heard of on an *etnoturismo* jaunt to **Caleta Condor** (p256).

2 Trek the otherworldly landscapes of La Araucanía's volcanically altered national parks: **Reserva Nacional Malalcahuello-Nalcas** (p232) and **Parque Nacional Conguillío** (p230).

3 Shred powder driving your own dogsled on a majestic seven-day Andean crossing with **Aurora Austral Patagonia Husky** (p235) near Villarrica.

4 Push your adrenaline to the limit every day of the week in **Pucón** (p237)

and **Puerto Varas** (p259).

5 Glissade down **Volcán Villarrica** (p243) beneath its fuming crater.

6 Hike or horse trek deep into the Río Cochamó Valley to the granite playground at impossibly gorgeous **La Junta** (p271).

7 Burn a day at the romantic and spectacular **Termas Geométricas** (p246).

8 Sleep in a fairy-tale hotel inside **Huilo-Huilo Reserva Natural Biosfera** (p253).

History

As the Spanish conquistadores pushed their way south from present-day Santiago, they were motivated by stories of precious metals and the possibility of a large, docile indigenous workforce. The land of La Araucanía and the Lakes District would be the ideal territory to continue the imperial dream. Or maybe not. The Mapuche waged one of the fiercest and most successful defenses against the European invaders anywhere in the Americas, and the Spanish were not able to settle south of the Río Biobío until the mid- to late 19th century.

Germans were recruited to settle the Lakes District, leaving their mark on architecture, food, manufacturing and dairy farming. Today millions of national and international tourists, plus wealthy Santiago refugees looking for country homes, are doing more than anybody to continue to tame and colonize the once wild lands. Real-estate prices are skyrocketing and the several hundred thousand remaining Mapuche are being pushed further and further into the countryside. Tourism, logging and salmon farming – despite a near-collapse in the late 2000s – are driving the future of the region.

In 2007, the Lakes District was subdivided and Chile's 14th region, Los Ríos, was created with Valdivia as its capital, returning to the city the power it had held up until 1974, when the military junta deemed it second class during a regional restructuring and stripped it of its designation as an administrative capital.

ⓘ Getting There & Away

Most visitors enter this region by bus or plane from Santiago. All of the major cities also have airports. By the time you get to Puerto Montt you are pretty far from Santiago and the short flight will save you a lot of time on the bus. Puerto Montt is also the ferry terminus for the Patagonian ferries, the most popular of which takes travelers back and forth to Puerto Natales.

THE INDOMITABLE MAPUCHE

Chile's largest indigenous group, the Mapuche (*che* meaning 'people' and *mapu* meaning 'of the land'), is the first and only indigenous nation on the continent whose sovereignty and independence was legally recognized, but they have exhausted generations in fighting to keep it that way.

The Mapuche first successfully fought off the marauding Inka empire, only to take on a sustained 300-year attack by the Spanish. They used the Río Biobío as a natural frontier and resisted colonization until the 19th century. It was the longest and hardest-fought indigenous defense in the Americas. By its end, the nation's once vast territory of 100,000 sq km was reduced to a mere 5000 sq km of *reducciones* (settlements).

The Mapuche signed the Treaty of Killin with the colonizing Spaniards in 1641 (the document solidified the territorial autonomy of the Mapuche and 28 others over two centuries of diplomatic relations). Yet, in the late 1800s, the Chilean and Argentine military massacred an estimated 100,000 Mapuche. From 1965 to 1973, land reform improved the situation for the Mapuche, but the military coup of 1973 reversed many of these gains. Between the restoration of democracy in 1989 and 2015, the Mapuche people made limited progress in their continuing fight for reparations and the return of their lands. However, most of the court rulings granting them land were effectively overturned by powerful business interests.

Various human rights organizations, as well as the Special Rapporteur of the UN, have widely reported the imposition of assimilation policies, and protests in Temuco are nearly a daily affair. In 2010 a series of hunger strikes were organized by Mapuche leaders in response to the Chilean government's efforts to prosecute some of the Mapuche community's more violent wings, such as the Coordinadora Arauco-Malleco (CAM). The government has accused it of using occupation, death threats and arson as tactics in the ongoing dispute.

The battle continues: Mapuches have been accused by the Chilean government of setting several deadly wildfires in Araucanía, which killed seven firefighters in 2012, as well as arson retaliations for the controversial death of Matías Catrileo, a Mapuche university student killed by police during Chilean student protests, in 2013.

ⓘ Getting Around

La Araucanía, Los Ríos and the Lakes District have an excellent network of buses: big buses, minibuses, vans, minivans and pretty much anything else that you can imagine. Bus transportation is the easiest and most low-maintenance way to get around. To get to some of the smaller and more remote towns, it may be necessary to backtrack to the closest city in order to find the correct bus. The roads are accessible for rental cars. There are taxis and occasionally *colectivos* (shared taxis) within all of the larger towns that cannot be covered on foot.

LA ARAUCANÍA

Temuco

🗗 045 / POP 262,530

With its leafy, palm-filled plaza, its pleasant Mercado Municipal and its intrinsic link to Mapuche culture, Temuco is the most palatable of Sur Chico's blue-collar cities to visit. The city is the former home of Pablo Neruda, one of most influential poets of the 20th century, who once called it the Wild West.

◉ Sights

**Museo Regional de
La Araucanía** MUSEUM
(www.museoregionalaraucania.cl; Av Alemania 084; adult/child CH$600/300; ⊙ 9:30am-5:30pm Tue-Fri, 11am-5pm Sat, 11am-2pm Sun) Housed in a handsome frontier-style building dating from 1924, this small but vibrant regional museum has permanent exhibits recounting the history of the Araucanían peoples before, during and since the Spanish invasion in its newly renovated basement collection, including an impressive Mapuche dugout canoe.

Be sure to check out the small Fundación Chol-Chol boutique, a nonprofit Fair Trade organization working with 600 rural Mapuche women to offer top-quality weaving and textiles made entirely by hand.

🛏 Sleeping

Temuco is not fundamentally a tourist town. Budget options around the train station and Feria Pinto are inexpensive and downright dirty. The neighborhood between the Plaza de Armas and the university has higher-quality budget options and is more secure at night for women.

Hospedaje Tribu Piren GUESTHOUSE $
(🗗 045-298-5711; www.tribupiren.cl; Prat 69; r per person without bathroom CH$15,000; 🅿@🛜) The young English-speaking owner at this traveler's *hospedaje* (budget accommodations) makes this a great choice for foreigners. Everything is clean and polished, and rooms, some of which open out onto a small terrace, offer cable TV and central heating. Alvaro, the owner, also guides snow-sport tours in the winter.

Hospedaje Klickmann GUESTHOUSE $
(🗗 045-274-8297; www.hospedajeklickmann.cl; Claro Solar 647; r per person with/without bathroom CH$16,500/13,800; 🅿@🛜) This clean and friendly family-run *hospedaje* is barely a hiccup from several bus companies.

Hostal Callejón Massmann GUESTHOUSE $$
(🗗 045-248-5955; www.hostalcm.cl; Callejón Massmann 350; r from CH$45,000; 🅿🛜) Single travelers get shafted on room prices, but it's otherwise hard to find fault with this new midrange choice in a lovely home that evokes the architecture of the countryside. The 10 rooms feature stylish furnishings and duvets and there's a lovely backyard patio, all with the advantage of being within walking distance of the best restaurants and nightlife.

🍴 Eating & Drinking

Temuco's best restaurants and bars are along Av Alemania and Av San Martín between Theirs and Trizano on Temuco's west side – catch *colectivos* marked 'Av Alemania' heading west on Manuel Montt. Cheap and lively eats can be had at the **Mercado Municipal** (cnr Bulnes & Portales; ⊙ 10am-7pm Mon-Fri, 11am-5pm Sun) and the dynamic **Feria Pinto** (Av Barros Arana; meals CH$2000-3000; ⊙ 8am-7pm), where vendors churn out *cazuelas* (stews), *sopapillas con queso* (traditional fried dough with cheese), empanadas, seafood stews and other tasty dishes.

★ Tradiciones Zuny CHILEAN $
(Tucapel 1374; meals CH$2000-4000; ⊙ 12:30-4:30pm Mon-Fri) Temuco's best-kept secret is an underground locals' haunt specializing in the fresh, simple food of the countryside served out of an indigenous-themed home. It's hard to find – look for the colorful duck/basketball mural – but the cheap, Chilean-Mapuche organic fusion cuisine is a showstopper. You're welcome.

Temuco

Temuco

⊙ Sights

🛏 Sleeping

🍴 Eating

🍷 Drinking & Nightlife

🛍 Shopping

Gohan Sushi   JAPANESE $$
(www.gohan.cl; España 390; rolls CH$2950-6950; ⊙1-3pm & 8pm-midnight Mon-Fri, 1:30-3:30pm & 8pm-midnight Sat; 🛜) This innovative and trendy sushi spot gets the job done with an extensive list of funky rolls and shrimp dishes. There's a **branch** (www.gohan.cl; Vicuña Mackenna 531) too.

La Pampa   STEAKHOUSE $$
(www.lapampa.cl; Av San Martín 0137; steaks CH$9200-14,000; ⊙noon-4pm & 8pm-midnight Mon-Sat, to 3:30pm Sun; 🛜) The best beef in the region is further south, but this high-style, two-story steakhouse is the Temuco hot spot for carnivores.

La Fuente   BAR
(Av San Martín 0265; sandwiches CH$4800-6500; ⊙12:30-11:30pm Mon-Sat; 🛜) Chase tasty gourmet sandwiches – try El Patagónico or El Alemán – with rarer Chilean craft beers.

🛍 Shopping

Temuco is great for Mapuche woolen goods (ponchos, blankets and pullovers), pottery and musical instruments, such as *zampoñas* (panpipes) or drums. The best spot in town is the Mercado Municipal.

ⓘ Information

Keep an eye out for pickpockets in *centro*, especially Mercado Municipal and Feria Pinto. Snatch-and-grab thievery has also been reported on the Cerro Ñielol hike. ATMs and exchange houses are plentiful all around Plaza de Armas Aníbal Pinto.

Conaf (☑ 045-229-8149; Bilbao 931; ⊘ 9am-1pm & 2-5:30pm Mon-Thu, to 4:30pm Fri) Mainly administrative offices, but has maps of the regional parks at the information booth.

CorreosChile (www.correos.cl; cnr Diego Portales & Prat; ⊘ 9am-7pm Mon-Fri, to 1pm Sat) Postal services.

Hospital Hernán Henríquez Aravena (☑ 045-255-9000; www.hhha.cl; Manuel Montt 115; ⊘ 24hr) Six blocks west and one block north of Plaza de Armas Aníbal Pinto.

Sernatur (☑ 045-240-6200; www.sernatur.cl; cnr Bulnes & Claro Solar; ⊘ 9am-2pm & 3-6pm Mon-Fri, 10am-2pm Sat) Well-stocked national tourist info.

Tourist Information Kiosk (☑ 045-297-3628; www.temucochile.com; Mercado Municipal; ⊘ 9am-6pm Mon-Sat, 10am-2pm Sun Jan-Feb, 9am-6pm Mon-Fri, to 2pm Sun Mar-Dec) Temuco operates two helpful city tourism kiosks. Free city tours on Tuesday, Friday and Saturday leave from the plaza location (☑ cell 6238-0660; Plaza de Armas; ⊘ 9am-6pm Mon-Fri, 10am-2pm Sat, 9am-noon Sun Jan-Feb, 9am-6pm Mon-Fri, 10am-2pm Sat Mar-Dec) at 9:45am.

ⓘ Getting There & Away

AIR

Temuco's shiny new **Aeropuerto de La Araucanía** (☑ 045-220-1900; www.aeropuertoaraucania.cl; Longitudinal Sur Kilómetro 692, Freire) is located near Freire, 20km south of the city. **LAN** (☑ 600-526-2000; www.lan.com; Bulnes 687; ⊘ 9am-1:30pm & 3-6:30pm Mon-Fri, 10am-1pm Sat) and **Sky Airlines** (☑ 045-275-7300; www.skyairline.cl; Bulnes 677; ⊘ 9am-7pm Mon-Fri, 10am-1pm Sat) fly seven times daily between them to Santiago (from CH\$62,586).

BUS

Temuco is a major transport hub. Long-haul bus services run from the **Terminal Rodoviario** (☑ 045-222-5005; Pérez Rosales 01609), located at the northern approach to town. Companies have ticket offices around downtown.

Bus lines serving main cities located along the Panamericana include: **Tur-Bus** (☑ 045-268-6604; www.turbus.cl; Claro Solar 625) and **Pullman Bus** (☑ 045-221-2137; www.pullman.cl; Claro Solar 611), both of which offer frequent services to Santiago and the latter to Valparaíso/Viña del Mar; **Cruz del Sur** (☑ 045-273-0315; www.busescruzdelsur.cl; Claro Solar 599), which is also set up at **Manuel Montt 290** (☑ 045-273-0315; www.busescruzdelsur.cl; Manuel Montt 290) and serves the island of Chiloé; and **Igi Llaima/Nar-Bus** (☑ 045-240-7700; www.igillaima.cl; Balmaceda 995), whose buses will pass by their Balmaceda station if you buy tickets there but otherwise originate at Miraflores 1535.

The latter heads to Neuquén (3am on Monday, Thursday and Saturday, and 8am on Tuesday, Wednesday, Friday and Sunday) and San Martín de los Andes, Argentina (7am daily), among others. **Andesmar** (☑ 045-225-8626; www.andesmar.com; based at the Rodoviario, offers the only departure for Bariloche from Temuco (CH\$28,000, eight hours, Tuesday and Saturday, 10:15am) – otherwise you'll need to get to Osorno.

The **Terminal de Buses Rurales** (☑ 045-221-0494; Av Aníbal Pinto 32) serves local and regional destinations. For Parque Nacional Conguillío's three entrances, Nar-Bus goes to Melipeuco eight times per day Monday to Saturday (CH$1900, two hours, 8am to 6:30pm) and considerably less often on Sunday. Vogabus runs hourly to Cherquenco (CH$1400, 1½ hours, 8am to 8:30pm), from where it's a 17km walk or hitchhike to the ski lodge at Los Paraguas; and **Buses Curacautín Express** (☑ cell 5699-3525) heads off for Curacautín seven times per day (CH$1500, every 30 minutes, 6:30am to 9pm), with just three departures on Sunday.

Buses JAC (☑ 045-299-3117; www.jac.cl; cnr Av Balmaceda & Aldunate), with its own terminal, offers the most frequent service to Villarrica and Pucón, plus services to Santiago, Lican Ray and Coñaripe.

Buses Bio Bio (☑ 045-265-7876; www.buses-biobio.cl; Lautaro 854) operates hourly services to Los Angeles and Concepción; as well as Chillán (4:45pm daily) and Lonquimay (CH$4300, three hours, 7am, 1:15pm, 5:15pm and 7pm).

Sample travel times and starting fares are as follows (prices fluctuate with the quality of the bus/class and season):

DESTINATION	COST (CH$)	DURATION (HR)
Castro	12,000	9
Chillán	8500	4
Concepción	7900	4½
Curacautín	1500	2
Neuquén (Ar)	17,000	12
Osorno	5300	4
Pucón	2900	2
Puerto Montt	6700	5
San Martín de Los Andes (Ar)	21,000	6
Santiago	12,000	9
Valdivia	4000	3
Valparaíso/ Viña del Mar	19,000	10
Villarrica	2000	1½

❶ Getting Around

Colectivo 11P and 111 Express go from downtown (Claro Solar) to the bus terminal (CH$450 to CH$600). A taxi from *centro* should cost CH$2300. A taxi to the airport will cost around CH$15,000. The most economical airport option is **Transfer Temuco** (☑ 045-233-4033; www.transfertemuco.cl; CH$5000), a reliable door-to-door shuttle service.

Parque Nacional Conguillío

Llaima means 'Blood Veins' in Mapudungun and that is exactly what tourists who were visiting **Parque Nacional Conguillío** (adult/child CH$4500/2500), and its towering Volcán Llaima (3125m), saw on New Year's Day 2008. The centerpiece of this Unesco Biosphere Reserve (and the Geoparque Kütralcura within) is one of Chile's most active volcanoes. Since 1640 Llaima has experienced 35 violent eruptions. Eruptions as recently as 2008 spewed fiery lava 300m into the air and created a 20km-long plume of billowing smoke that forced Chile's National Forestry Corporation (Conaf) to evacuate 43 trapped tourists as well as 11 of its own employees from the park; an additional 40 people were evacuated when a second eruption occurred. The Mapuche believe this impressive flamethrower is a living spirit, who is coughing up (a lot!) the earth's imbalances as punishment.

Despite the fire spitting, this wonderful park, which was created in 1950 primarily to preserve the araucaria and 608 sq km of alpine lakes, deep canyons and native forests, is open. The gray-brown magma that has accumulated over the years is to blame for the dramatic vistas and eerie lunarscape atmosphere – at its most dramatic, perhaps, in late April when the leaves are in full autumn bloom.

You can access Parque Nacional Conguillío from three directions. The first, and shortest (80km), is directly east of Temuco via Vilcún and Cherquenco; this accesses the ski resorts at Sector Los Paraguas, but doesn't access (by road) the campgrounds, main visitor center and trailheads. All of those are best reached by taking the more northern route from Temuco via Curacautín (120km).

The park's southern entrance, also 120km from Temuco, is accessed via Melipeuco. From here a road heads north through the park to the northern entrance also accessing the trailheads and campgrounds. It's passable heading south by most normal cars in high season (after Conaf grates the road); other times of year and heading the opposite direction, where there are many more gravely inclines, things can get very dicey between Laguna Captren and Laguna Conguillío.

Activities

Hiking

The 2008 eruption coughed up lava to the southeast into Sector Cherquenco, sparing all of the park's designated trails. One of Chile's finest short hikes, the **Sierra Nevada trail** (7km, three hours one way) to the base of the Sierra Nevada, leaves from the small parking lot at Playa Linda, at the east end of Laguna Conguillío. Climbing steadily northeast through dense coigüe forests, the trail passes a pair of lake overlooks; from the second and more scenic overlook, you can see solid stands of araucarias beginning to supplant coigües on the ridge top.

Conaf discourages all but the most experienced hikers from going north on the **Travesía Río Blanco** (5km, five hours one way), an excursion detailed in Lonely Planet's *Trekking in the Patagonian Andes*. A guide is essential.

Near the visitors center, the **Sendero Araucarias** (0.8km, 45 minutes) meanders through a verdant rainforest. At Laguna Verde, a short trail goes to La Ensenada, a peaceful beach area. The **Cañadon Truful-Truful trail** (0.8km, 30 minutes) passes through the canyon, where the colorful strata, exposed by the rushing waters of Río Truful-Truful, are a record of Llaima's numerous eruptions. The nearby **Los Vertientes trail** (0.8km, 30 minutes) leads to an opening among rushing springs.

Climbing

Experienced mountaineers can tackle Volcán Llaima from **Sector Los Paraguas** on the west side of the park, where there is a *refugio* (rustic shelter) on the road from Cherquenco, or from Captrén on the north side. Although you do not need a climbing permit, you must register your plans with Conaf and sign a release waiving them of responsibility.

It's more orthodox to summit from the Captrén side, where you remain in full view of park rangers the entire route.

Skiing

Centro de Ski Las Araucarias   SKIING
(☑ 045-227-4141; www.skiaraucarias.cl; half-/full-day lift tickets CH$19,000/24,000) Sector Los Paraguas has just three ski runs, but it's a tranquil and scenic area to enjoy a day on the slopes. Ski and snowboard rental costs CH$15,000 per day.

OFF THE BEATEN TRACK

PARQUE NACIONAL TOLHUACA

As the early morning mist burns off from the surrounding hill country, gaggles of parrots can sometimes be spotted lingering on the dusty road that leads to the 64-sq-km **Parque Nacional Tolhuaca** (☑ 045-229-8210; www.parquenacionaltolhuaca.blogspot.com; foreigner/Chilean CH$3500/2500) – a clear indication you're on the road less traveled. One of the park system's best-kept secrets, mainly because it's harder to get to than nearby Conguillío, Tolhuaca is located northeast of Temuco, on the north bank of the Río Malleco.

The park offers trekking over elevations changing from 850m around Laguna Malleco to 1830m on the summit of Cerro Colomahuida; the 2806m Volcán Tolhuaca is beyond the park's southeast boundaries.

Sleeping

Centro de Ski Las Araucarias has four options right on the mountain. Contact the ski center for bookings.

Sendas Conguillío   CAMPING, CABAÑAS $
(www.parquenacionalconguillio.cl; camping per site CH$5000-40,000, cabañas from CH$90,000) Sendas Conguillío runs five campgrounds inside the park around the south shore of Laguna Conguillío and the northwest shore of Laguna Captrén on a concession from Conaf. Accommodations include a special camping sector set aside for backpackers (campsites CH$5000). There are more comfortable cabins as well.

★ **La Baita**   BOUTIQUE LODGE $$
(☑ 045-258-1073; www.labaitaconguillio.cl; s/d CH$48,000/61,000, cabañas 4/6 people CH$58,000/70,000; ☺) ✿ Spaced amid pristine forest, this is an ecotourism project just outside the park's southern boundary. It's home to eight attractive cabins with slow-burning furnaces, solar-powered electricity and hot water; an extremely cozy, incense-scented lodge and restaurant with six rooms complete with granite showers and design-forward sinks; and a pleasant massage room, outdoor hot tub and sauna.

SUR CHICO PARQUE NACIONAL CONGUILLÍO

It's owned by adorable, hippie-esque former singer Isabel Correa, who entertains guests over wine and yoga when she is not in Santiago. Mountain bikes, kayaks and trekking are all at the ready. La Baita is located 16km from Melipeuco and 60km from Curacautín.

❶ Information

Centro de Información Ambiental (www. geachile.sernageomin.cl; Laguna Conguillío; ⊗ 8:30am-9:30pm Dec 16-Mar, 8:30am-1pm & 2:30-6pm Apr-Dec 15) Conaf's Centro de Información Ambiental, 8km from Guardería Captrén, offers a variety of programs mainly in the summer (January and February), including slideshows and ecology talks, hikes to the Sierra Nevada and outings for children. Good trail maps and a wealth of information on Geoparque Kütralcura are available.

❶ Getting There & Away

To reach Sector Los Paraguas, Vogabus, at Temuco's Terminal de Buses Rurales, runs hourly to Cherquenco (CH$1400, 1½ hours, 8am to 8:30pm), from where it's a 17km walk or hitch-hike to the ski lodge at Los Paraguas.

For the northern entrance at Laguna Captrén, Buses Curacautín Express (p232) has four departures from Curacautín Monday and Friday only (CH$800, one hour, 6am, 9am, 2pm and 6pm); and two departures on Tuesday, Wednesday and Thursday (6am and 6pm). The bus will drop you at the park border at Guardería Captrén, where it's a 12km walk to the park entrance.

In winter the bus will go as far as conditions allow. Other options from Curacautín include a taxi for CH$25,000, lugging a bike on the bus or a day tour from Hostal Epu Pewen for CH$80,000 per person all in.

For the southern entrance at Truful-Truful, **Nar-Bus** (🖉 045-211-611; www.narbus.cl) in Temuco runs eight buses daily to Melipeuco (CH$1900, two hours).

Curacautín

🖉 045 / POP 16,508

Curacautín is the northern gateway to Parque Nacional Conguillío. There are more services here than in Melipeuco and a pleasant step-up in traveler accommodations has leveled the playing field a bit, though you'll still be happier if you base yourself along the road to Lonquimay, a more central location for the area's three parks.

🛏 Sleeping & Eating

Hostal Epu Pewen   HOSTEL **$**
(🖉 045-288-1793; www.epupewen.cl; Manuel Rodríguez 705; dm CH$9000, d CH$26,000; 🅿@🛜) This excellent hostel run by an adorable half-Mapuche couple is clean and comfortable and features all sorts of indigenous touches, like bathroom and wall tiles patterned with *kultrün* (ceremonial drums), and non-conventional design elements (*raulí* wood sink stands). There's bike rental (full-day CH$12,000) and all park treks and activities can be organized. English and French spoken.

Terra Cafe   CAFE **$**
(Arturo Prat 539; meals CH$3500-7900; ⊗9am-9pm Mon-Thu, to 1am Fri-Sat; 🛜) This cute cafe's aspirations outshine the town by a long-shot, with a daily changing chalkboard menu of well-presented mains that includes a few curve balls like Thai-style salmon ceviche. There's good espresso and desserts. On weekends, it stays open late as Curacautín's most pleasant watering hole for the cocktail-inclined.

❶ Information

Tourist Office (🖉 045-288-2102; www. destinocuracautin.cl; Manuel Rodríguez s/n; ⊗8:30am-9pm Jan-Feb, 8:30am-6pm Mon-Sat, 9:30am-1:45pm Sun Mar-Dec) Has brochures and information on the park and accommodations in town.

❶ Getting There & Away

The bus terminal is directly on the highway to Lonquimay. **Buses Bio Bio** (🖉045-288-1123; www.busesbiobio.cl) heads to Temuco via Lautaro (CH$1500, 1½ hours), the quickest route, daily at 8pm, and 7:55am and 1:15pm Monday to Friday. **Buses Curacautín Express** (🖉045-225-8125) goes to Temuco via Lautaro (CH$1500, 1½ hours, every 30 minutes, 5:45am to 8:30pm). **Tur-Bus** (🖉045-268-6629; www.turbus.cl; Serrano 101) has two direct buses per day to Santiago (CH$9100 to CH$21,000, 8:50pm and 9:15pm).

For accommodations on the road to Lonquimay, **Buses Flota Erbuc** (🖉 cell 7632-5232) goes to Malalcahuello six times daily and can drop you anywhere along the route (CH$800).

Reserva Nacional Malalcahuello-Nalcas

Reserva Nacional Malalcahuello-Nalcas (adult/child CH$1000/500) is a combined reserve of 303 sq km just north of the town of Malalcahuello, en route to Lonquimay, and extends almost to the border of Parque Nacional Tolhuaca. Though off the main park circuit, Malalcahuello-Nalcas offers one of the most dramatic landscapes in all of Sur Chico, a charcoal desertscape of ash and sand that looks like the Sahara with a nicotine addiction.

For tourist information, the **Cámara de Turismo** (www.malalcahuello.org) has an excellent website.

◉ Sights & Activities

Though not an ambitious hike, the trek to **Cráter Navidad** (1.5km, two hours), which last blew on Christmas Day 1988, takes in this otherworldly atmosphere – not unlike Mars with its desolate red hues reflecting off the soils of magma and ash – and the magnificent backdrop of Volcán Lonquimay, Volcán Tolhuaca and Volcán Callaqui off in the distance.

The most easily accessible trail is **Piedra Santa** (7.5km, five hours), which is the beginning stretch of the longer Laguna Blanca trail. From Piedra Santa, **El Raleo** (3.5km, two hours) branches off and leads through coigüe forest and introduced pine. The trail starts near the small Conaf **information center** (cell 9545-2224; Camino Internacional Km82) near the road to the hamlet of Malalcahuello along the highway to Lonquimay. Wild camping is permissible along the trails.

Nalcas' western boundary abuts Volcán Tolhuaca, while Volcán Lonquimay marks the division between the two reserves. In Nalcas, **Sendero Tolhuaca** (40km, one day one way) is accessible only from **Sendero Laguna Blanca** (40km, two days one way), which traverses the western flank of Volcán Lonquimay and ends in a spectacular aquamarine lake at the foot of Volcán Tolhuaca outside the park's western boundary. There is a great view of both volcanoes. An old logging road connects the trail west to **Termas Malleco** (045-24-1111; www.termasmalleco.cl; r per person full-board CH$79,000) and Laguna Verde in Parque Nacional Tolhuaca (the trails may be hard to find; guides are recommended).

Corralco Mountain & Ski Resort   SKI RESORT
(02-2206-0741; www.corralco.com; half-/full-day lift tickets CH$25,900/34,900; 🛜) There's better skiing here than in Conguillío, with numerous runs, prettier scenery and new infrastructure which includes the new 64-room Valle Corralco Hotel & Spa, opened in 2013,

with excellent rooms (full-board doubles in high season from CH$253,684), a bar and restaurant (as well as two makeshift cafes on the mountain in high season) and spa.

To get here, the turnoff is 2km east of Malalcahuello on the road to Lonquimay. Rentals run CH$32,000.

Sled Chile   SNOWMOBILING
(cell 9541-3348; www.sledchile.com) This upstart adventure specialist offers customized, high-adrenaline backcountry tours by snowmobiles and/or splitboards.

Cañón del Blanco   HOT SPRINGS
(cell 7668-4925; www.canondelblanco.cl; admission CH$10,000; ⏰11am-7pm Mon-Thu, to 10pm Fri-Sun Mar-Nov, 11am-11pm Mon-Thu, to midnight Fri-Sun Dec-Feb) Located 16km down the same gravel road as Andenrose is this new hot springs, with well-done pools in a gorgeous forest setting.

🛏 Sleeping & Eating

This area has seen explosive growth of late, especially along the road to Corralco, now with its fair share of lodges, *cabañas,* backcountry adventure agencies and ski outfitters.

Andenrose   LODGE $$
(cell 9869-1700; www.andenrose.com; Camino Internacional Km68.5; s/d from CH$35,000/45,000, apt & cabaña from CH$55,000; 🅿️🐕🛜) The Bavarian-styled Andenrose along the Río Cautín is built from organic wood and is full of exposed brick and southern German hospitality (Hans, the enthusiastic owner, is quite the firecracker). Recent renovations have left two rooms, three fully equipped apartments and two *cabañas,* the latter set spectacularly among a field of lavender and daisies.

The nightly three-course meals are serious business (hope for veal goulash/späetzle pairing or pork medallions) and there's a rich breakfast. They also arrange excellent horseback riding, jeep tours and excursions in the area.

Suizandina Lodge   LODGE $$
(045-197-3725; www.suizandina.com; Camino Internacional Km83; campsite per person CH$8000, dm CH$18,000, s/d/tr from CH$39,000/54,000/64,000; 🅿️@🛜) The heavily German-staffed Suizandina is run by a hospitable Swiss-Chilean couple. Cleanliness is next to godliness in the roomy lodgings (fantastic bathrooms) and it's well stocked with wine and mini-küchens (sweet

German-style cakes). The menu goes all out with excellent Swiss specialties like *rösti* (hashbrowns), fondue and raclette (a type of cheese that is melted and poured over potatoes).

There's an emphasis on massages and horseback riding as the owner is a physiotherapist horse lover. A good source for backcountry skiing as well.

La Esfera RESTO-BAR $$
(www.vorticechile.com; Km69.5 de la Ruta Internacional, Vórtice Eco-Lodge; menu CH$9000-11,000; ⊙8am-midnight, bar till 2am Fri-Sat; 🌐) It's worth popping into the atmospheric wooden domo at this outdoor adventure complex for the Andino Mapuche fusion cuisine of Ariel Ñamcupil, a Pewenche chef doing surprisingly great-value gourmet grub. Ñamcupil and his team forage for many of their own indigenous ingredients and specialties include traditionally smoked meats and fish and unusual desserts like beet or hazelnut/ *rosa mosqueta* ice cream.

ⓘ Getting There & Away

Heading east of Malalcahuello, the road passes through the narrow, one-way 4527m Túnel Las Raíces, a converted railway tunnel from 1930 that emerges into the drainage of the upper Biobío and has sealed its place in history as the longest tunnel in South America. The road eventually reaches 1884m Paso Pino Hachado, a border crossing that leads to the Argentine cities of Zapala and Neuquén.

Malalcahuello-Nalcas is best accessed on a tour or by taxi from Curacautín (CH$25,000), though road conditions have improved to the point that visiting with a non-4WD is possible.

Melipeuco

☑ 045 / POP 5590

Melipeuco, the southern gateway to Parque Nacional Conguillío, is 90km east of Temuco via Cunco. If you're looking to base yourself nearer the park than Temuco, this is a good spot for day trips, though you're better off going all the way to truly absorb the otherworldly atmosphere of Conguillío.

⌕ Tours

Sendero Aventuras Andes OUTDOOR ADVENTURES
(☑cell 9055-2284; www.senderoaventurasandes. cl; Pedro Aguirre Cerda 384) Based at Hostal Sendero Andes; can line up climbs of Volcán Llaima (CH$85,000 for up to four

people), visits to the caldera and glacier at Sollipulli (CH$70,000 for up to five people), day trips into the park (CH$40,000 to CH$60,000) and spectacular canyoning trips to Alpehue Geysers (CH$80,000 for up to four people).

🛏 Sleeping

Hostal Sendero Andes GUESTHOUSE $
(☑045-258-1306; www.senderoaventurasandes. cl; Pedro Aguirre Cerda 384; r per person without bathroom CH$16,000; 🅿 @ 🌐) Top choice to bed down is this friendly hostel with an inviting bar and restaurant (good burgers!) that feels like a mountain lodge. The creaky hardwood floors lead to respectable rooms upstairs that are more typical of small-town Sur Chico.

The English-speaking owner, Fernando, wants to move his whole operation to the countryside – just in case you show up and nobody is home.

ⓘ Information

There is a BancoEstado ATM on Pedro Aguirre Cerda.

Tourist Office (☑045-258-1075; Pedro Aguirre Cerda s/n; ⊙8:30am-1pm & 2-7pm Tue-Sun Jan-Feb, to 5:30pm Mar-Nov) Friendly tourist information.

ⓘ Getting There & Away

From Temuco's Terminal de Buses Rurales, Nar-Bus has eight buses daily Monday to Saturday to Melipeuco (CH$1900, two hours). Service drops off considerably on Sunday.

Villarrica

☑ 045 / POP 49,184

Unlike Pucón, its wild neighbor across windswept Lago Villarrica, Villarrica is a real living and breathing Chilean town. While not as charming, it's more down to earth than Pucón, lacks the bedlam associated with package tour caravans, and has more reasonable prices and a faded-resort glory that attracts travelers of a certain lax disposition.

The new *costanera* (lakeshore boardwalk), a post-2010 Concepción earthquake project, is impressive and they have done a fine job with the new artificial black sand beach, Chile's first. Considering you can book all the same activities here as in Pucón, it makes for an agreeable alternative for those seeking less in-your-face tourism.

Villarrica

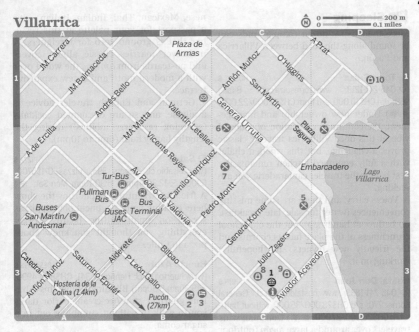

◉ Sights & Activities

Villarrica's new *costanera* and beach, Playa Pucará, is idyllic for strolling. Grab some *mote con huesillo* (a drink made with wheatberries and peaches) from one of the vendors and take a walk.

Museo Histórico Municipal MUSEUM
(Av Pedro de Valdivia 1050; ⊘ 9am-1pm & 2:30-6pm Mon-Fri) **FREE** Mapuche artifacts (including jewelry, musical instruments and rough-hewn wooden masks) are the focus of the Museo Histórico Municipal, behind the tourist office.

★ Aurora Austral Patagonia Husky DOG SLEDDING
(☑ cell 8901-4518; www.auroraaustral.com; Camino Villarrica–Panguipulli Km19.5) Located about 19km from Villarrica on the road to Lican Ray is this German-run husky farm, where you'll find over 50 of the cutest Siberian and Alaskan huskies you ever did see, ready to take you on the ride of your life. In winter, there are day trips (CH$65,000) and a seriously epic seven-day Andean crossing (CH$2,100,000 all-inclusive).

In summer, there are 6km rides with a barbecue (CH$33,000) and husky trekking on Volcán Villarrica (CH$48,000). True

Villarrica

dog lovers can sleep out here as well in three extremely nice cabins (CH$40,000 to CH$60,000). Four to 12-week volunteers are also accepted.

✦ Festivals & Events

Muestra Cultural Mapuche CULTURAL
In January. Features local artisans, indigenous music and ritual dance.

🛏 Sleeping

More than half a dozen campgrounds can be found along the road between Villarrica and Pucón.

La Torre Suiza   HOSTEL $
(☑045-241-1213; www.torresuiza.com; Bilbao 969; dm CH$10,000, s/d from CH$18,000/22,000; 🅿🛜) Under new ownership and management, the continued cultivation of a hostel vibe at this once Villlarrica traveler classic proves a challenge, but this wooden chalet with a fully equipped kitchen remains the best bet for the traveler camaraderie you are seeking.

Voices carry, and there are some missing conveniences (water for sale, late breakfast, no bathroom handsoap), but the old school crunchiness of the place has its charms and the friendly new owners are (hopefully) working on it.

Hostal Don Juan   INN $
(☑045-241-1833; www.hostaldonjuan.cl; General Körner 770; s/d CH$28,000/35,000, without bathroom CH$20,000/27,000; @🛜) Don Juan wins travelers over around a large *fogón* (outdoor oven), which was designed by the friendly owner, and offers fabulous volcano views from some rooms on the 2nd floor.

Hostería de la Colina   INN $$
(☑045-241-1503; www.hosteriadelacolina.com; Las Colinas 115; s/d CH$69,000/72,000, ste CH$105,000; 🅿@🛜) This smart *hostería* (inn) and restaurant is set on meticulously manicured and lush grounds on a hill with stupendous views just southwest of town. New US-expat owners have taken over with cautioned restraint from the previous American owners after 25 years and haven't missed a beat.

Rooms in the main house are classically inclined while the two independent suites offer more privacy and contemporary decor. Little afternoon surprises include snacks of smoked salmon or organic venison salami. The restaurant's limited seasonal, daily changing menu – excellent organic venison, hazelnut-crusted trout, 12 flavors of homemade ice cream – is one of Sur Chico's best and worth the drive up alone.

🍴 Eating

⭐ The Travellers   RESTO-BAR $
(www.thetravellers.cl; Valentín Letelier 753; mains CH$4250-8500; ⊙9am-4am Mon-Sat; 🛜) Chinese, Mexican, Thai, Indian, Italian – it's a passport for your palette at this resto-bar that is ground zero for foreigners. A makeover marries classic album covers and postcards from *amigos* the world over with a modern motif and a new expansive terrace.

German and English traveler advice is available, and so are discounted cocktails (stunning raspberry mojitos!) during the lengthy happy hour (6pm to 10pm).

El Sabio   PIZZA $
(www.elsabio.cl; Zegers 393; pizzas CH$5700-6900; ⊙12:30-4pm & 6:30-10pm Mon-Sat; 🛜) A friendly Argentine couple runs the show here, creating fantastic, uncut oblong pizzas served on small cutting boards. Forget everything you thought you knew about pizza in Chile.

Huerto Azul   DESSERTS $
(www.huertoazul.cl; Henríquez 341; CH$800-4990; ⊙9:30am-9:30pm) Blindingly blue, this fabulous gourmet store/ice-cream parlor dares you to walk in without stumbling out in a sugar coma.

Artisanal marmalade and chutney line the walls; an extensive line of house-made Belgian chocolate bars fill display cases; and locals line up outside for Italian-style gelato, also made on the premises (try the antioxidant-laced *maqui,* the world's new *açaí*).

Brazas   CHILEAN $$$
(www.brazas.cl; General Körner 145; mains CH$8600-15,550; ⊙12:30-4pm & 6:30-11:30pm Dec-Feb, 12:30-4pm & 6:30-11:30pm Mon-Sat, to 4pm Sun Mar-Nov; 🛜) This upscale choice has everything: postcard-framed volcano sunsets right out the bay windows, above-and-beyond service for Sur Chico and, most importantly, the grub to accompany it all. There's an emphasis on serious steaks, but the rest of the gourmet menu shouldn't be ignored – especially the caramelized slab of succulent pork ribs, falling off the bone between stolen lake glances.

🛍 Shopping

There is a high concentration of *artesanías* (handicrafts) surrounding the tourist office – look out for Mapuche figures carved from laurel wood and *raulí* wood bowls at **Centro Cultural Mapuche** (cnr Pedro de Valdivia & Zegers; ⊙10am-11pm), **Feria Artesanal** (Acevedo 565; ⊙10am-midnight

Jan-Feb, to 9pm Mar-Dec) and **Pueblito Arte-sanal** (cnr Prat & Körner; ☺10am-midnight Jan-Feb, to 9pm Mar-Dec).

ℹ Information

Banks with ATMs are plentiful near the corner of Pedro Montt and Av Pedro de Valdivia.

Hospital Villarrica (San Martín 460; ☺24hr) Small hospital in town.

Oficina de Turismo (☑ 045-220-6619; www.visitvillarrica.cl; Av Pedro de Valdivia 1070; ☺8:30am-1pm & 2:30-6pm Mon-Fri, 10am-4pm Sat-Sun) Municipal office that has helpful staff and provides many brochures.

CorreosChile (www.correos.cl; Anfión Muñoz 315; ☺9am-1pm & 2:30-6pm Mon-Fri, 9am-12:30pm Sat) Postal services.

ℹ Getting There & Around

Villarrica has a main (mostly regional) **bus terminal** (Av Pedro de Valdivia 621); most long-distance companies have separate offices nearby. Long-distance fares are similar to those from Temuco (an hour away), which has more choices for southbound travel. From the terminal – really just a parking lot – **Buses Vipu-Ray** (☑ cell 6835-5798) goes to Pucón every 25 minutes (6:50am to 9:15pm). **Buses Coñaripe** (☑ cell 7125-8183) departs throughout the day to Lican Ray (CH$800, 45 minutes, 6:50am to 8:55pm) and Coñaripe (CH$1100, one hour, 6:50am to 8:55pm). **Buses Villarrica** (☑ 045-241-4468) heads to Temuco (every 30 minutes, 6:40am to 8pm).

From their respective terminals, **Buses JAC** (☑ 045-246-7775; www.jac.cl; Bilbao 610) goes to Pucón every 30 minutes and Temuco every 20 minutes; Puerto Montt and Puerto Varas at least twice a day (8:40am and 4:45pm) and Valdivia six times daily.

Tur-Bus (☑ 045-220-4102; www.turbus.cl; Anfión Muñoz 657), **Pullman Bus** (☑ 045-241-4217; www.pullman.cl; cnr Anfión Muñoz & Bilbao) and Buses JAC offer the most frequent services to Santiago, the former with two nightly departures to Viña del Mar/Valparaíso (8:15pm and 8:45pm) and two to Chillán as well (10am and 12:15pm).

For Argentine destinations, **Igi Llaima** (☑ 045-241-2753; www.igillaima.cl), in the main terminal, leaves at 9am Monday to Saturday and 11:30am Sunday for San Martín de los Andes and to Zapala and Neuquén with a switch in Junín. **Buses San Martín** (☑ 045-241-9673; Pedro León Gallo 599) does the same route Tuesday to Sunday at 8am.

Sample travel times and starting fares are as follows (prices fluctuate with the quality of the bus/class and season):

DESTINATION	COST (CH$)	DURATION (HR)
Chillán	10,200	5
Los Angeles	8200	4
Pucón	800	¾
Puerto Montt	8600	5
San Martín de los Andes (Ar)	12,000	5
Santiago	23,000	10
Temuco	1800	1
Valdivia	4300	3
Viña del Mar/ Valparaíso	16,100	15

Pucón

☑ 045 / POP 22,081

Pucón is firmly positioned on the global map as a mecca for adventure sports, its setting on beautiful Lago Villarrica under the smoldering eye of the volcano of the same name sealing its fate as a world-class destination for adrenaline junkies. Once a summer playground for the rich, Pucón is now a year-round adventure machine catering to all incomes, especially in February (a time to avoid, if possible), when it is absolutely overrun. The town receives alternating floods of package tourists, Santiago holidaymakers, novice Brazilian snowboarders, adventure-seeking backpackers, new age spiritualists and mellowed-out ex-activists turned eco-pioneers.

While its popularity can be off-putting for some, Pucón boasts the best small-town tourism infrastructure south of Costa Rica. That means quality accommodations, efficient tourism agencies, myriad activities and excursions, vegetarian restaurants, falafel, microbrews and hundreds of expat residents from the world over.

Like every other place in the region, the crowds do trickle in winter and skiing and snowboarding become the focus. In summer, if you're not hiking it, jumping off of it, riding it or climbing it, you'll likely find yourself planted on Pucón's gorgeous black-sand beach, tucked behind the Gran Hotel Pucón – blink and you'll swear you're in the tropics!

🏃 Activities

It's easy to overdose on adrenaline before actually doing any activity in Pucón – the wealth of adventure operators lining Av O'Higgins

SUR CHICO PUCÓN

Pucón

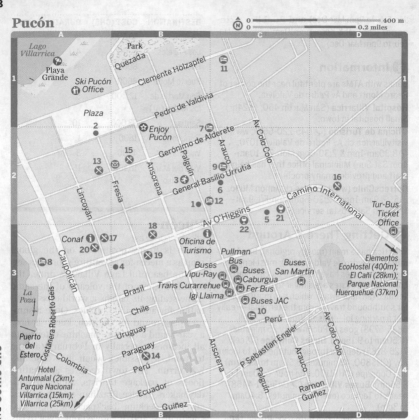

and the bounty of activities on offer in and around Pucón can easily overwhelm. The standards, climbing Villarrica and rafting Río Trancura, are offered by many, but consider some of the other activities – those that allow you to appreciate the area away from the masses, such as horseback riding, renting a bike, snowshoeing or exploring some of the smaller nature reserves on foot.

Horseback Riding

There are a few spectacular options for horse treks in this region. Most rides take in various environments and may include stopovers so riders can meet with local *huasos* (cowboys) or Mapuche communities. Half- and full-day rides hover around CH$24,000 to CH$49,000 depending on the grade of difficulty, number of people going and location exclusivity.

Mountain Biking

Mountain bikes can be rented all over town. Daily rental prices are negotiable

but shouldn't be more than CH$8000 to CH$10,000 unless it is a brand-new bike with full suspension.

The most popular route is the Ojos de Caburgua Loop. Take the turnoff to the airfield about 4km east of town and across Río Trancura. It's a dustbowl in summer, though, and tends to irritate all but the most hard-core riders. Extensions off the same route include the Lago Caburgua to Río Liucura Loop and the full Río Trancura Loop. Two other popular trails that are close to town are Correntoso and Alto Palguín Chinay (to the Palguín hot springs). It's also possible to tackle the volcano on a downhill run (CH$40,000).

Any bike-rental agencies will be able to give you more details and should provide a decent trail map. You'll pay slightly more, but **Freeride Pucón** (☎ 045-244-1055; Urrutia 484B; half-day/full-day CH$8000/12,000; ☉ 9am-8pm Dec-Feb, to 7:30pm Mar-Nov) has the best bikes and maintenance in town.

Pucón

Rafting & Kayaking

Pucón is known for both its river sports and the quality of the rafting and kayaking infrastructure. Most of the larger travel agencies run rafting trips. The rivers near Pucón and their corresponding rapids classifications are: the Lower Trancura (III), the Upper Trancura (IV), Liucura (II–III), the Puesco Run (V) and Maichín (IV–V). When negotiating a rafting or kayaking trip, recognize that the stated trip durations often include transportation, not just the time spent on the water. Prices can range from CH$10,000 full-day rentals to CH$50,000 excursions depending on the season, the number of people per raft or kayaking trip, the company and the level of challenge. Many of the rivers are swollen in the winter and closed for most sports, although it is still possible to raft or kayak in some.

Rock Climbing

Cerduo, at the foot of Volcán Villarrica, offers 40 different climbing routes ranging from 5.8 to 5.12d. There's sport climbing as well as traditional, all surrounded by native forest. For more intense and physically demanding routes, head to pristine Las Peinetas near the Argentine border, where climbs consist of five to six pitches and can last up to 12 hours. It is a three-hour hike-in to where the climbing commences. For experienced and certified guides, check out Summit Chile, where, in addition to advanced options, owner Claudio Retamal has opened up five routes at Cerduo for all skill levels.

👉 Tours

Most of the tour operators are on Av O'Higgins or within a half block. Prices are similar throughout, but quality of service can vary. In summer, seasonal operators pop up on all corners, but are not as established as those listed here – you are advised to stick to these for most activities.

★ Aguaventura   OUTDOOR ADVENTURE
(☑045-244-4246; www.aguaventura.com; Palguín 336; ⏱8:30am-10pm Dec-Mar, to 8:30pm Apr-Nov) This friendly French-owned agency is your one-stop shop, offering highly skilled volcano guides (beer after!) and also specializing in snow sports and kayaking, but can book it all. It also rents everything for the mountain, water and snow (including GoPro); and books flights and ferries too. Ask co-owner Vincent about Japanese-style capsule dorms at his new hostel, French Andes.

Summit Chile   MOUNTAINEERING, ROCK CLIMBING
(☑045-244-3259; www.summitchile.org; Urrutia 585; ⏱10am-8pm Nov-Mar, till 6pm Apr-Oct) Started by internationally certified Claudio Retamal, a former Chilean climbing champion and the most experienced guide on the volcano. He can also take you up the other volcanoes – Lanín, Llaima and Lonquimay – as well as offering rock climbing, throwing in some geology and natural history along the way. Advanced/backcountry skiers should ask about skiing *up* Villarrica.

Elementos   CULTURAL TOUR
(☑cell 5689-3491; www.elementos-chile.com; Pasaje Las Rosas 640) 🌿 A good bet for *etnotourism,* merging nature and culture with an eco-slant, this German-run agency runs half- to multiday trips delving deeper into Mapuche culture, including cooking lessons with Mapuche chefs, visits to *rukas* and meet-and-greets with Mapuche medicine men, with a few waterfalls and Andean lagoons thrown in. Discounts for booking online or via WhatsApp.

Bike Pucón
MOUNTAIN BIKING

(☑cell 9579-4818; www.bikepucon.com) Offers thrilling 17km to 20km downhill rides spread among six trails of very slippery volcanic terrain, single-track and old fire roads. It's not for novices – you can make it on limited experience, but don't expect not to kiss some ash at one point or another.

Kayak Pucón
KAYAKING

(☑cell 9716-2347; www.kayakpucon.net; Av O'Higgins 211; ⊙9am-9pm Nov–mid-Mar) This well-regarded kayak operator offers three-day kayak courses (CH$180,000) as well as multiday expeditions for more experienced boaters. Half-day ducky (one-person inflatable boats) tours on Class III rapids are a good option for those with less kayak experience (CH$20,000) and there's rafting for kids as well.

Canyoning Pucón
CANYONING

(☑cell 9294-6913; www.canyoningpucon.cl) The recommended agency for canyoning offers half-day trips for CH$39,000 to Pillan (October to March) and Nevados (December to April) canyons.

Politur
RAFTING

(☑045-244-1373; www.politur.cl; Av O'Higgins 635; ⊙8:30am-8:30pm) This is the go-to agency for rafting.

Free Tour Pucón
WALKING TOUR

(☑cell 4305-5479; www.freetourpucon.com; ⊙11am Wed-Sun Dec-Mar) **FREE** Javier is your enthusiastic, English-speaking guide on this great two-hour walking tour that goes beyond belays and backpacks. No need for reservations in high-season – just turn up at the plaza in front of the church.

🛏 Sleeping

While Pucón has plenty of places to stay, prices are higher than in other cities (even for the budget options). Reservations are absolutely necessary in advance in January and February, but aren't a problem in winter. Note that due to the nature of early rise tourism here, breakfast is often not included.

★ iécole!
HOSTEL $

(☑045-244-1675; www.ecole.cl; Urrutia 592; dm with/without bedding CH$10,000/8000, d/tr CH$30,000/36,000, s/d/tr without bathroom CH$18,000/20,000/30,000; @🕾) 🌱 The eco-conscious iécole! is a travel experience in itself. It's a meeting point for conscientious travelers and a tranquil and artsy hangout that has long been Pucón's most interesting place to stay. Rooms are small, clean and comfortable, but walls are thin and voices carry within the leafy grounds, so it's not a wild party hostel.

Expansion plans and renovations are in the works and the excellent vegetarian restaurant is one of Chile's best (mains CH$2500 to CH$4500). These guys were preaching sustainability, conservation and eco-everything nearly two decades before anyone else in Chile.

Chili Kiwi
HOSTEL $

(☑045-244-9540; www.chilikiwihostel.com; Roberto Geis 355; dm from CH$9000, r without bathroom from CH$24,000; 🕾) Sitting on prime lakeside real estate, this is Pucón's most sociable hostel, run by an enthusiastic Kiwi-Dutch partnership packing years of globetrotting experience from which to draw their traveler-centric ideas. There are various dorms and private options (converted vans, tree houses, cabins), the best of which are in the main house, and an overload of kitchens and bathrooms throughout.

Elementos EcoHostel
HOSTEL $

(☑045-244-1750; www.elementos-chile.com; Pasaje Las Rosas 640; dm CH$800, s/d CH$29,000/32,000, without bathroom CH$20,000/23,000; **P**@🕾) 🌱 An easy 15-minute walk from Centro brings you to this sustainable German-run choice, operated by the eco-tourism folks at Elementos. There are green touches throughout (LED lighting, natural cleaning products made in-house, biodegradable soaps), a few very spacious privates and rustic dorms. The wonderful breakfast is fueled by fiercely local artisanal products (CH$3500).

Hospedaje Victor
GUESTHOUSE $

(☑045-244-3525; www.hostalvictor.cl; Palguín 705; dm CH$10,000, r CH$30,000; @🕾) If you value actual sleep, Victor stands out for cleanliness and a warm atmosphere conducive to rest.

La Bicicleta
HOSTEL $$

(☑045-244-4583; labibicletapucon@gmail.com; Palguín 361; dm CH$13,000, s/d CH$35,000/38,000, s/d without bathroom CH$16,000/36,000; @🕾) Run by a friendly Chileno from Viña del Mar, this subtly stylish spot gets great reviews from travelers. There is a bar and a restaurant in front (guests can claim a 10% discount) though a recent fire has left José, the immediately likable owner, with quite a rebuilding project. There's a great 2nd-floor back patio for sipping afternoons away with pints of Stella.

Bambu Lodge B&B $$
(☎ cell 6802-9145; www.bambulodge.com; Camino a Volcán Km4.2; s/d CH$40,000/60,000; @) For those looking to stay away from the madness but still enjoy all that Pucón has to offer, or perhaps those who are traveling a bit more romantically but are still budget-conscious, this discerning four-room B&B in a woodsy spot on the road to the volcano is a wonderful find.

The French owner has imported much of the decor from Morocco, and service is as personalized as possible: it's just Guillaume and his Chilean girlfriend, Beatriz, tending to your solitude. A taxi from town is CH$6000.

Hostel Etnico HOSTEL $$
(☎ 045-244-2305; www.etnicohostel.com; Colo Colo 36; dm from CH$9000, s/d CH$30,000/40,000, without bathroom CH$20,000/24,000; 🚭@🛜🏊) 🍃 Eco-conscious Chilean owners have jump-started this hostel housed in a former monastery, applying their sustainable knowledge (these folks drove the length of Chile in a veggie oil–powered bus) everywhere you turn: organic compost/recycling, solar-enhanced energy, a solar-powered DJ soundsystem etc.

There's a huge backyard with newly installed party domo and guests can cook with fresh produce plucked straight from the greenhouse.

Hotel Antumalal BOUTIQUE HOTEL $$$
(☎ 045-244-1011; www.antumalal.com; Camino Pucón–Villarrica Km2; s/d from CH$185,000/220,000; 🅿@🛜🏊) This testament to Bauhaus architecture on the road to Villarrica is built into a cliffside above the lake. From its tree-bark lamps to araucaria-clad walls, it instills a sense of location while being wildly and wonderfully out of place.

Its huge slanting windows give unbeatable views of Lago Villarrica from the swanky common areas and all the minimalist rooms offer fireplaces; some have fern- and moss-covered raw rock for the internal walls. The restaurant does advanced Chilean cuisine, with many ingredients plucked right from the organic vegetable patch, just a drop in the bucket of the property's 12 hectares of gardens.

Aldea Naukana BOUTIQUE HOTEL $$$
(☎ 045-244-3508; www.aldeanaukana.com; Gerónimo de Alderete 656; r from CH$98,000; 🅿🛜) A wonderful clash of native hardwoods and volcanic stone forms the backbone of this nine-room boutique hotel, the sleekest option in Pucón proper. Besides the wonderfully comfortable rooms, there is a small sauna (included in rates) and a chargeable rooftop hot tub with expectedly stupendous volcano views. The restaurant specializes in unusual (for southern Chile) Asian fusion with mixed results.

🍴 Eating

Pucón is the undisputed king of culinary variety in southern Chile.

Trawen CHILEAN, FUSION $
(www.trawen.cl; Av O'Higgins 311; mains CH$3600-10,300; 🕘8:30am-midnight; 🛜) 🍃 This time-honored favorite does some of Pucón's best gastronomic work for the price, boasting innovative flavor combinations and fresh-baked everything. Highlights include excellent home-style breakfasts, bacon-wrapped venison, *merkén*-grilled octopus and salads from their own certified-organic gardens, the first in southern Chile. Creative types tend to congregate here, along with hopheads – it boasts the town's best craft beer selection.

Latitude 39° AMERICAN $
(www.latitude39.cl; Gerónimo de Alderete 324; burgers CH$4600-6100; 🕘11am-11pm; 🛜) California transplant owners fill a clearly appreciated gringo niche at this newly expanded homesick remedy of a restaurant. Juicy American-style burgers are a huge hit: try the Grand Prix (caramelized onions, bacon, peanut butter) or the Buddha (Sriracha mayo, Asian slaw, popcorn shrimp), but there's also fat breakfast burritos, fish tacos, BLTs and everything else you might be missing.

It has also evolved into the foreigner happy hour hot spot for beer and camaraderie.

Menta Negra CAFE $
(www.emporiomentanegra.cl; O'Higgins 772; set meals CH$5500; 🕘10am-11:30pm, closed Sun Apr-Nov) On a sunny day, it's hard to beat plopping yourself down on this artsy emporium's patio for good home-cooked meals and views of a rare breed in Pucón: to nature, not development.

La Picada
CHILEAN $

(Paraguay 215; set lunch CH$3500; ◷noon-3:30pm, closed Sun Mar-Nov) This local's secret is out: an underground eatery in someone's living room serving fuss-free set lunches (salads, *pastel de choclo*, *cazuelas*, pasta). No sign. Knock to gain entrance.

El Castillo
INTERNATIONAL $$

(✆cell 8901-8089; Camino a Volcán Km8; mains CH$3800-7900; ◷noon-9pm Dec-Feb, noon-6pm or with reservation Apr-Nov) Along the volcano road and with optimal Ansel Adams–like views of the beast itself, this volcanic stone and wood space warmed by a Russian stove is a requisite stop for those with wheels. Chef Zoe does homey gourmet with an emphasis on game – wild rabbit, venison stew, wild boar – that stunningly satiates the urge for something different.

La Maga
STEAK $$

(www.lamagapucon.cl; Gerónimo de Alderete 276; steak CH$9900-14,700; ◷1-4pm & 8-11pm Dec-Mar, closed Mon Mar-Nov) There is a *parrilla* (steakhouse) for every budget in Pucón, but this Uruguayan steakhouse stands out for its *bife de chorizo* (steak), house-cut fries and onion-heavy chimmichurri. It's not the cheapest, but this is one of Sur Chico's best grills.

Viva Perú
PERUVIAN $$

(www.vivaperudeli.cl; Lincoyán 372; mains CH$6500-14,900; ◷noon-midnight Dec-Mar, noon-4pm & 7:30-11:30pm Apr-Nov; 🖥) This intimate Peruvian restaurant does all the classics and does them well: ceviche (raw fish and onions marinated in citrus juices and spices), *tiradito* (onion-free ceviche), *chicharónes* (deep-fried pork rinds) and *ají de gallina* (creamy chicken stew with cheese, peppers and peanuts). They even serve Peru's famous Chinese fusion *chifa* dishes.

Pizza Cala
PIZZA $$

(Lincoyán 361; pizzas CH$3700-15,000; ◷noon-midnight; 🖥) The best pizza in town is spit from a massive 1300-brick oven by an Argentine-American pizza maker who grows his own fresh basil. In winter, it's the only warm restaurant in town.

★ La Fleur de Sel
FRENCH $$$

(✆045-197-0060; www.termaspeumayen.cl; Camino Pucón Huife Km28; mains CH$8200-14,500; ◷1-4pm & 7-9pm, closed Mon mid-Mar–mid-Dec) Basque-country chef Michel Moutrousteguy offers a Mapuche-infused French menu that's well worth the trip to Termas Peumayen (for the food, not the service), 32km east of Pucón, even if you don't plan on getting wet. It's meat heavy, but much more than typical *parrilla* fare, and has slowly built up a reputation in the region as *the* gourmet destination for foodies.

A three-course menu plus entrance to the hot springs runs CH$22,000. Peumayan is reachable by car or five times daily from Pucón with Fer Bus (CH$1500).

Supermercado Eltit
SELF-CATERING $

(Av O'Higgins 336; ◷8:30am-10pm Sun-Thu, to 10:30pm Fri-Sat) Grocery store; also changes US cash and has an ATM.

🍷 Drinking & Nightlife

The bar scene in Pucón, like Puerto Varas, changes more often than a baby's diapers.

Mama's & Tapas
BAR, CLUB

(Av O'Higgins 597; cocktails CH$3500-5500; ◷10am-5am Dec-Mar, from 6pm Apr-Nov) Known simply as 'Mama's,' this is Pucón's long-standing bar of note. It boasts an all-wood wall and ceiling space designed by an acoustic engineer to sonically seize your attention. It doesn't get going until the wee hours, when it morphs into a club.

La Vieja Escuela
CLUB

(Colo Colo 450; ◷8:30pm-3:30am Mon-Thu, to 5am Fri-Sun; 🖥) Aiming to shake up the status quo of Pucón's nightlife, this dark and sexy bar/club/live music venue – 'The Old School' – caters to sophisticated thirtysomethings who've outgrown the guide versus backpacker pick-up game. Blood-red velvet seats emanate Victorian overtones and the whole place is in a class all its own. Expect DJs and live rock.

ℹ Information

Petty theft is on the rise in Pucón, especially in the areas around the beach. Bikes and backpacks are the biggest targets, but you can't leave anything in your vehicle overnight. Use prudence.

There are several banks with ATMs up and down Av O'Higgins.

Conaf (✆045-244-3781; Lincoyán 336; ◷8:30am-6:30pm Mon-Fri) The best-equipped Conaf in the region.

CorreosChile (www.correos.cl; Fresia 183; ◷9am-1pm & 2:30-6pm Mon-Fri, 9am-noon Sat) Postal services.

Hospital San Francisco (www.hospitalpucon.cl; Uruguay 325; ◷24hr) Medical services.

Oficina de Turismo (✆045-229-3001; www.municipalidadpucon.cl; cnr Av O'Higgins & Palguín; ◷8:30am-7pm) Has stacks of brochures and usually an English speaker on staff.

ⓘ Getting There & Away

AIR

At the time of writing, flights to Pucón were no longer operating, though this could change in the future. Otherwise, Temuco's new Aeropuerto de La Araucanía (p229), 103km northeast, is the closest runway with flights.

BUS

Bus transportation to and from Santiago is best with **Tur-Bus** (☑045-244-3328; www.turbus.com; Av O'Higgins 910; ☺9am-7pm), with a ticket office in town and their own station east of the center, and **Pullman Bus** (☑045-244-3331; www.pullman.cl; Palguín 555), in the center. Both offer a few daily departures to Viña del Mar/Valparaíso. **Buses JAC** (☑045-299-3183; www.jac.cl; cnr Uruguay & Palguín) goes to Temuco throughout the day as well as points south (Osorno, Puerto Varas, Puerto Montt) twice daily (8am and 4:15pm). For Valdivia, JAC has six daily buses. **Buses Vipu-Ray** (☑cell 6835-5798; Palguín 550) and **Trans Curarrehue** (☑045-262-5168; Palguín 550) have continuous services to Villarrica and Curarrehue. **Buses Caburgua** (☑cell 9838-9047; Palguín 555) has six daily buses to Parque Nacional Huerquehue (CH$2000, 45 minutes) between 8:30am and 5:10pm. From the same station, **Fer Bus** (☑cell 9047-6382; Palguín 555) goes to Termas Los Pozones (CH$1500), Termas Peumayen (CH$1500) and Santuario El Cañi (CH$700) five times daily between 7am and 5:30pm (less on Sunday).

Buses San Martín (☑045-244-2798; Av Colo Colo 612) offers departures Tuesday, Thursday and Saturday at 8:30am and Wednesday, Friday and Sunday at 9:05am to San Martín de los Andes, Argentina and Neuquén (CH$27,000, 12 hours) via Junín. **Igi Llaima** (☑045-244-4762; cnr Palguín & Uruguay) plies the same route Monday to Saturday at 9:45am and Sunday at 12:15pm.

Sample travel times and starting fares are as follows (prices fluctuate with the quality of the bus/class and season):

DESTINATION	COST (CH$)	DURATION (HR)
Curarrehue	1000	¾
Puerto Montt	9500	5
San Martín de los Andes (Ar)	12,000	5
Santiago	31,000	9½
Temuco	2900	1
Valdivia	4500	3
Valparaíso/ Viña del Mar	16,000	12½
Villarrica	800	½

ⓘ Getting Around

Pucón itself is very walkable. A number of travel agencies rent cars and prices can be competitive, especially in the low season, though prices tend to climb on weekends.

Parque Nacional Villarrica

Parque Nacional Villarrica is one of the most popular parks in the country because of its glorious mix of volcanoes and lakes. Its proximity to Pucón, with all of the town's tourism infrastructure, also makes Villarrica an unusually accessible park for everyone from bus-trippers to climbers, skiers and hardcore hikers.

The highlights of the 630-sq-km park are the three volcanoes: Villarrica (2847m) – which erupted briefly but spectacularly in March 2015 (p245) – Quetrupillán (2360m) and, along the Argentine border, a section of Lanín (3747m). The rest of Lanín is protected in an equally impressive park in Argentina, from where it may be climbed.

Due to the 2015 eruption, information regarding activities in the park is particularly vulnerable to change at the moment – please check the situation on the ground ahead of your visit.

🏃 Activities

Climbing

The hike up to the smoking, sometimes lava-spitting crater of Volcán Villarrica is a popular full-day excursion (around CH$35,000 to CH$50,000 not including the chairlift fee of CH$9000), leaving Pucón between 6am and 7am depending on the season. You do not need prior mountaineering experience, but it's no Sunday stroll and can challenge even seasoned trekkers. Conditions are most difficult in fall when snow levels are depleted. It is important to use reliable equipment and choose an outfitter whose guides are properly trained.

Note that bad weather may delay organized ascents for days. Climbs are sometimes cancelled altogether or may be required to turn back partway. Check cancellation policies carefully, but know that less reputable operators may take you partway up on days when they know the weather won't hold, just so they don't have to return the money as per your agreement.

SUR CHICO PARQUE NACIONAL VILLARRICA

Around Pucón

Experienced mountaineers may prefer to take a taxi or bus to the ski area and tackle the volcano without a tour. Most folks ride the ski lift to the top of Chair 5 and start from there. Ascents without a tour group are officially discouraged and should only be done by two or more experienced hikers under clear conditions. Solo climbers must have a mountaineering license and obtain permission from Conaf in Pucón before setting out for the park, as well as pay a CH$4000 volcano-ascension fee (already included in group tour prices). Obligatory gear includes crampons, ice axe/pick and helmet; these can be rented for around CH$7000 if you don't have your own. It is also possible to ski down from June to December.

Hiking

The most accessible sector of the park, Rucapillán, is directly south of Pucón along a well-maintained road and takes in the most popular hikes up and around Volcán Villarrica.

The trail **Challupen Chinay** (23km, 12 hours) rounds the volcano's southern side, crossing through a variety of scenery to end at the entrance to the Quetrupillán sector. This sector is easily accessed via the road that goes to Termas de Palguín. However, if you plan to continue through to Coñaripe, the road south through the park requires a high-clearance 4WD even in good weather.

A 32km combination of hikes, with a couple of camping areas, links to the Puesco sector, near the Argentine border, where there is public transportation back to Curarrehue and Pucón (or you can make connections to carry on to Argentina).

Those traversing the volcano (as opposed to climbing it) will be charged a CH$8000 fee.

Skiing

Ski Pucón

SKIING

(☎ 045-244-1901; www.skipucon.cl; Clemente Holzapfel 190, Pucón office at Enjoy Tour, Gran Hotel Pucón; full-day lift ticket adult/child CH$30,000/25,000; ⏰ 9am-5pm Jul–mid-Oct) Ski Pucón is not on a par with Valle Nevado, Termas de Chillán, Portillo or the other resorts to the north, but it is the most developed ski area in La Araucanía and the Lakes District. Plus, where else do you get to ski on a live, smoking volcano? The views from the mid-mountain lodge almost single-handedly make the lift ticket worth the price.

The ski area is mainly for beginners, with a bit of steeper terrain for intermediates. However, skiing out of bounds just to the left or right of the lifts offers a range of more challenging options for experienced skiers and snowboarders.

The weather at the ski area tends to be different from the town of Pucón. Look at how the smoke from the crater is blowing to gauge how windy it will be. Rentals are available on the mountain (CH$13,000), but are less expensive (and often better quality) in town. Almost every agency and a number of hotels send minivans (from CH$10,000) up to the base lodge. Other than briefly losing it's access to water, the resort was unaffected by the 2015 Villarrica eruption.

❶ Getting There & Away

Taxis to the volcano base (CH$15,000 to CH$20,000), your own car or a tour are the only ways to get to the park (although fit mountain bikers can make it too).

Río Liucura Valley

Heading east out of Pucón, the wishbone road splits into two valleys. Highlights of the Río Caburgua Valley to the north include Lago Caburgua and its wonderful Playa Blanca (24km away), as well as the waterfall-heavy Ojos del Caburgua. To the northeast, the Camino Pucón–Huife road leads to myriad hot springs, the El Cañi nature sanctuary and views of the silver-ribbon Río Liucura that cuts through its

---

SAFETY ON VOLCÁN VILLARRICA

Summiting Volcán Villarrica is far and away the number-one excursion in Pucón, but at time of writing, volcano ascensions had been suspended due to the dramatic fireworks show put on by Pucón's definitive landmark on March 3, 2015. Around 3am, Villarrica briefly roared to life, spitting lava spectacularly up to 3km skyward for all the town to see.

Precautionary evacuation orders were issued for a 10km radius around the volcano as a social media frenzy ensued. By dawn Pucón and the surrounding communities were all but shut down. It was Villarrica's first major eruption since 1984 and, though short and sweet, altered the crater and surrounding landscape to an extent that was still being assessed during this guide's production. In anticipation of the eruption, volcano ascensions had already been stopped a month prior; though they should be resumed by the time you read this, the smoking and rumbling was continuing off and on through April as this guide went to print, leaving everyone wondering if the volcano might blow again. It's best to check on the situation ahead of your visit both with the recommended agencies as well as Sernageomin (www.sernageomin.cl), the official government agency for monitoring volcanic activity. If Villarrica is still out of commission, summits are possible on nearby volcanoes Quetrupillan, Llaima and Lanin.

Once the all clear to climb Villarrica is given, by all means, do it! But reaching the summit is never a guarantee and if the weather turns, responsible agencies will always turn back, no questions asked. Others press on and the consequences sometimes have been fatal. Crampons and ice axes are required on the snow and it can be treacherous and frightening at times. Nearly 20,000 people per year climb the volcano, which some local experts say is far too many.

Moral of the story: summiting this roaring monster is a truly unforgettable experience, but choosing your agency wisely is key. Fundamentally, you will get what you pay for and it is worth spending CH$5000 to CH$10,000 more for safety, insurance and to not be treated like part of a cattle drive to the top. If you have any doubts about commitment to safety, walk on. And don't hesitate to peruse the tourist complaint book on offer at the Oficina de Turismo in Pucón.

DON'T MISS

TERMAS GEOMÉTRICAS

If all that climbing, trekking, paddling and cycling have left your bones rattled and your muscles begging for mercy, you're in luck. Pucón's environs are sitting on one of the world's biggest natural Jacuzzis: **Termas Geométricas** (www.termasgeometricas.cl; adult/child 11am-noon & 6-8pm CH\$20,000/10,000, noon-6pm CH\$24,000/12,000; ⊙10am-11pm Dec 21-Mar 21, 11am-8pm rest of year). Hot springs are as common as adventure outfitters around here, but Termas Geométricas stands out above the crowd. For couples and design aficionados, this Asian-inspired, red-planked maze of 17 beautiful slate hot springs set upon a verdant canyon over a rushing stream is simply gorgeous.

There are two waterfalls and three cold plunge pools to cool off and a cafe heated by *fogón* (outdoor oven) and stocked with natural chicken soup and real coffee. If it weren't for the Spanish, you'd think it was Kyoto.

It's located 15km north of Coñaripe. Transport is available from Coñaripe as well as day trips from Pucón (around CH\$35,000 including admission). Note that a 4WD is best if you are driving yourself, though the gravel approach from Coñaripe is passable in a normal vehicle in good conditions.

---

richly verdant valley. Both roads eventually link back up with the road that goes to Parque Nacional Huerquehue.

The nature sanctuary **El Cañi** (www.santuariocani.cl; Km21; admission with/without guide CH\$15,000/4000) is proof that concerned citizens can make a difference and affect conservation of old-growth forests. When logging interests threatened the area in 1991, Fundación Lahuen, a small cluster of concerned folks with start-up funding from Ancient Forests International, formed to purchase the land and develop a drop-dead-gorgeous park with an emphasis on education and scientific research. This success story is now a reserve that protects some 500 hectares of ancient araucaria forest, all of which has been turned over to, and is now successfully maintained by, a local guide association, **Cañe Guides Group** (✆cell 9837-3928; contacto@santuariocani.cl).

A **hiking trail** (9km, three hours) ascends the steep terrain (the first 3km very steep) of lenga and araucaria to arrive at Laguna Negra. On clear days the lookout – another 40 minutes – allows for spectacular views of the area's volcanoes. In winter, when the underbrush is covered in snow, the area is particularly gorgeous. All hikers must go with a guide except in summer when the trail is easier to find.

An alternative route, which detours around the steepest part, starts along the road to Coilaco; a guide is required. Camping and accommodations are now available at **La Loma Pucón** (✆cell 8882-9845; www.lalomapucon.cl; Santuario El Cañi; camping per person CH\$3000; dm CH\$4000, d CH\$20,000),

operated by Rod Walker, an environmental education legend in Chile.

Arrangements to visit El Cañi can be made at ¡école! (p240) in Pucón or at the entrance to the park. Alternatively, **Buses Caburga** (✆098-038-9047; Uruguay 540) can drop you at the park entrance. It has services several times per day (CH\$700, 30 minutes).

Parque Nacional Huerquehue

Startling aquamarine lakes surrounded by verdant old-growth forests ensure wonderful **Parque Nacional Huerquehue** (adult/child CH\$4500/2500; ☒Buses Jac to/from Pucón in morning & afternoon) is one of the shining stars of the south and a standout in the Chilean chain of national parks. The 125-sq-km preserve, founded in 1912, is awash with rivers and waterfalls, alpine lakes and araucaria forests, and a long list of interesting creatures, including the pudú (the world's smallest deer) and *arañas pollitos* (tarantula-like spiders that come out in the fall).

The trails here are well marked and maintained and warrant multiple days of exploration, but a day trip from Pucón, about 35km to the southwest, is a must for those in a bigger hurry. Stop off at Conaf's **Centro de Informaciones Ambientales** (✆cell 6157-4809; p.huequehue@gmail.com; ⊙10:30am-2:30pm & 4:30-7:30pm) at the entrance for hiking maps and park info.

🏃 Activities

The **Los Lagos trail** (7km, four hours round-trip) switchbacks from 700m to 1300m through dense lenga forests with rushing waterfalls, then enters solid stands of araucaria surrounding a cluster of pristine and placid lakes. Most hikers turn back at Lago Verde and Laguna el Toro, the largest of the cluster, but continuing on to the lookout at **Mirador Renahue** will give hikers their just rewards with a spectacular view into the canyon. It is not as spectacular, however, as **Cerro San Sebastián** (16km, seven hours round-trip), which starts from the park entrance and climbs from 700m to 2000m. From the top, on a clear day, you can see eight volcanoes and 14 lagoons. Many consider this to be the best trek in all of La Araucanía.

🛏 Sleeping

Camping accommodations are at the Conaf-managed 22-site **Lago Tinquilco** (campsites CH$15,000) and at **Renahue** (campsites CH$15,000) on the Los Huerquenes trail. There are also a few private options in the vicinity of Tinquilco, where you can also park your car for CH$1000.

Refugio Tinquilco　　　　　LODGE $$
(📞cell 9539-2728; www.tinquilco.cl; camping CH$15,000, dm CH$14,000, d with/without bathroom CH$35,900/28,900, cabin CH$50,000; 🕐closed Jun-Aug) Refugio Tinquilco, on private property at the Lago Verde trailhead 2km past the park entrance, is a luxe two-story lodge offering much more than a bed, a meal and a quiet place to get away from it all – it's an experience. After hiking, be sure to submit yourself to the addictive forest sauna/plunge-pool treatment (CH$12,000).

Your host, Patricio, turns out home-style Chilean cuisine with welcome touches, such as French-press coffee and an extensive wine list, and is a helluva guy to share a bottle of Carmenere with. He also produces a field guide to the park that is leaps and bounds beyond anything published by Conaf. Designed by an architect, a writer, an engineer and an Emmy-nominated documentary filmmaker, it's the kind of place people lose themselves for a week and lost souls find their way. Breakfast is included; lunch or dinner is CH$8500.

ℹ Getting There & Away

Buses Caburgua (📞 098-038-9047; Uruguay 540, Pucón) has regular services that run to and from Pucón three times a day (CH$2000, one hour) through the summer, less in winter; purchase tickets in advance. Most agencies and outfitters offer organized excursions.

Curarrehue

📞 045 / POP 6624
The Mapuche stronghold of Curarrehue, which is located 40km west of the Argentine border, isn't much to look at, but it has begun a slow rise to fame for its excellent museum and wealth of *etnoturismo* opportunities. The small pueblo counts 80% of the population as Mapuche and is the last town of note before the border with Argentina.

◉ Sights & Activities

Aldea Intercultural Trawupeyüm　MUSEUM
(Héroes de la Concepción 21; adult & child CH$500; 🕐9am-8pm Mon-Fri, from 11am Sat & Sun Jan-Feb, 9am-6pm Tue-Sun Mar-Dec) A sparse but excellent museum of Mapuche culture housed in a modern interpretation of a mountain *ruka*, a traditional circular Mapuche dwelling oriented to the east.

Patragon　　　　　　　CULTURAL
(📞cell 9441-5769; www.patragon.cl) Offers fascinating tours in the area that include Mapuche cooking classes and lunch in a traditional *ruka;* great new *cabañas* (CH$100,000).

🛏 Sleeping & Eating

Hostal Quechupehuen　　HOSPEDAJE $
(📞045-197-1540; www.quechupehuen.cl; O'Higgins 470; r per person without bathroom CH$12,000; 🅿🛜) This well-located spot on the main road through town is walking distance from the museum and named for the five araucaria trees sprouting from its well-manicured front lawn. Accommodations are spread throughout an atmospheric 65-year-old home.

★**Cocina Mapuche Mapu Lyagl**　　　　MAPUCHE $
(📞cell 8788-7188; anita.epulef@gmail.com; Camino al Curarrehue; menu CH$5600; 🕐1-6pm Dec-Feb, by reservation only Apr-Nov; 🍴) Mapuche chef Anita Epulef turns seasonal ingredients into adventurous vegetarian Mapuche tasting menus. You can sample such indigenous delicacies as *Mullokiñ* (bean puree rolled in quinoa), sautéed *piñoñes,* the nut of the araucaria tree (in season only!) and roasted corn bread with an array of salsas – all excellent and unique. For those with extra time, Anita also offers half-day cooking

courses. You'll find her on the right-hand side of the main road just before the town entrance.

ℹ Information

Tourism Office (www.curarrehue.cl; O'Higgins s/n; ⊘9am-7pm mid Dec–mid-Mar, 9am-5:20pm Mon-Thu, to 4:20pm Fri mid-Mar–mid-Dec) Small but helpful tourist information along the main road through town.

ℹ Getting There & Away

Trans Curarrehue (p243) offers continuous services between Pucón and Curarrehue Monday to Friday (CH$1000, 45 minutes, 6:45am to 9:15pm), slightly scaled back on weekends.

LOS RÍOS

Valdivia

☑ 063 / POP 154,432

Valdivia was crowned the capital of Chile's newest Región XIV (Los Ríos) in 2007 after years of defection talk surrounding its inclusion in the Lakes District despite its geographical, historical and cultural differences. It is the most important university town in southern Chile and, as such, offers a strong emphasis on the arts, student prices at many hostels, cafes, restaurants and bars, Chile's best craft beer culture and a refreshing dose of youthful energy and German effervescence.

⊙ Sights & Activities

Av Costanera Arturo Prat (known simply as Prat) is a major focus of activity, but the most important public buildings are on Plaza de la República. To the west, the Puente Pedro de Valdivia crosses the river to Isla Teja, a leafy suburb that is the site of the Universidad Austral and many trendy restaurants and bars. The Valdivia region is also home to Sur Chico's newest national park, Parque Nacional Alerce Costero, which protects 24,000 hectares of the coastal alerce trees which give the park its name. It's located 137km southwest of the city.

★ **Cervecería Kunstmann**   BREWERY
(☑063-229-2969; www.laerveceria.cl; Ruta T-350 950; pitchers CH$7650-8250, mains CH$2700-9950; ⊘noon-midnight; ☎) On Isla Teja at Km5 on the road to Niebla, you'll find the

south's best large-scale brewery. Tours leave hourly from noon to 11pm (CH$10,000; November to March) and include a takeaway glass mug and a 300mL sampling of the Torobayo unfiltered, available only here, straight from the tank.

Unless you're a beer-history nut, the cost of the tour is better spent on sampling your way through the 10 or so beers on offer here, chased with hearty German fare that includes lots of pork chops, späetzle, sauerkraut and apple sauce. There isn't a German in sight, and it's nearly overflowing with tourists and tour buses, but you could do worse than drinking away an afternoon here. Bus 20 from Carampangue to Isla Teja (CH$550) can drop you off – a good idea even if you have wheels.

Museo Histórico y Antropológico   MUSEUM
(Los Laureles 47; admission CH$1500; ⊘10am-8pm Jan 5-Feb, 10am-1pm & 2-6pm Mar-Jan 4) Housed in a fine riverfront mansion on Isla Teja, this museum is one of Chile's finest. It features a large, well-labeled collection from pre-Columbian times to the present, with particularly fine displays of Mapuche Indian artifacts and household items from early German settlements.

On the same grounds, you'll find the sparse **Museo de Arte Contemporáneo** (www.macvaldivia.cl; admission CH$1500; ⊘10am-1pm & 3-7pm Tue-Sun) and, in a neighboring mansion, the science- and nature-oriented **RA Philippi Museo de la Exploración** (admission CH$1500); admission for the latter can be purchased together with Museo Histórico for CH$2500.

Feria Fluvial   MARKET
(Av Prat s/n; ⊘7am-4pm) A lively riverside market south of the Valdivia bridge, where vendors sell fresh fish, meat and produce. Waterfront sea lions have discovered the Promised Land here – a place where they can float around all day and let tourists and fishmongers throw them scraps from the daily catch. To get closer to the sea lions, walk up the Costanera another 200m.

Parque Saval   PARK
Parque Saval on Isla Teja has a riverside beach and a pleasant trail that follows the shoreline of Laguna de los Lotos, covered with lily pads. It's a good place for birdwatching.

Torreón del Barro   TOWER
(Av Costanera Arturo Prat s/n) A couple of turrets can be seen around town: east of the

bus terminal, the Torreón del Barro is from a Spanish fort built in 1774, while the **Torreón de los Canelos** (cnr Yerbas Buenas & General Lagos) dates from the 17th century.

☞ Tours

Valdivia's main and traditional tourist attraction is the boat cruise that plies the rivers to visit the 7th-century Spanish fortifications at Corral, Niebla and Isla Mancera. Largest and most intact is the Castillo de Corral, consisting of the Castillo San Sebastián de la Cruz (1645), the gun emplacements of the Batería de la Argolla (1764) and the Batería de la Cortina (1767). Fuerte Castillo de Amargos, a half-hour walk north of Corral, lurks on a crag above a small fishing village.

Located on the north side of the river, Fuerte Niebla (1645) allowed Spanish forces to catch potential invaders in a crossfire. The broken ramparts of Castillo de la Pura y Limpia Concepción de Monfort de Lemus (1671) are the oldest remaining ruins. Isla Mancera's Castillo San Pedro de Alcántara (1645) guarded the confluence of the Valdivia and the Tornagaleones, and later it became the residence of the military governor.

Each tour says it's different, but most take the same route, stopping at Corral and Isla Mancera for 45 minutes to one hour each, and all include lunch and *onces* (afternoon tea). To reach Niebla under your own steam – a fine day trip with its coastal northern California beach-town vibe – see Getting Around (p252).

Reina Sofia CRUISE
(☎063-220-7120; CH$16,000-18,000) A recommended (albeit a bit pushy) outfitter for Valdivia's boat cruises. It departs from Puerto Fluvial at the base of Arauco at 1:30pm daily.

✯ Festivals & Events

Bierfest/Oktoberfest BEER
Kunstmann-organized suds festival every January; newly inaugurated Oktoberfest in Parque Saval.

Noche de Valdivia CULTURAL
The largest happening is Noche de Valdivia, on the third Saturday in February, which features decorated riverboats and fireworks.

🛏 Sleeping

For most of the year students from the Universidad Austral monopolize the cheapest lodging, but many of these same places

vigorously court travelers during summer. There are cheaper, dingier *hospedajes* near the bus terminal along Av Ramón Picarte and Carlos Anwandter.

★ Airesbuenos Hostel & Permacultura HOSTEL $
(☎063-222-2202; www.airesbuenos.cl; Garcia Reyes 550; dm CH$10,000, r CH$28,000; @🤚) 🌿 Valdivia's best hostel is run by a friendly Northern Californian who has turned this long-standing traveler mainstay into Sur Chico's most eco-friendly sleeps. Solar-heated showers, rainwater catchment, permaculture, vertical gardens, compost, Egyptian bamboo towels – it's all here. Besides the sustainability, you'll find comfy, colorful dorm rooms and simple, well-done private rooms that are a little on the small side.

Breakfast boasts real coffee and housemade granola. It's a five-minute walk to the river and bus station. You may be charged a small fee if you dawdle too long after checkout.

Hostel Bosque Nativo HOSTEL $
(☎063-243-3782; www.hostelnativo.cl; Pasaje Fresia 290; dm CH$10,000, s/d CH$19,000/26,000, without bathroom CH$17,000/22,000; @🤚) This hostel, run by a sustainable forestry management NGO, is a wooden den of comfort hidden away down a gravel residential lane a short walk from the bus station.

It's not without issues: device-heavy travelers will be frustrated with the dire lack of outlets in the dorms; there are no bathroom hand towels and, oddly, toilet paper is *outside* the stalls in common bathrooms (and there's limited English). But the private rooms are some of Valdivia's best value and it's one of the city's coziest.

Hostal Totem GUESTHOUSE $
(☎063-229-2849; www.turismototem.cl; Carlos Anwandter 425; s/d/tr CH$25,000/30,000/39,000; @🤚) Of the ample choices along residential thoroughfare Carlos Anwandter, this 11-room guesthouse is the best bang for the *peso*. Clean rooms, a friendly French- and English-speaking upstart owner and a sunny breakfast room make up for the lack of antiquated character, though the hardwood floors in this old house squeak with the best of 'em.

Hostal Torreón HISTORIC HOTEL $$
(☎063-221-3069; hostaltorreon@gmail.com; Pérez Rosales 783; s/d CH$30,000/40,000, without bathroom CH$25,000/30,000; 🅿🤚) This rickety old mansion tucked away off the

Valdivia

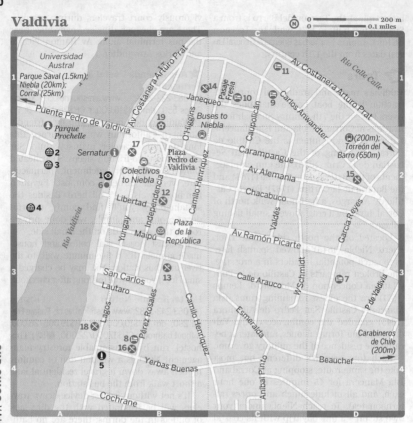

street prides itself on uneven flooring – it's survived two massive earthquakes! – and is notable for its antiquated character. The antique-laden common areas are a nod to the house's lengthy past while 2nd-floor rooms offer more light and less dampness than the basement options. It's relatively pricy, though. Breakfast is CH$5000.

Hotel Encanto del Río HOTEL **$$**
(☑ 063-222-4744; www.hotelencantodelrio.cl; Av Costanera Arturo Prat 415; s/d CH$49,000/69,000; ℙ☜) This midrange hotel is along a quieter and trendier stretch of the river. It's laden with indigenous weavings and Botero reprints on the walls, giving it some extra character, and the feeling you're sleeping in someone's home with the services of a hotel. River-view rooms have small patios that look straight across the Río Calle Calle...to a factory, unfortunately.

✖ Eating & Drinking

Isla Teja across the river from the city is the latest ubertrendy neighborhood for restaurants. For inexpensive seafood, head to the top floor of the **Mercado Municipal** (Prat s/n; mains CH$2500-4000; ☺9am-9pm), where you'll find hearty homespun meals for between CH$2500 to CH$4000.

The main concentration of nightlife is on tiny but lively Esmeralda – take your pick. Most of the hot spots serve good food as well, so you can settle in for the evening. **Casino Dreams Valdivia** (www.mundodreams.cl; Carampangue 190; admission CH$3000; ☺noon-6pm Mon-Thu, to 7pm Fri, to 5pm Sun), the city's glitzy hotel/casino complex, is also an option with trendy sushi and a glamy discotheque.

★La Última Frontera RESTO-BAR **$**
(Pérez Rosales 787; sandwiches CH$2800-4400; ☺10am-2am Mon-Sat; ☜☑) You'll find one-stop traveler nirvana at this bohemian

Valdivia

resto-bar with a vibe unmatched in the whole of Sur Chico. Hidden quietly away in a restored mansion, you'll find a load of outside-the-box sandwiches, fresh juices and local craft beer – 12 or so on draft (start with Cuello Negro Stout) and a few more stragglers in bottles.

At night, it morphs into the best bar for miles and miles courtesy of the town's hip artistic front. Lose yourself in one of the art-saturated rooms or knock back a cold one on the new patio and deck. Don't miss it.

Café Moro   CHILEAN $
(Paseo Libertad 174; menu CH$3100; ⊗9:30am-10pm Mon-Fri, 11am-10pm Sat; 🛜) An excellent spot for a supervalue set-menu lunch. It draws an age-defying and eclectic mix of intellectual hipsters and WWF think-tank scientists from Valdivia's Centro de Estudios Científicos, and turns to drinking as evenings progress.

Entrelagos   CAFE $
(www.entrelagos.cl; Pérez Rosales 640; sandwiches CH$3100-6400; ⊗9am-9pm Mon-Fri, 10am-9:30pm Sat, 11am-9pm Sun) This classic salón

de té (tea house) is where Valdivians talk about you behind your back over delicious *café cortados* (espresso with milk), cakes, sandwiches and crepes. Hearty set menus and toasted sandwiches draw those looking for something more filling (or perhaps just escapists – the Parisian-style seating couldn't be more un-Chilean). On Sunday, there's little else.

La Calesa   PERUVIAN $$
(www.lacalesa.cl; O'Higgins 160; mains CH$6900-10,500; ⊗lunch Wed-Sun, dinner Tue-Sat; 🛜) This restaurant serves Peruvian staples, such as garlic-roasted chicken and *lomo saltado* (stir-fried beef with spices, onions, tomatoes and potatoes). The pisco sours are memorable as is the *suspiro*, a Peruvian dessert made from *manjar* (Chilean milk caramel) and meringue and laced with pisco.

La Cave del Buho   RESTO-BAR $$
(Av Alemania 660; mains CH$5900-9600; ⊗7:30pm-1am Mon-Sat; 🛜) If you like to mix your drinking with a step-up in food, this dark, candlelit resto-bar off the beaten path is a good bet. The handwrittten menu specializes in filets and there's an extensive cocktail to list to go with it. It gets going on the later end on weekends (after 10pm), when locals pile into the Middle Earth-inspired space.

Santo Pecado   RESTO-BAR $$
(Yungay 745; cocktails CH$2400-5900, mains CH$3900-8900; ⊗12:30-3pm & 7pm-midnight Mon-Fri, 8pm-12:30am Sat; 🛜) Notable not only for such missing-in-action culinary flavors as Camembert, leeks and a monster *tortilla española,* but, weather-permitting, unstoppable river views from its waterfront back patio. Get here early for summer sunsets – there are only seven tables.

ℹ Information

Downtown ATMs are abundant.

Carabineros de Chile (☑063-250-3085; www.carabineros.cl; Beauchef 1025) Police station.

Clínica Alemana (www.alemanavaldivia.cl; Beauchef 765; ⊗24hr) Better, faster and closer than the public hospital.

CorreosChile (www.correos.cl; O'Higgins 575; ⊗9am-7pm Mon-Fri, 9:30am-1pm Sat) Postal services.

Información Turística (☑063-222-0498; www.munivaldivia.cl; ⊗8am-9:30pm) At the bus terminal.

Sernatur (☑063-223-9060; www.turismolosrios.cl; Prat s/n; ⊗9am-9pm) Provides very helpful advice.

SUR CHICO VALDIVIA

❶ Getting There & Away

AIR

Aeropuerto Pichoy (☎ 063-227-2294) is situated 32km from Valdivia on Ruta 5.

LAN (☎ 600-526-2000; www.lan.com; Maipú 271; ☺ 9am-1pm & 3:30-6pm Mon-Fri, 10am-1pm Sat) Flies to Santiago once daily from CH\$162,778.

Sky Airlines (☎ 063-222-6280; www.skyairline.cl; Chacabuco 308; ☺ 9am-7pm Mon-Fri, 10am-1pm Sat) Sky Airlines flies direct to Santiago (from CH\$63,678) on Friday and Sunday only. Otherwise, flights to the capital route via Concepción (from CH\$40,678).

BUS

Valdivia's centrally located **Terminal Valdivia** (☎ 063-222-0498; www.terminalvaldivia.cl; Anfión Muñoz 360), along the northeast side of the *costanera* at Anfión Muñoz, was undergoing a major modernization at time of research. Leave your luggage at the *Custodia de Equipaje* (CH\$1500; open 7am to 11pm).

The terminal offers frequent buses to destinations on or near the Panamericana between Puerto Montt and Santiago, especially with **Tur-Bus** (☎ 063-221-2430; www.turbus.cl), **Pullman Bus** (☎ 063-220-4660; www.pullman.cl) and **Cruz del Sur** (☎ 063-221-3840; www.buscruzdelsur.cl), the latter with the most frequent services to Chiloé. For Viña del Mar/Valparaíso, Tur-Bus heads out twice daily at 8:30pm and 8:45pm.

Regional bus carriers include **Buses Pirihueico** (☎ 063-221-3804) to Panguipulli (every 45 minutes, 6:45am to 8pm); **Bus Futrono** (☎ 063-220-2227) to Futrono (frequent, 6:20am to 8:10pm); and **Buses JAC** (☎ 063-221-3754; www.busjac.cl) to Villarrica, Pucón and Temuco. Officeless **Ruta 5** (☎ 063-231-7040) goes to Lago Ranco at 12:05pm and 4:10pm Monday to Saturday; and on 7:45pm Sunday. Otherwise JAC has a daily 7:05pm bus.

Andesmar (☎ 063-222-4665; www.andesmar.com) goes to Bariloche, Argentina direct daily at 8:45am on Monday, Tuesday, Wednesday, Saturday and Sunday; a few other bus services also leave from Osorno. **Buses San Martín** (☎ 063-222-4665) goes to San Martín de los Andes Wednesday, Friday and Sunday at 6am. To get to Neuquén, switch in Junín.

Sample travel times and starting fares are as follows (prices fluctuate with the quality of the bus/class and season):

DESTINATION	COST (CH\$)	DURATION (HR)
Bariloche (Ar)	21,000	7
Castro	9500	7
Futrono	2500	2
Lago Ranco	3100	2
Neuquén (Ar)	41,900	12
Osorno	5000	2
Panguipulli	2900	2¼
Pucón	4500	4
Puerto Montt	5000	3½
San Martín de los Andes (Ar)	13,000	8
Santiago	34,000	12
Temuco	4200	3½
Valparaíso	35,600	13
Villarrica	4300	3
Viña del Mar	35,600	13

❶ Getting Around

To and from the airport, **Transfer Aeropuerto Valdivia** (☎ 063-222-5533) provides an on-demand minibus service (CH\$3500), but the most economical way is catching any Buses Pirihueico bus to Panguipulli at the bus terminal, which will drop you at the airport (CH\$1000, 6:30am to 8pm Monday to Friday, from 7:15am Saturday, 8:20am to 8:30am Sunday). A taxi from the bus terminal costs CH\$16,000 to CH\$18,000.

From the bus terminal to Plaza de la República, head to the south end of the terminal and up the escalators to the 3rd-floor exit onto Carlos Anwandter, where you can take any green or yellow *colectivo* (CH\$500) or bus 3 (CH\$45), which will drop you on Chacabuco, one block north of the plaza.

For Niebla, take **colectivos** (cnr Yungay & Chacabuco; CH\$1000) or **buses** (Carampangue; CH\$550). From the Muelle Niebla, small boats go back and forth to Corral every 20 minutes or so from 8am to 9pm (CH\$800) and ply the waters to Isla Mancera every 20 minutes a few times daily (CH\$300; 9am, 12:30pm, 2:30pm and 5:30pm Monday to Saturday, 10:30am, noon and 4pm Sunday). There is also a larger **ferry** (☎ 063-228-2743; www.barcazas.cl) that can carry cars to Corral (pedestrians CH\$650, cars CH\$4370; every hour, 8am to midnight).

THE LAKES DISTRICT

The Lakes District, named for its myriad glacial lakes that dot a countryside otherwise characterized by looming, snow-capped volcanoes, otherworldly national parks and serene lakeside villages, is one of Chile's most picturesque regions. Outdoor

HUILO-HUILO RESERVA NATURAL BIOSFERA

The mostly paved road from Lago Pirihueico, 101km east of Valdivia and 80km south of Villarrica, to Puerto Fuy parallels the scenic Río Huilo Huilo, which tumbles and falls through awe-inspiring scenery to the impressive **Huilo-Huilo Reserva Natural Biosfera** (02-2887-3500; www.huilohuilo.com; Camino Internacional Panguipulli–Valdivia Km55; excursions CH$2500-55,000). This conservation project, begun in 2000, encompasses 1000 sq km of private land that has been developed for low-impact ecotourism and falls within a much larger Unesco biosphere reserve. There is a wealth of excursions, a fantastic museum and microbrewery and a bevy of lodging for all budgets, including four spectacularly insane and surreal hotels. The beautiful reserve, owned and managed by Fundación Huilo-Huilo, is especially well-known for its endemic species, including the Darwin's frog, pudú, *monito del monte* (little mountain monkey), 111 species of birds, 35 species of ferns (second only to Archipiélago Juan Fernández) and, most importantly, the endangered huemal (South Andean deer), which is being reproduced here by the Fundación with startling success.

The reserve offers numerous outdoor adventures (trekking, climbing, mountain biking, horseback riding, rafting, kayaking and ice trekking), but you need a guide to enter everywhere but the stunning 37m **Salto de Huilo Huilo**. Nonguests can arrange guides at the **Centro de Excursiones** (02-2887-3500; www.huilohuilo.com; 8am-9:30pm Jan-Feb, 9am-7:30pm Apr-Mar) inside La Montaña Magica. The stone-domed **Museo de Volcanes** (adult/child CH$2000/1000; 11am-8pm Dec-Mar, 10am-5pm Apr-Nov) is Sur Chico's most impressive archaeological museum, covering native Chilean indigenous cultures, including one of the best Mapuche ornament collections in existence, an impressive lantern, padlock and iron collection, a re-creation of the 2010 Copiapó mine rescue and a prehistoric mastodon tusk, which they claim is one of only four in the world.

La Montaña Mágica (02-2887-3500; www.huilohuilo.com; s/d CH$127,925/172,550; P@) is a Frodo-approved spire with a fountain spewing from the top and full of kitschy furniture and supernatural design touches. The less-intimate **Nothofagus Hotel & Spa** (02-2887-3500; www.huilohuilo.com; s/d CH$127,925/172,550; P@) is a Gaudí-inspired inverted cone suspended in the treetops with a restaurant serving international and Chilean cuisine with indigenous touches. The newest accommodation is the mushroom-inspired **Reino Fungi Lodge** (02-2887-3500; www.huilohuilo.com; s/d from CH$127,925/172,550;). Nearby, the exclusive **Nawelpi Lodge** (02-2887-3500; www.huilohuilo.com; s/d all-inclusive 3-night packages CH$1,240,580/1,783,280; P) offers 12 expansive cabins with luxurious furnishings, volcanic slate fireplaces and outstanding terraces overlooking the Río Fuy. More down-to-earth accommodations in the park include **Camping Huilo-Huilo** (02-2887-3500; www.huilohuilo.com; camping per person CH$6000), with electricity, nice bathrooms with hot water and thermal bathtubs carved from the wooden patio deck, and the **Canopy Village** (02-2887-3500; www.huilohuilo. com; cabañas 2/6 people from CH$30,000/70,000), with raised cabins connected by a wooden walkway, a kitchen for guest use and outstanding views of Volcán Mocho.

From Puerto Fuy, the ferry **Hua-Hum** (063-197-1871; www.barcazas.cl) carries passengers and vehicles to and from Puerto Pirihueico (1½ hours) once daily from March to December (1pm) and three times in January and February (8am, 1pm and 6pm). Automobiles cost CH$16,390 to CH$24,590, pedestrians pay CH$800 and bicycles CH$3275. The *Hua-Hum* can only fit 22 vehicles, so make reservations.

Budget travelers without wheels can still enjoy all that Huilo-Huilo has to offer. There are seven or so buses per day from Monday to Saturday (only two on Sunday) to Huilo-Huilo from Panguipulli (CH$2200, 2¼ hours) and more affordable accommodations in the small hamlet of Neltume, 3km from the park's reception.

adventurers congregate around pretty Puerto Varas, the region's most touristy town and the jumping-off point for most of the area's attractions, be they horseback riding or rock climbing in the Cochamó Valley, lake lingering around Lagos Llanquihue, Puyehue or Todos los Santos, or flashpacking through any number of impressive national parks.

THE LAKES OF LA ARAUCANÍA & LOS RÍOS

Chile's Región XIV may be named for its rivers, but it wasn't shortchanged on beautiful lakes, either. While not as heavily visited as those in Los Lagos, there are some gems here, and they're a good bet if you'd rather holiday with Chileans than fellow countrymen.

Lago Ranco

When it comes to southern Chilean lakes, Lago Ranco, 124km from Valdivia, is a true sleeper: though not heavily visited or well-known outside Chile, it's a glistening sapphire hideaway bound by lush mountains and peppered with verdant islands. For whatever reason, tourism hasn't dug in its heels here yet, so it's great if you want to escape the crowds and get away with your best friend's spouse or hunker down to finish that screenplay, but bad if you want to eat or sleep well while you're doing it.

In one circuit around this cerulean lake you can enjoy majestic views of the Andes, simple working towns, high-end fishing resorts and Mapuche communities. On the north shore of Lago Ranco, 102km from Valdivia via Paillaco, Futrono is a dusty old town with a frontier feel. It is the main service center for the lake and the Mapuche community on Isla Huapi.

Lago Panguipulli

At the northwest end of Lago Panguipulli, the town of **Panguipulli** is a quiet spot with awkward beach access, a lively main street and a totally odd Swiss-style church founded by Capuchin monks. You won't starve here – there are also a surprising number of restaurants and it has become a playground for the upwardly mobile in recent years.

Little more than two streets at the east end of Lago Panguipulli, the cute hamlet **Choshuenco** has a sweeping beach with views that are a study in serenity, with crystal waters and rolling hills of green. It's a relaxing base for hikes, or a good place to rest before or after the Lago Pirihueico crossing between here and Argentina. This lake stands out as the region's most stunning.

Lago Calafquén

Some 82% of this gorgeous lake sits in Los Ríos and Coñaripe (only the bit around Lican Ray falls is in La Araucanía) in the shadow of one of Chile's most active volcanoes (Villarrica), and it's the most popular and liveliest lake town in the region. Its black-sand beaches and easy access to a number of the smaller hot springs – 14 in all – attract the summer crowds and it's a far more pleasant spot to stay than Liquiñe if you're looking to sooth your aching muscles in a little *agua caliente* (warm water).

At the east end of Coñaripe, the main drag, Av Guido Beck Ramberga, intersects Ruta 201, the international highway to Junín de los Andes in Argentina; the westbound fork leads to Panguipulli and the southeast to Termas de Coñaripe, Termas Geométricas (p246; the area's finest), Liquiñe and the border crossing at Paso Carirriñe. The road heading north of Coñaripe leads to a number of rustic hot springs and the southern boundary of Parque Nacional Villarrica.

Osorno

☑ 064 / POP 151,913

Osorno (the city, not the volcano) is a bustling place and the commercial engine for the surrounding agricultural zone. Though it's an important transportation hub on the route between Puerto Montt and Santiago and the Hulliche communities of the Osorno coast, most visitors do not spend a lot of time here.

🛏 Sleeping & Eating

You'll find plenty to eat along the main drag, Juan Mackenna, in the blocks east and west of Plaza de Armas. At the Mercado Municipal, hearty meals go for CH$2000 to CH$5000.

Hostel Vermont   HOSTEL $
(☑064-224-7030; www.hostelvermont.cl; Toribio Medina 2020; dm CH$12,000, s/d without bathroom CH$20,000/30,000, cabins s/d/q CH$25,000/35,000/50,000; @ 🛜) Osorno's first decent

hostel is run by a bilingual snowboarder who named the hostel after her stint near Burlington, Vermont. It's everything you want in a hostel: friendly, clean and well-equipped (as well as some things you don't want: creaky old floors mixed with rowdiness means it gets sleep-deprivingly loud).

From the bus station, walk two blocks south to Juan Mackenna, five blocks east to Buenos Aires and one and a half blocks south to Toribio Medina.

Hotel Villa Eduviges   HOTEL **$$**
(☑ 064-223-5023; www.hoteleduviges.cl; Eduviges 856; s/d/tr from CH$25,000/40,000/55,000; ℙ☎) Midrange and comfortable, Eduviges wins props for being in the minority in Región X, allowing singles to sleep in a double bed without paying for a double. The relaxed setting in a residential area south of the bus terminal bodes well, with spacious, somewhat old-fashioned rooms, private bathrooms and kind management.

ℹ Information

You'll find ATMs on Plaza de Armas.
Tourist Information Kiosk (☑ 064-221-8740; Plaza de Armas; ⊙9am-7pm mid-Dec–mid-Mar, 9am-1pm & 3-6pm Mon-Fri, from 10am Sat mid-Mar–mid-Dec) On Plaza de Armas.

ℹ Getting There & Away

AIR

Aeropuerto Carlos Hott Siebert (☑ 064-224-7555; Cañal Bajo) is 7km east of downtown, across the Panamericana via Av Buschmann. **LAN** (☑ 600-526-2000; www.lan.com; Eleuterio Ramírez 802; ⊙9am-1pm & 3-6:30pm Mon-Fri, 9:30am-1pm Sat) flies once daily to Santiago at 2pm (from CH$186,000).

BUS

Long-distance buses use the main **Terminal de Buses** (☑ 064-221-1120; Errázuriz 1400). Most services going north on the Panamericana start in Puerto Montt, departing about every hour, with mainly overnight service to Santiago. Good options include **Pullman Bus** (☑ 064-231-8529; www.pullman.cl), **Tur-Bus** (☑ 064-220-1526; www.turbus.cl) and **Cruz del Sur** (☑ 064-223-2778; www.busescruzdelsur.cl).

For Valparaíso/Viña del Mar, try Tur-Bus (10:45pm). **Buses JAC** (☑ 064-255-3300; www.jac.cl) is your best bet for Valdivia, Temuco and Pucón. **Ruta 5** (☑ 064-231-7040) goes to Lago Ranco (CH$2500, two hours, 10:15am and 5:45pm, also 12:20pm Monday to Friday). Cruz del Sur has the most departures south and on to the island of Chiloé. **Buses Pirihueico** (☑ 064-

ℹ TO THE AIRPORT

There is no public transport to the airport, but any Entre Lagos–bound bus can drop you at the airport entrance, 300m from the terminal (CH$600). That beats a CH$6000 taxi!

223-3050) goes to Panguipulli via Valdivia (CH$3500, 1¾ hours).

For Chilean Patagonia, **Queilen Bus** (☑ 064-226-0025; www.queilenbus.cl) heads to Coyhaique (12:35pm Monday and Wednesday) and **Trans Austral** (☑ 064-223-3050) goes to Futaleufú (CH$25,000, 10 hours, 8am Tuesday and Saturday). For Punta Arenas, try Queilen Bus (12:20pm Monday and Friday), **Turibús** (☑ 064-223-2778; 12:45pm Tuesday, Thursday and Saturday) or Pullman Bus (noon Monday and Saturday).

Buses to Bariloche, Argentina, include **Bus Norte** (☑ 064-223-2778; www.busnortechile.cl) at 10:30am, **Via Bariloche** (☑ 064-226-0025; www.viabariloche.com.ar) at 4:30pm and **Andesmar** (☑ 064-223-3050; www.andesmar.com) at 10:15am and 10:30am, plus 2:30pm January and February. All Bariloche-bound buses stop in Villa Angostura, Argentina (from CH$15,000, four hours). For Zapala or Neuquen, Argentina, direct buses leave from Temuco.

There is a small *custodia* for left luggage (CH$900-1800; open 7:30am to 10:30pm).

Sample travel times and starting fares are as follows (prices fluctuate with the quality of the bus/class and season):

DESTINATION	COST (CH$)	DURATION (HR)
Ancud	6200	4
Bariloche (Ar)	16,000	5
Concepción	12,300	9
Coyhaique	40,000	20
Pucón	8400	4
Puerto Montt	2200	1¾
Punta Arenas	42,000	28
Santiago	20,000	12
Temuco	5800	3½
Valdivia	3600	1¾
Valparaíso/ Viña del Mar	29,900	14

Also departing from the main bus terminal are several trips daily to places around Lago Llanquihue at the foot of Volcán Osorno.

Other local and regional destinations leave from the **Terminal Mercado Municipal** (Errázuriz btwn Arturo Prat & Cristóbal Colón) in front of the new Mercado Municipal. **Expreso Lago**

HUILLICHE HOLIDAY

The indigenous Huilliche communities of Osorno's gorgeous coast are sitting on an *etnoturismo* gold mine and have only just started to realize it. Fresh off an idea planted by a decade of sustainable tourism research by the WWF (World Wildlife Fund), these off-the-beaten-path communities are beginning to embrace visitors. You can immerse yourself in their way of life over multiday trips that involve some of Chile's most stunning beaches, Valdivian forest treks, and rural homestays around San Juan de la Costa and **Territorio Mapa Lahual** (www.mapulahual.cl), an indigenous protected zone that stretches south into Río Negro province.

In San Juan de la Costa, a series of five magnificent *caletas* (bays) are accessible by car and could be visited as day trips from around Osorno for those short on time. **Bahía Mansa**, **Pucatrihue** and **Maicolpué** are villages where dolphins and sea lions practically swim to shore and women scramble about wild, rugged beaches collecting *luga* and *cochayuyo*, two types of seaweed that help fuel the local economy. On either side are the two best *caletas*, **Manzano**, 20km north of Bahía Mansa, and **Tril-Tril**, 7km south of Bahía Mansa.

Going deeper requires more logistics and planning, but the rewards are spectacular. **Caleta Condor**, part of Territorio Mapa Lahual and accessible only by a two-hour boat ride (or two-day trek) from Bahía Mansa or a nine-hour 4WD/trekking/boat combo from Río Negro, is an impossibly gorgeous bay completely off the grid – communication with the outside world here is via VHF radio! If the weather is clear, arriving here is miraculous: as you enter via the scenic and translucent Río Cholcuaco from the Pacific, you are greeted with an idyllic combination of nature (moss-strewn thatches of land that line the river like wild putting greens, flush with horses and seabirds, backed by hillsides peppered with beautiful *luma* and *arrayán* trees) and nurture (10 families call this piece of paradise home on a permanent basis, and several have a bed waiting for you). It all culminates at the river's end on a sandbar strip of out-of-place *tropicália* that separates the river beach and the ocean beach.

If you just want to sleep in a breathtaking spot, you can make your own way to Caleta Condor. Boat trips can be arranged in San Juan de la Costa. Boatman Rubén Pailapichún runs **Paseos Náuticos Lafken Mapu Lahual** (☎ cell 8418-5727, cell 7871-6874; maitecbg@gmail.com; per 8 people CH$180,000), which leaves from the pier in Bahía Mansa daily at 8am from December to March or by reservation the rest of the year (though sea conditions prevent most departures in winter). If you can't get in touch with him, you'll find his wife at **Comida Rápida Doña Mary** near the Huilliche statue overlooking the beach in Maicolpué. The best of the four homestay options, with an elevated position affording spectacular views, is **Hospedaje Don Florentín** (r without bathroom CH$12,000, meals CH$5000). But if you want to truly experience all that a visit here has to offer, you'll need to arrange a tour. **Mawidan Tour Chile** (☎ cell 7771-7275; www.mawidan.com; Camino Cheuquemo Km1, Río Negro) ✐ has the best relationships with local communities and the best logistical support.

It is feasible to make your way to the coast and use the excellent Argentine-run **Hostería Miller** (☎064-255-0277; www.hosteriamiller.com; Maicolpué; s/d without bathroom CH$25,000/35,000, tr/q CH$45,000/55,000; P☎) in Maicolpué as a base. Here you can sip on Don Ruben's meticulously prepared pisco sours while ogling Peale's and Commerson's dolphins right from your window. From Osorno, minibuses depart hourly to Bahía Mansa, Pucatrihue and Maicolpué (CH$1800, 1½ hours) from the Feria Libre Ráhue (p256).

Puyehue (☎ 064-224-3919; www.expresola-gopuyehue.wix.com/buses-expreso) goes to Termas Puyehue/Aguas Calientes (CH$2200, 1½ hours, hourly, 6:40am to 7pm) and Entre Lagos (CH$1400, one hour, every 10 minutes, 6:50am to 7:15pm). **Buses Río Negro** (☎ 064-223-6748) goes to Caleta Condor via Río Negro (CH$1200, 45 minutes, every 10 minutes).

To get to the Huilliche communities of San Juan de la Costa (CH$1800, 1¾ hours) – Bahía Mansa, Pucatrihue and Maicolpué – minibuses depart every hour from the **Feria Libre Ráhue** (cnr Chillán & Temuco). Catch bus 1, 6 or 10 from the northeast corner of Errázuriz and Cristóbal Colón (CH$400).

Parque Nacional Puyehue

Volcán Puyehue, 2240m tall, blew its top the day after the earthquake in 1960, turning a large chunk of dense, humid evergreen forest into a stark landscape of sand dunes and lava rivers. **Parque Nacional Puyehue** (www.parquepuyehue.cl) FREE protects 1070 sq km of this contrasting environment, and it is one of the more 'developed' of the country's national parks, with a ski resort and several hot-spring resorts within its boundaries.

There are also several hikes that explore more pristine areas of the national park. Aguas Calientes is the main sector of the park, with the hot-springs resort and Conaf's Centro de Información Ambiental.

The park's western border is about 75km east of Osorno via the paved Ruta 215, which continues through the park, following the course of the Río Golgol to the Argentine border.

Aguas Calientes

The **hot springs** (www.termasaguascalientes.cl; day use without/with meals CH$12,500/28,000) resort of Aguas Calientes is overrun with Chilean families and gets crowded in the summer months. On offer are typical spa services, individual tubs, a very hot indoor pool and a large shallow cement pool by the side of the river. However, you can access the free **Pocitos Termas** 80m across the Colgante bridge from the Conaf parking lot.

Another way to get your heart rate up is to hike the enjoyable **Sendero El Pionero**, a steep 1800m nature trail that ends with splendid views of Lago Puyehue, the valley of the Río Golgol and Volcán Puyehue.

🛏 Sleeping

Cabañas Aguas Calientes   CABAÑAS $$
(☏064-223-1710; www.termasaguascalientes.cl; Ruta 215, Camino Antillanca Km76; camping per site CH$20,000, 2-/8-person cabin from CH$120,000/180,000, 2-/4-person domos without bathroom CH$65,000/90,000; P@@🛜🏊) The only lodging option. Its A-frame cabins are stacked up along the hillside like a well-planned miniature village, and they are remarkably comfortable, with plush beds, full kitchens, hot showers and wood stoves (and some with hot tubs, though they lack privacy). Comfortable riverside domos back up against the pleasant, somewhat rushing river. Rates include spa facilities and breakfast.

Parque Nacional Puyehue

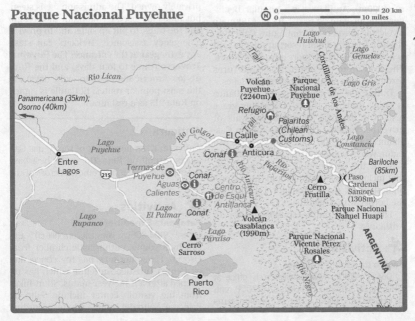

BEERVANA!

If you're within 100km of Osorno and a beer lover, you'll want to readjust your itinerary to visit this improvised temple of suds, **Cervecería Artesenal Armin Schmid** (cell 8294-1818; Ruta 215 Km12; beer CH$1600-2400, mains CH$4900-8100; 1-10pm Mon-Fri, from noon Sat), the South's most interesting craft brewery, located 12km outside of Osorno on Ruta 215 toward Entre Lagos and the border with Argentina.

Bavarian transplant Armin Schmid brews stunning Märzen, Pils and Doppelbock (and an off-menu Light) in a private home and serves them in a wonderful makeshift frontyard *biergarten*. There is requisite German food (*bratwurst, leberkäse*) and surprisingly good thin-crust pizzas. To find it, head out on Ruta 215 from Osorno. Shortly after the small village of Las Lumas, look for it on the righthand side of the road – it's announced by a small, easy-to-miss sign flanked by blue-and-white checkered Bavarian flags. A taxi costs CH$8000 from the city center. *¡Prost!*

Information

Centro de Información Ambiental (064-197-4572; 9am-1pm & 2-6pm) Conaf's Centro de Información Ambiental houses an informative display on Puyehue's natural history and geomorphology.

Getting There & Away

Expreso Lago Puyehue (p255) goes to Aguas Calientes (CH$2200, 1½ hours, hourly, 6:40am to 7pm) from Osorno's Mercado Municipal.

Antillanca

On the southwest slope of Volcán Casablanca (1990m), Antillanca is a popular beginner/intermediate ski resort. It's just 18km up a volcanic gravel road from Aguas Calientes. It has a friendly small-resort ambience, but is not challenging for more advanced skiers. The road up to the resort twists and turns through scenic areas and past glassy lakes.

During the no-snow months Antillanca is rather drab, but the resort's saving grace rests with its trails, especially the walk or drive (per vehicle CH$6000) to Volcán Casablanca's Crater Rayhuen, and Cumbre Mirador, where you can drink in a spectacular view of the surrounding mountain range that includes four volcanoes and the region's highest point, Cerro Tronador (3470m), on the border with Argentina.

There is no public transportation to Antillanca.

Activities

Centro de Esquí Antillanca   SKIING
(064-224-2010; www.skiantillanca.cl; office at O'Higgins 1073, Osorno; lift tickets CH$27,000, rentals CH$26,000-29,000) The ski season runs from early June to September. The ski area has five surface lifts and 460m of vertical drop. The resort includes an outrageously overpriced hotel open year-round with typical ski-resort trimmings.

El Caulle

Two kilometers west of Anticura, the privately owned **El Caulle** (cell 9920-3244; www.elcaulle.com; entrance CH$10,000) is the southern entrance for the trek across the magnificently desolate plateau at the western base of Volcán Puyehue. While officially within park boundaries, the access land is privately owned. The admission fee is steep, but funds are used to maintain the *refugio* and the trails, to put up signs and to provide emergency assistance. Trekkers can stash any extra gear at the entrance. The **Puyehue Traverse** (three to four days) and the **Ruta de los Americanos** (six to eight days) are the most popular routes. El Caulle is signed on Ruta 215 as a restaurant.

Anticura

Anticura, 17km northwest of the Aguas Calientes turnoff on Ruta 215, is the best base for exploring the more remote sectors of the park.

Activities

Patagonia Expeditions   TREKKING
(cell 9104-8061; www.anticurachile.cl) Co-run by a young, enthusiastic climber from Osorno, Patagonia now has the concession on Centro Turístico Anticura, which has reopened after a three-year hiatus. Short hikes from the visitors center include Salto de Princesa, Salto del Indio – where, according

to legend, a lone Mapuche hid to escape *encomienda* (colonial labor system) service in a nearby Spanish gold mine – and Repucura, which ends back up on Ruta 215 (buses come careening down the highway; walk on the opposite side).

There's also a 4km steep hike up to a lookout point. Excursions from here include climbing Volcán Casablanca (1960m; CH$35,000); Volcán Puyehue (2240m; CH$70,000, or CH$90,000 along with 2011 Puyehue eruption crater), nocturnal waterfall visits and multiday treks. A restaurant serves three meals a day (CH$6000). There is also a Cordón Caulle eruption photo exhibition here.

🛏 Sleeping

Camping Catrué   CAMPING, CABAÑAS **$$**
(📞 cell 9104-8061; www.anticurachile.cl; camping CH$3500, dm CH$8000, cabañas for 2 CH$35,000, cabañas for 4/6 CH$42,000/52,000) Patagonia Expeditions runs the hostel-vibey Camping Catrué, which now offers 18 woodsy sites with tree-trunk picnic tables, electricity and bathrooms with hot water. Cabins have been refurnished and are fully equipped, two of which have been converted into dorms.

ⓘ Getting There & Away

There are two buses to Anticura per day (1½ hours, noon and 4pm) from Osorno's Terminal Mercado Municipal with **Buses Carlos** (📞 cell 9408-8453, cell 7265-9780), but by reservation only. Fares vary from CH$3500 (three or more passengers) to CH$6000 (under three passengers). Otherwise, catch any bus to Aguas Calientes, from where Patagonia Expeditions offers a pick-up service for CH$5000.

Any bus heading to Anticura can drop off trekkers at El Caulle.

Puerto Varas

📞 065 / POP 37,942

Two menacing, snowcapped volcanoes, Osorno and Calbuco, stand sentinel over picturesque Puerto Varas and its scenic Lago Llanquihue like soldiers of adventure, allowing only those on a high-octane quest to pass. Just 23km from Puerto Montt but worlds apart in charm, scenery and options for the traveler, Puerto Varas has been previously touted as the 'next Pucón,' but unlike its kindred spirit to the north, Puerto Varas has been able to better manage its rise as a go-to destination for outdoor adventure sports, and, as a result, avoids some of the tourist-package onslaught that besieges Pucón.

There is great access to water sports here – kayaking and canyoning in particular – as well as climbing, fishing, hiking and even skiing. While Puerto Varas gets packed in the summer, it receives many more independent travelers than Pucón. It basically shuts down in the winter except for a few hearty skiers and mountaineers.

With all of the conveniences of Puerto Montt just a short trip away, Puerto Varas is a top choice for an extended stay and also makes a good base for exploring the region. Some find it too touristy, but its juxtaposition of German heritage and contemporary Chilean adrenaline is both beautiful and addictive.

⊙ Sights

Puerto Varas' well-maintained German colonial architecture gives the town a distinctive middle-European ambience.

SUR CHICO PUERTO VARAS

ⓘ BETWEEN TWO LAKES & A HARD PLACE

Entre Lagos ('Between Lakes') is a slow-paced lakeside town 50km east of Osorno on Ruta 215, on the southwest shore of Lago Puyehue and north of Lago Rupanco. It's a tranquil alternative to Osorno, especially if you're on your way to Parque Nacional Puyehue embarking on the Puyehue traverse from El Caulle. It's also the first town of significance after crossing the border on the road from Bariloche. Most folks move on to Osorno to catch buses further afield, but you'll find a few hospitable guesthouses and limited traveler infrastructure here if you can't be bothered to carry on.

A popular place to base yourself within striking distance of Entre Lagos and all things Puyehue is the French-run **Lodge El Taíque** (📞 064-297-0980; www.lodgeeltaique.cl; Sector El Taíque Puyehue; s/d CH$47,000/64,000, cabins from CH$70,000; 🅿🛜), located 8km off Ruta 215 between Entre Lagos and Agua Calientes. You'll find a stylish lodge and gourmet restaurant with postcard views of Volcán Osorno, Volcán Puntiagudo and Lago Rupanco and vivid attention to detail.

Iglesia del Sagrado Corazón   CHURCH
(cnr San Francisco & Verbo Divino; ☺hours vary)
The imposing and colorful 1915 Iglesia del
Sagrado Corazón, overlooking downtown
from a promontory, is based on the Marien-
kirche of the Black Forest, Germany.

Paseo Patrimonial   ARCHITECTURE
Many notable constructions in town are
private houses from the early 20th century.
Grab a city map at the tourist information
office, which highlights the Paseo Patrimonial, a suggested walking tour of historic
homes listed as Monumentos Nacionales.

🏃 Activities

Nearby lakes, mountains, rivers and fjords
provide a variety of activities. There is *a
ciclovia* (bike lane) nearly circling Lago
Llanquihue in its entirety.

Rafting, Canyoning & Kayaking
Opportunities abound for rafting and kayaking. Río Petrohué's blue waters churn
up Class III and IV rapids. Half-day rafting
trips run around CH$35,000 (5½ hours to-
tal, two hours river time). All-day kayaking
in the Reloncaví Fjord is about CH$70,000.
For multiday sea kayaking expeditions, try **Al
Sur** (☎065-223-2300; www.alsurexpeditions.com;

SUR CHICO PUERTO VARAS

Puerto Varas

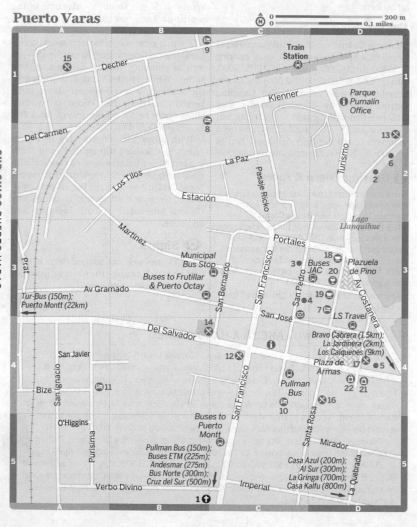

0   200 m
0   0.1 miles

cnr Aconcagua & Imperial) or **Yak Expediciones**
(☑cell 8332-0574; www.yakexpediciones.cl).

Ko'Kayak
RAFTING, CANYONING

(☑065-223-3004; www.kokayak.cl; San Pedro 311; ☺8am-8pm Oct-Apr, 9am-7pm May-Sep) A long-standing favorite for rafting, offering half-day rafting trips for CH$35,000 with two departures daily, full-day/two-day sea kayaking for CH$70,000/160,000 and half-day canyoning (CH$40,000).

Fly-Fishing
There are loads of places to cast a line, but knowing just where the best spots are will require some local knowledge.

Tres Ríos Lodge
FISHING

(☑065-271-5710; www.tresrioslodge.com; ☎) For trout and salmon on Río Petrohué, trophy browns on Río Maullin and fly-fishing in the Lakes District (day trips, lodge stays or road trips throughout Patagonia), call John Joy at Tres Ríos Lodge, who also runs the Tradicion Austral B+B in town.

Puerto Varas

Horse Trekking
The best spot for a horse trek is the Río Cochamó Valley.

Campo Aventura
HORSEBACK RIDING

(☑cell 9289-4318; www.campoaventura.cl) Campo Aventura offers multiday treks, often in conjunction with some hiking, rafting or kayaking. The most popular is a three-day jaunt that traverses the valley from its riverside lodge to its mountain lodge in the Río Cochamó Valley with as much emphasis on culture as nature. All guides are trained as Wilderness First Responders (WFR). English spoken.

☞ Tours
Easy day tours include Puerto Montt/Puerto Varas (CH$15,000), Frutillar/Llanquihue (CH$17,000), Puella/Saltos de Petrohué (CH$34,000), Volcán Osorno (CH$18,000) and around the lake. Day tours to Chiloé are also offered, but most of your tour is spent in transportation and you do not get a quality experience of the island. **Pionero del Lago** (☑cell 9229-6043; pionerodellago@gmail.com; Santa Rosa s/n; adult/child CH$10,000/6000) offers two daily catamaran trips on the lake as well.

★ Secret Patagonia
OUTDOORS

(☑065-223-2921; www.secretpatagonia.com; San Pedro 311; ☺8am-8pm Oct-Apr, 9am-7pm May-Sep) This eco-sensitive collective marries four smaller outfitters – La Comarca, Ko'Kayak, Birds Chile and OpenTravel – which specialize in dramatic and custom-tailored adventure trips to less explored areas of the Río Puelo Valley, Cochamó Valley and beyond.

Highlights include hiking in Cochamó Valley, extensive mountain-bike trips (including an epic 12-day single-track ride from Bariloche to Puerto Varas), remote French retreats on Isla Las Bandurrias in Lago Las Rocas, multiday horseback-riding/cultural farmstay trips between Argentina and Chile, and trips to Parque Tagua Tagua. Their newest opus: drinking and biking (not in that order, mind you!). The Bike & Beer tour is a good-fun 30km bike ride along the lake, culminating in a craft brew tasting at Chester Beer. Groups are never more than 12 strong and everyone here is dedicated to giving travelers a unique off-the-beaten-path experience while keeping their carbon footprint at bay. Also rents full-suspension mountain bikes.

DAY TRIPS ON LAGO LLANQUIHUE

Puerto Varas might boast a distinct lack of diversions in town, but there are plenty of beautiful spots around the lake that make for excellent day trips once your adrenaline can't go any higher.

Frutillar

Picturesque Frutillar is an enchanting lakeside retreat right up the coastline from Puerto Varas. There is an attractive pier, a long, drawn-out lakeside beach and, above all, quaint German architecture and küchen aplenty. It is home to the impressive **Teatro del LagoSur** (Teatro del Lago; ☎ 065-242-2900; www.teatrodellago.cl; Av Philippi 1000), an amazing 12-years-in-the-making, US$25-million world-class performing arts center that single-handedly put Frutillar on the global cultural map when it opened in 2010. The striking copper-roofed structure is a thing of beauty in itself, flanked against the lake with postcard views of four volcanoes. The theater hosts events throughout the year, but is the focal point of the town's world-renowned **Semana Musical de Frutillar** (www.semanasmusicales.cl), a 10-day music festival held every winter. Daily 45-minute tours start at noon throughout the year (CH$3500).

Another must-stop in town is the **Museo Histórico Alemán** (www.museosaustral.cl; cnr Pérez Rosales & Prat; admission CH$2500; ⏱9am-7:30pm), which is considered the best museum on German colonialism in the region.

For lunch, try **Se Cocina** (☎ cell 8972-8195; www.secocina.cl; Km2 a Quebrada Honda; mains CH$9500; ⏱1-3pm & 7:30-10:30pm Tue-Sun Jan-Mar & Jul), **Melí** (☎ 065-242-0766; www.emporiomeli.com; Camino Punta Larga Km1; menu CH$8900-10,900; ⏱12:30-4pm & 7-11pm Mon-Sat, 10am-6pm Sun; ☎) or **Lavanda Casa de Té** (☎ cell 9269-1684; www.lavandacasadete.cl; Km1.5 a Quebrada Honda; menu CH$13,000; ⏱1-8pm Jan-Feb, closed Mon Apr-Dec), three of the most interesting restaurants in the area. The town is a peaceful place to spend the night as well, though with scant budget options it caters more to affluent and mature travelers.

Minibuses to Frutillar depart Puerto Varas (p267) every 10 minutes throughout the day (CH$900). Buses back leave Frutillar from a small parking lot on Jorge Montt near Av Philippi.

Puerto Octay

Cute and quaint, Puerto Octay (ock-tie), 56km north of Puerto Varas, isn't heavily visited, but is actually one of the most stunningly located towns on Lago Llanquihue. On a banner clear-blue day, the surrounding countryside here, especially along the road

Birds Chile
BIRDWATCHING

(☎ 065-223-1820; www.birdschile.com; Santa Rosa 161, Club de Yates; ⏱10am-1pm & 3:30-7pm Dec-Mar) ✏ Excellent and expert birdwatching tours are on offer with Raffaele Di Biase, who, in addition to being the foremost naturalist in the area, is an all-around great guy to spend a day with while outdoors. Italian and English spoken.

Vive SUP
STAND-UP PADDLE

(☎ cell 8475-7830; www.vivesup.cl; Santa Rosa s/n; per hour rentals/classes CH$5000/8000; ⏱10am-7pm Dec-Feb) Stand-up paddleboarding enthusiast Eduardo divides his time between Portland, USA, and Puerto Varas and can get you supping on the water. He offers excursions (one a sunset trip to Laguna Escondida and another more advanced trip on the Río Petrohué), classes and rentals.

TurisTour
OUTDOORS, GUIDED TOUR

(☎ 065-243-7127; www.turistour.cl; Del Salvador 72; ⏱7:30am-7pm Mon-Fri, 7am-2pm & 5-7pm Sat & Sun) Runs the Cruce de Lagos, a bus-and-boat combo transport trip through the majestic lakes and mountains of the Pérez Rosales Pass to Bariloche, Argentina, and vice versa. The total fare is US$280, although there are seasonal discounts and a 50% discount for children. There are daily departures throughout the year, but the 12-hour trip requires a mandatory overnight in Peulla in winter (May to August).

Reservations must be made at least a day in advance. However, if you're only going as far as Peulla, tickets may be purchased at the Petrohué dock. Consider bringing your own food for the first part of the trip, as some feel meals aboard the catamaran to Peulla from Frutillar, is absolutely unforgettable with no-filter-necessary views across pastoral farmlands in all directions. It can serve as a good escape from more touristy towns to the south as well.

The tranquil streets, perched on a hillside above the lake, yield interesting 1800s German settler architectural treasures around every turn, making for a nice tour of historic homes and buildings and giving the town a supremely sedate and picturesque colonial air. Some of our favorite buildings include Casa Wulf No 2 (1926), Hotel Haase (1894) and Casa Werner (1910). It is the oldest town on the lake settled by Germans. It's worth checking the tourism office for a possible tour map of historical homes. Pop into the **Museo de Puerto Octay** (Independencia 591, 2nd fl; admission CH$1000; ⊙ 10:15am-1pm & 3-5pm) as well, a small but well-done museum inside the historic 1920 Casa Niklitschek telling the story of Puerto Octay via antiques.

For lunch, don't miss all-you-can-eat **Rancho Espantapájaros** (www.espantapajaros. cl; Quilanto, Km5 desde Puerto Octay a Frutillar; buffet CH$15,000, sandwiches CH$3200-3500; ⊙ 10am-10pm Dec-Mar, to 5:30pm Mon-Thu, to 10pm Fri & Sat, to 7pm Sun Apr-Nov; 🐾), one of the best restaurants on the lake, located 7km outside Puerto Octay on the road to Frutillar. It packs in the crowds for the main attraction, succulent *jabalí* (wild boar, fatty but fantastic) cooked on 3.5m spits across a giant *fogón* (outdoor oven) behind the buffet.

If you feel like staying over, Chilean-Swiss **Zapato Amarillo** (☎ 064-221-0787; www.zapatoamarillo.cl; Ruta 55 Km2.5, La Gruta; dm CH$13,000, s/d CH$30,000/40,000, without bathroom CH$25,000/34,000; 🅿🐾) is an all-time favorite, nestled away on a small farm, approximately 2km north of town toward Osorno.

Puerto Octay's **bus terminal** (cnr Balmaceda & Esperanza) has regular service to Puerto Varas (CH$1400), among other places.

Puerto Fonck

If Chile was tropical and the black beach at Puerto Fonck was white, these would be sought-after sands indeed. Instead, this hidden spot, tucked away down a long gravel road 22km east of Puerto Octay on the road from Puerto Varas, only caters to a few Chileans in the know. On a clear summer day, the dramatic volcano views over a tranquil bay make it a splendid beach to kill a day around the lake.

Access is by 4WD or foot only. Any Puerto Varas/Puerto Octay–bound bus can drop you off at the turnoff. From there, you'll have to leg it the last 2.5km to the beach.

and in Peulla are expensive and dull. You must also pay an AR$23 boarding fee (cash only in Argentine pesos, Chilean pesos, US dollars, euros or Brazilian reais) for Parque Nacional Nahuel Huapi in Argentina. Also runs numerous day trips in the region.

🛏 Sleeping

Puerto Varas is well equipped with beds for all budgets, and many places can also book all the adventures in the area. *Hospedajes* fill up fast in January and February, so make sure you make a reservation.

For camping or calmer accommodations, head around the lake or to Ensenada.

Margouya Patagonia HOSTEL $
(☎ 065-223-7695; www.mapatagonia.com; Purisima 681; dm CH$9000, s/d without bathroom CH$18,000/25,000; 🅿@🐾) This spacious

and historic 1932 home is on the town's list of patrimonial heritage sites. It's the nicest hostel in town, offering quieter and much larger rooms and bathrooms for better prices than most spots and a whole lot of French-Chilean hospitality. Big, bright dorms hold nine beds only.

It also has its own in-house Spanish school and tour agency for activities in the area and good-value bike rentals. There is no breakfast.

Hostel Melmac Patagonia HOSTEL $
(☎ 065-223-0863; www.melmacpatagonia.com; Santa Rosa 608 Interior; dm CH$13,000, s/d from CH$35,000/39,500; @🐾) This intimate hostel in perfectly located new digs is decked out with all the modern fixings – right down to the artisanal homebrew beer fridge, which goes down

nicely on the front porch (first beer free!), and Wall-E, the Roomba cleaning robot.

It's also the only hostel we have ever stumbled across with rooms boasting bathtubs stocked with relaxing bath salts – perfect after a day of hiking! Alfonso, the friendly Argentine-Colombian owner, is one of the few that charges solo travelers a single price for a private room (gracias!).

Casa Margouya HOSTEL $
(☎065-223-7640; www.margouya.com; Santa Rosa 318; dm CH$10,000, s/d without bathroom CH$18,000/24,000; @🛜) This French-owned, excellently located hostel is smaller than average and fosters a friendly communal vibe between its guests (it's vaguely hippie...and loud).

Galpon Aíre Puro GUESTHOUSE $$
(☎cell 9979-8009; www.galponairepuro.com; cnr Decher & Independencia; s/d CH$34,000/48,000, ste CH$60,000; P@🛜) American expat Vicki Johnson – chef, chocolatier and purveyor of life's finer things – has transformed this massive 1920s potato storage barn into her very own den of good taste, expanding and moving her artisan chocolate shop and cafe here and offering eight spacious guest rooms for more independently minded travelers above a hip commercial office space.

Huge rooms with vaulted ceilings, fabulous stone bathrooms and an inviting common space and guest kitchen evoke a homespun sense of community that only Vicki can pull off. An optional gourmet breakfast runs CH$6000.

Casa Azul HOSTEL $$
(☎065-223-2904; www.casaazul.net; Manzanal 66; dm CH$10,000, d CH$34,000, s/d without bathroom CH$18,000/26,000; @🛜) It's hard to find fault with this impeccably kept German-Chilean operation set in a quieter residential neighborhood just outside downtown. The superbly tranquil garden and koi pond (with bonsai trees) immediately calm your nerves, in any case. Rooms are spacious, in excellent condition and there's an expansive guest kitchen and common area with cool furniture fashioned from tree branches.

Some say there are too many rules (men should pee sitting down?), but it's all for maintaining staunch German efficiency and cleanliness – hard to complain about that. Breakfast is an extra CH$3500.

Casa Kalfu B&B $$
(☎065-275-1261; www.casakalfu.cl; Tronador 1134; s/d CH$63,000/69,000; P@🛜) Since Casa Azul was taken, the Chilean-Argentine couple that runs this excellent midrange choice opted for Kalfu (Mapudungun for blue) instead. And what a big, bright, beautiful blue it is. The home is a renovated 1940s chalet that now holds 17 rooms, simply and minimally decorated with large *oveja* (natural wool) wall hangings by renowned local artist Kika Xicota.

The owners are very hands-on, giving it a more personal feel than many others in town, and the house is perched just high enough for lake views from its pleasant terrace.

Compass del Sur B&B $$
(☎065-233-2044; www.compassdelsur.cl; Klenner 467; camping CH$9000, dm CH$12,000, s/d CH$32,000/42,000, without bathroom CH$27,000/30,000; P@🛜) This charming colonial house with Scandinavian touches and very friendly staff sits above the main area of town, accessed by a staired walking street. It has comfortable beds and some new rain-style showers that please the flashpacker crowd who dominate the scene here.

★ Los Caiquenes B&B $$$
(☎cell 8159-0489; www.hotelloscaiquenes.cl; Camino a Ensenada Km9.5; r from CH$70,000; P🛜❄) This lakeshore boutique B&B 9km from Puerto Varas on the road to Ensenada is a shabby chic escape for settling in for the long haul. The extremely cozy common area and kitchen boasts big bay windows with lake views and an enticing fireplace; discerning rooms are just as seductive, all hardwood floors, snug bedding and wonderful bathrooms.

It's an easy-to-love retreat with a particular emphasis on personalized service and gourmet gluttony.

🍴 Eating

The dining scene here is second only to Pucón in Sur Chico, but only the strong survive winter, so restaurant turnover is high. Fancier spots tend to congregate on the *costanera,* both north and south of the *centro.*

★ La Gringa AMERICAN $
(www.lagringa.cl; Imperial 605; mains CH$3500-7900; ⊙8am-8pm Mon-Fri, from 10am Sat; 🛜) 🍃 Evoking the rainy-day cafes of the American Pacific Northwest, this charming spot run by an adorable Seattleite dishes up scrumptious

muffins and baked goods, creative sandwiches (pulled pork with coffee glaze) and beautiful CH$6500 lunch menus (1pm to 4pm). Browse excellent wines and gourmet artisanal fare for great picnic options as well.

Naomi sources locally and organic where possible, and it all goes down so very nicely inside the historic Casa Bechthold. In the evenings, the attached and intimate Mercado 605 goes deeper into Nouveau Chilean cuisine (mains CH$6900 to CH$11,500) with mixed results.

Donde El Gordito   CHILEAN, SEAFOOD $
(San Bernardo 560; mains CH$3900-8000; ⊙noon-4:30pm & 6:30-10pm, closed Jun) This down-to-earth local's favorite is an intimate seafooder in the Mercado Municipal. It does wonderful things with crab sauce. It's rich but excellent.

The Office   CAFE $
(San Juan 425, 2nd fl; sandwiches CH$1990-5390; ⊙8:30am-8:30pm Mon-Fri, to 10pm Sat; 🛜) Overlooking the plaza, this artsy cafe does messy gourmet sandwiches big enough to share, along with organic coffee and good-value steaks, in a stylish, multiroom environment.

Café Dane's   CAFE $
(Del Salvador 441; mains CH$4450-7800; ⊙7:30am-11:30pm; 🛜) This local favorite sums up the hybrid history of the region within its walls: küchen and empanadas, Alpen architecture and Spanish menus, *apfelstrudel* (apple strudel) and *pastel de choclo* (maize casserole). It's one of the few open early on Sunday. Try the *empanada de horno* (beef, egg, onions and olives), gargantuan sandwiches and hot dogs, or the insanely moist *tres leches* cake with *manjar* (milk caramel).

El Patio de Mi Casa   CHILEAN $
(Decher 830; mains CH$4800-7000; ⊙12:30-3pm & 7:30-11pm Mon-Sat, to 4pm Sun) This classy neighborhood Chilean is true to its name: it's hidden away on the back patio of the chef's home. Amid creative and cutesy decor touches like kindling as wall art, sophisticated regional fare (mostly *lomo* and *merluza* various ways) are served in a spot that feels like a local's secret.

★ La Jardinera   GASTROPUB $$
(www.lajardinera.cl; Blanco Encalada 1160; mains CH$7000-8500; ⊙1-3:30pm Mon & Tue, 1-3:30pm & 8-11pm Wed-Sat; 🛜) Featuring one of the most eclectic menus in town, the friendly

Chilean couple running this cozy spot in a transformed home learned the art of fish and chips, shrimp green curry and – wait for it – warm sticky toffee pudding (prunes substituted for dates) during a five-year London culinary stint.

But it's not all imported recipes. Vibrant local fusion – wild mushroom ravioli with *piñones* (pine nuts), pistachio-crusted trout – makes an appearance as well. Great spot.

La Marca   STEAK $$
(www.lamarca.cl; Santa Rosa 539; steaks CH$5200-12,900; ⊙noon-11pm) This is *the* spot in Puerto Varas for devout carnivores to delight in serious slabs of perfectly grilled beef. You won't find any obnoxious *rancho* decor here – it's all very subtle and stylish with sweet service to boot. The small filet (300g) carries some heft and is seasoned just right.

Order a bottle of reasonably priced Carmenere and save room for the sinful churros, some of the best you'll ever have.

Casavaldés   CHILEAN $$$
(📱cell 9079-3938; Santa Rosa 40; mains CH$5300-11,300; ⊙12:30-4pm & 7-11pm; 🛜) Though a bit cramped, Puerto Varas' most intimate, interesting and best seafooder beckons lake and Calbuco views. Highlights of the innovative menu include divine crab-stuffed *piquillo* peppers and a long list of fresh fish preparations, accented by the perfectly pleasant kick of the *donostiarria* (olive oil, garlic, red chilli and vinegar). Reservations recommended.

🎷 Drinking & Entertainment

Caffé El Barrista   CAFE
(www.elbarista.cl; Martínez 211; coffee CH$1400-2800, sandwiches CH$3500-6800; ⊙8am-1am; 🛜) This Italian-style Palestinian-Chilean coffeehouse serves the best brew in Sur Chico bar none, and draws a healthy lunch crowd for its excellent CH$6800 menus and a selection of tasty sandwiches. As night falls, it morphs into the most consistent bar in town, drawing heavily from the gaggles of guides and expats in town.

Cafe Mawen   CAFE
(cnr Diego Portales & Santa Rosa; coffee CH$1100-2800; ⊙7:45am-10:30pm Mon-Fri, 9:30am-11pm Sat & Sun; 🛜) In new digs in a big, beautiful lakeview home, Chilean-owned Mawen is the town's *other* great coffee spot, with more of a local vibe, a family-friendly atmosphere and great java.

Bravo Cabrera
RESTO-BAR

(www.bravocabrera.cl; Vicente Pérez Rosales 1071; ☺7pm-1:30am Mon-Thu, 1pm-4am Fri & Sat, 2-6pm Sun; 🐾) Named after a Patagonian Robin Hood who stole beef from the rich and threw barbecues for the poor, this fashionable resto-to-bar is where you'll find upper-class local color downing craft beers, trendy cocktails and great pub grub (mains CH$4800 to CH$7900). It's a great place to escape the tourist onslaught and see how the other half of PV lives. A late-night taxi back to *centro* costs CH$1500.

Garage
BAR

(Martínez 220; ☺hours vary) Attached to the Copec gas station, Garage caters to an art-sy, alternative crowd, staying up later than it should and hosting everything from im-promptu jazz sessions to all-out Colombian *cumbia* shakedowns...when it's open (complaints about erratic hours by its devout local following are not unfounded).

🛍 Shopping

Artisan chocolate, gourmet wares and outdoor adventure gear are popular purchases in Puerto Varas. Check out **Feria Artesanal** (Del Salvador; ☺11am-7:30pm) for souvenirs.

Fundación Artesanías de Chile HANDICRAFTS (www.artesaniasdechile.cl; Del Salvador 109; ☺9am-8:45pm Mon, Wed, Fri & Sat, 10:30am-1:30pm & 2:30-6:45pm Tue, Thu & Sun) 🍃 A not-for-profit foundation offering beautiful Mapuche textiles as well as high-quality jewelry and ceramics from all over southern Chile.

ℹ Information

Carabineros de Chile (☎065-276-5100; www.carabineros.cl; San Francisco 241) Police station.

Clínica Alemana (www.alemanapv.cl; Otto Bader 810; ☺24hr) Near Del Salvador's southwest exit from town.

CorreosChile (www.correos.cl; San José 242; ☺9am-1pm & 3-6pm Mon-Fri, 9:30am-1pm Sat) Postal services.

Parque Pumalín Office (☎065-225-1910; www.pumalinpark.org; Klenner 299; ☺9am-6pm Mon-Fri) Though the park is found in Northern Patagonia, this is the official tourism office for Parque Pumalín.

Tourist Office (☎065-236-1146; www. ptovaras.cl; Del Salvador 320; ☺8:30am-9:30pm Aug-May, to 7:30pm Apr-Jul) Helpful, with brochures and free maps of the area.

ℹ Getting There & Around

AIR

LAN (☎600-526-2000; www.lan.com; Av Gramado 560; ☺9am-1:30pm & 3-6:30pm Mon-Fri, 9am-1:30pm Sat) and **Sky Airlines** (☎065-223-4252; San Bernardo 430; ☺9am-1pm & 3-6:45pm Mon-Fri, 10am-12:45pm Sat) have offices in town but fly from Puerto Montt. From the Puerto Montt airport, taxis cost approximately CH$20,000.

BUS

Most long-distance bus services from Puerto Varas originate in Puerto Montt. Buses leave from two terminals, one for **Cruz del Sur** (☎065-223-6969; www.busescruzdelsur.cl; San Francisco 1317; ☺office 7am-9:30pm) and Bus Norte's Bariloche departures, and the other **Tur-Bus** (☎065-223-3787; www.turbus.cl; Del Salvador 1093; ☺office 7am-11:10pm Mon-Fri, 7am-1:50pm & 4:30-11:10pm Sat-Sun) station just outside *centro*, which also serves JAC and Inter. At time of research, several companies were departing from Ramón Rosas near San Francisco (ETM, Bus Norte and Pullman), and Andesmar from the corner of Andrés Bello and San Francisco, but this is subject to change once the construction of the new Gimnasio Municipal is finished (check ahead before departure). A few companies sell tickets through their individual offices around downtown.

For Osorno, Valdivia and Temuco, Cruz del Sur has several departures daily; it also goes to Chiloé seven times per day and Punta Arenas on Tuesday, Thursday and Saturday (11:25am). For Santiago, **Buses ETM** (☎065-223-0830; www. etm.cl; Ramón Rosas 1017, office; ☺8:30am-10:30pm) – less stops – **Bus Norte** (☎065-223-4298; www.busnortechile.cl; Andrés Bello 304, 2nd fl, office) – less stops and wi-fi – and **Pullman Bus** (☎065-223-3462; www.pullman. cl; San Francisco 1004, office; ☺9am-1:30pm & 2:30-10pm) offer the best services. Pullman also has an in-town **office** (San Pedro 519; ☺hours vary) but it only seems to open when the wind blows just so. **Buses JAC** (☎065-238-3800; www.jac.cl; Walker Martínez 230; ☺9am-2:30pm & 4:30-6:30pm Mon-Fri, 9am-1:30pm Sat), whose in-town office also represents Tur-Bus, goes to Temuco (10:10am and 6:50pm), Villarrica/Pucón (9:20am, 2:55pm and 5:25pm) and Valdivia (8:40am, 10:10am and 7:20pm). For Viña del Mar/Valparaíso, Pullman has a nightly bus at 8pm, as does Buses ETM (8:45pm) and Tur-Bus (9:10pm).

For Bariloche (Argentina), Cruz del Sur/Bus Norte goes daily at 8:50am and again on Thursday only at 11:15am. **Andesmar** (☎065-228-0999; www.andesmar.com; cnr San Francisco & Andrés Bello) goes there on Monday, Tuesday, Thursday and Saturday at 8:40am (travelers without a Chilean ID can only make advance purchases at their office in Puerto Montt – at least until foreigners can make online bus ticket purchases). **LS Travel** (☏ 065-223-2424; www. lstravel.com; San José 128; ☉ 8am-8pm) offers more exclusive daily shuttles (US$150, 7:30am) and shuttle/boat combos (US$230, 7:15am) with touristy stops along the way.

Starting long-distance bus fares from Puerto Varas (prices fluctuate with the quality of the bus/class and season):

DESTINATION	COST (CH$)	DURATION (HR)
Ancud	5000	2½
Bariloche (Ar)	15,000	6
Castro	6500	4½
Osorno	2000	1¼
Pucón	9300	5½
Punta Arenas	40,000	18
Santiago	25,000	12
Temuco	6500	6
Valdivia	4500	3½
Viña del Mar/ Valparaíso	30,000	15

MINIBUS

Minibuses to and from Ensenada, Petrohué and Puerto Montt leave regularly from a small stop (cnr Walker Martínez & San Bernardo), though for Puerto Montt it's easier to catch them on the 600 block of San Francisco alongside the new shopping mall. Minibuses to Cochamó and Río Puelo also pass here 20 minutes or so after leaving Puerto Montt (p279). For Frutillar and Puerto Octay, buses depart from a small stop (Av Gramado) near San Bernardo.

Regional minibus fares from Puerto Varas:

DESTINATION	COST (CH$)	DURATION (HR)
Cochamó	2500	3
Ensenada	1200	1
Frutillar	900	½
Petrohué	2500	1½
Puerto Montt	800	¼
Puerto Octay	1400	1¼
Río Puelo	4000	1½

Ensenada

☏ 065 / POP 1623

Rustic Ensenada, 45km along a picturesque shore-hugging road from Puerto Varas, is really nothing more than a few restaurants, *hospedajes* and adventure outfitters, but it's a nice natural setting in full view of three majestic beasts: Volcán Osorno, Volcán Calbuco and Volcán Puntiagudo. Staying in Ensenada instead of Puerto Varas has a few advantages: if you plan to climb or ski Osorno, you can save an hour of sleep by overnighting here (and if the weather turns, you won't have come quite as far for nothing). Volcán Calbuco is also within striking distance, just to the south of Ensenada. And between them is the breathtaking Parque Nacional Vicente Pérez Rosales, the entrance of which sits just outside town.

🛏 Sleeping & Eating

Casa Ko B&B **$$**
(☏ cell 7703-6477; www.casako.com; Camino a Ensenada Km37; s/d CH$38,000/45,000, s/d without bathroom from CH$22,000/25,000; @ 🛜) A young and artsy French couple run this cultured choice, completely renovated and homey for this price range. Artists are invited annually in exchange for leaving behind a creation, so the six-room home is filled with random creative goodness and a throwback vibe – all under the nose of super Osorno and Calbuco views.

You can trek the latter volcano direct from the front door and home-cooked dinners served family-style are CH$12,000.

Hamilton's Place GUESTHOUSE **$$**
(☏ cell 8466-4146; hamiltonsplaceensenada@gmail. com; Camino a Ensenada Km42; s/d CH$40,000/ 49,000, without bathroom CH$22,000/35,000; P 🛜) A friendly Canadian-Brazilian couple run this show situated close to Ensenada but down an isolated residential street that feels a world away. Tastefully decorated rooms have excellent beds, give off a woodsy feel and boast premium Osorno and Calbuco views. Eloa, a Brazilian chef, makes revelatory homemade bread and more substantial meals for guests, including Brazilian specialties like *feijoada* (a black bean and pork stew) and *moqueca* (seafood stew) on occasion.

Latitude 42° INTERNATIONAL **$$**
(☏ 065-221-2030; www.southernchilexp.com; Ruta 225 Km42, Yan Kee Way Lodge; mains CH$6500-9800; ☉ noon-6pm, dinner by reservation only; 🛜) 🍽 Despite a revolving door of chefs, the restaurant at this high-end American-owned fly-fishing lodge is one of the best dining destinations on the lake and far and away the best in Ensenada, with a menu that spans several continents (aged steaks, German pork

OH NO, CALBUCO!

Following on from Volcán Villarrica a month before, Volcán Calbuco, just south of Ensenada, blew its top rather dramatically on April 22, 2015. The violent sub-plinian eruption, of which there have only been 300 recorded in history, resulted in no fatalities but threatened livestock and even thousands of salmon from the nearby farms. A red alert was declared and immediate evacuation orders were issued for 4000 people within a 20km radius of the volcano. Residents didn't need the order, though; things got ugly real fast when a massive plume of gases, ash and pyroclastics rose several kilometers into the air, draping the area in volcanic fallout and sending locals fleeing with whatever they could grab. Though Calbuco is considered one of Chile's three most dangerous volcanoes, this was its first eruption in 42 years. Damages were yet to be assessed when this book went to press but some of our recommendations in this guide may have been affected so check before you travel.

chops, coq au vin, duck confit, local fish) and ingredients that are often foraged from their own organic farm. Impressive wine list and volcano views.

❶ Getting There & Away

Minibuses frequently shuttle between Ensenada and Puerto Varas (CH$1200, 50 minutes). There is no public transportation between Ensenada and Las Cascadas, a distance of 22km on the road to Puerto Octay.

Parque Nacional Vicente Pérez Rosales

In this park of celestial lakes and soaring volcanoes, Lago Todos Los Santos and Volcán Osorno may be the standouts, but they're actually just part of a crowd. One lake leads to the next and volcanoes dominate the skyline on all sides of this storied pass through the Andes range. The needle-point of Volcán Puntiagudo (2493m) lurks to the north and craggy Monte Tronador (3491m) marks the Argentine border to the east. From the higher levels you can see where lava flows pinched off rivers and lakes, detouring them into new bodies of water.

Established in 1926, the 2510-sq-km Pérez Rosales was Chile's first national park, but its history goes back much further. In pre-Columbian times Mapuche traveled the 'Camino de Vuriloche,' a major trans-Andean route they managed to conceal from the Spaniards for more than a century after the 1599 uprising. Jesuit missionaries traveled from Chiloé, continuing up the Estero de Reloncaví and crossing the pass south of Tronador to Lago Nahuel Huapi, avoiding the riskiest crossings of the region's lakes and rivers.

The park is open year-round, depending on weather conditions. There is a Conaf **visitor center** (☑ 065-221-2036; www.conaf.cl; ⊙ 8:30am-1pm & 2-5:30pm Mon, to 6:30pm Tue-Sun) for basic info at Laguna Verde.

Volcán Osorno

Volcán Osorno (2652m), rivaled only by Volcán Villarrica, is a perfect conical peak towering above azure glacial lakes. It retains its idyllic shape due to the 40 craters around its base – it's there that the volcano's eruptions have taken place, never at the top.

🏃 Activities

You can spend a day trekking under its nose for around CH$18,000 from Puerto Varas, but if you want to summit the volcano, costs run CH$150,000 for one person and drops CH$10,000 per person for two or more people (including snow and ice-climbing gear); it's a full day starting at 5am (3:30am from Puerto Varas). The trip is technical and not for the unfit. Weather determinations are made the evening prior and there are no refunds after that point. Trips up Volcán Calbuco (2003m), the region's most active volcano, run CH$140,000 for one person and drops CH$10,000 per person for two or more people.

Independent climbers must obtain Conaf permission, providing detailed personal qualifications as well as lists of equipment and intended routes.

Moyca Expediciones   CLIMBING
(☑ cell 7790-5679; San Pedro 210; ⊙ 8:30am-8:30pm Jan-Mar, 8:30am-1pm & 3:30-6:30pm Apr-Dec) This Puerto Varas–based outfitter comes highly recommended for summiting Volcán Osorno (2652m) or Volcán Calbu-

co (2003m), but the three companies that climb all share the same seven or so guides.

Centro de Ski y Montaña Volcán Osorno
SKIING

(☑ 065-566-624; www.volcanosorno.com; half-/full-day lift tickets CH$19,000/24,000) Centro de Ski y Montaña Volcán Osorno has two lifts for skiing and sightseeing and has recently undergone an expansion of its restaurant and rental shop. It has ski and snowboard rentals (from CH$19,000) and food services on the mountain year-round.

Expanded summer options include taking the ski lift up for impossibly scenic views at 1420m (CH$10,000) or 1670m (CH$14,000). You can descend a little faster via ziplines (CH$18,000 to CH$22,000).

🛏 Sleeping

Refugio Teski
GUESTHOUSE $

(☑ 065-256-6622; www.teski.cl; dm with bedding/sleeping bag CH$15,000/12,000, r without/with bathroom CH$35,000/47,000; 🛜) Just downhill from the ski slopes, the spruced-up Refugio Teski offers unparalleled access to the mountain. It's a spectacular spot to stay as you can have the outstanding views of Lago Llanquihue and the surrounding mountains all to yourself once the tourist buses depart in the late afternoon.

With 24 hours notice, rent out a mountainside hot tub (CH$40,000 for three hours, including a pisco sour and finger food), take advantage of two-for-one happy hour drinks at sunset and make a night of it.

ℹ Getting There & Away

To get to the ski area and the *refugio,* take the Ensenada–Puerto Octay road to a signpost about 3km from Ensenada and continue driving 10km up the lateral. It's well worth your money renting a car and driving up the paved road, taking in spectacular views flanked by Osorno on one side, Calbuco on the other and Lago Llanquihue down below. There are no transportation services to or from the slopes for anyone except package-tour buyers.

Petrohué

People may come for the ferry cruise to Peulla, but Petrohué's majestic lakeside setting and serenity tend to convince visitors to stay a little longer. Tourism feels a bit forced here, but once the package tour onslaught leaves or you get yourself across the lake to the *hospedajes,* it feels like a world away. It's only 20 minutes from Ensenada down a reasonable ash road, so it has similar advantages in an infinitesimally prettier locale.

Parque Nacional Vicente Pérez Rosales

◉ Sights & Activities

From Conaf's woodsy Camping Playa Petrohué just beyond the paid parking area (you can park for free here), a dirt track leads to **Playa Larga**, a long black-sand beach much better than the one near the hotel. From the beach, **Sendero Los Alerces** heads west to meet up with **Sendero La Picada**, which climbs past Paso Desolación and continues on to Refugio La Picada on the volcano's north side. Alternatively, follow Los Alerces back to the hotel. Trips to **Isla Margarita**, a wooded island with a small interior lagoon, cost CH$5000 for up to four in a small fishing boat. Boatsmen also linger to take folks on a 30-minute lake navigation (CH$15,000 for up to five people).

Saltos del Petrohué WATERFALL
(admission CH$1500; ⊙ 8:30am-8pm) Six kilometers southwest of Petrohué, the Saltos del Petrohué is a rushing, frothing waterfall raging through a narrow volcanic rock canyon carved by lava. Anyone wondering why the rafting trips don't start from the lake will find the answer here, although experienced kayakers have been known to take it on (though we'd like to see the canyoners try it).

A new well-done visitor center houses a cafe and handicrafts shops. Try to arrive after 9:15am, once the TurisTur day tour bus brigade has departed.

🛏 Sleeping & Eating

Hospedaje Esmeralda GUESTHOUSE $
(✆ cell 6225-6230, cell 9839-2589; rosabur6@ hotmail.com; campsite/r per person without bathroom CH$7000/10,000; @) Like mother, like son: this wooden lodge on stilts is a nearly upscale budget option run by the son of matriarch Küschel, who owns the cheaper *hospedaje* a few hundred meters down the shore. There's a beautiful breakfast room (add CH$3500) with broad windows sucking up the lake views. If you call ahead, they will provide transport from the dock for free.

Hospedaje Küschel CAMPGROUND, GUESTHOUSE $
(✆ cell 5791-2870; campsite/r per person CH$5000/8000) You're in the thick of it with the pigs and chickens at this run-down farmhouse across the lake (reached by boat at the dock for CH$500 to CH$1000), but you are situated right on the lake (from where your startlingly good home-smoked trout dinner comes). Breakfast is included; dinner or lunch runs CH$6000.

Petrohué Hotel & Cabañas LODGE $$$
(✆ 065-221-2025; www.petrohue.com; Ruta 225 Km60; s/d from CH$115,430/157,080, cabins for 4 people CH$148,750; P@ 🛜 🞀) In a gorgeous stone and wood-gabled building replete with a tower, this high-end adventure lodge deserves a visit. Its abundant skylights and the roaring fires in the lounge make it a romantic place to relax, read a book or cuddle up. The rooms, rich in wood, have beds piled high with blankets and are scattered with candles.

The restaurant is open to the general public and the adventure outfitter here arranges climbing, rafting and canyoning excursions and has kayaks for rent. The equally luxe *cabañas* sit on the lakeshore.

ℹ Getting There & Away

Minibuses run from Puerto Varas to Petrohué (CH$2500) throughout the year.

Cochamó

✆ 065 / POP 3908

The Chilote-style, alerce-shingled Iglesia Parroquial María Inmaculada stands picturesque and proud against a backdrop of milky-blue water along the road to Cochamó, forming one of the most stunning spots throughout the region and the gateway to the upper Río Cochamó Valley. In addition to its made-over *costanera,* some vibrant new accommodations choices are now vying for your attention as well, doing their best to graduate Cochamó to more than just the spot where you put your kayaks in the water on a day trip from Puerto Varas.

🏃 Activities

Southern Trips HORSEBACK RIDING
(✆ cell 8407-2559; www.southern-trips.com; Pueblo Hundido) Locally run Southern Trips, on the main road, offers five-hour (CH$40,000) to 11-day (CH$960,000) horse-trekking trips in the area as well as horses and pack horses to La Junta (per horse CH$30,000, 65kg maximum).

🛏 Sleeping & Eating

Las Bandurrias Eco Hostal GUESTHOUSE $
(✆ cell 9672-2590; www.hostalbandurrias.com; Sector el Bosque s/n; dm CH$14,000, s/d without bathroom CH$25,000/32,000) 🍃 The friendly Swiss-Chilean owners at this newly built eco-guesthouse will grab you in town to

introduce you to their fairy-tale sleeps, the best and most sustainable choice. The bathrooms and guest kitchen are great, and composting and solar-heating are the norm. House-made breads (including Swiss *tresse*) and horseback rides with their own horses are highlights.

Book ahead as there are only three rooms, and prepare to fight for the outdoor bench space overlooking the fjord.

Patagonia Nativa   GUESTHOUSE $
(☑cell 9316-5635; www.patagonianativa.cl; Av Aerodromo s/n; dm CH$13,000, r without/with bathroom CH$30,000/39,000) One of several worthwhile options that have opened above town, with views over the Reloncaví Fjord that would make a postcard throw in the towel. Owner Christian speaks enough English and has built a cozy cabin-like guesthouse that still smells of pine. He runs kayak trips as well. CH$2000 for a towel seems outrageous, however.

Hospedaje Maura   GUESTHOUSE $
(☑cell 9334-9213; www.hostalmaura.cl; J Molina 77; r per person without bathroom CH$15,000) The cozy in-town choice with charming owners, good beds and very low ceilings. Hop from the guest kitchen to the outdoor hot tub and sauna and call it a night.

Campo Aventura   LODGE $
(☑cell 9289-4318; www.campoaventura.cl; campsites per person CH$5000, r per person CH$35,000, r per person full board CH$50,000) Campo Aventura sleeps 15 in three splendid rooms and one cabin at its riverside camp at Cochamó, which is both US owned and managed. Here you'll find lovely meals (breakfast and lunch CH$5000, dinner CH$10,000) as well as a beautiful camping area at the river's edge.

La Ollita   CHILEAN $$
(Av Cochamó 91; mains CH$3800-9500; ⊙noon-midnight) Paint us unimpressed with Cochamó's most popular restaurant, which goes to a lot of trouble to infuse olive oil with garlic and *merkén* (yet still serves the same old bread to dip in it) and on our visit delivered the fish a mangled mess. The pisco sours and terrace views of Volcán Yates are nice, however.

ℹ Information

Municipal Office (☑cell 9442-3583; www.municochamo.cl; Av Cochamó s/n; ⊙8:30am-1pm & 2:30-5:30pm Mon-Fri) Provides a very useful Cochamó hiking map, brochure, bus schedule and list of official lodgings and contact numbers. At time of writing, this office and the town library next door boasted the town's only wi-fi signals, but foreigners can more easily connect to this one, especially on weekends. Network: turismo municipal. Password: turismo2014 (they told us they had no plans to change it!).

ℹ Getting There & Away

Buses Río Puelo (p279) leaves Puerto Montt for Cochamó (CH$2500, 2½ hours) at 7:15am, 7:45am and 4pm (3pm on Sunday). Transhar (p279) goes at 12:15pm and 3:30pm Monday to Saturday and 2:15pm on Sunday. All services stop in Puerto Varas and Ensenada and continue on to Río Puelo (CH$4000).

Cochamó Valley

With its impressive granite domes rising above the verdant canopy and colossal alerce trees dominating the rainforest, some tout the spectacular Cochamó Valley as the Chilean Yosemite. It's near here where the glacial waters of the Lakes District give way to the saltwaters of the 80km Estero de Reloncaví, a fjord that forms the gateway to Northern Patagonia. The region's popularity is growing fast, especially with the rock climbers – each year new climbing routes and trails open (more than 300 climbs and six full-day hikes to date) with more climbers clambering around the valley to reach them. The area is indeed a beautiful spot worthy of multiple days and tourism has not yet overwhelmed the area, so go now before it *does* turn into Yosemite.

The road to the trailhead begins just before the Río Cochamó bridge to Campo Aventura, but most folks grab a taxi from town or drive themselves this first 7km to the trailhead (you can park at the last house on the right for CH$1500).

La Junta

From Cochamó, a splendid 12km trek that goes through the deep Valdivian rainforest and along the Río Cochamó brings you to La Junta, an impressive valley situated under the watch of massive granite domes jutting from the top of the surrounding mountains. Unless they build a road here, it should remain a gorgeous and serene spot and nearly everyone who goes up for a day wishes they had allotted more time to enjoy the supreme scenery and outstanding trekking. In January, the *tábanos* (horseflies) can be relentless.

PARADISE LOST?

The raw beauty of Reloncaví fjord, Cochamó and the Río Puelo Valley is in jeopardy: construction of a controversial run-of-the-river hydroelectric (ROR) project was green-lighted in 2014, giving **Mediterráneo S.A.** (www.centraldepasadamediterraneo.cl) permission to break ground where the nearby Ríos Manso and Torrentoso converge. The project would include some 40 miles of high-tension power cables, some of which would cut right across the fjord in front of Cochamó and Lago Tagua Tagua in the Puelo Valley. Environmental activists, the indigenous Cayún community, local property owners and small business operators are digging in for a fight. Mediterráneo has already punched back, touting hundreds of new jobs and the use of underground machinery to minimize flora and fauna impact.

The outcome remains to be seen, but Chilean environmentalists have won before: a similar green-lighted hydroelectric project, HidroAysén – now famously known for the battle cry '¡Patagonia Sin Represas!' – was declared nonviable by President Michelle Bachelet after years of protests. For more information, see **Río Puelo Sin Torres** (www.puelosintorres.org).

Secret Patagonia in Puerto Varas runs three- to eight-day treks (CH$360,000 to CH$800,000 per person including meals, lodging and load horses). It can take you up to the 900m viewpoint at Arco Iris through three types of native forest, with wine and cheese to boot.

🛏 Sleeping & Eating

Refugio Cochamó　　　　　LODGE **$**
(www.cochamo.com; campsites per person CH$2500, dm CH$15,000, d without bathroom CH$39,000; @) The impressive Refugio Cochamó, in La Junta valley, is a fantastic gringo-Argentine climber-run cabin with wood-fired showers, water straight from the Trinadad waterfall and homemade pizza (from CH$9000). Ask about their very own homebrew, Tábano Pale Ale, whose production was temporarily on hold. It's open from November to April.

To reach it, you'll need to hike approximately 10km, then continue past the first pulley system stretching across the Río Cochamó (this one takes you to Campo Aventura). Continue 10 minutes to the pampa of Camping La Junta, and follow signs to the Refugio Cochamó's pulley system. Reservations through website only.

Campo Aventura
Mountain Lodge　　　　　LODGE **$$**
(☎cell 9289-4318; www.campoaventura.cl; campsites per person CH$5000, dm CH$10,000, r per person full board CH$50,000) Run by the most established outfitter in the area, Campo Aventura, this candlelit converted farmhouse on 80 hectares has four bedrooms

and a four-bed bunkhouse, wood-fired showers and a dining room with a central woodstove. A sundeck has superb Arco Iris views.

The delightful Chilean caretakers pamper guests with mountain hospitality and hearty home-cooked food – pork and lamb *asados*, chicken and lentil *cazuelas* and the like. Nice touches like wine, homemade bread and filtered coffee are available.

Río Puelo

The road from Cochamó continues along the Estero de Reloncaví another 31km through to Río Puelo, a little hamlet that's bound for growth as a new land-lake route into Argentina develops. Under the watchful eye of Volcán Yates and the jade-hued Río Puelo, it's a serene and photogenic spot that makes for a great base for exploration further afield into the Río Puelo Valley.

🛏 Sleeping & Eating

Most decent accommodations are in Puelo Alto, 2km east of the center.

Camping Río Puelo　　　　CAMPGROUND **$**
(☎cell 6769-2918; www.cabalgatasriopuelo.cl; Puelo Alto; campsites per person CH$4000, r per person CH$13,000, cabaña d/tr/q CH$30,000/40,000/50,000; P🛜) This basic campground offers lovely Andes views, improved bathrooms and wi-fi. The friendly owner, a bit of a multilinguist, has a few well-equipped *cabañas* that may function as *hospedaje*s when not rented. Call ahead.

★ **Domo Camp** HOTEL **$$**
(🖊cell 6802-4275; www.andespatagonia.cl; Puelo Alto; d/tr/q CH$50,000/60,000/70,000, cabaña CH$50,000; 🅿@🛜) Each of these geodesic domes connected by planks through native forest has its own fireplace for warmth, and cozy mattresses and sleeping bags are provided. Unlimited use of the soothing outdoor hot tub on the premises is included in domo rates and there's a great *quincho* for BBQs. The agency here arranges excursions for guests and nonguests alike.

Restaurant Tique CHILEAN **$$**
(mains CH$4700-7200; ⊙9am-9pm Dec-Mar, 11:30am-3pm Apr-Nov; 🛜) Located at the Domo Camp, this is the best spot to eat in town. Coca runs a rustic kitchen but the meals are home prepared and excellent.

❶ Information

Tourist Office (🖊065-256-2551, ext 114; www.municochamo.cl; Santiago Bueras s/n; ⊙8:30am-2pm & 3-5:30pm Mon-Fri) This small plaza tourist office inside the municipalidad has a map and basic info on local treks, rustic family lodgings and guides.

❶ Getting There & Away

There are five daily departures to and from Puerto Montt (CH$4000, four hours), stopping in Puerto Varas, Ensenada and Cochamó (less on Sunday). From the village, the road banks inland to El Canelo on Lago Tagua Tagua. In January and February, **Transportes Puelche** (🖊065-227-0709; www.navierapuelche.cl; cars CH$7000, pedestrians CH$1050) operates the 45-minute lake crossing to the road's extension three times daily at 7:45am, 9am and 1pm, returning at 8:15am, noon and 4:30pm (the first departure drops out the rest of the year). The road then parallels the river 32km to Llanada Grande. Vehicles show up an hour before departure to get in line.

Río Puelo Valley

🖊065
Like a country lass of modest origins, the Río Puelo Valley remains unfazed by that massive industry called tourism, offering authentic, off-the-grid adventures. An eco-tourism surge here in recent years has thus far warded off proposed hydroelectric dams (which would flood most of the valley), but the threat continues to linger. Fishing, trekking and horseback riding are king here and each offers days of satiating adventures in the area.

Llanada Grande & Beyond

After the lake crossing at Tagua Tagua, the gravel road continues by mountainsides peppered with patches of dead coigüe trees (killed by fire but tragically pretty) and lands still traversed by gaucho families on horseback. This is Llanada Grande – you are now out of bounds, though the area has seen a steady stream of new *hospedajes*, camping and fishing lodges. The road is being slowly forged all the way to Argentina (it now goes as far as Segundo Corral), though whether Argentina will continue it remains up in the air.

Most treks start in Llanada Grande and take different routes along the valley, including unforgettable jaunts to Lago Azul and Argentina. Inquire at Campo Eggers about a system of pioneer homes and rustic B&Bs in place for travelers to continue east from here, making your treks and horseback rides feel a little less touristy and a little more cultural.

🛏 Sleeping & Eating

Campo Eggers GUESTHOUSE **$**
(🖊065-256-6644; agroturelsalto@gmail.com; r per person without bathroom incl breakfast & dinner CH$35,000; 🅿🛜) An invaluable choice in an impeccably clean and sensibly furnished log home owned by spirited Blanca Eggers, who can set up accommodations in pioneer homes and B&Bs all the way to Lago Puelo in Argentina. Breakfast, *onces* and dinner (and wine!) are included and often involve traditional lamb or wild-boar *asado*.

The animal-packed farm's postcard setting in front of the 1200m El Salto waterfall is a destination in itself, but it can be too quiet if it's not a full house.

❶ Getting There & Away

The two earliest departures from Puerto Montt to Río Puelo continue on to the ferry at El Canelo on the north side of Lago Tagua Tagua, where ferries leave three times a day in January and February (7:30am, 9am and 1pm). At Puerto Maldonado, on the south side, a bus to Llanada Grande (CH$800) waits for the 1pm ferry *only* (and passes Llanada Grande around 10:15am to return for the noon ferry). To return, ferries leave Puerto Maldonado three times a day in high season (8:15am, noon and 4:30pm; only the last two depart the rest of the year). The first morning departure each way drops off the rest of the year.

Puerto Montt

☑ 065 / POP 218,858

Say what you will about Puerto Montt (locals certainly don't hold back, with *Muerto Montt,* meaning 'Dead Montt,' topping the list), but if you choose to visit southern Chile's ominous volcanoes, its celestial glacial lakes and its mountainous national parks, you will most likely be visiting the capital of the Lakes District and the region's commercial and transportation hub.

Puerto Montt's most redeeming quality besides its plethora of exit points is that it has become a fine spot for a meal (several of the region's best restaurants are here). Still, most folks, including those who on occasion become endeared of Puerto Montt's unpolished working-class Chilean atmosphere, make their way to Puerto Varas instead.

◉ Sights

Puerto Montt doesn't offer much for lingering – it's really a large transit town.

Casa del Arte Diego Rivera GALLERY
(www.culturapuertomontt.cl; Quillota 116; ⊙9am-1pm & 3-6:30pm Mon-Fri) FREE This is a joint Mexican-Chilean project finished in 1964. The upstairs Sala Hardy Wistuba specializes in works by local artists, sculptors and photographers. Also houses a small cafe and an excellent boutique.

Iglesia Catedral CHURCH
(Urmeneta s/n) Built entirely of alerce in 1856, this church, located on the Plaza de Armas, is the town's oldest building and one of its few attractive ones.

🛏 Sleeping

Puerto Montt is a business town and port rather than a destination in itself and most travelers spend little more than one night here as a transportation hub. Most of the budget places listed are within a few blocks of the bus station. If arriving at night, stay alert; petty thievery isn't uncommon.

Casa Perla GUESTHOUSE $
(☑ 065-226-2104; www.casaperla.com; Trigal 312; camping per person CH$6000, dm CH$10,000, r per person without bathroom CH$12,000; @ 🛜) This welcoming family home's matriarch, Perla, will have you feeling like a sibling. English and German are spoken. All bathrooms are shared and guests can use the kitchen, where Perla makes jam and homemade bread on the wood-burning stove. It's the coziest, knickknack-filled choice in this neighborhood.

Hospedaje Vista al Mar GUESTHOUSE $
(☑065-225-5625; www.hospedajevistaalmar.cl; Vivar 1337; s/d CH$25,000/35,000, without bathroom CH$15,000/28,000; @ 🛜) This family-run favorite is one of nicest of the residential guesthouses, decked out in great-condition hardwoods with spick-and-span bathrooms, rooms with cable TV and wonderful bay

---

PARQUE TAGUA TAGUA

Carved out of virgin Valdivian rainforest 15km east of Puelo, **Parque Tagua-Tagua** (☑065-223-4892; www.parquetaguatagua.cl; adult/child CH$5000/3500) is southern Chile's latest park. A private initiative funded by Universidad Mayor in Santiago and managed by Mitico Puelo Lodge and Miralejos Chile Adventure, the park preserves 3000 hectares of previously unseen alerce forest along with two lakes, Lago Alerce and Lago Quetrus, bounded by granite mountains. Trekking and climbing are big draws here, as is birdwatching and the chance of spotting pudú (small deer), puma and condors.

There are three basic but well-made alerce *refugios* (rustic shelters) with bathrooms, solar panels and wood-burning stoves in the park, built along its 20km of trails that traverse rivers via well-built wooden bridges. The park has a limited capacity established by the fragility of its ecosystem and visits are possible by reservation only.

To get here, catch the once-a-day Lago Tagua-Tagua–bound bus from Puerto Montt (7:45am) or Puerto Varas (8:20am), which meets the ferry at the edge of Lago Tagua-Tagua. Make sure you have called ahead to park officials, who will meet you on the other side of the Tagua-Tagua ferry crossing (Puerto Maldonado) for the final 10-minute boat ride to the park.

views. Eliana fosters a family-friendly atmosphere – helpful to the nth degree – and breakfast goes a step beyond for Chile: yogurt, whole-wheat breads, cakes, muffins and (sometimes) real coffee. Maybe if you beg?

Colores del Puerto
GUESTHOUSE $
(☑065-248-9360; www.coloresdelpuerto.cl; Pasaje Schwerter 207; r per person without bathroom CH$17,000; ☎) Tomás, a friendly, classical music–loving amateur artist, offers four rooms with shared bathrooms and views inside his well-appointed home not more than 100m from the Navimag office and port, which is the real coup here.

House Rocco Backpacker
GUESTHOUSE $
(☑065-227-2897; www.hospedajerocco.cl; Pudeto 233; dm/s/d CH$12,000/25,000/30,000; ☎) This Chilean-American traveler's mainstay five blocks from the Navimag has a large sunny kitchen, warm wooden walls and floors and feather duvets. Home-cooked breakfasts of sweet crepes with *manjar* and real coffee are pluses, but it's a little rougher around the edges than the competition. Veronica, the good-hearted owner, is selling if you're interested in shining it up.

★ Tren del Sur
DESIGN HOTEL $$
(☑065-234-3939; www.trendelsur.cl; Santa Teresa 643; s/d CH$31,800/41,800; P@☎) This boutique hotel in the old neighborhood of Modelo is full of furniture (headboards, wardrobes) fashioned from rescued railway trestles. The high-style lobby is cozy and follows the principles of feng shui. The 17 rooms, a step down from the high-design common areas, offer private bathrooms and central heating and are entered from a skylit hallway visible through newly installed windows.

The in-house Slow Food restaurant, Anden, has limited choices but is excellent (mains CH$8500 to CH$8900).

✖ Eating

For Navimag provisions, you'll find both **Santa Isabel** (Diego Portales 1040) and **Bigger** (Diego Portales 1800), two large supermarkets, across from the bus terminal.

Sanito
CHILEAN $
(www.sanito.cl; Copiapó 66; menu CH$4000; ⊙9am-8pm Mon-Fri; ☎☑) Puerto Montt's best bet for healthy and homey food, served up fresh daily in an artistic atmosphere. Each day, there's a soup, salad or entrée menu (includes juice and coffee/tea) and à la carte salads and sandwiches (CH$2800 to CH$3500), all served up with a funky soundtrack that bounces from Arcade Fire to '70s soul.

Puerto Fritos
SEAFOOD $
(Presidente Ibañez 716, Mercado Municipal Presidente Ibañez; mains CH$2800-6700; ⊙9:30am-5:30pm Mon-Sat, 10am-6pm Sun; ☎) Forget touristy Angelmó! All of Puerto Montt is laid out before you at this cute and unassuming local's secret with the best views in town. It's well worth the CH$3000 taxi ride for excellent *caldillo de mariscos* (seafood soup; CH$4200 to CH$4900) and ceviches (CH$4700 to CH$6500), all of which are served fresh directly from the colorful market downstairs.

On Sunday, seafood and Sauvignon Blanc is the Golden Ticket – there is little else to see, eat or do in the city.

★ Chile Picante
CONTEMPORARY CHILEAN $$
(☑cell 8454-8923; www.chilepicanterestoran.cl; Vicente Pérez Rosales 567; menu CH$8500; ⊙11:30am-3:30pm & 7:30-10:30pm Mon-Sat; ☎) Chef Francisco Sánchez Luengo is on to something at this intimate and playful gourmet hot spot that's an ambitious (uphill) walking distance from most of the budget sleeps. With expansive city and sea views as the backdrop, Luengo offers just a few choices in his daily-changing, three-course menu, all delicately presented yet bursting with the flavors of the market that day.

There's a fascinating emphasis on out-of-the-box preparations of native ingredients – *nalca* (Chilean rhubarb), *cochayuyo* (giant kelp), *michuña* (a native Chiloé potato) etc. Reservations recommended.

★ Cotelé
STEAK $$
(☑065-227-8000; www.cotele.cl; Juan Soler Manfredini 1661, Pelluco; steaks CH$7500-10,000; ⊙1-3:30pm & 8-11:30pm Mon-Sat; ☎) This *quincho* (barbecue hut) steakhouse has a long-standing reputation for its meticulous grillmen who honor the meat with Picasso-level focus. Julio, who has been manning the open hearth here through various changes since 2002, isn't shy about letting you know he has skills. Fair enough: the top-end Angus cuts (sirloin, rib-eye and filet) are riveting.

The amicable South African owner sources his best cuts from a private farmer who oversees the beef from birth to butcher; steaks work from a base of CH$2000 and are priced per kilo from there (Julio will bring

Puerto Montt

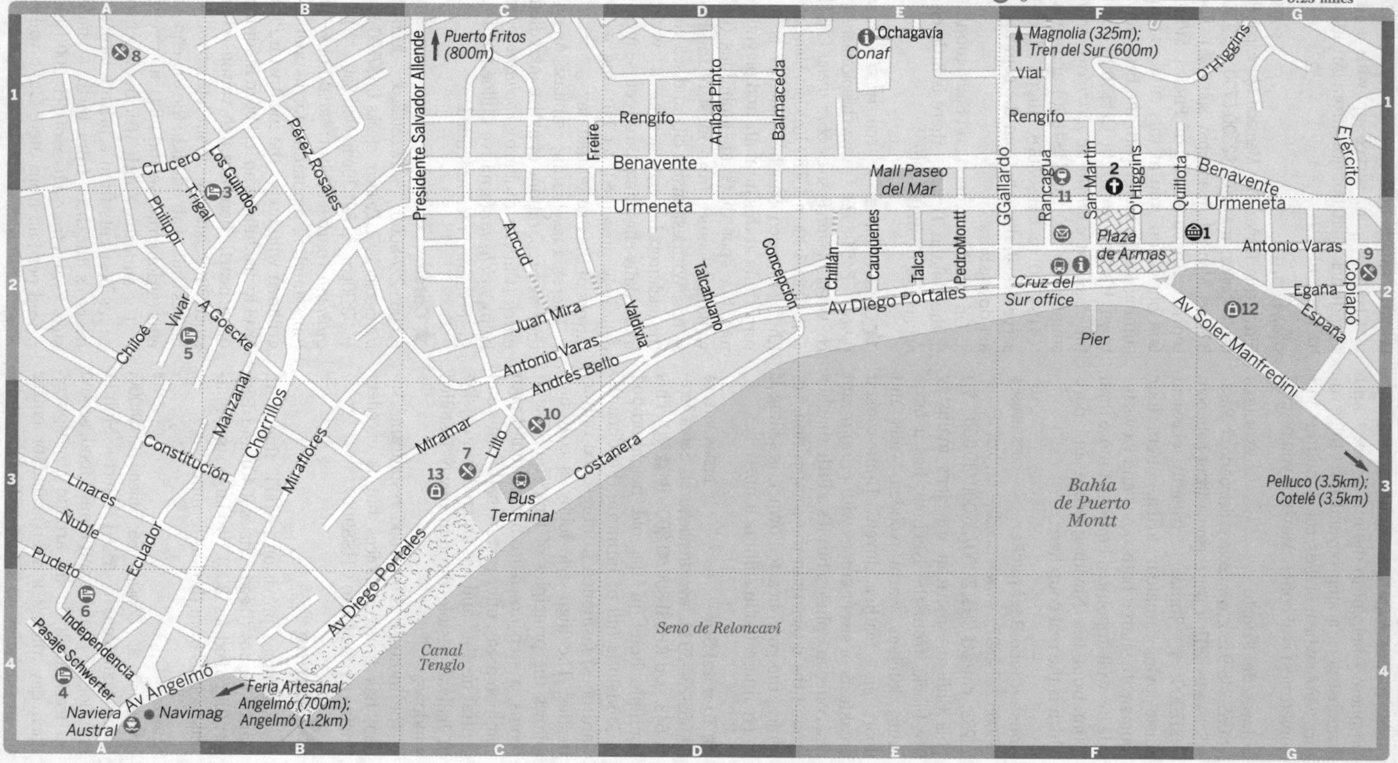

Map labels (street names and features):

- Ejército
- Copiapó
- 9
- Antonio Varas
- Egaña
- España
- Benavente
- Urmeneta
- Av Soler Manfredini
- Pelluco (3.5km); Cotelé (3.5km)
- Quillota
- 1
- 12
- O'Higgins
- Plaza de Armas
- San Martín
- 2
- Pier
- Bahía de Puerto Montt
- Magnolia (325m); Tren del Sur (600m)
- Vial
- Rengifo
- Rancagua
- 11
- Cruz del Sur office
- GGallardo
- PedroMontt
- Talca
- Mall Paseo del Mar
- Ochagavía Conaf
- Cauquenes
- Av Diego Portales
- Chillán
- Balmaceda
- Concepción
- Seno de Reloncaví
- Aníbal Pinto
- Rengifo
- Benavente
- Urmeneta
- Talcahuano
- Valdivia
- Freire
- Juan Mira
- Andrés Bello
- Ancud
- Costanera
- Antonio Varas
- 10
- Bus Terminal
- Lillo
- Miramar
- 7
- 13
- Puerto Fritos (800m)
- Presidente Salvador Allende
- Canal Tenglo
- Av Diego Portales
- Pérez Rosales
- Los Guindos
- Crucero
- Trigal
- A Goecke
- 3
- 5
- Philippi
- Vival
- Chiloé
- Manzanal
- Chorrillos
- Miraflores
- Feria Artesanal Angelmó (700m); Angelmó (1.2km)
- 8
- Constitución
- Ecuador
- Linares
- Ñuble
- Pudeto
- 6
- Independencia
- Pasaje Schwerter
- Av Angelmó
- 4
- Naviera Austral
- Navimag

Puerto Montt

the pre-cooked slabs to the table and cut to order) and are served with roasted breadsticks with a fiery *merkén* paste, *sopaipillas* (fried bread) with *pebre* (coriander, chopped onion, olive oil, garlic and spicy peppers) and potatoes. Perfect order: 350g Angus filet with green peppercorn sauce. In Pelluco, it can be easily reached by buses from the terminal marked Chamiza/Pelluco (CH$400) or taxi (CH$4000). Reservations are a good idea, especially Thursday through Sunday – there's just 10 tables.

🍷 Drinking

There are several low-rent spots for a drink around the plaza and a good selection of trendier, ever-changing bars on Rengifo between Baquedano and Salvador Allende. There is also a concentration of popular clubs in Pelluco, though Chile's new zero tolerance drink driving law has dampened the party out that way a bit.

Magnolia   CAFE
(Luis Ross 460; coffee CH$1200-2800; ⊙8am-11pm Mon-Fri, 11am-8pm Sat; 🖥) 🍴 Cute little cafe tucked away inside Casa del Diamante, which also houses an organic/natural grocery store and Bikram yoga center.

Boule Bar   BAR
(Benavente 435; ⊙6pm-3am Mon-Fri, 8pm-4am Sat) Old *Rolling Stone* covers and other musical propaganda dot this classic, multi-

roomed bar lit with candles and featuring several tables and a bar rack made from tree bark. It's a good spot to carry on late into the evening with a crowd that appreciates a smart soundtrack. A long list of cocktails are 50% off until 11pm nightly.

🛍 Shopping

Along busy, diesel-fume-laden Av Angelmó is a dizzying mix of streetside stalls (selling artifacts, heaps of smoked mussels, cochayuyo – edible sea plant – and mysterious trinkets), crafts markets and touristy seafood restaurants with croaking waiters beckoning you to a table. Enjoy the frenzy, but keep on going.

The best-quality crafts and food are found at the end of the road at the picturesque fishing port of Angelmó, about 3km west of downtown. It is easily reached by frequent local buses and *colectivos*.

For bigger purchases, **Mall Paseo Costanera** (Illapel 10; ⊙10am-9pm Mon-Sat, from 11am Sun) is the city's best shopping mall.

ℹ Information

EMERGENCY
Carabineros de Chile (📞065-276-5158; www. carabineros.cl; Guillermo Gallardo 517; ⊙24hr) Police station.

MEDICAL SERVICES
Clínica Los Andes (www.clinandes.cl; Av Bellavista 123; ⊙24hr) Best private medical services in town.

MONEY
There are more banks along Antonio Varas near Plaza de Armas than there are in Switzerland. You'll find money exchange houses clustered around Diego Portales and Guillermo Gallardo.

POST
CorreosChile (www.correos.cl; Rancagua 126; ⊙9am-7pm Mon-Fri, 9am-noon Sat) One block west of the plaza.

TOURIST INFORMATION
Conaf (📞065-248-6102; Ochagavía 458; ⊙9am-12:45pm & 2:30-5:30pm Mon-Thu, to 4:30pm Fri) Can provide details on nearby national parks.

Sernatur (📞065-222-3016; www.sernatur. cl; San Martín 80; ⊙8:30am-5:30pm Mon-Fri, 9am-3pm Sat) On the west side extension of Plaza de Armas and at arrivals in the airport (⊙9am-6pm Mon-Fri). Stocks a wealth of brochures, but little English is spoken.

CHILE'S SALMON SAGA

Salmon was first imported to Chile about a century ago. It wasn't until the mid-1980s that salmon farming in submerged cages was developed on a massive scale. Nowadays, Chile is the world's second-largest producer of salmon, right on the tail of Norway. Puerto Montt is the epicenter of the farming and exportation industry, where, in the late 2000s, billions of dollars in investment were pushing the farming operations further south into Patagonia as far as the Strait of Magellan and the industry was expected to double in size and growth by 2020, overtaking Norway. By 2006 salmon was Chile's third-largest export (behind copper and molybdenum) and the future looked endlessly bright. Then the bottom dropped out.

Coupled with the global recession, Chile's salmon industry was hit hard with a sudden outbreak of Infectious Salmon Anemia (ISA), first detected in 2007 at a Norwegian-owned farm, with disastrous consequences. Between 2005 and 2010, annual Atlantic salmon production dropped from 400,000 to 100,000 tonnes; 26,000 jobs in Puerto Montt and around were lost (along with US$5 billion) and many players in the salmon service industry went bankrupt. Chile found itself in complete salmon panic – an increase in crime in Puerto Montt and the doubling of suicide rates didn't help matters. But there had been signs. Veritable mountains of organic waste from extra food and salmon feces had led to substantial contamination and depletion of other types of fish; and sanitation issues and pen overcrowding were serious industry concerns for many years.

Environmentalists, including the environmental organization **Oceana** (www.oceana. org) and Doug Tompkins (founder of Parque Pumalín), have expressed their concerns about the negative effects of the salmon industry directly to the Chilean government. **Fundación Terram** (www.terram.cl), which closely monitors the industry, has published reports over a range of topics from working conditions to environmental damage.

By 2012 salmon began making a comeback, mainly thanks to an insatiable emerging market in Brazil, which temporarily overtook the USA to become the world's second-largest global consumer of farmed Chilean salmon behind Japan in 2010. By 2014, salmon had fully rebounded, overtaking molybdenum to become Chile's second-largest export by value and topping $4 billion in sales, mainly thanks to now realigned appetites in the United States (33%), Japan (22%) and Brazil (13%).

Though the crisis appears to be officially over, concerns are not. A recent report by El Servicio Nacional de Pesca y Acuicultura (Sernapesca), Chile's government aquaculture watchdog and compliance agency, found that the Chilean salmon industry uses more antibiotics than any other country (an astonishing 993,000 pounds in 2013). Among them are quinolones, a family of antibiotics that are not approved for use in aquaculture in the USA and elsewhere due to their negative effect on the human immune system.

As an aside, it should be noted that all the quality salmon in Chile is exported, so if it's on menus in country, it's probably one of two scenarios: it's downgraded (ie defective or not fit for export) or 'wild,' which really just means it has escaped from a farm (or was spawned from an escaped bloodline).

¡Buen provecho!

TRAVEL AGENCIES

Andina del Sud (☏ 065-222-8600; www.andi-nadelsud.com; Antonio Varas 216, Edificio Torre del Puerto, suite 907; ☺9am-7pm Mon-Fri) Represents TurisTour for the Cruce de Lagos bus-ferry combo trip to Argentina.

ℹ Getting There & Away

AIR

Aeropuerto El Tepual (☏065-229-4161; www. aeropuertoeltepual.cl) Located 16km west of the city.

LAN (☏ 600-526-2000; O'Higgins 167, Local 1-B; ☺9am-1:30pm & 3-6:30pm Mon-Fri, 9:30am-1:30pm Sat) Flies three to four times daily to Punta Arenas (one-way fares from CH$170,000), twice daily to Balmaceda/Coyhaique (one-way fares from CH$110,000) and up to 10 times daily to Santiago (one-way fares from CH$180,000). The cheap and quick flight to Castro lifts off Monday, Wednesday, Friday and Saturday (fares from CH$6683).

However, you can fly one way for up to 75% less if you buy a round-trip ticket and simply don't turn up for the return leg.

Sky Airlines (☑ 600-600-2828; www. skyairline.cl; cnr San Martín & Benavente; ☺9am-7pm Mon-Fri, 10am-1pm Sat) Flies to Punta Arenas twice daily (one-way fares from CH$85,093) and three to four times to Santiago (one-way fares from CH$83,193). Considerably cheaper than LAN.

Aerocord (☑ 065-226-2300; www.aerocord.cl; Aeródromo La Paloma) For Chaitén, Aerocord flies Twin Otters and similar Monday to Saturday at 9:30am, and Monday and Tuesday at 11:45am (CH$50,000).

Pewen Services Aéreos (☑ 065-222-4000; www.pewenchile.com; Aeródromo La Paloma) Pewen Services Aéreos flies Monday to Saturday (CH$50,000, 9:30am and 11:30pm) and offers charters for up to nine passengers with a week's notice.

BUS – REGIONAL

Puerto Montt's modern waterfront **bus terminal** (☑ 065-228-3000; www.terminalpm.cl; cnr Av Diego Portales & Lillo) is the main transportation hub for the region, and it gets busy and chaotic – watch your belongings or leave them with the *custodia* (per 24 hours CH$1200 to CH$2400) while sorting out travel plans. In summer, trips to Punta Arenas and Bariloche can sell out, so book in advance.

Regional minibuses, including Puerto Varas (CH$800, 25 minutes), Frutillar (CH$1300, one hour) and Puerto Octay (CH$1800, two hours), leave frequently from the northern front of the terminal. **Buses Río Puelo** (☑ cell 7408-9199) leaves for the villages of Ralún (CH$2000, two hours), Cochamó (CH$2500, 2½ hours) and Río Puelo (CH$4000) at 7:15am, 7:45am and 4pm (3pm on Sunday). The first two morning departures carry on all the way to Lago Tagua Tagua. **Transhar** (☑ 065-225-4187) goes at 12:15pm and 3:30pm Monday to Saturday, 2:15pm on Sunday.

BUS – LONG-DISTANCE

Bus companies, all with offices at the bus terminal, include **Cruz del Sur** (☑ 065-248-3144; www.busescruzdelsur.cl) with frequent services to Chiloé; **Tur-Bus/Tas-Choapa** (☑ 065-249-3402; www.turbus.cl), with daily service to Valparaíso/Viña del Mar; **Igi Llaima** (☑ 065-225-9320; www.igillaima.cl); and **Pullman Bus** (☑ 065-251-6561; www.pullman.cl). All of these services go to Santiago, stopping at various cities along the way; **Buses Fierro** (☑ 065-228-9024; www.busesfierro.cl) has an 8:45pm 'direct' service (CH$15,000, 12 hours). **Buses ETM** (☑ 065-225-6253; www.etm.cl) and **Bus Norte** (☑ 065-225-2783; www.busnorte.cl) also offer nightly service to Valparaíso/Viña del Mar.

For long-haul trips to Punta Arenas via Argentina, **Queilen Bus** (☑ 065-225-3468; www. queilenbus.cl) heads out Monday and Friday at 3pm; Cruz del Sur goes Tuesday, Thursday and Saturday at 11:10am; and Pullman Bus goes Saturday at 10:30am. The former goes to Coyhaique on Tuesday at 4pm and Friday at 10:35am (CH$36,000, 22 hours).

For Bariloche, Argentina, Cruz del Sur travels Thursday and Sunday at 8:30am and 10:45am; **Via Bariloche** (☑ 065-223-3633; www.viabariloche.com.ar) goes at 3pm daily; **Andesmar** (☑ 065-228-0999; www.andesmar.com) heads out Wednesday, Friday and Sunday at 8:15am; and **Trans Austral** (☑ 065-227-0984; www. transaustral.com) leaves Monday and Thursday at 10:15am and Wednesday and Friday at 10am.

Kemelbus (☑ 065-225-6450; www.kemelbus. cl) has daily 6am and 8am departures to Chaitén (CH$10,000) that stop at Parque Pumalín; otherwise, catch more frequent buses to Hornopirén (CH$6000, four hours, 8am, 1pm, 4:45pm and 6pm) and switch there.

Sample travel times and starting fares are as follows (prices fluctuate with the quality of the bus/class and season):

DESTINATION	COST (CH$)	DURATION (HR)
Ancud	4500	2½
Bariloche (Ar)	18,000	6
Castro	6200	4
Chaitén	14,000	9½
Concepción	15,000	10
Coyhaique	36,000	24
Osorno	2500	1½
Pucón	9500	5½
Punta Arenas	45,000	32
Quellón	8000	6
Santiago	27,000	12-14
Temuco	6700	5
Valdivia	5000	3½
Valparaíso/ Viña del Mar	23,000	15
Villarrica	8800	5

BOAT

Puerto Montt is the main departure port for Patagonia. At the port, you can find ticket offices and waiting lounges for both Navimag and Naviera Austral, housed inside the same building. Both companies are primarily commercial transporters, so don't expect thread counts and Dom Pérignon.

Auto-passenger ferries from Pargua, 62km southwest of Puerto Montt, go to Chacao (30 minutes), on the northern tip of Chiloé, every 30 minutes or so. Fares are CH$600 for passengers (included in bus fares to Chiloé) or CH$10,600 per car, no matter how many passengers.

Navimag (☑ 065-243-2361; www.navimag. com; Angelmó 1735; ⊘ 9am-1pm & 2:30-6pm Mon-Fri, 11am-1pm Sat) Navimag's ferry *Eden*, which sails on Friday from Puerto Montt to Puerto Natales and back on Friday (boarding Thursday evening), is the most popular route, a stunning three-night journey through Chile's fjords; book passage at Navimag offices in Santiago, Puerto Montt, Puerto Natales or via the website.

High season is from November to March and low season is April to October. Prices for the trip include full board (vegetarian meals can be requested). Per-person fares vary according to the view and whether it is a private or shared bathroom (ranging from the upper-deck AAA room with an en suite bathroom for US$1050 based on double occupancy to the least-attractive C class, with no views and shared bathrooms, for US$450).

Cars are CH$290,000 extra. Bicycles and motorcycles can also be carried along for an additional cost. Travelers prone to seasickness should consider taking medication prior to the 12-hour crossing of Golfo de Penas, which is exposed to rolling Pacific swells – particularly in winter. The southern route includes passage by the glacier Pio XI, the largest in South America (it's as big as Santiago), though there are more beautiful and photogenic glaciers along the route.

Navimag also sails the ferry *Evangelista* to Puerto Chacabuco Wednesday and Saturday at midnight. Per-person fares for the 24-hour journey range from CH$35,000 to CH$74,000. Small cars cost CH$160,000. The return journey departs Puerto Chacabuco on Tuesday and Friday at 6pm.

Naviera Austral (☑ 065-227-0430; www. navieraustral.cl; Angelmó 1673; ⊘ 9am-1pm & 3-7pm Mon-Fri, 10am-1pm Sat) Naviera Austral sails the *Dom Baldo* Monday, Thursday and Friday to Chaitén year-round. The trip takes nine hours and usually runs overnight and is less than comfortable. Prices are CH$16,000 per seat, from CH$31,000 for a berth and CH$88,000 for vehicles.

Cruceros Skorpios (☑ 065-227-5646; www. skorpios.cl; Av Angelmó 1660; d incl meals & alcohol from US$4000; ⊘ 8:30am-12:30pm & 2:30-6:30pm Mon-Fri) A legitimate cruise that calls itself 'semi-elegant.' Its most popular trip sails the *MV Skorpios II* to Laguna San Rafael with departures on Saturday from Puerto Montt from September to April. The five-day round-trip cruise stops at its exclusive hot-springs resort, Quitralco, and the Chiloé archipelago.

ⓘ Getting Around

Andrés Tour (☑ 065-225-6611; www.andrestur. com) services the airport from the bus terminal (CH$2500). Catch the shuttle two hours before your flight's departure (don't cut it close with the shuttle departure time – they are fined if they sit in their assigned gate longer than a few minutes and they *will* leave without you!). It also offers door-to-door service from the airport to Puerto Montt (per person CH$15,000) and Puerto Varas (oddly, CH$15,000 for two people).

Taxis to most places around town run CH$3000 or so; to the airport, CH$12,000. *Coletivos* and minibuses ply the *costanera* and around for CH$400 to CH$500.

Europcar (☑ 065-236-8216; Antonio Varas 162; ⊘ 8am-7pm Mon-Fri, to 1:30pm Sat) With 24 hours notice, Europcar can help get the permission certificate (CH$64,000 plus taxes) to take rental vehicles into Argentina.

Chiloé

Best Places to Eat

➡ Mercadito (p295)

➡ Rucalaf Putemún (p296)

➡ La Cocinería Dalcahue (p290)

➡ Hostalomera (p295)

➡ Mar y Canela (p296)

Best Places to Sleep

➡ EcoLodge Chepu Adventures (p288)

➡ Palafito del Mar (p295)

➡ Palafito 1326 (p295)

➡ Palafito Cucao Hostel (p299)

➡ Isla Bruja Lodge (p296)

Why Go?

When the early-morning fog shrouds misty-eyed and mis-understood Chiloé, it's immediately apparent something different this way comes. Isla Grande de Chiloé, the continent's fifth-largest island, is home to a fiercely independent, seafaring people who developed culturally and historically in defiance of Santiago.

Immediately apparent are changes in architecture and cuisine: *tejuelas*, the famous Chilote wood shingles; *palafitos* (houses mounted on stilts along the water's edge); the iconic wooden churches (16 of which are Unesco World Heritage sites); and the renowned meat, potato and seafood stew, *curanto*. A closer look reveals a rich spiritual culture that is based on a distinctive mythology of witchcraft, ghost ships and forest gnomes.

All of the above is weaved among landscapes that are wet, windswept and lush, with undulating hills, wild and remote national parks, and dense forests, giving Chiloé a distinct flavor unique in South America.

When to Go
Ancud

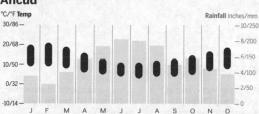

Feb The clearest skies of the year in Chiloé, but you'll still need a poncho.

Sep–Mar Magellanic and Humboldt penguins breed in Monumento Natural Islotes de Puñihuil.

Dec–May Best time of year to catch endangered blue whales off Chiloé's northwest coast.

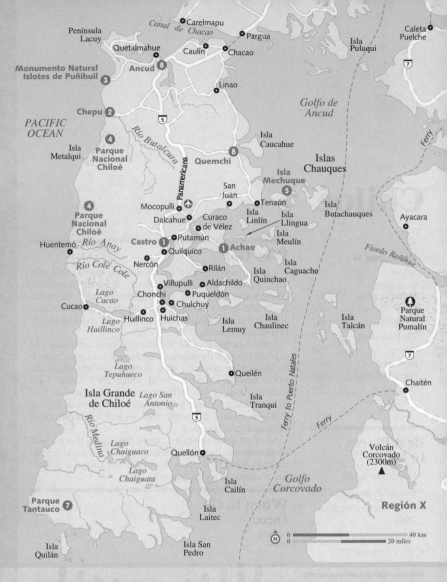

Map labels:

Caleta Puelche

Canal de Chacao — Carelmapu — Pargua

Península Lacuy — Quetalmahue — Caulín — Chacao

Isla Puluqui

Monumento Natural Islotes de Puñihuil — Ancud

Linao

Golfo de Ancud

Chepu

PACIFIC OCEAN

Río Butalcura — Panamericana

Quemchi

Isla Caucahue

Isla Mechuque — Islas Chauques

Isla Metalqui — Parque Nacional Chiloé

San Juan

Mocopulli — Dalcahue — Curaco de Vélez

Tenaún

Isla Butachauques — Ayacara

Parque Nacional Chiloé

Castro — Putamún — Quilquico — Achao

Isla Linlín — Isla Llingua — Isla Meulín

Huentemó — Río Anay

Río Cole Cole — Nercón — Rilán

Isla Quinchao — Isla Caguache

Fiordo Reñihue

Parque Natural Pumalín

Villupulli — Aldachildo — Chonchi — Puqueldón — Chulchuy — Huillinco — Huichas

Lago Cucao — Cucao

Isla Talcán

Lago Huillinco

Isla Lemuy — Isla Chaulinec

Chaitén

Lago Tepuhueco

Isla Grande de Chiloé — Lago San Antonio

Queilén

Ferry to Puerto Natales

Isla Tranqui

Río Medina — Lago Chaiguaco — Quellón

Volcán Corcovado (2300m)

Ferry

Golfo Corcovado

Región X

Lago Chaiguata

Isla Cailín

Parque Tantauco

Isla Laitec

Isla San Pedro

Isla Quilán

N — 0 — 40 km — 0 — 20 miles

Chiloé Highlights

1 Genuflect in awe at the interiors of Chiloé's Unesco-listed wooden churches, especially in **Achao** (p291) and **Castro** (p292).

2 Wake up with the sun on a kayak trip in misty **Chepu** (p288).

3 Spy Magellanic and Humboldt penguins at the wild and rugged **Monumento Natural Islotes de Puñihuil** (p287).

4 Hike along the raging and wild west coast in **Parque Nacional Chiloé** (p298).

5 Wander the picturesque roads of **Isla Mechuque** (p289), an idyllic microcosm of Chiloé on a mini-island.

6 Hit the outdoor hot tub with wine in hand in one of Chiloé's **remote lodges** (p296).

7 Lose yourself on a hut-to-hut trek through **Parque Tantauco** (p299).

8 Tear into a bowl of *curanto*, Chiloé's most traditional dish, in restaurants such as **Kuranton** (p286) and **El Chejo** (p288).

History

The islands were first populated by the Chono people, who were pushed toward the Archipelago de Aisén as the Mapuche invaded from the north. The Spaniards took full possession of Chiloé in 1567, some five years after a smallpox epidemic killed much of the indigenous population. A measles epidemic in 1580 further weakened the native influence.

During the wars of independence, Chiloé was a Spanish stronghold; the Spanish resisted criollo attacks in 1820 and 1824 from heavily fortified Ancud, until their final defeat in 1826. In 1843 the schooner *Ancud* left the shores of Chiloé full of islanders, who stuck out four months of sailing to lay Chilean claim to Magallanes at Fuerte Bulnes. The later wool and ranching booms in Magallanes were built on the backs of migrant Chilote labor. Their cultural influence is still felt in the far southern regions.

Chiloé itself stayed off the radar until the 1850s when its proximity to the new Puerto Montt gave the islands increasing commercial importance. It took another century to establish a road running the length of the main island. Fishing was and is the main industry, but is now heavily dominated by salmon and shellfish farming. Tourism has increased significantly during the last two decades.

ℹ️ Getting There & Away

The most popular route for travelers is the frequent **ferry** (www.navieracruzdelsur.cl; car/pedestrian CH$10,600/600) between Pargua, on the mainland 62km southwest of Puerto Montt, and Chacao, a small town of little interest at the northeast corner of Isla Grande de Chiloé, but that is all set to change over the coming years. Construction on the controversial Puente Chacao, a 2.6km suspension bridge – the largest of its kind in Latin America – linking Chiloé with the mainland, is scheduled to begin in 2015 and be operational by 2020. Until then, bus fares to/from the mainland include the half-hour ferry crossing. LAN Airlines operates one daily flight from Santiago to Castro via Puerto Montt five days a week.

ℹ️ Getting Around

The easiest way to get around Chiloé is the bus. Buses connect every major destination on the main island with some frequency and link up with ferries to smaller islands. It is also easy to explore with a car, which allows you to visit some of the more remote parts of this land. You can rent a car in Ancud or Castro, or bring one over from the mainland on the ferry.

Ancud

📞 065 / POP 40,800

Ancud was once a rather wealthy place with gracious buildings, *palafitos* and a railway line. But the earthquake of 1960 decimated the town. Today, version 2.0, though rather quaint, is a sprawling city only peppered with occasional native architecture leading down to the spectacular waterfront, which glistens throughout the better part of each summer day.

Ancud's coup is in its natural surroundings, and for those who want a taste of Chiloé but don't have time to dig as deep as Castro, its spectacular nearby coastline, excellent seafood, cozy hostels and proximity to Monumento Natural Islotes de Puñihuil make it an easy-to-digest base for exploring a less-beaten-path corner of Chiloé.

⊙ Sights

★ **Centro de Visitantes Inmaculada Concepción** MUSEUM

(www.iglesiasdechiloe.cl; Errázuriz 227; suggested donation CH$500; ⊙10am-7pm Dec-Feb, to 6pm Mar-Nov) Don't even think about visiting Chiloé's Unesco churches without first stopping in at this excellent museum housed in the former Convento Inmaculada Concepción de Ancud (1875). It's home to wooden scale models of all 16 churches, which show the workings of the intricate interior woodwork of each.

You'll also find an interesting museum shop, artisan shop and cafe. No English signage or information is available yet, but if you dig Chiloé churches, it has produced a well-done coffee-table book available in the shop.

★ **Museo Regional de Ancud** MUSEUM

(Museo Chilote; www.museoancud.cl; Libertad 370; adult/child CH$600/300; ⊙10am-7:30pm Jan & Feb, to 5:30pm Tue-Fri, to 2pm Sat & Sun Mar-Dec) The excellent Museo Regional Aurelio Bórquez Canobra, casually referred to as Museo Chilote, offers fantastic displays tracking the history of the island, including a full-sized replica of the *Ancud,* which sailed the treacherous fjords of the Strait of Magellan to claim Chile's southernmost territories.

Fuerte San Antonio FORTRESS

(cnr Lord Cochrane & Baquedano; ⊙8:30am-9pm Mon-Fri, 9am-8pm Sat & Sun) FREE During the wars of independence, Fuerte San Antonio was Spain's last Chilean outpost. At the

Ancud

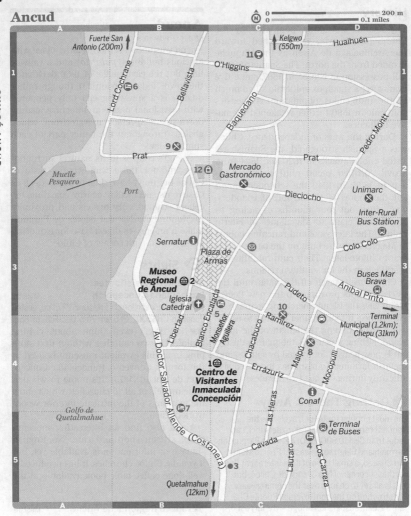

Fuerte San
Antonio (200m)

Kelgwo
(550m)

Huaihuén

O'Higgins

11

Lord Cochrane

6

Bellavista

Baquedano

Pedro Montt

Prat

Prat

9

Muelle
Pesquero

Port

12

Mercado
Gastronómico

Dieciocho

Unimarc

Inter-Rural
Bus Station

Colo-Colo

Sernatur

Plaza de
Armas

**Museo
Regional 2
de Ancud**

Buses Mar
Brava

Aníbal Pinto

Pudeto

Iglesia
Catedral

Blanco Encalada

Monseñor
Aguilera

5

Chacabuco

Ramírez

10

Terminal
Municipal (1.2km);
Chepu (31km)

Libertad

Errázuriz

Maipú

8

Mocopulli

**1
Centro de
Visitantes
Inmaculada
Concepción**

Las Heras

Conaf

Golfo de
Quetalmahue

Av Doctor Salvador Allende (Costanera)

7

Cavada

Lautaro

4

Los Carrera

Terminal
de Buses

3

Quetalmahue
(12km)

northwest corner of town, late-colonial cannon emplacements look down on the harbor from the early-19th-century remains of the fortress. There's a somewhat secluded beach, Playa Gruesa, behind the north wall.

☞ Tours

Many folks around town run minibus tours to see the penguins at Monumento Natural Islotes de Puñihuil for around CH$17,000.

Austral Adventures OUTDOORS
(☎065-262-5977; www.austral-adventures.com; Av Costanera 904) 🍃 This is the go-to agen-

cy for English-speaking tours from Ancud, including extended nature-centric jaunts to see the penguins and whales, kayaking on the bay and birdwatching – always with a fierce eco-slant and more elaborate than the cookie-cutter tours. American owner Britt Lewis is impossibly nice and knowledgeable.

🛏 Sleeping

Chiloé Turismo Rural HOMESTAY $
(www.chiloeturismorural.cl) 🍃 Chiloé's agro-tourism association organizes excursions to farming and fishing communities, as well as private homes that offer meals and lodging

Ancud

in several small towns and rural outposts. Pick up a catalog at Sernatur.

★ **13 Lunas Hostel** HOSTEL $
(☏065-262-2106; www.13lunas.cl; Los Carrera 855; dm from CH$10,500, s/d 19,000/33,000, all incl breakfast; ₱@☞) ✈ The best option for migrating backpackers, this helpful hostel can't be missed, situated directly across from the Cruz del Sur bus terminal: its bright-green-and-yellow motif screams artsy Chiloé. Owner Claudio is young, enthusiastic and speaks English. The lovely hostel oozes coziness with bright hardwoods, beacons of natural light, hotel-level bathrooms, a grassy lawn and a wonderful terrace with views.

Solar-heated water and active recycling give it an eco-edge as well. Avoid less-atmospheric basement rooms if possible.

Hostal Lluhay GUESTHOUSE $
(☏065-262-2656; www.hostal-lluhay.cl; Lord Cochrane 458; s/d/tr incl breakfast CH$15,000/ 29,000/38,000; ₱@☞) The best antique kitsch and character for the price goes to Lluhay, which wins over visitors with its very welcoming owners. Don't be surprised if they start feeding you delicious homemade *küchen* (sweet, German-style cakes), pouring you cocktails by the fireplace or knocking out a few bars on the piano.

Chil-Hué GUESTHOUSE $$
(☏065-262-5977; www.chil-hue.com; Playa Lechagua; r from CH$50,000, casita CH$90,000) For those with extra pesos and a penchant for solitude, this is Ancud's best bet. Your hosts are Britt from Austral Adventures and his wife, Sandra – a gourmet Peruvian chef and Ashtanga yoga instructor – who have built just three lodgings on their property on an isolated beach 6km south of Ancud.

The namesake tower offers two stylish apartments with kitchenettes (pluck your organic greens straight from the adjacent garden), but sea views are obstructed. The real coup is the isolated beachfront *casita*, where it's just you and the dolphins in the bay. This remote and rustic getaway with style and food (meals run CH$3500 to CH$15,000) is only for certain souls. You know who you are.

Hostal Mundo Nuevo HOSTEL $$
(☏065-262-8383; www.hostalmundonuevo.com; Costanera 748; dm CH$13,000, s/d/q CH$32,000/ 43,000/54,000, s/d without bathroom CH$24,000/ 34,000, all incl breakfast; @☞) This Swiss-owned midrange masquerading as a hostel is just a hop, skip and a jump from Cruz del Sur's bus station. It boasts postcard-perfect sunset views over the Bay of Ancud from a big, comfortable bench on its naturally lit front porch as well as the 12 private rooms and a six-bed dorm. The new outdoor hot tub (from CH$12,000 for up to eight guests) is well worth reserving a few hours in advance.

✗ Eating & Drinking

Tucked away off Dieciocho is a series of downhome market stalls doing *cazuela* (meat and vegetable stew), *chupe* (fish casserole) and set lunch menus for around CH$2000 to CH$5000.

Retro's Pub RESTO-BAR $
(Ramírez 317; mains CH$4300-9000, pizza CH$9000-12,500; ☉noon-2am Mon-Fri, 8pm-4am Sat; ☞) Inside this cozy home, Ancud's most timeless bar spreads itself among several rooms. The menu is chock-full of Tex-Mex, as well as killer burgers the size of Kansas (fork required) on sourdough-reminiscent buns, stone-cooked pizza, sandwiches and pasta – everything made from scratch, everything a great homesickness remedy.

Q'ilú RESTO-BAR $
(www.qiluurestobar.blogspot.com; Ramírez 278; mains CH$3600-8000; ☉10am-1am Mon-Thu, til 2am Fri-Sat; ☞) This stylish resto-bar does

CURANTO: CHILOÉ'S CULINARY COUP

No words can quite prepare you for the first moment a piping hot bowl of *curanto* lands on the table in front of you, but 'What did I get myself into?' comes to mind. Rest assured, however, your slack jaw will come in handy when it's time to shove all that food in. Chiloé's most traditional dish is of unknown origins, but historically its preparation harkens back to the earth ovens of Polynesian culinary ancestry.

Traditionally *curanto* was made by heating up stones in a hole in the ground and waiting until they crackle, then directly piling on shellfish, pork and chicken, followed by *nalca* (a rhubarb-like plant) or *pangue* (a native plant of Chile) leaves and damp cloths before the whole shebang was covered in dirt and grass and left to simmer for nearly two hours.

They still prepare it this traditional way, called *curanto al hoyo*, in a few places around the island, including **Restaurant Quetalmahue** (www.restaurantequetalmahue.es.tl; curanto CH$9000 Dec-Feb; ☺10am-7pm) in Quetalmahue, a small fishing village 12km from Ancud (high season only unless you are a big group with advanced reservations). If you can't make it there (*curanto* ready from 2pm to 4pm; a taxi runs a negotiable CH$10,000 or so round-trip from Ancud with waiting), the next best thing – minus the pit and dirt – is Kuranton (p286) in Ancud and El Chejo (p288) in Quemchi.

a well-executed and tasty-valued *menú del día* (CH$3500; until 1pm) in a hardwood-heavy atmosphere that doubles – as is usually the case in Ancud – as a great place for a drink.

Kuranton CHILEAN, SEAFOOD $
(Prat 94; curanto CH$7000; ☺11am-10pm) This year-round classic has an extensive menu of underwhelming seafood, but it's really all about the *curanto*, Chiloé's gastronomic bombshell. This hearty stew of mussels, clams, chicken, pork and three types of potatoes is a meal fit for hibernation.

El Embrujo de Chiloé CAFE $
(Maipú 650; coffee CH$900-2500, sandwiches CH$1800-3500; ☺9am-8pm Mon-Fri, 11am-2pm Sat; 🐾) This cozy cafe is always packed with discerning locals, sipping decent cappuccinos or catching a quick sandwich on the cheap. There's a playful witchcraft undercurrent and it feels more Chilote than elsewhere.

Club Social Mehadier BAR
(Baquedano 469; beers CH$2500; ☺noon-2am, closed Sun) A Temuco nightlife veteran has opened Ancud's most interesting and classiest new bar, housed in a restored shingled Chilote house that once hosted a social club of the same name in the '60s and '70s. There's craft beer on draft – Cuello Negro and Kross – and Victorian-like sofas and decor to lounge on. Pizza and pasta are served.

🛍 Shopping

Kelgwo CLOTHING
(www.kelgwo.cl; Costanera Norte 200; ☺8am-5pm Mon-Fri) This boutique, housed in a crumbling home in Arena Gruesa, does naturally dyed, high-quality woven coats, dresses, scarfs, shawls and tops that put a gorgeous modern take on Chiloé's age-old weaving traditions.

Mercado Municipal MARKET
(Prat, cnr Dieciocho & Libertad; ☺8:30am-9pm Mon-Sat, to 7:30pm Sun) Has an abundance of craft stalls.

ℹ Information

Conaf (☎065-262-7520; Errázuriz 317; ☺9am-12:50pm & 2:30-5:30pm Mon & Wed, to 12:50pm & 2:30-4:30pm Fri) National park info.

Hospital de Ancud (www.hospitalancud.gov.cl; Almirante Latorre 301; ☺24hr) Located at the corner of Pedro Montt.

CorreosChile (www.correos.cl; cnr Pudeto & Blanco Encalada; ☺9am-6pm Mon-Fri, 9:30am-12:30pm Sat)

Sernatur (☎065-262-2800; www.sernatur.cl; Libertad 665; ☺8:30am-7pm Mon-Fri, 9:30am-7pm Sat & Sun Dec-Feb, to 6pm Mon-Thu, 8:30am-5pm Fri Mar-Nov; 🐾) This is the only formal national tourist office on the island; very helpful staff, brochures, town maps, lists of accommodations and wi-fi.

ℹ Getting There & Away

Ancud has three bus terminals. **Cruz del Sur** (☎065-262-2265; www.busescruzdelsur.cl; ☺6:30am-10pm Mon-Sat, 7am-10pm Sun) owns and operates the main **Terminal de Buses** (cnr Los Carreras & Cavada), which offers the most departures to Chiloé's more southerly towns, with departures about every hour, and to cities on the Panamericana to the north (including two daily departures to Santiago). It's a five-minute walk from the waterfront and downtown. A taxi to/from the terminal to Av Costanera in downtown costs CH$2000. **Queilen Bus** (☑ 065-262-1140; www.queilenbus.cl) and **Pullman Bus** (☑ 065-262-0800) operate out of the old **Terminal Municipal** (Anibal Pinto 1200), 1.5km from the center, most economically reached by flagging down a black-and-yellow *colectivo* on Dieciocho (CH$350).

Cruz del Sur buses go to Punta Arenas every Tuesday, Thursday and Saturday at 8:30am. Queilen Bus heads out Monday at 7:45am. However, travelers going to most southerly regions beyond Chiloé and to Bariloche, Argentina, will do better to take buses from Puerto Montt.

Sample starting fares in high season are as follows (prices can fluctuate with company and the quality of the bus/classes):

DESTINATION	COST (CH$)	DURATION (HR)
Castro	1500	1½
Concepción	23,000	12
Dalcahue	1700	¾
Osorno	6200	4
Puerto Montt	4500	2
Puerto Varas	5000	1½
Punta Arenas	45,000	32
Quellón	4000	3
Santiago	17,000	16
Temuco	10,500	8
Valdivia	8300	6

Chiloé's more rural destinations to the east, as well as afternoon buses to Chepu, the gateway to the northern end of Parque Nacional Chiloé, are serviced by buses that leave from the small **inter-rural bus station** on Colo Colo. The schedule is posted near the bathroom (if not, ask at the administration office); simply buy tickets on the bus.

In high season, **Buses Mar Brava** (☑ 065-262-2312), departing from the 300 block of Aníbal Pinto, heads to Pumillahue, near Monumento Natural Islotes de Puñihuil, at 6:45am (Monday to Friday, returning 8am), noon (Monday & Friday, returning 1:30pm) and 2pm (Saturday, returning 3:30pm) and 3pm (Tuesday, Wednesday and Thursday, returning 4:30pm). The bus will drop you at Piedra Run crossroads, from which it is a 2km walk to the beach (follow the paved road). In low season, service drops off substantially.

Monumento Natural Islotes de Puñihuil

Three islands off the coast of Puñihuil, on the Pacific Ocean, are breeding grounds for Magellanic and the near-extinct Humboldt penguins, and a haven for blue whales. The entire area is protected as a natural monument and a no-fishing zone is enforced in the area. The best time of year to go for the penguins is when they are breeding, from September to March (you might otherwise be out of luck). Several travel agencies in Ancud organize excursions to the site, or you can grab a Mar Brava bus from central Ancud on your own (except Sunday).

No matter how you arrive, your transportation will drive right out onto a magnificent rugged beach. **Ecoturismo Puñihuil** (☑ cell 8317-4302; www.pinguineraschiloe.cl; adult/child CH$6500/3500) represents three of the six licensed operators and runs 20 or so trips per day with three local fishing boats between 10am and 6pm to take tourists out for a closer (but quick) look at the penguins (if they're full, walk on down the beach for other options). All-weather gear is provided. Boats can fill up in high season – it's best to book ahead at Austral Adventures in Ancud. When weather permits, it also does whale-watching and sea-lion trips.

The road to Puñihuil is paved, so managing all of this with a sustainable slant is the area's most pressing challenge.

Quemchi

☑ 065

On a clear summer day, the snowcapped mountains of southern Chile loom in the distance over misty Quemchi, topping off an already impressive view from the sea wall of this sleepy little town. Quemchi's waterfront is an ideal place to lose yourself for a day, strolling along the bay and passing the hours in one of Chiloé's best restaurants – El Chejo. It has the highest change in tides (7m) on the island, which makes for a surreal scene of beached fishing boats while the water's out.

Rural buses make the trip to Ancud and Castro (CH$1500, 1½ hours to either destination) every 20 to 45 minutes from 6:45am to 7pm. On Sunday, there are only three to Castro (12:30pm, 3:30pm and 5:50pm) and four to Ancud (9:30am, 4pm, 5pm and 5:45pm). Buses leave from the library (where

ECOLODGE CHEPU ADVENTURES

Previously difficult to access and lacking infrastructure, **Chepu**, the northern sector of Parque Nacional Chiloé, 38km southwest from Ancud, remains Chiloé's sanctuary of pristine beauty. Arriving here gives you a sense of discovery. You'll find stunning coastline, gorgeous rivers and 128 species of birds, totally untapped by mass tourism thus far, but changing sooner rather than later (the road is slated to be paved in the near future).

In a breathtaking spot overlooking the confluence of three rivers and 140 sq km of sunken forest (a phenomena created by by the 1960 Valdivia earthquake, which sunk the ground some 2m, allowing salt water to enter the area and kill the trees), consummate hosts Fernando and Amory at **EcoLodge Chepu Adventures** (☑cell 9379-2481; www. chepu.cl; Camino a Chepu Km 13.2; dm CH$56,000, d CH$161,000, all incl kayak at dawn & half board; 🅿@🛜) 🗡 have labored for years creating the ultimate eco nirvana. Not only have they built their nearly self-sufficient lodge and home *twice* in one of Chile's most breathtaking spots, but their constant innovation and adaptability to the surrounds is a testament to sustainable will that has earned green accolades the world over (the lodge was an innovation finalist in the 2014 World Travel & Tourism Council Tourism for Tomorrow Awards and was named Chile's most sustainable small business as well, among many others).

It is here where you can take in mystical self-guided kayak trips at dawn through the surreal landscape of the Río Puntra (nonguests CH$20,000 per person) – as one traveler put it, it's like paddling into a Pink Floyd album cover! But these Santiago escapees also know their way around organic cuisine, wine and barbeque. Rustic accommodations made from wood-alternative recycled fiber feature solar and wind-generated electricity power and unique water consumption software. Options include two Argentine-style *dormis* (mini sleeping rooms) and four upscale eco-cabañas. Camping is also available.

Although the most untouched northern sector of Parque Nacional Chiloé is also near here, there is no reasonable trail maintenance. You can access the park's borders by a 30-minute boat ride from Chepu and a two-hour coastal hike, but it stops short of the park. There's a small *refugio* for camping at the end of the trail, but getting keys from Conaf is difficult. From there, in theory, you can hike another three hours to Río Pescado, but you'll need a machete and it's really not worth it.

Buses Peter (☑cell 8383-1172) has two buses on Monday, Wednesday and Friday from Ancud to Chepu. The 6:30am bus picks up folks at the Petrobras gas station on the corner of Prat and Goycolea (it drives by slowly, flag it down!), while the second, at 4pm, leaves from the inter-rural bus station. Buses return to Ancud at 7:45am and 5:45pm (CH$1800, one hour). If coming by bus, ignore the creative marketing of the competition, telling you EcoLodge is full or otherwise undesirable.

you'll also find a fussy Banco de Chile ATM). Check at the Cruz del Sur sales office around the corner on Yungay for complete published schedules.

🛏 Sleeping & Eating

Hospedaje Costanera   GUESTHOUSE $
(☑065-269-1230; ray.paredes.d@gmail.com; Diego Bahamonde 141; per person without bathroom CH$10,000, s/d from CH$20,000/22,000; 🅿🛜)
It isn't the only game in town, but it boasts the best sea views (though some are obstructed by electrical wires) and prime location 50m from El Chejo. Ask for one of the front rooms to get a glimpse, but avoid No 3 as there is no room for luggage!

★**El Chejo**   CHILEAN $
(Diego Bahamonde 251; mains CH$3000-5000; ⏰9am-midnight; 🛜) A family-run treasure. El Chejo is no gourmet restaurant, it offers honest food prepared with love by a family that fawns over its patrons. There's no menu – you get what's good that day.

That could mean starting with the excellent *empanada de centolla* (a fried pastry filled with king crab) followed by a choice of several locally caught fish, all washed down with a sampling of Chilote fruit liqueurs (try the *murtado*, a medicinal berry). Some complain it's greasy, but service is still brimming with Chilote personality. *Curanto al hoyo* (curanto prepared in the traditional way in an earth oven) is served Sundays in high season (CH$4500).

Barlovento's
CHILEAN $

(Yungay 08; meals CH$3000-7000; ⊘10am-6pm Mon-Thu, to 2am Fri-Sat, to 10pm Sun; ☎) Like others in town, this menu-less seaview bar and restaurant serves what's fresh that day. The food is typical – empanadas, congrio, salmon – and service is friendly. It's the best spot for a beer as well, including the sporadic craft brew hidden among the Escudos in the fridge.

Isla Mechuque

☑ 065

The further you venture into Chiloé's smaller islands, the more it feels as if you've traveled back in time. Isla Mechuque is only 45 minutes by boat from Tenaún, but feels like it's caught in a bygone era. A part of the Islas Chauques – considered Chiloé's most beautiful island chain – Mechuque is small but stunning. There are two museums, *tejuela* homes, a splendid viewpoint, a picturesque bridge, famous *curanto al hoyo* and *palafitos* – it's like a mini Chiloé offering all of the larger archipelago's attractions condensed down into an area that makes for an easy and memorable day trip.

If you want to spend the night, the new **Hospedaje Maria Humilde** (☑cell 9012-6233; r per person without bathroom CH$15,000) is a perfectly reasonable option.

Several boats make the trip from Dalcahue's fishing dock each week. **Ingrid Andrea** (☑cell 9408-7842) departs at noon on Tuesdays; **Ultima Esperanza** (☑cell 9525-9605) and **Doña Luisa II** (☑cell 9444-0123) both depart at 1pm Wednesdays and the latter again at 4pm on Thursday; and the **Doña Luisa** (☑cell 9376-4088) leaves Saturdays at 12:30pm. Returns are available

at 7am Monday, Tuesday and Friday; and 7:30am Thursday. The fare ranges between CH$2000 and CH$3500 depending on the boat.

Other departures may be available the rest of the week except Sunday, but a tour with Turismo Pehuén in Castro is the easiest way to explore Mechuque.

Dalcahue

☑ 065

In Huilliche, Dalcahue means 'Dalca's Place' and it is named after the boats (*dalcas*) constructed by Chiloé's first inhabitants. It's a feisty town facing the inner sea of the island and is famous for its vibrant Sunday crafts fair. It's also the jumping-off point for Isla Quinchao, one of archipelagic Chile's more accessible and interesting islands, and Isla Mechugue.

◉ Sights

Nuestra Señora de Los Dolores
CHURCH

Founded in 1849, this church is another one of the island's 16 Unesco World Heritage sites (take special note of the painting behind the entrance door; the juxtaposition of Jesus with Chiloé's mythological characters was used as Jesuit propaganda to convert the indigenous inhabitants). A complete restoration is due to finish by late 2015.

Crafts Fair
MARKET

(⊘9am-6pm Dec-Feb, to 5pm Sun Mar-Nov) You'll find the island's most authentic arts and crafts here, dominated by sweaters, socks, and hats woven from *oveja* (wool) and dyed with natural pigments made from roots, leaves and iron-rich mud. It's open daily but at its best on Sundays, when all the surrounding islands participate.

CHILOÉ'S ICONIC WOODEN CHURCHES

Chiloé once boasted more than 150 gorgeous wooden *iglesias* (churches) and *capillas* (chapels), one of the region's main attractions; today, some 60 or so remain, 16 of which are Unesco World Heritage sites. They are almost all built in a similar fashion with a single tower in the front, slanted side roofs, arched entrances and attractive wooden shingles. Some boast amazing exteriors, some gorgeous surroundings, but the truly triumphant moment comes when you step inside – the interiors are completely unorthodox if your comparison is European or North American cathedrals. Count Achao, Castro, Tenaún, Colo and Aldachildo are among our favorites.

For tours to some of the island's less accessible churches, contact Chiloétnico (p293) in Castro.

WORTH A TRIP

TENAÚN

Tiny Tenaún is rural – 37km northeast along a gravel road from Dalcahue – but there are two very compelling reasons to visit. The magnificent **Iglesia de Nuestra Señora del Patrocinio** (1837), for which the town is named (Tenaún means 'three mounts'), is one of Chiloé's Unesco stunners, meticulously restored down to the last shingle. Its three magnificent blue towers, in stark contrast to almost any other church you will ever see, appear to be reflecting the cerulean blue sea that sits right across the street on orders from God Himself. Its distinctive stars and trimmings add to the surreal architecture.

Hospedaje Mirella (✆ cell 9647-6750; mirellamontana@gmail.com; r with/without bathroom incl breakfast CH$14,000/12,000; @ 🛜), located next to the church and part of the Agroturismo Network, makes it worth staying in Tenaún. The indomitable Mirella is an exceptional cook and is serious about making sure her guests enjoy the multicourse meals she prepares (CH$4000 to CH$8000). She does *curanto al hoyo*, great seafood empanadas, *cazuelas* or whatever fresh catch the fisherman grab that day. Try to call ahead. On a clear day, you can see Volcán Corcovado across the Gulf of Ancud from her front porch. She can also arrange boats to Isla Mechugue for up to four people (CH$30,000 return, 45 minutes).

On weekdays, there are over 15 buses between Castro and Tenaún (CH$1600, 1½ hours, 7:45am to 8pm), half that on Saturday and just three on Sunday (9:10am, 4:10pm and 6pm), stopping in Dalcahue (CH$800) along the way. **Expresos Tenaún** (✆ cell 9875-6960) is a good source for up-to-date timetables of all buses. The (almost correct) schedule is posted on the window of Minimercado Ita (not Anita) on the main road through town.

🛏 Sleeping & Eating

Hostal Encanto Patagon
GUESTHOUSE $

(✆ 065-264-1651; www.hostalencantopatagon. blogspot.com; Perdro Montt 148; dm per person CH$8000, r without bathroom per person CH$10,000, all incl breakfast; P @ 🛜) You'll need to sleep on a boat to get closer to the sea than this rambling, 100-year-old Chilota treasure of a home. Hardwood floors throughout and common areas chock full of antiquated charm are highlights, as is Cecilia and her home-cooked local meals (CH$3000).

Hostal Lanita
GUESTHOUSE $

(✆ 065-264-2020; www.lanitahostal.blogspot.com; O'Higgins 50B; r without bathroom per person incl breakfast from CH$13,000; P 🛜) This great-value B&B is just a block from the sea. There's a massive kitchen for guest use (lunch and dinner only) and shared-bath-only rooms are clean with comfortable beds and cozy down comforters. Ana, a friendly Valparaiso transplant, whips up a great little breakfast.

★ La Cocinería Dalcahue
CHILEAN $

(mains CH$2000-6000; ⏱ 9am-7pm) Tucked behind the crafts market, this is the place to go for a true taste of local color. It's a collection of kitchenette stalls run by grandmotherly types dishing up *curanto* and *cazuela*, pounding out *milcao* (potato bread) and dosing out Chilota sweets. Plop yourself down at the counter – locals prefer Doña Lula (No 8), her *cazuela* with beef and *luche* (algae) is outstanding – but go with your gut.

Dalca
CHILEAN $

(Calle Acceso Rampla s/n; mains CH$2500-8900; ⏱ 10am-midnight Mon-Sat, 11am-7:30pm Sun; 🛜) Dalcahue's top seafooder, doing excellent steamed fresh fish (*al jugo*, CH$3900) and *caldillo de mariscos* (shellfish stew, CH$2300), among others.

Refugio de Navagantes
CAFE $

(www.refugiodenavagantes.cl; San Martín 165; items CH$1700-3500; ⏱ 8am-11pm Dec 15-Feb, 1-8pm Wed-Sun Mar-Dec 14; 🛜) You could glide right past this perfectly shingled gem on the Plaza de Armas catering to Dalcahue's bold and beautiful, who come for excellent espresso, high-quality teas, wraps and desserts. The upstairs lounge monopolizes the scene.

Casita de Piedra
CAFE $

(Pedro Montt 144; items CH$900-2800; ⏱ 10:30am-2pm & 3:30-8pm Tue-Sat, to 7pm Sun; 🛜) This wonderful cafe houses a very stylish crafts shop on the 1st floor and an atmospheric waterfront spot for espresso, quiche, sandwiches and great lemon meringue pie on the 2nd floor.

ℹ Information

There is a BancoEstado ATM on Freire near the Copec gas station.

ℹ Getting There & Away

There is no bus terminal in Dalcahue. **Buses Dalcahue** runs buses to Castro (CH$800, 30 minutes) and Mocopulli (CH$600), for airport access, every 15 minutes from a stop on Freire in front of Supermercado Otimarc between Henriquez and Eugenin. You can also catch buses at various points up and down the main street of Freire. **Cruz del Sur** (☎065-264-1050; San Martín 102; ⊘8:30am-1pm & 2:30-7pm Mon-Sat) has two buses per day to Ancud (CH$1700) and Puerto Montt (CH$6000) leaving at 9:10am and 3:15pm; there's an extra 7pm departure on Sunday. Buses depart from the office on San Martín right next to the church. Buses between Castro and Tenaún (CH$800) pass here several times per day. Catch them along the main street.

Ferries for Isla Quinchao leave continuously between 6am and 1am. Pedestrians go free, but try and time it so you cross with an Achao-bound bus as you'll need to be on it once you get to the other side. Cars cost CH$5000 (round trip). Boats also leave here for Isla Mechuque (p289) several days per week – the schedule is available at the Aramda de Chile office in the white building near the fishing dock.

Isla Quinchao

☑065

The elongated island of Quinchao, easily accessed via a short ferry crossing from Dalcahue, is a hilly patchwork of pasturelands punctuated by small villages. A good road runs the length of the island and carries you through the island's most popular destinations, Curaco de Vélez and Achao. On a clear day, you have spectacular views to Chiloé to the west and the snowcapped mountains of Northern Patagonia to the southeast.

Curaco de Vélez

An unexpected treasure lies in wait in the form of lovely Curaco de Vélez, the first town you come to along the main road from the ferry dock on Isla Quinchao. A superbly tranquil town, it's well worth spending an afternoon strolling the streets here, taking in the fascinating two- and three-story ornately shingled wooden homes and eight traditional water mills for which the town is known.

Don't miss the underground crypt of War of the Pacific hero Galvarino Riveros Cárdenas – he's buried right in the square!

The buses that run frequently between Achao and Dalcahue stop in Curaco.

Achao

When the early-morning fog rolls into the village of Achao, 22km southeast of Dalcahue, it can be an eerie sight, leaving no doubt you are in a remote Chilote seaside town. Though it lacks some of the indisputable charm and stillness of Curaco, Achao, too, is a worthwhile stop for its landmark church and outstanding architecture – not to mention stupendous views across to mainland Chile on a clear day. People from nearby islands come to Achao to sell their wares and produce, creating quite a buzz of activity along its small jetty and adjacent Feria Artisanal.

There is a BancoEstado ATM at the corner of Delicias and Velesquez.

◉ Sights

★**Iglesia Santa María de Loreto** CHURCH
(⊘11am-12:45pm Tue-Sat, 2-4pm Sun) Achao's 18th-century Jesuit church, Iglesia Santa María de Loreto, on the south side of the Plaza de Armas, is Chiloé's oldest (1740) and also a Unesco World Heritage site. Crowned by a 25m tower, it has alerce shingles and is held together by wooden pegs rather than nails. The church has been slowly restored, with new wood juxtaposing the old, but its restoration has remained faithful to the original design.

Museo de Achao MUSEUM
(cnr Delicias & Amunátegui; admission CH$300; ⊘10am-7pm Dec-Mar) Museo de Achao highlights aspects of the Chono people of Achao and other indigenous groups in Chiloé. Wood products, weavings, stones and plants used for tinting materials are all elegantly presented with informative material (in Spanish).

Grupo Artesanal Llingua MARKET
(cnr Serrano & Ricardo Jara; 10am-4pm Mon, Thu & Fri) The Grupo Artesanal Llingua, artisans from the nearby Isla Llingua, have a well-stocked market of their crafts including woven coffee cups, handbags and breadbaskets. It's only open on days when the ferry comes over from Isla Llingua.

🛏 Sleeping & Eating

In the busy summer season everything can get booked up and most places close down during the winter. If you're not fussed about seaviews, pop into Restaurante El Medan on Serrano as well.

Hospedaje Plaza　　　　GUESTHOUSE $
(☑065-266-1283; Amunátegui 20; s/d incl breakfast CH$8000/16,000, without bathroom CH$7000/14,000) A friendly family home that is right on the plaza. It's kind of like staying at grandma's house.

Mar y Velas　　　　CHILEAN, SEAFOOD $
(Serrano 2; mains CH$4500-8000; ⊘9am-1am) Overlooking the bustling jetty (and usually a thick blanket of intimidating fog) is this recommended seafood restaurant with an extensive menu and flirtatious servers. Try the house-style fish smothered in cheese, sausage and mussels.

ℹ Getting There & Away

The **bus terminal** (cnr Miraflores & Zañartu) is a block south of the church. Buses run daily to Dalcahue (CH$1200), Castro (CH$1600) and Curaco de Velez (CH$700) every 15 to 30 minutes. **Queilen Bus** (☑065-266-1345; www.queilenbus. cl; Bus Terminal; ⊘6:30-7am, 10am-1pm, 2-6pm & 9:30-10pm Mon-Fri, 10-11am Sun) also goes to Puerto Montt (CH$7000) Monday to Saturday at 7am, and 1pm Sunday. **Marorl Bus** (☑cell 9905-6884; Bus Terminal) goes at 6:30am Monday to Saturday and 11am on Sunday.

Castro

☑065 / POP 41,600

Using some poetic license here, if there is one place to call Chiloé cosmopolitan, it's Castro, where all the idiosyncrasies and attractions of Chiloé are nicely packaged in the Big City. At times loud and boisterous like some working class towns in Chile, the capital of the archipelago somehow retains its local Chilote character side by side with a dash of modern development, comfortable tourism infrastructure and a burgeoning trendy side. Just 85km south of Ancud, it is located in the dead center of the island, making it the main transportation hub and a perfect base for exploring attractions further afield. The city sits on a bluff above its sheltered estuary lined with distinctive *palafito* houses.

The earthquake in 1960 destroyed the port, the railway and the town hall as well as some *palafitos,* but Castro rebounded and turned itself into an easily digestible destination that's navigable on foot. Perhaps the greatest single attraction is simply walking down the streets and around the central plaza, soaking up all of Castro's curious energy.

⊙ Sights

Castro is the best place to see the *palafitos*. From the street, they resemble any other house in town, but the backsides jut over the water and, at high tide, serve as piers with boats tethered to the stilts. This truly singular architecture – technically illegal – can be seen along six areas in town. The postcard view from land is the **Puente Gamboa Mirador** just west of centro.

★ Iglesia San Francisco de Castro　　　　CHURCH
(San Martín; ⊘9:30am-10pm Jan & Feb, to 12:30pm & 3:30-8:30pm Mar-Dec) Italian Eduardo Provasoli chose a marriage of neo-Gothic and classical architecture in his design for the elaborate Iglesia San Francisco, one of Chiloé's Unesco gems and finished in 1912 to replace an earlier church that burned down (which had replaced an even earlier church that had burned down).

The church is an unconventional visual delight – yellow with violent and mauve trim. Inside, the varnished-wood interior is stunning. It is best to visit on a sunny day – if you are lucky enough – as the interior is more charming illuminated by the rows of stained-glass windows.

Iglesia Nuestra Señora de Gracia de Nercón　　　　CHURCH
(Nercón; ⊘10am-12:30pm & 1:30-6:30pm) Just 4km south of Castro is another of Chiloe's Unesco-recognized churches, restored in 2012. Built from cypress and larch wood between 1887 and 1888, its prominent 25m tower can be viewed from Ruta 5. Notable interiors include an all-wood sculpture of St Michael with a demon and columns painted to look like marble. A small visitor's center is next door, giving this church better tourism infrastructure than most. It's a CH$2500 taxi ride from central Castro.

Museo Regional de Castro　　　　MUSEUM
(Esmeralda 255; ⊘9:30am-7pm Mon-Fri, 9:30am-6:30pm Sat, 10:30am-1pm Sun Jan & Feb, 9:30am-1pm & 3-6:30pm Mon-Fri, 9:30am-1pm Sat Mar-Dec) FREE This museum, half a block from Plaza de Armas, houses a well-organized collection

MYTHOLOGICAL CREATURES OF CHILOÉ

For centuries Chiloé's distinctive mythology swirled through the foggy towns, blew from one island to the next and gave form to the culture of the Chilote people. Outside the commercial centers, these traditional beliefs are still very much alive today. The beliefs, syncretic with the island's Catholicism, weave a story of the creation of the island, tales of destruction on the stormy seas and warnings about straying from the 'clean' way of life.

Brujos (*broo*-hos) The center of Chiloé's mythology, *brujos* are warlocks with black-magic powers, bent on corrupting and harming normal Chilote folks. They are based in a secret location (most likely a cave) near Quicaví.

Cai-Cai Vilú (kai-kai-vee-*loo*) The Serpent God of the Water who waged a battle against Ten-Ten Vilú (Serpent God of the Earth) for supremacy over the domain. Cai-Cai Vilú eventually lost but was successful in covering enough territory with water that Chiloé stayed separated from the mainland.

El Caleuche (el-ka-le-*oo*-che) A glowing pirate ship piloted by singing, dancing *brujos*. Their melodious songs draw commercial vessels into *El Caleuche's* trap. It is capable of sailing into the wind and navigating under the water's surface.

Fiura (fee-*oo*-ra) A short, forest-dwelling hag with a ravenous sexual appetite and breath that causes sciatica in humans and is enough to kill smaller animals.

Invunche (een-*voon*-che) The grotesque guardian of the cave of the *brujos*. Invunche was born human, but the *brujos* disfigured him as he grew: turning his head 180 degrees, attaching one leg to his spine and sewing one of his arms under his skin. He eats human flesh and cat's milk, and is extremely dangerous.

Pincoya (peen-*koi*-a) A naked woman of legendary beauty who personifies the fertility of the coasts of Chiloé and its richness of marine life. On the rocky shores she dances to her husband's music. The way that she faces determines the abundance of the sea harvest.

Ten-Ten Vilú (ten-ten-vee-*loo*) Serpent God of the Earth.

Trauco (*trow*-ko) A repugnant yet powerful gnome who can kill with a look and fell trees with his stone hatchet. He is irresistible to young virgins, giving them impure erotic dreams and sometimes even a 'mysterious' child out of wedlock.

Viuda (vee-*oo*-da) Meaning 'the widow,' Viuda is a tall, shadowy woman dressed in black with milk-white bare feet. She appears in solitary places and seduces lonely men. The next day she abandons them where she pleases.

La Voladora (la-vo-la-*do*-ra) A witch messenger, who vomits out her intestines at night so that she is light enough to fly and deliver messages for the *brujos*. By the next morning, she swallows her intestines and reassumes human female form.

---

of Huilliche relics, musical instruments, traditional farm implements and Chilota wooden boat models, and exhibits on the evolution of Chiloé's towns. Its black-and-white photographs of the 1960 earthquake help you to understand the impact of the tragic event.

🖝 Tours

★ **Chiloétnico**   CULTURAL, ADVENTURE TOURS
(☎ 065-630-951; www.chiloetnico.cl; Ernesto Riquelme 1228) This highly recommended trilingual (fluent English and German) agency

is doing the right things in the right places. Jata runs great mountain-biking and hiking trips to Parque Nacional Chiloé, Parque Tantauco and nearby islands; and cultural trips out to some of Chiloé's more obscure Unesco churches on the less-trampled secondary islands where tourism is still a novelty.

Also rents camping gear and bikes.

Chiloé Natural   KAYAKING
(☎ cell 6319-7388; www.chiloenatural.com; Pedro Montt 210) 🖉 This extremely friendly, environmentally conscious agency specializes in kayaking, both as rentals (CH$5000 per

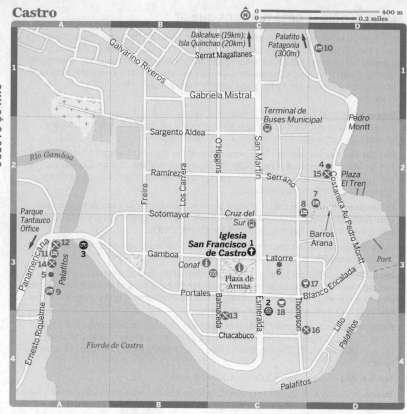

hour) as well as half-/multiday trips around Castro and further afield (from CH$3500 per person).

Turismo Pehuén WILDLIFE, GUIDED TOURS
(☑065-263-5254; www.turismopehuen.cl; Latorre 238) Highly regarded agency that organizes multiday tours to nearby islands such as Mechuque (from CH$50,000) and Parque Nacional Chiloé (from CH$31,000); also the official office for Naveira Austral in Castro.

✺ Festivals & Events

Festival Costumbrista CULTURAL
(☉Feb) Castro celebrates Festival Costumbrista in mid-February. It is a week-long party with folk music and dance, as well as traditional foods.

🛏 Sleeping

Castro offers a variety of affordable choices, mostly along San Martín and O'Higgins,

their immediate side streets, and the eastern end of Sotomayor, which turns into the wide concrete staircase called Barros Arana with a high concentration of *hospedajes* (budget accommodations).

Hostal Cordillera GUESTHOUSE $
(☑065-253-2247; www.hostalcordillera.cl; Barros Arana 175; r per person without bathroom CH$15,000, s/d CH$18,000/35,000, all incl breakfast; @🛜) Weather dragging you down? The firecracker owner here will smother you with motherly love and put a big smile on your face at this traveler's hub. You'll get some sea views, large bathrooms (two newly renovated ones upstairs), comfy beds, electric heaters and cable TV. There's a pleasant little deck out back where you can take in the water views over a few drinks. Also conveniently rents cars.

Hospedaje Mirador GUESTHOUSE $
(☑065-263-3795; maboly@yahoo.com; Barros Arana 127; r per person without bathroom

Castro

CH$14,000, s/d CH$25,000/35,000; $\boxed{P}$@🛜) One of the better Barros Arana choices, Mirador has some seaside views, fantastic bathrooms (by Chiloé standards), hearty breakfasts, a welcoming atmosphere and off-site parking.

Hostalomera　　　　　　　　　HOSTEL $
(☑ cell 9386-2454; www.hostalomera.com; Balmaceda 241; dm CH$8000; @🛜) Though primarily a restaurant, this artsy spot offers the best budget dorms in town.

Palafito Hostel　　　　　　　　HOSTEL $$
(☑ 065-253-1008; www.palafitohostel.com; Ernesto Riquelme 1210; dm CH$15,000, s/d CH$30,000/42,000; $\boxed{P}$@🛜) This flashpackers hostel sitting on Palafitos Gamboa with spiritual views over the Fiordo de Castro revolutionized Castro when it opened in 2008 and was the catalyst for turning the city into a hip destination. You pay more for a dorm here, but the quality (and lockers) outweighs the difference, with great breakfasts, dreamy views and a cabin-cool feel throughout.

Private parking runs CH$2000 per night but you can find spots on the street.

Palafito del Mar　　　　　BOUTIQUE HOTEL $$
(☑065-263-1622; www.palafitodelmar.cl; Pedro Montt 567; r from CH$50,000; 🛜) Of all the stylish *palafito* options in Castro, this minimalist, seven-room hotel along the northern *palafitos* boasts an important caveat: all rooms have pleasant terraces with full or partial seaviews, ready for you to kick your feet up with a bottle of Carménère. Cozy showers and bright mañío and tepú hardwoods throughout give it a stylish edge as well.

Palafito 1326　　　　　　BOUTIQUE HOTEL $$
(☑065-253-0053; www.palafito1326.cl; Ernesto Riquelme 1326; s/d incl breakfast from CH$52,000/62,000; @🛜) Following a Chilote design aesthetic carved entirely from tepú and cypress woods, this *palofito* design hotel has 12 smallish rooms with high-style touches like wool throws from Dalcahue. The fjord-view rooms make you feel like you're sleeping over wetlands.

✗ Eating

★ Hostalomera　　　　　　　　CHILEAN $
(www.hostalomera.com; Balmaceda 241; menu CH$2800; ⊙1-5pm Mon-Sat & 7-10pm Tue-Sat; 🛜) You can't eat this well in this cool kind of atmosphere for this price anywhere. How it can be done without bleeding money is an extraordinary question, but this art-fueled lunch hot spot offers five exceptional home-cooked choices per day, including an appetizer and juice for a wallet-friendly CH$2800.

The entirety of Castro – all races, religions, creeds and classes – converge amid tagged walls and seriously good food. The secret is out.

Café del Puente　　　CAFE, BREAKFAST $
(Ernesto Riquelme 1180b; mains CH$1200-5200; ⊙9am-9pm Tue-Sun; 🛜) Cure the breakfast blues (and more)! This atmospheric baby-blue cafe-teahouse over the water does everything you're missing: eggs, bacon, French toast, muesli, whole wheat bread... and does it well. Afternoon tea and classy sandwiches throughout the day.

★ Mercadito　　　CONTEMPORARY CHILEAN $$
(www.elmercaditodechiloe.cl; Pedro Montt 210; mains CH$6400-8200; ⊙1-4pm & 8-11pm Mon-Wed; 🛜) This wonderfully whimsical spot is the place in Castro proper for foodies. Creative takes calling on the wares of local farmers produce outstanding dishes that

CHILL AWAY: BEST OFF THE BEATEN PATH ESCAPES

Chiloé's raw beauty is everywhere, but escaping to some of the island's more remote corners is even more poetic. Here are a few far-flung top-end lodges and guesthouses that truly hide themselves away among the island's remote and rugged nature.

Tierra Chiloé (☎065-277-2080; www.tierrachiloe.com; Bahía Pullao, San José, Rilán Peninsula; full-board 2-night packages s/d US$1650/2300; P🕏@🛜) Formerly La Refugia, this dramatic upscale shelter on the edge of Chiloé's most important wetlands was purchased by Tierra Hotels in 2014, becoming the latest in a growing list of remote boutique lodges that includes properties in San Pedro de Atacama and Torres del Paine. The building, a striking, environmentally unobtrusive marriage of native woods (certified alerce wood, the sacred wood of the Mapuche; *Ulmo*, Chilean honey wood; and *mañío*) with unfinished concrete, frames the stunning countryside with 3m-high windows throughout the rooms and common area. A long hallway that seemingly narrows to a trapezoidal window – an architectural illusion only adding to this building's wonder – leads to the 12 rooms. Rates include meals, drinks and all excursions, which include trekking, horseback riding, sailing and kayaking.

Isla Bruja Lodge (☎cell 7732-7142; www.islabrujalodge.com; Estero Paildad, Comuna de Queilén; d/tr incl breakfast from CH$68,000/78,000; P@🛜) Hidden way away on the shores of the Palidad estuary southwest of Queiién, 15km or so from Ruta 5, a young Chilean-American couple have turned their cozy home into a wonderful and tasteful getaway. Homespun hospitality abounds, whether by Francisco and Marie or their domesticated sheep Torpé, who was abandoned by her mother and raised here. Hardwoods throughout the home give off a cabin-in-the-woods feel and you can see dolphins in the estuary right from the comforts of the outdoor hot tub (included in the price along with kayaks and bikes). It's popular with sailors, who ride right up.

Espejo de Luna (☎cell 7431-3090; www.espejodeluna.cl; Km 35 de la ruta Chonchi-Queiién; r per person incl lunch & dinner CH$93,000; P🛜) A massive sideways ship forms the reception and restaurant at this extremely cozy eco getaway 7km from Queiién. Four bungalows of various shapes and sizes are spread about 3 hectares, connected by wooden walkways wrapped in recycled fisherman's nets for grip. Each has a Mapudungun name – The Wisemen, the Family, the Lovers– the latter of which those seeking romance and solitude could tuck themselves away in for a week without coming up for air, except to visit the supremely private outdoor hot tub, hidden away in an arrayán forest.

present painstaking choices: crab phyllo dough wraps doused in vermouth, tempura hake over mashed fava beans, stuffed shells with surf clams in pil-pil sauce. Dishes tend towards the rich side, but it's worth it.

★ **Rucalaf Putemún**　　　　FUSION $$
(☎cell 9579-7571; www.rucalafputemun.cl; Km 3.6 de la Ruta a Rilán; mains CH$6800-8000; ⊙1-4pm & 8-11pm) In tiny Putemún (7km outside Castro on the way to the Rilan Peninsula and Dalcahue) is one of Chiloé's destination restaurants. In a colorful and cozy cabin-like room, tasteful regional art surrounds scrumptious contemporary Chilean gourmet food – red-wine-doused osso buco, *merluza* with blue cheese and white wine, organic wines – served by adorable staff in a rustic-refined atmosphere.

Save room for dessert: the *suspiro* of *murta com membrillo* (Chilean guava with quince) is both unique and to die for! A taxi from Castro costs CH$5000.

Mar y Canela　　CONTEMPORARY CHILEAN $$
(Ernesto Riquelme 1212; mains CH$7200-9200; ⊙1:30-4pm & 8-10pm Dec-Feb, closed Sun Mar-Nov; 🛜) Mar y Canela raised the bar on creative cuisine in Chiloé when it opened a few years back. Now this staunchly local and seasonal *palafito* bistro has competition, but it still offers one of the most innovation menus on the island. Also home to Castro's best crafts shop, Pura Isla.

Sacho　　　　　　　　SEAFOOD $$
(Thompson 213; mains CH$4200-10,000; ⊙noon-3:30pm & 8-11pm Tue-Sat, to 3:30pm Sun; 🛜) If you lived in Castro a decade ago, Sacho

was the only spot for a cultured meal. While an ever-evolving culinary scene emerges around it, this long-standing seafood staple with views has dug in its heels and held on. The atmosphere is semirefined (orange tablecloths, linen napkins) and there are loads of fresh fish preparations to choose from.

Drinking

Almud Bar
BAR

(Serrano 325; craft beer CH$2500-4000; ⊙6:30pm-2am Mon-Thu, 7:30pm-3:30am Fri, from 8:30pm Sat) The best proper bar in Castro – named after Chiloé's unit of measurement for potatoes – offers a wide range of cocktails, craft beers, sparking wines and some bar grub for it all to be chased by.

★Palafito Patagonia
CAFE

(Pedro Montt 651; coffee CH$1200-2200; ⊙9am-9pm Dec-16 Feb, noon-9pm Tue-Sat Mar-Dec 15; 🎧) This wonderful cafe-gallery takes coffee very seriously – Intelligentsia is served, one of North America's best – and is a pristine spot for a caffeine jolt, light bites and postcard views from its naturally lit lounge and breezy patio on the increasingly stylish northern *palafitos*. A very hip couple runs the show, which features regional art exhibitions as well.

Ristretto Café
CAFE, BAR

(Blanco 264; items CH$1200-2450; ⊙10am-10pm Mon-Fri, from 10:30am Sat; 🎧) An extensive coffee, tea and tapas menu and 25 or so beers, ensuring it's a nice spot for a drink as well.

Information

ATMs can be found at the numerous banks on or around the Plaza de Armas.

Conaf (☑065-253-2501; Gamboa 424; ⊙9am-1pm & 2-6pm Mon-Thu, to 5pm Fri) The official Chilean parks department has a limited amount of information in Spanish and English on Parque Nacional Chiloé.

CorreosChile (www.correos.cl; O'Higgins 388; ⊙9am-1:30pm & 3-6pm Mon-Fri, 9:30am-12:30pm Sat) On the west side of Plaza de Armas.

Hospital de Castro (www.hospitalcastro.gov.cl; Freire 852)

Parque Tantauco Office (☑065-263-3805; www.parquetantauco.cl; Panamericana Sur 1826; ⊙9am-6pm Jan & Feb, to 6pm Mon-Fri Mar-Dec) The official office of Parque Tantauco.

Tourist Information (☑065-254-7706; www. visitchiloe.cl; Plaza de Armas; ⊙10am-9pm Jan & Feb, to 7pm Mar-Dec) A large kiosk stocking some helpful brochures and maps.

✈ Getting There & Around

AIR

Castro's newish Aerodrómo Mocopulli, located 20km north of town, finally connects Chiloé with the rest of the country via commercial flights. **LAN** (☑065-263-2866; www.lan.com; O'Higgins 412; ⊙9am-1pm & 3-6:15pm Mon-Fri, 9:30am-1:15pm Sat) flies from Santiago via Puerto Montt five days a week on a varying schedule throughout the year.

BUS

Centrally located Castro is the major hub for bus traffic on Chiloé. There are two main bus terminals. The rural station, **Terminal de Buses Municipal** (San Martín), has the most services to smaller destinations around the island and some long-distance services. Buses to Mocopulli (CH$600), Dalcahue (CH$800), Chonchi (CH$800), Isla Quinchao (CH$1400 to CH$1600) and Tenaún (CH$1500) all leave from here as well as Quemchi. **Queilen Bus** (☑065-253-2103; www.queilenbus.cl) and an office representing Cruz del Sur and others also operates out of here to most destinations of importance, including Punta Arenas (Monday, Wednesday and Friday in high season, 6:25am).

Buses Ojeda (☑cell 6760-8846) and **Union Express** (☑cell 6668-3531) offer the most departures from here for Cucao and Parque Nacional Chiloé on the west coast, 15 times per day between them (CH$1800, 8:30am to 5:45pm). Sit on the right side for the most outstanding views of Lago Cucao.

The second terminal, the main depot of **Cruz del Sur** (☑065-263-5152; www.buscruz delsur.cl; San Martín 486), focuses on transportation to the main Chilote cities, Quellón and Ancud, and long-distance services, including including Punta Arenas (Tuesday, Thursday and Saturday, 7am) and Bariloche (Thursday and Sunday, 6:45am).

Starting sample fares and times are as follows (prices may fluctuate with the quality of the bus/classes):

DESTINATION	COST (CH$)	DURATION (HR)
Ancud	1500	1½
Bariloche (AR)	21,200	13
Concepción	25,000	13
Puerto Montt	6200	3¾
Quellón	2000	2
Quemchi	1500	1½
Santiago	31,000	16
Temuco	12,000	10
Valdivia	9500	7
Punta Arenas	41,000	36

BOAT

Naveira Austral (☎ 065-263-5254; www.navieraustral.cl; Latorre 238) Summer ferries to/from Chaitén depart Sunday at midnight in January and February. Fares range from CH$12,000 (seat) to CH$25,700 (berth with window). Vehicles cost CH$82,000.

Parque Nacional Chiloé

Running back from the pounding Pacific coastline, and over extensive stands of native evergreen forest, the 430-sq-km **Parque Nacional Chiloé** (☎ 065-297-0724; adult/child CH$1500/750; ⏱ 9am-8:30pm Dec-Mar 15, to 6:30pm Mar 16-Nov) is located only 30km west of Chonchi and 54km west of Castro. The park teems with Chilote wildlife, ranging from 110 different types of bird, to foxes and the reclusive pudú (the world's smallest deer), which inhabits the shadowy forests of the contorted tepú tree. Within the park and situated along the eastern perimeter are a number of Huiliche indigenous communities, some of which are involved with the management of campsites within the park.

The park comprises three sections. The northern sector is called **Chepu** and includes Isla Metalqui (and its sea-lion colony) and is not truly accessible without a machete and a pioneering spirit. In addition, Metalqui is highly restricted because of ecological concerns and can only be visited with special arrangements from the parks service. The middle sector, **Abtao**, is restricted by Conaf and accessible only by an 18km hike from the Pichihué property. The more accessible southern sector, **Chanquín**, contains the majority of the eight official hikes in the park, ranging from quick jaunts to 25km slogs.

Visitors are at the mercy of Pacific storms, so expect lots of rain. The mean annual rainfall at Cucao, the park's main epicenter near the southern Chanquín sector, is 2200mm, and anyone planning more than an hour-long walk should have water-resistant footwear, woolen socks and a decent rain jacket. Insect repellent is not a bad idea, either. There is a **Conaf visitor center** (⏱ 9am-8:30pm Dec-Mar 15, to 6:30pm Mar 16-Nov) 1km past the bridge from Cucao with park info in five languages. The center covers flora and fauna extensively and it also houses a small museum.

Cucao is your last chance to pick up supplies, although you will find better prices and wider selections in Chonchi or Castro.

Sights & Activities

The raw beauty of this national park is best appreciated on foot, and there are several hikes that can easily hold your attention for a day or two. The **Sendero Interpretivo El Tepual**, a short 1km nature trail built with tree trunks, branches and short footbridges, loops through dense, gloomy forest. The **Sendero Dunas de Cucao** starts from the visitor center and heads 2km through a remnant of coastal forest to a ocean viewpoint and a long, white sandy beach.

Day hikers can follow the coast north on a 3km trail to **Lago Huelde** or a shorter 1.5km trek to **Playa Cucao**, a roaring Pacific beach. The most popular route is the **Sendero Chanquín-Cole Cole**, a 25km hike (about five hours one way) located along the coast, past Lago Huelde to Río Cole Cole. Lots of people set out to make this hike and back in one day, but nobody usually makes it further than the indigenous settlement at Huentemó, where there are basic camping facilities as well as a *refugio* for CH$4000 per person (equipped with a kitchen) and a local *hospedaje*. The hike extends another 8km north to **Río Anay**, passing through a stand of arrayán to arrive at another rustic *refugio* in reasonable shape. Keep in mind, you take the gravel highway about 6km past the visitors center before it dead-ends on the beach (near the end of this highway, you'll find one of your last chances for food: El Arco de Noé Café).

In Cole Cole, Conaf-run camping is CH$1500 per person and there's also a basic *refugio* with a kitchen and bathroom for CH$2000 per person.

Tours

Palafito Trip ADVENTURE TOUR (☎ cell 9884-9552; www.palafitotrip.cl; Sector Chanquín, Palafito Cucao Hostel) Can arrange kayaking, horseback riding and trekking in and around Parque Nacional Chiloé. Also rents bikes (per day CH$16,000).

Sleeping & Eating

Most accommodations and restaurants are in Sector Chanquín, just past the bridge from Cucao.

Camping y Cabañas del Parque CAMPGROUND $ (☎ 065-971-027; www.parquechiloe.cl; dm CH$12,000, campsites per person CH$5000, cabins from CH$48,000; 🅿🛜) Under concession from

---

WORTH A TRIP

THE PRESIDENT'S PARK

Among the world's 25 biodiversity hot spots, **Parque Tantauco** (☑065-263-3805; www.parquetantauco.cl; Panamericana Sur 1826, Castro; adult/child CH$3500/500) – created and owned by Chilean business magnate and former president Sebastián Piñera, and run by his foundation (Fundación Futura) – is a private nature reserve encompassing 130km of trails throughout 1180 sq km west of Quellón. The park is home to native otters, Darwin foxes and pudús (small deer, indigenous to Chile), as well as both the world's largest mammal (blue whales) and its smallest marsupial (*monito del monte* or 'little mountain monkey'), and is a very worthwhile off-the-beaten-track find for hiking, camping and watching wildlife. Spending time here usually means you are isolated with nature, sharing air with way more Valdivian temperate rainforest than The North Face set (access is limited to eight trekkers per day).

Tantauco is the only place outside of Torres del Paine that you traverse a park by hut-to-hut hiking over multiday treks (there are three- and five-day options). Along the way, there are basic **refugios** (r per person CH$8000) and an absolutely wonderful and welcomed **guesthouse** (r with/without bathroom incl breakfast CH$60,000/50,000; ☎) in Inío, a fascinating fishing village at the bottom of Chiloé where the trek ends. From Inío, you'll need to charter a plane (CH$180,000, maximum three passengers) or, in high season, a boat to Quellón (per person CH$60,000).

For more information, check out the the park's office in Castro.

Conaf, this well-equipped camping and cabin complex lies about 100m beyond the visitors center and into the park. The cabins are surprisingly nice, with stylish furnishings, running water, hot showers, firewood and all the modcons. Dorms are low season only.

There is great little **cafe** (mains CH$1500-7900; ⏰9am-6:30pm Dec 15-Mar, 10am-6pm Apr-Dec 14; ☎) on site that is not only great for fueling up for a hike but handles reception as well.

Cucao Home   GUESTHOUSE $
(☑cell 5400-5944; cucaohome@gmail.com; Laura Vera, Cucao; dm CH$7000, s/d without bathroom CH$15,000/30,000; ℗@☎) A young upstart from Puerto Natalas has rented this traditional budget option in Cucao (formerly Hospedaje Paraiso) and given it a backpacker-friendly makeover. There's a small cafe and it has the cheapest dorm beds in town. It's inside a faded pink house a few hundred meters before the bridge and offers a fantastic river view.

Hospedaje Chucao   GUESTHOUSE $
(☑cell 9787-7319; Huentemó; r per person without bathroom incl breakfast CH$8000) Simple *hospedaje* for crashing at Huentemó.

⭐**Palafito Cucao Hostel**   HOTEL $$
(☑065-297-1164; www.hostelpalafitocucao.cl; Sector Chanquín; dm CH$15,000, s/d/tr CH$40,000/50,000/70,000, all incl breakfast; ℗@☎) This equally chic sister hotel of Palafito 1326 and

Palafito Hostel in Castro offers by far the best and most comfortable bed in Cucao, whether you lay your head in the stylish private rooms or equally fashionable six-bed dorm.

It's a beautiful hotel on the Lago Cucao, with a cozy common area and kitchen, and a lovely wraparound terrace with outstanding views and an outdoor hot tub.

Parador Darwin   GUESTHOUSE $$
(☑cell 6350-9051; www.paradordarwincucao.cl; Sector Chanquín; s/d incl breakfast CH$40,000/46,000; ⏰closed Apr-Oct; @☎) A tragic fire and a death in the family has upended what once was Cucao's most interesting option and one of Chiloé's best restaurants. Now under concession to the owner of Turismo Pehuen in Castro, the rooms have been done up, new black ceramic bathrooms added and a snug common area converted from the old garage. It's still comfortable, but there's no restaurant and its soul will be missed.

⭐**El Arrayán**   CHILEAN $
(Sector Chanquín; mains CH$3000-7000; ⏰1-10pm, closed Jun & Jul; ☎) A lovely couple runs what is easily Cucao's best restaurant, a welcoming spot where everything from the pisco sours to sophisticated versions of Chilean staples are made from scratch in-house. Octopus, shrimp, fresh fish and beef dishes are chased by good wines in a room warmed by the massive dining room *parrilla*. Good desserts, too.

ℹ️ Getting There & Away

Cucao is 54km from Castro and 34km west of Chonchi via a bumpy gravel road, passable in all but the most inclement weather. There is regular bus service between Cucao and Castro (CH$1800, 7:30am to 6:30pm).

Quellón

While it's the southern terminus for one of the world's great highways (the Panamericana Hwy, also known as Hwy 5) and a salmon epicenter, Quellón is for the most part an unsophisticated town, one you're likely only to see coming or going from the ferry to Chaitén.

If you come in on the ferry and have had enough traveling for a day, there are some excellent eats, but a general drunken-sailor sentiment about the place makes Quellón a get in, get out town. Don't wander west of the Naveira Austral office on the *costanera* or around the bus station, especially at night.

For cash, there is a Banco de Chile at Juan Ladrilleros 315.

🛏️ Sleeping & Eating

Hotel El Chico Leo
HOTEL $$

(☎065-268-1567; ligorina@hotmail.com; Costanera Pedro Montt 325; r per person without bathroom CH$9000, r CH$15,000-28,000; 🅿️🛜) El Chico Leo is cramped, but it's the obvious and most comfortable choice, though the low-ceilinged bathrooms pose a serious challenge for taller travelers. The justifiably popular restaurant is known for its seafood, especially the ginormous *curanto* (CH$5500), which easily feeds two.

Taberna Nos
SPANISH $

(O'Higgins 150; tapas CH$2000-6000; ⊗8pm-4am Mon-Sat; 🛜) If you spend one night in Quellón, it should be at this local secret run by a Spanish music aficionado. Inside a residential black house, there are excellent tapas and drinks in a bar that's way too cool for its address.

Isla Sandwich
CAFE $

(Juan Ladrilleros 190; sandwiches CH$3500-6500; ⊗10:30am-9pm Mon-Fri, noon-8pm Sat; 🛜) This tiny cafe is Quellón's safe haven for sophisticates. You'll find great espresso and tea and a wealth of huge gourmet sandwiches. Requisite lunch stop.

Ask about pleasant rooms above for CH$18,000.

ℹ️ Getting There & Away

Buses to Castro (CH$200, two hours, 6:40am to 7:30pm) leave from **bus terminal** (📲065-268-1284; cnr Pedro Aguirre Cerda & Miramar), where you'll also find the the Cruz del Sur ticket office. There are also services to Puerto Montt (CH$8000, 6:40am to 6:10pm) and Temuco (CH$13,000, 9:10am).

Naviera Austral (📲065-268-2207; www.navieraustral.cl; Pedro Montt 457; ⊗9am-1pm & 3-7pm Mon-Fri, 10am-1pm & 4-10pm Sat) Sails the *Don Baldo* to Chaitén on Thursday at 3am throughout the year. Passengers cost CH$12,000 (seat) to CH$25,700 (berth with window) and vehicles CH$82,000. The *Barcaza Jacaf* also sails to Puerto Chacabuco on Wednesday and Saturday at 11pm throughout the year. Prices run CH$15,500 for a seat CH$125,100 for a vehicle). The trip takes 28 hours.

Northern Patagonia

Best Places to Eat

➡ Mamma Gaucha (p319)

➡ Cocinas Costumbristas (p305)

➡ Ruibarbo (p320)

➡ Dalí (p320)

➡ Mi Casita de Té (p314)

Best Places to Stay

➡ Fundo Los Leones (p314)

➡ Bordebaker Lodge (p328)

➡ Destino No Turistico (p327)

➡ Terra Luna (p327)

➡ Patagonia House (p319)

Why Go?

For a century, Northern Patagonia has been the most rugged and remote part of continental Chile, the place where scant pioneers quietly set forth a Wild West existence. While life here may still be tough for its residents, it doesn't lack for scenery. Exuberant rainforest, scrubby steppe and unclimbed peaks crowd the horizon, but the essence of this place is water, from the clear cascading rivers to the turquoise lakes, massive glaciers and labyrinthine fjords.

Southbound visitors often bypass Northern Patagonia on a sprint to Torres del Paine, but its backcountry treasures are pay dirt to the adventurous traveler.

The mostly gravel Carretera Austral rumbles from Puerto Montt to Villa O'Higgins, some 1200km south. Ferry connections are required for northerly roadless stretches where mountains meet the sea. Though sections north of Coyhaique are now being paved, the iconic challenge of driving the rest still remains.

When to Go
Coyhaique

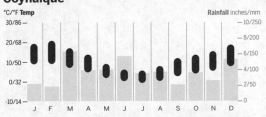

Nov–Mar Warmest months and the best bus connections on the Carretera Austral.

Feb Festival Costumbrista celebrates pioneer culture; parties in most small towns.

Jul–Aug Blue sky days around Coyhaique, with nearby skiing and snowshoeing.

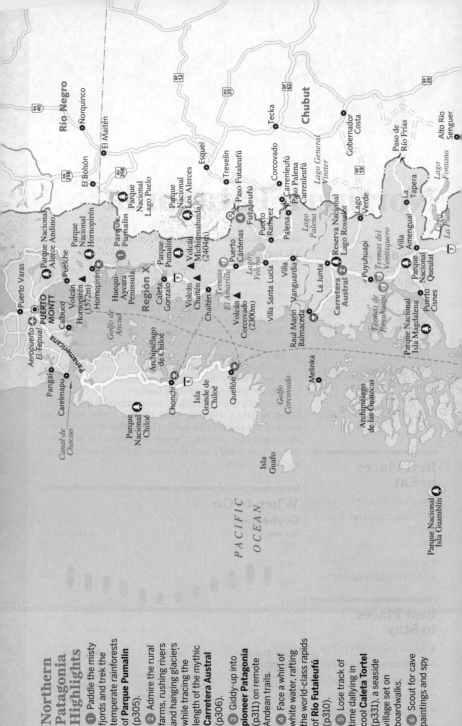

Northern Patagonia Highlights

1 Paddle the misty fjords and trek the temperate rainforests of **Parque Pumalín** (p305).

2 Admire the rural farms, rushing rivers and hanging glaciers while tracing the length of the mythic **Carretera Austral** (p306).

3 Giddy-up into **pioneer Patagonia** (p311) on remote Andean trails.

4 Face a whirl of white water, rafting the world-class rapids of **Río Futaleufú** (p310).

5 Lose track of time dallying in cool **Caleta Tortel** (p331), a seaside village set on boardwalks.

6 Scout for cave paintings and spy

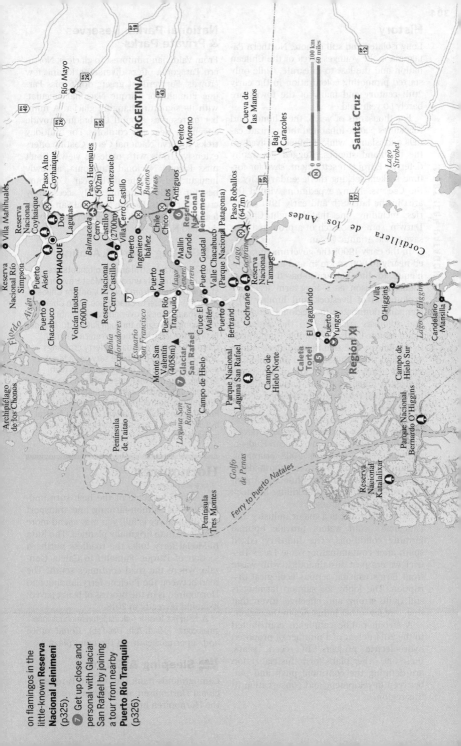

on flamingos in the little-known **Reserva Nacional Jeinimeni** (p325).

7 Get up close and personal with Glaciar San Rafael by joining a tour from nearby **Puerto Río Tranquilo** (p326).

History

Long isolated and still remote, Northern Patagonia is the youngest area of the Chilean nation and the last to integrate. Chile only started promoting colonization in the early 20th century and many of the towns are barely 50 years old.

For thousands of years, the Chonos and Alacalufes people inhabited the intricate canals and islands, while Tehuelches lived on the mainland steppes. Rugged geography deterred European settlement, save for fortune seekers seeking the legendary 'City of the Caesars.' Many expeditions visited the area in the late 18th and early 19th centuries, including one that brought Charles Darwin, some in search of a protected passage to the Atlantic Ocean.

In the early 1900s the government granted nearly 10,000 sq km in and around Coyhaique to the Valparaíso-based Sociedad Industrial Aisén as a long-term lease for exploitation of livestock and lumber. The company dominated the regional economy, and colonists trickled into the region to claim remote lands for farming. Encouraged by a Chilean law that rewarded clearance with land titles, the Sociedad and colonists burned nearly 30,000 sq km of forest and destroyed much of Aisén's native southern beech in fires that raged for nearly a decade in the 1940s.

The region is sparsely populated, most notably south of Coyhaique, an area devastated by the 1991 eruption of Volcán Hudson. As with Volcán Chaitén's 2008 eruptions, it dumped tons of ash over thousands of square kilometers in both Chile and Argentina, ruining cropland and killing livestock by burying pasture grasses.

Salmon farming is a major industry and Patagonia's cold waters provide optimal farming conditions. The industry edged south after contaminating some Lakes District waters past sustainability, with waste from farms causing serious ecological disruption. The lobby for salmon farming is still quite strong and effective, given that there are few other industries in the region.

A strong public campaign contributed to the 2014 defeat of a number of proposed hydroelectric projects. In recent years, these and other plans for industrialization are defining the continual push and pull between development and conservation in this region.

National Parks, Reserves & Private Parks

From Valdivian rainforest to glaciers, Northern Patagonia offers diverse parks and few crowds. For verdant green, don't miss Parque Pumalín or Parque Nacional Queulat, with its signature hanging glacier. A number of reserves around Coyhaique provide adventure near city comforts. For multiday treks, Reserva Nacional Cerro Castillo offers extensive trails with majestic views. Don't miss Parque Nacional Patagonia, a newly inaugurated private park near Cochrane best for wildlife-watching. Only accessed by cruises or boats, Parque Nacional San Rafael features the magnificent glaciers of Campo de Hielo Norte.

❶ Getting There & Around

The Carretera Austral and its offshoots are remote and mostly unpaved. Most travelers start with a ferry from Puerto Montt or Chiloé to Chaitén or Puerto Chacabuco; fly to Chaitén or Coyhaique; or go overland via Argentina, accessing the region through Futaleufú. In order to drive the length of the Carretera Austral, there are several mandatory ferry crossings. Some bus routes only have services a few days per week, with fewer in low season. In high season, long-distance buses often fill up early in their route and refuse standing passengers. Hitchhiking, not recommended by Lonely Planet, is possible along the Carretera Austral, but difficult for groups or travelers with a lot of luggage.

Hornopirén

◪ 065 / POP 2500

Few take advantage of the lush surroundings of this salmon-farming and transport hub. If the ferry is full, you may spend more time here than originally planned. The Ruta Bi-Modal ferry links the roadless northern section of Parque Pumalín to Caleta Gonzalo, where the road continues south. The road between the Puelche ferry landing and Hornopirén is in the process of being paved; it should be ready in 2018.

A **tourist kiosk** (oficinadeturismohualaihue@ gmail.com; ◷9am-7pm Dec-Feb), Conaf office and supermarket are at the main plaza.

⌕ Sleeping & Eating

Campgrounds flank the road to Parque Nacional Hornopirén, including a large site at the Hornopirén bridge.

Hotel Hornopirén
HOTEL $

(☑065-221-7256; Carrera Pinto 388; s/d without bathroom CH$15,000/28,000, d CH$35,000; @ 🛜) With well-worn Patagonian character, water views and the assuring presence of Señora Ollie.

Cabañas Lahuan
CABINS $$

(☑065-221-7239; www.turismolahuan.com; Calle Cahuelmo 40; 5-/8-person cabins CH$70,000/ 100,000; 🛜) Lovely two-story cabins with wood stoves, grills and big picture windows facing the harbor. There are kayaks for guest use and the owners take groups on all-day excursions to the lovely and remote Termas Porcelanas, 1½-hours by boat, with food included (CH$58,000 per person).

★ Cocinas Costumbristas
SEAFOOD $

(cnr O'Hlggins & Cordillera; mains CH$6000; ⊗8:30am-9pm Mon-Sat, 10am-5pm Sun) Eating in these market-style shops is like a visit to your Chilean grandma. The fried *merluza* (hake) comes fresh, crisp and oversized, though you probably won't want to share. There's also seafood stews and surprisingly good steak.

❶ Getting There & Away

Kemelbus (☑in Puerto Montt 065-225-6450) has four buses daily to and from Puerto Montt (CH$4000, four hours). The bus ticket includes the fee for the ferry across the narrow Estuario de Reloncaví. Departing Puerto Montt at 6am and 8am, passengers can also continue on to Parque Pumalín or Chaitén (CH$10,000, ten hours), via the Ruta Bi-Modal; bus tickets include ferry costs.

Less than one hour south of Puerto Montt, the **Naviera Puelche ferry** (☑ in Puerto Montt 065-227-0761; www.navierapuelche.cl; bicycle/ car CH$2700/9500; ⊗7am-8pm) makes the 30-minute crossing from Caleta La Arena to Puelche. Ferries leave every half-hour in high season, with extended hours in summer.

Between Hornopirén and Parque Pumalín, **Naviera Austral** (☑in Puerto Montt 065-227-0430; www.taustral.cl; Angelmó 2187, Puerto Montt; per passenger/car CH$10,000/64,000) travels the Ruta Bi-Modal, a new system which coordinates two ferry crossings with a short 15km land stretch between them; passengers pay only once. In total, the trip between Hornopirén and Caleta Gonzalo lasts five hours. From the first week of January to the end of February there are two trips daily at 9:30am and 2pm. Summer is busy, so reserve one week ahead online, or with a direct bank deposit including passport information for all passengers and the vehicle license plate. Public buses also do the route.

ALERCE

Waterproof and nearly indestructible, the valuable alerce shingle once served as currency for the German colonists in the south. Known as *lahuan* in Mapuche, *Fitzroya cupressoides* ranks among the oldest and largest tree species in the world, with specimens reaching almost 4000 years old. This 40m to 60m jolly evergreen giant plays a key role in temperate rainforests, though its prime value as a hardwood (and surefire shelter in a rainy climate) means it was logged to near extinction. It is no longer legal to harvest live trees, but you can see alerce shingles on Chilote houses and the real deal deep in the Lakes District and Northern Patagonian forests.

Parque Nacional Hornopirén

The obscure **Parque Nacional Hornopirén** `FREE` protects a lush wilderness of alpine terrain. Trails to and in the park are marked but at times hard to follow. Still, it offers great scenery and backcountry escapes, though there's no public transportation that comes here. If planning on making an overnight hike, check in with Conaf before departing town.

About 6km south of Hornopirén, the road forks. The right fork eventually leads to the end of the road at Pichanco. Continue walking another 8km from here along a faintly marked trail to the park's entrance. Three kilometers on, Lago General Pinto Concha has a pristine beach where wild camping is possible.

Parque Pumalín

☑065

Verdant and pristine, this 2889-sq-km **park** (www.pumalinpark.org) `FREE` encompasses vast extensions of temperate rainforest, clear rivers, seascapes and farmland. A remarkable forest-conservation effort, stretching from near Hornopirén to south of Chaitén, Parque Pumalín attracts international visitors in great numbers. Created by American Doug Tompkins, it's Chile's largest private park and one of the largest private parks in the world. Alongside forest preservation, there's

ROAD TRIP!

Ranking among the world's ultimate road trips, the **Carretera Austral** runs 1240 mostly unpaved kilometers alongside ancient forests, glaciers, pioneer farmsteads, turquoise rivers and the crashing Pacific. Completed in 1996, it required an initial investment of US$300 million, took more than 20 years to build and cost 11 workers their lives. Pinochet's quest to cut a road through Aisén was not based on common sense or a pragmatic plan, it arguably had more to do with the symbolism of a highway that tied together the disparate regions of the country.

Highway is a glorified name for it – part of the adventure is simply navigating sections of gargantuan ruts and potholes. Yet travelers are drawn here in part because the route is not lined with Shell stations and Starbucks. Don't skimp on planning and a good dose of prudence. Top off your tank whenever you see a gas station as the next may be far. If you like your food green, bring fresh fruit and produce – the local selection can be severely lacking.

To the north of the Carretera Austral, ferry service is inadequate for the amount of traffic and only runs regularly during summer. Especially in winter, rock slides are common and landslides may close sections of the road for days. In the south, the road sits barely 1m above the flood-prone Río Baker, the mightiest Chilean river.

Beware the 'company trucks', usually white pickups that charge at full speed, their drivers always anxious to finish a day's work. Also watch out for cyclists and motorcyclists for whom the Carretera Austral has become a popular challenge and true badge of courage.

Lastly, isolation makes this region expensive. Be prepared for costs 20% above the rest of Chile. Go prepared:

➡ Get your vehicle checked out prior to departure.

➡ When possible, reserve ferry crossings in advance.

➡ Organize your cash (few towns have ATMs, and BancoEstado takes only MasterCard).

➡ Drive during the day, as there are no streetlights and curves are not marked with reflectors.

➡ Carry extra food, water and even gas, as a breakdown or empty tank can leave you marooned.

➡ Always carry a *neumático* (spare tire) and make sure the vehicle has *una gata* (a car jack).

➡ Take your time and enjoy the scenery – high-speed turns on loose gravel roads are a recipe for disaster.

➡ Stop if someone looks like they might need help.

➡ Give trucks a wider berth on gravel – broken windshields are endemic to the Carretera Austral.

If crossing into Argentina, start your trip with all papers in order, permission to take a rental vehicle out of the country and the required insurance. Extra fuel, meat, produce and dairy products can't cross borders. All of the larger towns listed in Northern Patagonia have some sort of gas station.

---

been experimentation with agricultural uses such as bee keeping, organic farming and animal husbandry in an innovative park model. For Chile it's a flagship conservation project, with well-maintained roads and trails, extensive infrastructure and minimal impact.

After the 2008 eruption of Volcán Chaitén, the park closed for several years. It reopened in 2011, adding a spectacular trail to the new volcano.

Since the ferry usually requires advance reservations, many people access the park from Chaitén in the south. Caleta Gonzalo, the ferry landing, features cabins and a cafe. A new visitor center is being implemented in the current *guardaparques* (ranger) station 20km south of Chaitén. Fires are prohibited in the park.

🏃 Activities

Check with an information center before finalizing your hiking plans as conditions are changeable.

Sendero Cascadas (a three-hour round-trip) is an undulating climb through dense forest that ends at a large waterfall. The river crossing about an hour into the hike can be dangerous at high water.

About 12km south of Caleta Gonzalo, the marked route to **Laguna Tronador** is not so much a trail as it is, often literally, a staircase. Beginning as a boardwalk, it crosses a rushing stream on a *pasarela* (hanging bridge) before ascending a series of wooden stepladders where the soil is too steep and friable for anything else. After about an hour's climb, at the saddle, there's a *mirador* (lookout platform) with fine views of Volcán Michinmahuida above the forest to the south. The trail then drops toward the lake, where there's a two-site campground with sturdy picnic tables (one set on a deck) and a latrine.

One kilometer further south, only a few minutes off the highway to Chaitén, **Sendero los Alerces** crosses the river to a substantial grove of alerce trees, where interpretive signs along the way explain the importance of conserving these ancients. At **Cascadas Escondidas**, 14km south of Caleta Gonzalo, a one-hour trail leads from the campground to a series of waterfalls.

The most popular route – for a good reason – heads to the **Volcán Chaitén Crater Trail**. The 5-hour round-trip ascends the blast path to view the puffing crater. The lower sections teem with vegetation while the upper reaches are barren and beautiful. The trail is 800m with a 250m change in altitude, a pyroclastic Mt St Helen's–style trail through forest that burned through heat, not fire. It's near Puente Los Gigos.

At **Michinmahuida**, 33km south of Caleta Gonzalo, a 12km trail leads to the base of the volcano.

In the park's newest sector some 20km south of Chaitén, a flat, open 10km trek to **Ventisquero Amarillo** starts at the Ventisquero campground toward the base of the Michinmahuida Glacier; cross the river at its widest point, closer to the campground.

👉 Tours

Currently the only way to access some of the isolated northern reaches of the park is by boat. A few Puerto Varas–based operators organize boating and kayaking trips through the fjords and to otherwise inaccessible hot springs. In Chaitén, Chaitur has information on local guides who take hiking groups to the volcano.

Al Sur Expeditions　　　　BOATING
(☎ 065-223-2300;　www.alsurexpeditions.com) Specializes in sea kayaking and provides boat transportation to the remote Cahuelmo Hot Springs.

Ko'Kayak　　　　KAYAKING
(☎ cell 9310-5272;　www.kokayak.cl) Reputable multiday sea-kayak expeditions to Pumalín Park, stopping at the hot springs along the way. French- and English-speaking guides.

🛏 Sleeping & Eating

Information centers and the park website have details on all of the campgrounds, some of which are at trailheads.

🛏 North Parque Pumalín (boat access only)

Camping Cahuelmo　　　　CAMPGROUND $
(☎ 065-225-0079; North Pumalín; campsites per person CH$3000) Cahuelmo has hot springs (CH$5000) and six good tent spaces at the southeast corner of the Cahuelmo Fjord, accessed by boat via Hornopirén or Leptepu. Advance reservations are required.

🛏 Península Huequi-Aycara

Avellano Lodge　　　　LODGE $$
(☎ 065-257-6433, cell 9641-4613; www.elavellanolodge.com; Ayacara; per person half-board CH$35,000; @ 🌐) Just outside of the park on the peninsula, this hardwood lodge offers an unbeatable combination of access to the park, service and comfort. All-inclusive hiking, fly-fishing and sea-kayaking tours, including transfer from Puerto Montt, are available.

🛏 Main Parque Pumalín

The following camping options are listed from north to south.

Camping Río Gonzalo　　　　CAMPGROUND $
(Caleta Gonzalo; campsites per person CH$2500) On the shores of Reñihué Fjord, this walk-in campground has a shelter for cooking, firepits and bathrooms with cold showers.

Caleta Gonzalo Cabañas　　　　CABINS $$$
(reservas@parquepumalin.cl; s/d/t/q CH$70,000/85,000/105,000/125,000) Cozy cabins (without

kitchen facilities) that overlook the fjord, with cool loft beds for kids.

Café Caleta Gonzalo
CAFE $$

(mains CH$8000; ⊗9am-10pm) The park's only restaurant is this attractive cafe with a huge fireplace. Fresh bread, local honey and organic vegetables put it a notch above average. Homemade oatmeal cookies, honey or picnic boxes are available to go.

Camping Tronador
CAMPGROUND $

(campsites free) Free campsites at the basin of the stunning amphitheater lake on Tronador trail, 1½ hours from the trailhead.

Fundo del Río Cabañas
CABINS $$$

(reservas@parquepumalin.cl; 2-4-person cabins CH$65,000-125,000) Tucked into farmland, these private cabins with kitchen facilities have sea or valley views. Firewood included.

Cascadas Escondidas
CAMPGROUND $

(covered campsites CH$7500) Features platform sites with roof at the trailhead to Cascadas Escondidas.

Lago Negro
CAMPGROUND $

(campsites per person CH$2500, covered campsites CH$7500) Large campground close to the lake.

Lago Blanco
CAMPGROUND $

(covered campsites CH$7500) Twenty kilometers south of Caleta Gonzalo and 36km north of Chaitén, Lago Blanco has a few covered sites and great views of the lake. Make sure you hike the short distance to the *mirador* for a better view. There is excellent fishing in the lake, but you'll need to get a permit from a ranger station.

Camping El Volcán
CAMPGROUND $

(campsites per person CH$2500, covered campsites CH$7500) At the southern end of the park before Chaitén, 2.5km before the southern-entrance ranger station, this big camping zone has car camping and information.

Sector Amarillo
CAMPGROUND $

(campsites per person CH$2500) This newest sector south of Chaitén occupies former farmland beyond the Termas El Amarillo, with great views and flat, open sites in three separate areas. It is a couple of days' hiking from other areas or accessible by car.

❶ Information

Two **Centros de Visitantes** (www.parquepumalin.cl; Caleta Gonzalo & El Amarillo; ⊗9am-7pm Mon-Sat, 10am-4pm Sun) have park brochures,

photographs and environmental information as well as regional artisan goods for sale. For more information before arriving, contact the Pumalín office in **Puerto Varas** (☎065-250-079; Klenner 299; ⊗9am-5pm Mon-Fri) or the **USA** (☎415-229-9339; 1606 Union St, San Francisco). The website has updated information.

In the El Amarillo sector, **Puma Verde** (Carretera Austral s/n; showers CH$1000; ⊗10am-8:30pm) is a park-run general store and gas station – the last one before La Junta. It sells an excellent selection of regional artisan products and reasonably priced provisions, including eggs and produce.

❶ Getting There & Away

The **Naviera Austral** (☎065-270-431; www.taustral.cl; passenger/car CH$10,000/64,000) ferries sail from Caleta Gonzalo to Hornopirén (five to six hours) twice daily in high season. Bus-boat combos from Puerto Montt can drop visitors in the park on the way to Chaitén.

Chaitén

☎065 / POP 4000

When an unknown volcano decided to wake up on May 2, 2008, this quiet village underwent a total siege. Locals were able to evacuate, but suffered years of uncertainty as the government formed a response. Residents resisted the initial government decision to move the town 10km north, in the coastal enclave of Santa Bárbara, and have rebuilt their shingled town with pride.

Chaitén is the major transport hub for the northern Carretera Austral. Flights and ferries from Puerto Montt and Chiloé arrive here, and it's the starting point for many bus routes south. It's also the main service town for Parque Pumalín.

If you arrive by ferry, the port is a 10-minute walk northwest of town. Chaitén is 56km south of Caleta Gonzalo and 45km northwest of Puerto Cárdenas.

🏃 Activities

Termas El Amarillo
HOT SPRINGS

(admission CH$3700) Overly popular in summer with one large cement soaking pool and two smaller, hotter tubs, overlooking Río Michinmahuida. It's 25km southeast of Chaitén, on a spur north off the Carretera Austral. Fanatics can camp at a private site 1km away.

Lago Yelcho
FISHING

A brilliant blue under glacial peaks, and fed by the raging Río Futaleufú, the 110-sq-km Lago Yelcho is adored by anglers. The small

VOLCÁN CHAITÉN WAKES UP

No one even considered it a volcano, but that changed quickly. On May 2, 2008, Volcán Chaitén, 10km northeast of its namesake town, began a month-long eruption with a 20km-high column of ash.

During the first week, successive explosions emitted more than a cubic kilometer of rhyolitic ash. The rampage caused flooding and severe damage to homes, roads and bridges, decimated thousands of livestock and spewed ash as far as Buenos Aires. Chaitén's 4000 inhabitants were evacuated. The government sanctioned relocating the town slightly northwest to the village of Santa Barbara (Nuevo Chaitén), but later improvements in the old town infrastructure has had locals returning to recover their homes in Chaitén.

Located in Parque Pumalín, the volcano is easily viewed from sections of the main park road that show forests on the volcano's northeastern flank calcified by pyroclastic flows. The crater has yawned open to 3km in diameter, hosting within it a new complex of quickly formed rhyolitic domes. For stunning views of the smoking crater, hike to the ridge top of the crater trail (p307). Go early or late in the day during summer, as there's little shade on the trail.

The park reopened in 2011, thanks to park rangers who have worked tirelessly in its recovery. Volcán Chaitén remains under constant monitoring by Sernageomin (www.sernageomin.cl), the government agency of geology and mining.

port of Puerto Cárdenas (62km south of Chaitén) has modest lodging choices in the summer only, and lodges that provide fishing boats and guides.

Ventisquero Yelcho   HIKING
A 2½-hour hike to a large hanging glacier. Camping is possible near the parking lot, where there is also a *quincho* (barbecue hut) and bathrooms. There are glacier views throughout the hike along the riverbanks. If short on time, hike one hour in for good views. It's 15km south of Puerto Cárdenas. Puente Ventisquero (Glacier Bridge) is the starting point.

Tours

Chaitur   TOUR
(☑065-273-7249, cell 7468-5608; www.chaitur.com; O'Higgins 67) The best source local information, English-speaking Nicholas dispatches most of the buses and arranges bilingual guided visits to Pumalín, Yelcho glacier, Termas El Amarillo and beaches with sea-lion colonies. Guided hikes to the Volcan Chaitén Crater Trail offer detailed scientific information. Also rents bikes (CH$10,000/day).

Sleeping & Eating

Doña Collita   GUESTHOUSE $
(☑cell 8445-7500; Diego Portales 54; per person without bathroom CH$12,000, d CH$27,000) An immaculate, old-fashioned *hospedaje* (guesthouse) with spotless rooms and a stern hostess. Cold feet take heart: it's one

of the few options on the Carretera Austral where the heat is always cranking.

Cielo Mar Camping   CAMPGROUND $
(☑cell 7468-5608; www.chaitur.com; O'Higgins & Corcovado; campsites per person CH$5000; @) Backyard campsites and hot-water showers, right in the center of town.

★**Cocinerías Costumbristas**   SEAFOOD $
(Portales 258; meals CH$3000-6000; ⊗8:30am-midnight) Apron-clad señoras in tiny kitchens serve up piping-hot seafood empanadas, fish platters and fresh *paila marina* (shellfish soup). Come early because it fills up fast with locals.

Cafe Pizzeria Reconquista   PIZZERIA, CAFE $
(☑cell 6671-4081; Diego Portales 269; pizza CH$6800; ⊗9am-3pm & 7-11pm Mon-Fri, 12:30-3pm & 7-11pm Sat) A good bet for thin-crust pizzas, also serving sandwiches and scrambled-egg breakfasts, this shiny cafe has a handful of gleaming indoor picnic tables and considerate staff.

Restobar el Volcán   CHILEAN $$
(☑cell 8186-9558; Pratt 65; mains CH$8000; ⊗9am-midnight) A friendly restaurant/bar housed in a rambling shingled home. In summer, local produce and housemade jams and juices (try *nalca*, a Patagonian relative of rhubarb) spiff up a typical menu of regionally-sourced fish, meat and sandwiches. Breakfast is also served.

❶ Information

BancoEstado (cnr Libertad & O'Higgins) Has an ATM and poor exchange rates for cash.

Hospital de Chaitén (☑ 065-731-244; Av Ignacio Carrera Pinto; ⊙24hr) Emergency is open 24 hours.

Tourist Kiosk (cnr Costanera & O'Higgins; ⊙9am-9pm Jan-Feb) Has leaflets and a list of accommodations.

❶ Getting There & Away

AIR

A new airport is slated for 2015 near Santa Bárbara, between Pumalín and Chaitén. Both **Aerocord** (☑ in Puerto Montt 065-226-2300; www.aerocord.cl; Costanera s/n) and **Pewen** (☑ in Puerto Montt 065-222-4000; www.pewenchile.com) fly to Aerodromo La Paloma in Puerto Montt (one-way CH$50,000, 45 minutes). Both fly daily (except Sundays), usually mid-morning.

BOAT

Ferry schedules change, so confirm online before making plans. In summer, the **Naviera Austral** (☑ 065-273-1272; www.navieraustral.cl; Corcovado 266; passenger seat/bunk/car CH$16,000/35,000/88,000) auto-passenger ferry *Don Baldo* sails three times a week to Puerto Montt (nine hours) and twice weekly to Quellón (six hours) and Castro, Chiloé (five hours).

BUS

Transportation schedules and operators for the Carretera Austral change frequently. Departures are from the main **Chaitur Bus Terminal** (☑cell 7468-5608; www.chaitur.com; O'Higgins 67). Kemelbus goes to Puerto Montt (CH$10,000, nine hours) daily at 10am and noon. Buses Becker goes to Coyhaique on Wednesday and Sunday at 12pm, stopping in Villa Santa Lucía (where offshoots lead to Futaleufú and Palena), La Junta and Puyuhuapi along the way. The current paving of this route means there may be delays and closures through 2018; ask for updates at the terminal.

Buses Cardenas goes to Futaleufú daily at 1pm and to Palena daily at noon. **Buses Cumbres Nevadas** goes to Palena and Futaleufú daily at 4pm and 7pm. Currently many bus routes offer subsidized fares for all passengers, but in the future discounts may be for residents only.

DESTINATION	COST (CH$)	DURATION (HR)
Coyhaique	CH$24,000	9-10
Futaleufú	CH$2000	3½
La Junta	CH$12,000	4
Palena	CH$2000	4
Puyuhuapi	CH$15,000	5
Villa Santa Lucía	CH$1000	2

Futaleufú

☑ 065 / POP 1800

The Futaleufú's wild, frosty-mint waters have made this modest mountain town famous. Not just a mecca for kayaking and rafting, it also boasts fly-fishing, hiking and horseback riding. Improved roads and growing numbers of package-tour visitors mean it isn't off the map anymore – just note the ratio of down puffs to woolen mantas. That said, it's still a fun place to be. December and March, on either end of the summer rush, are more peaceful times to be here.

The town of Futaleufú, a small 20-block grid of pastel-painted houses 155km southeast of Chaitén, is mainly a service center to the Argentine border, only 8km away, and a bedroom community for boaters. Many visitors hop the border to the nearby Argentine towns of Trevelín and Esquel, and to Argentina's Parque Nacional Los Alerces.

🏃 Activities

The Futa or Fu, as it's known, is a technical, demanding river, with some sections only appropriate for experienced rafters. Depending on the outfitter you choose and the services included, rafting the Futaleufú starts at CH$40,000 per person for a half-day section known as Bridge to Bridge with Class IV and IV-plus rapids. A full-day trip for experienced rafters only goes from Bridge to Macul, adding two Class V rapids, starting at CH$60,000.

Ideal for families, rafting trips on the Class III Río Espolón cost about CH$15,000 for the five-hour trip. Novice kayakers can try this river or head to Lago Espolón for a float trip.

Bio Bio Expeditions　　　　　　　　OUTDOORS
(☑ 022-196-4258, US toll free 1-800-246-7238; www.bbxrafting.com) A pioneer in the region, this ecologically minded group offers river descents, horse treks and more. It is well established but may take walk-ins.

Expediciones Chile　　　　　　　　OUTDOORS
(☑ 065-562-639; www.exchile.com; Mistral 296) A secure rafting operator with loads of experience. Specializes in week-long packages but offers kayaking, mountain biking and horseback riding as well.

H2O Patagonia　　　　　　　　　　RAFTING
(☑ cell 5340-1257; www.h2opatagonia.com) A US-based adventure company that can coordinate

DON'T MISS

PIONEER PATAGONIA

When winds roar sidelong and rains persist, take refuge by the wood stove, drink a round of *maté* (tea) and *echar la talla* (pass the time) with the locals. Rural Patagonia offers a rare and privileged glimpse of a fading way of life. To jump-start their slack rural economy, government and nonprofit initiatives have created local guide and homestay associations.

These family enterprises range from comfortable roadside *hospedajes* and farmstays to wild country multiday treks and horseback-riding trips through wonderland terrain. Prices are reasonable – starting from CH$15,000 per day for lodging and CH$20,000 per day for guide services. Pack horses or riding are extra and only Spanish is spoken.

Travelers can link with rural homestays and guide services through Casa del Turismo Rural (p317) in Coyhaique or the **Municipalidad de Cochamó** (☑065-350-271; www.cochamo.cl; Plaza) in Río Puelo. Some of the best opportunities around the Carretera Austral are in Bahía Murta, Cerro Castillo, La Junta, and Palena. In Sur Chico, head to Llanada Grande. It's best to book a week or more in advance, as intermediaries have to make radio contact with the most remote hosts. That's right – no phones, no electricity, no worries.

Another good resource, **Discover Patagonia Circuit** (www.undiscoveredpatagonia. com) is an innovative government-funded project that offers travelers original DIY circuits in rural Aysen to download, written in English and Spanish.

your entire trip, including luxurious accommodations on its ranch.

Patagonia Elements　　　　　　RAFTING
(☑cell 7499-0296; www.patagoniaelements.com; Cerda 549) With competent Chilean guides, also offers kayak classes, fly-fishing and horseback riding.

🛌 Sleeping

Las Natalias　　　　　　　HOSTEL $
(☑cell 9631-1330; http://hostallasnatalias.info; dm CH$10,000, d/tr CH$24,000/30,000, d without bathroom CH$20,000) Named for four generations of Natalias, this welcoming spot is a great deal for backpackers with tips on outdoor options. There's plenty of shared bathrooms, a large communal area, mountain views and a guest kitchen. It's a 10-minute walk from the center. Follow Cerda and signs for the northwest outskirts of town; it's on the right after the hill climb.

Martín Pescador B&B　　　　　B&B $
(☑065-272-1279; Balmaceda 603; s/d CH$15,000/20,000, 6-person cabin CH$55,000; ☜) Behind the restaurant, this cozy home with adobe-style walls and attractive furnishings is a steal. The two-bedroom cabins with narrow staircases are rustic and stylish, with kitchenettes. Mitch, the owner, also works as a freelance outdoor guide.

Adolfo's B&B　　　　　　　B&B $
(☑065-272-1256; pettyrios@gmail.com; O'Higgins 302; d CH$30,000, per person without bathroom CH$10,000; @) The best bargain digs in town

are in this warm wood-finish home run by a hospitable family. Breakfast includes eggs, homemade bread and coffee cake.

Posada Ely　　　　　　　GUESTHOUSE $
(☑065-272-1205; posada.ely.futaleufu@gmail.com; Balmaceda 409; s/d CH$15,000/30,000; P☜) These well-kept rooms sit under the sure guardianship of Betty, a dyed-in-the-wool local who makes a mean rosehip jam, served with a breakfast of fresh bread, eggs, juice, tea and more. Cable TV is available.

Cara del Indio　　　　　　CAMPGROUND $
(☑sat phone 02-1962-4240; www.caradelindio. cl; campsite per person CH$3000, cabañas from CH$35,000; ☺Nov-April) With a spectacular riverfront setting, this adventure base camp (also offering rafting) is run by Luis Toro and his family. Cabins come in various sizes on the 10km spread. Sites have access to hot showers, an outdoor kitchen and a wood-burning sauna. Guests can dine on site or purchase homemade items.

It's 15km from Puerto Ramiréz and 35km from the Carretera Austral.

Camping Puerto Espolón　　CAMPGROUND $
(☑cell 7721-9239; www.lagoespolon.cl; campsite per person CH$5000, cabins from CH$35,000; ☺Jan & Feb; ☜) A gorgeous setting on a sandy riverbank flanked by mountains, just before the entrance to town. Campers have hot showers. Hosts Anibal and Elma also offer *asados* (barbecues; CH$10,000 per person), meals and discounts for longer stays.

★ **La Antigua Casona** INN $$

(☑065-272-1311; silvanobmw@gmail.com; Rodriguez 215; d/tr CH$50,000/60,000; 🐾) Every polished detail of this refurbished settler's barn expresses the loving attention of its Italian and Chilean owners. Rooms sport a lovely, nature-themed decor with hand-painted birds and quilted beds. For passers-by, there's an inviting cafe with a shaded terrace attended by Silvano, an afficionado of local history.

La Gringa Carioca B&B $$

(☑065-272-1260, cell 9659-9341; Sargento Aldea 498; d CH$60,000) A rustic setting with a sweeping garden area with hammocks and lovely windowbox seats in an old, lived-in house. Adriana, the Brazilian hostess, speaks multiple languages and proves helpful with local tips. Breakfasts include farm eggs and real coffee. The downside is old installations and outdated bathrooms.

Hostería Río Grande HOTEL $$

(☑065-272-1320; O'Higgins 397; s/d/tr CH$40,000/55,000/65,000; 🅿🐾) This comfortable shingled lodge caters to sporty gringos who, between raft trips, can pump iron in the attached weight room. Expect bright, carpeted rooms with portable heaters and low-slung beds in deep frames. It also features a small pub with a grassy terrace.

Uman Lodge LODGE $$$

(☑065-272-1700; http://umanlodge.cl; Fundo La Confluencia; d US$460; 🐾🏊) This panorama of converging rivers rates amongst Patagonia's best views. *Uman* means lodging in Mapundungun, and the place longs for a native connection beyond the hardwoods. Tastefully modern, it's sheathed in glass walls and alerce shingles with 16 luxury rooms, all with views. Amenities include on-site adventure tours and an indoor-outdoor pool. It's 2.5km from town, with a steep gravel approach.

Hotel El Barranco HOTEL $$$

(☑065-272-1314; www.elbarrancochile.cl; O'Higgins 172; s/d CH$99,000/110,000; @🏊) At this elegant lodge on the edge of the grid of town, rooms are snug with carved woodwork, colonial accents and big beds. Service could be more attentive, but it is the most ambient option in town. There's also a swimming pool and outdoor excursions.

✗ **Eating**

Since most supplies have to be trucked in from afar, fresh vegetables can be in short supply.

Rincón de Mama CHILEAN $

(☑065-272-1208; O'Higgins 465 alley; mains CH$6000; ⊙11:30am-2:30pm & 6:30-10pm Mon-Sat) This homespun restaurant with citrus colors and plastic tablecloths is one of the better deals in town for home-cooked meals and friendly service. It's on the second floor of a rambling alleyway house.

Martín Pescador CHILEAN $$

(☑065-721-279; Balmaceda 603; mains CH$8000; ⊙dinner) Serving regional delicacies on a changing menu, such as chicken with morel mushrooms, or salmon carpaccio, this exclusive eatery with a roaring log fire is perfect for a special dinner. There's a good wine selection and a four-course meal option (CH$16,000).

🛈 **Information**

BancoEstado (cnr O'Higgins & Manuel Rodríguez) Bring all the money you'll need; this is the only choice for changing money. The ATM takes only MasterCard.

Post Office (Manuel Rodríguez)

Tourist Office (O'Higgins 536; ⊙9am-9pm) Helpful, with information on cabins, activities and descriptions of local treks.

🛈 **Getting There & Away**

Buses Becker (☑065-272-1360; www.busesbecker.com; cnr Balmaceda & Pratt; ⊙9am-1pm & 3-7pm) goes to Coyhaique (CH$24,000, 10 hours) every Friday via Villa Santa Lucía (two hours), La Junta and Puyuhuapi. **Cumbres Nevadas** goes north to Chaiten (CH$3000, 3½ hours) at 11am and 2pm from Monday to Saturday. **Frontera Sur** travels to Palena (CH$1200, two hours) three times per week.

TransAustral (☑065-721-360; cnr Balmaceda & Pratt) goes at 8am on Wednesday and Sunday to Puerto Montt (CH$25,000, 12 hours via Argentina). The same office also sells air and ferry tickets originating from Chaitén to Puerto Montt, worth buying in advance.

International buses (☑065-272-1458; Cerda 436, Telefonica office; CH$2500) to the Argentine border currently leave on Mondays and Fridays at 9am. The **Futaleufú border post** (⊙8am-8pm) is far quicker and more efficient than the crossing at Palena, opposite the Argentine border town of Carrenleufú.

There's now a gas station, though if you're crossing the border it's cheaper in Argentina.

Palena

A quiet mountain town on its namesake turquoise river, Palena's draw is exploring its verdant valleys on foot or horseback, where you'll find remnants of pioneer lifestyle and real hospitality. The rodeo, held on the last weekend in January, and the week-long Semana Palena, in late February, feature cowboy festivities and live music.

On the plaza, the **tourism office** (☎065-274-1221; www.municipalidadpalena.cl; Piloto Pardo s/n; ☺9am-8pm Mon-Sat, to 6pm Sun) arranges horse packing, rafting and fishing trips with local guides. Allow some lead time before your trip, since some rural outfitters must be reached by radio. It can also connect adventurers to the wonderful Casanova family farm **Rincón de la Nieve** (☎cell 8186-4942; rincondelanieve@hotmail.com; Valle Azul; per person CH$15,000), accessed via hiking or horseback riding. Chill there or continue on a truly incredible five-day round-trip ride to remote Lago Palena; arrange in advance.

With two locations, in Palena and El Malito, **Aventuras Cordilleranas** (☎065-284-1377, cell 5761-9207; El Malito bridge; s CH$12,000) is run by a friendly family who also offer kayaking and floating on Río Palena. Contact in advance. If arriving from the west, have the bus drop you off 22km before Palena for El Malito.

Buses Cumbres Nevadas goes to Chaitén (CH$2000, four hours) daily.

La Junta

☎067

With the slow feel of a Rocky Mountain backwater, La Junta is a former *estancia* (grazing ranch) that formed a crossroads for ranchers headed to market. Midway between Chaitén and Coyhaique, it's also an important transfer point for north–south connections, with solid lodging options. Unmistakable with its centerpiece monument to Pinochet, it now serves as a major fuel and rest stop for travelers, replete with old-fashioned hardware stores and a rocky butte bookending town.

At the end of January, the **Fiesta del los Rios** celebrates the two rivers that converge here, with free floating trips, barbecues and folk performances. There is no bus terminal here; ask locals the schedules and catch a bus passing by.

🏃 Activities

Visitors can take float trips on Río Palena, go fly-fishing or hike in area reserves. Brown, rainbow and Chinook trout abound at Reserva Nacional Lago Rosselot and Lago Verde.

Yagan Expeditions   ADVENTURE TOURS
(☎067-231-4352; www.yaganexpeditions.com; Calle 5 de Abril # 350) Small tour operator providing horseback riding, trekking and hot-springs trips, as well as kayaking on Lago Rosselot.

Termas del Sauce   HOT SPRINGS
(☎cell 9454-2711; Camino a Raul Marin Balmaceda, Km17; per person CH$4000; ☺10am-8:30pm) Private hot springs with pleasant but rustic pools and camping on a brook 17km out of town toward Raúl Marín Balmaceda.

🛏 Sleeping & Eating

Pension Hospedaje Tía Lety   GUESTHOUSE $
(☎cell 8763-5191; Varas 596; r per person CH$15,000; ☎) A friendly family setting, with bulky beds in well-kept rooms. Breakfast, with homemade küchen, jam and bread, is filling.

Hostería Mirador del Río   FARMSTAY $
(☎cell 6177-6894; www.miradordelrio.cl; Camino a Raul Marin Balmaceda, Km6; r per person incl breakfast CH$15,000) For a welcome retreat from the dusty Carretera Austral, get outside of town to this charming farmhouse. The family is lovely and breakfast satisfies with homemade jam and bread hot out of the woodstove. Guests can also float down the mellow Río Palena in a kayak or rafts.

Alto Melimoyu Hotel   B&B $$
(☎067-231-4320; www.altomelimoyu.cl; Carretera Austral 375; s/d without bathroom CH$33,000/48,000, s/d 35,000/51,000; ☎) A design B&B with rental bikes and kayaks and connections to local tours. Guests cozy up by the fire on the wide-wale corduroy couch and enjoy big breakfasts around communal tables handmade by locals. It's on the Carretera Austral, though set back enough to almost forget it's there. A wooden hot tub and sauna are rented by the hour.

Terrazas de Palena   B&B $$
(☎cell 9415-4274; www.terrazasdelpalena.cl; Carretera Austral s/n; d/q apt CH$55,000/85,000, 2-/5-person cabin CH$50,000/80,000; ☺) With sweeping views, these cubist cabins and apartments with woodstove provide a nice, tranquil spot to regroup. There's also a restaurant in the works, excursions and airport transfers. Located 2km north of La Junta.

★ Espacio y Tiempo   LODGE $$$
(☎067-231-4141; espacioytiempo.cl; Carretera Austral s/n; s/d/tr US$102/148/192; ☎) This well-heeled and comfortable lodge relaxes

visiting anglers and travelers with classical music, sprawling green gardens and a well-stocked bar. Rooms feature muted tones and top-quality mattresses. Further perks include private porches and an abundant buffet breakfast with real coffee. The hosts happily arrange local excursions.

The on-site restaurant is popular with locals; specialties include local elk, but there are also enticingly big bowls of salad.

★ **Mi Casita de Té**　　　　CHILEAN $
(☑cell 7802-0488; Carretera Austral s/n; set menu CH$6000; ☺8:30am-midnight) A community fixture where doting Eliana and her daughters cook and serve abundant, fresh meals and even espresso. In summer there are lovely salads with organic lettuce and fresh rhubarb juice. Any time, the beef *cazuela* (stew), with corn cobs, fresh peas and cilantro, is deeply satisfying Chilean comfort food.

❶ Information

Conaf (☑ 067-231-4128; cnr Patricio Lynch & Manuel Montt) Has details on nearby parks and reserves.

Tourist Kiosk (cnr Portales & 1era de Noviembre; ☺9am-9pm Mon-Fri, 10:30am-7:30pm Sat & Sun) On the plaza, with information on buses, lodgings and activities.

Puyuhuapi
☑067

Tucked into the Jurassic scenery of overgrown ferns and nalca plants, this quaint seaside village is the gateway to Parque Nacional Queulat and Termas de Puyuhuapi, a prestigious hot-springs resort. In 1935 four German immigrants settled here, inspired by explorer Hans Steffen's adventures. The town sits at the northern end of the Seno Ventisquero, a scenic fjord that's part of the larger Canal Puyuhuapi.

The agricultural colony grew with Chilote textile workers whose skills fed the success of the 1947 German **Fábrica de Alfombras** (www.puyuhuapi.com; Aysen s/n; tours per group CH$5000), which sells its high-end handmade carpets online.

There's free wi-fi on the plaza.

🏃 Activities

Termas del Ventisquero　　　HOT SPRINGS
(☑067-231-4686；　www.termasventisqueropuyuhuapi.cl; admission CH$17,000; ☺9am-11pm Dec-Feb, reduced winter hr) Located roadside on the Carretera Austral, 6km south of Puyuhuapi, with one big pool and three small pools facing the sound. The water is 36°C to 40°C and there are adequate changing rooms with showers and lockers.

WORTH A TRIP

EXPLORE THE LOST COAST

The long-isolated coastal village of **Raul Marín Balmaceda** finally has road access and it's well worth the detour. At the mouth of the Río Palena, a new watershed preserve, it's teeming with wildlife, such as otters, sea lions and austral dolphins. For the best marine life, paddle out in a kayak or take a boat tour. The village has wide sandy streets and grassy paths to a lovely beach.

From La Junta, buses depart on Monday, Wednesday and Friday at 8:30am. You can make the nearly two-hour drive on a decent gravel road. There's an obligatory ferry crossing (free): day-trippers, note that it's only open until 7pm. There's also a weekly ferry to Quellon, Chiloé.

Los Lirios (☑cell 6242-0180; violaloslirios@gmail.com; r per person with/without bathroom from CH$12,000/10,000) In the village, Los Lirios offers a comfortable homestay.

Born in Patagonia (☑cell 7769-0375; born.ricardo@gmail.com; s/d 30,000/50,000) On the water, Born in Patagonia has just two lovely B&B rooms, reservation only. Its owner Ricardo is a tested sea captain offering week-long charter expeditions in the channels in a gorgeous handbuilt catamaran.

Fundo Los Leones (☑cell 6597-3986, cell 7898-2956; www.fundolosleones.cl; s/d cabin CH$96,000/129,000; @) A wonderful ecotourism option, Fundo Los Leones provides the ultimate retreat (reservations only) in tiny shingled cabins on the Pitipalena Fjord. It also offers meals with organic ingredients from the farm and excursions by kayak and boat.

Experiencia Austral ADVENTURE TOURS
(☑cell 7766-1524, cell 8258-5799; www.expe-
rienciaustral.com; Otto Uebel 36) Adventure
tours led by the amicable Adonis. Offerings include kayaking the fjord, hiking in
the Parque Nacional Queluat (CH$30,000)
and trips to Isla Magdalena. Rents bicycles (CH$2000/hr) and sit-on-top kayaks
(CH$6000/hr).

🛏 Sleeping & Eating

Day visitors to the hot springs often lodge in
town, but reserve ahead in summer.

Hostal Comuyhuapi GUESTHOUSE $
(☑cell 7766-1984; comuyhuapi.cl; Llautureo 143;
dm/d CH$10,000/30,000; 🛜) A solid bargain
option, this annex to a family home has decent doubles and dorm area, though kitchen
use is extra (CH$1000).

★Ecocamp Arrayanes CAMPGROUND $
(☑067-252-6906, cell 8549-3679; www.camping
arrayanes.com; campsite per person CH$5000,
covered campsite CH$25,000) A lovely beach
and campground 5km north of town with a
covered dining area. Reddish arrayan trees
shade the beach, there's hiking trails, volcanic caves and kayak options, which make it
worthwhile for day use (CH$4000).

Camping La Sirena CAMPGROUND $
(☑067-232-5100, cell 7880-6251; Costanera
148; campsite per person CH$4000) Sites are
cramped, but there are tent shelters, bathrooms and hot showers. Enter via the road
passing the playground to the water.

★Casa Ludwig GUESTHOUSE $$
(☑067-232-5220; www.casaludwig.cl; Uebel 202;
s/d without bathroom from CH$18,000/30,000, s/d
CH$25,000/48,000; ⊙Oct-Mar) A historic land-
mark, this classic home is elegant and snug,
with roaring fires in the sprawling living
room and big breakfasts at the communal
table. Prices correspond to room size. The
English- and German-speaking owners can
help with tour arrangements.

Cabañas Aonikenk CABINS $$
(☑067-232-5208; www.casaturismorural.cl; Ham-
burgo 16; s/d from CH$25,000/40,000, apt from
CH$45,000, cabin for 4/5 people CH$60,000; 🛜)
Hosted by the amicable Veronica, these all-
wood cabins have local log furniture, snug
white bedding and small balconies. Apartments have kitchens and the cafe offers refuge on a rainy day. Good breakfasts.

Los Mañíos del Queulat CAFE $
(☑cell 7664-9866; mains CH$6000; ⊙10:30am-
10pm) An attentive family-run cafe serving
sandwiches, abundant set lunches and an
appealing selection of homemade desserts.

El Muelle SEAFOOD $$
(☑cell 7654-3598; Otto Ubel s/n; mains CH$5000-
8000; ⊙noon-10pm Tue-Sun) If the *merluza*
(hake) on your plate were any fresher, it
would still be in the fjord. Despite slow ser-
vice, it's worth hunkering down to a big sea-
food meal served with mashed potatoes or
crisp fries. The shingled house surrounded
by overgrown flowerbeds sits in front of the
police station.

ℹ Information

Tourist Office (www.puertopuyuhuapi.cl; Otto
Uebel s/n; ⊙10am-1:30pm & 3-8pm Fri-Wed)
Facing the park, Patagonia's best public infor-
mation center has comprehensive information
on lodgings, hot springs and restaurants,
thanks to helpful Almendra. Offers maps to the
town walking circuit.

ℹ Getting There & Away

The road around Puyuhuapi, between La Junta
and Parque Nacional Queluat, is under construc-
tion until 2025, with sections closed to traffic
during established hours. Check with tourism
offices and hotels for closure information and
schedules, and be prepared for delays.

Buses that run between Coyhaique and
Chaitén will drop passengers in Puyuhuapi. Buy
your return ticket as far ahead as possible, as
demand exceeds availability in summer. **Buses
Becker** (☑067-232-167) goes to Chaitén on
Tuesdays at 8am and Futaleufú on Saturdays at
8am; both buses pass through La Junta. **Terra
Austral** (Nido de Puyes supermarket) and **Agui-
las Patagonicas** (☑in Coyhaique 067-221-1288;
www.aguilaspatagonicas.cl) leave at 6am daily
for Coyhaique.

DESTINATION	COST (CH$)	DURATION (HR)
Chaitén	15,000	5
Coyhaique	12,000	4-5
Futaleufú	15,000	6
La Junta	2000	1

Termas de Puyuhuapi

Chile's leading hot-springs resort, **Termas
de Puyuhuapi Hotel & Spa** (☑067-232-
5117, 067-232-5103; www.puyuhuapilodge.com; d
US$150, all-inclusive per person per day US$390)

WORTH A TRIP

ISLA MAGDALENA

An island sanctuary with hot springs and trails, **Parque Nacional Isla Magdalena** makes an engaging trip for adventurers, but there is little infrastructure from Conaf and boat hire is expensive. One option is to visit with Experiencia Austral (p315) in Puyuhuapi. Acces is via Puerto Cisnes, an industrial salmon-farming area 35km west of the Carretera Austral linked by a paved road. Buses from La Junta (CH$5000, three hours) arrive here daily.

sits in a lush forest on the western shore of the Seno Ventisquero. The only access is by boat. Buildings combine the rustic look of Chilote *palafitos* (houses on stilts) with Bavarian influences, but some standard rooms lack pizzazz. Package vacationers make up most of the clientele. Packages may include boating trips to Glaciar and Laguna San Rafael. Those paying a room and breakfast rate only have access to outdoor pools. Stays may require a two-night minimum.

Three outdoor baths, including a fern-shaded hot-mud lagoon, sit right by the water, allowing visitors to soak and steam away then jump into the cool sound. The indoor spa is more elaborate but less ambient. Families frequent its cold-water pools, Jacuzzis and one large pool with different jets. Spa treatments and massages cost extra.

Day use is not offered in high season (Jan & Feb) or during high occupancy. Day-trippers get use of the outdoor pools (CH$50,000), transportation and lunch. Food is served at the hotel restaurant and a cheaper cafe.

Access via boat from the Bahía Dorita mainland dock, 13km south of Puerto Puyuhuapi. Launches (CH$10,000) leave between 10am and 6pm.

Parque Nacional Queulat

The 1540-sq-km **Parque Nacional Queulat** (admission CH$4000; ☉ 8:30am-5:30pm) is a wild realm of rivers winding through forests thick with ferns and southern beech. When the sun is out it's simply stunning, with steep-sided fjords flanked by creeping glaciers and 2000m volcanic peaks. The park straddles the Carretera Austral for 70km, midway between Chaitén and Coyhaique.

Created in 1983, the park is extremely popular but its far-flung location keeps it within reach of few. Visitors are challenged by the almost constant rain (up to 4000mm per year) and impenetrable foliage. Despite its impressive size, hiking trails are few. Conaf has struggled to maintain trailhead signs, most of which are either hidden by the aggressive growth or missing.

The **Centro de Información Ambiental** (☉ 8:30am-5:30pm), 22km south of Puerto Puyuhuapi and 2.5km from the road, at the parking lot for the Ventisquero Colgante, is the main center to the park and where admission fees are collected. It has well-organized, informative displays of plants and glacial activity, and rangers can help with hiking plans.

🏃 Activities

Near the information center, there's a quick walk to a lookout of the **Ventisquero Colgante**, the main attraction. You can also take the bridge across Río Ventisquero and follow a 3.2km trail along the crest of a moraine on the river's north bank for great glacier views. At **Laguna de Los Tempanos**, there are boat cruises (CH$12,000 for four, summer only) to the glacier.

North of the southern entrance, at Km170, a damp trail climbs the valley of the **Río de las Cascadas** through a dense forest of delicate ferns, copihue vines, tree-size fuchsias, podocarpus and lenga. The heavy rainfall percolates through the multistoried canopy. After about half an hour, the trail emerges at an impressive granite bowl where half a dozen waterfalls drop from hanging glaciers.

Twenty kilometers south of the information center, **Sendero Bosque Encantado** is a 4km roundtrip to an overlook of an impressive waterfall and its transparent pool. Park near Chucao bridge. Continuing on, the road zigzags treacherously up the Portezuelo de Queulat between Km175 and Km178, with outstanding views of the Queulat Valley.

Top-notch **fishing** can be found at the larger streams, such as the Río Cisnes, and the glacial fingers of Lago Rosselot, Lago Verde and Lago Risopatrón.

🛏 Sleeping

Camping Ventisquero   CAMPGROUND **$**
(campsites CH$6000) Near the Ventisquero Colgante, 10 attractive private sites have covered barbecues, picnic tables and hot

showers. Firewood is available. Sites are a bit rocky for pitching multiple tents.

Camping Angostura CAMPGROUND **$**
(Lago Risopatrón; campsites CH$6000) Located in a sopping rainforest, 15km north of Puerto Puyuhuapi, but the facilities are good, with firepits and hot showers.

❶ Getting There & Away

Buses connecting Chaitén and Coyhaique will drop passengers here. In summer, don't arrive late in the day to camp – spots fill in the morning and there's no onward transportation. Buy tickets for your onward bus ahead in Puyuhuapi, if possible.

Around Parque Nacional Queulat

After Parque Nacional Queulat, the road splits at the turn-off for Puerto Cisnes. From here to Coyhaique it's all paved. **Villa Amengual** is a pioneer village with a Chilote-style shingled chapel, basic family-run lodgings and basic services. It's at the foot of 2760m Cerro Alto Nevado.

An excellent option for fly-fishing or horseback riding just past the turnoff for **Puerto Aisén, Los Torreones** (✆cell 9829-3263, cell 9873-9031; Camino Turistico; d CH$80,000, half-day horseback riding CH$25,000) is a comfortable lodge in the bucolic countryside along the Río Simpson. From Coyhaique it's 42km to the Camino Turístico; take your first left.

A further 13km south of Villa Mañihuales, the Carretera Austral splits. The highway southwest to Puerto Aisén and Puerto Chacabuco is also paved. Access to Coyhaique takes an incredibly scenic route crossing the Andes through primary forest thick with ferns and lianas.

Coyhaique

✆067 / POP 59,000

The cow town that kept growing, Coyhaique is the regional hub of rural Aisén, urbane enough to house the latest techie trends, mall fashions and discos. All this is plopped in the middle of an undulating range, with rocky humpback peaks and snowy mountains in the backdrop. For the visitor, it's the launch pad for far-flung adventures, be it fly-fishing, trekking the ice cap or rambling the Carretera Austral to its end at Villa O'Higgins.

For those fresh from the rainforest wilderness of northern Aisén, it can be a jarring relapse into the world of semi trucks and subdivisions. Rural workers come to join the timber or salmon industries and add to the growing urban mass. In February 2012, massive citizen protests shut down the region and highlighted problems with poor public services and the high cost of living in Patagonia. The movement, known as Fuerza Aysén, expressed a growing frustration with the central government that remains unresolved.

At the confluence of the Río Simpson and Río Coyhaique, the sprawling city center has its plaza at the heart of a pentagonal plan.

◎ Sights & Activities

Mirador Río Simpson LOOKOUT
For prime river vistas, walk west on JM Carrera to this viewpoint.

Lago Elizalde LAKE
One of many serene mountain lakes surrounding Coyhaique and great for trout fishing, kayaking or simply time at the beach. It's just 33km from Coyhaique. Buses depart from the bus terminal.

☞ Tours

Casa del Turismo Rural CULTURAL TOUR
(✆cell 7954-4794; www.casaturismorural.cl; Plaza de Armas; ☺10:30am-7:30pm Mon-Fri, 2-6pm Sat) This organization networks visitors to rural homestays and local guide services for a grassroots approach to trekking, fishing and horseback riding. Also offers city tours and *asados* (barbecues).

GeoSur Expediciones ADVENTURE TOUR
(✆cell 9264-8671; www.patagonialearning.com; Símon Bolívar 521) Adventure and regional culture specialists offering multiday treks to Cerro Castillo or Jeinimeini-Chacabuco (US$800-1200), kayaking, hiking or country day trips at their adventure center located 57km south of Coyhaique.

Alma Patagonica TREKKING
(✆cell 7618-3588; www.almapatagonica.cl; Serrano 621) Trekking guide Hugo Castaneda guides four-day backpacking trips around Cerro Castillo (per person CH$350,000), glacier trips on the same mountain and shorter trips around Coyhaique.

Coyhaique

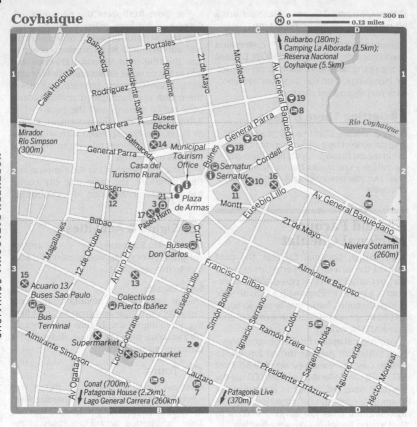

Coyhaique

🏂 Activities, Courses & Tours
1	Casa del Turismo Rural	B2
2	GeoSur Expediciones	B4
3	Navimag	B2

🛏 Sleeping
4	El Reloj	D2
5	Hostal Español	D4
6	La Estancia Cabañas	D3
7	Patagonia Hostel	B4
8	Raices B&B	C1
9	Residencial Mónica	B4

✖ Eating
10	Café Confluencia	C2
11	Cafe de Mayo	C2

12	Café Holzer	B2
13	Carnes Queulat	B3
14	Casino de Bomberos	B2
15	Dalí	A3
16	La Ovejita	C2
17	Mamma Gaucha	B2

🍷 Drinking & Nightlife
18	Bajo Marquesina	C2
	Café Confluencia	(see 10)
19	Cerveceria Arisca	C1
20	Piel Roja	C2

🛍 Shopping
21	Feria Artesanal	B2

Aventura Tehuelche ADVENTURE SPORTS
(☎cell 5681-2848; aventuratehuelche@gmail.com) Guides climbs to Los Avellanos and treks around Cerro Castillo, offering day trips (CH$50,000) from the village and a three-day trek (CH$350,000) that includes guide, porter, equipment and transport from Coyhaique.

🛏 Sleeping

Patagonia Hostel
HOSTEL $

(☑cell 6240-6974; www.patagonia-hostel.com; Lautaro 667; dm/d CH$14,000/34,000; @🛜) A welcoming German-run hostel. The rooms are stylish and minimal, but splurge with 2m-long beds and huge pillows. Tea is always available and breakfast includes fruit, cheese, salami and jam. Also offers tour services and bike rentals (CH$15,000/day).

Kooch Cabins
HOSTEL $

(☑067-252-7186; julietasotocristi@gmail.com; Camino Piedra del Indio 2; 2-/6-person cabin CH$28,000/50,000; @) Two smart cabin options on a suburban street, with down duvets and bright colors. It's 200m from the turnoff to Piedra del Indio, 10 blocks from the plaza.

Hostal Español
GUESTHOUSE $

(☑067-242-580; www.hostalcoyhaique.cl; Aldea 343; s/d CH$25,000/35,000; @) Tasteful and modern, this ample wooden house has 10 rooms with fresh quilted bedding, central heating and a personal touch. Service is great and there's a comfortable living room to put your feet up by the crackling fire.

Residencial Mónica
GUESTHOUSE $

(☑067-223-4302; Lillo 664; r per person CH$12,000) Well-attended and warm, this prim '60s-style home is always full.

★Patagonia House
BOUTIQUE HOTEL $$

(☑067-221-1488, cell 7659-9963; www.patagonia-house.com; Campo Alegre s/n; s/d/ste US$110/120/160, 3-person cottage US$160) Set apart from the bustle of downtown Coyhaique, this comfortable countryside lodging offers great service and top amenities with understated modern style. Spacious rooms feature garden views, beautiful photographs and organic toiletries. Breakfasts are extensive and their gourmet dinners (CH$17,000) with vegetarian choices are a godsend after a long day on dusty roads. It's 3km from the center. The owner Ruth also runs a travel agency specializing in Patagonian wildlife safaris and tailor-made trips.

Patagonia Live
GUESTHOUSE $$

(☑067-223-0892, cell 9886-7982; www.hostal-patagonialive.cl; Lillo 826; s/d/tw CH$28,000/39,000/45,000; 🛜) 🌿 Victor warmly welcomes guest into his immaculate suburban home with a guest breakfast nook. Rooms are comfortable and modern. With discounts for carbon offsets and a list of local artists who welcome visits.

Raices B&B
B&B $$

(☑067-221-0490, cell 9619-5672; www.raicesbedandbreakfast.com; Baquedano 444; s/d CH$49,000/69,000; P🛜) A central lodging with a tasteful, minimalist ethos. Comfortable beds are set in large rooms accented by raw wood and rustic fireplaces or space heaters. The busy location translates to some noisy rooms.

La Estancia Cabañas
CABINS $$

(☑067-250-193; cabanasla@hotmail.com; Colón 166; s/d/tr cabins CH$30,000/40,000/50,000; 🛜) These rustic, well-spaced cabins fill a quiet orchard of apple trees. Two-story cabins have tiled floors, wood stoves and kitchenettes. It's a great deal for small groups.

El Reloj
BOUTIQUE HOTEL $$$

(☑067-223-1108; www.elrelojhotel.cl; Av General Baquedano 828; s/d US$90/125; @) Comfortably upscale, this lovely lodging is actually a renovated warehouse. Old rustic remnants blend with a smart, clean design. Think cypress walls, colonial furniture and a cozy stone fireplace. Rooms are quiet, with those upstairs boasting better light and views. The restaurant is highly regarded.

Camping La Alborada
CAMPGROUND $

(☑067-223-8868; Km 1 Coyhaique-Puerto Aysén; campsite per person CH$4000) Only 1km from the city, this campground has exceptionally clean and sheltered sites (with roofs), lots of bathrooms and individual sinks, hot showers, fire pits and electricity.

🍴 Eating

The two large supermarkets that are situated side by side on Lautaro are ideal for self-caterers.

★Mamma Gaucha
PIZZA $

(☑067-221-0721; www.mammagaucha.cl; Paseo Horn 47; mains CH$5000-9000; ⏱10am-1:30am Mon-Sat) Fusing Patagon lore with a sophisticated palette and reasonable prices, Mamma Gaucha could please the fussiest road warrior. Cane ceilings and whitewashed barnboard walls create a down-home setting. Start with fresh-mint lemonade, organic wine or a pint of La Tropera. The mainstay are clay-oven pizzas, but the homemade pastas and salad bowls filled with local produce are just as worthy.

Those with wheels could venture to their sister outlet and brewery, La Tropera, on the outskirts of town.

Café Confluencia INTERNATIONAL $
(067-224-5080; 21 de Mayo 544; mains CH$4000-7000; closed Sun) A chic eatery serving lovely oversized salads, healthy mains and the occasional stir fry or taco. Mint pisco sours are the standout, but tea and fresh juices are good daytime fixes.

Café Holzer CAFE $
(www.holzer.cl; Dussen 317; cakes CH$2000; 9:30am-9pm Tue-Fri, Sat & Sun 10am-9pm;) This tiny cafe with a grassy front patio is a local favorite for sweets and caffeine. Cakes and tarts are flown in from a reputable Santiago bakery. Real coffee is served and you can also sample a gourd of *maté* to see what all the buzz is about.

Cafe de Mayo CAFE $
(cell 9709-8632; 21 de Mayo 543; mains CH$3000-6000; 9am-10pm;) A meeting spot specializing in espresso drinks, farm egg breakfasts or filling staples like *pastel de choclo* (maize casserole). There's also sandwiches, cheeseboards and home-made cakes. With shady outdoor tables or a cozy indoors with hanging teapots and fireplace.

Casino de Bomberos CHILEAN $
(067-223-1437; Parra 365; mains CH$5000; 12pm-3:30pm) Call it a cultural experience – this classic but windowless eatery packs with locals downing seafood plates or steak and eggs.

La Ovejita CAFE $
(cnr Lillo & Moraleda; mains CH$2000-5000; 9:30am-9:30pm Mon-Sat;) Settle down in this inviting nook with a pot of Dilmah tea and some goodies from the dessert case, like the chocolate made on-site. Sandwiches like almond chicken or cured ham with chive cream cheese cure you of the same-old, same-old.

★Dalí GOURMET $$
(cell 8198-2906; Lautaro 82; mains CH$10,000; 8:30pm-11pm Mon-Sat) A happy surprise, dining in this chef's home is a special event. There's no menu, just a few well-attended candlelit tables. Chef Cristian employs seasonal seafood, game and fresh local produce in innovative combinations, to delicious effect. Start with a calafate sour and end with an airy raspberry meringue.

Ruibarbo CONTEMPORARY $$
(067-221-1826; Baquedano 208; mains CH$700-13,000; 7:30am-8:30pm Mon-Fri, 8:30am-7pm) For wonderful, drawn-out lunches by the wood-stove. Highlights include appetizers like baked razor clams with bubbling cheese or smoked salmon mixed with greens and plums. There's also pisco sours and affordable set menus for lunch. Don't skip the rhubarb crème brûlée – the owner is an inventive pastry chef.

Carnes Queulat PARRILLA $$
(067-225-0507; www.carnesqueulat.cl; Ramón Freire 327; mains CH$5000-8000; 1-3:30pm & 7:30-11pm) Tucked away down a gravel alleyway, this friendly plain-Jane place happens to serve the best steaks in the region. *Carne a las brasas* – meat attentively grilled over wood fire – is the worthy house specialty, best matched with some piping-hot homemade empanadas and the secret-recipe pisco sour.

Drinking & Entertainment

Coyhaique has a surprisingly active nightlife in the summer months.

Cerveceria Arisca BREWPUB
(Baquedano 400; sandwiches CH$5000; 12:30-3pm & 7:30-11:30pm Tue-Sat) Artisan beer in a cheerful, modern space. Wash it down with ceviche or homemade shredded lamb sandwiches with mint chimichurri.

Bajo Marquesina SPORTS BAR
(067-221-0720; bajo.marquesina@gmail.com; 21 de Mayo 306; 5pm-midnight Tue-Fri, 1:30-10pm Sat & Sun) Lovers of football, unite! With vintage photos of Patagonian cowboys playing footie and jerseys from clubs all over Chile, this sports pub and dedicated football (soccer) museum has wonderful relics of bygone eras, best enjoyed if you can get the friendly owner chatting.

Piel Roja BAR
(Moraleda 495; 6pm-5am) Rumbling late-night life with local youth and the occasional adventure guide. Upstairs becomes a romping dance floor in the wee hours.

Café Confluencia CAFE
(067-224-5080; 21 de Mayo 548) Two-for-one drink specials and live music on the weekends featuring a range of rock-and-roll bands and Latin acts turn this cool cafe into a crowded nightspot come 1am.

Shopping

Feria Artesanal MARKET
(Plaza de Armas) Artisan goods, woolens and wood carvings; shop No 15 has particularly good original paintings and crafts.

ℹ Information

Along Condell, between the plaza and Av Baquedano, are a number of banks with ATMs. Get cash here; it is one of the few stops on the Carretera Austral with Visa ATM access.

Cabot (☑ 067-223-0101; General Para 177) A general service travel agency.

Conaf (☑ 067-221-2109; Av Ogaña 1060; ⊙ 9am-8pm Mon-Sat, 10am-6pm Sun) Provides information on the area's parks and reserves.

Hospital Regional (☑ 067-221-9100; Ibar 68; ⊙ 24hr) Emergency is open 24 hours.

Municipal Tourism Office (☑ 067-221-1253; Plaza de Armas; ⊙ 9am-1pm & 3-7pm Thu-Tue) English-speaking, helpful with excursion and accommodations information.

Police (☑ 067-221-5105; Baquedano 534)

Post Office (Lord Cochrane 202) Near Plaza de Armas.

Sernatur (☑ 067-223-3949; www.recorreaysen. cl; Bulnes 35; ⊙ 9am-9pm Mon-Fri, 10am-9pm Sat & Sun summer) A helpful office with lists of activity, lodging and transportation options and costs. Regional information is also available.

Turismo Prado (☑ 067-223-1271; 21 de Mayo 417; ⊙ 9am-6pm) Changes currency.

ℹ Getting There & Away

AIR

LAN (☑ 600-526-2000; Parra 402) Has several daily flights (most leaving in the morning) to Puerto Montt (CH$100,000) and Santiago (CH$214,000) from the Balmaceda airport; note that rates can be deeply discounted if purchased in-country.

Sky Airline (☑ 067-240-827; www.skyairline.cl; Arturo Prat 203) Flights from Santiago stop at Balmaceda on the way to Punta Arenas.

Aerocord (☑ 067-224-6300; www.aerocord. cl; Parra 21, Coyhaique) Flies small craft to Villa O'Higgins (CH$28,000) on Monday and Thursday at 10am. Charter flights are available to Raul Marin Balmaceda, Parque Nacional Laguna San Rafael and Chile Chico.

BOAT

Ferries and cruises to Puerto Montt, Chiloé and Parque Nacional Laguna San Rafael leave from Puerto Chacabuco, one hour west of Coyhaique by bus; the closest regional offices are in Coyhaique.

Travelers to Chile Chico can purchase ferry tickets in town at Naviera Sotramin (p458), the ferry that crosses Lago General Carrera between Puerto Ingeniero Ibáñez and Chile Chico almost daily, saving drivers a lot of time on bad roads. If you're driving, make reservations a week out in summer.

BUS

Buses operate from the **bus terminal** (☑ 067-225-8203; cnr Lautaro & Magallanes) and separate offices. Schedules change continuously; check with **Sernatur** (☑ 067-233-949; Bulnes 35) for the latest information. Busing in and out of Coyhaique is just about as confusing as getting around the plaza. Companies and departures vary on demand, and unless noted leave from the terminal.

DESTINATION	COST (CH$)	DURATION (HR)
Chaitén	24,000	9-11
Chile Chico	6000	3½ with ferry
Cochrane	13,000	7-10
Futaleufú	20,000	8-9
La Junta	10,000	6
Puerto Montt	30,000	23
Puyuhuapi	8000	5

Companies serving destinations north:

Aguilas Patagonicas (☑ 067-221-1288; www. aguilaspatagonicas.cl) La Junta, Puyuhuapi and Puerto Cisnes, leaving at 3pm daily.

Transaustral (☑ 067-223-2067) Osorno and south to Comodoro Rivadavia, Argentina, for connections to Punta Arenas.

Buses Becker (☑ 067-223-2167; www.buses-becker.com; General Parra 335) Runs services twice weekly to Puyuhuapi, La Junta, Villa Santa Lucía and Chaitén. To Futaleufú on Saturdays.

Transportes Terra Austral (☑ 067-225-4355) Puyuhuapi and La Junta.

Queilen Bus (☑ 067-224-0760) Osorno, Puerto Montt, Santiago and Chiloé via Argentina.

Companies serving destinations south:

Acuario 13/Buses Sao Paulo (☑ 067-252-2143, cell 9874-8022) Cochrane at 8am on Tuesday, Thursday and Saturday.

Buses Don Carlos (☑ 067-223-1981; Cruz 63) Serves Villa Cerro Castillo, Puerto Río Tranquilo, Puerto Bertrand and Cochrane.

Colectivos Puerto Ibáñez (cnr Prat & Errázuríz) Door-to-door shuttle to Puerto Ingeniero Ibáñez (CH$3500, 1½ hours).

ℹ Getting Around

TO/FROM THE AIRPORT

Door-to-door shuttle service (CH$5000) to Balmaceda airport, 50km southeast of town; leaves two hours before flight departure. Take any airport transfer or call **Transfer Velasquez** (☑ 067-225-0413) for pick-up service.

CAR & BICYCLE

Car rental is expensive and availability limited in summer. However, it's a popular option since public transportation is infrequent and focused on major destinations. Shop around for the best price and, if possible, reserve ahead. Try **Traeger** (☑ 067-223-1648; www.traeger.cl; Av General Baquedano 457), with its own repair shop and tow service, or **Los Andes Patagónicos** (☑ 067-223-2920; Horn 48). **Figon** (☑ 067-223-4616; Simpson 888) rents and repairs bicycles.

Reserva Nacional Coyhaique

Draped in lenga, ñire and coigue, the 21.5-sq-km Reserva Nacional Coyhaique has small lakes and Cerro Cinchao (1361m). The park is 5km from Coyhaique (about 1½ hours on foot), with views of town and Cerro Mackay's enormous basalt columns in the distance. Take Baquedano north, across the bridge, then go right at the gravel road, a steep climb best accessed by 4WD.

From the park entrance, it's 2.5km to the Casa Bruja sector, where you'll find campsites (CH$5000 per site) with fire pits, hot water, showers and bathrooms. Hike 4km through coigue and lenga forests to Laguna Verde, with picnic sites and camping with basic facilities. Hiking trails also lead to Laguna Los Sapos and Laguna Venus.

Reserva Nacional Río Simpson

Rocky elephant buttes flank the lazy curves of Río Simpson in a broad valley 37km west of Coyhaique. Straddling the highway to Puerto Chacabuco, the 410-sq-km Reserva Nacional Río Simpson is an easily accessed scenic area that is popular with anglers and summer soakers. Conaf's Centro de Visitantes (admission CH$1000; ⊙10am-4pm Mon-Sat, 11am-2pm Sun), on the Coyhaique–Puerto Aisén road, has a small natural-history museum and botanical garden. A short walk leads to Cascada de la Virgen, a shimmering waterfall on the north side of the highway.

Five kilometers east of the Centro de Visitantes, Camping San Sebastián (campsites per group CH$7000) has sheltered sites and hot showers. Near the confluence of the Río Simpson and Río Correntoso, 24km west of Coyhaique, Camping Río Correntoso (☑ 067-232-005; campsites per group CH$7000) has 50 spacious riverside sites in a bucolic setting. The showers are rustic, but hot.

From Coyhaique there are frequent buses for Puerto Aisén.

Monumento Natural Dos Lagunas

Near Paso Alto Coyhaique on the Argentine border, this 181-hectare wetland reserve (admission CH$2000) hosts diverse birdlife, including swans, coots and grebes. It's an ecological transition zone from southern beech forest to semiarid steppe. Orchids abound. A short hiking trail goes to Laguna El Toro while a longer loop flanks the northern edge of Laguna Escondida. Near the entrance there's a self-guided nature trail (1km) and picnic area. While the park lacks regular public transportation, Coyhaique's branch of Conaf may be able to offer suggestions for getting there.

Parque Nacional Laguna San Rafael

Awesome and remote, this national park (entry CH$4000) brings visitors face to face with the 30,000-year-old San Valentín glacier in Chile's northern ice field. Established in 1959, the 12,000-sq-km Unesco Biosphere Reserve is a major regional attraction. The park encompasses peaty wetlands, pristine temperate rainforest of southern beech and epiphytes, and 4058m Monte San Valentín, the southern Andes' highest peak. Scientific interest centers on the extreme fluctuation in water level of the glacier-fed lagoon.

Until recently, getting here was expensive and time consuming. Most visitors arrived by cruise, shifting to smaller craft and rubber rafts to approach the glacier's 60m face. Unfortunately, this approach permits only a few hours at the glacier without exploring the surrounding trails.

A new 77km gravel road travels Valle Exploradres from Puerto Río Tranquilo to Bahía Exploradores. The new route makes day trips possible from Río Tranquilo: outfitters provide a necessary boat crossing to continue on from where the road ends. Stay overnight to hear the sighs, splintering and booms of calving ice.

There is camping (per site CH$5000) near the Conaf office by the airstrip. Five rustic campsites have water and bathrooms. Fires are not allowed and no food is available at the park.

⟁ Tours

The following ships sail from Puerto Chacabuco and Puerto Montt. Check website's for departures and student/senior discounts.

Emtrex
GLACIER TOUR

([✏]cell 8259-4017; www.exploradores-sanrafael.
cl; per person day trip/overnight CH$140,000/
220,000) Run by a knowledgeable adventure-travel group, these excursions provide
access to the glacier in an open Zodiac boat
(passengers are provided with flotation
suits). Overnights are spent in a well-heeled
base camp in the park. Day trips start at
Km75 on the Valle Exploradores road.
Longer excursions feature hiking.

Destino Patagonia
GLACIER TOUR

([✏]cell 9158-6044; www.destinopatagonia.cl; per
person full day CH$140,000) This tour picks up
participants at Km77 on the Valle Exploradores road (overland transfers from Puerto
Río Tranquilo extra). It visits the San Rafael
Glacier in a covered boat. Includes lunch
and whiskey on millennial ice.

Cruceros Skorpios
CRUISE

([✏]in Santiago 02-477-1900; www.skorpios.cl;
6-day, 5-night cruise d occupancy from US$4400)
The luxuriant *Skorpios II* sails from Puerto
Montt, spending all of the third day at the
glacier. A highlight is the stop at Quitralco,
Skorpios' private hot-springs resort. On the
return it visits the island of Chiloé.

Navimag
FERRY

([✏]067-223-3306; www.navimag.com; Paseo Horn
47-D, Coyhaique; ferry to Puerto Montt passenger/
vehicle from CH$35,000/160,000) Sailing the
lovely fjords and islands of Patagonia, the
Puerto Chacabuco to Puerto Montt ferry
takes 24 hours. Cabins range from individual bunks in shared rooms to private doubles.

Catamaranes del Sur
CRUISE

([✏]067-235-1112; www.catamaranesdelsur.cl; JM
Carrera 50, Puerto Chacabuco; glacier day trip per
person CH$190,000) Runs a 12-hour day trip
from Puerto Chacabuco on the *Catamaran
Chaitén* and the smaller *Iceberg Expedition,* with deep discounts in low season.
Daytime travel ensures fjord views, but less
time at the glacier face. There's also lodging
at the exclusive but nondescript Loberías del
Sur and visits to its private park Aikén.

Reserva Nacional
Cerro Castillo

Cerro Castillo's basalt spires are the crowning centerpiece of **Reserva Nacional Cerro Castillo** (admission CH$2000) a sprawling
1800-sq-km mountain reserve of southern
beech forest, 75km south of Coyhaique. The
park boasts fine fishing and hiking, along
with little foot traffic. Its namesake, the
2700m triple-tier Cerro Castillo, is flanked
by three major glaciers on its southern
slopes. Hikers can complete a segment of
Sendero de Chile with the 16km trail to
Campamento Neozelandés. Another recommended four-day trek (described in Lonely
Planet's *Trekking in the Patagonian Andes*)
leaves from Km75, at the north end of the reserve, and goes to Villa Cerro Castillo at the
south end via a high route passing glaciers,
rivers and lakes.

Conaf operates a sheltered **campground**
(tent CH$3500) at Laguna Chaguay, 67km
south of Coyhaique. It has bathrooms and hot
showers. Backcountry camping is also possible. Before going into the backcountry, check
in with the ranger to avoid seasonal hazards.

Buses can leave passengers at the turnoff
to the ranger station and campground.

Villa Cerro Castillo

Under the sparkly five-karat face of Cerro
Castillo, pioneer town Villa Cerro Castillo has
a congenial dusty-heeled feel. It's a good base
to explore the reserve and a short distance
from the Carretera Austral, 10km west of the
Puerto Ingeniero Ibáñez junction. The town's
Festival Costumbrista, usually held in February, offers an authentic take on Patagonian
rodeo and draws artists and artisans from all
over Chile and Argentina. The helpful **tourist
office** (cnr Carretera Austral & O'Higgins; [⊙]10am-
1pm & 2pm-6pm Jan-Feb) has information.

The clean family lodging **Cabañas
Don Niba** ([✏]cell 9474-0408; Los Pioneros 872; d CH$25,000, s/d without bathroom
CH$9000/18,000) dishes out whopping
breakfasts, horseback riding, *asados* and
hikes. **Baqueanos de la Patagonia** ([✏]cell
6513-6226, cell 7898-8550; www.baqueanos-
delapatagonia.cl; Camino sector Arroyo el Bosque;
camping per person CH$4000) offers camping
with hot showers, barbecues and bikes. They
also lead good horseback treks and practice
domo racional, a gentle taming method.

You can't miss **La Cocina de Sole** ([✏]cell
9839-8135; Carretera Austral s/n; sandwiches
CH$4000; [⊙]8:30am-8pm), a roadside bus
painted in swirling pastels, serving enormous steak sandwiches and juices. For satisfying sit-down meals, **La Querencia** ([✏]cell
9503-0746; O'Higgins 522; set menu CH$5000;
[⊙]8am-8pm) and **Villarica** ([✏]cell 6656-0173;

O'Higgins 592; mains CH$4000-7000; ⊗8am-10pm daily) cook homemade set lunches.

Buses heading north to Coyhaique or south to Puerto Río Tranquilo pass daily.

Puerto Ingeniero Ibáñez

☑ 067 / POP 3000

On the north shore of Lago General Carrera, sleepy Puerto Ingeniero Ibáñez serves as a transit station for ferry goers, although new sport-climbing routes are making it a hot stop for climbers. Clobbered in Volcán Hudson's 1991 eruption, it has since recovered.

Ferries to Chile Chico, on the lake's south shore, leave from here. If local handicrafts interest you, ask around for pottery artist Señora Marta Aguila or weaver and herbal-remedy specialist Señora Juana Vega. It's that informal. Locals can also point you to cave paintings or the stunning Río Ibañez falls.

Around 1.5km after the turnoff to Ibáñez, **La Casona** (☑ cell 7106-3591; senderospatagonia@gmail.com; dm/s/d with shared bathroom CH$12,000/15,000/30,000, d CH$40,000, camping per person CH$5000) offers friendly, electric pink farmhouse lodgings and camping, ideal for cyclists or hikers. Campers will find friendly faces at countryside **Maitenal Camping** (☑ cell 8389-2832; Camino a Levican, Km10; campsites per person CH$2500, dm CH$6000), with good installations, including showers, lamb for barbecues and artisan beer. Host Lillian is a certified guide and her German husband Gerald maintains the on-site climbs (suitable for all levels). To get there, follow past the waterfall to Levican and take the right-hand offshoot at km10.

Ferry **Naviera Sotramin** (☑ 067-252-6992; www.sotramin.cl; General Carrera 202; passenger/automobile CH$2100/18,650) crosses Lago General Carrera almost daily; arrive 30 minutes predeparture. Get current ferry schedules online. To Coyhaique, **Buses Acuña** (☑ 067-225-1579) goes almost daily (CH$5000, two hours) when the ferry from Chile Chico arrives.

Chile Chico

☑ 067 / POP 4600

Bordering Argentina, this pint-sized orchard town occupies the windy southern shore of Lago General Carrera. It is linked to Chile by ferry or a roller-coaster road dotted with gold and silver mines. Locals traditionally earned their living from raising livestock and farming, but have since turned to mining. Rumor has it that wi-fi is soon coming to town.

Hikers shouldn't miss the Reserva Nacional Jeinimeni, 60km away, with solitary treks in an arid wonderland of flamingo-filled turquoise mountain lagoons. Travelers can cross easily to Los Antiguos, Argentina, and onward to Ruta 40 and points south.

Traveling the abrupt curves of Paso Las Llaves, west from Chile Chico to the junction with the Carretera Austral, is one of the region's highlights. Scary and stunning, it hits blind corners and steep inclines on loose gravel high above the lake. There's no guardrails, so drivers should proceed with caution.

◎ Sights & Activities

Casa de la Cultura　　　　　　　　MUSEUM
(☑ 067-241-1355; cnr O'Higgins & Lautaro; ⊗9am-1pm & 3pm-6pm Mon-Fri) **FREE** Features works by regional artists and a 2nd-floor assemblage of local artifacts, including minerals and fossils. Outside, the restored *El Andes* was built in Glasgow, Scotland, to navigate the Thames, but was brought here to transport passengers and freight around the lake.

Expeditions Patagonia　　　ADVENTURE TOURS
(☑ cell 8464-1067; www.expeditionspatagonia.com; O'Higgins 333, Galeria Municipal; ⊗9am-1pm & 2:30-8pm) Run by Ferdinando Georgia, a reputable guide and graduate of Escuela de Guias (a rigorous training program in Coyhaique), this outfitter does trekking in Jeinimeni, multiday trips and mountaineering expeditions.

Patagonia Xpress　　　　　ADVENTURE TOUR
(☑ cell 9802-0280; www.patagoniaxpress.cl; O'Higgins 333, Galería Municipal #4; all-day multisport CH$92,000; ⊗9am-1pm & 3pm-6pm) Mountain biking and hiking adventures in Reserva Nacional Jeinimeni, where they also do drop-offs (CH$30,000 per person). Friendly staff.

🛏 Sleeping & Eating

Ñandu Camp　　　　　　　　　HOSTEL $
(☑ cell 6779-3390; www.nanducamp.com; O'Higgins 750; dm CH$12,000; 🐾) Ample dorm lodging in an octagonal space with guest kitchen. The mountaineering owners are developing huts in Reserva Nacional Jeinimeni and offer extensive information for trekkers, as well as transfers to the park.

Hospedaje Brisas del Lago　　GUESTHOUSE $
(☑ 067-241-1204; brisasdellago@gmail.com; Manuel Rodríguez 443; s/d apt CH$25,000/35,000, s/d without bathroom CH$15,000/25,000) There are a number of good-sized rooms, both clean and comfortable, and cute cabins squeezed into the backyard strewn with flowerbeds.

Kon Aiken GUESTHOUSE $
(☑ 067-241-1598; Pedro Burgos 6; campsites per person CH$4000, r per person CH$12,000, 7-person cabin from CH$30,000) A handy lodging with a family atmosphere, sometimes chaotic. The kind owners sell firewood, share the bounty of local produce and organize the occasional *asado* or salmon bake. A row of poplars blocks the winds for campers.

★**Hostería de la Patagonia** GUESTHOUSE $$
(☑067-241-1337, cell 8159-2146; hdelapatagonia@gmail.com; Camino Internacional s/n; camping per person CH$4000, per person without bathroom CH$15,000, s/d/tr CH$35,000/50,000/61,000, cabin CH$50,000; ☏) Descendants of Belgian colonists run this sweet farmhouse with horses, historic memorabilia and a garden hot tub (extra). The 1st floor rooms are all renovated, with central heating. The cabin is actually a restored boat with kitchen – charming though landlocked. They serve dinner and are very helpful with travel plans. Look for the yellow roof, leaving town toward Argentina.

La Posada del Río HOTEL $$
(☑ cell 9452-0759, cell 9647-0968; www.posadadelriolodge.com; Camino Internacional, Km5; s/d/tr US$66/88/111) On the open steppe with sweeping views, this boxy newcomer has bright, attractive rooms and breakfasts with orange juice and *medialunas* (croissants).

Restaurante Facundo CHILEAN $$
(☑067-241-1452; Manuel Rodriguez 243; mains CH$8000; ☉noon-3:30pm & 7-11pm) A bustling restaurant with lake views and rustic details. Service is slow but portions of roast potatoes, salad and lamb or salmon are enormous.

ℹ Information

BancoEstado (González 112; ☉ 9am-2pm Mon-Fri) Changes US cash only and has reasonable rates, but collects a commission on all traveler's checks. The ATM only takes MasterCard.
Conaf (☑ 067-241-1325; Blest Gana 121; ☉10am-6pm Mon-Fri, 11am-4pm Sat) For information on Reserva Nacional Jeinimeni.
Oficina de Información Turística (☑ 067-241-1338; www.chilechico.cl; cnr O'Higgins & Blest Ghana; ☉ 8am-1pm & 2pm-5pm Mon-Fri) Excellent area information.
Post Office (Manuel Rodríguez 121)

ℹ Getting There & Away

There's a Copec gas station.

BOAT

An almost-daily ferry run by **Naviera Sotramin** (☑067-223-7958; www.sotramin.cl; Muelle Chile Chico; passenger/automobile CH$2000/17,700) crosses Lago General Carrera to Puerto Ingeniero Ibáñez, a big shortcut to Coyhaique. If driving, make reservations a week out in summer. Arrive 30 minutes pre-departure.

BUS

A number of shuttle buses cross the border to Los Antiguos, Argentina (CH$2000, 20 minutes), just 9km east. Shuttles, which coordinate with buses that run directly to El Chaltén, leave from O'Higgins 420. From Los Antiguos, travelers can make connections in Argentina to Perito Moreno, El Chaltén and southern Argentine Patagonia.

Bus routes are run by private individuals subject to applying for the government concession, so providers and schedules can vary from year to year.

To Puerto Guadal (CH$7000, 2½ hours), **Seguel** (☑ 067-243-1214; O'Higgins 394) and **Buses Eca** (☑ 067-243-1224) go Monday to Friday at 4pm or 5pm. To Puerto Río Tranquilo (CH$14,000, four hours), Costa Carrera has service on Tuesday and Friday at 11am. To Cochrane (CH$14,000, four hours), **Fernando Varas** (☑ cell 7756-8234) goes on Monday and Friday at 8am.

Buses Acuña (☑ 067-225-1579; Rodríguez 143) and **Buses Carolina** (☑ 067-241-1490; ferry office) go to Coyhaique (CH$5000, 3½ hours) with a ferry-bus combination; reserve ahead. You will first take the Naviera Sotramin Ferry to Puerto Ibáñez.

Reserva Nacional Jeinimeni

Turquoise lakes and the rusted hues of the steppe mark the rarely visited **Reserva Nacional Jeinimeni** (admission CH$2000) 52km southwest of Chile Chico. Its unusual wonders range from cave paintings to foxes and flamingos. In the transition zone to the Patagonian steppe, it covers 1610 sq km. Through-hikers can link to Valle Chacabuco via a three-day mountain traverse; for details ask at Parque Nacional Patagonia.

Three private **camping areas** (per site CH$5000) are on the banks of the startlingly blue Lago Jeinimeni, about 400m from the Conaf office. **Sendero Lago Verde** takes visitors on a three-hour, 10km-round-trip hike to a gemstone lake. For park access, 4WD is necessary because Río Jeinimeni cuts across the road, causing sporadic flooding conditions. Day-trippers should leave early enough to cross on the way back before 4pm.

Beginning at Sendero Lago Verde, the four-day (45km) backpacking route to Aviles Valley in Futuro Parque Nacional Patagonia in **Paso de la Gloria** is gaining interest, though the logistics are not easy (transfers must be arranged ahead). The route requires navigational skills and mountain expertise, as there are minimal markings and many river crossings.

Operator **Patagonia Huts** (☑cell 6779-3390; hiking packages per person per day US$250) offers all-inclusive mountain guide service, with stays at a new private *refugio* in the park.

En route to the reserve, about 25km south of Chile Chico, an access road leads to **Cueva de las Manos**, Tehuelche cave paintings less impressive than their Argentine counterpart of the same name. Reaching the cave requires a steep uphill climb (unmarked) best done with a guide.

Puerto Río Tranquilo

☑067

A village of shingled houses on the windy western shores of Lago General Carrera, Puerto Río Tranquilo is a humble pit stop in a growth spurt. For many travelers, it's just a fuel stop, but growing outdoor opportunities have put it on the map. It's the closest access point to Capilla de Marmol's cool marble caves. More recently it's become the launch point for more budget-minded tours to the stunning Glaciar San Rafael. There's no ATM.

◉ Sights & Activities

Due to the invasive didymo algae, boats and kayaks need permits, which are available at the Capitanía.

Capilla de Mármol   LANDMARK
(Marble Chapel) Well worth the detour, these sculpted geological formations are accessible by boat on Lago General Carrera. Trips (from CH$40,000 for five passengers) only go out in calm boating conditions. If you're driving, continue 8km south of town to the tour boats at Bahía Manso. It's directly across from the caves and at a shorter boating distance.

Valle Exploradores   DRIVING TOUR
This new east–west road heads toward Laguna San Rafael, but stops short at a water crossing. Gorgeous but rough, it is still a worthy driving or biking detour, crowded with glaciers and overgrown nalca plants. Keep an eye out for the **Glaciar Exploradores Overlook** (CH$1500 trail fee) at Km52. Day-trippers to Glaciar San Rafael meet their outfitters at the end of the road.

⌂ Sleeping & Eating

Residencial Darka   GUESTHOUSE $
(☑cell 9126-5292; Arrayanes 330; r per person CH$13,000) Family-run, with clean rooms. The pastels and lace provide a good dose of kitsch.

Camping Pudu   CAMPGROUND $
(☑cell 8920-5085; www.puduexcursiones.cl; campsites per person CH$6000; ☺Dec-Mar) Attractive beach camping with hot showers, laundry service and sauna (CH$12,000), 1km south of Puerto Río Tranquilo. Offers tourist info.

★El Puesto   INN $$
(☑cell 6207-3794; www.elpuesto.cl; Pedro Lagos 258; s/d/tr US$131/184/210; ☎) This smart 10-room hotel pampers with woolen slippers, hand-woven throws and rockers. There's a swing set for kids. The English-speaking owners run reputable ice treks on Glaciar Exploradores, kayaking and other services. Dinner (CH$15,000) is available with reservations; they also offer massage and rent local cabins.

Campo Alacaluf   INN $$
(www.campoalacaluf.com; Km44, Valle Exploradores; camping per person CH$3000, d/tr CH$46,000/60,000, d/tr without bathroom CH$28,000/42,000) This rural stone lodging is the sole option in remote Valle Exploradores (located roughly midway). The German owners also offer showers for campers (CH$1500), meals (from CH$8000), and lunchboxes with homemade bread. Reserve via the website.

Cervecería Río Tranquilo   BREWPUB $
(☑cell 9895-5577; Carretera Austral s/n; sandwiches CH$5000) Facing the tourism kiosk, this pub makes Arisca beer onsite, served alongside lamb sandwiches on homemade bread.

ℹ Information

Tourism Kiosk (Av Costanera s/n; ☺10am-1pm & 2-6:30pm Tue-Sun Dec-Mar) Has information about lodging, alternate transportation (including vans to Valle Exploradores) and tours to the Capilla de Mármol.

Casa del Turista (☑cell 5189-3146; cnr Av Costanera & Pedro Lagos; ☺9am-noon & 4-9pm) Organizes adventure tours and boat trips to Glacier San Rafael.

ℹ Getting There & Away

Regular buses between Coyhaique (CH$10,000) and Cochrane (CH$8000) will drop off and pick up passengers here. Minibus **Vidal** (☑cell 9932-9896) travels to Coyhaique twice weekly. Coyhaique-bound buses usually pass at around 10am. Those heading further south pass between 1pm and 2pm. To Chile Chico (CH$14,000), the bus passes at around 2pm on Wednesday and Sunday.

Cruce el Maitén

Cruce el Maitén is little more than a fork in the road where an eastern route branches alongside Lago General Carrera to Chile Chico. With a new adventure center on the lake, reputable tour operator **Pared Sur** (☑cell 9345-6736, in Santiago 022-207-3525; www.paredsur.cl; Bahía Catalina) has deluxe camping and packages for biking, kayaking, rafting and canopy tours. Lakeside **Hacienda Tres Lagos** (☑067-241-1323; www.haciendatreslagos.com; Km274; s/d from US$280/312; @중) offers elegant accommodations, fishing trips and amenities that aim to please all, namely an art gallery, zip line, sauna, Jacuzzi and cafe.

Puerto Guadal

Windy but damn postcard beautiful, Puerto Guadal is located at the southwest end of Lago General Carrera on the road to Chile Chico, 13km east of the Carretera Austral. The village appears to hold siesta at all hours, but cool accommodations, nearby fossil hikes and glaciers can keep a visitor very entertained.

Adventure outfitter **Kalen** (☑067-243-1289, cell 8811-2535; turismokalenpatagonia@gmail.com; Los Alerces 557; ⊙9am-9pm) is run by reputable guide Pascual Diaz. He offers horseback riding, glacier trips (CH$60,000) and hikes to a beautiful fossil bed (CH$25,000 per person) with a four-person minimum. Contact in advance, as the office closes during outings.

🛏 Sleeping

Destino No Turistico   HOSTEL, CAMPGROUND $
(☑cell 8756-7545; www.destino-noturistico.com; Camino Laguna La Manga, Km 1; campsites per person CH$5500, dm/d CH$12,000/28,000) 🦮 With rave reviews, ecocamp and hostel Destino No Turistico provides a lovely countryside getaway. Owners Rocio and Marcelo are active educators, teaching off-grid living and sharing their innovations. The hostel is impeccable, with comfortable beds, each with its own reading lamp, in addition to solar showers, kitchen use and composting toilets. It's situated 1.5km from town, an uphill walk. A pickup may be possible for multiple-day stays. Cars should park outside the entrance gate.

⭐ Terra Luna   CABINS $$$
(☑067-243-1263; www.terra-luna.cl; campsites per person CH$5000, 2-person huts CH$36,000, d/tr/q from CH$77,000/95,000/105,000; 중🐾) Lakeside adventure lodge Terra Luna pre-

sents the option of perfect repose or an adrenaline rush. Lodgings vary from smart apartments to cabins and excellent treehouses, with the tempting extra of a lakefront wood-fired hot tub. The restaurant serves a set menu of chef-prepared meals nightly. Adorable budget-oriented huts with kitchen and campsites suit budget travelers, though spots are few. With sprawling grounds, there is also a play area, kayaks and zip lines. Run by Azimut, a French-owned guide service, there are frequent excursions like glacier visits and hikes by jet boat, canyoning and overnighting on the Campo de Hielo Norte. It's 1.5km from Puerto Guadal toward Chile Chico.

ℹ Getting There & Away

Buses leave from **ECA** (☑067-243-1224; Las Magnolias 306), heading north to Coyhaique (CH$11,000) Wednesdays and Sundays at around 8am. Bus services that are southbound pass the crossroads just outside of town, to Cochrane (CH$5000) starting at around 2pm.

Seguel (☑067-231-1214; Los Notros 560) services Chile Chico (CH$7000, three hours) on Mondays and Thursdays at about 7am. Check locally for other bus servcies; the website of Destino No Turistico usually has updated information.

Puerto Bertrand & the Baker River

☑067 / POP 1500
On the bank of the ultramarine blue Lago Bertrand below the snow-covered San Valentín and Campo de Hielo Norte, Puerto Bertrand is a show of contrasts. Weathered shingle homes overgrown with rose blossoms and high-end fishing lodges share the space of this humble stop. Bertrand occupies the southeast shore of the lake, situated 11km south of Cruce el Maitén. It is also the base for rafting Río Baker, Chile's most voluminous river. The Río Baker flows from Lago Bertrand, running parallel to the Carretera Austral south toward Cochrane. Lodges and a museum flank this scenic strip.

◉ Sights & Activities

⭐ **La Confluencia**   LANDMARK
(The Confluence) Don't miss this viewpoint, where Chile's most powerful river, the Baker, froths into a broad, behemoth cascade before merging with the milkier, glacial-fed Río Nef in a swirling contrast of mint and electric blue. It's 12km south of Puerto Bertrand. Park roadside and follow the 800m trail.

Museo Pioneros del Baker　　MUSEUM
(www.fundacionriobaker.cl; Carretera Austral s/n; ⊙ by request) **FREE** In a pioneer house, this adorable new cultural museum packs in engaging details, from Patagonian sayings to pioneer relics and molds of animal tracks. It's all in Spanish. For the key, go to the caretaker's house out back. It's located roadside between Puerto Bertrand and the entrance to Valle Chacabuco.

Baker Patagonia Aventura　　RAFTING
(🖉 cell 8817-7525; www.bakerpatagonia.com; half-day trips CH$28,000) Leads five-day and one-day (Class III) raft trips on the Río Baker. The office faces Lago Bertrand.

🛏 Sleeping & Eating

Hostería Puerto Bertrand　　GUESTHOUSE $
(🖉 cell 9219-1532; Costanera s/n; r per person without bathroom CH$12,000, cabin CH$45,000) Above the general store, this rickety wood home has a cozy atmosphere with soft armchairs and lace-covered tables. Shop around for a room with ventilation.

Patagonia Green Baker　　CABINS $$
(🖉 cell 9159-7757, in Santiago 02-196-0409; www.greenlodgebaker.com; Carretera Austral s/n; d CH$60,000; 2-/3-/4-person cabins CH$60,000/75,000/90,000) These two-story cabins are a pleasant enough stop. Riverside, the complex features a hot tub, restaurant and activities like kayaking and horseback riding. Cabins have direct TV and phones. It's 3km south of Puerto Bertrand.

★ Bordebaker Lodge　　CABINS $$$
(🖉 in Santiago 022-585-8464; www.bordebaker.cl; Carretera Austral s/n; d US$260) A tasteful design hotel with rustic touches, Bordebaker has a two-story main lodge connected by boardwalk to modern cabins. Each overlooks a sublime stretch of the emerald Baker River. The lodge offers tours with local operators and organic chef-made meals (dinner US$40). It's 8km south of Puerto Bertrand.

Valle Chacabuco (Parque Nacional Patagonia)

Eighteen kilometers north of Cochrane, this reformed *estancia* (grazing ranch) is home to flamingo, guanaco, huemul (endangered Andean deer), puma, viscacha and fox. Conservacion Patagonica, the NGO behind the Patagonia National Park project, began this initiative in 2004. Now

dubbed the Serengeti of the Southern Cone, the 690-sq-km Valle Chacabuco features Patagonian steppe, forests, mountains, lakes and lagoons. The park stretches from the Río Baker to the Argentine border. In a private vehicle, it's possible to cross here at Paso Roballos.

It's still a national park in the making. Combining this valley with Reserva Nacional Jeinimeni to the north and Reserva Nacional Tamango to the south will eventually result in a 2400-sq-km park worthy of one day rivaling Torres del Paine.

Major rehabilitation, with the help of many volunteers, has reinstated the valley as an important wildlife corridor. Already foxes and herds of guanaco are easily spotted. Studies underway in the park look at grasslands ecology and track huemul populations. The park's roaming population consists of around 120 huemules, out of a worldwide population of 2000. The park is still adding trails and campgrounds.

🏃 Activities

Lagunas Altas Trail　　HIKING
This 23km trail ascends from the Westwind Camping site (near park headquarters) toward a southern ridge and heads east across open terrain and around small gemstone lakes before winding down toward the administration buildings, with spectacular views of the Chacabuco Valley, San Lorenzo, and the northern Patagonian ice field. It's a long day hike; bring plenty of water.

Aviles Valley Trail　　HIKING
A gorgeous 16km loop through open steppe. It starts at the Stone House Camping site (25km up valley from the main park headquarters). Continue for a three- to four-day (about 45km) backpack to Jeinimeni National Reserve near Chile Chico, but get detailed information first, as the reserve is far from town, with no public transportation.

Valley Drive　　WILDLIFE WATCHING
The 72km drive from the Río Baker to the Argentine border climbs through steppe, with flamingos in lagoons and foxes crossing the road. Drive slowly and pull out only where there's room.

☞ Tours

Guided Tours　　TOUR
(half-day 6-person group US$150) An official park guide offers excellent birdwatching tours, guided tours and treks, in English and Spanish. Book far in advance.

🛏 Sleeping & Eating

Visitors can also lodge in nearby Cochrane.

Westwind Camping   CAMPGROUND **$**
(campsite per person CH$5000) In the valley, this large, grassy campground features eight covered cook shelters and a bathhouse with hot solar showers. Sites are first-come, first-served. It's 4km from the administrative area.

Stone House Camping   CAMPGROUND **$**
(campsite per person CH$5000) Part way up the valley drive, it's about 25km from the administrative area. The bathrooms are housed in a historic stone outpost left over from the park's days as a sheep *estancia*.

**The Lodge at
Valle Chacabuco**   BOUTIQUE HOTEL **$$$**
(reservas@vallechacabuco.cl; s/d US$350/500; ☉ mid-Oct–Apr) Classic and refined, this beautiful stone lodge was modeled on English architecture in southern Argentina. Patterned tiles, handsome wood and large photographic nature prints foster a warm ambience. There are just 10 guest rooms, mostly doubles with some bunks for families. Advance reservations required.

El Rincón Gaucho   INTERNATIONAL **$$**
(set lunch/dinner CH$10,000/17,000) In the park administration area, this handsome bar and restaurant provides an ambient setting for lunch or dinner. An onsite greenhouse supplies most of the fresh produce and local lamb is served. In addition to a set menu, there's sandwiches, takeout lunches and tea.

ℹ Information

Visitors can go to **Park Headquarters** (☑ in Puerto Varas 065-297-0833; www.conservacionpatagonica.org; ☉ 8am-6pm Mon-Sat) for trail maps and information. The **official blog** (www.conservacionpatagonica.org/blog) offers more information about the project and the region. Contact the website to take part in the extensive volunteer program.

ℹ Getting There & Away

The entrance to the park is 18km north of Cochrane. Look for the sign for Entrada Baker. Buses between Cochrane and Coyhaique can drop passengers at the entrance, but the administrative area is 11km further east on the main road to Paso Roballos.

A 12-passenger van can be booked through the park for transfers to Cochrane (CH$50,000) or within the park; arrange far in advance. In

Cochrane, **El Chilotito** (☑ cell 5648-6019; Teniente Merino 200) offers reasonable transfers (4-passenger truck CH$30,000) and park tours.

Cochrane

☑ 067 / POP 2900

An old ranching outpost, Cochrane is the southern hub of the Carretera Austral. With plans for nearby hydroelectric dams scrapped, the speculative boom has ended and the village has reverted to its languorous state. Though seemingly oblivious to tourism, Cochrane is the gateway to the new Parque Nacional Patagonia, Reserva Nacional Tamango, and fishing destination Lago Cochrane. It's also the best place for information along this lonely stretch of road and a last-chance stop to fill up the tank.

◉ Sights & Activities

Calluqueo Glacier   NATURE
This glacier descending from the southeast flanks of Mt San Lorenzo has only recently become a tourist attraction. It requires boat access and a guide.

Mercado Municipal   MARKET
(cnr Pioneros & Vicente Previske; ☉ 9am-7pm Mon-Fri) A covered market with artisan crafts in addition to local produce sold on Mondays, Wednesdays and Fridays.

**Patagonia Adventure
Expeditions**   ADVENTURE TOURS
(☑ cell 8182-0608; www.adventurepatagonia.com; Sol de Mayo Ranch) A pioneering high-end adventure outfitter adding scientific support and education to the mix, with a Wilderness Experience Center under construction. Meanwhile, there's fixed dates for horseback treks through Aysen Glacier Trail and ice-to-sea floating on the Río Baker. The base is four hours from Cochrane; contact first via email.

Lord Patagonia   TREKKING
(☑ cell 8267-8115; www.lordpatagonia.cl; Lago Brown 388; full-day CH$50,000) Guide Jimmy Valdes takes groups to Glaciar Calluqueo on trekking day trips and overnights.

🛏 Sleeping & Eating

Residencial Cero a Cero   GUESTHOUSE **$**
(☑ 067-252-2158, cell 7607-8155; ceroacero@gmail.com; Lago Brown 464; d CH$30,000, r per person without bathroom CH$10,000; 🛜) A log home that has ample space, this is a comfortable option with good beds and a cozy interior.

Latitude 47 GUESTHOUSE $
(☑cell 8252-2118; Lago Brown 564; r per person without bathroom CH$10,000) A selection of narrow upstairs rooms with single beds and kitchen use. The more recently constructed rooms with bathroom, in an independent area, are worthy upgrades.

Cabañas Sol y Luna CABINS $$
(☑cell 8157-9602; xmardonestorres@hotmail.com; Camino a la Reserva Tamango; 4-person cabins CH$55,000; @) Nice, and well equipped, these cabins help you achieve a needed rest, 1km outside town. There's a sauna and hot tubs.

Restaurant Ada's CHILEAN $
(☑cell 8399-5889; Teniente Merino 374; mains CH$5500; ☺12pm-10pm) Serving crisp whole fish or tender beef, bottles of wine, salads and potatoes, these big meals add up to a good deal. Service is attentive too.

Café Tamango CAFE $
(☑cell 9158-4521; Esmeralda 464; mains CH$5000; ☺9am-7:30pm Mon-Sat; ☑) Everything looks good in this cafe, from the homemade candies and chestnut ice cream to sandwiches, lentil burgers and couscous served with garden lettuce. There's outdoor seating.

Nacion Patagonia CAFE
(☑cell 9988-7766; Las Golondrinas 198; ☺hr vary) Ideal for a coffee and a conversation, this eclectic cafe also doubles as a cultural information center.

ℹ️ Information

BancoEstado (Esmeralda 460) ATM accepts MasterCard only.

Conaf (☑067-522-164; Río Nef 417; ☺10am-6pm Mon-Sat)

Hospital (☑067-522-131; O'Higgins 755; ☺24hr) Emergency is open 24 hours.

Post Office (Esmeralda 199; ☺9am-3pm Mon-Fri, 11am-2pm Sat)

Tourist Kiosk (www.cochranepatagonia.cl; Plaza de Armas; ☺9am-1pm & 2-9pm Jan-Mar) With bus schedules, fishing guides and taxi information. In the off-season there's tourist information in a municipal building near the plaza.

ℹ️ Getting There & Away

Buses go daily to Coyhaique, usually at 8am. Companies include **Buses Don Carlos** (☑067-252-2150; Prat 334), **Buses Acuario 13** (☑067-252-2143; Río Baker 349) and **Sao Paulo** (☑067-252-2143; Río Baker 349).

Various companies provide morning or evening service to Caleta Tortel. Those include **Buses Aldea** (☑067-522-143; Río Baker 349), **Pachamama** (☑cell 9411-4811), Bus Patagonia and Acuario 13. For Villa O'Higgins (CH$8000), **Buses Catalina** (☑067-252-2333, cell 8429-

---

THE TOMPKINS LEGACY

Ecobarons – the wealthy philanthropists recycling their greenbacks into green causes – have stamped an indelible presence on Southern Cone conservation and none more so than US entrepreneurs Douglas and Kris Tompkins. With holdings in Chile and Argentina, the couple has conserved over two million acres of land – more than any individual in history. While they started in the trenches of retail (she as CEO of Patagonia, he as founder of The North Face and Esprit), they have turned their industry toward rewilding key ecosystems.

It started in 1991 with Parque Pumalín, a Rhode Island–sized conservation project cobbled together from small Patagonian farms abutting ancient forest. Then in 2004, Kris Tompkins purchased a run-down *estancia* (grazing ranch) near Cochrane. Intensive sheep ranching had resulted in the widespread desertification of the ranch, which had ceased turning a profit. Its major rehabilitation has recast it as an important wildlife corridor between two other parks. Known as Valle Chacabuco (Parque Nacional Patagonia), the 690-sq-km park features Patagonian steppe, forests, mountains, lakes and lagoons.

Re-creating a home on the range was never so hard won. To restore grasslands, invasive plant species that proliferated with livestock were ripped out by hand. Over 644km of fencing was removed so native guanaco and huemul could return – and they did.

The Tompkins' sweeping land purchases initially stirred up suspicion and regional resentment in Chile. Yet as time goes by, much of the initial criticism has died down. Easing the public's misapprehension, national parks Corcovado and Yendegaia have already been donated to the state. More recently, the couple was presented with the 2015 Kiel Institute Global Economy Prize for their conservation efforts. Many Chileans now find the parks to be valuable national assets. The donations have even inspired copycats, like former Chilean president Sebastian Piñera's Parque Tantauco in Chiloé.

8970; Las Golondrinas 398) departs at 8am on Thursday and Sunday.

Chile Chico is served by **Turismo Baker** (☑ 067-252-2020; cnr Steffan & Golondrinas, correos) three days per week, with stops in Puerto Bertrand and Puerto Guadal.

To Valle Chacabuco, the Confluencia and Glaciar Calluqueo, **Turismo Cochrane Patagonia** (☑ cell 8256-7718, cell 7450-2323; www. turismocochranepatagonia.com; park day trip CH$30,000) offers private vans, with a minimum of passengers, but sells out well in advance.

DESTINATION	COST (CH$)	DURATION (HR)
Caleta Tortel	7000	2½
Chile Chico	15,000	4
Coyhaique	14,000	7-10
Villa O'Higgins	8,000	6

Reserva Nacional Tamango

Boasting Chile's largest population of endangered huemul deer, **Reserva Nacional Tamango** (admission CH$3500; camping per site CH$5000) protects a 70-sq-km transition zone to the Patagonian steppe. Huemul are notoriously shy, but the chances of sighting one are better here than anywhere else. At the entrance, trails (1.5km to 7km in length) lead to Laguna Elefantina, Laguna Tamanguito and 1722m Cerro Tamango. The reserve is located 6km northeast of Cochrane; there is no public transportation to the entrance. At the corner of Colonia and San Valentín, hikers can take Pasaje No 1 north and then east to access trails to the entrance. Cochrane's Conaf office may have trail maps available.

Caleta Tortel

☑ 067 / POP 320

A network of creaky boardwalks tracing the milky waters of the glacier-fed sound, Caleta Tortel feels fabled. There are no roads. Dedicated as a national monument, this fishing village cobbled around a steep escarpment is certainly unique. Seated between two ice fields at the mouth of Río Baker, it was first home to canoe-traveling Alacalufes (Qawashqar); colonists didn't arrive until 1955. Still isolated but more outwardly social than other Patagonians, locals live off tourism and cypress-wood extraction. Dependence on a small turbine means that the town has water and electricity shortages in big droughts. Use water sparingly. If you're here to disconnect, you can enjoy the fact that there's no wi-fi yet.

The road stops at the edge of town, near the El Rincon sector. Boardwalks and staircases lead to the center and past, to the sector of Playa Ancha. Water taxis help people get around town, but it's best to take minimal luggage keeping in mind all of the staircases.

◉ Sights & Activities

Imposing glaciers like Glacier Montt (Campo de Hielo Sur) and Glacier Steffens (Campo de Hielo Norte) can only be reached by boat. Motorized boat trips for eight to 10 people cost around CH$300,000. Some excursions include hiking or horseback riding. Rates are divided by the number of passengers and departures are dependent on weather.

Paz Austral   GLACIER TOUR
(☑ cell 9579-3779; www.entrehielostortel.cl) Trips to Glacier Steffens and Reserva Katalalixar (on demand) and the mouth of the Río Baker and Isla Los Muertos (daily).

Destinos Patagonia   GLACIER TOUR
(☑ cell 7704-2651; claudio.landeros@live.cl; per person 2-day package CH$200,000) Boat *Qawasqar* visits both glaciers and Isla los Muertos.

Junquillo   HIKING
Above the Rincon sector of Tortel, this three-hour round-trip offer views of the Baker estuary and canals.

🛏 Sleeping & Eating

Playa Ancha Camping   CAMPGROUND $
(Playa Ancha; campsites free) Camping is free but primitive with a stunning rivermouth setting. No services.

Brisas del Sur   GUESTHOUSE $$
(☑ cell 5688-2723; valerialanderos@hotmail.com; Playa Ancha sector; d CH$35,000, r per person without bathroom CH$12,000; 🖥) Señora Valería puts guests at ease in snug rooms with lovely beach views.

Residencial Estilo   GUESTHOUSE $$
(☑ cell 8255-8487; zuri1_67@hotmail.com; d/ste CH$40,000/60,000, r per person without bathroom CH$15,000) Alejandra's well-kept wooden house with bright colors and tidy doubles with down duvets.

★ Entre Hielos   B&B $$$
(☑ cell 9579-3779; www.entrehielostortel.cl; s/d US$118/150; 🖥) A lovely cypress home located at the top of a steep staircase, this wonderful lodging boasts both modern style and family

warmth, with a two-night minimum. Breakfast includes real coffee and homemade jams. Chef-prepared dinners may include local beef or salmon from the Río Baker. There's a great selection of wines. Also runs boat tours.

Sabores Locales CHILEAN $$
(☑ cell 9087-3064; mains CH$6000-10,000; ☺ 1pm-1am; ☑) Maritza cooks up a storm of tasty soups, smoked salmon and ceviche dishes in this cute cafe with vegetarian options.

❶ Information

Tourism Kiosk (www.municipalidaddetortel. cl; ☺ 9am-11pm Tue-Sun) Helpful with some English-speaking staff. At the entry to the village, where buses stop.

❶ Getting There & Away

All buses depart from a stop next to the tourism kiosk in the upper entrance to the village since there is no motorized access to town. There are three bus companies serving Cochrane (CH$7000, three hours). **Buses Aldea** (☑ cell 6232-2798) departs four days per week at various hours. Pachamama (p330) goes six times per week and Buses Patagonia goes three times per week. Currently, there is no public transportation to Villa O'Higgins (four hours), but this may change so check with the Tourism Kiosk.

Charging per trip, not per person, boat taxis leave from the Rincon sector for the center (CH$4500), Playa Ancha (CH$7000) and Isla de los Muertos (CH$50,000); they also do tours of the bay (CH$10,000). One provider is **Sergio Ganga** (☑ cell 9677-1755).

South to Villa O'Higgins

Wild stretches of rushing rivers and virgin forest flank the curvy road south of El Vagabundo and the access road to Caleta Tortel. The Carretera Austral demands constant attention here with sectors of washboard road and potential slides. It's best to travel in a high-clearance vehicle.

At **Puerto Yungay**, a **government ferry** (www.barcazas.cl) hauls passengers and four cars to the east end of Fiordo Mitchell at Río Bravo, at 10am, noon and 6pm (free, one hour) from December to March, with trips twice daily in low season. Return trips from the Villa O'Higgins side leave at 11am, 1pm and 7pm. Drivers should arrive early. Pass the time with a scrumptious empanada from the kiosk. After the ferry crossing, another 100km of rugged road leads to the north end of a narrow arm of Lago O'Higgins (known as Lago San Martín on the Argentine side).

Villa O'Higgins

☑ 067 / POP 612
The last stop on the Carretera Austral, this mythic village is alluring in its isolation. First settled by the English (1914–16), the outpost attracted few Chileans – the road didn't arrive until 1999. The spectacular surroundings can be explored on horseback or foot, and there's world-class fishing. A growing number of trekkers and cyclists are crossing over from El Chaltén, Argentina. Plans to create road access to Argentina via Entrada Mayer and add a strip of road between Candelaria Mansilla and Lago del Desierto (which would still require ferry use) will greatly facilitate travel to and from Argentina. Almost no one uses addresses but locals are happy to point you in the right direction. There's no ATM here so bring all the cash you will need.

⌖ Tours

**Villa O'Higgins
Expediciones** ADVENTURE TOUR
(☑ 067-243-1821, cell 8210-3191; www.villaohiggins. com) Guided horseback riding or trekking trips are available with advance booking through Hans Silva's full-service company, which also rents bikes.

Robinson Crusoe GLACIER TOUR
(☑ 067-243-1822; www.villaohiggins.com; Carretera Austral s/n; glacier tour CH$88,000; ☺ 9am-1pm & 3-7pm Mon-Sat) Departing from Puerto Bahamondez, catamaran *La Quetru* tours to Glaciar O'Higgins, with drop-offs at Candelario Mansilla (CH$42,000) for those hiking to Argentina. Available around November through March.

🛏 Sleeping & Eating

★ **El Mosco** HOSTEL $
(☑ 067-243-1819; www.patagoniaelmosco.blogspot.com; Carretera Austral Km1240; campsites per person CH$5000, dm CH$9000, d CH$45,000, s/d without bathroom CH$18,000/30,000) Friendly and full-service, this buzzing outpost hosts loads of cyclists, trekkers and even the odd conventional traveler. It's all about the service, and Orfelina nails it with motherly care. There's a collection of area topographical maps and worthwhile extras include a private wooden hot tub and a Finnish sauna.

Ecocamp Tsonek CAMPGROUND $
(☑ cell 7892-9695; www.tsonek.cl; Carretera Austral s/n; campsites per person/cyclist CH$4000/3000; ☎) 🏕 A conservation project in a beautiful

ARGENTINA VIA THE BACK DOOR

Gonzo travelers can skirt the southern ice field to get from Villa O'Higgins to Argentina's Parque Nacional Los Glaciares and El Chaltén. The one- to three-day trip can be completed between November and April. Bring all of your provisions, plus your passport and rain gear. Travel delays due to bad weather or boat problems do happen. Travel with extra food and extra pesos. The trip goes as follows:

➡ Take the 8am bus from Villa O'Higgins to Puerto Bahamondez (CH$1000).

➡ Take catamaran *La Quetru* (CH$42,000, four hours) from Villa O'Higgins to Candelario Mansilla. It goes one to three times a week, mostly on Saturdays with some Monday or Wednesday departures. Candelario Mansilla has basic lodging, guided treks and pack-horse rental. Pass through Chilean customs and immigration here.

➡ Trek or ride to Laguna Redonda (two hours). Camping is not allowed.

➡ Trek or ride to Laguna Larga (1½ hours). Camping is not allowed.

➡ Trek or ride to the north shore of Lago del Desierto (1½ hours). Camping is allowed. Pass through Argentine customs and immigration here.

➡ Take the ferry from the north to the south shores of Lago del Desierto (US$30, 2¼ hours). Another option is to hike the coast (15km, five hours). Camping is allowed. Check current ferry schedules with Argentine customs.

➡ Grab the shuttle bus to El Chaltén, 37km away (US$28, one hour).

For more information, consult **Robinson Crusoe** (☑067-431-821, 067-431-822; www.villaohiggins.com) in O'Higgins or Rancho Grande Hostel (p370) on the Argentine side.

beech forest with tent platforms (and some loaner tents), composting toilets, hot solar showers and kitchen. It's the dream project of El Pajarero, a talented birdwatching guide.

Hospedaje Rural GUESTHOUSE $
(☑067-243-1805; sector Candelario Mansilla; r per person without bathroom CH$8000, campsites per person CH$2500) If you're reaching for the final, final frontier, check out this lodging in the southernmost sector of Candelario Mansilla, reached by ferry. Dinner (CH$6000) and breakfast (CH$3000) are extra. Host Don Ricardo can help you explore area trails to glaciers, lakes and rivers.

Hospedaje Patagonia GUESTHOUSE $
(☑067-431-818; Río Pascua & Lago Christie; s/d without bathroom CH$12,000/24,000, s CH$20,000) A selection of simple, clean doubles in a rambling house. Meal or tea service may be possible.

Robinson Crusoe Lodge LODGE $$$
(Deep Patagonia; ☑cell 9357-8196, in Santiago 02-334-1503; www.robinsoncrusoe.com; Carretera Austral Km1240; d US$220; ☎) Alone in the upscale niche, this modern prefab construction is made warm with colorful Andean throws and comfortable sofas. While the hotel overshoots the value of a comfy king-sized bed, it does offer nice amenities like varied buffet breakfasts and wooden-tub Jacuzzis.

El Campanario CHILEAN $
(Lago O'Higgins 72; set menu CH$4500) Good-value home-cooked meals, though you may have to wait a while.

Entre Patagones CHILEAN $$
(☑067-243-1810; Av Carretera Austral s/n; mains CH$8000-10,000) This faux-rustic log restaurant and bar serves up tasty and abundant meals of salmon and salad or barbecue specialties. Call ahead to ensure service; it's at the entrance to town. It also rents cabins.

🔒 Shopping

Taller Marcela Stormesani ART STUDIO
(☑cell 6679-7125; pintaconusurpacion.blogspot. com; Lago Cisnes s/n; ⊗hr vary) The workshop of Marcela Stormesani makes an interesting visit, with her colorful, locally themed paintings and beautiful crafts by local artists.

ℹ Information

Information Kiosk (Plaza Cívica; ⊗8:30am-1pm & 2:30-7pm Nov-March) May have trekking maps.

ℹ Getting There & Away

Twice weekly flights to Coyhaique (CH$28,000, 1½ hours) are offered by Aerocord (p321), but fill up fast. Catch buses on the Carretera Austral, since the new bus terminal has yet to be inaugurated. Buses Catalina goes to Cochrane (CH$8000, six hours) on Friday and Monday at 8am. Frequency changes in low season.

Southern Patagonia

Best Places to Eat

➡ The Singular Restaurant (p351)

➡ Mi Rancho (p365)

➡ La Marmita (p342)

➡ La Aldea (p351)

➡ Afrigonia (p351)

Best Places to Stay

➡ Ilaia Hotel (p341)

➡ Bories House (p349)

➡ We Are Patagonia (p348)

➡ Tierra Patagonia (p361)

➡ Refugio Grey (p360)

Why Go?

Pounding westerlies, barren seascapes and the ragged spires of Torres del Paine – this is the distilled essence of Patagonia. The provinces of Magallanes and Última Esperanza boast a frontier appeal perhaps only matched by the deep Amazon and remote Alaska. Long before humans arrived on the continent, glaciers chiseled and carved these fine landscapes. Now it's a place for travelers to hatch their greatest adventures, whether hiking through rugged landscapes, seeing penguins by the thousands or horseback riding across the steppe.

Parque Nacional Torres del Paine is the region's star attraction. Among the finest parks on the continent, it attracts hundreds of thousands of visitors every year, even some towing wheeled luggage (though we don't recommend it). Throughout the region, it's easy and worthwhile to travel between Argentina and Chile. Included in Southern Patagonia are the highlights of Argentine Patagonia.

When to Go
Punta Arenas

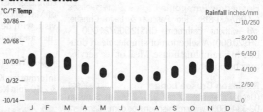

Dec–Feb Warmest months, ideal for *estancia* (grazing ranch) visits and backpacking.

Mid-Oct–early Mar Coastal fauna, including penguins and marine birds, abounds.

Mar–Apr Blasting summer winds start to die down and brilliant fall colors come in.

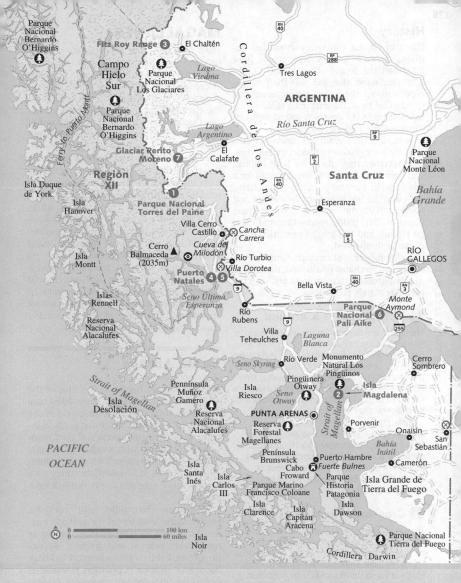

Southern Patagonia Highlights

1 Discover the remote backside of **Parque Nacional Torres del Paine** (p353).

2 Join the march of the penguins on **Isla Magdalena** (p345).

3 Hike under the toothy **Fitz Roy Range** (p368) near El Chaltén, Argentina's trekking capital.

4 **Ride the range** (p346) and eat a traditional *asado* (barbeque) at a working ranch outside Puerto Natales.

5 Enjoy a local microbrew, massage and lovely meals in **Puerto Natales** (p346) after time in Torres del Paine.

6 Explore the gnarled volcanic steppe of the little-known **Parque Nacional Pali Aike** (p345).

7 Check out the cool blue contours of 15-story **Glaciar Perito Moreno** (p367) in Argentina.

History

Caves in Última Esperanza show that humans, known as the Aonikenk people, have inhabited the region since 10,000 BC. In 1520 Ferdinand Magellan was the first European to visit the region. Development was spurred by the California gold rush, which brought trade via the ships sailing between Europe, California and Australia.

In the late 19th century, *estancias* formed, creating a regional wool boom that had massive, reverberating effects for both Chilean and Argentine Patagonia. Great wealth for a few came at the cost of native populations, who were all but wiped out by disease and warfare. With the opening of the Panama Canal in 1914, traffic reduced around Cabo de Hornos and the area's international importance diminished.

Today fisheries, silviculture, small oil reserves and methanol production, in addition to a fast-growing tourism industry, keep the region relatively prosperous.

❶ Getting There & Around

The easiest way to get to Southern Patagonia is to fly from Santiago or Puerto Montt to Punta Arenas. There are many flights daily and less-frequent flights from a few other major Chilean cities. Other transportation options include the Navimag ferry from Puerto Montt to Puerto Natales, or a long bus trip from Puerto Montt that goes to Argentina and then back over to Punta Arenas.

Unlike other parts of Patagonia, the roads around Punta Arenas are paved and smooth. Buses to major destinations are frequent but should be booked ahead in summer. Travelers must fly or take a ferry to get to Porvenir or Puerto Williams. Be aware that schedules change frequently.

❶ Crossing into Argentina

Transportation between Argentina and Chile is frequent and easy, with crossing the border a normal daily occurrence for locals, on par with a trip to the bank. The Chilean entry fee (US$132 for Canadian residents, US$117 for Australians) is valid for the life of the passport.

Do not cross the border where there are no officials to stamp you through or you will risk expulsion. The most-used border crossings are at Cancha Carrera, between Torres del Paine and El Calafate, and Monte Aymond, between Punta Arenas and Río Gallegos.

Frequent buses link Puerto Natales with the Argentine towns El Calafate and El Chaltén, and Punta Arenas with Ushuaia. If you travel from Ushuaia to Chile's Isla Navarino by boat, make sure to visit customs at the airport.

MAGALLANES

Hard to believe, but this rugged, weather-battered land has actually been inhabited for hundreds, if not thousands, of years. While modern inhabitants have little in common with the natives who once paddled the channels in canoes and hunted guanacos, they still remain cut off from the rest of the continent by formidable mountains and chilly waters. A supreme sense of isolation (and hospitality) is what attracts most visitors to Magallanes. The only way to get here from the rest of Chile is by air or sea, or by road through Argentine Patagonia.

While the capital, Punta Arenas, offers all of the conveniences of a major Chilean city, its surroundings are raw and desolate. Here visitors will find the end-of-the-world pioneer feeling to be recent and real.

Magallanes' modern economy depends on commerce, petroleum development and fisheries. Prosperity means it has some of the highest levels of employment and school attendance, and some of the best-quality housing and public services in Chile.

Punta Arenas

📞 061 / POP 130,136

A sprawling metropolis on the edge of the Strait of Magellan, Punta Arenas defies easy definition. It's a strange combination of the ruddy and the grand, witnessed in the elaborate wool-boom mansions and port renovations contrasted with windblown streams of litter and urban sprawl. Set at the bottom of the Americas, it is downright stingy with good weather – the sun shines through side-long rain.

Magellanic hospitality still pervades local culture, undeterred (or perhaps nurtured by) nature's inhospitality. The city is remarkably relaxed and friendly. Recent prosperity, fed by a petrochemical industry boom and growing population, has sanded down the city's former roughneck reputation. It would be nice if it were all about restoration, but duty-free shopping and mega-malls on the city outskirts are the order of the future.

Easy connections to Tierra del Fuego, Torres del Paine and Argentina and good travelers' services make Punta Arenas a convenient base. A growing volume of cruise-ship passengers and trekkers has effectively replaced yesteryear's explorers, sealers and sailors.

History

Little more than 150 years old, Punta Arenas was originally a military garrison and penal settlement conveniently situated for ships headed to California during the gold rush in later years. Compared to the initial Chilean settlement at Fuerte Bulnes, 60km south, the town had a better, more protected harbor and superior access to wood and water. English maritime charts dubbed the site Sandy Point, and thus it became known as its Spanish equivalent.

In its early years Punta Arenas lived off natural resources, including sealskins, guanaco hides and feathers, as well as mineral products (including coal and gold), guano, timber and firewood. The economy took off in the last quarter of the 19th century, after the territorial governor authorized the purchase of 300 purebred sheep from the Falkland Islands. This successful experiment encouraged sheep ranching, and by the turn of the century nearly two million animals grazed the territory.

The area's commercial and pastoral empires were built on the backs of international immigrant labor, including English, Irish, Scots, Croats, French, Germans, Spaniards, Italians and others. Many locals trace their family origins to these diverse settlers. The many mansions created by the wealthy are now hotels, banks and museums.

⊙ Sights & Activities

Plaza Muñoz Gamero, also known as the Plaza de Armas, is the center of town. Street names change on either side of the plaza, but street addresses fronting the plaza bear the name Muñoz Gamero. Landmarks, restaurants and lodgings fan out from here. Both Av España and Av Bulnes are main thoroughfares to the north of the city (the latter accesses the large duty-free shopping area known as the Zona Franca).

Plaza Muñoz Gamero   PLAZA
A central plaza of magnificent conifers surrounded by opulent mansions. Facing the plaza's north side, **Casa Braun-Menéndez** (☑061-224-1489; admission CH$1000; ⊙10:30am-1pm & 5-8:30pm Tue-Fri, 10:30am-1pm & 8-10pm Sat, 11am-2pm Sun) houses the private Club de la Unión, which also uses the tavern downstairs (open to the public). The nearby **monument** commemorating the 400th anniversary of Magellan's voyage was donated by wool baron José Menéndez in 1920. Just east is the former **Sociedad Menéndez Behety**, which now houses Turismo Comapa. The **cathedral** sits west.

Museo Regional de Magallanes   MUSEUM
(Museo Regional Braun-Menéndez; ☑061-224-4216; www.museodemagallanes.cl; Magallanes 949; admission CH$1000; ⊙10:30am-5pm Wed-Mon, closes at 2pm May-Dec) This opulent mansion testifies to the wealth and power of pioneer sheep farmers in the late 19th century. The well-maintained interior houses a regional historical museum (ask for booklets in English) and original exquisite French-nouveau family furnishings, from intricate wooden inlaid floors to Chinese vases. In former servants' quarters, a downstairs cafe is perfect for a pisco sour while soaking up the grandeur.

SOUTHERN PATAGONIA PUNTA ARENAS

ENIGMATIC PATAGONIA: CHATWIN'S MASTERPIECE

In 1977 the late English writer Bruce Chatwin penned *In Patagonia,* an indispensable companion for the Patagonian traveler.

Chatwin's fascination with Patagonia began in childhood, when he coveted a giant sloth pelt from his eccentric seafaring relative Charley Milward, who resided in Punta Arenas. He was intrigued by the seemingly out-of-place immigrant communities, such as the Patagonian Welsh, and cowboys-in-exile Butch Cassidy and the Sundance Kid. A six-month journey through Patagonia resulted in Chatwin's masterpiece at the age of 37. It tells of travels south from Buenos Aires to his final destination, Cueva del Milodón – the one-time home of the prehistoric sloth.

Chatwin mixed fluid storytelling, intriguing regional history, personal portraits and old-fashioned travel memoir, tossing one last controversial ingredient into the pot: fiction. *In Patagonia* reads primarily as a nonfiction travel memoir, yet subjects have challenged and contradicted events depicted in the book. There's no acknowledgement that any of the stories were fabricated. Many of the conversations and characters that Chatwin reported as true were just figments of his imagination. But that's not to say that the real Patagonia is less peculiar.

Punta Arenas

★ **Cementerio Municipal** CEMETERY
(main entrance at Av Bulnes 949; ⊙ 7:30am-8pm)
FREE Among South America's most fascinating cemeteries, with both humble immigrant graves and flashy tombs, like that of
wool baron José Menéndez, a scale replica
of Rome's Vittorio Emanuele monument,
according to Bruce Chatwin. See the map
inside the main entrance gate.

It's an easy 15-minute stroll northeast
of the plaza, or catch any *taxi colectivo*
(shared taxi with specific route) in front of
the Museo Regional Braun-Menéndez on
Magallanes.

Museo Naval y Marítimo MUSEUM
(☑ 061-220-5479; www.museonaval.cl; Pedro
Montt 981; adult/child CH\$1200/600; ⊙ 9:30am-
12:30pm & 2-5pm Tue-Sat) A naval and maritime museum with historical exhibits that
include a fine account of the Chilean mission that rescued Sir Ernest Shackleton's
crew from Antarctica. The most imagina-
tive display is a replica ship complete with
bridge, maps, charts and radio room.

Museo Regional Salesiano MUSEUM
(☑ 061-222-1001; Av Bulnes 336; adult/12yr
& under CH\$2500/200; ⊙ 10am-12:30pm &
3-6pm Tue-Sun) Especially influential in

Punta Arenas

settling the region, the Salesian order collected outstanding ethnographic artifacts, but their museum touts their role as peacemakers between the Yaghan, Ona and settlers.

Instituto de la Patagonia MUSEUM
(Av Bulnes 01890) Pioneer days are made real again at the Patagonian Institute's **Museo del Recuerdo** (☑061-220-7056; www.umag. cl; admission CH$2500; ☺8:30am-11am & 2:30-6pm Mon-Fri), part of the Universidad de Magallanes. On display are a collection of antique farm and industrial machinery, a typical pioneer house and shearing shed, and a wooden-wheeled shepherds' trailer. The library has historical maps and a series of historical and scientific publications. Any *taxi colectivo* that is heading to the Zona Franca will drop you across the street.

Reserva Forestal Magallanes PARK
(☺daylight hours) **FREE** Great hiking and mountain biking through dense lenga and coihue, 8km from town.

☞ Tours

Worthwhile day trips include tours to the Seno Otway *pingüinera* (penguin colony; see p345), 48km to the north. Tours (CH$15,000) leave at 4pm daily October through March, weather permitting.

Visits to the town's first settlements at Fuerte Bulnes and Puerto Hambre leave at 10am (admission CH$12,000). Both tours can be done in one day; by sharing a rental car and going at opposite times visitors can avoid the strings of tour groups. Most lodgings will help arrange tours – if they don't run their own operation.

Torres del Paine tours are abundant from Punta Arenas, but the distance makes for a very long day; it's best to organize transport from Puerto Natales.

If you have the time, a more atmospheric alternative to Seno Otway is the thriving Magellanic penguin colonies of Monumento Natural Los Pingüinos (p345) on Isla Magdalena. Five-hour ferry tours (adult/child CH$30,000/15,000) land for an hour at the island and depart the port on Tuesday, Thursday and Saturday, December through

INDECENT EXPOSURE

In the mid-1980s British scientists at Halley Station in Antarctica noticed that their ozone-measuring instrument seemed to have gone wrong – ozone levels were vastly lower than had ever been recorded before. Unfortunately, it was not their instrument that had gone wrong, but the ozone itself – ozone levels over Antarctica in springtime were dropping to a fraction of the regular amount.

Soon after, they isolated the culprit: chlorofluorocarbons (CFCs), which are manmade gases used in aerosols, refrigeration, air-conditioning, industrial solvents, asthma inhalers and fire control. Most of the time CFCs are innocuous, but in the Antarctic springtime the combination of very cold temperatures and the return of sunshine to the polar region allow the CFCs to rapidly gobble up the stratospheric ozone, resulting in the famed ozone hole. As spring progresses, Antarctic temperatures start to warm, and the ozone begins to recover, only to be depleted again when the next spring arrives.

Ozone protects the Earth's surface from UV radiation, the stuff that causes sunburn and skin cancer, among other things. The ozone hole has impacted Southern Patagonia more than any other inhabited area on earth, particularly during spring when the ozone hole is at it's worst. Visitors, especially children, should wear brimmed hats and sunglasses, and slather on the sunscreen.

The 1987 Montreal Protocol banned CFCs, and Antarctic ozone levels are finally beginning to recover, but it will take another couple of decades to get back to normal. Unfortunately, many of the gasses that are now used in place of CFCs are greenhouse gasses, adding to the warming of our planet.

Jocelyn Turnbull, atmospheric scientist

February. Confirm times in advance. Book tickets through **Turismo Comapa** (061-220-0200; www.comapa.com; Magallanes 990) and bring a picnic.

Tours also go to destinations such as Parque Nacional Pali Aike.

Kayak Agua Fresca KAYAKING
(cell 9655-5073; www.kayakaguafresca.com; half-day tour CH$50,000) On the rare day in Punta Arenas when winds are calm and the sea is glass, the sea kayaking can be spectacular. There's no office; see the website for information.

Solo Expediciones TOUR
(061-271-0219; http://soloexpediciones.com; Nogueira 1255) This agency offers an Isla Magdalena penguin tour with faster semi-rigid boats (other tours take the ferry). They also plan to offer whale watching day trips in the marine park Francisco Coloane.

Turismo Aonikenk GUIDED TOUR
(061-222-8616; www.aonikenk.com; Magallanes 570) Recommended English-, German- and French-speaking guides. Offers Cabo Froward treks, visits to the king penguin colony in Tierra del Fuego, and cheaper open expeditions geared at experienced participants. Also has information on Estancia Yendegaia.

Turismo Laguna Azul BIRDWATCHING
(061-222-5200; www.turismolagunaazul.com; Magallanes 1011; tour CH$48,000) If you are keen to see the king penguins on Tierra del Fuego, this agency makes a very long day trip of it, leaving before 8am and returning by 9pm. Much of the trip is getting there. Beware that you may not get a guide or lunch (bring your own) and entrance to the private Reserva Onaisin is extra (CH$12,000).

Turismo Pali Aike GUIDED TOUR
(061-261-5750; www.turismopaliaike.com) Recommended tour company.

Whale Sound WHALE WATCHING
(061-222-1076; www.whalesound.com; Lautaro Navarro 1163; per person 3-night, 4-day package US$1500; Nov-Apr) Supports science with sea expeditions to the remote Coloane Marine Park. Packages range from two days/one night to four days/five nights with lodging both in domes and at Hostería Faro San Isidro.

Patagonia Backroads MOTORCYCLE TOUR
(061-222-1111, cell 8393-6013) For those who dream of Che's *Motorcycle Diaries* trip. Operator Aníbal Vickacka runs reputable 10-day BMW motorcross (or 4WD) tours of Patagonia.

⚒ Festivals & Events

Winter Solstice   CULTURAL
The longest night of the year is celebrated on June 21.

Carnaval de Invierno   CULTURAL
At the end of July with fireworks, parades and good cheer.

🛏 Sleeping

On the cruise-ship circuit, Punta Arenas has a plethora of hotels but few bargains. Foreigners are not required to pay the additional 18% IVA charge if paying with US cash or credit card. Off-season (mid-April to mid-October) prices drop. Rates include breakfast.

Hospedaje Magallanes   B&B $
(☑ 061-222-8616; www.aonikenk.com; Magallanes 570; dm/d w shared bathroom CH$14,000/34,000; @ 🛜) A great inexpensive option run by a German-Chilean couple who are also Torres del Paine guides with an on-site travel agency. With just a few quiet rooms, there are often communal dinners or backyard barbecues by the climbing wall. Breakfast includes brown bread and strong coffee.

Hostal Fitz Roy   GUESTHOUSE $
(☑ 061-224-0430; www.hostalfitzroy.com; Navarro 850; d CH$30,000, 5-person cabin CH$35,000, dm/d without bathroom CH$10,000/25,000; @) This country house in the city offers rambling, good-value rooms and an inviting, old-fashioned living room to pore over books or sea charts. Rooms have phones and TVs.

Hostal Bustamante   HOTEL $
(☑ 061-222-2774; www.hostalbustamante.cl; Jorge Montt 847; s/d CH$25,000/30,000) This quaint, slightly creaky wooden house boasts a sweeping staircase and a leafy breakfast room. Doubles are basic affairs with cable TV; each has a small private bathroom, many with gleaming new shower stalls that were recently added.

Hostel Keoken   GUESTHOUSE $
(☑ 061-224-4086; www.hostelkeoken.cl; Magallanes 209; s/d with shared bathroom CH$20,000/28,000, s/d CH$30,000/38,000; @) Increasingly popular with backpackers, Hostel Keoken features comfortable beds topped with fluffy white down comforters and homemade pastries for breakfast. The center of town is a few minutes away on foot.

Hostal Independencia   GUESTHOUSE $
(☑ 061-222-7572; www.hostalindependencia.cl; Av Independencia 374; campsites per person/dm CH$2000/7000; @ 🛜) One of the last die-hard backpacker haunts with cheap prices and bonhomie to match. Despite the chaos, rooms are reasonably clean and there are kitchen privileges, camping and bike rentals.

Al Fin del Mundo   HOSTEL $
(☑ 061-271-0185; www.alfindelmundo.cl; O'Higgins 1026; dm/s/d without bathroom CH$10,000/15,000/25,000; 🛜) On the 2nd and 3rd floors of a musty downtown building, these rooms are cheerful but due for updates. All share bathrooms with hot showers and a large kitchen, as well as a living area with a large TV, pool table and DVD library. Has bikes for rental (CH$1000/hr).

★ Ilaia Hotel   BOUTIQUE HOTEL $$
(☑ 061-272-3100; www.ilaia.cl; Carrera Pinto 351; s/d/tr from US$100/132/184; P 🛜) Playful and modern, this high-concept boutique hotel is run with family warmth. Sly messages are written to be read in mirrors, rooms are simple and chic and an incredible glass study gazes out on the Strait. Offers a shuttle to yoga class and healthy breakfasts with chapati bread, homemade jam, avocados, yogurt and more. But you won't find a television.

Hotel Patagonia   HOTEL $$
(☑ 061-222-7243; www.patagoniabb.cl; Av España 1048; s/d/tw CH$30,000/40,000/50,000; P 🛜) A solid midrange option offering no-nonsense rooms with crisp white linens and simple style. Service could be a few degrees warmer. It's accessed via a long driveway behind the main building.

Hotel Plaza   HOTEL $$
(☑ 061-224-1300; www.hotelplaza.cl; Nogueira 1116; s/d US$105/130; 🛜) This converted mansion boasts vaulted ceilings, plaza views and historical photos lining the hall. Inconsistent with such grandeur, the country decor is unfortunate. But service is genteel and the location unbeatable.

Hostal La Estancia   GUESTHOUSE $$
(☑ 061-224-9130; www.estancia.cl; O'Higgins 765; d CH$48,000, dm/s/d without bathroom CH$12,500/20,000/38,000; @ 🛜) An old downtown house with big rooms, vaulted ceilings and tidy shared bathrooms. Long-time owners Alex and Carmen are eager to help with travel plans. There's a book exchange, kitchen use, laundry and storage.

Hotel Dreams del Estrecho
LUXURY HOTEL $$$

(✉ toll-free 600-626-0000; www.mundodreams.com/detalle/dreams-punta-arenas; O'Higgins 1235; d/ste US$169/201; P@🖥❄) Parked at the water's edge, this glass oval highrise brings a little Vegas to the end of the world. It's a glittery atmosphere, with spacious and luxuriant rooms, but the show-stopper is the swimming pool that appears to merge with the ocean. There's also a spa, casino and swank restaurant on site.

Hotel Cabo De Hornos
BUSINESS HOTEL $$$

(✉061-224-2134; www.hoteles-australis.com; Plaza Muñoz Gamero 1025; d/tr US$240/300; @🛈) This smart business hotel begins with a cool interior of slate and sharp angles, but rooms are relaxed and bright, with top-notch views. Service is good and the well-heeled bar just beckons you for a nightcap. The on-site restaurant is well-regarded too.

Eating

Local seafood is an exquisite treat: go for *centolla* (king crab) between July and November or *erizos* (sea urchins) between November and July.

Café Almacen Tapiz
CAFE $

(✉cell 8730-3481; www.cafetapiz.cl; Roca 912; mains CH$5000; ⊙9am-9:30pm; 🛈) Cloaked in alerce shingles, this lively cafe makes for an ambient coffee break. In addition to gorgeous layer cakes, there's salads and pita sandwiches with goat cheese, meats or roasted veggies.

Mercado Municipal
MARKET $

(21 de Mayo 1465; ⊙8am-3pm) Fish and vegetable market with cheap 2nd-floor *cocinerías* (eateries), a great place for inexpensive seafood dishes.

La Mesita Grande
PIZZERIA $

(✉061-224-4312; O'Higgins 1001; mains CH$3000-6000; ⊙12pm-11:30pm) If you're homesick for Brooklyn, La Mesita Grande might do the trick. This mod exposed-brick pizzeria serves them up thin and crisp, with organic toppings and pints of local brew. Save room for their homemade ice cream. The original outlet is in Puerto Natales.

Kiosco Roca
SNACKS $

(Roca 875; snacks CH$500; ⊙7am-7pm Mon-Fri, 8am-1pm Sat) An irresistible stop, with locals patiently waiting for counter stools and U of Chile paraphernalia plastering the walls.

They only turn out bite-sized sandwiches with chorizo or cheese or both, best paired with a banana milkshake.

Los Inmigrantes
CAFE $

(✉061-222-2205; www.inmigrante.cl; Quillota 559; mains CH$5000; ⊙noon-8pm) In the historic Croatian neighborhood, this cafe serves decadent cakes in a room full of interesting relics from Dalmatian immigrants.

Lomit's
DINER $

(Menéndez 722; mains CH$4000; ⊙10am-2:30am) Chile's answer to the sidecar diner is this atmospheric cafe where cooks flip dripping made-to-order burgers at a center-stage griddle. Portions are generous but the service dallies.

Fuente Hamburg
CHILEAN $

(✉061-224-5375; Errázurriz 856; mains CH$2500-6000; ⊙10:30am-8:30pm Mon-Fri, to 3pm Sat) Shiny barstools flank a massive grill churning out quickie bites. Grab a *churrasco* (thin-sliced beef) topped with tomatoes and green beans, served with fresh mayo on a soft bun.

★ La Marmita
CHILEAN $$

(✉061-222-2056; www.marmitamaga.cl; Plaza Sampaio 678; mains CH$6000-12,000; ⊙12:30-3pm & 6:30-11:30pm Mon-Sat; 🖉) This classic bistro enjoys wild popularity for its lovely, casual ambiance and tasty fare. Besides fresh salads and hot bread, hearty dishes such as casseroles or seafood hark back to grandma's cooking, Chilean style. With good vegetarian options and takeout service.

Damiana Elena
CHILEAN $$

(✉cell 6122-2818; Magallanes 341; mains CH$7000-10,000; ⊙7-11pm Mon-Sat) This elegant restaurant is in a romantic old house, off the beaten path in a residential neighborhood. The detour is usually worth it.

La Cuisine
FRENCH $$

(✉061-222-8641; O'Higgins 1037; mains CH$8000-9000) If you're craving veggies beyond the trusted potato, this plain-Jane French restaurant is a good bet. Seafood dishes come with sauteed vegetables, green salad or ratatouille. There's also homemade pâté and wine by the glass is cheap.

Okusa
CHILEAN $$

(cnr O'Higgins & Av Colón; mains CH$6500-9000; ⊙noon-3pm & 7pm-midnight Mon-Sat, to 4pm Sun) A beautiful, rambling old home with period furniture, Okusa offers hearty fare, with oversized slabs of salmon, lamb and bubbling casseroles. The service can be lax.

Remezón GOURMET $$$
(☑ 061-224-1029; www.patagoniasalvaje.cl; 21 de Mayo 1469; mains CH$5000-15,000; ☺ lunch & dinner) An innovative mainstay with homey atmosphere. Garlic soup made with fragrant beef broth is a good starter, even shared. Game dishes are the house specialty, but the delicate *merluza negra* (black hake) shouldn't be missed, served with *chupe de espinaca* (spinach casserole).

Sotito's SEAFOOD $$$
(☑ 061-224-3565; O'Higgins 1138; mains CH$7000-15,000; ☺ noon-3pm & 7-11pm Mon-Sat, to 4pm Sun) This seafood institution is popular with moneyed locals and cruise-ship travelers in search of a classy king crab feast. The decor may not be inspiring but the cuisine doesn't disappoint. The upstairs room has an expanded, cheaper menu that includes pastas (from CH$5000).

Secreto de la Patagonia SELF-CATERING
(Sarmiento 1029) Locally-made artisan chocolates, goat cheese and preserved meats, worthy as gifts or park treats.

Unimarc SUPERMARKET
(Bories 647) A large, well-stocked supermarket.

Pachamama SELF-CATERING
(☑ 061-222-6171; Magallanes 619A) Bulk trail-mix munchies and organic products.

🍷 Drinking

La Taberna BAR
(Casa Braun-Menéndez, Plaza Muñoz Gamero; ☺ 7pm-2am Mon-Fri, to 3am Sat & Sun) This dark and elegant subterranean bar, with polished wood fixtures and cozy nooks reminiscent of an old-fashioned ship, is a classic old boys' club. The rooms fill with cigar smoke later in the evening, but the opportunity to sip pisco sours in this classy mansion shouldn't be missed.

Jekus PUB
(O'Higgins 1021; ☺ 6pm-3am) A restaurant that serves as a popular meeting spot for drinks, with happy hours, karaoke and soccer on the tube.

Klub CLUB
(☑ cell 9435-8247; http://klubpuntaarenas.blog-spot.com; Bories 655; admission incl 1 free drink CH$3000) Tiki torches warm up this most southerly dance club and, if you're lucky, there's an occasional live rock band.

☆ Entertainment

Cine Estrella CINEMA
(Mejicana 777) Shows first-run movies.

🛍 Shopping

The Art Corner ARTS & CRAFTS
(☑ cell 8904-5392; Errázuriz 910, 2nd fl) The workshop and store of talented local artist Andrea Araneda. A great place for innovative handmade gifts, with crafts, gorgeous woolens and paintings focused on Magellanic themes.

Zona Franca DUTY FREE
(Zofri; Km3.5 Norte Zona Franca Punta Arenas; ☺ Mon-Sat) The duty-free zone is a large, polished conglomeration of shops that is worth checking out if you're looking for electronics, outdoor gear, computer accessories or camera equipment. *Colectivos* (shared taxis) shuttle back and forth from downtown along Av Bulnes throughout the day.

ℹ Information

Travel agencies in the center along Roca and Lautaro Navarro change cash and traveler's checks. All are open weekdays and Saturday, with a few open on Sunday morning. Banks with ATMs dot the city center. Sernatur has a list of recommended doctors.

Conaf (☑ 061-223-0681; Bulnes 0309; ☺ 9am-5pm Mon-Fri) Has details on the nearby parks.

Hospital Regional (☑ 061-220-5000; cnr Arauco & Angamos)

Information Kiosk (☑ 061-220-0610; Plaza Muñoz Gamero; ☺ 8am-7pm Mon-Sat, 9am-7pm Sun Dec-Feb) South side of the plaza.

Police (☑ 061-224-1714; Errázuriz 977)

Post Office (Bories 911) Located one block north of Plaza Muñoz Gamero.

Sernatur (☑ 061-224-1330; www.sernatur.cl; Navarro 999; ☺ 8:30am-8pm Mon-Fri, 10am-6pm Sat-Sun) With friendly, well-informed, multilingual staff and lists of accommodations and transportation. Reduced hours in low season.

ℹ Getting There & Away

The tourist offices distribute a useful brochure that details all forms of transport available.

AIR

Punta Arenas' airport (PUQ) is 21km north of town. DAP offers Antarctica tours (full day US$5500), charter flights over Cabo de Hornos and to other Patagonian destinations, including Ushuaia and Calafate.

LanChile (☎ 061-224-1100; www.lan.com; Bories 884) Flies several times daily to Santiago (CH$162,000 round-trip) with a stop in Puerto Montt (CH$153,000) and on Saturday to the Falkland Islands (round-trip CH$530,000).

Sky Airline (☎ 061-271-0645; www.skyairline.cl; Roca 935) Flies daily between Santiago and Punta Arenas, with a stop either in Puerto Montt or Concepción.

Aerovías DAP (☎ 061-261-6100; www.aeroviasdap.cl; O'Higgins 891) From November to March, flies to Porvenir (CH$55,000 round-trip) Monday through Saturday several times daily, and to Puerto Williams (CH$143,000 round-trip) Monday through Saturday at 10am. Luggage is limited to 10kg per person.

BOAT

Transbordador Austral Broom (☎ 061-258-0089; www.tabsa.cl) Operates three ferries to Tierra del Fuego from the Tres Puentes ferry launch. The car/passenger ferry to/from Porvenir (CH$6200/39,800 per person/vehicle, 2½ to four hours) usually leaves at 9am but has some afternoon departures; check the current online schedule. From Punta Arenas, it's faster to do the Primera Angostura crossing (CH$1600/13,900 per person/vehicle, 20 minutes), northeast of Punta Arenas, which sails every 90 minutes between 8:30am and 11:45pm.

Broom sets sail for Isla Navarino's Puerto Williams (reclining seat/bunk CH$98,000/137,000 including meals, 30 hours) three or four times per month on Thursday only, returning Saturday.

Cruceros Australis (☎ in Santiago 02-442-3110; www.australis.com; ☺ Sep-May) Runs luxurious four- and five-day cruises to Ushuaia and back. Turismo Comapa handles local bookings.

BUS

Buses depart from company offices, most within a block or two of Av Colón. Buy tickets several hours (if not days) in advance. The **Central de Pasajeros** (☎ 061-224-5811; cnr Magallanes & Av Colón) is the closest thing to a central booking office. Daily destinations and companies include the following:

DESTINATION	COST (CH$)	DURATION (HR)
Osorno	30,000	30
Puerto Natales	6000	3
Río Gallegos	12,000	5-8
Río Grande	25,000	7
Ushuaia	30,000	10

Bus Sur (☎ 061-261-4224; www.bus-sur.cl; Av Colón 842) Puerto Natales.

Buses Fernández/Buses Pingüino (☎ 061-224-2313; www.busesfernandez.com; Sanhueza 745) Puerto Natales and Río Gallegos.

Buses Ghisoni (☎ 061-224-0646; www.busesbarria.cl; Av España 264) Comfortable buses to Río Gallegos and Ushuaia.

Buses Pacheco (☎ 061-224-2174; www.busespacheco.com; Av Colón 900) Puerto Natales, Río Gallegos and Ushuaia.

Tecni-Austral (☎ 061-222-2078; Navarro 975) Río Grande.

Cruz del Sur (☎ 061-222-7970; www.buscruzdelsur.cl; Sanhueza 745) Puerto Montt, Osorno and Chiloé.

ⓘ Getting Around

TO/FROM THE AIRPORT

Buses depart directly from the airport to Puerto Natales. **Transfer Austral** (☎ 061-272-3358; www.transferaustral.com) runs door-to-door shuttle services (CH$3000) to/from town to coincide with flights. Buses Fernández does regular airport transfers (CH$3000).

BUS & TAXI COLECTIVO

Taxi colectivos, with numbered routes, are only slightly more expensive than buses (about CH$400, or a bit more late at night and on Sundays), far more comfortable and much quicker.

CAR

Cars are a good option for exploring Torres del Paine, but renting one in Chile to cross the border into Argentina gets expensive due to international insurance requirements. If heading to El Calafate, it is best to rent your vehicle in Argentina.

Punta Arenas has Chilean Patagonia's most economical rental rates, and locally owned agencies tend to provide better service. Recommended **Adel Rent a Car/Localiza** (☎ 061-222-4819; www.adelrentacar.cl; Pedro Montt 962) provides attentive service, competitive rates, airport pickup and good travel tips. Other choices include **Hertz** (☎ 061-224-8742; O'Higgins 987) and **Lubag** (☎ 061-271-0484; Magallanes 970).

Around Punta Arenas

Monumentos Históricos Nacionales Puerto Hambre & Fuerte Bulnes

Two national monuments make up **Parque del Estrecho de Magallanes** (Parque Historia Patagonia; ☎ 061-272-3195; www.phipa.cl; Km56 Sur; admission CH$12,000; ☺ 9:30am-6:30pm). Founded in 1584 by Pedro Sarmiento de Gamboa, 'Ciudad del Rey don Felipe' was one of Spain's most inauspicious and short-lived South American outposts. Its inhabitants

PENGUIN COLONIES

You don't have to trek to Antarctica for a sizable dose of happy feet. Two substantial Magellanic penguin colonies are easily reached from Punta Arenas. If you have time to make a day of it, we recommend the larger (60,000 breeding pairs) and more interesting **Monumento Natural Los Pingüinos** on Isla Magdalena in the Strait of Magellan and accessible only by boat.

Easier to reach is **Seno Otway** (Otway Sound; admission CH$6000, road toll CH$1000; ⏰8am-6:30pm), with about 6000 breeding pairs, located around an hour northwest of the city. Tours to Seno Otway usually leave in the afternoon; however, visiting in the morning is best time of the day for photography because the birds are mostly backlit in the afternoon. Arrive via private vehicle or tour. If driving independently, pay attention as you head north on Ruta 9 (RN 9) – it's easy to miss the small sign indicating the turnoff to the penguin colony. It's worth noting that it's close to the airport.

struggled against the elements and starved to death at what is now known as **Puerto Hambre** (Port Hunger).

In May 1843, Chilean president Manuel Bulnes sent the schooner *Ancud,* manned by Chilotes and captained by John Williams, a former English officer, to Magallanes to occupy this southern area, then only sparsely populated by indigenous peoples. Four months later on September 21, when the *Ancud* arrived at Puerto Hambre, Williams declared the area Chilean territory and began to establish camp on a hilltop, dubbed **Fuerte Bulnes.** The exposed site, lack of portable water, rocky soil and inferior pasture soon made his colony abandon the site and move northward to a more sheltered area, called Sandy Point by the settlers and Lacolet by the Tehuelche.

There are trails, a visitors center and lookouts. A new museum and cafe are under construction. A paved road runs 60km south from Punta Arenas to the restored wooden fort, where a fence of sharpened stakes surrounds the blockhouse, barracks and chapel. There isn't any scheduled public transportation but several tour companies make half-day excursions to Fuerte Bulnes and Puerto Hambre.

Cabo Froward

The most southerly point on the continent, Cabo Froward (Cape Froward) is 90km south of Punta Arenas and accessible by a two-day hike along wind-whipped cliffs. At the cape, a 365m hill leads to an enormous cross, originally erected by Señor Fagnano in 1913; the latest one was erected in 1987 for Pope John Paul II's visit. Camping is possible along the trail. Ask about guided hikes at any of the tour companies in Punta Arenas or Puerto Natales–based Erratic Rock.

Faro San Isidro, about 15km before Cabo Froward, is a lighthouse near the base of Monte Tarn (830m). This rugged area is home to prolific birdlife and some good hiking. It's also a launch point for humpback whale–watching trips to Isla Carlos III in **Parque Marino Francisco Coloane,** Chile's first marine park. Humpbacks and minke whales feed seasonally here between December and May. Package stays are available at **Hostería Faro San Isidro** (✆cell 9349-3862, cell 9640-7968; www.hosteriafarosanisidro.cl; d per person CH$40,000; 2-day packages per person CH$215,000; ⏰Oct-Apr), including transport from Punta Arenas and activities, such as kayaking and hiking.

Parque Nacional Pali Aike

Rugged volcanic steppe pocked with craters, caves and twisted formations, Pali Aike means 'devil's country' in Tehuelche. This desolate landscape is a 50-sq-km **park** (www.conaf.cl/parques/parque-nacional-pali-aike; adult/child under 12yr CH$1000/free) along the Argentine border. Mineral content made lava rocks red, yellow or green-gray. Fauna includes abundant guanaco, ñandú, gray fox and armadillo. In the 1930s Junius Bird's excavations at 17m-deep **Pali Aike Cave** yielded the first artifacts associated with extinct New World fauna such as the milodón and the native horse *Onohippidium.*

The park has several trails, including a 1.7km path through the rugged lava beds of the **Escorial del Diablo** to the impressive **Crater Morada del Diablo;** wear sturdy shoes or your feet could be shredded. There are hundreds of craters, some four stories

SOUTHERN PATAGONIA AROUND PUNTA ARENAS

high. A 9km trail from Cueva Pali Aike to **Laguna Ana** links a shorter trail to a site on the main road, 5km from the park entrance.

Parque Nacional Pali Aike is 200km northeast of Punta Arenas via RN9, Ch 255 and a graveled secondary road from Cooperativa Villa O'Higgins, 11km north of Estancia Kimiri Aike. There's also access from the Chilean border post at Monte Aymond. There is no public transport, but Punta Arenas travel agencies offer full-day tours.

ÚLTIMA ESPERANZA

With a name that translates to Last Hope, the once-remote Última Esperanza fills the imagination with foreboding. Storms wrestle the vast expanse and the landscape falls nothing short of grand; after all, Parque Nacional Torres del Paine and part of the Southern Patagonian Ice Field are in the backyard. Often lumped together with neighboring Magallanes, Última Esperanza is a separate southern province. While it can still be a challenging place to travel in winter, it is no longer so far off the beaten path. In fact, the tourism boom has transformed parts of it from rustic to outright decadent; still, there's something for everyone here.

Puerto Natales

✆ 061 / POP 18,000

A formerly modest fishing port on Seno Última Esperanza, Puerto Natales has blossomed into a Gore-Tex mecca. The gateway to Parque Nacional Torres del Paine, this town is reaping the benefits of its business savvy: boutique beers and wine tastings are overtaking tea time, and gear shops have already replaced the yarn sellers. The town now feeds off tourism, and it's an all-you-can-eat feast with unwavering demand. While some sectors cater to international tastes, there's appeal in Natales' corrugated-tin houses strung shoulder to shoulder and cozy granny-style lodgings. Most notably, in spite of a near-constant swarm of summer visitors, the town still maintains the glacial pace of living endemic to Patagonia.

Puerto Natales sits on the shores of Seno Última Esperanza, 250km northwest of Punta Arenas via Ruta 9, and has some striking views out over the mountains. It is the capital of the province of Última Esperanza and the southern terminus of the ferry trip through the Chilean fjords.

⊙ Sights

Museo Histórico   MUSEUM
(✆ 061-241-1263; Bulnes 28; admission CH$1000; ⊙ 8am-7pm Mon-Fri, 10am-1pm & 3-7pm Sat & Sun) A crash course in local history, with archaeological artifacts, a Yaghan canoe, Tehuelche bolas and historical photos.

Mirador Dorotea   TRAIL
(admission CH$5000) A day hike through a lenga forest on private land to splendid views of Puerto Natales and the glacial valley. Less than 10km from Natales. Dorotea is the large rocky outcrop just off Ruta 9.

⅍ Activities

Turismo Fjordo Eberhard   ADVENTURE TOUR
(Estancia Puerto Consuelo; ✆ cell 9380-1080; www.fiordoeberhard.com; Km23 Norte; 2hr horseride CH$28,000) Surrounded by tranquil fjords and looming mountains, this gorgeous *estancia* offers horseback riding and kayaking.

Pingo Salvaje   HORSE RIDING
(✆ cell 6236-0371; www.pingosalvaje.com; Estancia Laguna Sofía; 3hr horseride CH$33,000; ⊙ Oct-Apr) This lovely *estancia* getaway offers horseback riding and condor-spotting. You can stay over in a comfortable shared cabin (CH$15,000 per person, bring a sleeping bag) or campsite (CH$4000 per person) under a stand of trees, outfitted with grills, tables and hot showers. It's 30km from Puerto Natales; transport costs CH$10,000 per person.

Mandala Andino   SPA
(✆ cell 9930-2997; mandalaandino@yahoo.com; Bulnes 301; massages from CH$18,000; ⊙ 10am-10pm Nov-Mar) A recommended full-service wellness center with spot-on massages, tub soaks and various pampering treatments. Also sells interesting gifts and local crafts.

Patagom Lila   YOGA
(✆ cell 6140-7857; www.yogapatagomlila.com; Galvarino 345) ✎ Wonderful yoga teacher Susanne offers classes in English, German and Spanish in both a downtown house and a spectacular rural dome with views of the Seno Última Esperanza, where you will also find permaculture courses, yoga vacations and Thai and singing bowl massages. She also brings alternative therapies into the local community.

Encuentro Gourmet   COOKING CLASS
(✆ cell 6720-3725; reservas@encuentrogourmet.com; Bories 349; CH$25,000; ⊙ 10:30am or 7:30pm) A French expat teaches classic

Chilean dishes such as lamb stew or *chupe de centolla* (king crab casserole); includes group lunch or dinner.

☞ Tours

Antares/Big Foot Patagonia ADVENTURE TOUR
(✆061-241-4611; www.antarespatagonia.com; Pedro Montt 161) Specializing in Torres del Paine, Antares can facilitate climbing permits and made-to-order trips. They also have the park concession for Lago Grey activities including Glacier Grey ice trekking and kayak trips.

Baqueano Zamora HORSE RIDING
(✆061-261-3530; www.baqueanozamora.cl; Baquedano 534) Runs recommended horseback-riding trips and wild horse viewing in Torres del Paine.

Chile Nativo ADVENTURE TOUR
(✆061-241-1835, cell 9078-9168; www.chilenativo.cl; Eberhard 230, 2nd fl) Links visitors with local gauchos, organizes photo safaris and can competently plan your tailor-made dream adventures.

Erratic Rock ADVENTURE TOUR
(✆061-241-4317; www.erraticrock.com; Baquedano 719) ✔ Guides bare-bones Torres del Paine trips plus alternative options and rents gear. Alternative treks include Cabo Froward, Isla Navarino and lesser-known destinations.

Fortaleza Expediciones ADVENTURE TOUR
(✆061-261-3395; www.fortalezapatagonia.cl; Tomás Rogers 235) Knowledgeable operator; rents camping gear.

Turismo 21 de Mayo GUIDED TOUR
(✆614420 ; www.turismo21demayo.com; Eberhard 560) Organizes day-trip cruises and treks to the Balmaceda and Serrano glaciers.

✮ Festivals & Events

Festival de Cine de la Patagonia FILM FESTIVAL
(⊙mid-Feb) This is a week-long outdoor film festival.

🛏 Sleeping

Options abound, most with breakfast, laundry and discounted rates in the low season. Reserve ahead if arriving on the ferry. Hostels often rent equipment and help arrange park transport.

The Singing Lamb HOSTEL $
(✆061-241-0958; www.thesinginglamb.com; Arauco 779; dm US$22-30, d US$80; @🛜) ✔ A clean

and green hostel with compost, recycling, rainwater collection and linen shopping bags. Dorm rooms are priced by the number of beds (maximum nine) and shared spaces are ample. Nice touches include central heating and homemade breakfasts. To get here, follow Raimírez one block past Plaza O'Higgins.

Hostal Dos Lagunas GUESTHOUSE $
(✆cell 8162-7755; hostaldoslagunas@gmail.com; cnr Barros Arana & Bories; dm/d CH$12,000/ $30,000; 🛜) Natales natives Alejandro and Andrea are attentive hosts, spoiling guests with filling breakfasts, steady water pressure and travel tips. Among the town's most longstanding lodgings, the place is spotless.

4Elementos GUESTHOUSE $
(✆cell 9524-6956; www.4elementos.cl; Esmeralda 811; d CH$30,000, dm/s/d/q without bathroom CH$12,000/20,000/25,000/40,000; 🛜) ✔ A pioneer of Patagonian recycling, the passionate mission of this spare guesthouse is educating people about proper waste disposal. The hostel itself produces zero waste. Guests enjoy Scandanavian breakfasts made with care. Guide service, park bookings and greenhouse tours are available. By reservation only, as it isn't always open.

Lili Patagonico's Hostal HOSTEL $
(✆061-241-4063; www.lilipatagonicos.com; Arturo Prat 479; dm CH$10,000, d with/without bathroom CH$32,000/24,000; @🛜) A sprawling house with a climbing wall, a variety of dorms and colorful doubles with newer bathrooms and down comforters.

Hostal Nancy GUESTHOUSE $
(✆061-241-0022, dorm 061-241-4325; www.nateslodge.cl; Raimírez 540; dm CH$9000, s/d/tr CH$15,000/32,000/36,000; 🛜) Praised for its adoptable hostess Nancy, this family guesthouse recently remodeled, adding TVs and bathrooms in all rooms. There are still kitchen privileges in the annex across the street. It's a family environment with twin or double beds available with shared bath.

Yaganhouse HOSTEL $
(✆061-241-4137; www.yaganhouse.cl; O'Higgins 584; dm CH$12,000, d with/without bathroom CH$32,000/27,000; 🛜) Typical of local houses-turned-hostel, with funky additions. There are a few single rooms (CH$15,000, shared bath) and homey living spaces with colorful throws and rugs, laundry service and equipment rental.

Puerto Natales

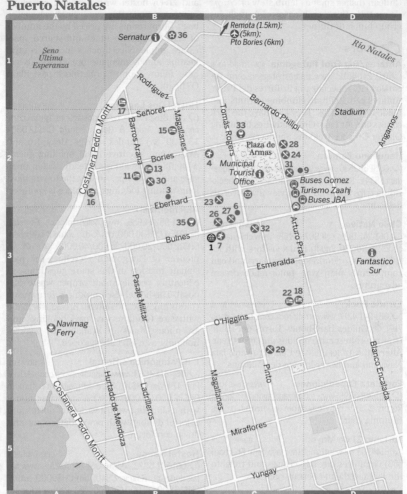

Residencial Bernardita GUESTHOUSE **$**
(☎061-241-1162; www.residencialbernardita.cl; O'Higgins 765; s/d with shared bathroom CH$15,000/25,000; ☎) Guests highly recommend Bernardita's quiet rooms with central heating and mismatched granny decor. Choose between rooms in the main house or more private ones in the back annex. There's also kitchen use and breakfast.

★ **We Are Patagonia** B&B **$$**
(☑ cell 7389-4802; www.wearepatagonia.com; Galvarino 745; r with/without bathroom CH$40,000/35,000; ☎) A lovely art hotel with minimal-

ist Nordic charm, central heating and homespun charms. Mantras stenciled on the walls provide some not-so-subliminal positive messaging. The breakfast of champions includes real coffee, fruit, oatmeal and whole wheat bread. It's located in a small house.

Kau B&B **$$**
(☑061-41-4611; www.kaulodge.com; Costanera Pedro Montt 161; d CH$60,000; ☎☒) ✿
With a mantra of simplicity, this aesthetic remake of a box hotel is cozy and cool. Thick woolen throws, picnic-table breakfast seating and well-worn, recycled wood

lic, also selling organic chocolate, teas and gluten-free options. Also rents cars.

Temauken Hotel
B&B **$$**

(☎ 061-241-1666; www.temauken.cl; Calle Ovejero 1123; s/d/tr CH$45,000/55,000/75,000; 🛜) A cheerful and elegant choice well away from the center, this newer three-story stilted home is plush and modern, with an ample, light-filled living room, panoramic sea views and gourmet meals.

Erratic Rock II
B&B **$$**

(☎ 061-241-4317; www.erraticrock2.com; Benjamin Zamora 732; d CH$40,000, tr without bathroom CH$42,000; @🛜) Billed as a 'hostel alternative for couples', this cozy home offers spacious doubles with throw pillows and tidy bathrooms. Breakfasts in the bright dining room are abundant.

★ The Singular Hotel
BOUTIQUE HOTEL **$$$**

(☎ 061-241-4040, bookings in Santiago 02-387-1500; www.thesingular.com; RN9, Km1.5; d US$414, d incl full board & excursions US$1360; P @ 🛜 🏊) A regional landmark reimagined, the Singular is a former meatpacking and shipping facility on the sound. Heightened industrial design, like chairs fashioned from old radiators in the lobby, mixes with vintage photos and antiques. The snug glass-walled rooms have water views and a well-respected bar/restaurant (alongside the museum, open to the public) serves fresh local game.

Guests can use the spa with pool and explore the surroundings by bike or kayak. It's located in Puerto Bories, 6km from the center.

Bories House
INN **$$$**

(☎ 061-241-2221; www.borieshouse.com; Puerto Bories 13-B; d/tr US$150/195, cottage US$350; 🛜) 🖉 Located outside of Puerto Natales in nearby Puerto Bories, this lovely new option has all the elegance of an English country house with sweeping views of the sound. There's a comfortable den area and just a few rooms, with bold fabric headboards and sturdy wooden furniture. Dinners are available with advance notice.

Indigo Patagonia
BOUTIQUE HOTEL **$$$**

(☎ 061-241-3609; www.indigopatagonia.com; Ladrilleros 105; d/ste with spa US$279/329; @🛜) Hikers will head first to Indigo's rooftop Jacuzzis and glass-walled spa. Materials like eucalyptus, slate and iron overlap the modern with the natural to interesting effect, though rooms tend to be small. The star

lend casual intimacy. Rooms boast fjord views, central heating, bulk toiletries, and safe boxes. **The Coffee Maker** espresso bar boasts killer lattes and staff have tons of adventure information on tap.

Amerindia
B&B **$$**

(☎ 061-241-1945; www.hostelamerindia.com; Barros Arana 135; d CH$45,000, without bathroom CH$35,000, 6-person apt CH$80,000; ⊘ closed Jul; @🛜) An earthy, tranquil retreat with a wood stove, beautiful weavings and raw wood beams. Guests wake up to cake, eggs and oatmeal in a cozy cafe open to the pub-

Puerto Natales

here is the fjord in front of you, which even captures your gaze in the shower. The hotel is part of Chile's upscale Noi hotel chain.

Hotel IF Patagonia   BOUTIQUE HOTEL **$$$**
(☑ 061-241-0312; www.hotelifpatagonia.com; Magallanes 73; s/d US$140/150; ⓟ🛜) 🍴 With brimming hospitality, IF (for Isabel and Fernando) is minimalist and lovely. Its bright, modern interior includes wool throws, down duvets and deck views of the fjord. There's also a garden sauna and wooden hot tub.

Remota   LODGE **$$$**
(☑ 061-241-4040, bookings in Santiago 02-387-1500; www.remota.cl; RN9, Km1.5; s/d US$300/350; all-inclusive from US$1950; @🛜🛅) Unlike most hotels, this one draws your awareness to what's outside: silence broadcasts gusty winds, windows echo old stock fences and a crooked passageway imitates *estancia* sheep corridors. Though rooms are cozy, there's a feeling of isolation here and service can be cool.

Weskar   HOTEL **$$$**
(☑ 061-241-4168; www.weskar.cl; RN9, Km5; d from US$160; @🛜) Just outside of town on the coastal road of the sound, this wooden lodge boasts big views, cozy nooks and a variety of rooms. Prices are high for the homespun, mismatched style, but shoulder season

rates offer good value. There's a buffet-style breakfast and their upscale restaurant has garnered acclaim.

🍴 Eating

La Mesita Grande   PIZZA **$**
(☑ cell 6141-1571; www.mesitagrande.cl; Arturo Prat 196; pizza CH$5000-7000; ⊙12:30-3pm & 7-11:30pm Mon-Sat, 1-3pm & 7-11:30pm Sun) Happy diners share one long, worn table for outstanding thin-crust pizza, quality pasta and organic salads.

Cafe Kaiken   CHILEAN **$**
(☑ cell 8295-2036; Baquedano 699; mains CH$5000-7000; ⊙1-3:30pm & 6:30-11pm Mon-Sat) With just five tables and one couple cooking, serving and chatting up customers, this is as intimate as it gets. The owners moved here to get out of the Santiago fast lane, so you'd best follow their lead. Dishes like slow-roasted lamb or homemade smoked-salmon stuffed ravioli are well worth the wait. Arrive early to claim a spot.

El Bote   CHILEAN **$**
(☑ 061-241-0045; Bulnes 380; set menu CH$3500; ⊙noon-11:30pm Mon-Sat) A haven for Chilean comfort food, this unpretentious restaurant dishes out roast chicken, seafood casseroles and homemade soups in addition to more expensive game dishes featuring guanaco

and venison. For dessert, go with the classic chestnuts in cream.

Cangrejo Rojo CAFE **$$**
(☑061-241-2436; Santiago Bueras 782; mains CH$6000-8500; ☉1:30-3pm & 5:30-10pm Tue-Sun) Unfathomably friendly and reasonable, this cute corrugated tin cafe serves pies, ice cream, sandwiches and hot clay pot dishes like seafood casserole or lamb chops. To get here, follow Baquedano four blocks south of Plaza O'Higgins to Bueras.

El Living CAFE **$**
(www.el-living.com; Arturo Prat 156; mains $4000-6000; ☉11am-10pm Mon-Sat Nov–mid-April; ✍) Indulge in the London lounge feel of this chill cafe, one of Natales' first. There's fresh vegetarian fare (plus vegan, gluten-free), stacks of European glossies and a hidden backyard with outdoor tables.

G Sushi SUSHI **$**
(☑061-241-4653; Pinto 552; mains CH$4500-7300; ☉11:30am-3:30pm & 7-11:30pm Mon-Sat) Delicious sushi, wok dishes and artisan beers are served up in a stylish refurbished home located a few blocks away from the commercial center. Also delivers.

Creperia FRENCH **$**
(☑cell 6657-8348; Bulnes 358; mains CH$4000-7000; ☉12:30-3pm & 5-11pm Mon-Sat) A bright nook with savory and sweet crepes, teas and coffee drinks. Factors like local produce and sought-after Nutella help you to break out of that meat-and-potato rut.

Masay SANDWICHES **$**
(☑061-241-5008; Bulnes 427; mains CH$3000-5000; ☉11am-midnight) Nothing fancy, just good Chilean sandwiches on white buns and swift service.

La Aldea MEDITERRANEAN **$$**
(☑cell 6141-4027; www.aldearestaurant.cl; Barros Arana 132; mains CH$7000-10,000; ☉7-11pm Wed-Mon) Chef Pato changes the offerings daily, but the focus is fresh and Mediterranean. Think grilled clams, lamb tagine and quinoa dishes.

Asador Patagónico PARRILLA **$$**
(☑061-241-3553; Arturo Prat 158; mains CH$7000-10,000; ☉12:30-3pm & 7-11:30pm) If trekking left you with a mastodon appetite, this upscale Argentine-style grill serves flame-seared lamb, steak and salads, as well as sweetbreads, alongside quality wines.

★**The Singular Restaurant** CONTEMPORARY **$$$**
(☑061-272-2030; Puerto Bories; mains CH$6000-14,000; ☉8am-11pm) The perfect port in a storm, part supper club of yore, part modern bistro, with exquisite food and attentive service. Leather sofas and polished wood meet bare beams and stark views of the sound. Chef Pasqualetto reinvigorates local ingredients: the freshest ceviche, tender lamb medallions and lovely salads come with original sides and fine Chilean wines. Vegetarian options excel.

Afrigonia FUSION **$$$**
(☑061-241-2877; Eberhard 343; mains CH$10,000-14,000; ☉12:20-3pm & 6:30-11pm) Outstanding and wholly original, you won't find Afro-Chilean cuisine on any NYC menu. This romantic gem was dreamed up by a hard-working Zambian-Chilean couple. Fragrant rice, fresh ceviche and mint roasted lamb are prepared with succulent precision. Make reservations.

🍷 Drinking

Baguales BREWERY
(www.cervezabaguales.cl; Bories 430; ☉6pm-2:30am; ☎) Climber friends started this microbrewery as a noble quest for quality suds and the beer (crafted on-site) does not disappoint. A 2nd-floor addition seeks to meet the heavy demand. The gringo-style bar food is just so-so.

Por Que no te Callas BAR
(☑061-241-4942; Magallanes 247; ☉7pm-1:30am Mon-Sat, to 2am weekends) For a local vibe, you can't go wrong with a bar called 'Why don't you shut up.' It's friendlier than the name implies and even a bit gentrified. Besides a pool table, there's live music ranging from bossa nova to rock on weekends. Drinks like the fernet-based *caballo negro* come sized to do damage.

Base Camp BAR
(☑061-241-4658; Baquedano 731; ☉6pm-2am) Debut your park tall tales at this gringo hideout. With pub trivia nights and occasional live music.

☆ Entertainment

Centro Cultural Galpon Patagonia CULTURAL CENTER
(Pedro Montt 16; ☉10am-1pm & 3-7pm Tue-Sun) **FREE** This new cultural center and tea house occupies a revamped 1920 warehouse

with exposed beams and worn floorboards. Features art exhibits, theater, dance and music.

ℹ️ Information

Most banks in town are equipped with ATMs. The best bilingual portal for the region is www.torresdelpaine.cl.

Conaf (☑ 061-241-1438; Baquedano 847; ⊙ 8:30am-12:45pm & 2:30-5:30pm Mon-Fri) National parks service administrative office.

Fantastico Sur (☑ 061-261-4184; www.fantasticosur.com; Esmeralda 661; ⊙ 9am-1pm & 3-6pm Mon-Fri) Runs Refugios Torres, El Chileno, Los Cuernos in Torres del Paine and offers park tours, guiding and trek planning services, including a popular self-guided option.

La Hermandad (Bulnes 692) Decent rates on cash and traveler's checks.

Hospital (☑ 061-241-1582; Pinto 537)

Municipal Tourist Office (☑ 061-261-4808; Plaza de Armas; ⊙ 8:30am-12:30pm & 2:30-6pm Tue-Sun) In the Museo Histórico and the Rodoviario (bus station), with regionwide lodgings listings.

Post Office (Eberhard 429)

Sernatur (☑ 061-241-2125; infonatales@sernatur.cl; Pedro Montt 19; ⊙ 9am-7pm Mon-Fri, 9:30am-6pm Sat & Sun) With useful city and regional maps and a second plaza location in high season.

Turismo Comapa (☑ 061-241-4300; www.comapa.com; Bulnes 541; ⊙ 9am-1pm & 3-7pm Mon-Fri, 10am-2pm Sat) Navimag ferry and airline bookings; also runs *refugios* in Torres del Paine.

Vertice Patagonia (☑ 061-241-2742; www.verticepatagonia.com; Bulnes 100) Runs Refugios Grey, Dickson and Paine Grande, as well as Camping Perros, in Torres del Paine.

ℹ️ Getting There & Away

AIR

Puerto Natales' small airport is currently closed, but may reopen pending an airstrip expansion.

BOAT

For many travelers, a journey through Chile's spectacular fjords aboard the **Navimag Ferry** (☑ 061-241-1421, Rodoviario 061-241-1642; www.navimag.com; Pedro Montt 308; 2nd office in the Rodoviario; ⊙ 9am-1pm & 2:30-6:30pm Mon-Fri) becomes a highlight of their trip. This four-day and three-night northbound voyage has become so popular it should be booked well in advance. You can also try your luck. To confirm when the ferry is due, contact Turismo Comapa or Navimag a couple of days before your esti-

mated arrival date. There is now a second office in the Rodoviario (bus station).

The ferry leaves Natales early on Friday and stops in Puerto Edén (or Glaciar Pía XI on southbound sailings) en route to Puerto Montt. It usually arrives in Natales in the morning of the same day and departs either later that day or on the following day, but schedules vary according to weather conditions and tides. Disembarking passengers must stay on board while cargo is transported; those embarking have to spend the night on board.

High season is November to March, mid-season is October and April and low season is May to September. Fares vary according to view, cabin size and private or shared bathroom, and include all meals (request vegetarian meals when booking) and interpretive talks. Bring water, snacks and drinks anyway. Per-person high season (Nov-Mar) fares range from US$450 for a bunk berth to US$2100 for a triple-A cabin; students and seniors receive a 10% to 15% discount. Check online for current schedules and rates.

BUS

Buses arrive at the **Rodoviario** (Bus Terminal; Av España 1455), a bus terminal on the town outskirts, though companies also sell tickets at their downtown offices. Book at least a day ahead, especially for early-morning departures. Services are greatly reduced in the low season.

Buses leave for Torres del Paine two to three times daily at around 7am, 8am and 2:30pm. If you are headed to Mountain Lodge Paine Grande in the low season, take the morning bus to meet the catamaran. Tickets may also be used for transfers within the park, so save your stub. Schedules change, so double-check them before heading out.

Companies and destinations include the following:

DESTINATION	COST (CH$)	DURATION (HR)
El Calafate	15,000	5
Punta Arenas	6000	3
Torres del Paine	8000	2
Ushuaia	36,000	13

Bus Sur (☑ 061-261-4220; www.bus-sur.cl; Baquedano 668) Punta Arenas, Río Gallegos and Ushuaia.

Buses Fernández/El Pingüino (☑ 061-241-1111; www.busesfernandez.com; cnr Esmeralda & Ramírez) Torres del Paine and Punta Arenas. Also goes direct to Puerto Natales from the airport.

Buses Gomez (☑ 061-241-5700; www.busesgomez.com; Arturo Prat 234) Torres del Paine.

Buses JBA (✆061-241-0242; Arturo Prat 258) Torres del Paine.

Buses Pacheco (✆061-241-4800; www.bus-espacheco.com; Ramírez 224) Punta Arenas, Río Grande and Ushuaia.

Cootra (✆061-241-2785; Baquedano 244) El Calafate daily at 8:30am.

Turismo Zaahj (✆061-241-2260; www.turismozaahj.co.cl; Arturo Prat 236/270) Torres del Paine and El Calafate.

❶ Getting Around

Many hostels rent bikes. Car rental rates are generally better in Punta Arenas. Try **Emsa/Avis** (✆061-261-4388; Eberhard 577). Drivers should know that there are two routes into Torres del Paine; the more direct gravel one goes via Lago Toro. **Reliable Radio Taxi** (✆061-241-2805; cnr Arturo Prat & Bulnes) can even be counted on for after-hours deliveries.

Cueva del Milodón

In the 1890s, German pioneer Hermann Eberhard discovered the partial remains of an enormous ground sloth in a cave 25km northwest of Puerto Natales. The slow-moving, herbivorous *milodón,* which stood nearly 4m tall, was supposedly the motivating factor behind Bruce Chatwin's book *In Patagonia.* The 30m-high **Cueva del Milodón** (cuevadelmilodon.cl; adult/child 12yr & under CH$4000/500) pays homage to its former inhabitant with a life-size plastic replica of the animal. It's not exactly tasteful, but still worth a stop to appreciate the grand setting and ruminate over its wild past. An easy walk leads up to a lookout point.

Torres del Paine buses pass the entrance, which is 8km from the cave proper. There are infrequent tours from Puerto Natales; alternatively, you can hitch or share a *taxi colectivo* (CH$20,000). Outside of high season, bus services are infrequent.

Parque Nacional Bernardo O'Higgins

Virtually inaccessible, O'Higgins remains an elusive cache of glaciers. As it can be entered only by boat, full-day excursions (CH$75,000, lunch included) to the base of Glaciar Serrano are run by Turismo 21 de Mayo (p347).

You can access Torres del Paine via boat to Glaciar Serrano. Passengers transfer to a Zodiac (a motorized raft), stop for lunch at Estancia Balmaceda and continue up Río Serrano, arriving at the southern border of the park by 5pm. The same tour can be done leaving the park, but may require camping near Río Serrano to catch the Zodiac at 9am. The trip, which includes park entry, costs CH$100,000 with Turismo 21 de Mayo.

Parque Nacional Torres del Paine

Soaring almost vertically more than 2000m above the Patagonian steppe, the granite pillars of Torres del Paine (Towers of Paine) dominate the landscape of what may be South America's finest national park. Before its creation in 1959, the park was part of a large sheep *estancia,* and it's still recovering from nearly a century of overexploitation of its pastures, forests and wildlife.

Most people visit the park for its one greatest hit but, once here, realize that there are other attractions with equal wow power. We're talking about azure lakes, trails that meander through emerald forests, roaring rivers you'll cross on rickety bridges and one big, radiant blue glacier. Variety spans from the vast openness of the steppe to rugged mountain terrain topped by looming peaks.

Part of Unesco's Biosphere Reserve system since 1978, the park is home to flocks of ostrich-like rhea (known locally as the ñandú), Andean condor, flamingo and many other bird species. Its star success in conservation is undoubtedly the guanaco, which grazes the open steppes where pumas cannot approach undetected. After more than a decade of effective protection from poachers, these large, growing herds don't even flinch when humans or vehicles approach. The puma population is also growing, and huemul (an endangered Andean deer) have been spotted in Valle Frances.

When the weather is clear, panoramas are everywhere. However, unpredictable weather systems can sheath the peaks in clouds for hours or days. Some say you get four seasons in a day here, with sudden rainstorms and knock-down gusts part of the hearty initiation. Bring high-quality foul-weather gear, a synthetic sleeping bag and, if you're camping, a good tent. It is always wise to plan a few extra days to make sure that your trip isn't torpedoed by a spot of bad weather.

The crowning attraction of this 1810-sq-km park is its highly developed infrastructure, which makes it possible to do the

Parque Nacional Torres del Paine

Parque Nacional Torres del Paine

whole 'W' hike while sleeping in beds, eating hot meals, taking showers and even drinking the random cocktail. It's essential to make reservations ahead of time.

If you want to sleep in hotels or *refugios* (rustic shelters), you must make reservations in advance. Plan a minimum of three to seven days to enjoy the hiking and other activities. Guided day trips on minibuses from Puerto Natales are possible, but permit only a glimpse of what the park has to offer.

At the end of 2011, a raging fire burned over 16,000 hectares. The fire took weeks to contain, destroyed old forest, killed animals and burned several park structures. An international visitor was charged with accidentally setting the fire while trying to start an illegal campfire. The hiker denied setting the fire but paid a US$10,000 fine and agreed to help with reforestation efforts. Chile has since enacted a stricter 'Ley del Bosque' (forest law) to protect parks and Conaf has started to actively remove visitors found breaking park guidelines. The affected area, mostly between Pehoé and Refugio Grey, is essentially the western leg of the 'W' trek.

Be conscientious and tread lightly – you are among hundreds of thousands of yearly guests.

🏃 Activities

Hiking

Torres del Paine's 2800m granite peaks inspire a mass pilgrimage of hikers from around the world. Most go for the Paine Circuit or the 'W' to soak in these classic panoramas, leaving other incredible routes deserted. The Paine Circuit (the 'W' plus the backside of the peaks) requires seven to nine days, while the 'W' (named for the rough approximation to the letter that it traces out on the map) takes four to five. Add another day or two for transportation connections.

Most trekkers start either route from Laguna Amarga. You can also hike from Administración or take the catamaran from Pudeto to Lago Pehoé and start from there; hiking roughly southwest to northeast along the 'W' presents more views of black sedimentary peaks known as Los Cuernos (2200m to 2600m). For more detailed information of the following hikes, see Lonely Planet's *Trekking in the Patagonian Andes*.

As more trekkers arrive in the shoulder season, they should be aware of early-season and foul-weather route closures. Trekking alone, especially on the backside of the circuit, is inadvisable, and may soon be regulated by Conaf. Tour operators in Puerto Natales offer guided treks, which include all meals and accommodations at *refugios* or hotels. Per person rates decrease significantly in groups.

In a move to emphasize safety in the park, Conaf requires all visitors to sign a contract upon entering. The document details park regulations and explains the penalties of breaking them.

The 'W'

Most people trek the 'W' from right to left (east to west), starting at Laguna Amarga – accessible via a twice-daily 2½-hour bus ride from Puerto Natales. But hiking west to east – especially between Lago Pehoé and Valle Francés – provides superior views of Los Cuernos. To start the 'W' from the west, catch the catamaran across Lago Pehoé, then head north along Lago Grey or Campamento Italiano, from which point excellent (and pack-free) day hikes are possible. Going this direction, the hike is roughly 71 kilometers in total. The following segments are some of the most memorable; all distances are one way.

Refugio Las Torres to Mirador Las Torres (8km, four hours) A moderate hike up Río Ascencio to a treeless tarn beneath the eastern face of the Torres del Paine for the closest view of the towers. The last hour is a knee-popping scramble up boulders (covered with knee- and waist-high snow in winter). There are camping and *refugios* at Las Torres and Chileno, with basic camping at Campamento Torres. In summer stay at Campamento Torres and head up at sunrise to beat the crowds.

Refugio Las Torres to Los Cuernos (12km, seven hours) Hikers should keep to the lower trail as many get lost on the upper trail (unmarked on maps). There's camping and a *refugio*. Summer winds can be fierce.

Los Cuernos/Lago Pehoé to Valle Francés (10km, five hours) In clear weather, this hike is the most beautiful stretch between 3050m Cerro Paine Grande to the west and the lower but still spectacular Torres del Paine and Los Cuernos to the east, with glaciers hugging the trail. Camp at Italiano and at Británico, right in the heart of the valley, or at the valley entrance at Camping Francés.

The W

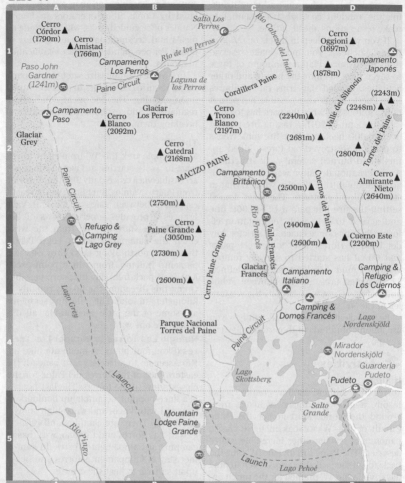

SOUTHERN PATAGONIA PARQUE NACIONAL TORRES DEL PAINE

Valle Francés to Mountain Lodge Paine Grande (13km, five hours) From Campamento Británico, the trail heads downhill out of Valle Francés, over a hanging bridge toward Mountain Lodge Paine Grande. The spectacular Cuernos loom overhead on the right, and Lago Skottsberg is passed on the left. The ferry dock is just before the *refugio* and campground.

Mountain Lodge Paine Grande to Refugio Lago Grey (10km, four hours one way from Lago Pehoé) A relatively easy trail with a few challenging downhill scampers. The glacier lookout is another half-hour's

hike away. It has camping and *refugios* at both ends. This is the primary area which burned in 2011, so expect ash, burned forest and areas in recovery.

Mountain Lodge Paine Grande to Administración (16km, five hours) Up and around the side of Lago Pehoé, then through extensive grassland along Río Grey. Not technically part of the 'W,' but after completion of the hike, cut out to the Administración to avoid backtracking to Laguna Amarga. Mountain Lodge Paine Grande can radio in and make sure that you can catch a bus from the

(map)

deep mud and snow. There's one basic *refugio* at Los Perros; the other option is rustic camping.

Many hikers start the Paine Circuit by entering the park (by bus) at Laguna Amarga, then hike for a few hours to Refugio and Camping Chileno. From this point, the circuit continues counterclockwise, ending in Valle Francés and Los Cuernos. The Paine Circuit is closed during winter.

The following segments are some of the most memorable; all distances are one way.

Refugio Lago Grey to Campamento Paso (10km, four hours heading north, two hours going south) Hikers might want to go left to right (west to east), which means ascending the pass rather than slipping downhill.

Campamento Paso to Campamento Los Perros (12 km, four hours) This route has plenty of mud and sometimes snow. Don't be confused by what appears to be a campsite right after crossing the pass; keep going until you see a shack.

Campamento Los Perros to Campamento Dickson (9km, around 4½ hours) A relatively easy but windy stretch.

Campamento Lago Dickson to Campamento Serón (19km, six hours) As the trail wraps around Lago Paine, winds can get fierce and the trails vague; stay along the trail furthest away from the lake. On the way, Campamento Coiron has been closed since the 2005 fire.

Campamento Serón to Laguna Amarga (15km, four to five hours) You can end the trek with a chill-out night and a decent meal at Refugio Las Torres.

Other Overnight Hikes

From Guardería Lago Grey, a four-hour trail follows Río Pingo to Conaf's Camping Zapata, from where hikes (about another 1½ to two hours) continue to a lookout with impressive views of **Glaciar Zapata** and **Lago Pingo**. Because of ongoing studies of wildlife and fossil beds, hiking in this pristine area is authorized only for groups traveling with a Conaf-approved guide.

From Guardería Laguna Amarga a four-hour hike leads to **Laguna Azul**. The camping area on the northeastern shore closed after a wildfire; check with Conaf about its current status. After another two-hour hike north the trail reaches **Lago Paine**. Meeting up with the Paine Circuit trail on the

Administración back to Puerto Natales. You can also enter the 'W' this way to hike it east to west.

The Paine Circuit

For solitude, stellar views and bragging rights over your compadres doing the 'W,' this longer trek is the way to go. This loop takes in the 'W', plus the backside between Refugio Grey and Refugio Las Torres; the total distance is roughly 112 kilometers. The landscape is desolate yet beautiful. **Paso John Gardner** (the most extreme part of the trek) sometimes offers knee-

AVOID THE MULTITUDES

➡ Most hikers go up to the Torres around 8am and down at 4pm. With full summer light, you can go against traffic by starting a couple of hours earlier or later; inquire about the times of sunset/sunrise at your *refugio* or *guardaparques* (ranger station).

➡ Hike the less-crowded Full Circuit.

➡ Join a multiday trip kayaking Río Serrano or horseback riding; you'll get a completely different perspective and incredible views.

➡ Hike in the shoulder season but prepare for brisk weather. March can be excellent in the park. Winter can be stunning, though extra skills are required.

other side of the lake is made impossible by the river.

From the Administración, the three-hour hike to Hostería Pehoé is an easy, mainly flat trail with great views. For more solitude and birdwatching, a four-hour hike branches east after crossing Río Paine, zigzags up the skirt of the Sierra del Toro to access a string of lakes, ending with **Laguna Verde**. There is no camping, but those inclined could splurge for a night at Hostería Mirador del Payne.

Day Hikes

Walk from Guardería Pudeto, on the main park highway, to **Salto Grande**, a powerful waterfall between Lago Nordenskjöld and Lago Pehoé. Another easy hour's walk leads to **Mirador Nordenskjöld**, an overlook with superb views of the lake and mountains.

For a more challenging day hike with tranquility and gorgeous scenery, try the four-hour trek to **Lago Paine**; its northern shore is only accessible from Laguna Azul.

Kayaking & Floating

A great way to get up close to glaciers, Big Foot Patagonia (p347) leads 2½-hour tours (per person CH$55,000) of the iceberg-strewn Lago Grey several times daily in summer. Family-oriented floating trips that take rafts down the mild Río Serrano are run by Fantastico Sur (p352).

Cruise

From Hotel Lago Grey (p361), a daily sightseeing cruise (CH$55,000 per person) approaches Glacier Grey in a three-hour round-trip excursion. Contact the hotel for reservations.

Horseback Riding

Due to property divisions within the park, horses cannot cross between the western sections (Lagos Grey and Pehoé, Río Serrano) and the eastern part managed by Fantastico Sur/Hotel Las Torres (Refugio Los Cuernos is the approximate cut off). Baqueano Zamora (p347) runs excursions to Laguna Azul, Valle Frances, Dickson glacier and more remote locations, with one-day (US$60) and multiday options.

Hotel Las Torres (p361) is part of an *estancia* that comprises the eastern area of the park; it offers full-day horseback-riding trips around Lago Nordenskjöld and beyond.

Ice Trekking

A fun walk through a sculpted landscape of ice, and you don't need experience to go. Antares' Big Foot Patagonia (p347) is the sole company with a park concession for ice hikes (CH$90,000) on Glacier Grey, using the Conaf house (former Refugio Grey) as a starting point. The five-hour excursion is available from October to May, in high season at 8:30am and 2:30pm.

Rock Climbing

Rock climbers can contact Puerto Natales outfitters for customized multiday trips. There are not a lot of beginner routes here.

Self-supported climbers must have accident insurance and get permission from the **Dirección de Fronteras y Límites** (Difrol; ☏ 02-671-4110; www.difrol.cl; Bandera 52, 4th fl, Santiago); this day errand in Santiago takes up to 10 days from the Gobernación de Ultima Esperanza in Puerto Natales. Ask for dates with a time cushion to avoid paying a separate fee each time you enter the park. With these two documents, climbers can obtain a climbing permit at park headquarters.

Avoid delays by arranging the permissions with a climbing outfitter, such as Antares in Puerto Natales, before arrival in the country.

Mountain Biking

Trails newly authorized for mountain biking include Laguna Azul and Cañon de Perros. Check with outfitters in Puerto Natales about this new option.

🛏 Sleeping

Make reservations! Arriving without them, especially in high season, limits you to camping. Travel agencies offer reservations, but it's best to deal directly with the various management companies. Listings feature high-season rates. Phone numbers listed are for Puerto Natales offices.

Refugios & Domos

If you are hiking the 'W' or the Paine Circuit, you will be staying in *refugios, domos* ('domes,' also known as yurts) or campsites along the way. It is essential to reserve your spot and specify vegetarian meals in advance. Try to do this as soon as you book your trip.

Refugio rooms have four to eight bunk beds each, kitchen privileges (for lodgers and during specific hours only), hot showers and meals. If you don't bring a sleeping bag, a rental or bedding is extra (from CH$4500 to CH$24,000). Meals are also extra (CH$7500 to CH$15,000). Should a *refugio* be overbooked, staff provide all necessary camping equipment. Most *refugios* close by the end of April. *Domos* are either cloth or plastic permanent camp structures with bunks or cots. Their operating season may be shorter.

Guests should use resources wisely and conserve water and electricity. There are no plugs in rooms, so bring a solar charger or extra batteries to charge electronics.

Accommodations may require photo ID (ie a passport) upon check-in. Photocopy your tourist card and passport for all lodgings in advance to expedite check-in. Staff can radio ahead to confirm your next reservation. Given the huge volume of trekkers, snags are inevitable, so practice your Zen composure.

Accommodations are listed (roughly) counterclockwise from Refugio Las Torres to Lago Dickson, following the 'W' trail. Rates listed are basic – if you want bed linens (versus your own sleeping bag), it's extra.

Ecocamp DOME $$$
(✍in Santiago 022-923-5950; www.ecocamp. travel; 5-day hiking package US$1777) Part of a package tour, these domes range from basic, with shared composting bathrooms, to deluxe versions with heat, private bathroom and canopied beds. They're linked by boardwalks to dining, bar and yoga areas with a cozy, social atmosphere. Guided activities include hiking, fly-fishing and kayaking.

SOUTHERN PATAGONIA PARQUE NACIONAL TORRES DEL PAINE

TREKKING LIGHTLY

Some 200,000 tourists visit Torres del Paine each year and with the park headlining life adventure lists everywhere, its popularity will only grow. And there is sure to be an impact. Already, in the high season of January and February, trails have traffic jams and campgrounds resemble Woodstock. In that peace-and-love spirit, we offer some trip tips:

➡ Don't drink bottled water, since the bottles become a recycling nightmare (trash is taken out on pack horses, if you can imagine). Instead opt to bring a purifier or use tablets.

➡ Pack out all garbage, as little scavengers, mainly mice, love to make merry in campgrounds.

➡ Respect the official camp zones and hike only in designated areas.

➡ Don't make campfires, they're illegal.

➡ Be extremely mindful of fire from cigarettes, camp stoves, lighters etc. In 2005 and 2011 fires attributed to backpackers destroyed large parts of the park.

➡ Stay friendly. Park regulars have noted that as traffic increases the community feeling diminishes. But it doesn't have to be that way. So say hi to your fellow hikers and let the fleet-footed ones pass.

To help you can volunteer with trail maintenance, biological studies or an animal census with nonprofit **AMA Torres del Paine** (www.amatorresdelpaine.org). Alternatively, make donations through the **Torres del Paine Legacy Fund** (https://supporttdp.org), which aids park reforestation and recycling in Puerto Natales, organized by the nonprofit Sustainable Travel.

Refugio Las Torres
LODGE **$**

(☎ 061-261-4184; www.fantasticosur.com; dm US$53, incl full board US$109; ☺ Sep-Apr; @) An ample, attractive base camp with 60 beds and the added feature of a comfortable lounge, restaurant and bar. In high season, a nearby older building is put into use to handle the overflow, at discounted rates.

Refugio Chileno
CABIN **$**

(☎ 061-261-4184; www.fantasticosur.com; dm US$53, incl full board US$109; ☺ Oct-Mar) Nearest to the fabled towers, Chileno is one of the smallest refugios, with 32 beds and a small provisions kiosk. It's run on wind energy and toilets use composting biofilters.

Refugio Los Cuernos
CABIN **$**

(☎ 061-261-4184; www.fantasticosur.com; dm US$53, incl full board US$109; 2-person cabin US$177, incl full board $289; ☺ Sep-Apr) Filling fast, this mid-'W' location tends to bottleneck with hikers going in either location. But with eight beds per room, this small lodge is more than cozy. New separate showers and bathrooms for campers relieve some of the stress. For a deluxe option, cabins with shared bath offer privacy, with access to a piping-hot wooden hot tub.

Domos Los Cuernos
DOME **$**

(☎ 061-261-4184; www.fantasticosur.com; dm US$63, incl full board US$119; ☺ Sep-Mar, varies) Next to Refugio Los Cuernos.

Domos El Francés
DOME **$$**

(☎ 061-261-4184; www.fantasticosur.com; dm US$69, incl full board US$125; ☺ Oct-Mar, varies) New domes with dining hall located at Camping Francés, a 40-minute walk from Los Cuernos. Each has four bunks, central heating and individual bathrooms with showers. More private 'cubos' (shelters) are under construction.

Mountain Lodge Paine Grande
CABIN **$**

(☎ 061-241-2742; www.verticepatagonia.cl; dm from US$50, incl full board US$95; @) Though gangly, it's nicer than most dorms, with sublime Los Cuernos views in all rooms. Its year-round presence is a godsend to cold, wet winter hikers, though meals are not available in winter (May to September). There's on-site camping, a kiosk with basic kitchen provisions and a more deluxe version of camping in domes.

Between Lago Grey and Valle Francés, it's a day hike from either and also accessible by ferry across Lago Pehoé.

Refugio Grey
HUT **$**

(☎ 061-241-2742; www.verticepatagonia.cl; dm from US$35, incl full board US$80; ☺ year-round) Inland from the lake, this deluxe trekkers' lodge features a decked-out living area with leather sofas and bar, a restaurant-grade kitchen and snug bunkrooms that house 60, with plenty of room for backpacks. There's also a general store, and covered cooking space for campers.

It runs in winter without meal service (May to September).

Domos El Seron
DOME **$**

(☎ 061-261-4184; www.fantasticosur.com; dm US$36, incl full board US$113) Located at Camping Seron.

Refugio Lago Dickson
CABIN **$**

(☎ 061-241-2742; dm US$35, incl full board US$80; ☺ Nov-Mar) One of the oldest refugios and smallest, with 30 beds, in a stunning setting on the Paine circuit, near Glaciar Dickson.

Camping

The park has both fee camping, with some services, and free camping.

Camping at the *refugios* costs CH$4000 to CH$8500 per person. *Refugios* and some *domos* rent equipment – tent (CH$9500 per night), sleeping bag (CH$5500) and mat/pad (CH$2000) – but potential shortages in high season make it prudent to pack your own gear. Small kiosks sell expensive pasta, soup packets and butane gas, and cook shelters (at some campgrounds) prove useful in foul weather.

Campgrounds generally operate from mid-October to mid-March, though those on the backside of the Paine Circuit may not open until November due to harsher weather. The decision is made by Conaf.

It's crucial to reserve ahead. For bookings, Vertice Patagonia looks after Camping Grey, Lago Dickson, Perros and Paine Grande. Fantastico Sur owns Camping Las Torres, Chileno, Francés, Los Cuernos and Serón.

Sites on the trekking routes which are administered by Conaf are free but very basic. They do not rent equipment or offer showers. These include: Campamento Británico, Campamento Italiano, Campamento Paso, Campamento Torres and Camping Guardas. Other private campgrounds include Pehoé (☎ in Punta Arenas 061-224-9581; http://campingpehoe.com; per person CH$9000) and Río Serrano.

Rodents lurk around campsites, so don't leave food in packs or in tents – hang it from a tree instead.

Hotels

When choosing lodgings, pay particular attention to location. Lodgings that adjoin the 'W' offer more independence and flexibility for hikers. Most offer multiday packages.

Cheaper hotels occupy the sector of **Pueblito Río Serrano**, just outside the park on the gravel road from Puerto Natales. Banked on the S-curves of Río Serrano, there's stunning views of the entire Paine massif though reaching the principal trailheads requires transport.

★ Tierra Patagonia   LODGE $$$
(☑ in Santiago 022-207-8861; www.tierrapatagonia.com; d per person 3 nights incl full board & transfers from US$2150; @ ⚡ ☀) Sculpted into the sprawling steppe, this sleek luxury lodge is nothing if not inviting, with a lively living room and circular bar focused on a grand fire pit and a beautiful oversized artist's rendition of a park map. Large, understated rooms enjoy panoramas of the Paine Massif. All-inclusive rates include airport transfer, daily excursions, use of spa, meals and drinks.

Located on Cerro Guido *estancia*, the hotel's ranch-focused activities are a strong asset. It's on Lago Sarmiento, just outside the national park about 20km from Laguna Amarga.

Awasi   LODGE $$$
(☑ in Santiago 022-233-9641; www.awasipatagonia.com; 3-night all-inclusive per person US$2970; ☎) The appetite for upscale lodges in Paine does not abate. Awasi enters the mix with modern, understated style and a remote location that drinks in the wild surroundings. Twelve villas with individual hot tubs surround a main lodge offering fine dining, lounge areas and wi-fi. Villas are connected by radio. It's sheepskin-chic and well-attended, with quality individually-tailored tours included.

It's located outside the park, on the northeast side of Lago Sarmiento. Travel time might require a little patience: it's a good distance by gravel road from the main attractions, though transfers are provided.

Hotel Lago Grey   HOTEL $$$
(☑ 061-271-2100; www.lagogrey.cl; booking address Lautaro Navarro 1061, Punta Arenas; s/d US$153/185; @ ☎) Open year-round, this tasteful hotel has snug white cottages linked by raised boardwalks. The new deluxe rooms are lovely, featuring lake views and sleek modern style. The cafe (open to the public) overlooks the grandeur. Boat tours visit the glacier, stopping at the Conaf office on the other side of Lago Grey to pick up and drop off passengers.

Explora   HOTEL $$$
(☑ in Santiago 022-395-2800; www.explora.com; d per person 4 nights incl full board & transfers from US$3000; @ ☀) These upscale digs sit perched above the Salto Chico waterfall at the outlet of Lago Pehoé. Views of the entire Paine massif pour forth from every inch of the hotel. The spa features a heated lap pool, sauna and open-air Jacuzzi. Rates include airport transfers, full gourmet meals and a wide variety of excursions led by young, affable, bilingual guides.

Hotel Las Torres   HOTEL $$$
(☑ 061-261-7450; www.lastorres.com; booking address Magallanes 960, Punta Arenas; s/d from US$284/327; ☉ closed Jun; ☎) ✔ A hospitable and well-run hotel with international standards, spa with Jacuzzi and good guided excursions. Most noteworthy, the hotel donates a portion of fees to nonprofit park-based environmental group AMA. The buffet serves organic vegetables from the greenhouse and organic meat raised on nearby ranches.

Hostería Mirador del Payne   INN $$$
(☑ 061-222-8712; www.miradordelpayne.com; s/d/tr US$200/245/265) On the Estancia El Lazo in the seldom-seen Laguna Verde sector, this comfortable inn is known for its serenity, proximity to spectacular viewpoints and top-rate service – but not for easy access to the most popular trails. Activities include birdwatching, horseback riding and sport fishing. Call to arrange a ride from the road junction.

Hostería Pehoé   HOTEL $$$
(☑ 061-272-2853; http://altopehoe.cl; s/d/t from US$138/155/200) On the far side of Lago Pehoé, linked to the mainland by a long footbridge. Pehoé enjoys five-star panoramas of Los Cuernos and Paine Grande, but it's poor value with dated rooms reminiscent of a roadside motel. The restaurant and bar are open to the public.

Hostería Lago del Toro   INN $$$
(☑ 061-222-3351; www.lagodeltoro.com; Pueblito Río Serrano; d/superior US$170/205; @) Sandwiched between two behemoth hotels, this

more intimate charmer has fresh carpeted rooms and a warm fire to greet guests. The house, with a corrugated-iron face, resembles an old-fashioned inn, with macramé lace decor and dense wood furniture.

Hotel Cabañas del Paine   CABIN $$$
(☑ 061-273-0177; www.cabanasdelpaine.cl; Pueblito Río Serrano; s/d/tr US$264/275/308) On the banks of the Río Serrano, these cabin-style rooms stand apart as tasteful and well integrated into the landscape with great views.

ℹ Information

Parque Nacional Torres del Paine (www. parquetorresdelpaine.cl; high/low season CH$18,000/10,000) is open year-round, subject to your ability to get there. Unfortunately, Conaf's new National Parks Pass (CH$10,000) does not include entrance here.

Transportation connections are less frequent in the low season, lodging and services are more limited and winter weather adds additional challenges to hiking. Yet the months of November and March are some of the best times for trekking, with fewer crowds and windy conditions usually abating in March. Check the opening dates of all the services you will require in advance (they change based on the weather in any given year). The website **Torres del Paine** (www.torresdelpaine.com) also has useful information.

The main entrance where fees are collected is **Portería Sarmiento**. **Conaf Centro de Visitantes** (☉ 9am-8pm Dec-Feb), located 37km from Portería Sarmiento, has good information on park ecology and trail status. **Administración** is located also here. There is a small cafeteria at **Pudeto** and another in the works at the southern tip of Lago Grey.

Erratic Rock (p347) features a good backpacker equipment list on its website. It also holds an excellent information session every day at 3pm at its Puerto Natales Base Camp location; go for solid advice on everything from trail conditions to camping. Fantastico Sur (p352) also provides information sessions at 10am and 3pm daily in its Puerto Natales office.

The best trekking maps, by JLM and Luis Bertea Rojas, are widely available in Puerto Natales.

ℹ Getting There & Away

Parque Nacional Torres del Paine is 112km north of Puerto Natales. An unpaved alternative road from Puerto Natales to the Administración provides a shorter, more direct southern approach via Pueblito Río Serrano.

Argentina is nearby but there is no direct transportation from the park. About 40km south of the main park entrance, the seasonal border crossing of Cancha Carrera accesses Argentina at Cerro Castillo. Going to El Calafate from the park on the same day requires joining a tour or careful advance planning, since there is no direct service. Your best bet is to return to Puerto Natales.

ℹ Getting Around

Shuttles (CH$2800) drop off and pick up passengers at Laguna Amarga, at the catamaran launch at Pudeto and at Administración.

Catamaran **Hielos Patagónicos** (☑ 061-241-1380; info@hielospatagonicos.com; one-way/round-trip CH$15,000/24,000) leaves Pudeto for Mountain Lodge Paine Grande at 9:30am, noon and 6pm December to mid-March, at noon and 6pm in late March and November, and at noon only in September, October and April.

Another launch travels Lago Grey between Hotel Lago Grey and Refugio Lago Grey (CH$45,000, 1½ to two hours) a couple of times daily; contact Hotel Lago Grey for current schedules.

ARGENTINE PATAGONIA

Patagonia die-hards won't want to miss the Argentine side, and why not? With easy access to wilderness and a well-developed tourism infrastructure, it combines well with a trip to Chilean Patagonia. In contrast to the Chilean side, here the mountains are surrounded by vast tracts of steppe and plains. Personality-wise it also provides contrast: Argentines are notably more gregarious, a trait that even carries over to competition among tour operators, dining habits and nightlife.

El Calafate

☑ 02902 / POP 16,700
Named for the berry that, once eaten, guarantees your return to Patagonia, El Calafate hooks you with another irresistible attraction: Glaciar Perito Moreno, 80km away in Parque Nacional Los Glaciares. The glacier is a magnificent must-see but its massive popularity has encouraged tumorous growth and rapid upscaling in the once-quaint Calafate. At the same time, it's a fun place to be, with a range of traveler services. The town's strategic location between El Chaltén and Torres del Paine (Chile) makes it an inevitable stop for those in transit.

The main strip, Av Libertador, is dotted with cutesy knotted-pine constructions of souvenir shops, chocolate shops, restaurants and tour offices. Beyond, main-street pretensions melt away quickly; muddy roads lead to ad-hoc developments and open pastures.

January and February are the most popular and costly months to visit, but shoulder-season visits are growing steadily.

⊙ Sights & Activities

★ Glaciarium   MUSEUM
(☑497912; www.glaciarium.com; adult/child AR$185/90; ⊙9am-8pm Sep-May, 11am-8pm May-Aug) Unique and exciting, this gorgeous museum illuminates the world of ice. Displays and bilingual films show how glaciers form, along with documentaries on continental ice expeditions and stark meditations on climate change. Adults suit up in furry capes for the *bar de hielo* (AR$100 including drink), a blue-lit below-zero club serving vodka or fernet and Coke in ice glasses.

⌖ Tours

Some 40 travel agencies arrange excursions to the glacier and other local attractions, including fossil beds and stays at regional *estancias*, where you can hike, ride horses or relax. Tour prices for Glaciar Perito Moreno (around AR$120-1050 per person) don't include the park entrance fee. Ask agents and other travelers about added benefits, such as extra stops, boat trips, binoculars or multilingual guides.

★ Glaciares Sur   ADVENTURE TOUR
(☑495050; www.glaciarsur.com; 9 de Julio 57; per person US$225-250) Get glacier stunned *and* skip the crowds with these recommended day tours to the unexplored end of Parque Nacional Los Glaciares. Small groups drive to Lago Rocas with an expert multilingual guide to view Glaciar Frias. The adventure option features a four-hour hike, the culture option includes a traditional *asado* (barbecue grill) and off-hour visits to Glaciar Perito Moreno.

Cal-tur   TOUR
(☑491368; www.caltur.com.ar; Libertador 1080) Specializes in El Chaltén tours and lodging packages.

Chaltén Travel   TOUR
(☑492480, 492212; www.chaltentravel.com; Libertador 1174) Recommended tours to Glaciar Perito Moreno, stopping for wildlife viewing (binoculars provided); also specializes in RN40 trips. Outsources some excursions to Always Glaciers (www.alwaysglaciers.com).

ⓘ INFLATION WARNING
Because of rampant inflation in Argentina, prices may be higher than listed and increase at a faster rate than normal. Check current exchange rates at www.xe.com.

Overland Patagonia   TOUR
(☑492243, 491243; www.glaciar.com) Operates out of both Hostel del Glaciar Libertador and Hostel del Glaciar Pioneros; organizes the alternative glacier trip, which includes hiking and navigating the lake.

⌸ Sleeping

Rates and availability fluctuate widely by season; high season is January and February, but can extend from early November to April. Most hostels offer pickup from the bus terminal.

Hostal Schilling   GUESTHOUSE $
(☑491453; http://hostalschilling.com; Paradelo 141; dorm AR$170, d w shared bathroom AR$440, s/d/tr AR$460/520/630; ☎) Good value and centrally located, this friendly guesthouse is a good choice for travelers. Much is due to the family owners, Cecilia, Marcelo and Raimiro, who look after guests with a cup of tea or help with logistical planning. When we visited it was mid-renovation, so rooms vary widely, the best are well lit and roomy. It also has multiple living rooms and a restaurant.

Las Cabañitas   CABIN $
(☑491118; www.lascabanitascalafate.com; Valentín Feilberg 218; 2-person cabins AR$600, dm/d/tr without bathroom AR$200/480/800; ⊙closed Jul; @☎) A restful spot with snug storybook A-frames with spiral staircases leading to loft beds and apartments. Guests have kitchen privileges. The energetic owner Gerardo also provides worthy meals, lunch boxes and helpful information. Nice touches include English lavender in the garden, a barbecue area and guest cooking facilities.

Hostel del Glaciar Libertador   HOSTEL $
(☑492492; www.glaciar.com; Libertador 587; dm US$20, s/d US$76/84; @☎) The best deals here are dorm bunks with thick covers. Behind a Victorian facade, modern facilities include a top-floor kitchen, radiant floor heating, new computers and a spacious common area with a plasma TV glued to sports channels.

El Calafate

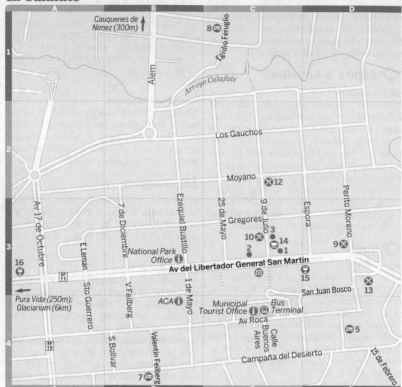

America del Sur HOSTEL $
(✆493525; www.americahostel.com.ar; Puerto Deseado 151; dm AR$250, d/q AR$540/600; @☎) This backpacker favorite has a stylish lodge setting with heated floors and views. Doubles are pleasant and uniform. It's a well-staffed social scene that boasts fun times, including nightly barcecues with salad buffet in high season.

Cauquenes de Nimez B&B $$
(✆492306; www.cauquenesdenimez.com.ar; Calle 303, No 79; s/d/tr US$93/100/135; ✳☎) ⬛
Both modern and rustic, Gabriel's welcoming two-story lodge offers views of flamingos on the lake (from November through summer). Smart rooms decorated with corduroy duvets and nature photography also feature lock boxes and TVs. Personalized attention is a plus, as is the complimentary tea time with lavender muffins, and free bikes (donations support the nature reserve).

Hosteria La Estepa BOUTIQUE HOTEL $$
(✆493551; www.hosterialaestepa.com; Libertador 5310; s/d US$90/110, deluxe US$110/130; @☎) Guests happily tuck into this snug. rustic lodging with panoramic lake views and farm antiquities. Of the 26 rooms, a handful have water views, the deluxe versions have small living areas. A sprawling 2nd-floor social area is strewn with regional maps and board games. The restaurant serves homemade meals. It's 5km west of the town center, toward the national park.

Miyazato Inn B&B $$
(✆491953; www.interpatagonia.com/miyazatoinn; Egidio Feruglio 150, Las Chacras; s/d US$80/90; ℙ@) Resembling a simple Japanese inn, this elegant B&B wins points for personalized service. Breakfast include sweets and *medialunas*, and excursionists get a hot thermos of coffee or tea to go. It's a five-minute walk away from the center of town.

SOUTHERN PATAGONIA EL CALAFATE

Eating

For picnic provisions, small shops selling fresh bread, fine cheeses, sweets and wine are found on the side streets perpendicular to Av Libertador. Head to **La Anónima** (cnr Libertador & Perito Moreno) for cheap takeout and groceries.

Viva la Pepa CAFE $
(☑491880; Amado 833; mains AR$50-90; ⊙lunch & dinner) Decked out in children's drawings, this cheerful cafe specializes in crepes, but also offers great sandwiches with homemade bread (try the chicken with apple and blue cheese), fresh juice and gourds of *maté*.

La Fonda del Parillero PARRILLA $
(9 de Julio 29; mains AR$37-57; ⊙10am-12am) Skip the pretension and dine at this busy grill with a few sidewalk tables and take-out, particularly good if your hunger strikes late

at night. In addition to steaks, it also offers homemade pastas, pies and a variety of empanadas.

★ Mi Rancho ARGENTINE $$
(☑490540; Moyano 1089; mains US$90-130; ⊙noon-3:30 & 8pm-midnight) Inspired and intimate, with the owners themselves cooking and serving oversized osso buco, delicious braided pastas stuffed with king crab, divine salads and sweetbreads with wilted spinach on toast. For dessert, chocolate fondant or passionfruit semifreddo are both worth the calorie hit, and more. In a tiny brick pioneer house with space for few. Reserve a few days ahead.

Pura Vida ARGENTINE $$
(☑493356; Libertador 1876; mains AR$90-140; ⊙7:30-11:30pm Thu-Tue; ☑) Featuring the rare treat of Argentine home cooking, this offbeat, low-lit eatery is a must. Its longtime owners are found cooking up buttery spiced chicken pot pies and filling wine glasses. For vegetarians, brown rice and wok veggies or various salads are satisfying. Don't skip the decadent chocolate brownie with ice cream, steeped in warm berry sauce. Reserve ahead.

La Tablita PARRILLA $$
(☑491065; www.la-tablita.com.ar; Rosales 24; mains AR$100-150; ⊙lunch Thu-Tue, dinner daily) Steak and spit-roasted lamb are the stars

at this satisfying *parrilla,* popular beyond measure for good reason. For average appetites a half-steak will do, rounded out with a good malbec, fresh salad or garlic fries.

Drinking

Sholken
BREWPUB

(Libertador 1630; ☺8pm-2am) After a day in the wind and sun, this snug brewpub is a godsend. Beer is brewed on-site and the tiny kitchen (mains AR$80) churns out heaping trays of meats and cheeses and spicy beef empanadas. For vegetarians, the endive salad with walnuts, blue cheese and passionfruit dressing is excellent.

Librobar
PUB

(Libertador 1015) Upstairs in the gnome village, this hip bookshop-bar serves coffee, bottled beers and pricey cocktails. Peruse the oversized photography books on Patagonian wildlife or bring your laptop and take advantage of the free wi-fi.

el ba'r
CAFE

(9 de Julio s/n; ☺breakfast & lunch) This trendy patio cafe is the hot spot for you and your sweater-clad puppy to order espresso, *submarinos* (hot milk with melted chocolate bar), green tea or sandwiches (mains around AR$60).

ℹ Information

Withdraw your cash before the weekend rush – it isn't uncommon for ATMs to run out on Sundays. If you are headed to El Chaltén, consider getting extra cash here.

Most agents deal exclusively with nearby excursions and are unhelpful for other areas.

ACA (Automóvil Club Argentino; ☑491004; cnr 1 de Mayo & Roca) Argentina's auto club; good source for provincial road maps.

Banco Santa Cruz (Libertador 1285) Changes travelers checks and has an ATM.

Hospital Municipal Dr José Formenti (☑491001; Roca 1487)

Municipal Tourist Office (☑491466, 491090; www.elcalafate.gov.ar; cnr Rosales & Libertador; ☺8am-8pm) Has town maps and general information. There's also a kiosk at the bus terminal (☑491090; www.elcalafate.gov.ar; cnr Libertador & Rosales; ☺8am-8pm); both have some English-speaking staff.

National Park Office (☑491545; Libertador 1302) Offers brochures and a decent map of Parque Nacional Los Glaciares. It's better to get info here than at the park.

Post Office (Libertador 1133)

Thaler Cambio (Libertador 963; ☺10am-1pm Mon-Fri, 5:30-7:30pm Sat & Sun) Usurious rates for travelers checks, but open weekends.

Tiempo Libre (☑491207; www.tiempolibreviajes.com.ar; Gregores 1294) Books flights.

ℹ Getting There & Away

AIR

The modern **Aeropuerto El Calafate** (ECA; ☑491230, 491220) is 23km east of town off RP 11; the departure tax is US$38.

Aerolíneas Argentinas (☑492814, 492816; Libertador 1361) flies every day to Bariloche or Esquel (US$300), Ushuaia (US$185), Trelew (US$250), and Aeroparque and Ezeiza in Buenos Aires (AR$240).

LADE (☑491262; Jean Mermoz 168) flies a few times a week to Ushuaia and Buenos Aires.

Lan (☑495548; 9 de Julio 57) flies to Ushuaia weekly (round-trip US$530).

BUS

El Calafate's hilltop **bus terminal** (Roca s/n) is easily reached by a pedestrian staircase from the corner of Av Libertador and 9 de Julio. Book ahead in high season, as outbound seats can be in short supply.

Destinations include the following:

DESTINATION	COST (AR$)	DURATION (HR)
Bariloche	1290	31
El Chaltén	220	3½
Puerto Natales (Chile)	350	5
Río Gallegos	285	4

For Río Gallegos, buses go four times daily, contact **Taqsa** (☑491843)or **Sportman** (☑492680) Connections to Bariloche and Ushuaia may require leaving in the middle of the night and a change of buses in Río Gallegos.

For El Chaltén, buses leave daily at 8am, 2pm and 6pm. Both **Caltur** (☑491368; www.caltur.com.ar; Libertador 1080) and Chaltén Travel (p363) go to El Chaltén and drive RN 40 to Bariloche in summer.

For Puerto Natales, **Cootra** (☑491444) and **Turismo Zahhj** (☑491631) depart at 8am and 8:30am daily, crossing the border at Cerro Castillo, where it may be possible to connect to Torres del Paine.

ℹ Getting Around

Airport shuttle **Ves Patagonia** (☑494355; www.vespatagonia.com) offers door-to-door service (one way/roundtrip AR$90/170).

There are several car-rental agencies at the airport. **Localiza** (☑491398; www.localiza.com.ar;

Libertador 687)and **Servi Car** (☎492541; www.servi4x4.com.ar; Libertador 695) offer car rentals from convenient downtown offices.

Perito Moreno & Parque Nacional Los Glaciares (South)

Among the Earth's most dynamic and accessible ice fields, **Glaciar Perito Moreno** is the stunning centerpiece of the southern sector of **Parque Nacional Los Glaciares** (admission AR$215, collected after 8am). The glacier measures 30km long, 5km wide and 60m high, but what makes it exceptional in the world of ice is its constant advance – up to 2m per day, causing building-sized icebergs to calve from its face. In some ways, watching the glacier is a very sedentary park experience, but it manages to be nonetheless thrilling.

The glacier formed as a low gap in the Andes and allowed moisture-laden Pacific storms to drop their loads east of the divide, where they accumulated as snow. Over millennia, under tremendous weight, this snow has recrystallized into ice and flowed slowly eastward. The 1600-sq-km trough of Lago Argentino, the country's largest single body of water, is unmistakable evidence that glaciers were once far more extensive than today.

Visiting the Moreno Glacier is no less an auditory than visual experience, as huge icebergs on the glacier's face calve and collapse into the **Canal de los Témpanos** (Iceberg Channel). From a series of catwalks and vantage points on the Península de Magallanes, visitors can see, hear and photograph the glacier safely as these enormous chunks crash into the water. The glacier changes appearance as the day progresses (the sun hits the face of the glacier in the morning).

◉ Sights & Activities

Hielo y Aventura   ICE TREKKING, CRUISE
(☎02902-492205, 02902-492094; www.hieloyaventura.com; Libertador 935, El Calafate) Conventional cruise Safari Nautico (AR$120, one hour) tours Brazo Rico, Lago Argentino and the south side of Canal de los Témpanos. Catamarans crammed with up to 130 passengers leave hourly between 10:30am and 4:30pm from Puerto Bajo de las Sombras. If it's busy, buy tickets in advance for afternoon departures.

To hike on the glacier, try minitrekking (AR$670, under two hours on ice) or the longer and more demanding Big Ice (AR$1070, four hours on ice). Both involve a quick boat ride from Puerto Bajo de las Sombras, a walk through lenga forests, a chat on glaciology and then an ice walk using crampons. Children under eight are not allowed; reserve ahead and bring your own food. Don't forget rain gear: it's often snowing around the glacier and you might get wet and cold quickly on the boat deck.

Solo Patagonia S.A.   CRUISE
(☎02902-491115; www.solopatagonia.com; Libertador 867, El Calafate) Offers the All Glacier tour (AR$720) from Punta Bandera, visiting Glaciar Upsala, Glaciar Spegazzini and Glaciar Perito Moreno. If icebergs are co-operating, boats may allow passengers to disembark at Bahía Onelli to walk 500m to iceberg-choked **Lago Onelli**, where the Onelli and Agassiz glaciers merge. Its other all-day tour, Rivers of Ice, takes in glaciers Upsala and Spegazzini (AR$480).

Cerro Cristal   HIKING
A rugged but rewarding 3½-hour hike, with views of Glaciar Perito Moreno and the Torres del Paine on clear days. The trail begins at the education camp at La Jerónima, just before the Camping Lago Roca entrance, 55km southwest of El Calafate along RP15.

Cabalgatas del Glaciar   HORSEBACK RIDING
(☎02902-495447; www.cabalgatasdelglaciar.com) Day and multiday riding or trekking trips with glacier panoramas to Lago Rocas and Paso Zamora on the Chilean border. Also available through Caltur.

⌂ Sleeping & Eating

★ Camping Lago Roca   CAMPGROUND $
(☎02902-499500; www.losglaciares.com/campinglagoroca; per person AR$120, cabin dm per 2/4 people AR$500/750) This full-service campground with restaurant-bar, located a few kilometers past the education camp, makes an excellent adventure base. The clean concrete-walled dorms provide a snug alternative to camping. Hiking trails abound, and the center rents fishing equipment and bikes and coordinates horseback riding at the nearby Estancia Nibepo Aike.

Estancia Cristina   ESTANCIA $$$
(☎02902-491133, in Buenos Aires 011-4803-7352; www.estanciacristina.com; d 2 nights incl full board & activities US$1200; ☼Oct-Apr) Locals in the

know say the most outstanding trekking in the region is right here. Lodging is in bright, modern cabins with expansive views. A visit includes guided activities and boating to Glaciar Upsala. Accessible by boat, it's at Punta Bandera, off the northern arm of Lago Argentino.

❶ Getting There & Away

The Moreno Glacier is 80km west of El Calafate via paved RP 11, passing through the breathtaking scenery around Lago Argentino. Bus tours are frequent in summer; or you can simply stroll down Av Libertador. Buses to the glacier leave El Calafate (AR$200 round-trip) in the early morning and afternoon, returning around noon and 7pm.

El Chaltén & Parque Nacional Los Glaciares (North)

📞 02962 / POP 1630

The **Fitz Roy Range**, with its rugged wilderness and shark-tooth summits, is the trekking capital of Argentina. Occupying the northern half of Parque Nacional Los Glaciares, this sector offers numerous well-marked trails with jaw-dropping scenery – when the clouds clear, that is. The town effectively closes down in winter and services are few during the muddy shoulder seasons.

At the entrance to the northern sector, the ragtag village of El Chaltén serves the thousands of visitors who make summer pilgrimages to explore the range. This is a frontier town: it was slapped together in 1985 to beat Chile to the land claim. As Argentina's youngest town, it still has to sort out details like banks (there are no ATMs), roads and zoning, but services continue to evolve rapidly.

◉ Sights & Activities

Before heading out, stop by the park ranger office for updated trail conditions.

Laguna Torre   HIKING

If there's little wind and clear skies, make this hike (three hours one way) a priority, since the toothy Cerro Torre is the most difficult local peak to see on normal blustery days. There are two trail options from town. They merge before reaching **Mirador Laguna Torre**, a crest with up-valley views to the extraordinary 3128m rock spire of Cerro Torre, above a sprawling mass of intersecting glaciers.

It's worth pushing on an extra 40 minutes to make camp at **Campamento De Agostini** and further soak in the wonderful setting.

Laguna de los Tres   HIKING

One of the most popular destinations, this strenuous hike reaches a high alpine tarn (four hours one way). There are free backcountry campsites at Laguna Capri. The lovely glacial **Laguna de los Tres** sits in close view of 3405m Cerro Fitz Roy.

Loma del Pliegue
Tumbado & Laguna Toro   HIKING

A gentle hike heading southwest from the park ranger office, this trail (four to five hours one way) is the only route that allows views of both Cerros Torre and Fitz Roy at once. Prepare for strong winds and carry extra water.

Lago del Desierto & Chile   HIKING

Some 37km north of El Chaltén is Lago del Desierto, near the Chilean border – a nice day-hike for rainy days with no visibility of the Fitz. A 500m trail leads to an overlook with lake and glacier views. A popular way to get to Chile is crossing the border here.

☞ Tours

Most come for the hiking, but don't discount other outdoor opportunities.

Casa de Guias   MOUNTAINEERING

(📞 493118; www.casadeguias.com.ar; Lago del Desierto s/n, El Chaltén) Friendly and professional, with English-speaking guides certified by the Argentine Association of Mountain Guides (AAGM). It specializes in small groups. Offerings include mountain traverses, ascents for the very fit and rock-climbing classes.

Fitzroy Expediciones   MOUNTAINEERING

(📞 493178; www.fitzroyexpediciones.com.ar; Av San Martín 56, El Chaltén) Runs glacier-trekking excursions on Viedma Glacier, a five-day itinerary that includes trekking in the Fitz Roy and Cerro Torre area, as well as other excursions. Note that Fitzroy Expediciones does accept credit cards, unlike most businesses in town.

Patagonia Aventura   ADVENTURE TOUR

(📞 493110; www.patagonia-aventura.com; Av San Martín 56, El Chaltén) Offers ice trekking

THE ERASURE OF GLACIERS

Ribbons of ice, the raw magnificence of glaciers is boggling to behold, whether they've been stretched flat in sheets or sculpted by weather and fissured by pressure. Some of the best places to see, hike or climb these massive conglomerations of ice, snow and rock are here in Patagonia.

During the last ice age, nearly a third of the earth's landmass was under glaciers – today they only cover about 10%. Yet hundreds dot the Patagonian landscape. The most accessible can be found in Argentina's Parque Nacional Los Glaciares (home of the famous Perito Moreno glacier), Chile's Torres del Paine and Bernardo O'Higgins national parks, along the Beagle Channel and Chile's Patagonian fjords.

Glaciers are much more complex than simple mounds of frozen water. These rivers of ice flow downslope due to gravity, which deforms their layers as they move. Melted ice mixes with rock and soil on the bottom, grinding it into a lubricant that allows the glacier to slide along its bed. Debris from the bed is forced to the side, creating features called moraines. Movement also causes cracks and deformities called crevasses. As snow falls on the accumulation area, it compacts to ice.

When accumulation outpaces melting, the glacier advances; when there's more melting or evaporation, the glacier recedes. Since 1980, global warming has contributed greatly to widespread glacial retreat. Current global ice mass loss is resulting in a rise in sea level, of which 60% can be attributed to the retreat of small ice caps and glaciers, such as those in Chile and Argentina.

While the Perito Moreno glacier is advancing, it is an anomaly among the rest of Patagonia's glaciers. Most northern Patagonian glaciers are thinning at a rate of 2m per year; over the past decade some have been retreating hundreds of meters per year. Scientists believe the change is both a product of rising temperatures and a drier climate overall.

Glaciers will play a crucial role in the future of our world. Changes to the atmosphere affect the health of glaciers and changes to glaciers, in turn, affect the health of the atmosphere. The melting of glaciers around the world will have significant changes on the sea level. And, as we head into a period of less and less potable water, we should remember that 75% of the world's fresh water is contained in glaciers.

Carolyn McCarthy with contributions by Ursula Rick

(AR$780, two hours) and ice climbing (AR$1000, all day) on Glaciar Viedma with cruise ship access. Tours do not include transportaion to Puerto Bahía Túnel (AR$90), where excursions depart.

El Chaltén

Mountain Guides MOUNTAINEERING
(☑ 493329; www.ecmg.com.ar; Av San Martín 187, El Chaltén) Licensed guides do ice-field traverses, trekking and mountaineering. Rates decrease significantly with group size.

Las Lengas BUS TOUR
(☑ 493023; Viedma 95, El Chaltén) Minibus service to Lago del Desierto (AR$150, two hours), leaving El Chaltén at 8am, 12pm and 3pm daily. At the south end of the lake, travelers can dine in the inviting restaurant at **Hostería El Pilar** (☑ 493002; www.hosteriaelpilar.com.ar).

🛏 Sleeping

Reservations should be made at least one month in advance for the January-to-February high season, or bring a tent: campgrounds are a sure bet.

Albergue Patagonia HOSTEL $
(☑ 493019; www.patagoniahostel.com.ar; Av San Martín 392; s/d/tr AR$700/750/900, dm/s/d without bathroom AR$170/450/500 ; ⊙ Sep-May; @ 🛜) A gorgeous and welcoming wooden farmhouse with helpful staff. Dorms in a separate building are spacious and modern, with good service and a humming atmosphere. The B&B features rooms with private bathrooms, kitchen use and a sumptuous buffet breakfast at Fuegia Bistro. It also rents bikes.

Inlandsis GUESTHOUSE $
(☑ 493276; www.inlandsis.com.ar; Lago del Desierto 480; s AR$520-650, d AR$550-680; ⊙ Oct-Apr) This small, relaxed brick house offers

economical rooms with bunk beds (some are airless, check before booking) or larger, pricier doubles with two twin beds or a queen-sized bed. It also has bilevel cabins with bathtubs, kitchens and DVD players.

Condor de Los Andes
HOSTEL $

(🖉 493101; www.condordelosandes.com; cnr Río de las Vueltas & Halvor Halvorsen; dm AR$200-230, s/d AR$660; @🖥) This homey hostel has the feel of a ski lodge, with worn bunks, warm rooms and a roaring fire. The guest kitchen is immaculate and there are comfortable lounge spaces.

Rancho Grande Hostel
HOSTEL $

(🖉493092; www.ranchograndehostel.com; Av San Martín 724; dm AR$130, s/d/tr AR$400/460/520; @🖥) Serving as Chaltén's Grand Central Station (Chaltén Travel buses stop here), this bustling backpacker factory has something for everyone, from bus reservations to internet (extra) and cafe service. Clean four-bed rooms are stacked with blankets, and bathrooms sport rows of shower stalls. Private rooms have their own bathrooms and free breakfast.

Camping El Refugio
CAMPGROUND $

(🖉493221; Calle 3 s/n; campsites per person AR$60, dm A$90) This private campground is attached to a basic hostel – hot showers for campers are included in the fee. Sites are exposed and there is some sparse firewood (fires are OK).

Camping El Relincho
CAMPGROUND $

(🖉493007; www.elrelinchopatagonia.com.ar; Av San Martín 545; campsites per person/vehicle AR$75/30, 4-person cabin AR$1000) A private campground, with wind-whipped and exposed sites.

★Nothofagus B&B
B&B $$

(🖉493087; www.nothofagusbb.com.ar; cnr Hensen & Riquelme; s/d/tr AR$640/680/800, without bathroom AR$500/550/700; ⊘Oct-Apr; @🖥) 🖋 Attentive and adorable, this chalet-style inn offers a toasty retreat with hearty breakfast options. Practices which earn them the Sello Verde (green seal) include separating organic waste and replacing towels only when asked. Wooden-beam rooms have carpet and some views. Those with hallway bathrooms share with one other room.

Senderos Hostería
B&B $$

(🖉493336; www.senderoshosteria.com.ar; Perito Moreno s/n; s/d/ste from US$150/170/220) This contemporary, corrugated tin home offers wonderful amenities for trekkers seeking creature comforts. The on-site restaurant serves exquisite gourmet meals with excellent wines and attentive service, a real perk when you've spent from a day outdoors. Smart rooms have soft white sheets, firm beds, lock boxes and occasional Fitz Roy views.

Posada Lunajuim
INN $$

(🖉493047; www.lunajuim.com; Trevisán 45; s/d/tr US$95/115/140; 🖥) 🖋 Combining modern comfort with a touch of the off-beat, this welcoming inn gets good reviews from guests. The halls are lined with the owner's monochrome sculptures and textured paintings, and a stone fireplace and library provide a rainy-day escape. Nice touches include DIY box lunches and a buffet breakfast.

✕ Eating & Drinking

Groceries, especially produce, are limited and expensive. Bring what you can from El Calafate.

La Lucinda
CAFE $

(🖉493202; Av San Martín 175; mains AR$90; ⊘7am-midnight; 🖋) With homemade soups and stews, hot sandwiches (including good vegetarian options) and a selection of coffee, tea and wine. This artsy, sky-blue cafe is friendly and almost always open – a godsend when the weather is howling. Breakfast is served too.

La Chocolatería
CAFE $

(🖉493008; Lago del Desierto 105; chocolate & coffee drinks AR$60; ⊘Nov-Mar) This irresistible chocolate factory tells the story of local climbing legends on the walls. It makes for an intimate evening out, with options ranging from spirit-spiked hot cocoa to wine and fondue.

★La Cervecería
BREWPUB $$

(🖉493109; Av San Martín 320; mains AR$100-125; ⊘noon-midnight) That après-hike pint usually evolves into a night out in this humming pub with *simpatico* staff and a feisty female beer master. Savor a stein of unfiltered blond pilsner or turbid bock with pasta or *locro* (a spicy stew of maize, beans, beef, pork and sausage).

El Muro
ARGENTINE $$

(🖉493248; Av San Martín 912; mains AR$90-200; ⊘dinner) For ribsticking mountain food (think massive stir-fry, lentil stew or trout with crisp grilled veggies), head to this tiny outpost at the end of the road. Portions are abundant and desserts – such as warm apple pie or bread pudding – should practically be mandatory.

Techado Negro
CAFE $$

(☑493268; Av Antonio Rojo; mains AR$60-130; ☺7am-12am) 🍴 With local paintings on the wall, bright colors and a raucous, unkempt atmosphere in keeping with El Chaltén, this homespun cafe serves up abundant, good-value and sometimes healthy Argentine fare. Think squash stuffed with *humita* (sweet tamale), brown rice vegetarian dishes, soups and pastas. It also offers box lunches.

Patagonicus
PIZZA $$

(☑493025; Av MM De Güemes 57; pizza AR$80-160; ☺11am-midnight Oct-April) The best pizza in town, with 20 kinds of pizza, salads and wine served at sturdy wood tables surrounded by huge picture windows. Cakes and coffee are also worth trying.

Fuegia Bistro
INTERNATIONAL $$$

(☑493243; Av San Martín 342; mains AR$90-250; ☺dinner Mon-Sat) Favored for its warm ambience and savory mains, this upscale eatery boasts good veggie options and a reasonable wine list. Try the homemade pasta with ricotta, spinach and fresh mushrooms, or trout with lemon.

La Tapera
TAPAS $$$

(☑493195; Antonio Rojo 74; mains AR$95-220; ☺lunch & dinner) This ambient eatery specializes in tapas but wintry staples such as pumpkin soup and grilled steak are also good options. On cold days, you can sit so close to the open fireplace that you'll have to peel off a layer.

Estepa
PATAGONIAN $$$

(☑493069; cnr Cerro Solo & Av Antonio Rojo; mains AR$100-250; ☺noon-1am) Local favorite Estepa cooks up consistent, flavorful dishes such as lamb with calafate sauce, trout ravioli or spinach crepes.

ℹ️ Information

Newspapers, cell phones and money exchange have yet to hit El Chaltén, but there's now mercurial satellite internet, a gas station and an ATM. Surf www.elchalten.com for a good overview of the town.

Chaltén Travel (☑493092; www.chaltentravel.com; cnr Av MM De Güemes & Lago del Desierto) Books airline tickets and bus travel on RN40.

Municipal Tourist Office (☑493370; comfomelchalten@yahoo.com.ar; Terminal de Omnibus; ☺10am-10pm) Friendly and extremely helpful, with lodging lists and good information on town and tours. English is spoken.

Park Ranger Office (☑493024, 493004; pnlgzonanorte@apn.gov.ar; donations welcome; ☺9am-8pm Dec-Feb, 10am-5pm Mar-Nov) Many daytime buses stop for a short bilingual orientation at this visitor center, just before the bridge over the Río Fitz Roy. Park rangers distribute a map and town directory and do a good job of explaining Parque Nacional Los Glaciares' ecological issues. Climbing documentaries are shown at 2pm daily – great for rainy days. Open 10am-5pm low season.

Puesto Sanitario (☑493033; AM De Agostini 70) Provides basic health services.

Viento Oeste (☑493200; Av San Martín 898) Sells books, maps and souvenirs and rents a wide range of camping equipment, as do several other sundries shops around town.

ℹ️ Getting There & Away

El Chaltén is 220km from El Calafate via paved roads.

All buses go to the new bus terminal, located near the entrance to town. For El Calafate (AR$220, 3½ hours), **Chaltén Travel** (☑493092, 493005; Av San Martín 635) has daily departures at 7:30am and 6pm in summer. **Cal-tur** (☑493079; Av San Martín 520) and **Taqsa** (☑493068; Av Antonio Rojo 88) also make the trip, but neither company will take advance reservations. Service is less frequent in the low season.

Las Lengas (☑493023; www.transporte laslengas.com.ar; Antonio de Viedma 95)runs shuttles directly to El Calafate Airport (AR$200) in high season. It also has minivans to Lago Desierto (AR$200 round-trip), Hostería El Pilar (AR$80 one-way) and Río Eléctrico (AR$60 one-way).

Hikers can make it to Chile through an overland crossing via Lago del Desierto (p333). The trip takes one to three days.

1. Valle Chacabuco (Parque Nacional Patagonia; p328)
Once an *estancia* (grazing ranch), this park is host to an array of wildlife, including guanaco.

2. Coyhaique (p317)
This rural town is scenically located amid rocky humpback peaks and undulating mountains.

3. Parque Nacional Laguna San Rafael (p322)
Experience the majesty of 30,000-year-old glaciers in this remote park.

2

3

1. Parque Nacional Torres del Paine (p353)

From azure lakes to snow-capped peaks, awe-inspiring views abound.

2. Parque Pumalín (p305)

Encompassing temperate rainforest, clear rivers, seascapes and farmland, this pristine park is a remarkable conservation effort.

3. Río Futaleufú (p310)

Take to the rapids on this demanding river, a mecca for kayaking and rafting.

Tierra del Fuego

Best Places to Eat

➡ Kalma Resto (p393)

➡ La Picada de los Veleros (p385)

➡ María Lola Restó (p393)

➡ Club Croata (p381)

Best Places to Sleep

➡ Hostería Yendegaia (p380)

➡ Refugio El Padrino (p385)

➡ Lakutaia Lodge (p385)

➡ Lodge Deseado (p382)

➡ Antarctica Hostel (p391)

Why Go?

At the southern extreme of the Americas, the immense Fuegian wilderness, with its slate-gray seascapes, murky crimson bogs and wind-worn forests, endures as awesome and irritable as in the era of exploration. Shared by Chile and Argentina, this area is also lovely and wild. The remote Chilean side consists of hardscrabble outposts, lonely sheep ranches, and a roadless expanse of woods, lakes of undisturbed trout and nameless mountains.

In contrast, the Argentine side lives abuzz. Antarctica-bound cruisers arriving in Ushuaia find a lively dining scene and dozens of outfitters poised at the ready. Take a dogsled ride, boat the Beagle Channel or carve turns at the world's southernmost resort. When you tire of the hubbub, cross the Beagle Channel to the solitary Isla Navarino.

Uninhabited groups of islands peter out at Cabo de Hornos (Cape Horn). And if Tierra del Fuego is not remote enough, Antarctica remains just a boat ride away.

When to Go
Porvenir

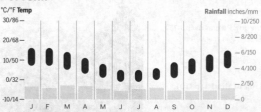

Nov–Mar Warm but windy, best for hiking, penguin-watching and *estancia* visits.

Mid-Nov–mid-Apr Fishing season on the Atlantic coast and Chile's remote Lago Blanco.

Jul–Sep Optimal for skiing, snowboarding or dog sledding in Ushuaia.

History

In 1520, when Magellan passed through the strait that now bears his name, neither he nor any other European explorer had any immediate interest in the land and its people. Seeking a passage to the Spice Islands of Asia, early navigators feared and detested the stiff westerlies, hazardous currents and violent seas that impeded their progress. Consequently, the Selk'nam, Haush, Yaghan and Alacalufes people who populated the area faced no immediate competition for their lands and resources.

These groups were hunters and gatherers. The Selk'nam, also known as Ona, and the Haush subsisted primarily on hunting guanaco and dressing in its skins, while the Yaghan and Alacalufes, known as 'Canoe Indians,' lived on fish, shellfish and marine mammals. The Yaghan (also known as the Yamaná) consumed the fungus dubbed Indian bread which feeds off southern beech. Despite inclement weather, they wore little clothing, but constant fires kept them warm. European sailors termed the region 'Land of Fire' for the Yaghan campfires they spotted along the shoreline.

European settlement brought the rapid demise of the indigenous Fuegians. Darwin, visiting the area in 1834, wrote that the difference between the Fuegians and Europeans was greater than that between wild and domestic animals (as a result, he has few fans here). On an earlier voyage, Captain Robert Fitzroy of the *Beagle* had abducted a few Yaghan, whom he returned after several years of missionary education in England.

No European power took any real interest in settling the region until Britain occupied the Falkland Islands (Islas Malvinas) in the 1770s. However, the successor governments of Chile and Argentina felt differently. The Chilean presence on the Strait of Magellan beginning in 1843, along with increasing British evangelism, spurred Argentina to formalize its authority at Ushuaia in 1884. In 1978 Chile and Argentina nearly went to war over claims to three small disputed islands in the Beagle Channel. International border issues in the area were not resolved until 1984 and are still the subject of some discussion.

National Parks, Reserves & Private Parks

On Isla Grande, Parque Nacional Yendegaia became Chile's newest park in 2014, though it's still virtually inaccessible. Isla Grande is also home to Parque Nacional Tierra del Fuego, Argentina's first shoreline national park. Parque Nacional Cabo de Hornos is usually reached by air tours or cruises.

ℹ Getting There & Away

The most common overland route is the Chilean ferry crossing at Punta Delgada. Roads within Chilean Tierra del Fuego are largely rough and unpaved. Chile is in the process of building a road to the southern end of the island. So far, it links with Lago Fagnano, on the Argentine side, but a 4WD vehicle is required. Those renting a car will need special documents and extra insurance to cross into Argentina; most rental agencies can arrange this paperwork given advance notice.

Visitors can hop on a short flight from Punta Arenas to Porvenir. Most travelers enter the region at Ushuaia (Argentina), a major transportation hub with planes, ferries and buses that access many regional destinations, including Punta Arenas, and Chile's Isla Navarino.

ℹ Getting Around

Half the island is Argentine; have your passport ready for border crossings. Those traveling by bus can make connections through Punta Arenas or cities in southern Argentina.

CHILEAN TIERRA DEL FUEGO

Foggy, windy and wet, Chile's slice of Tierra del Fuego includes half of the main island of Isla Grande, the far-flung Isla Navarino and a group of smaller islands, many of them uninhabited. Home to only 7000 Chileans, this is the least-populated region in Chile. Porvenir is considered the main city, though even that status could be considered an overstatement. These parts can't help but exude a rough and rugged charm and those willing to venture this far can relish its end-of-the-world emptiness. Increasingly, anglers are lured to the little-known inland lakes, and adventurers to the wild backcountry of Parque Nacional Yendegaia.

Chile's long-standing plans to develop the region are finally under way. Tourism will eventually ramp up as the road from Estancia Vicuña to PN Yendegaia nears completion (slated for 2021) and a public airport is added. In future years, a direct crossing to Isla Navarino from nearby Chilean Tierra del Fuego is expected.

Tierra del Fuego Highlights

1 Trek around the jagged peaks and sculpted landscapes on the five-day circuit of **Dientes de Navarino** (p383).

2 Explore the ancient Fuegian forests of **Parque Nacional Tierra del Fuego** (p394).

3 Splurge on fresh local seafood in one of Argentina's best **restaurants** (p392).

4 Skirt the scenic cliffs of Bahía Inútil while driving the empty back roads around **Porvenir** (p380).

5 Speed through frozen valleys on a **dog-sledding tour** (p389) near Ushuaia.

6 Cruise the Strait of Magellan via **ferry** (p385), admiring glaciers and remote lighthouses.

7 Ski and snowboard with sublime views at the world's southernmost resort, **Cerro Castor** (p389).

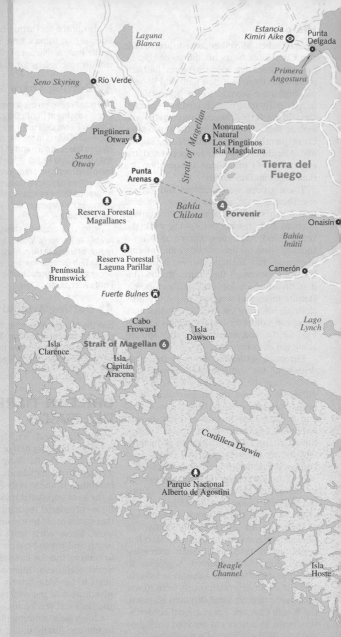

Laguna Blanca

Estancia Kimiri Aike

Punta Delgada

Seno Skyring

Río Verde

Primera Angostura

Pingüinera Otway **1**

Monumento Natural Los Pingüinos Isla Magdalena

Seno Otway

Punta Arenas

Tierra del Fuego

Reserva Forestal Magallanes

Bahía Chilota

4 Porvenir

Onaisín

Bahía Inútil

Reserva Forestal Laguna Parillar **2**

Camerón

Península Brunswick

Fuerte Bulnes **7**

Cabo Froward

Isla Dawson

Lago Lynch

Isla Clarence

Strait of Magellan 6

Isla Capitán Aracena

Cordillera Darwin

Parque Nacional Alberto de Agostini **2**

Beagle Channel

Isla Hoste

Strait of Magellan

Bahía Chilota

PACIFIC OCEAN

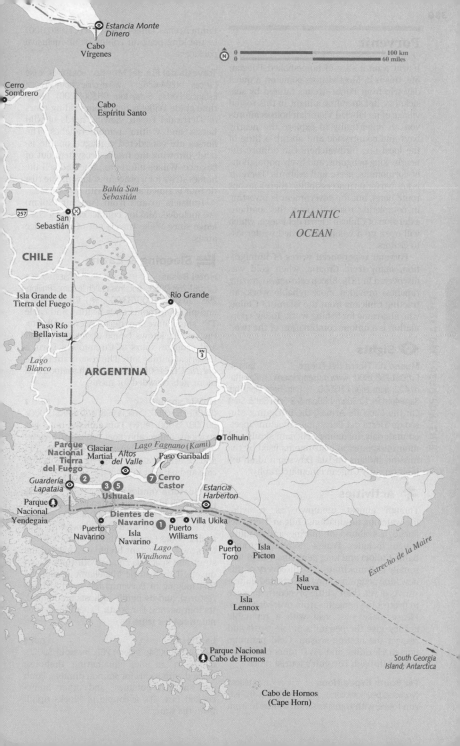

Estancia Monte
Dinero
Cabo
Vírgenes

0   100 km
0   60 miles

Cerro
Sombrero

Cabo
Espíritu Santo

Bahía San
Sebastián

ATLANTIC

OCEAN

257

San
Sebastián

CHILE

Isla Grande de
Tierra del Fuego

Río Grande

Paso Río
Bellavista

Lago
Blanco

ARGENTINA

RN
3

Tolhuin

Parque
Nacional   Glaciar   Lago Fagnano (Kami)
Tierra   Martial   Altos
del Fuego   del Valle   Paso Garibaldi

Guardería   ②   ⑦   Cerro
Lapataia   ③ ⑤   Castor
             Ushuaia   Estancia
Parque   Harberton
Nacional   Dientes de
Yendegaia   Navarino   ①   Villa Ukika
      Puerto   Isla   Puerto
      Navarino   Navarino   Williams

Lago   Puerto   Isla
Windhond   Toro   Picton

Isla
Nueva

Isla
Lennox

Isla
Mendez

Estrecho de la Maire

Parque Nacional
Cabo de Hornos

South Georgia
Island; Antarctica

Cabo de Hornos
(Cape Horn)

Porvenir

🗹 061 / POP 5907

If you want a slice of home-baked Fuegian life, this is it. Most visitors come on a quick day trip from Punta Arenas tainted by sea-sickness. But spending a night in this rusted village of metal-clad Victorian houses affords you an opportunity to explore the nearby bays and countryside and absorb a little of the local life; birdwatchers can admire the nearby king penguins, and lively populations of cormorants, geese and seabirds. Porvenir is known for its inaccessibility (there's no bus route here), but the government is investing in completing roads through the southern extension of Chilean Tierra del Fuego, which will open up a whole untouched wilderness to visitors.

Porvenir experienced waves of immigration, many from Croatia, when gold was discovered in 1879. Sheep *estancias* (grazing ranches) provided more reliable work, attracting Chileans from the island of Chiloé, who also came for fishing work. Today's population is a unique combination of the two.

◎ Sights

Museo de Tierra del Fuego   MUSEUM
(🗹 061-258-1800; www.museoporvenir.cl; Zavattaro 402; admission CH$500; ◎ 8am-5pm Mon-Thu, 8am-4pm Fri, 10:30am-1:30pm & 3-5pm Sat & Sun) On the Plaza de Armas, the intriguing Museo de Tierra del Fuego has some unexpected materials, including Selk'nam skulls and mummies, musical instruments used by the mission Indians on Isla Dawson and an exhibit on early Chilean cinematography.

🏃 Activities

Though almost unknown as a wild-life-watching destination, Chilean Tierra del Fuego has abundant marine and birdlife, which includes Peale's dolphins around Bahía Chilota and king penguins, found seasonally in Bahía Inútil. The discovery of this new king penguin colony has created quite a stir. As of yet, there's little procedure in place to protect the penguins from over-visitation. Please make your visit with a reputable agency, give the penguins ample berth and respect the nesting season. Gold panning, horseback riding and 4WD tours can be arranged through Porvenir's tourist office.

Far South Expeditions   OUTDOORS
(www.fsexpeditions.com) High-end naturalist-run tours, with transportation available from

Punta Arenas. Offers transport (CH$80,000) to the king penguin colony or all-inclusive packages.

Travesia del Fin del Mundo   HORSEBACK RIDING
(🗹 cell 4204-0362; wilke_chile@hotmail.com; Estancia Porfin; 8-day tour CH$500,000) Long-time guide Wilke is developing riding tours of Tierra del Fuego, viewing herds of wild horses and visiting remote ranches. The horses are considered a plague on the island, throwing the fragile ecosystem out of balance. Wilke's efforts to tame and sell the horses strive for a peaceful solution. The rustic tour is aimed at riders with experience.

Transfers to and from Porvenir (80km) are included. Making contact can be a challenge since Wilke travels out of cell service areas.

🛏 Sleeping & Eating

Hotel Rosas   GUESTHOUSE $
(🗹 061-258-0088; hotelrosas@chile.com; Philippi 296; s/d CH$23,000/33,000; ☜) Eleven clean and pleasant rooms offer heating and cable TV; some have wonderful views. Alberto, the owner, knows heaps about the region and arranges tours to Circuito del Loro, a historical mining site. The restaurant (*plato del día* CH$4600), serving fresh seafood and more, gets crowded for meals.

Hotel España   HOTEL $
(🗹 061-258-0160; Croacia 698; s/d/tr AR$18,000/ 30,000/35,000; ℗☜) This ambling hotel has spacious, impeccably kept rooms with views of the bay. Rooms have Berber carpets, TVs and central heating. There is a downstairs cafe and parking in the back.

★Hostería Yendegaia   B&B $$
(🗹 061-258-1919; www.hosteriayendegaia.com; Croacia 702; s/d/tr CH$25,000/40,000/50,000; ☜) Everything a B&B should be, with naturalist books (some authored by the owner) to browse, abundant breakfast, views of the strait and spacious rooms with thick down duvets. This historic Magellanic home (the first lodging in Porvenir) has been lovingly restored, and its family of hosts are helpful. Its tour agency, Far South Expeditions, runs naturalist-led trips.

La Chispa   CAFE $
(🗹 061-258-0054; Señoret 202; mains CH$3000-6000) In an old aquamarine firehouse packed with locals for salmon dinners, lamb and mashed potatoes, and other home-cooked fare. It's a couple of blocks uphill from the water.

Porvenir

Club Croata SEAFOOD **$$**
(☑ 061-258-0053; Señoret 542; mains CH$4000-10,000; ☺ 11am-4pm & 7-10:30pm Tue-Sun) Formal to the verge of stuffy, this restaurant serves good seafood at reasonable prices, in addition to Croat specialties, such as pork chops with *chucrut* (sauerkraut). The pub is open to 3am.

ℹ Information

Banco de Estado (cnr Philippi & Croacia) Has a 24-hour ATM.

Hospital (☑ 061-258-0034; Wood, btwn Señoret & Guerrero)

Post Office (Philippi 176) Faces the plaza.

Tourist Office (☑ 061-258-0098, 061-258-0094; www.muniporvenir.cl; Zavattaro 434; ☺ 9am-5pm Mon-Fri, 11am-5pm Sat & Sun) Information is also available at the handicrafts shop on the *costanera* (seaside road) between Philippi and Schythe.

ℹ Getting There & Away

A good gravel road (Ruta 257) runs east along Bahía Inútil to the Argentine border at San Sebastián; allow about four hours. From San Sebastián (where there's gas and a motel), northbound motorists should avoid the heavily traveled and rutted truck route directly north and instead take the route from Onaisín to the petroleum company town of Cerro Sombrero, en route to the crossing of the Strait of Magellan at Punta Delgada–Puerto Espora.

Aerovías DAP (☑ 061-261-6100; www.aeroviasdap.cl; cnr Señoret & Philippi) Aerovías DAP flies three times daily to Punta Arenas on weekdays and twice daily on Saturdays. There's fewer flights between April and October.

Transbordador Austral Broom (☑ 061-258-0089; www.tabsa.cl; passenger/vehicle Porvenir-Punta Arenas CH$6200/39,800)

Porvenir

◉ Sights
1 Museo de Tierra del Fuego C1

◉ Sleeping
2 Hostería Yendegaia B1
3 Hotel España B1
4 Hotel Rosas C1

◉ Eating
5 Club Croata.. C1
6 La Chispa C1

South of Porvenir

POP 420

On the southern shore of the bay, **Camerón** is a large *estancia* owing its name to a pioneer sheep farming family from New Zealand. Here, the municipal tourist office may have information on latest developments.

If you are heading to Argentine Tierra del Fuego via the San Sebastián crossing, stop in at welcoming family-run teahouse **Nona Nina** (☑ 061-274-4349; www.nonanina.cl; Ruta 257, Km 87, Estancia Miriana; from CH$2500; ☺ hours vary) at Estancia Miriana for real coffee and loose-leaf teas served with homemade bread, rhubarb jam and sumptuous pies and cakes.

Located south of Bahía Inútil (the Useless Bay), the region of **Timaukel** occupies the southern section of Chilean Tierra del Fuego. It is eagerly trying to reinvent itself as an ecotourism destination – a far rosier option than being logged by US-based Trillium Corporation, which was the plan some years back. Few roads lead into this region, with even less public transportation.

ADVENTURES IN SOUTHERN TDF

South of Camerón, access to Chilean Tierra del Fuego once petered out into stark, roadless wilderness and the rugged Cordillera Darwin. But the Ministry of Public Works is working hard to create access to these southern points and develop future tourism destinations. Currently projects are under way to create a link to Ushuaia via Lago Fagnano. In the future the same road will continue to provide access to Parque Nacional Yendegaia.

For now there's at least one worthy destination on the road. **Lodge Deseado** (✆061-9165-2564; www.lodgedeseado.cl; 2-/3-person cabin US$310/370) marks a cozy spot to reel in wild trout, kick back in cool modern cabins and swap stories with the engaging owner Ricardo. It's located on Lago Deseado. Kayaks and bicycles are available to guests at no charge, and you can also book fly-fishing packages.

A 4WD is required for this ultraremote region. The road to the western shore of Lago Fagnano is a rough five-hour-plus journey in summer. An earlier offshoot connects to the Argentine side via mountain pass Río Bellavista, which is only open from December through March. Check with local police stations (known as *carabineros* in Chile) about the state of roads before heading out.

To the south, the cherished fly-fishing getaway **Lago Blanco** is accessible only by car, and the only accommodations on offer are the nearby exclusive fishing lodges.

Parque Nacional Yendegaia

Serene glacier-rimmed bays and native Fuegian forest comprise this 1500-sq-km **national park** (www.conaf.cl), Chile's newest, over a third of which was donated in 2014 by the Yendegaia Foundation. Located in the Cordillera Darwin, it is a strategic wildlife corridor between Argentina's Parque Nacional Tierra del Fuego and Chile's Parque Nacional Alberto de Agostini.

Partially a one-time *estancia* comprising 400 sq km, it is still in the process of removing livestock and rehabilitating trails. The Vicuña–Yendegaia road through the park will be finished in 2021. Trails and visitor infrastructure are in the works. For now only wild camping (without toilets or services) is possible. Unfortunately, access is difficult and expensive. Visitors should plan to camp and be completely self-supported. There are no provisions available here and there is no on-site phone contact.

Transbordadora Austral Broom's ferry between Punta Arenas and Puerto Williams will drop passengers off only if given advance notice. Be aware of ferry dates and have reservations, as there is only weekly service in each direction, and weather delays could alter pick-up times or dates.

Isla Navarino

✆061 / POP 2300

For authentic end-of-the-earth ambience, this remote outpost wins the contest without even campaigning. Isla Navarino is a rugged backpacker's paradise. Located south across the Beagle Channel from Ushuaia, its mostly uninhabited wilderness hosts a rugged terrain of peat bogs, southern beech forest and jagged, toothy spires known as Dientes de Navarino, also a famed trekking route. By a quirk, the island is considered by Santiago to be part of Chilean Antarctica, not Chilean Tierra del Fuego or Magallanes. The naval settlement of Puerto Williams is the only town on the island, the official port of entry for vessels en route to Cabo de Hornos and Antarctica, and home to the last living Yaghan speaker.

A permanent European presence was established on the island by mid-19th-century missionaries who were followed by fortune-seekers during the 1890s gold rush. Current inhabitants include the Chilean navy, municipal employees and octopus and crab fishers. The remaining mixed-race descendants of the Yaghan people live in the small coastal village of Villa Ukika.

Puerto Williams

✆061 / POP 2262

Those stationed here might feel marooned, but for travelers Puerto Williams smarts of great adventure. Yet not much happens here. In town, action means the wind hurtling debris while oblivious cows graze on the plaza and yards are stacked roof-deep in firewood. With transportation expensive and irregular,

Williams feels cut off, but complaints that it's a forgotten burg are far more common from locals than its few tourists, who recognize buried treasure when they see it.

In a renovation boom, the village is adding coastal lookouts and walkways, paved roads and modern gas installations. It centers around a green roundabout and a concrete slab plaza called the Centro Comercial. Walk a few minutes from town and you will be in moss-draped lenga forest, climbing steeply above the tree line. The coast is lovely for bike rides, with many quiet coves and stands of forest worth exploring.

The island's 150km of trails are gaining international attention, though at points are poorly marked and challenging. If hiking, take a companion, get directions from locals before heading out and register with the *carabineros* (police).

⊙ Sights

Museo Martín Gusinde MUSEUM
(cnr Araguay & Gusinde; donation requested; ⊘9am-1pm & 3-6:30pm Tue-Fri, 3-6:30pm Sat & Sun, reduced hours off-season; 🛜) An attractive museum honoring the German priest and ethnographer who worked among the Yaghans from 1918 to 1923. Focuses on ethnography and natural history. Public wi-fi is available in the library.

Club de Yates Micalvi LANDMARK
(⊘late Sep-May) A grounded German cargo boat, the *Micalvi* was declared a regional naval museum in 1976 but found infinitely better use as a floating bar, frequented by navy men and yachties. Unfortunately, the bar isn't open to the general public.

Kipa-Akar CULTURAL BUILDING
(📞061-9417-8823; Villa Ukika; ⊘sporadic) A modest crafts shop that sells Yaghan-language books, jewelry and knives made of scavenged whale bone. Opens only for groups with 24-hour advance notice. Call Agrupación de Artesanos Yagan.

Yelcho LANDMARK
Near the entrance to the military quarters is the original bow of the ship that rescued Ernest Shackleton's Antarctic expedition from Elephant Island in 1916.

🏃 Activities

Mountain biking is a great way to see the island, which has a gravel coastal road on its northern face. Lakutaia Lodge offers trekking and horseback-riding (CH$30,000 for three hours) excursions, available to nonguests. The last weekend of the month, a free ferry visits Puerto Toro, a seasonal fishing village. Visitors can sign up at the Municipality; spots are limited.

★Dientes de Navarino HIKING
This trekking circuit offers impossibly raw and windswept vistas under Navarino's toothy spires. Beginning at the Virgin altar just outside of town, the five-day, 53.5km

TIERRA DEL FUEGO ISLA NAVARINO

LEAVE IT TO BEAVERS

Forget guns, germs and steel. Canadian beavers have colonized Tierra del Fuego and Isla Navarino using only buck teeth and broad tails.

It all goes back to the 1940s, when Argentina's hapless military government imported 25 pairs of beavers from Canada, hoping they would multiply and generate a lucrative fur industry in this largely undeveloped area. Without natural predators, the beavers did multiply, but once felted beaver hats lost their fashion appeal the industry collapsed.

Today up to 100,000 beavers inhabit Tierra del Fuego and the surrounding islands, where they are officially considered a plague. Beavers' damaging effects are many. Flooding from beaver dams destroys roads and meadows, ruining infrastructure and creating havoc for livestock. Loggers compete with the rodents for wood, and risk losing their livelihoods. A sole beaver couple has the chewing power to create their own lake, felling hundreds of trees. Beavers can also pass giardia into water supplies where it works its black magic on human intestines.

Busy beavers have already made their way across the Strait of Magellan from where they could spread to the rest of the South American continent. With the help of global grants, conservationists, scientists and forestry officials are in a rush to eradicate populations, at an estimated cost of US$35 billion. Only then will reforestation be feasible.

Following a young scientist couple who have made the beavers their life mission, the Chilean documentary *Los Castores* debuted to acclaim in Chilean film festivals in 2014, with distribution pending.

DIENTES PRIMER

While growing in popularity, the Dientes de Navarino hiking circuit requires more navigational skills and backcountry know-how than Torres del Paine. Out here, you're essentially on your own. Before going:

➡ Consider whether you prefer naturalist guides or local guides and porters.

➡ When choosing a guide, ask about first-aid certification, language skills and the extent of their experience.

➡ Remember that planes allow only minimum luggage. You may have to rent gear and buy most of your food on the island. Dry goods are well stocked, but bring energy bars if you need them.

➡ Make a plan B for bad weather – which might mean a change in destination, a postponement or extra time.

➡ Register at the police station (for safety reasons) before starting your trek.

route winds through a spectacular wilderness of exposed rock and secluded lakes. Fit hikers can knock it out in four days in the (relatively) dry summer months. Markings are minimal: GPS, used in conjunction with marked maps, is a handy navigational tool.

Winter hikes are only recommended for experienced mountaineers. For detailed trekking routes, refer to Lonely Planet's *Trekking in the Patagonian Andes*.

Cerro Bandera HIKING
With expansive views of the Beagle Channel, this four-hour round trip covers the first approach of the Navarino Circuit. The trail ascends steeply through lenga to blustery hillside planted with a Chilean flag.

Lago Windhond HIKING
This remote lake is a lesser known, but worthy, alternative to hiking the Dientes circuit, with sheltered hiking through forest and peat bogs. The four-day round trip is a better bet if there's high winds. For route details, ask at Turismo Shila or go with a guide.

✆ Tours

Fuegia & Co TOUR
(✆cell 7876-6934; fuegia@usa.net; Ortiz 049) For guided trekking or logistical support, Denis Chevallay guides in French, German and English and has a wealth of knowledge. Guiding includes porter support and a satellite emergency phone. Day trips to archaeological sites are also available.

Turismo SIM BOAT TOUR
(www.simexpeditions.com; Cape Horn per person US$1750; ◷Nov-Apr) For yacht tours, contact this warm German and Venezuelan couple. Wolf and Jeanette run reputable sailing

trips (reserve well in advance) to the Beagle Channel, Cape Horn, South Georgia Islands and Antarctica.

Lancha Patriota BOATING
(✆061-262-1367; askhila1@yahoo.es; 6-person boat per day US$300) Fishing trips and tailor-made nautical excursions are available through captain Edwin Olivares.

Wulaia Expeditions BOAT TOUR
(✆cell 6193-4142; www.ptowilliams.cl/Wulaia_Expediciones.html; Yelcho 224; 6-person charter US$800; ◷9am-1pm & 3-7pm Mon-Sat) A fiberglass boat ride to historic Wulaia Bay, a site of Yaghan ritual where Darwin landed in the *Fitzroy*. The full-day trip with up to three hours of boating includes an hour-long walk.

Parque Etnobotánico Omora ECOTOUR
(www.omora.org) Open for scientist-led tours by reservation only with Lakutaia Lodge. Trails feature plant names marked in Yaghan, Latin and Spanish. On the road to the right of the Virgin altar, 4km (an hour's walk) toward Puerto Navarino.

🛏 Sleeping

Lodgings often offer meals, best arranged in advance, and can arrange tours of the island or airport transfers.

Residencial Pusaki GUESTHOUSE $
(✆cell 9833-3248; pattypusaki@yahoo.es; Piloto Pardo 222; s/d CH$12,500/27,000) With legendary warmth, Patty welcomes travelers into this cozy home with comfortable, carpeted rooms with private bathrooms. Patty also organizes group dinners, which are also available to nonguests.

Refugio El Padrino HOSTEL $
(☑061-262-1136, cell 8438-0843; Costanera 276; dm CH$12,000) Friendly and conducive to meeting others, this clean, self-service hostel doubles as a social hub hosted by the effervescent Cecilia. The small dorm rooms are located right on the channel.

Hostal Miramar GUESTHOUSE $
(☑061-272-1372; www.hostalmiramar.wordpress.com; Muñoz 555; d with/without bathroom CH$30,000/25,000; ☎) Señora Nuri hosts guests in her lovely, light-filled home with great views of the Beagle Channel. Dinners are available with advance notice.

Hostal Paso Mckinlay GUESTHOUSE $
(☑cell 7998-7595; www.hostalpasomckinlay.cl; Piloto Pardo 213; dm/s/d CH$12,000/15,000/30,000; ☎) Run by the friendly family of an artisan fisherman, this lodging has clean remodeled rooms with cable TV. There's kitchen use and laundry service, but the best feature is fresh fish available for dinners in-house.

Hostal Coiron GUESTHOUSE $
(☑061-262-1127; hostalcoiron@hotmail.com; Maragaño 168; per person with shared/private bathroom CH$12,000/15,000) A tidy little home with a lovely yard for lounging. Rooms are mostly fitted with single beds and thick down covers.

Lakutaia Lodge HOTEL $$$
(☑061-262-1733; www.lakutaia.cl; s/d/tr US$200/250/300) About 3km east of town toward the airport, this modern lodge offers respite in a lovely, rural setting. There is a full-service restaurant and the library contains history and nature references. Its only disadvantage is its isolation; you might leave without getting much of a feel for the quirky town. Can arrange transportation from Punta Arenas. Also offers excursions hiking the Navarino Circuit, heli-fishing and trips to Cape Horn.

✖ Eating & Drinking

Of the few supermarkets, Simon & Simon is the best, with fresher vegetables, fast food and great pastries.

★ La Picada de los Veleros CHILEAN $
(☑cell 9833-3248; Piloto Pardo 222; meals CH$5000-11,000; ☺dinners by reservation) Family-style dinners are served to a menagerie of travelers, visiting workers and whoever makes a dinner reservation. Patty is a genius with fresh seafood preparations. The jovial environment at Residencial Pusaki is best enjoyed if you can speak some Spanish. A bottle of wine is always welcome on the table.

Puerto Luisa Cafe CAFE $
(☑cell 9934-0849; Costanera 317; snacks CH$3000; ☺10am-8pm Mon-Fri, 7am-8pm Sat Nov-Mar) Next to the dock, this welcoming haven offers espresso drinks, chocolates and pies in a cozy setting of oversized chairs with great sea views.

El Alambique ITALIAN, PUB $
(☑cell 5714-2087; Piloto Pardo 217; set menu CH$5500; ☺noon-2:30pm Mon-Fri, 8pm-1am Tue-Sat) Covered in murals, this homespun pub delivers good homemade pastas (and pizzas on all-you-can-eat Fridays). It's the only venue with a pub atmosphere at night.

La Picada del Castor CAFE $
(☑061-262-1208; Plaza de Ancla; mains CH$4000-8000; ☺noon-3pm & 6-11pm Mon-Sat, 11am-5pm Sun) A simple eatery serving sandwiches and set menus, with *chupe de centolla* (crab casserole) in season.

❶ Information

Near the main roundabout, the Centro Comercial contains the post office, Aerovías DAP and call centers. Chile Express can change US dollars. Bring cash: the ATM at Banco de Chile has a tendency to run out on holidays and weekends.

Municipal Tourist Information (☑cell 8383-2080; turismo@imcabodehornos.cl; cnr Piloto Pardo & Arturo Prat; ☺8am-1pm & 2-5pm Mon-Fri) The best tourist information stop in Chile. Offers city maps, day trek maps, as well as weather and route conditions for Lago Windhond and Dientes de Navarino treks. With multilingual service. Located in a small kiosk.

Turismo Shila (☑cell 7897-2005; www.turismoshila.cl; O'Higgins 220) Very helpful stop for trekkers. Offers local guides, camping rentals, bicycle rentals (CH$5000 per day), snowshoes, fishing gear and GPS maps. Also sells boat tickets and can arrange charter flights to Ushuaia.

❶ Getting There & Away

Puerto Williams is accessible by plane or boat though inclement weather can produce delays. Allow for a cushion of extra travel time to get on or off the island. Options from Punta Arenas, Chile include the following:

Aerovías DAP (☑061-262-1051; www.aeroviasdap.cl; Plaza de Ancla s/n) Flies to Punta Arenas (CH$65,000, 1¼ hours) daily Monday to Saturday from November to March, with fewer winter flights. Reserve ahead since there's high demand. DAP flights to Antarctica may make a brief stopover here.

Transbordador Austral Broom (☑061-272-8100; www.tabsa.cl) A ferry sails from the Tres Puentes sector of Punta Arenas to Puerto Williams four times a month on Thursdays, with departures from Puerto Williams back to Punta Arenas on Saturdays (reclining seat/bunk CH$98,000/137,000 including meals, 38 hours). Only bunk berths can be reserved ahead, the seats are reserved for locals until the last minute, although you can request one and will usually get it. Travelers rave about the trip: if the weather holds there are glacier views on the trip from Punta Arenas and the possibility of spotting dolphins or whales between December and April. From Puerto Williams, the glaciers are passed at night.

Options from Ushuaia, Argentina change frequently. Turismo Shila keeps tabs on the current offerings and offers reservations:

Ushuaia Boating (☑ in Argentina 02901-436-193; www.ushuaiaboating.com.ar; one way US$130; ⊘ service Mon-Sat) A sporadic service which usually goes daily in high season with Zodiac boats. Tickets include a sometimes bumpy and exposed 40-minute crossing plus an overland transfer to/from Puerto Navarino. Note: inclement weather often means cancellations and indefinite postponement.

Turismo Akainij (☑ 061-262-1173; www.turismoakainij.cl; Centro Comercial Sur 156) Can arrange charter flights to Ushuaia.

Cabo de Hornos & Surrounding Islands

If you've made it to Isla Navarino or Ushuaia, you've nearly reached the end of the Americas at Cabo de Hornos (Cape Horn). This small group of uninhabited Chilean islands has long been synonymous with adventure and the romance of the old days of sailing, although sailors usually dreaded the rough and brutally cold trip.

The cape was 'discovered' in January 1616 by Dutchmen Jakob Le Maire and Willem Schouten aboard the *Unity*. They named the cape for their ship *Hoorn*, which had accidentally burned at Puerto Deseado on the Argentine Patagonian coast. Horn Island, of which the famous cape forms the southernmost headland, is just 8km long. The cape itself rises to 424m, with striking black cliffs on its upper parts. Aerovías DAP has charter flights above Cabo de Hornos that don't land. Potential visitors can also charter a sailboat trip with Turismo SIM.

The South Shetland Islands at the northern end of the Antarctic Peninsula are one of the continent's most visited areas, thanks to the spectacular scenery, abundant wildlife and proximity to Tierra del Fuego, which lies 1000km to the north across the Drake Passage. The largest of the South Shetlands, King

George Island, has eight national winter stations crowded onto it. Chile established Presidente Eduardo Frei Montalva station in 1969. Ten years later Chile built Teniente Rodolfo Marsh Martin station less than 1km across the Fildes Peninsula from Frei station. The human population fluctuates between 10 and 20, while the estimated penguin population is around two to three million.

As part of Chile's policy of trying to incorporate its claimed Territorio Chileno Antártico into the rest of the country as much as possible, the government has encouraged families to settle at Frei station, and the first of several children was born there in 1984. Today the station accommodates a population of about 80 summer personnel in sterile, weatherproofed houses.

For sailing options, see the Tours section of Puerto Williams.

☞ Tours

All transportation is weather-dependent, although ships are more likely to do the trip in rough conditions than the small airplanes. Plan for the possibility of delays and if you can't wait, don't plan on a refund. Check with Hotel Lakutaia for last-minute specials from Puerto Williams.

Antarctica XXI   TOUR
(☑ Punta Arenas 061-261-4100; www.antarcticaxxi.com; 7 days/6 nights double occupancy per person US$10,800) Runs the only air-cruise combo, flying from Punta Arenas to Chile's Frei station on King George Island, with a transfer to the 46-passenger ship *Grigoriy Mikheev* for cruising the South Shetlands and peninsula region. Programs vary in length. It's a member of IAATO, a body that mandates strict guidelines for responsible travel to Antarctica.

Cruceros Australis   CRUISE
(☑ in Santiago 022-442-3115; www.australis.com; 3 nights & 4 days per person in low/high season from US$1440/2298; ⊘ late Sep-early Apr) Luxurious three- to four-night sightseeing cruises from Ushuaia to Punta Arenas, with the possibility to disembark at Cape Horn.

Aerovías DAP   TOUR
(☑ 061-222-3340; www.dap.cl; ⊘ Nov-Apr) Flies from Punta Arenas to Frei station on King George Island (three hours). One- and two-day programs include tours to Villa Las Estrellas, sea lion and penguin colonies and other investigation stations on the island. Flights to Cabo de Hornos can also be chartered. Check the website for updated departure dates and prices.

ARGENTINE TIERRA DEL FUEGO

In contrast to its Chilean counterpart, this side of the island is bustling, modern and industrial. Argentina's half of the Fuegian pie boasts a paved highway and two major cities with growing economies. That doesn't mean that nature isn't grand here. There are historical *estancias,* excellent Atlantic coast fly-fishing opportunities, and Antarctic access via Ushuaia. The Cordillera Darwin rises 2500m above Ushuaia, flush with trails and excellent skiing in the winter. Dog sledding and sailing outings offer an alternative to the usual Patagonian fare of trekking and toasting to a hard-day's walk. The island is home to Parque Nacional Tierra del Fuego, Argentina's first shoreline national park.

Ushuaia

☑02901 / POP 57,000

Gone are the days when this former missionary outpost and penal colony had to woo or shackle its occupants to stay put. Now a bustling port and adventure hub, Ushuaia draws hundreds of thousands of willing visitors yearly. The city occupies a narrow escarpment between the Beagle Channel and the snowcapped Martial Range. Though remote, it is plugged into modern commerce with a critical mass of shops, cafes and restaurants. While not quite the southernmost city in the world, Ushuaia is the southernmost city of size.

The city caters well to visitors, and its dazzling outdoor options include hiking, sailing, skiing, dog mushing and kayaking.

Also nearby, the spectacular Parque Nacional Tierra del Fuego, with thick stands of native lenga, is a must-see.

Tierra del Fuego's comparatively high wages draw Argentines from all over to resettle here, and some locals lament the loss of small-town culture. Meanwhile, expansion means haphazard development advancing in the few directions the mad geography allows.

◉ Sights

Paralleling the Beagle Channel, Maipú becomes Malvinas Argentinas west of the cemetery, then turns into RN 3, continuing 12km to Parque Nacional Tierra del Fuego. To the east, public access ends at Yaganes, which heads north to meet RN 3 going north toward Lago Fagnano. Most visitor services are on or within a couple blocks of San Martín, a block inland from the waterfront.

The tourist office distributes a free city-tour map with information on the historic houses around town. The 1894 **Legislatura Provincial** (Provincial Legislature; Av Maipú 465) was the governor's official residence. The century-old **Iglesia de la Merced** (cnr Av San Martín & Don Bosco) was built with convict labor. **Casa Beban** (cnr Av Maipú & Plúschow; ☉11am-6pm) was built in 1911 using parts ordered from Sweden, and sometimes hosts local art exhibits.

★**Museo Marítimo & Museo del Presidio**   MUSEUM

(☑02901-437481; www.museomaritimo.com; cnr Yaganes & Gobernador Paz; admission AR$150; ☉9am-8pm) Convicts were transferred from Isla de los Estados (Staten Island) to Ushuaia in 1906 to build this national prison, which

TIERRA DEL FUEGO USHUAIA

A PIONEER'S GUIDE TO TIERRA DEL FUEGO

It was a childhood too fabulous for fiction. E Lucas Bridges grew up with the Beagle Channel as his backyard, helped his dad rescue shipwrecked sailors and learned survival from the native Yaghan and Selk'nam (Ona) people. His memoir *Uttermost Part of the Earth* fed Bruce Chatwin's boyhood obsession with Patagonia. Now, after decades out of print, this 1947 classic has been rereleased in English.

Bridges' tale starts with his British father establishing an Anglican mission in untamed Ushuaia. *Little House on the Prairie* it wasn't. After the family traded the missionary life for pioneering, founding Estancia Harberton (p395), Bridges' father died. As a young adult, Bridges tried adventuring with the Selk'nam, which meant surviving on lean guanaco meat, crossing icy rivers and negotiating peace between quarreling factions.

Measles epidemics and sparring with hostile colonists wreaked havoc on Tierra del Fuego's native peoples. By the time the book was first published, their population had nose-dived to less than 150. *Uttermost Part of the Earth* captures the last days of these hardy civilizations and one island's transformation from virgin wilderness to a frontier molded by fortune seekers, missionaries and sheep ranchers.

ANTARCTICA: THE ICE

For many travelers, a journey to Antarctica represents a once-in-a-lifetime adventure. Despite its high price tag, it is much more than just a continent to tick off your list. You will witness both land and ice shelves piled with hundreds of meters of undulating, untouched snow. Glaciers drop from mountainsides and icebergs form sculptures as tall as buildings. The wildlife is thrilling, with thousands of curious penguins and an extraordinary variety of flying birds, seals and whales.

Over 90% of Antarctic-bound boats pass through Ushuaia. That translates to tens of thousands of tourists – a stunning contrast to the continent's population of 5000 (summer) or 1200 (winter) scientists and staff. As long as you've got two or three weeks to spare, hopping on board a cruise ship is not out of the question.

Some voyages take in the Falkland Islands and South Georgia; some go just to the Antarctic Peninsula; others focus on retracing historic expeditions. A small handful of visitors reach Antarctica aboard private vessels. All are sailboats (equipped with auxiliary engines).

The season runs from mid-October to mid-March, depending on ice conditions. Most voyages sell out. When shopping around, ask how many days you will actually spend in Antarctica, as crossing the Southern Ocean takes up to two days each way. Also ask how many landings there will be. The smaller the ship, the more landings there are per passenger (always depending on the weather). Tour companies charge anywhere from US$7000 to US$70,000, although some ships allow walk-ons, which can cost as little as US$5000.

Due to Ushuaia's proximity to the Antarctic Peninsula, most cruises depart from here. Last-minute bookings can be made through contacting Ushuaia Turismo (p391). Other travel agencies that are offering packages include **Rumbo Sur** (☑ 02901-421139; www.rumbosur.com.ar; Av San Martín 350), **All Patagonia** (☑ 02901-433622; www.allpatagonia.com; Juana Fadul 48) and Canal Fun (p389), though there are many more.

Check that your company is a member of IAATO (International Association Antarctica Tour Operators; www.iaato.org), which mandates strict guidelines for responsible travel to Antarctica. The following are just a few companies that go.

Adventure Associates (www.adventureassociates.com) Australia's first tour company to Antarctica, with many ships and destinations.

National Geographic Expeditions (www.nationalgeographicexpeditions.com) Highly recommended, with quality naturalists and experts, aboard the 148-passenger *National Geographic Explorer.*

Peregrine Adventures (www.peregrineadventures.com) This outfit offers unique trips that include visiting the Antarctic Circle, with options for kayaking and camping.

Quark Expeditions (www.quarkexpeditions.com) Three kinds of ships, from an icebreaker to a 48-passenger small ship for close-knit groups.

WildWings Travel (www.wildwings.co.uk) UK-based company that focuses on birdwatching and wildlife in Antarctica.

For more information and up-to-date information and articles check out www.70south.com. In Ushuaia consult the very helpful **Oficina Antárctica** (☑ 02901-430015; www.tierradelfuego.org/ar/antartida; Av Maipú 505) at the pier.

---

was finished in 1920. The cells, designed for 380 inmates, held up to 800 before closing in 1947. Famous prisoners include illustrious author Ricardo Rojasand and Russian anarchist Simón Radowitzky. The depiction of penal life is intriguing, but info is in Spanish only.

Museo Yamaná　　　　　　　　MUSEUM
(☑ 02901-422874; Rivadavia 56; admission AR$60; ☺10am-7pm) Small but carefully tended,

with an excellent overview of the Yamaná (Yaghan) way of life. Delves into their survival in harsh weather without clothing, why only women swam and how campfires were kept in moving canoes. Expertly detailed dioramas (also in English) show the bays and inlets of Parque Nacional Tierra del Fuego; coming here before a park visit offers new bearings.

Museo del Fin del Mundo   MUSEUM

(☑ 02901-421863; www.museodelfindelmundo.org.
ar; cnr Av Maipú & Rivadavia; admission AR$90;
⊙ 10am-7pm) Built in 1903, this former bank
contains exhibits on Fuegian natural history, stuffed birdlife, life of natives and early
penal colonies, and replicas of moderate interest. Guided visits are at 11am and 3:30pm.

🏃 Activities

Boating can be undertaken year-round.
Hiking possibilities should not be limited to
Parque Nacional Tierra del Fuego; the entire mountain range behind Ushuaia, with
its lakes and rivers, is a hiker's high. However, many trails are poorly marked or not
marked at all, and some hikers who have
easily scurried uphill have become lost trying to find the trail back down. Club Andino
Ushuaia has maps and good information.
In an emergency, contact the **Civil Guard**
(☑ 02901-22108, 103).

With the surrounding peaks loaded with
powder, winter visitors should jump at the
chance to explore the local ski resorts. Accessed from RN 3, resorts offer both downhill and cross-country options. The ski
season runs from June to September, with
July (winter vacation) the busiest month.

Cruceros Australis (p386) runs sightseeing cruises from Ushuaia to Punta Arenas.

Cerro Castor   SKIING

(☑ 02901-499301; www.cerrocastor.com; full-day
lift ticket adult/child AR$540/370; ⊙ mid-Jun–mid-
Oct) Fun and incredibly scenic, the largest
resort is 26km via RN 3 from Ushuaia, with
15 runs spanning 400 hectares and a number of lodges with cafes and even a hip sushi
bar. Rentals are available for skis, boards and
cross-country skis. Multiday and shoulder-
season tickets are discounted. Clear wind-
breaks are added to lifts on cold days.

Cerro Martial & Glaciar Martial   OUTDOORS

(⊙ 10am-4pm) The fantastic panoramas of
Ushuaia and the Beagle Channel are more
impressive than the actual smallish glacier.
You can arrive directly or an *aerosilla* (chairlift) can take you up from the ski run 7km
northwest of town. For the best views, hike
an hour above the chairlift terminus. A cozy
refuge offers coffee, desserts and beer at the
aerosilla base. Weather is changeable so take
warm, dry clothing and sturdy footwear.

Catch a taxi up the hill or jump aboard
one of the minivans (AR$60) to Cerro Mar-
tial that leave from the corner of Av Maipú
and Juana Fadul every half-hour from
8:30am to 6:30pm.

Tierra Mayor   SNOW SPORTS

(☑ 02901-430329; http://antartur.com.ar; RN 3,
Km3018; guided dog sledding US$45) Snowshoe
a beautiful alpine valley or dogsled with Siberian and Alaskan huskies bumping across
Tierra Mayor. For a memorable night, combine either with an evening bonfire (AR$650
to A$800). It also does guided snowcat rides.
It's 19km from Ushuaia via RN 3.

👉 Tours

Many travel agencies sell tours around the
region. You can go horseback riding, hiking,
canoeing, visit Lagos Escondido and Fagnano, stay at an *estancia* or spy on wildlife.

★ Compañía de
Guías de Patagonia   ADVENTURE TOUR

(☑ 02901-437753; www.companiadeguias.com.ar)
A reputable outfitter organizing excursions
in Parque Nacional Tierra del Fuego, full-day
treks and ice-hiking on Glaciar Vinciguerra,
and recommended three-day treks to Valle An-
dorra and Paso la Oveja. It also offers mountain biking, sea kayaking and Antarctica trips.

★ Tierra   ADVENTURE TOUR

(☑ 02901-15-486886; www.tierraturismo.com; Cam-
pos 36, 5C) 🖉 Doing active tours and unusual
tailored trips with aplomb, this agency was
created by former guides hoping to create a
more personalized experience. Partners Juan
and Nacho lead some of the tours themselves.
Options include a 4WD trip to Lago Fagnano
with boating and hiking (AR$700), treks in
Parque Nacional Tierra del Fuego (half-day
AR$380) and Estancia Harberton visits.

Canal Fun   ADVENTURE TOUR

(☑ 02901-435777; www.canalfun.com; Roca 136)
Run by hip young guys, these popular all-
day outings include hiking and kayaking
in Parque Nacional Tierra del Fuego, the
famous 4WD adventure around Lago Fagnano, and a multisport outing that includes
kayaking around Estancia Harberton and a
visit to the penguin colony.

Canopy Tours   ADVENTURE TOUR

(www.canopyushuaia.com.ar; Refugio de Montaña;
adult/child US$35/28; ⊙ 10am-5:15pm Oct-Jun)
Canopy tours run from the base of the *aerosilla* and offer an hour's worth of Tarzan
time, zipping through the forest with 11 zip-
line cables and two hanging bridges. The
highest cable is 8m.

Beagle Channel   BOAT TOUR

(cruise around AR$450) Navigating the Beagle
Channel's gunmetal-gray waters, with glaciers
and rocky isles in the distance, offers a fresh

Ushuaia

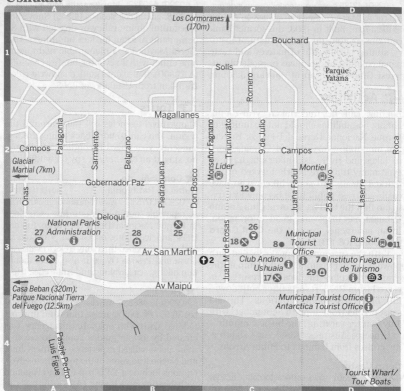

perspective and decent wildlife watching. Operators are found on the tourist wharf Maipú between Lasserre and Roca. Harbor cruises are usually four-hour morning or afternoon excursions to sea lion and cormorant colonies. The number of passengers, extent of snacks and hiking options may vary between operators. A highlight is an island stop to hike and look at *conchales,* middens or shell mounds left by the native Yaghan.

Patagonia Adventure Explorer   BOAT TOUR
(☑ 02901-15-465842; www.patagoniaadvent.com. ar; Tourist Wharf) Comfortable boats with snacks and a short hike on Isla Bridges. For extra adventure, set sail in the 18ft sailboat. Full-day sail trips with wine and gourmet snacks or multiday trips are also available.

Piratour   BOAT TOUR
(☑ 02901-435557; www.piratour.com.ar; Av San Martín 847) Runs 20-person tours to Isla Martillo for trekking around Magellanic and

Papúa penguins. There is also an office on the Tourist Wharf.

Che Tango   BOAT TOUR
(☑ 02901-15-517967; navegandoelfindelmundo@ gmail.com; Tourist Wharf; 🕸) With two 12-passenger boats, this tour includes a trek on Bridges Island and Beagle (what else?) beer on tap served for the cruise back to the harbor – very popular with the hostel crowd. No website, but has a Facebook page.

Tres Marías Excursiones   BOAT TOUR
(☑ 02901-436416; www.tresmariasweb.com; Tourist Wharf) The only outfitter with permission to land on Isla 'H' in the Isla Bridges natural reserve, which has shell mounds and a colony of rock cormorants. It takes only eight passengers.

Tolkar   GUIDED TOUR
(☑ 02901-431408, 02901-431412; www.tolkarturismo.com.ar; Roca 157) A helpful, popular, all-

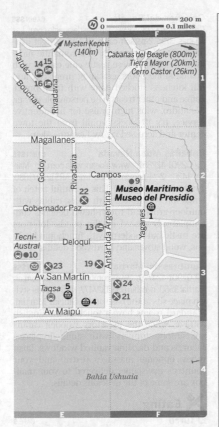

TIERRA DEL FUEGO USHUAIA

round agency, affiliated with Tecni-Austral
buses.

Turismo Comapa TOUR
(☏ 02901-430727; www.comapa.com; Av San
Martín 409) Confirm Navimag and Cruceros
Australis passages at this long-standing
agency, which also sells conventional tours
and boat transfer to Puerto Williams, Chile.

Ushuaia Turismo TOUR
(☏ 02901-436003; www.ushuaiaturismoevt.com.
ar; Gobernador Paz 865) Offers last-minute
Antarctica cruise bookings.

🛏 Sleeping

Reserve ahead from January to early March.
Check when booking for free arrival transfers. Winter rates drop a bit, and some places
close altogether. Most offer laundry service.

The municipal tourist office has lists of
B&Bs and *cabañas* (cabins), and also posts
a list of available lodgings outside after clos-

ing time. Hostels abound, all with kitchens
and most with internet access. Rates typically drop 25% in low season (April to October).

★ Antarctica Hostel HOSTEL $
(☏02901-435774; www.antarcticahostel.com; Antártida Argentina 270; dm AR$170, d/tr AR$450/
500; @ 🛜) This friendly backpacker hub delivers with a warm atmosphere and helpful
staff. The open floor plan and beer on tap
are plainly conducive to making friends.
Guests lounge and play cards in the common room and cook in a cool balcony kitch-
en. Cement rooms are clean and ample, with
radiant floor heating.

Los Cormoranes
HOSTEL **$**

(☑02901-423459; www.loscormoranes.com; Kamshen 788; dm AR$150-240, d/tr/q AR$580/650/720; @🛜) This friendly, mellow HI hostel is a 10-minute (uphill) walk north of the town center. Good, warm, six-bed dorms face outdoor plank hallways, some with private bathrooms. Modern doubles have polished cement floors and bright down duvets – the best is room 10, with bay views. The abundant breakfast includes toast, coffee, DIY eggs and fresh orange juice.

★ Galeazzi-Basily B&B
B&B **$$**

(☑02901-423213; www.avesdelsur.com.ar; Valdéz 323; s/d without bathroom US$46/70, 2-/4-person cabin US$110/140; @🛜) The best feature of this elegant wooded residence is its warm and hospitable family who will make you feel right at home. Rooms are small but offer a personal touch. Since beds are twin-sized, couples may prefer a modern cabin out back. It's a peaceful spot, and where else can you practice your English, French, Italian and Portuguese?

Mysten Kepen
GUESTHOUSE **$$**

(☑02901-430156, 02901-15-497391; http://mysten-kepen.blogspot.com; Rivadavia 826; d US$105; 🛜) If you want an authentic Argentine family experience, this is it. Hosts Roberto and Rosario still recount stories of favorite guests from years past, and their two-kid home feels busy and lived in, in a good way. Rooms have newish installations, bright corduroy duvets and handy shelving for nighttime reading. They also offer airport transfers and winter discounts.

La Casa de Tere B&B
B&B **$$**

(☑02901-422312; www.lacasadetere.com.ar; Rivadavia 620; d US$110, without bathroom US$80) Tere showers guests with attention, but also gives them the run of the place in this beautiful modern home with great views. Its three tidy rooms fill up fast. Guests can cook, and there's cable TV and a fireplace in the living room. It's a short but steep walk uphill from the town center.

Posada Fin del Mundo
B&B **$$**

(☑02901-437345; www.posadafindelmundo.com.ar; cnr Rivadavia & Valdéz; d/tr US$125/155, without bathroom AR$100/120) This expansive home exudes good taste and character, from the snug living room with folk art and expansive water views to the doddling chocolate Lab. Each of the nine rooms is distinct; the best are upstairs. Some are small but beds are long. Breakfast is abundant and there's also afternoon tea and cakes. Sometimes booked by entire ski teams in winter.

Cabañas del Beagle
CABIN **$$$**

(☑02901-432785; www.cabanasdelbeagle.com; Las Aljabas 375; 2-person cabin US$185, 4-night minimum) Couples in search of a romantic hideaway delight in these rustic chic cabins with heated stone floors, crackling fireplaces, and full kitchens stocked daily with fresh bread, coffee and other treats. The personable owner, Alejandro, wins high praise for his attentive service. It's 13 blocks uphill from the town center and accessed via Av Leandro Alem.

Cabañas Aldea Nevada
CABIN **$$$**

(☑02901-422851; www.aldeanevada.com.ar; Martial 1430; 2-/4-person cabins from AR$1230/1630, 2-night minimum; @🛜) This beautiful patch of lenga forest is dotted with 13 log cabins with outdoor grills and rough-hewn benches contemplatively placed by the ponds. Interiors are rustic but modern, with functional kitchens, wood stoves and hardwood details.

Cumbres del Martial
INN **$$$**

(☑02901-424779; www.cumbresdelmartial.com.ar; Martial 3560; d/cabin US$332/477; @🛜) This stylish place sits at the base of the Glaciar Martial. Standard rooms have a touch of the English cottage, while the two-story wooden cabins are simply stunners, with stone fireplaces, Jacuzzis and dazzling vaulted windows. Lush robes, optional massages (extra) and your country's newspaper delivered to your mailbox are some of the delicious details.

✖ Eating

El Turco
CAFE **$**

(☑02901-424711; Av San Martín 1410; mains AR$50-119; ⊙noon-3pm & 8pm-midnight) Nothing fancy, this dated Argentine cafe nonetheless charms with reasonable prices and swift bow-tied waiters game to try out their French on tourists. Standards include *milanesa* (breaded meat), pizzas, crispy fries and roast chicken.

Lomitos Martinica
ARGENTINE **$**

(☑02901-432134; Av San Martín 68; mains AR$70-100; ⊙11:30am-3pm & 8:30pm-midnight Mon-Sat) Cheap and cheerful, this greasy spoon with grill-side seating serves enormous *milanesa* sandwiches and offers a cheap lunch special.

Bodegón Fueguino
PATAGONIAN **$$**

(☑02901-431972; Av San Martín 859; mains AR$92-170; ⊙noon-2:45pm & 8-11:45pm Tue-Sun) The spot to sample hearty home-style Patagonian fare or gather for wine and appetizers. Painted peach, this century-old Fuegian home is cozied up with sheepskin-clad benches, cedar barrels and ferns. A *picada* (shared appetizer plate) for two includes eggplant, lamb brochettes, crab and bacon-wrapped plums.

María Lola Restó
ARGENTINE $$

(☑ 02901-421185; Deloquí 1048; mains AR$100-180; ☺ noon-midnight Mon-Sat) 'Satisfying' defines the experience at this creative cafe-style restaurant overlooking the channel. Locals pack this silver house for homemade pasta with seafood or strip steak in rich mushroom sauce. Service is good and portions tend toward humongous: desserts can easily be split. It's among few downtown restaurants with off-street parking.

Chiko
SEAFOOD $$

(☑ 02901-436024; Antártida Argentina 182; mains AR$58-190; ☺ noon-3pm & 7:30-11:30pm Mon-Sat) Great value, this popular 2nd-floor restaurant is a clear boon to seafood lovers. Crisp calamari rings, *paila marina* (shellfish stew) and fish dishes like *abadejo a pil pil* (pollock in garlic sauce) are done so right that you might not mind the slow service. An odd assemblage of Chilean memorabilia spells homesickness for the owners from Chiloé.

Almacen Ramos Generales
CAFE $$

(☑ 02901-4247317; Av Maipú 749; mains AR$152-180; ☺ 9am-midnight) With its quirky memorabilia and postings of the local environmental issues you never heard of, this former general store is a peek inside the real Ushuaia. Locals hold their pow-wows here. Croissants and crusty baguettes are baked by the French pastry chef. But there's also local beer on tap, a wine list, and light fare such as sandwiches, soups and quiche.

La Estancia
STEAK $$

(☑ 02901-431421; cnr Godoy & San Martín; mains AR$70-190; ☺ noon-3pm & 8-11pm) For authentic Argentine *asado* (barbecue grill) it is hard to beat this reliable, well-priced grill. There are many others along the main drag, but this is the one that consistently delivers. At night it's packed with locals and travelers alike, feasting on whole roast lamb, juicy steaks, sizzling ribs and heaping salads.

★ Kalma Resto
INTERNATIONAL $$$

(☑ 02901-425786; www.kalmaresto.com.ar; Antártida Argentina 57; mains AR$155-250; ☺ 8pm-midnight Tue-Sun, lunch by reservation only) This tiny chef-owned gem presents Fuegian staples like crab and octopus in a giddy new context. Black sea bass, a rich deep-sea dweller, wears a tart tomato sauce for contrast, there's roast lamb stews with earthy pine mushrooms and the summer greens and edible flowers are fresh from the garden.

La Anónima
SUPERMARKET $

(cnr Gobernador Paz & Rivadavia) A grocery store with cheap takeout.

🍷 Drinking

Geographically competitive drinkers should note that the southernmost bar in the world is not here but on a Ukrainian research station in Antarctica.

Dublin Irish Pub
PUB

(☑ 02901-430744; www.dublinushuaia.com; 9 de Julio 168) Dublin doesn't feel so far away with the lively banter and free-flowing drinks at this dimly lit foreigners' favorite. Look for occasional live music and be sure to try at least one of its three local Beagle beers.

Macario 1910
PUB

(☑ 02901-422757; www.macario1910.com; Av San Martín 1485; ☺ 6pm-late) A welcoming pub with a trans-Atlantic style of polished wood and leather booths. The tasty locally made Beagle beer flows on tap and above-average pub fare includes fresh tuna sandwiches on homemade bread and plates stacked with shoestring fries made from scratch. It's also good for cheap set meals (AR$25).

🔒 Shopping

Boutique del Libro
BOOKS

(☑ 02901-432117; 25 de Mayo 62; ☺ 10am-9pm) Outstanding selection of Patagonia and Antarctica-themed material, with literature, guidebooks and pictorials (also in English); there's an **Av San Martín** (☑ 02901-424750; Av San Martín 1120) branch.

ℹ Information

Several banks on Maipú and San Martín have ATMs.

Automóvil Club Argentino (ACA; www.aca.org.ar; cnr Malvinas Argentinas & Onachaga) Argentina's auto club; good source for provincial road maps.

Cambio Thaler (Av San Martín 209; ☺ 10am-1pm & 5-8pm Mon-Sat, 5-8pm Sun) Convenience equals slightly poorer exchange rates.

Club Andino Ushuaia (☑ 02901-422335; www.clubandinoushuaia.com.ar; Juana Fadul 50; ☺ 9am-1pm & 3-8pm Mon-Fri) Sells a map and bilingual trekking, mountaineering and mountain-biking guidebook. The club occasionally organizes hikes and can recommend guides. Unguided trekkers are strongly encouraged to register here or with the Municipal Tourist Office before hiking and after a safe return.

Hospital Regional (☑ 107, 02901-423200; cnr Fitz Roy & 12 de Octubre)

Immigration Office (☑ 02901-422334; Beauvoir 1536; ☺ 9am-noon Mon-Fri)

Instituto Fueguino de Turismo (Infuetur; ☑ 02901-421423; www.tierradelfuego.org.ar; Av Maipú 505) On the ground floor of Hotel Albatros.

Municipal Tourist Office (☎ 02901-432000; www.turismoushuaia.com; Av San Martín 674; ⊙ 5-9pm) Very helpful, with English- and French-speaking staff, a message board and multilingual brochures, as well as good lodging, activities and transport info. Also at the Airport (☎ 02901-423970; ⊙ during flight arrivals) and Pier (☎ 02901-437666; Prefectura Naval 470; ⊙ 8am-5pm).

National Parks Administration (☎ 02901-421315; Av San Martín 1395)

Post Office (cnr Av San Martín & Godoy)

ⓘ Getting There & Away

AIR

The best bet for Buenos Aires is Lan (round trip AR$1823). Purchase tickets through local travel agencies.

Aerolíneas Argentinas (☎ 0810-2228-6527; cnr Av Maipú & 9 de Julio) Aerolíneas Argentinas jets several times daily to Buenos Aires, sometimes stopping in Río Gallegos or El Calafate.

LADE (☎ 02901-421123; Av San Martín 542) LADE has flights to Buenos Aires, Comodoro Rivadavia, El Calafate and Río Gallegos.

BUS

Ushuaia has no bus terminal; buses stop at their individual offices. Book outgoing bus tickets as much in advance as possible; many readers have complained about getting stuck here in high season. Depending on your luck, long waits at border crossings can be expected.

Some destinations served:

DESTINATION	COST (AR$)	DURATION (HR)
Bariloche	1474	36
Calafate	789	18
Punta Arenas, Chile	650-1080	11
Río Gallegos	580	12
Río Grande	180	4
Tolhuin	115	2

Bus Sur (☎ 02901-430727; Av San Martín 245) Buses to Punta Arenas and Puerto Natales, Chile, three times weekly at 5:30am, connecting with Montiel. The office is in Comapa, which also does tours and ferries in Chile.

Lider (☎ 02901-442264; Gobernador Paz 921) Door-to-door minivans to Tolhuin and Río Grande six to eight times daily, with fewer departures on Sunday.

Montiel (☎ 02901-421366; Gobernador Paz 605) Door-to-door minivans to Tolhuin and Río Grande six to eight times daily, with fewer departures on Sunday.

Taqsa (☎ 02901-435453; Godoy 41) Buses to Río Grande at 5am via Tolhuin; to Punta Arenas and Puerto Natales, Chile, three-times weekly at 5am; to Río Gallegos, El Calafate and Bariloche daily at 5am.

Tecni-Austral (☎ 02901-431412, 02901-431408; Roca 157) Buses to Río Grande at 5am via Tolhuin; to Punta Arenas three times weekly; and to Río Gallegos daily at 5am.

ⓘ Getting Around

Taxis to/from the modern airport (USH), 4km southwest of downtown, cost AR$75.

There's a local bus service along Maipú.

Rental rates for compact cars, including insurance, start at around AR$750 per day; try **Localiza** (☎ 02901-430739; Sarmiento 81). Some agencies may not charge for dropoff in other parts of Argentine Tierra del Fuego.

Hourly ski shuttles (round trip AR$250) leave from the corner of Juana Fadul and Maipú to resorts along RN 3, from 9am to 2pm daily. Each resort also provides its own transportation from downtown Ushuaia.

Parque Nacional Tierra del Fuego

Banked against the channel, the hush, fragrant southern forests of Tierra del Fuego are a stunning setting to explore. West of Ushuaia by 12km, **Parque Nacional Tierra del Fuego** (admission AR$140, collected 8am-8pm), Argentina's first coastal national park, extends 630 sq km from the Beagle Channel in the south to beyond Lago Fagnano (also known as Lago Kami) in the north. However, only a couple of thousand hectares along the southern edge of the park are open to the public, with a miniscule system of short, easy trails that are designed more for day-tripping families than backpacking trekkers. The rest of the park is protected as a *reserva estricta* (strictly off-limits zone). Despite this, a few scenic hikes along the bays and rivers, or through dense native forests of evergreen coihue, canelo and deciduous lenga, are worthwhile. For truly spectacular color, come in the fall when hillsides of ñire burst out in red.

Birdlife is prolific, especially along the coastal zone. Keep an eye out for condors, albatross, cormorants, terns, oystercatchers, grebes, kelp geese and the comical, flightless orange-billed steamer ducks. Common invasive species include the European rabbit and the North American beaver, both of which are wreaking ecological havoc in spite of their cuteness. Gray and red foxes, enjoying the abundance of rabbits, may also be seen.

ESTANCIA HARBERTON

Tierra del Fuego's first *estancia* (grazing ranch), **Harberton** (☑ Skype estanciaharberton. turismo; www.estanciaharberton.com; adult/child under 10yr AR$140/free; half-board s/d/tr US$260/440/600, per person hostel US$50; ☉ 10am-7pm Oct 15-Apr 15) was founded in 1886 by missionary Thomas Bridges and his family. The location earned fame from a stirring memoir written by Bridges' son Lucas, titled *Uttermost Part of the Earth,* about his coming of age among the now-extinct Selk'nam and Yaghan people (see p387).

In a splendid location, the *estancia* is owned and run by Thomas Bridges' descendants. There's lodging and day visitors can attend guided tours (featuring the island's oldest house and a replica Yaghan dwelling), dine at the restaurant and visit the Reserva Yecapasela penguin colony. It's also a popular destination for birdwatchers.

On-site, the impressive **Museo Acatushún** (www.acatushun.com; entrance with estancia visit AR$140) houses a vast collection of mammal and bird specimens compiled by biologist Natalie Prosser Goodall. Emphasizing the region's marine mammals, the museum has inventoried thousands of mammal and bird specimens; among the rarest specimens is a Hector's beaked whale. Much of this vast collection was found at Bahía San Sebastián, north of Río Grande, where a difference of up to 11km between high and low tide leaves animals stranded. Confirm the museum's opening hours with the *estancia.*

Reserve well in advance as there are no phones at the *estancia,* though Skyping may be possible. With advance permission, free primitive camping is allowed at Río Lasifashaj, Río Varela and Río Cambaceres. Harberton is 85km east of Ushuaia via RN 3 and rough RC-j, a 1½- to two-hour drive one way. In Ushuaia, shuttles leave from the base of 25 de Mayo at Av Maipú at 9am, returning around 3pm. Day-long catamaran tours are organized by local agencies.

🏃 Activities

Just 3km from the entrance gate, the **Senda Pampa Alta** (5km) heads up a hill with impressive views from the top. A quick 300m further leads to a *senda* (trail) paralleling the Río Pipo and some waterfalls. A more popular saunter is along the **Senda Costera** (6.5km), accessed from the end of the Bahía Ensenada road. This trail meanders along the bay, once home to Yaghan people. Keep an eye out for shell middens, now covered in grass. The trail ends at the road, which leads 1.2km further to the **Senda Hito XXIV** (5km), a level trail through lenga forest along the northern shore of Lago Roca; this trail terminates at an unimposing Argentine–Chilean border marker. **Senda Cerro Guanaco** (8km) starts at the same trailhead, but climbs up a 970m hill to reach a great viewpoint.

After running 3242km from Buenos Aires, RN 3 takes its southern bow at gorgeous Bahía Lapataia. **Mirador Lapataia** (1km), connecting with **Senda del Turbal** (2km), winds through lenga forest to access this highway terminus. Other walks in this section include the self-guided nature trail **Senda Laguna Negra** (950m), through peat bogs, and the **Senda Castorera** (800m),

along which beaver dams, and possibly beavers themselves, can be spotted in the ponds.

🛏 Sleeping

The only fee-based campground and *refugio* is **Lago Roca** (☑ 15-412649; campsites per person/dm AR$40/80), 9km from the park entrance, open except when weather prohibits transport to the park. Both the campground and lodging offer hot showers, a good *confitería* (cafe offering light meals) and a tiny (expensive) grocery store. There is plenty of availability for camping at wild sites. Note that water at Lago Roca is not potable; boil it before using.

❶ Getting There & Away

Buses leave from the corner of Maipú and Juana Fadul in Ushuaia every 40 minutes in high season from 9am to 6pm, returning between 8am and 8pm. Depending on your destination, a round-trip fare is around AR$200, and you need not return the same day. Private tour buses are slightly more expensive. Taxis shared between groups can be the same price as bus tickets.

The most touristy and, beyond jogging, the slowest way to the park, **El Tren del Fin de Mundo** (☑ 02901-431600; www.trendelfindemundo.com.ar; adult/child plus park entrance fee AR$380/100) originally carted prisoners to work camps. It departs (sans convicts) from the

Estación del Fin de Mundo, 8km west of Ushuaia (taxis one way AR$80), three or four times daily in summer and once or twice daily in winter. The one-hour, scenic narrow-gauge train ride comes with historical explanations in English and Spanish. Reserve in January and February, when cruise-ship tours take over. You can take it one way and return via minibus. Hitchhiking is feasible, but many cars may already be full.

Tolhuin

☑ 02901 / POP 2000

Named for the Selk'nam word meaning 'like a heart,' Tolhuin is a lake town nestled in the center of Tierra del Fuego, 132km south of Río Grande and 104km northeast of Ushuaia via smooth pavement. This fast-growing frontier town of small plazas and sheltering evergreens fronts the eastern shore of Lago Fagnano, also known as Lago Kami. Most travelers tend to skip right over it, but if you are looking for a unique and tranquil spot, Tolhuin is well worth checking out.

A local highlight – and usually a stop on buses headed toward Ushuaia, **Panadería La Unión** (☑ 02901-492202; www.panaderialaunion.com.ar; Jeujepen 450, Tolhuin; snacks AR$15; ☺ 24hr) serves first-rate pastries and some decent empanadas. The best spot for basic lodgings and camping is **Camping Hain** (☑ 02964-15-603606; Lago Fagnano; campsite per person AR$65, 3-/6-person refugio AR$390/780), with grassy, sheltered sites, hot-water showers, a huge barbecue pit and *fogón* (sheltered fire pit and kitchen area). Roberto, the conscientious owner, can recommend local excursions and guides.

Río Grande

☑ 02964 / POP 70,042

The island's petroleum service center has an industrial feel and an addiction to urban sprawl, egged on by its duty-free status. But look further and you will find some of the world's best trout fishing and exclusive lodges that cater to serious anglers. If you didn't come with rod in hand, the longest that you will likely stay in windswept Río Grande is a scant hour to change buses to Ushuaia, 230km southwest.

Catering to high-end anglers, **Posada de los Sauces** (☑02964-432895; www.laposadadelossauces.com.ar; Elcano 839; d $850; @☎) fosters a lodge atmosphere, with fresh scents and woodsy accents. Opposite Casino Status, **Hotel Villa** (☑02964-424998; hotelvillarg@hotmail.com; Av San Martín 281; d/tr AR$550/625;

P@☎) has a popular restaurant, and a dozen spacious and stylish rooms. Hosting both ladies having tea and cake, and boys at the varnished bar downing beer and burgers, **Tante Sara** (Belgrano 402; mains AR$80-160) serves good cafe food, though service can be sluggish.

Most visitor services are along Avs San Martín and Belgrano. For tourist information, visit **Instituto Fueguino de Turismo** (Infuetur; ☑ 02964-426805; www.tierradelfuego.org.ar; Av Belgrano 319; ☺ 9am-9pm) on the south side of the plaza or the **Municipal Tourist Kiosk** (☑02964-431324; turismo@riogrande.gob.ar; ☺9am-8pm), a helpful kiosk on the plaza, with maps, *estancia* brochures and fishing details. **Mariani Travel** (☑02964-426010; mariani@marianitravel.com.ar; Rosales 281) books flights and represents nearby *estancias*.

❶ Getting There & Away

The **airport** (☑ 02964-420699) is off RN 3, a short taxi ride from town. **Aerolíneas Argentinas** (☑02964-424467) flies daily to Buenos Aires (one way US$250). **LADE** (☑ 02964-422968; Lasserre 445) flies a couple of times weekly to Río Gallegos (AR$265), El Calafate (AR$457) and Buenos Aires (AR$1091); prices are one way.

DESTINATION	COST (ARS)	DURATION (HR)
Punta Arenas, Chile	550	9
Río Gallegos	350	8
Tolhuin	115	2
Ushuaia	180	4

Transfer van companies at **Terminal Fuegina** (Finocchio 1194):

Bus Sur (☑ 02964-420997; www.bus-sur.cl; ticket office 25 de Mayo 712) Buses to Ushuaia, Punta Arenas and Puerto Natales, Chile, three times weekly at 5:30am, connecting with Montiel.

Buses Pacheco (☑02964-421554) Buses to Punta Arenas three times weekly at 10am.

Lider (☑02964-420003, 424-2000; www.lidertdf.com.ar; Moreno 635) Best option for Ushuaia and Tolhuin is this door-to-door minivan service, with several daily departures. Call to reserve.

Montiel (☑02964-420997; 25 de Mayo 712) Buses to Ushuaia and Tolhuin.

Taqsa/Marga (☑02964-434316) Buses to Ushuaia via Tolhuin.

Tecni-Austral (☑02964-434316; ticket office Moyano 516) Buses to Ushuaia via Tolhuin three times weekly at 8:30am; to Río Gallegos and Punta Arenas three times weekly.

Easter Island (Rapa Nui)

📖 032

Best Places to Eat

➡ Au Bout du Monde (p404)

➡ Te Moana (p405)

➡ Mikafé (p404)

➡ Tataku Vave (p404)

Best Places to Sleep

➡ Cabañas Ngahu (p402)

➡ Hare Noi (p403)

➡ Cabañas Christophe (p402)

➡ Camping Mihinoa (p402)

➡ Cabalgatas Pantu – Pikera Uri (p403)

Why Go?

Few areas in the world possess a more mystical pull than this tiny speck of land, one of the most isolated places on Earth. Here, it's hard to feel connected to Chile, over 3700km to the east, let alone the wider world. Endowed with the most logic-defying statues in the world – the strikingly familiar *moai* – Easter Island (Rapa Nui to its native Polynesian inhabitants) emanates a magnetic, mysterious vibe.

But Easter Island is much more than an open-air museum. Diving, snorkeling and surfing are fabulous. On land, there's no better ecofriendly way to experience the island's savage beauty than on foot, from a bike saddle or on horseback. But if all you want to do is recharge the batteries, a couple of superb expanses of white sand beckon.

Although Easter Island is world famous and visitors are on the increase, everything remains small and personable – it's all about eco-travel.

When to Go
Hanga Roa

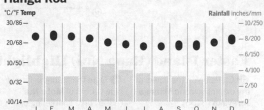

| | Jan–Mar Peak season. Highest prices and scarce hotels around February's Tapati Rapa Nui festival. | Jul–Aug Chilly weather, not ideal for beaches but a good time for hiking and horse-back riding. | Apr–Jun & Oct–Dec The shoulder season is not a bad time to visit; the climate is fairly temperate. |

HANGA ROA

POP 6700

Hanga Roa is the island's sole town. Upbeat it ain't, but with most sights almost on its doorstep and nearly all the island's hotels, restaurants, shops and services lying within its boundaries, it's the obvious place to anchor oneself. It features a picturesque fishing harbor, a couple of modest beaches and surf spots, and a few archaeological sites.

◉ Sights

Museo Antropológico Sebastián Englert   MUSEUM

(☎032-255-1020; www.museorapanui.cl; Tahai s/n; admission CH$1000; ⊗9:30am-5:30pm Tue-Fri, to 12.30pm Sat & Sun) This well-organized

EASTER ISLAND (RAPA NUI) HANGA ROA

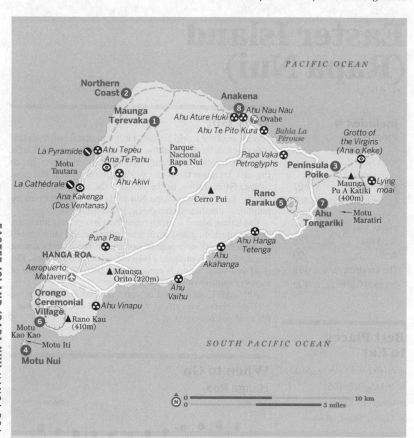

Easter Island (Rapa Nui) Highlights

❶ Clip-clop on the flanks of the extinct volcano **Maunga Terevaka** (p406).

❷ Hike along the ruggedly beautiful **northern coast** (p400).

❸ Seek solace on the mysterious **Península Poike** (p407).

❹ Ogle the stunning limpid blue waters of **Motu Nui** (p399) on a snorkeling or diving trip.

❺ Take a lesson in archaeology at **Rano Raraku** (p407), the 'nursery' of the *moai*.

❻ Ponder the island's mysterious past at **Orongo**

ceremonial village (p406), perched on the edge of Rano Kau.

❼ Watch the sun rise at the row of enigmatic statues at **Ahu Tongariki** (p407).

❽ Take a snooze under the swaying palms at **Anakena** (p407).

museum makes a perfect introduction to the island's history and culture. It displays basalt fishhooks, obsidian spearheads and other weapons, and a *moai* head with reconstructed fragments of its eyes, among others.

Caleta Hanga Roa & Ahu Tautira
ARCHAEOLOGICAL SITE

Your first encounter with the *moai* will probably take place at **Ahu Tautira** (Av Te Pito o Te Henua), which overlooks Caleta Hanga Roa, the fishing port in Hanga Roa at the foot of Av Te Pito o Te Henua. Here you'll find a platform with two superb *moai*.

Ahu Tahai
ARCHAEOLOGICAL SITE

Ahu Tahai is a highly photogenic site that contains three restored *ahu*. Ahu Tahai proper is the *ahu* in the middle, supporting a large, solitary *moai* with no topknot. On the north side of Ahu Tahai is Ahu Ko Te Riku, with a topknotted and eyeballed *moai*. On the other side is Ahu Vai Uri, which supports five *moai* of varying sizes and shapes. Along the hills are foundations of *hare paenga* (traditional houses resembling an upturned canoe, with a narrow doorway).

Ahu Akapu
ARCHAEOLOGICAL SITE

You'll find this *ahu* with a solitary *moai* along the coastline, north of Hanga Roa.

Caleta Hanga Piko & Ahu Riata
HARBOR

Easily overlooked by visitors, the little Caleta Hanga Piko is used by local fishers. Facing the *caleta* (bay), the restored Ahu Riata supports a solitary *moai*.

Iglesia Hanga Roa
CHURCH

(Av Tu'u Koihu s/n) The unmissable Iglesia Hanga Roa, the island's Catholic church, is well worth a visit for its spectacular wood carvings, which integrate Christian doctrine with Rapa Nui tradition. It also makes a colorful scene on Sunday morning.

Playa Pea
BEACH

For a little dip, the tiny beach at Playa Pea, on the south side of Caleta Hanga Roa, fits the bill.

🏃 Activities

Diving & Snorkeling

Scuba diving is increasingly popular on Easter Island. The strong points are the gin-clear visibility (up to 50m), the lack of crowds, the dramatic seascape and the abundance of pristine coral formations. The weak point is marine life, which is noticeable only in its scarcity.

DON'T MISS

TRADITIONAL DANCE SHOWS

If there's one thing you absolutely *have* to check out while you're on Easter Island it's a traditional dance show. The most reputable groups include the following.

Kari Kari (☑ 032-210-0767; Av Atamu Tekena s/n; tickets CH$15,000; ⊙ show 9pm Tue, Thu & Sat) This elaborately costumed and talented group performs island legends through song and dance at a venue on the main street.

Vai Te Mihi – Maori Tupuna (☑ 032-255-0556; Av Policarpo Toro s/n; ⊙ show 9pm Mon, Thu & Sat) Features excellent traditional dance shows. Front row seats cost CH$17,000.

Easter Island is diveable year-round. Water temperatures vary from as low as 20°C in winter to 26°C in summer. Most sites are scattered along the west coast. You don't need to be a strong diver – there are sites for all levels. A few favorites include **Motu Nui** and the very scenic La Cathédrale and La Pyramide.

Mike Rapu Diving Center
DIVING, SNORKELING

(☑ 032-255-1055; www.mikerapu.cl; Caleta Hanga Roa s/n; ⊙ 8am-5pm Mon-Sat) This is a well-established operator that offers introductory dives (CH$40,000), single-dive trips (CH$30,000) and courses. Prices drop by about 15% for more than three dives. Also runs snorkeling trips (CH$15,000) to Motu Nui three days a week.

Orca Diving Center
DIVING, SNORKELING

(☑ 032-255-0877; www.orcadivingcenter.cl; Caleta Hanga Roa s/n; ⊙ 8am-5pm Mon-Sat) This state-of-the-art outfit offers the full slate of diving adventures, including introductory dives (CH$50,000), single dives (CH$40,000), courses and packages, as well as snorkeling trips to Motu Nui (CH$25,000).

Surfing

Easter Island is hit with powerful swells from all points of the compass throughout the year, offering irresistible lefts and rights – mostly lava-reef breaks, with waves up to 5m. The most popular spots are scattered along the west coast. For beginners, there are a couple of good waves off Caleta Hanga Roa.

A handful of seasonal (usually from December to March) outfits based on the seafront offer surfing courses and also rent surfboards.

Hanga Roa

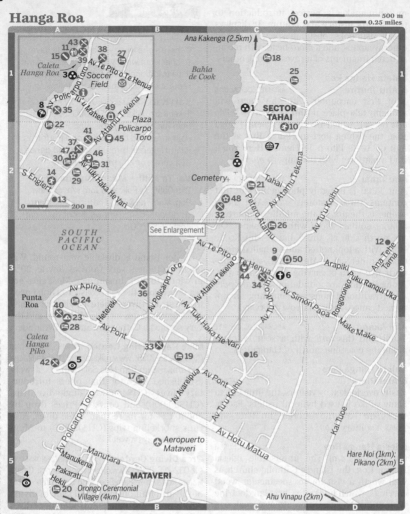

Hare Orca SURFING
(☏032-255-0877; Caleta Hanga Roa s/n; rental per half-day CH$10,000; ⊗8am-5pm Mon-Sat) This shop rents bodyboards, surfboards, stand-up paddle boards and snorkeling gear. Surfing lessons are also available.

Horseback Riding
A network of trails leading to some of the most beautiful sites can be explored on horseback – a typical Rapa Nui experience.

Cabalgatas Pantu HORSEBACK RIDING
(☏032-210-0577; www.rapanuipantu.com; Sector Tahai s/n; half-/full-day tour CH$30,000/70,000;

⊗daily by reservation) Offers guided trips that take in some of the sites near Hanga Roa or more remote places, such as Terevaka, Anakena and the north coast. Beginners welcome.

Hiking
You can take some fantastic trails through the island. A memorable walk is the way marked Ruta Patrimonial, which runs from Museo Antropológico Sebastián Englert up to Orongo ceremonial village (about four hours; 7km). Other recommended walks are the climb to Maunga Terevaka from near Ahu Akivi (about three hours) and the walk around Península Poike (one day). For

Hanga Roa

EASTER ISLAND (RAPA NUI) HANGA ROA

the walk between Ahu Tepeu and Anakena beach along the northern coastline, you'll need a guide because the path is not marked.

Cycling

Cycling is a superb way of seeing the island at your leisure, provided you're ready to come to grips with the winding roads around the southern parts. An easy loop is from Hanga Roa up to Ahu Tepeu, then east to Ahu Akivi and back to Hanga Roa (about 17km).

Makemake Rentabike   BICYCLE RENTAL
(☏ 032-255-2030; Av Atamu Tekena; per day CH$10,000; ☺9am-1pm & 4-8pm Mon-Sat, 9am-1pm Sun) Rents mountain bikes in tip-top condition. A helmet and a map are provided.

 Tours

We recommend joining an organized tour since you get the benefit of an English-speaking guide who will be able to explain

the cultural significance of the archaeological sites.

Plenty of operators do tours of the sites, typically charging CH$45,000 for a full day and CH$25,000 for a half-day. Entrance fees to Parque Nacional Rapa Nui (CH$30,000 or US$60) aren't included.

Aku Aku Turismo   CULTURAL TOUR
(☏ 032-210-0770; www.akuakuturismo.cl; Av Tu'u Koihu s/n; ☺8:30am-5pm) A well-established company that employs competent guides.

Kava Kava Tours   CULTURAL TOUR
(☏ cell 9352-4972; www.kavakavatour.cl; Ana Tehe Tama s/n; ☺by reservation) Run by a young, knowledgeable Rapanui lad who offers private, customized tours as well as hiking tours.

Kia Koe Tour   CULTURAL TOUR
(☏ 032-210-0852; www.kiakoetour.cl; Av Atamu Tekena s/n; ☺9am-1pm & 3-6pm) Has good credentials and uses knowledgeable guides.

TAPATI RAPA NUI

Easter Island's premier festival, the Tapati Rapa Nui, lasts about two weeks in the first half of February and is so impressive that it's almost worth timing your trip around it (contact the tourist office for exact dates). A genuine cultural event, it's a great chance for foreigners to immerse themselves in local culture. Expect a series of music, dance, cultural and sport contests between two clans that put up two candidates who stand for the title of Queen of the Festival. The most spectacular event is the Haka Pei: on the flanks of the Cerro Pui, a dozen male contestants run downhill on a makeshift sled at speeds that can reach 70km/h.

Rapa Nui Travel   CULTURAL TOUR
(☑ 032-210-0548; www.rapanuitravel.com; Av Tu'u Koihu; ☺ by reservation) Run by a Rapa Nui–German couple.

🛏 Sleeping

Unless otherwise stated, most places come equipped with private bathroom, and breakfast is included. Air-con is scarce but fans are provided in the hottest months. Airport transfers are included.

Camping Mihinoa   CAMPGROUND $
(☑ 032-255-1593; www.camping-mihinoa.com; Av Pont s/n; campsites per person CH$5000, dm CH$10,000, d CH$20,000-30,000; 🐾) You have options here: a clutch of well-scrubbed rooms (the dearer ones offer more privacy), several two- to six-bed dorms, some with their own bathroom, or a campsite on a grassy plot (no shade). The ablution block has hot showers (mornings and evenings). Perks include tent hire, wi-fi access (CH$5000 flat fee), a well-equipped communal kitchen and laundry service. Location is ace; you're just a pebble's throw from the seashore.

Hostal Raioha   CABIN $
(☑ cell 7654-1245, 032-210-0851; off Av Te Pito o Te Henua; s or d CH$40,000) Run by a friendly couple, this discreet number is a valid, safe and comfortable option that's great value for the town's center. The seven rooms are no-frills but well maintained and open onto a verdant garden. No breakfast is served but there's a communal kitchen. No wi-fi, but there's an internet cafe up the street.

Hostal Tojika   GUESTHOUSE $
(☑ cell 9358-0810; www.rapanuiweb.com/hostaltojika/hostal.htm; Av Apina s/n; dm/s CH$10,000/25,000, d CH$30,000-45,000; 🐾) A good bet for budgeteers, Hostal Tojika has several rooms that are all different, a five-bed dorm and a communal kitchen in a single building overlooking the sea. Some rooms lack natural light but the dorm is an excellent bargain. No breakfast is served but there's a small eatery at the entrance of the property.

★**Cabañas Christophe**   BUNGALOW $$
(☑ 032-210-0826; www.cabanaschristophe.com; Av Policarpo Toro s/n; d CH$60,000-90,000; 🐾) Hands-down the best-value option in Hanga Roa, this charming venue seduces those seeking character and comfort, with three handsomely designed bungalows that blend hardwoods and volcanic stones. They're spacious, well appointed – think king-size beds, kitchen facilities and a private terrace – and inundated with natural light. It's at the start of the Orongo trail, about 1.5km from the center. Reserve well in advance.

Cabañas Ngahu   CABIN $$
(☑ cell 9090-2774, cell 8299-1041; www.ngahu.cl; Av Policarpo Toro s/n; d CH$40,000-80,000; 🐾) A great choice where we encountered helpful service, friendly owners and happy guests. It consists of five well-equipped cabins of varying sizes and shapes, most with sea views. The casual atmosphere and prime sunset-watching make this the kind of place where you quickly lose track of the days. Good value (by Rapa Nui standards) considering the price and location. No breakfast.

Hare Swiss   BUNGALOW $$
(☑ 032-255-2221; www.hareswiss.com; Sector Tahai; s/d CH$52,000/75,000; 🐾) Run by a Rapanui-Swiss couple, this venture is a solid option, with three immaculate cottages perched on a slope overlooking the ocean. They come equipped with sparkling bathrooms, king-size beds, tiled floors, kitchen facilities and a terrace with sea views. It's a bit of a schlep from the center (you'll need a bike).

Tau Ra'a   HOTEL $$
(☑ 032-210-0463; www.tauraahotel.cl; Av Atamu Tekena s/n; s/d CH$75,000/90,000; 🐾) Here's one of the most commendable bets in the midrange category. The 16 rooms are spotless and flooded with natural light, and they come equipped with back-friendly beds and prim bathrooms. Alas, no sea views. The substantial breakfast is a plus, and there are plans to set up air-con. Bill, the Aussie owner, is a treasure trove of local information.

Its peerless location, just off the main drag, makes this an excellent base for roaming about town.

Aukara Lodge
CABIN $$

(☏ 032-210-0539, cell 7709-5711; www.aukara. cl; Av Pont s/n; s/d CH$40,000/65,000; ☏) A good pick, though the 'Lodge' bit is a gross misnomer. Where else could you find an establishment with an art gallery featuring various paintings and woodcarvings by Bene Tuki, the proprietor? The rooms themselves are nothing outstanding but spruce enough, and the shady garden is a great place to chill out. It's easy walking distance from the action. Bene's wife, Ana Maria, speaks excellent English and is very knowledgeable about the history of the island. Clearly a solid choice for the culturally and artistically inclined.

Cabañas Mana Nui
CABIN $$

(☏ 032-210-0811; www.mananui.cl; Sector Tahai; s/d CH$40,000/60,000; ☏) This well-run venture is a reliable bet. The seven adjoining rooms are nothing to crow about but the general feel of cleanliness, the location in a quiet area, and the million-dollar views over the ocean make it a steal. There are also two stand-alone cottages for self-caterers as well as a kitchen for guests' use.

Inaki Uhi
CABIN $$

(☏ 032-210-0231; www.inakiuhi.com; Av Atamu Tekena s/n; s/d CH$50,000/80,000; ☏) Can't speak a single word of Spanish? Here you'll be glad to be welcomed in flawless English by Alvaro Jr, who spent 15 years in Australia. The 15 smallish rooms, which have been thoroughly modernized, occupy two rows of low-slung buildings facing each other. No breakfast, but there are four shared kitchens. It's right on the main drag, close to everything. Alvaro Jr has plenty of experience in helping visitors with logistics and trip planning.

Aloha Nui
GUESTHOUSE $$

(☏ 032-210-0274; haumakatours@gmail.com; Av Atamu Tekena s/n; s/d CH$37,000/70,000) This agreeable place features six well-organized rooms and a vast, shared living room that opens onto a flowery garden. But the real reason you're staying here is to discuss Rapa Nui archaeology in flawless English with Josefina Nahoe Mulloy and her husband Ramon, who lead reputable tours. No wi-fi.

Vaianny
GUESTHOUSE $$

(☏ 032-210-0650; www.residencialvaianny.com; Av Tuki Haka He Vari; s/d CH$40,000/55,000; ☏) This well-established and central guesthouse is a good choice if you're counting the pennies, with basic but well-scrubbed rooms that are cluttered in a tiny garden area. There's a kitchen for self-caterers. The prime selling point here is the location, within hollering distance of some of the town's best bars and restaurants.

Hostal Petero Atamu
GUESTHOUSE $$

(☏ 032-255-1823; www.hostalpeteroatamu.com; Petero Atamu s/n; with/without bathroom s CH$40,000/25,000, d CH$60,000/40,000; ☏) Popular with Japanese backpackers, this guesthouse is a simple affair not too far from the center. Shoestringers will opt for the bare but acceptable rooms with shared bathroom, while wealthier travelers will choose the rooms with a private bathroom and a terrace; rooms 1, 2 and 3 are the best. There's a TV lounge and a kitchen.

★ Cabalgatas
Pantu – Pikera Uri
BUNGALOW $$$

(☏ 032-210-0577; www.rapanuipantu.com; Tahai s/n; d CH$110,000-125,000; ☏) A spiffing location plus decorative touches make this venture one of Hanga Roa's best retreats. Digs are in cute-as-can-be bungalows perched on a gentle slope overlooking the ocean; the Rito Mata and Uri offer the best sea views. They're all commodious, luminous and beautifully attired, and open onto a small corral where the owner, Pantu, gathers his horses every morning.

★ Hare Noi
BOUTIQUE HOTEL $$$

(☏ 032-255-0134; www.noihotels.com; Av Hotu Matua s/n; d CH$380,000; ☏☒) A top-drawer hotel, without the stiff upper lips. Digs are in wood and stone bungalows dotted on an alluring property not far from the airport. They are roomy, light-filled and judiciously laid out, with elegant furnishings, solid amenities and a private terrace. It's quite spread out so you can get a decent dose of privacy, and it features an excellent on-site restaurant. It's a bit far from the center, but bikes are available for free.

Altiplanico
HOTEL $$$

(☏ 032-255-2190; www.altiplanico.cl; Sector Tahai; s/d CH$205,000/230,000; @☏☒) The best thing about this well-run venture with a boutique feel is its excellent location on a gentle slope in Tahai. Try for bungalow 1, 2, 3, 10, 11 or 17, which have panoramic sea views. The 17 units are all sparkling clean and quirkily decorated, but they're fairly packed together and we found the rack rates somewhat inflated. The on-site restaurant is elegant but pricey (pizzas cost US$30).

Hanga Roa Eco
Village & Spa
LUXURY HOTEL $$$

(☑ 032-255-3700; www.hangaroa.cl; Av Pont s/n; s/d from CH$225,000/CH$300,000; ❋ ☎ ☷) ✎ Entirely renovated in 2012, this sprawling establishment is one of the best hotels on the island, with an array of creatively designed rooms and suites facing the sea. All units are built of natural materials and their layout is inspired by caves, with curving lines and shapes. The on-site restaurant serves refined food and the spa is a stunner. It's ecofriendly: there's a water and electricity saving system.

✖ Eating

For self-caterers, there are a couple of well-stocked supermarkets on Av Atamu Tekena.

★ Mikafé
CAFETERIA, SANDWICHES $

(Caleta Hanga Roa s/n; ice cream CH$1800-3200, sandwiches & cakes CH$3500-6000; ⊘ 9am-8:30pm Mon-Sat) Mmm, the *helados artesanales* (homemade ice creams)! Oh, the damn addictive banana cake! Other treats include panini, sandwiches, muffins and brownies. Also serves breakfast (from CH$3500).

Motu Hava Kafe
FAST FOOD $

(☑ cell 9301-5104; Caleta Hanga Roa s/n; mains CH$2500-7000; ⊘ 9am-7pm Mon-Sat) Blink and you'll miss the entrance of this funky little den overlooking the Caleta Hanga Roa. It whips up freshly prepared empanadas, sandwiches and delicious daily specials at wallet-friendly prices. Good breakfast too (from CH$2800). Takeaway is available.

Casa Esquina
FAST FOOD $

(☑ 032-255-0205; Av Te Pito o Te Henua; mains CH$5000-9000; ⊘ noon-11:30pm) A great-value option with a breezy terrace overlooking the church. Choose from pastas, pizzas, sandwiches, salads and (yes!) seriously authentic sushi. Wash it all down with a *jugo natural* (fruit juice).

Mara Pika
FAST FOOD $

(Av Apina s/n; mains CH$2500-6000; ⊘ 8am-8pm) You'll find no cheaper place for a sit-down meal in Hanga Roa. It's very much a canteen, but a good one, with friendly service and family-style Chilean cuisine, including empanadas and daily specials.

Caramelo
CAFETERIA $

(☑ 032-255-0132; Av Atamu Tekena s/n; mains CH$6500-8500; ⊘ 9:30am-9pm Mon-Sat) Caramelo is your spot for voluminous salads and gourmet sandwiches. It also features a tantalizing array of pastries and cakes as well as tea, coffee, smoothies and hot chocolate.

Moiko Ra'a
CAFETERIA $

(☑ 032-255-0149; Av Atamu Tekena s/n; snacks CH$2500-7000; ⊘ 9am-10pm daily; ✐) This delectable little cafeteria has a wide variety of cavity-inducing pastries, as well as excellent sandwiches, tarts and empanadas. Be sure to try the unctuous hot chocolate.

Tataku Vave
SEAFOOD $$

(☑ 032-255-1544; Caleta Hanga Piko s/n; mains CH$11,000-19,000; ⊘ noon-10pm Mon-Sat) Tucked behind the Caleta Hanga Piko, Tataku Vave is that easy-to-miss 'secret spot' that locals like to recommend, with a delightfully breezy terrace that's just meters from the seashore. Munch on superb fish dishes while the ocean crashes just feet away. Call ahead for free transportation from your hotel.

Au Bout du Monde
INTERNATIONAL $$

(☑ 032-255-2060; www.restaurantauboutdumonde.com; Av Policarpo Toro s/n; mains CH$11,000-18,000; ⊘ noon-2:30pm & 7-10:30pm Wed-Mon, closed Jun & Jul) In this agreeable venue run by a Belgian lady, every visitor ought to try the tuna in Tahitian vanilla sauce, the homemade tagliatelle or the organic beef fillet. Leave room for dessert – the Belgian chocolate mousse is divine.

Haka Honu
CHILEAN $$

(Av Policarpo Toro s/n; mains CH$11,000-16,000; ⊘ 12:30-10pm Tue-Sun) Fish dishes, steaks, homemade pasta, burgers and salads round out the menu at this well-regarded eatery blessed with unsurpassable ocean views.

Kanahau
SEAFOOD, CHILEAN $$

(☑ 032-255-1923; Av Atamu Tekena s/n; mains CH$10,000-16,000; ⊘ noon-11:30pm) Whether you satisfy yourself with ultrafresh tuna or try the *lomo kanahau* (beef with a homemade sauce), among a variety of hearty dishes, you'll be pleased with the careful preparation, attentive service and atmospheric decor.

Inkai
PERUVIAN $$

(☑ cell 7880-8886; Av Apina s/n; mains CH$12,000-16,000; ⊘ 12:30-10pm Wed-Mon) Growing weary of ceviche and beef? This seaside venue offers a great selection of Peruvian specialties, including a scrumptious *aji de gallina* (chicken breast in a mildly spicy creamy sauce). There's an inviting terrace with ocean views.

Kuki Varua
SEAFOOD, CHILEAN $$

(☑ 032-255-2072; Av Te Pito o Te Henua s/n; mains CH$9000-13,000; ⊘ noon-4pm & 7-10pm Wed-Mon) The Kuki Varua has a great selection of fish delivered daily from the harbor, including tuna and *mero* (grouper). The upstairs terrace is perfect for enjoying the cool, ocean breezes.

★ **Te Moana** CHILEAN $$$
(☎ 032-255-1578; Av Atamu Tekena s/n; mains CH$10,000-21,000; ☺12:30-11pm Tue-Sun) One of the most reliable options in Hanga Roa, this buzzy restaurant boasts a spiffing location, with an atmospheric veranda opening onto the ocean. It's renowned for its tasty meat and fish dishes. The Polynesian decor is another clincher, with woodcarvings and traditional artifacts adorning the walls.

La Taverne du Pêcheur FRENCH $$$
(☎ 032-210-0619; Caleta Hanga Roa s/n; mains CH$12,000-25,000; ☺noon-3pm & 6-11pm Mon-Sat) This French institution right by the harbor provides an enchanting, albeit expensive, dining experience with classic French fare with a Chilean twist – try the *thon Rossini* (tuna served with foie gras and flambéed with Cognac). The spiffing upstairs terrace is a great place to soak up the atmosphere of the seafront. Some readers have complained about grumpy service, though.

 Drinking & Nightlife

Most restaurants feature a bar section.

Te Moana BAR
(Av Atamu Tekena s/n; ☺12:30pm-midnight Mon-Sat) Come for the good fun, good mix of people and good cocktails.

Kopakavana Club BAR
(Av Te Pito o Te Henua s/n; ☺6pm-2am) You come here as much for a cocktail as for the trendy amosphere.

Toromiro BAR
(Av Atamu Tekena s/n; ☺10am-midnight Mon-Fri, 10am-2pm & 6pm-midnight Sat & Sun) A funky drinking spot in the center. Food is only so-so.

Marau BAR
(Av Atamu Tekena s/n; ☺5pm-midnight) Marau is the hangout of well-connected locals and serves devilishly good tropical potions.

Haka Honu BAR
(Av Policarpo Toro s/n; ☺12.30-10pm Tue-Sun) The outside terrace catches every wisp of breeze and is perfect for watching the world surf by.

Kanahau BAR
(Av Atamu Tekena s/n; ☺noon-11:30pm) Kick off the night with a strong pisco sour at this cheerful hangout decked in wood. Serves excellent *picoteos* (tapas), too.

Mikafé CAFE
(Caleta Hanga Roa s/n; ☺9am-8:30pm Mon-Sat) In search of a real espresso or a cappuccino? Mikafé is your answer.

LOCAL KNOWLEDGE

AHU TEPEU TO ANAKENA BEACH

If you want to experience Easter Island from a different perspective, consider exploring the coastline between Ahu Tepeu and Anakena beach. This wild area is extremely alluring: vast expanses of chaotic boulders, towering sea cliffs, barren landscapes and sensational ocean views. There are also plenty of archaeological sites dotted along the way as well as caves adorned with impressive petroglyphs. From Ahu Tepeu it takes six to seven hours to reach Anakena beach on foot. Then hitch back or arrange a taxi back to Hanga Roa. It's not marked and the archaeological sites are not signed; you'll definitely need a guide. Contact the tourist office or your lodging to secure one.

Pikano BAR
(cover CH$3000; ☺11pm-4am Wed & Fri) Not your average watering hole, Pikano is isolated on the road to Anakena about 3km from the airport. This multifaceted venue is very popular on Wednesdays and Fridays with an eclectic crowd gulping down glasses of beer or noshing on grilled meat while listening to live bands. Later in the night it morphs into a club.

🛍 **Shopping**

Hanga Roa has numerous souvenir shops, mostly on Av Atamu Tekena and on Av Te Pito o Te Henua.

Feria Artesanal ARTS, CRAFTS
(cnr Avs Atamu Tekena & Tu'u Maheke; ☺10am-8pm Mon-Sat) Good prices. Look for small stone or carved wooden replicas of *moai* and fragments of obsidian.

Mercado Artesanal ARTS, CRAFTS
(cnr Avs Tu'u Koihu & Ara Roa Rakei; ☺10am-8pm Mon-Sat) Across from the church. Has a bit of everything.

ℹ **Information**

BancoEstado (Av Tu'u Maheke s/n; ☺8am-1pm Mon-Fri) Changes US dollars and euros. There's also an ATM but it only accepts MasterCard.
Banco Santander (Av Policarpo Toro; ☺8am-1pm Mon-Fri) Currency exchange (until 11am), and has two ATMs that accept Visa and MasterCard. Credit-card holders can also get cash

advances at the counter during opening hours (bring your passport).

Farmacia Cruz Verde (Av Atamu Tekena; ⊗8:30am-10pm Mon-Sat, 9:30am-9pm Sun) Large and well-stocked pharmacy.

Hare Pc (Av Atamu Tekena s/n; per hr CH$1200; ⊗8:30am-2pm & 4-7pm Mon-Sat, 8:30am-2pm Sun; 🛜) Internet and wi-fi access.

Hospital Hanga Roa (📞032-210-0215; Av Simon Paoa s/n) Recently modernized.

Omotohi Cybercafé (Av Te Pito o Te Henua s/n; per hr CH$1000-1500; ⊗8:30am-10pm Mon-Fri, 9:30am-10pm Sat & Sun; 🛜) Internet and wi-fi access, and call center.

Police (📞133)

Puna Vai (Av Hotu Matua; ⊗8:30am-1:30pm & 3-8pm Mon-Sat, 9am-2pm Sun) This petrol station also doubles as an exchange office. Much more convenient than the bank (no queues, better rates, longer opening hours).

Sernatur (📞032-210-0255; www.chile.travel/en.html; Av Policarpo Toro s/n; ⊗9am-6pm Mon-Fri, 10am-1pm Sat) Has brochures, maps and lists of accommodations. Some staff speak English.

PARQUE NACIONAL RAPA NUI

Since 1935, much of Rapa Nui's land and all of the archaeological sites have been a **national park** (www.conaf.cl; adult/child CH$30,000/15,000; ⊗9am-4pm) administered by Conaf, which charges admission at Orongo and Rano Raraku that is valid for the whole park for five days as of the first day of entrance. You're allowed one visit to Orongo and one visit to Rano Raraku. There are ranger information stations at Orongo, Anakena and Rano Raraku.

🅞 Sights

🅞 Northern Circuit

North of Ahu Tahai, the road is rough. Your best bet is to explore the area on foot, on horseback or by mountain bike.

Ana Kakenga   CAVE
About 2km north of Tahai is Ana Kakenga, or Dos Ventanas. This site comprises two caves opening onto the ocean (bring a torch).

Ahu Tepeu   ARCHAEOLOGICAL SITE
This *ahu* has several fallen *moai* and a village site with foundations of *hare paenga* (elliptical houses) and the walls of several round houses, consisting of loosely piled stones.

Ana Te Pahu   CAVE
Off the dirt road to Akivi, Ana Te Pahu is former cave dwellings with an overgrown garden of sweet potatoes, taro and bananas. The caves here are lava tubes, created when rock solidified around a flowing stream of molten lava.

Ahu Akivi   ARCHAEOLOGICAL SITE
Unusual for its inland location, Ahu Akivi, restored in 1960, sports seven restored *moai*. They are the only ones that face toward the sea, but, like all *moai,* they overlook the site of a village, traces of which can still be seen. The site has proved to have astronomical significance: at the equinoxes, the seven statues look directly at the setting sun.

⭐**Maunga Terevaka**   MOUNTAIN
Maunga Terevaka is the island's highest point (507m). This barren hill is only accessible on foot or on horseback and is worth the effort as it offers sensational panoramic views.

Puna Pau   ARCHAEOLOGICAL SITE
The volcanic Puna Pau quarry was used to make the reddish, cylindrical *pukao* (topknots) that were placed on many *moai.* Some 60 of these were transported to sites around the island, and another 25 remain in or near the quarry.

🅞 Southwestern Circuit

Ana Kai Tangata   CAVE
This vast cave carved into black cliffs sports beautiful rock paintings. However, entrance is forbidden due to falling rocks.

⭐**Rano Kau & Orongo Ceremonial Village**   CRATER LAKE
Nearly covered in a bog of floating totora reeds, this crater lake resembles a giant witch's cauldron – awesome! Perched 400m above, on the edge of the crater wall on one side and abutting a vertical drop plunging down to the cobalt-blue ocean on the other side, **Orongo ceremonial village** (adult/child CH$30,000/15,000; ⊗9am-4pm) boasts one of the South Pacific's most dramatic landscapes. It overlooks several small *motu* (offshore islands), including Motu Nui, Motu Iti and Motu Kau Kau. Built into the side of the slope, the houses have walls of overlapping stone slabs, with an arched roof of similar materials, making them appear partly subterranean. Orongo was the focus of an island-wide bird cult linked to the god Makemake in the 18th and 19th centuries. Birdman petroglyphs are visible on a cluster of boulders between the cliff top and the edge of the crater. Orongo is either a steepish climb or a short scenic drive 4km from the center of town.

Ahu Vinapu
ARCHAEOLOGICAL SITE

Beyond the eastern end of the airport runway, a road heads south past some large oil tanks to this ceremonial platform, with two major *ahu*. One of them features neatly hewn, mortarless blocks akin to those found in Inka ruins. Both once supported *moai* that are now broken and lying facedown.

◉ Northeastern Circuit

★ Anakena
BEACH

Beach bums in search of a place to wallow will love this picture-postcard-perfect, white-sand beach. It also forms a perfect backdrop for **Ahu Nau Nau**, which comprises seven *moai,* some with topknots. On a rise south of the beach stands **Ahu Ature Huki** and its lone *moai,* which was re-erected by Norwegian explorer Thor Heyerdahl with the help of a dozen islanders in 1956.

Facilities include public toilets as well as food and souvenir stalls.

Ovahe
BEACH

This beach offers more seclusion than Anakena for wannabe Robinson Crusoes but is considered dangerous because of falling rocks.

Ahu Te Pito Kura
ARCHAEOLOGICAL SITE

Beside Bahía de La Pérouse, a nearly 10m long *moai* lies face down with its neck broken; it's the largest *moai* moved from Rano Raraku and erected on an *ahu*. A topknot – oval rather than round as at Vinapu – lies nearby.

Papa Vaka Petroglyphs
ARCHAEOLOGICAL SITE

About 100m off the coastal road (look for the sign), you'll find a couple of massive basaltic slabs decorated with carvings featuring a tuna, a shark, an octopus and a large canoe.

Península Poike
PENINSULA

At the eastern end of the island, this high plateau is crowned by the extinct volcano **Maunga Pu A Katiki** (400m) and bound in by steep cliffs. There are also three small volcanic domes, one of which sports a huge mask carved into the rock that looks like a giant gargoyle. Also worth looking for is a series of small *moai* that lie face down, hidden amid the grass, as well as the **Grotto of the Virgins** (Ana O Keke). It's worth crawling inside if you don't feel dizzy to admire a series of petroglyphs. The best way to soak up the primordial rawness of Península Poike is to take a day hike with a guide because the sights are hard to find.

> **ⓘ TICKETS FOR PARQUE NACIONAL RAPA NUI**
>
> Tickets for Parque Nacional Rapa Nui can be bought on arrival at the airport – look for the small booth. It's usually cheaper to pay in US dollars (US$60) than in Chilean pesos (CH$30,000). Children pay half price. Tickets are valid for five days as of the first day of entrance. It's also possible to buy them at **Conaf** (☑ 032-2100-827; www.conaf. cl; Sector Mataveri; tickets adult/child CH$30,000/15,000; ☉ 9am-4pm). Note that tickets are not sold at Orongo and Rano Raraku.

★ Ahu Tongariki
ARCHAEOLOGICAL SITE

The monumental Ahu Tongariki has plenty to set your camera's flash popping. With 15 imposing statues, it is the largest *ahu* ever built. The statues gaze over a large, level village site, with ruined remnants scattered about and some petroglyphs nearby; some figures include a turtle with a human face, a tuna fish and a birdman motif. The site was restored by a Japanese team between 1992 and 1995. A 1960 tsunami had flattened the statues and scattered several topknots far inland. Only one topknot has been returned to its place atop a *moai*.

★ Rano Raraku
ARCHAEOLOGICAL SITE

(adult/child   CH$30,000/15,000;   ☉ 9am-4pm)

Known as 'the nursery,' the volcano of Rano Raraku, about 18km from Hanga Roa, is the quarry for the hard tuff from which the *moai* were cut. You'll feel as though you're stepping back into early Polynesian times, wandering among dozens of *moai* in all stages of progress studded on the southern slopes of the volcano. At the top, the 360-degree view is truly awesome. Within the crater are a small, glistening lake and about 20 standing *moai*. On the southeastern slope of the mountain, look for the unique, kneeling Moai Tukuturi.

UNDERSTAND EASTER ISLAND

Easter Island Today

In 2008 Easter Island was granted a special status. It is now a *territoria especial* (special territory) within Chile, which means greater autonomy for the islanders. But independence is not the order of the day – ongoing economic reliance on mainland Chile renders this option unlikely in the foreseeable future.

The main claim is for the return of native lands. Indigenous Rapa Nui control almost no land outside Hanga Roa. A national park (designated in 1935) comprises more than a third of the island, and nearly all the remainder belongs to Chile. Native groups have asked the Chilean government and the UN to return the park to aboriginal hands. Since 2010 a land dispute has opposed one Rapa Nui clan to the owners of the Hanga Roa hotel.

The Rapa Nui are also concerned about the development and control of the tourism industry. Mass tourism it ain't, but the rising number of visitors – from about 30,000 10 years ago to approximately 95,000 tourists in 2014 – has had an impact on the environment.

The recent influx of mainland Chileans (mostly construction workers) has fostered tensions with some locals, who see mainland Chileans as 'troublemakers.' There are plans to establish tighter immigration controls for the island, similar to those in place in Ecuador's Galápagos Islands.

History

The first islanders arrived either from the Marquesas, the Mangarevas, the Cooks or Pitcairn Island between the 4th and 8th centuries.

The Rapa Nui developed a unique civilization, characterized by the construction of the ceremonial stone platforms called *ahu* and the famous Easter Island statues called

SUSTAINABLE TRAVEL

Easter Island is a superb open-air museum, but it's under threat due to the growing number of visitors. A few rules:

➡ Don't walk on the *ahu* (ceremonial stone platforms), as they are revered by locals as burial sites.

➡ It's illegal to remove or relocate rocks from any of the archaeological structures.

➡ Don't touch petroglyphs, as they're very fragile.

➡ Stay on designated paths.

➡ Motor vehicles are not allowed on Península Poike or Terevaka.

➡ Don't pitch your tent in the park.

moai. The population probably peaked at around 15,000 in the 17th century. Conflict over land and resources erupted in intertribal warfare by the late 17th century, only shortly before the arrival of Europeans, and the population started to decline. More recent dissension between different clans led to bloody wars and cannibalism, and many *moai* were toppled from their *ahu*. Natural disasters, such as earthquakes and tsunamis, may have also contributed to the destruction. The only *moai* that are left standing today were restored during the last century.

Contact with outsiders nearly annihilated the Rapa Nui people. A raid by Peruvian blackbirders (slavers) in 1862 took 1000 islanders away to work the guano (manure) deposits of Peru's Chincha islands. After intense pressure from the Catholic Church, some survivors were returned to Easter Island, but disease and hard labor had already killed about 90% of them. A brief period of French-led missionary activity saw most of the surviving islanders converted to Catholicism in the 1860s.

Chile officially annexed the island in 1888 during a period of expansion that included the acquisition of territory from Peru and Bolivia after the War of the Pacific (1879–84).

By 1897 Rapa Nui had fallen under the control of a single wool company, which became the island's de facto government, continuing the wool trade until the middle of the 20th century. In 1953 the Chilean government took charge of the island, continuing the imperial rule to which islanders had been subject for nearly a century. With restricted rights, including travel restrictions and ineligibility to vote, the islanders felt they were treated like second-class citizens. In 1967 the establishment of a regular commercial air link between Santiago and Tahiti, with Rapa Nui as a refueling stop, opened up the island to the world and brought many benefits to Rapa Nui people.

The People of Rapa Nui

Rapa Nui is a fairly conservative society, and family life, marriage and children still play a central role in everyday life, as does religion.

More than a third of the population is from mainland Chile or Europe. The most striking feature is the intriguing blend of Polynesian and Chilean customs. Although they will never admit it overtly, the people of Rapa Nui have one foot in South America and one foot in Polynesia.

LEARN HOW TO TELL YOUR AHU FROM YOUR MOAI

You don't need a university degree to appreciate the archaeological remains on Easter Island. The following explanations should suffice.

Ahu

Ahu were village burial sites and ceremonial centers and are thought to derive from altars in French Polynesia. Some 350 of these stone platforms are dotted around the coast. *Ahu* are paved on the upper surface with more or less flat stones, and they have a vertical wall on the seaward side and at each end.

Moai

Easter Island's most pervasive image, the enigmatic *moai* are massive carved figures that probably represent clan ancestors. From 2m to 10m tall, these stony-faced statues stood with their backs to the Pacific Ocean. Some *moai* have been completely restored, while others have been re-erected but are eroded. Many more lie on the ground, toppled over.

For several centuries, controversy has raged over the techniques employed to move and raise the *moai*. For many decades most experts believed they were dragged on a kind of wooden sledge, or pushed on top of rollers, but in the early 2000s archaeologists came to the conclusion that the *moai* were not dragged horizontally but moved in a vertical position using ropes. This theory would tally with oral history, which says that the *moai* 'walked' to their *ahu*. As you'll soon realize, it's a never-ending debate.

Topknots

Archaeologists believe that the reddish cylindrical *pukao* (topknots) that crown many *moai* reflect a male hairstyle once common on Rapa Nui.

Despite its unique language and history, contemporary Rapa Nui does not appear to be a 'traditional' society – its continuity was shattered by the near extinction of the population in the last century. However, although they have largely adapted to a Westernized lifestyle, Rapa Nui people are fiercely proud of their history and culture, and they strive to keep their traditions alive.

Arts

As in Tahiti, traditional dancing is not a mere tourist attraction but one of the most vibrant forms of expression of traditional Polynesian culture. A couple of talented dance groups perform regularly at various hotels. Tattooing is another aspect of Polynesian culture, and it has enjoyed a revival among the young generation since the late 1980s.

There are also strong carving traditions on Easter Island.

The Landscape

Easter Island is roughly triangular in shape, with an extinct volcanic cone in each corner – Maunga (Mt) Terevaka, in the northwest corner, is the highest point at 507m. The island's maximum length is just 24km, and it is only 12km across at its widest point. Much of the interior of Easter Island is grassland, with cultivable soil interspersed with rugged lava fields. Wave erosion has created steep cliffs around much of the coast, and Anakena, on the north shore, is the only broad sandy beach. Erosion, exacerbated by overgrazing and deforestation, is the island's most serious problem. To counteract the effects of erosion, a small-scale replanting program is under way on Península Poike.

SURVIVAL GUIDE

ⓘ Directory A–Z

ACCOMMODATIONS

If you come here from mainland Chile, be prepared for a shock. Despite a high number of establishments – about 150 when we visited – accommodations on Easter Island are pricey for what you get. All accommodations options are located in Hanga Roa except one luxury hotel. *Residenciales* (homestays) form the bedrock of accommodations on the island but there's a growing number of luxury options. At the other end of the scale, there are also a couple of camping grounds in Hanga Roa. Note that wild camping is forbidden in the national park.

PRACTICALITIES

→ *Mercurio,* the national daily newspaper, can be purchased at various shops in Hanga Roa.

→ Electricity is supplied at 240V, 50Hz AC.

→ Easter Island follows the metric system.

The following price ranges refer to a double room with private bathroom and breakfast.

$ less than CH$40,000
$$ CH$40,000–CH$80,000
$$$ more than CH$80,000

FOOD

The following price ranges refer to a standard main course.

$ less than CH$8000
$$ CH$8000–CH$15,000
$$$ more than CH$15,000

INTERNET ACCESS

You'll find internet cafes in Hanga Roa. Wi-fi is also available at most hotels and guesthouses but connections can be very slow at times.

MONEY

The local currency is the Chilean peso (CH$). A number of businesses on Rapa Nui, especially *residenciales,* hotels and rental agencies, accept US cash (and euros, albeit at a pinch). Travelers from Tahiti must bring US cash (or euros) as Tahitian currency is not accepted.

ATMs Easter Island has only three ATMs, one of which accepts only MasterCard. Don't rely solely on your credit card and make sure you keep some cash in reserve.

Credit cards Many *residenciales,* hotels, restaurants and tour agencies accept credit cards.

Moneychangers There are two banks and an exchange office in Hanga Roa. US dollars are the best foreign currency to carry, followed by euros. Note that exchange rates on Easter Island are slightly lower than those offered in mainland Chile.

Taxes All prices are inclusive of tax.

Tipping and bargaining Tipping and bargaining are not traditionally part of Polynesian culture.

OPENING HOURS

The following are normal opening hours for Easter Island.

Offices 9am to 5pm Monday to Friday
Restaurants 11am to 10pm Monday to Saturday

TELEPHONE

Easter Island's international telephone code is the same as Chile's (☑ 56), and the area code (☑ 032) covers the whole island. You'll find several private call centers in town. Entel offers GSM cell-phone service, and prepaid SIM cards are available for purchase. Ask your service provider about international roaming agreements and the charges involved.

TOURIST INFORMATION

Easter Island Foundation (www.islandheritage.org) Background information on the island.

Lonely Planet (www.lonelyplanet.com/chile/rapa-nui-easter-island) Has travel news and tips.

❶ Getting There & Away

AIR

The only airline serving Easter Island is **LAN** (☑ 032-210-0279; www.lan.com; Av Atamu Tekena s/n; ⊙ 9am-4:30pm Mon-Fri, to 12:30pm Sat). It has daily flights to/from Santiago and one weekly flight to/from Pape'ete (Tahiti). A standard economy round-trip fare from Santiago can range from US$550 to US$900.

SEA

Few passenger services go to Easter Island. A few yachts stop here, mostly in January, February and March. Anchorages are not well sheltered.

❶ Getting Around

Outside Hanga Roa, the entire east coast road and the road to Anakena are paved.

TO/FROM THE AIRPORT

The airport is just on the outskirts of Hanga Roa. Accommodations proprietors wait at the airport and will shuttle you for free to your hotel or *residencial.*

BICYCLE

Mountain bikes can be rented in Hanga Roa for about CH$10,000 per day.

CAR & MOTORCYCLE

Some hotels and agencies rent 4WDs for CH$40,000 to CH$60,000 for 24 hours depending on the vehicle. A word of warning: insurance is *not* available, so you're not covered should the vehicle get any damage. Don't leave valuables in your car. Scooters and motorcycles are rented for about CH$20,000 to CH$25,000 a day.

You can contact the following outfits.

Haunani (☑ 032-210-0353; Av Atamu Tekena s/n; ⊙ 9am-8pm Mon-Sat) On the main drag.

Insular Rent a Car (☑ 032-210-0480; www.rentainsular.cl; Av Atamu Tekena s/n; ⊙ 9am-8pm) Also rents mountain bikes.

Oceanic Rapa Nui Rent a Car (☑ 032-210-0985; www.rapanuioceanic.com; Av Atamu Tekena s/n; ⊙ 8am-8pm) On the main drag.

TAXI

Taxis cost a flat CH$2000 for most trips around town and CH$3000 to the airport.

EASTER ISLAND (RAPA NUI) SURVIVAL GUIDE

Understand Chile

Chile Today

In Chile, the ground is shifting, yet for once it's not another earthquake. Former president Michelle Bachelet is back at the helm, and she has made addressing inequality the mission of her administration. At the same time, Chile's steady growth spurt is showing signs of fatigue. Given the falling price of the country's number-one export, copper, many wonder if the country will see through massive reforms. One thing is certain for this small engine that could: the status quo is no longer enough.

Best on Film

Gloria (2013) A fresh and funny portrait of an unconventional 58-year-old woman.

The Maid (2009) A maid questions her lifelong loyalty.

Violeta Went to Heaven (2012) Biopic of rebel songstress Violeta Parra.

Motorcycle Diaries (2004) The road trip that made a revolutionary.

No (2013) Did an ad campaign really take down a dictator?

180° South (2010) Follows a traveler exploring untainted territory.

Best in Print

Deep Down Dark (Hector Tobar) The gripping story of the 33 trapped miners.

In Patagonia (Bruce Chatwin) Iconic work on Patagonian ethos.

Patagonia Express (Luis Sepúlveda) Masterful and funny end-of-the-world tales.

Twenty Love Poems and a Song of Despair (Pablo Neruda) A passionate classic.

Voyage of the Beagle (Charles Darwin) Observes native fauna and volcanoes.

Chilenismos: A Dictionary and Phrasebook for Chilean Spanish (Daniel Joelson) Translates local lingo.

Toward a Level Playing Field

The highest building on the continent, the 64-story Gran Torre Santiago, was completed in 2013, an irrefutable symbol of the country's newfound eminence. At around the same time, Chile became the first South American country to earn membership in the Organization for Economic Cooperation and Development (OECD). Yet there is room for improvement. Of all OECD members, Chile has the greatest levels of inequality.

One percent of the population holds half the country's wealth. The number of millionaires here doubled in the early 2000s, but those people living in poverty represent 14.4% of the population. Although poverty has declined by a third in the past decade, critics argue that much more can be done. The plan is to invest in public education and healthcare, two areas where the public has been clamoring for improvement.

Within a larger, controversial effort to revise the dictatorship-era constitution, Chile is also saying goodbye to binominal voting, a system that distorted votes by giving half of the representation in each district to the second-place coalition if it earned a third of the votes. Starting in 2017 the new system should help independent candidates get a foot in the door.

On the Rebound

Urban, poor, liberal, conservative – all of Chile is reaching for an upgrade. While its citizens negotiate the terms with some frustration, it helps to remember that Chile has been through so much in recent years. In February, 2010, an 8.8 earthquake hit off the central coast with the power of 10,000 Hiroshima bombs. With the ensuing tsunami, the events were responsible for hundreds of deaths and US$30 billion dollars in damage. Yet two months later, students returned to school, and the affected roads, ports and airports were back up. In large part the recovery depended on citizens who helped each other with no formal emergency response in place.

Months later, national solidarity strengthened as the country cheered on 33 miners trapped in the San José mine. While rescue crews worked against the clock, the workers survived 69 days underground, and emerged to both their families and the whole world watching.

Too bad there is no award for the most dogged country, because Chile would be a serious candidate.

New & Improved
Despite the challenges, Chile has been plodding toward progress, a country eager to redefine itself in so many ways. In the desert north, construction has begun on the European Extremely Large Telescope, or E-ELT, a cutting-edge space observatory that will examine the origin of the planets and search for water sources. Meanwhile, in the central city of Rancagua, a chapel by Antoni Gaudí is under way. Slated for 2017, the neo-baroque building will be the modernist's only design outside Spain.

Social progress is also on the agenda. Chile legalized civil unions for both same-sex and unmarried couples in January, 2015. Progressives hope that health reforms will legalize abortion, though opposition has been very vocal.

Chile's quest for connectivity continues, with road building reaching into the remotest regions of Patagonia and Tierra del Fuego. Longtime plans were finally approved for the largest suspension bridge in Latin America, which would connect the island of Chiloé to the Lakes District mainland.

Moving forward has also meant reassessing priorities. In 2014, the government rejected HidroAysén's controversial plans for a 3.2-billion-dollar hydroelectric project consisting of dams throughout Patagonia, though plans are still going forward for dams on the Ríos Manso, Puelo and Cuervo in the Lakes District and Patagonia, despite local opposition. Still, many hope that the government's about face over HidroAysén signals that Chile may finally be taking into account its greatest asset – nature.

Chile has both the driest desert in the world, with spectacular stargazing; 80% of the glaciers on the continent; and diverse, sparsely populated landscapes. It is no wonder experts forecast that it's on its way to becoming a leading adventure-travel destination.

POPULATION: **17 MILLION**

MEDIAN AGE: **33**

INTERNET USERS: **7 MILLION**

UNEMPLOYMENT: **6%**

LIFE EXPECTANCY: **78 YEARS**

INFLATION: **1.7%**

GDP: **$277 BILLION**

if Chile were 100 people
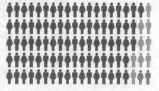

89 would be white
9 would be Mapuche
2 would be other

belief systems
(% of population)
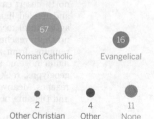

67 Roman Catholic
16 Evangelical
2 Other Christian
4 Other
11 None

population per sq km
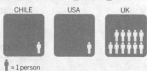

CHILE   USA   UK

≈ 1 person

History

With the oldest inhabited site in the Americas, Chile's astounding past is only starting to be unearthed and understood. Chile has come far from its first days as a backwater of the Spanish empire. Today's culture still bears the mark of having a small landowning elite, a long industry of mineral exploitation, and politics which both thwarted and strove for reform. Its ultimate resilience has led Chile to become one of the most stable and influential countries of Latin America.

The Chinchorro culture began mummifying their dead some 2000 years before the Egyptians. The oldest known mummy dates from around 5050 BC.

Beginnings

A small child's footprint left in a marshy field rocked the foundations of American archaeology during the 1980s. The 12,500-year-old print proved human habitation in Monte Verde, near Puerto Montt. Other evidence dated back as far as 33,000 years. These highly controversial dates negate the long-accepted Clovis paradigm, which stated that the Americas were populated via the Bering land bridge some 11,500 years ago, after which the Clovis people scattered southward. New theories suggest multiple entries, different routes or coastal landings by the first peoples. Following a landmark 1998 convention, the Monte Verde site was acknowledged as the oldest inhabited site in the Americas, although more recent discoveries, notably in New Mexico, date back as far as 40,000 years.

Early Cultures

Most pre-Columbian remains have been recovered in the north of Chile, preserved by the extreme desert aridity. The nomadic Chinchorro culture left behind the oldest known intentionally preserved mummies. In north desert canyons, Aymara farmers cultivated maize, grew potatoes and tended llama and alpaca; their descendants still practice similar agricultural techniques around Parque Nacional Lauca. Also in Chile's northern reaches, the Atacameño culture left remarkably well-preserved remains, from mummies to ornate tablets used in the preparation of hallucinogenic substances. The El Molle and Tiwanaku left enormous geoglyphs, rock etchings and ceramics, still visible in Chile's northern reaches. Meanwhile, Chango fisherfolk occupied northern coastal areas, and Diaguita peoples inhabited the inland river valleys.

TIMELINE	12,500 BC	1520	1535
	A child's footprint discovered in Monte Verde outside Puerto Montt – the oldest inhabited site in South America – disproves the supposed human migration across the Bering land bridge.	After his fleet faces mutiny and shipwreck, Ferdinand Magellan is the first European to sight Chilean territory on November 1, 1520 while sailing the strait now named for him.	Conquistador Diego de Almagro marches on Chile with 500 men, 100 African slaves and 10,000 Indian porters. Many freeze to death on Andean passes. Finding no riches, Almagro abandons his claim.

The invasive Inka culture enjoyed a brief ascendancy in northern Chile, but its rule barely touched the central valley and the forests of the south, where the sedentary farmers (Picunche) and shifting cultivators (Mapuche) fiercely resisted any incursions. Meanwhile the Cunco fished and farmed on the island of Chiloé and along the shores of the gulfs of Reloncaví and Ancud.

Invasion

In 1495, unbeknown to indigenous populations, the Americas were divided up by two superpowers of the day – Spain and Portugal. The papal Treaty of Tordesillas delivered all the territory west of Brazil to Spain. By the mid-16th century, the Spaniards dominated most of the area from Florida and Mexico to central Chile. Though few in number, the conquerors were determined and ruthless, exploiting factionalism among indigenous groups and intimidating native peoples with their horses and firearms. But their greatest ally was infectious disease, to which the natives lacked immunity.

The Spaniards' first ill-fated foray into northern Chile was led over frozen Andean passes in 1535 by Diego de Almagro. Though a failure, it laid the groundwork for Pedro de Valdivia's 1540 expedition. After surviving the parched desert, they reached Chile's fertile Mapocho Valley in 1541. After subduing local indigenous groups, Valdivia founded the city of Santiago on February 12. Six months later the indigenous peoples struck back, razing the town and all but wiping out the settlers' supplies. But the Spaniards clung on, and the population burgeoned. By the time of his death in 1553, at the hands of Mapuche forces led by the famous *caciques* (chiefs) Caupolicán and Lautaro, Valdivia had founded numerous settlements and laid the groundwork for a new society.

Colonial Chile

Lust for gold and silver was always high on the Spaniards' agenda, but they soon realized that the true wealth of the New World consisted of the large indigenous populations. The *encomienda* system granted

> Who knew that the ancients did drugs? Ancient Atacameños had a hallucinogenic habit, but all that remains are the accessories: mini spatulas, snuff boards, tubes, little boxes and woolen bags.

COLD HARD FACTS

Little is known about the Selk'nam (Ona) people who once inhabited Magallanes, but it is well documented that they withstood extreme temperatures wearing little or no clothing. On the **Chilean Cultural Heritage Site** (www.nuestro.cl), anthropologist Francisco Mena recounts, 'An investigator of the 19th century writes that he once met a naked man, and asked him how come he felt no cold. And the Selk'nam answered: My whole body has become face.' For more interesting historical anecdotes, explore the website, which also has an English version.

1535–1880	1540	1541	1548
The Arauco War marks the start of the Mapuches' 300-year resistance. Most meet Chile's revolt against the Spanish crown with indifference. The area south of the Río Biobío remains their stronghold.	After crossing the Atacama Desert and facing its blistering extremes, Pedro de Valdivia and a group of 150 Spaniards start a colony on the banks of the Río Mapocho.	Santiago is officially founded on September 11, despite fierce resistance by indigenous Araucanians, numbering around 500,000. The presence of colonists brings disease and death to the indigenous people.	Wine comes to Chile via missionaries and conquistadores. Jesuit priests cultivated early vineyards of rustic *pais* grapes; today Chile has more than 70 wineries and international distribution.

individual Spaniards rights to indigenous labor and tribute. It was easily established in northern Chile (then part of Peru) where the indigenous population were highly organized and even accustomed to similar forms of exploitation.

The Spaniards also established dominance in central Chile, but the semi-sedentary and nomadic peoples of the south mounted vigorous resistance. Feral horses taken from the Argentine pampas greatly aided the Mapuche, whose new mobility enhanced their ability to strike.

Despite the Crown's distant disapproval, Valdivia began rewarding his followers with enormous land grants. Such *latifundios* (estates) became an enduring feature of Chilean agriculture and society, with many intact as late as the 1960s.

Mestizo children of mixed Spanish and indigenous parentage soon outnumbered indigenous people, whose population declined after epidemics, forced-labor abuses and warfare. Chile's neo-aristocracy encouraged the landless *mestizo* population to attach themselves as *inquilinos* (tenant farmers) to large rural estates.

Caupolicán led the Mapuches in their first uprising against the Spanish conquistadores. It's believed he became a *toqui* (military leader) by holding a tree trunk for three days and nights and improvising a poetical speech to incite Mapuches to rebel against the Spanish.

Revolution

Independence movements sparked between 1808 and 1810 were born from the emergence of the *criollo* (creole) class – American-born Spaniards pushing for self-government. To facilitate tax collection, Madrid decreed that all Spanish trade pass overland through Panama rather than directly by ship. This cumbersome system hampered commerce and eventually cost Spain its empire.

During colonial times, Chile was judged to be a subdivision of the Lima-based Viceroyalty of Peru. Called the Audiencia de Chile, it reached from present-day Chañaral south to Puerto Aisén, plus the present-day Argentinean provinces of Mendoza, San Juan and San Luis. Chile developed in near isolation from Peru, creating a wholly distinct identity.

By the 1820s, independence movements were igniting throughout South America. From Venezuela, a *criollo* army under Simón Bolívar fought its way toward Peru. The Argentine liberator José de San Martín marched over the Andes into Chile, occupied Santiago and sailed north to Lima.

San Martín appointed Bernardo O'Higgins second-in-command of forces. O'Higgins, the illegitimate son of an Irishman who had served the Spaniards as Viceroy of Peru, became supreme director of the new Chilean republic. San Martín helped drive Spain from Peru, transporting his army in ships either seized from the Spaniards or purchased from Britons or North Americans seeking commercial gain. Thus it was that Scotsman Thomas Cochrane, a colorful former Royal Navy officer, founded and commanded Chile's navy.

Isabel Allende's historical novel *Inés of My Soul* is based on facts from the real-life *conquistadora* and former seamstress who fatefully trailed Pedro de Valdivia to the future Chile.

1553	1818	1834–35	1860
Conquistador Pedro de Valdivia is captured in the Battle of Tucapel, when 6000 Mapuche warriors attack Spanish forts in the south. Valdivia is bound to a tree and beheaded.	With independence movements sweeping the continent, Argentine José de San Martín liberates Santiago. Bernardo O'Higgins, the illegitimate son of an Irishman, becomes 'supreme director' of the Chilean republic.	HMS *Beagle* sails along Chile's coast with Charles Darwin on board; the planned two-year expedition actually lasts five, giving Darwin fodder for his later-developed theory of evolution.	French adventurer Orélie-Antoine de Tounens befriends Mapuche leaders and assumes the title King of Araucania and Patagonia. This seemingly protective act ends in his confinement to an insane asylum.

The Early Republic

Battered but buoyed by independence, Chile was a fraction of its present size, sharing ambiguous boundaries with Bolivia, Argentina and the hostile Mapuche nation south of the Río Biobío.

Politically stable, Chile rapidly developed agriculture, mining, industry and commerce. O'Higgins dominated politics for five years after formal independence in 1818, but the landowning elite objected to increased taxes, abolition of titles and limitations on inheritance. Forced to resign in 1823, O'Higgins went into exile in Peru.

Diego Portales was interior minister and de facto dictator until his execution following an 1837 uprising. His constitution centralized power in Santiago, limited suffrage to the propertied and established indirect elections for the presidency and senate. It lasted until 1925.

The end of the 19th century was an era of shifting boundaries. Treaties with the Mapuche (1881) brought temperate southern territories under Chilean authority. Chile focused much of its energy on northern expansion and the War of the Pacific. Forced to abandon much of Patagonia to Argentina, Chile sought a broader Pacific presence, and annexed the tiny remote Easter Island (also known as Rapa Nui) in 1888.

Chile may seem homogenous, but black culture dates back to early Arica where a black mayor was elected in 1620 (the viceroy of Peru later annulled the victory). Today *Foundación Oro Negro* preserves black cultural heritage.

HISTORY THE EARLY REPUBLIC

Civil War

Mining expansion created a new working class, as well as a class of nouveau riche, both of which challenged the political power of the landowners. The first political figure to tackle the dilemma of Chile's badly distributed wealth was President José Manuel Balmaceda, elected in 1886.

MINING FOR PROSPERITY

Chile's wealth and prosperity is owed in part to its wrangling of the north in 1879. In the five-year War of the Pacific (1879–84) Chile annexed vast areas of land from Peru and Bolivia. The battles began after Bolivia prohibited a Chilean company from exploiting the nitrate deposits in Atacama, then owned by Bolivia. Chile retaliated by seizing the Bolivian port of Antofagasta and wresting the Tacna and Arica provinces from Peru, thus robbing the Bolivians of all access to the Pacific. This fiercely fought campaign is still celebrated by Chileans with as much gusto as it is bitterly resented by Peruvians and Bolivians. And it's still a prickly thorn in their neighborly relations today.

Santiago's intervention proved a bonanza. The nitrate boom allowed Chile's high society to prosper. British, North American and German investors supplied most of the capital. Railroads revolutionized infrastructure, and the economy boomed. The addition of ports such as Iquique and Antofagasta only augmented Chile's success.

When the nitrate bubble eventually burst, copper, which still propels the Chilean economy, was there to replace it.

1879–84	1881	1885–1900	1888–1960s
Chile's active development of nitrate deposits in Peruvian and Bolivian territories leads to the War of the Pacific; Chile increases its territory by one-third after defeating both countries.	While focusing on northward expansion, Chile signs a treaty with Argentina conceding all of eastern Patagonia but retaining sovereignty over the Strait of Magellan.	British, North American and German capital turn the Atacama into a bonanza, as nitrates bring some prosperity, create an urban middle class and fund the government.	Chile annexes Easter Island and confines Rapa Nui people to Hanga Roa. The rest of the island becomes a sheep ranch, not reopening to its own citizens until the 1960s.

Balmaceda's administration undertook major public-works projects, revolutionizing infrastructure and improving hospitals and schools. In 1890, a conservative Congress voted to depose him.

Naval Commander Jorge Montt was elected to head a provisional government. In the ensuing civil war, Montt's navy controlled the ports and eventually defeated the government, despite army support for Balmaceda. Over 10,000 died and Balmaceda shot himself.

Twentieth Century

The Chilean economy took a hit for its crippling dependence on nitrates, which were being replaced by new petroleum-based fertilizers. The 1914 opening of the Panama Canal made the Cape Horn route, and its many Chilean ports, nearly obsolete.

After periods of poor leadership, several leftist groups briefly imposed a socialist republic and merged to form the Socialist Party. Splits divided the Communist Party, while splinter groups from radical and reformist parties created a bewildering mix of new political organizations. For most of the 1930s and '40s the democratic left dominated Chilean politics.

Meanwhile, the early 20th century saw North American companies gain control of the copper mines, the cornerstone – then and now – of the Chilean economy. WWII augmented the demand for Chilean copper, promoting economic growth even as Chile remained neutral.

Land Reform

In the 1920s, haciendas (large rural landholdings) controlled 80% of the prime agricultural land. *Inquilinos* remained at the mercy of landowners for access to housing, soil and subsistence. Even their votes belonged to landowners. Haciendas had little incentive to modernize, and production stagnated – a situation that changed little until the 1960s.

Reformist sentiment stirred fear in the old order. Conservative and liberal parties decided to join forces. Their candidate, Jorge Alessandri, son of former president Arturo Alessandri, scraped through the 1958 election with less than 32% of the vote. An opposition Congress forced Alessandri to accept modest land-reform legislation, beginning a decade-long battle with the haciendas.

The 1964 presidential election was a choice between socialist Salvador Allende and Christian Democrat Eduardo Frei Montalva, who drew support from conservative groups. Both parties promised agrarian reform, supported rural unionization and promised an end to the hacienda system. Allende was undermined by leftist factionalism and Frei won comfortably.

Robert Harvey's extremely readable *Liberators: South America's Struggle for Independence* (2002) tells the epic history of colonial Latin America through larger-than-life heroes and swashbucklers such as O'Higgins, San Martín and Lord Cochrane.

1890–91	1927	1938–46	1945
Tackling unequally distributed wealth and power with reforms, President José Manuel Balmaceda ignites congressional rebellion in 1890; it results in a civil war with 10,000 deaths and Balmaceda's suicide.	General Carlos Ibáñez del Campo establishes a de facto dictatorship, which will prove to be one of the longest lasting of 10 governments in the unstable decade.	Communists, socialists and radicals form the Popular Front coalition, rapidly becoming popular with the unionized working class and playing a leading role in the Chilean labor movement.	Poet and foreign consul Gabriela Mistral becomes the first Latin American and fifth woman to win the Nobel Prize (for literature). Her start was as a shy rural schoolmistress.

Christian Democratic Period

Committed to social transformation, the Christian Democrats attempted to control inflation, balance imports and exports and implement reforms. However, their policies threatened both the traditional elite's privileges and the radical left's working-class support.

The country's economy had declined under Alessandri's presidency, driving the dispossessed to the cities, where squatter settlements, known as *callampas* (mushrooms), sprang up almost overnight. Attacks increased on the export sector, then dominated by US interests. President Frei advocated 'Chileanization' of the copper industry (getting rid of foreign investors), while the Allende camp supported placing the industry under state control.

The Christian Democrats also faced challenges from violent groups such as the Movimiento de Izquierda Revolucionario (MIR; Leftist Revolutionary Movement), which began among upper-middle-class students in Concepción. Urban laborers joined suit, forming the allied Frente de Trabajadores Revolucionarios (Revolutionary Workers Front). Activism also caught on with peasants who longed for land reform. Other leftist groups supported strikes and land seizures by the Mapuche and rural laborers.

Frei's reforms were too slow to appease leftists and too fast for the conservative National Party. Despite better living conditions for many rural workers and gains in education and public health, the country was plagued by inflation, dependence on foreign markets and capital, and inequitable income distribution. The Christian Democrats could not satisfy rising expectations in Chile's increasingly militant and polarized society.

In Santiago's poor urban neighborhood of La Victoria, the protest murals by the BRP (Brigada Ramona Parra) have appeared since the 1940s, stirring up subversive thought. View them along Avenida 30 de Mayo.

Allende's Rise to Power

In this discomforting political climate, a new leftist coalition coalesced. With Allende at its head, the Unidad Popular (UP) was shaping a radical program that included the nationalization of mines, banks and insurance, plus the expropriation and redistribution of large landholdings. In the 1970 election, Allende squeezed 36% of the vote against the National Party's 35%, becoming the world's first democratically elected Marxist president.

But the country – and even Allende's own coalition – was far from united. The UP consisted of socialist, communist and radical parties conflicted over objectives. Allende faced an opposition Congress, a suspicious US government, and right-wing extremists who even advocated his overthrow by violent means.

Allende's economic program, accomplished by evading rather than confronting Congress, included the state takeover of many private enterprises and massive income redistribution. By increasing government spending, the new president expected to bring the country out of recession. This worked briefly, but apprehensive businesspeople and

1948–58	1952	1960	1964
The Communist Party is banned due to the spreading fear that its electoral base is becoming too strong amid the growing conservative climate of the Cold War.	Ibáñez returns, this time as an elected president promising to sweep out corruption. He revokes the Communist Party ban but sweeps himself out with plans for an auto-coup.	The strongest earthquake ever recorded takes place in southern Chile. It flattens coastal towns between Concepción and Chiloé and creates a tsunami that hits Hawaii and Japan.	On Easter Island, the Rapa Nui (native islanders) are granted full Chilean citizenship and the right to vote. Three years later commercial flights will open it up to the world.

landowners, worried about expropriation and nationalization, sold off stock, machinery and livestock. Industrial production nose-dived, leading to shortages, hyperinflation and black marketeering.

Peasants, frustrated with an agrarian reform, seized land and agricultural production fell. The government had to use scarce foreign currency to import food. Chilean politics grew increasingly polarized and confrontational, as many of Allende's supporters resented his indirect approach to reform. The MIR intensified its guerrilla activities, and stories circulated in Santiago's factories about new armed communist organizations.

Expropriation of US-controlled copper mines and other enterprises, plus conspicuously friendly relations with Cuba, provoked US hostility. Later, hearings in the US Congress indicated that President Nixon and Secretary of State Kissinger had actively undercut Allende by discouraging credit from international finance organizations and supporting his opponents. Meanwhile, according to the memoirs of a Soviet defector published in 2005, the KGB withdrew support for Allende because of his refusal to use force against his opponents.

Faced with such difficulties, the Chilean government tried to forestall conflict by proposing clearly defined limits on nationalization. Unfortunately, neither extreme leftists, who believed that only force could achieve socialism, nor their rightist counterparts, who believed only force could prevent it, were open to compromise.

Rightist Backlash

In 1915, German sailors scuttled the SMS *Dresden* in the harbor of Isla Robinson Crusoe after being attacked by the British Royal Navy. The infamous war cruiser had successfully avoided detection throughout WWI, only to be discovered because its sailors had joined a soccer match on shore.

In 1972 Chile was paralyzed by a widespread truckers' strike, supported by the Christian Democrats and the National Party. As the government's authority crumbled, a desperate Allende invited constitutionalist army commander General Carlos Prats to occupy the critical post of interior minister, and he included an admiral and an air-force general in his cabinet. Despite the economic crisis, results of the March 1973 congressional elections demonstrated that Allende's support had actually increased since 1970 – but the unified opposition nevertheless strengthened its control of Congress, underscoring the polarization of Chilean politics. In June 1973 there was an unsuccessful military coup.

The next month, truckers and other rightists once again went on strike, supported by the entire opposition. Having lost military support, General Prats resigned, to be replaced by the relatively obscure General Augusto Pinochet Ugarte, whom both Prats and Allende thought loyal to constitutional government.

On September 11, 1973 Pinochet unleashed a brutal *golpe de estado* (coup d'état) that overthrew the UP government and resulted in Allende's death (an apparent suicide) and the death of thousands of Allende supporters. Police and the military apprehended thousands of leftists,

1970 〉	1973 〉	1973–89 〉	1978 〉
Salvador Allende becomes the world's first democratically elected Marxist president; radical social reform follows; the state takes control of private enterprises alongside massive income redistribution.	A military coup on September 11, 1973, overthrows the UP government, resulting in Allende's death (an apparent suicide) and the death of thousands of his supporters.	General Augusto Pinochet heads a durable junta that dissolves Congress, bans leftist parties and suspends all others, prohibiting nearly all political activity and ruling by decree.	Chile and Argentina almost go to war over three small islands in the Beagle Channel. The Beagle Conflict is finally settled by papal mediation in 1979.

suspected leftists and sympathizers. Many were herded into Santiago's National Stadium, where they suffered beatings, torture and even execution. Hundreds of thousands went into exile.

The military argued that force was necessary to remove Allende because his government had fomented political and economic chaos and because – so they claimed – he himself was planning to overthrow the constitutional order by force. Certainly, inept policies brought about this 'economic chaos,' but reactionary sectors, encouraged and abetted from abroad, exacerbated scarcities, producing a black market that further undercut order. Allende had demonstrated commitment to democracy, but his inability or unwillingness to control factions to his left terrified the middle class as well as the oligarchy.

Military Dictatorship

Many opposition leaders, some of whom had encouraged the coup, expected a quick return to civilian government, but General Pinochet had other ideas. From 1973 to 1989, he headed a durable junta that dissolved Congress, banned leftist parties and suspended all others, prohibited nearly all political activity and ruled by decree. Assuming the presidency in 1974, Pinochet sought to reorder the country's political and economic culture through repression, torture and murder. The Caravan of Death, a group of military that traveled by helicopter from town to town, mainly in northern Chile, killed many political opponents, several of whom had voluntarily turned themselves in. Detainees came from all sectors of society, from peasants to professors. Around 35,000 were tortured and 3000 were 'disappeared' during the 17-year regime.

The CNI (Centro Nacional de Informaciones or National Information Center) and its predecessor DINA (Directoria de Inteligencia Nacional or National Intelligence Directorate) were the most notorious practitioners of state terrorism. International assassinations were not unusual – a car bomb killed General Prats in Buenos Aires a year after the coup, and Christian Democrat leader Bernardo Leighton barely survived a shooting in Rome in 1975. Perhaps the most notorious case was the 1976 murder of Allende's foreign minister, Orlando Letelier, by a car bomb in Washington, DC.

By 1977 even air-force general Gustavo Leigh, a member of the junta, thought the campaign against 'subversion' so successful that he proposed a return to civilian rule, but Pinochet forced Leigh's resignation, ensuring the army's dominance and perpetuating himself in power. By 1980 Pinochet felt confident enough to submit a new, customized constitution to the electorate and wagered his own political future on it. In a plebiscite with narrow options, about two-thirds of the voters approved the constitution and ratified Pinochet's presidency until 1989, though many voters abstained in protest.

Norwegian Thor Heyerdahl explored Easter Island while crossing the Pacific in the 1950s; it became the centerpiece of his theories about the South American origins of Polynesian civilization. For more details, read *Aku Aku* and *Kon Tiki*.

1980	1989	1994	1998
Pinochet submits a new, customized constitution to the electorate that will ratify his presidency until 1989. It passes, though many voters protest by abstaining from voting.	The Concertación para la Democracia (Consensus for Democracy) is formed of 17 parties. Its candidate, Christian Democrat Patricio Aylwin, ousts Pinochet in the first free elections since 1970.	The new president, Christian Democrat Eduardo Frei, ushers in a leftist era but struggles with a limiting constitution in which the military still holds considerable power.	Pinochet is arrested in the UK on murder charges relating to his regime. It's one of the first arrests of a dictator based on universal jurisdiction. Seven years of legal battles ensue.

Return to Democracy

Naturally occurring nitrate or 'saltpeter' created an early-20th-century boom. Today the Atacama Desert is home to 170 nitrate ghost towns – only one, María Elena, remains open.

The cracks in the regime began to appear around 1983, when leftist groups dared to stage demonstrations and militant opposition groups began to form in the shantytowns. Political parties also started to re-group, although they only began to function openly again in 1987. In late 1988, trying to extend his presidency until 1997, Pinochet held another plebiscite, but this time voters rejected him.

In multiparty elections in 1989, Christian Democrat Patricio Aylwin, compromise candidate of a coalition of opposition parties known as the Concertación para la Democracia (Concertación for short), defeated a conservative economist. Consolidating the rebirth of democracy, Aylwin's term was followed by another Concertación president, Eduardo Frei Ruiz-Tagle.

The Concertación maintained Pinochet's free-market reforms, but Pinochet's military senate appointees could still block other reform. Pinochet assumed a senate seat upon retirement from the army in 1997 – at least in part because it conferred immunity from prosecution in Chile.

This constitutional hangover from the dictatorship was finally swept away in July 2005 when the president was granted the right to fire armed-forces commanders and abolish unelected senators.

The Pinochet Saga

The Pinochet File by Peter Korn-bluh (2003) is a surprising and revealing look at US involvement in Chilean politics in the run-up to the military dictatorship of 1973 to 1989.

The September 1998 arrest of General Pinochet in London at the request of Spanish judge Báltazar Garzón, who was investigating deaths and disappearances of Spanish citizens in the aftermath of the 1973 coup, caused an international uproar.

Following the arrest, US president Bill Clinton released files showing 30 years of US government covert aid to undermine Allende and set the stage for the coup d'état. Pinochet was put under house arrest, and for four years lawyers argued whether or not he was able to stand trial for crimes committed by the Caravan of Death, based on his health and mental condition. Both the Court of Appeals (in 2000) and the Supreme Court (2002) ruled him unfit to stand trial. As a consequence of the court's decision – that he suffered from dementia – Pinochet stepped down from his post as lifetime senator.

It seemed the end of judicial efforts to hold him accountable for human rights abuses. But in 2004 Pinochet gave a TV interview in which he appeared wholly lucid. A string of court decisions subsequently stripped Pinochet of his immunity from prosecution as a former head of state. One of the key human rights charges subsequently brought against him revolved around his alleged role in Operation Condor, a coordinated

2000	2002	2002	2003
Defeating a former aide to Pinochet, the moderate leftist Ricardo Lagos is elected president, joining a growing breed of left-leaning governments elected across South America.	Chile loosens up – despite bitter cold, over 3000 eager citizens volunteer for artist Spencer Tunick's call for naked bodies for a now infamous outdoor Santiago photo shoot.	Portraying Chile's disaffected urban youth, the young novelist Alberto Fuget lands the cover of *Newsweek*; he claims the era of Latin American magic realism dead.	With the economy booming, Chile makes a controversial move and becomes the first South American country to sign a free-trade deal with the USA.

> **DOCUMENTING THE PINOCHET YEARS**
>
> ➡ Chilean Director Andrés Wood's hit *Machuca* (2004) depicts the bittersweet coming-of-age of two very different boys during the class-conscious and volatile Santiago of 1973.
>
> ➡ Epic documentary *La Batalla de Chile,* by Patricio Guzman, brilliantly chronicles the year leading up to the military coup of 1973. Filmed partly in secret on stock sent from abroad, the footage had to be smuggled out of Chile.
>
> ➡ March Cooper, Allende's translator, takes an insightful and poignant look at Chile's politics and society from the coup to today's cynical consumer society in *Pinochet and Me: A Chilean Anti-Memoir* (2002).

campaign by several South American regimes in the 1970s and 1980s to eliminate leftist opponents.

Chileans then witnessed a string of yo-yoing court decisions that first stripped his immunity, subsequently reversed the ruling, then again decided that he could stand trial. Revelations made in early 2005 about Pinochet's secret foreign bank accounts containing US$27 million added to the charges and implicated his wife and son. The judge investigating the bank accounts received death threats.

Despite the intense legal activity, Pinochet never reached trial. He died on December 10, 2006 at the age of 91. In Santiago's Plaza Italia, 6000 demonstrators gathered to celebrate, tossing confetti and drinking champagne, but there were also violent riots. Tens of thousands of Pinochet supporters attended his funeral and honored him as a patriot who gave Chile a strong economic future.

In 2014, a Chilean court made a landmark ruling to compensate 31 former dissidents who were tortured and detained on Dawson Island with a sum of US$7.5 million. If the ruling survives an appeal, it will be the first time that victims who were tortured under the dictatorship are compensated. In 2015, two former military intelligence officers were charged with the 1973 disappearance and death of two Americans – one of them, journalist Charles Horman, had inspired the 1982 movie *Missing*.

Watch the intense movie *Sub Terra* (2003) for a savage indictment of the exploitation, often at the hands of gringos, that used to go on in Chile's mining industry.

The Rise of the Left

The Concertación scraped through the 2000 elections for its third term in office. Its candidate, the moderate leftist Ricardo Lagos, joined a growing breed of left-leaning governments elected across South America, all seeking to put space between themselves and Washington. Lagos became an important figure in this shift in 2003 when he was one of the most determined members of the UN Security Council to oppose war in Iraq.

2004	2005	2006	2006
In a break with ultra-conservative Catholic tradition, Chile establishes the rights of its citizens to divorce; the courts are flooded with cases and proceedings backlog.	The senate approves more than 50 constitutional reforms to fully restore democracy, allowing the president to dismiss nonelected senators (known as 'senators for life') and military commanders.	Michelle Bachelet is elected the first female president of Chile and faces key crises: massive student protests seeking education reform and Santiago's traffic paralysis during transportation reform.	At the age of 91, General Augusto Pinochet dies, having never reached trial. He is denied a state funeral. At his burial, President Bachelet is noticeably absent.

In these years, Chile began to shed much of its traditional conservatism. The death penalty was abolished in 2001 and a divorce law was finally passed in 2004 (although the morning-after pill still provokes controversy). The arts and free press began once again flourishing, and women's rights were increasingly recognized in law.

The 2006 election of Michelle Bachelet, former minister of defense under Lagos, was a watershed event. Not only because she is a woman, but because as an agnostic, socialist single mother she represented everything that Chile superficially was not. Her father was an air-force general who died at the hands of Pinochet's forces; she was also detained and tortured but released, and lived in exile abroad. Her skill as a consensus builder helped her heal old wounds with the military and the public. For voters, she represented a continuum of the policies of Lagos, moving forward Chile's already strong economy.

Bachelet took the presidency with initially strong approval ratings, but increasing divisions within her coalition (La Concertación Democratica) made reforms difficult. She also was tested by emerging crises with no easy answer. An upgrade of urban buses to Transantiago abruptly consolidated and eliminated routes, leaving many riders stranded on the curb. The student protests of 2006–07 also put the government on the defensive. It took a massive natural disaster for the public to once again rally around Bachelet.

A Seismic Shift

In the early hours of February 27, 2010, one of the largest quakes ever recorded in history hit off the coast of central Chile. The 8.8 earthquake caused massive destruction, triggering tsunamis along the coast and in Archipiélago Juan Fernández and claiming 525 lives. Many homes and highways were destroyed, and insurance companies estimated billions of dollars worth of damages.

The strongest earthquake ever recorded, on May 22, 1960, measured between 8.6 and 9.5 on the Richter scale and rattled Chile from Concepción to southern Chiloé. The resulting tsunami wreaked havoc 10,000km away in Hawaii and Japan.

After some initial looting in affected areas, order quickly returned. Chile's Teletón, a yearly charity fundraising event, raised an unprecedented US$39 million for the cause. Several government officials faced charges for failing to warn Archipiélago Juan Fernández of the tsunami. Although there was debate about whether she should be considered responsible, ex-president Bachelet was ultimately not charged. Overall, the government was praised for its swift action in initial reparations. At the same time, the outpouring of solidarity demonstrated by the Chilean people was a boost to national pride.

Bachelet's tenure was nearly over at the time of the earthquake. After 20 years of rule by the liberal Concertacíon, Chile had elected conservative billionaire businessman Sebastián Piñera from the center-right Alianza por Chile. While Piñera took his oath of office, a 6.9 magnitude

2007	2009	2010	2010
Santiago's youth get radical, from a penchant for protest to the emergence of Pokemones – a short-lived trend of Goth-inspired youth who embrace in public kissing parties.	China displaces the US as the top trading partner of Chile; by the end of 2010 China's investment in Chile reached US$440 million.	On February 27, an 8.8 earthquake and tsunami claims 525 lives and creates massive destruction, with its epicenter 70 miles from the city of Concepción.	Inaugurated just 11 days post earthquake, billionaire businessman Sebastián Piñera becomes the first right-wing president since the Pinochet years. His first task is rebuilding Chile.

aftershock rocked Santiago. Liberal commentators, including novelist Isabel Allende, seized on this as a metaphor, but around the globe observers were curious about what the first right-wing government since Pinochet would herald.

The Rescue of Los 33

Six months after the massive earthquake, Chile rebounded onto the world stage when 33 miners became trapped 700m underground in the Atacama Desert. After 17 days they had been feared dead when a borehole broke through their emergency shelter. Miners relayed a scrawled message read live on TV by President Piñera himself: 'We are well in the shelter. The 33.'

After the hole came a tube and what the Chileans called *palomas* – messenger doves. In these capsules, videos and love letters went up, baked pies and medication went down. It was the line that connected the surface to the depths, life to a world devoid of it, and billions of viewers to 33 anxious souls. Awaiting the rescue, the miners' families and world media held vigil nearby, in the desert 45km north of Copiapó. World attention and an outpouring of public empathy encouraged the government to take over the flailing rescue, with help from NASA and private companies, but complications drew out the drama. On October 13, after enduring 69 days underground, the 33 were finally rescued.

The aftermath for the survivors has been difficult, with survivors suffering from PTSD (Post Traumatic Stress Disorder), financial woes and depression. The incident led to some long-overdue mining reforms, with the adoption of the International Labour Organization's (ILO) convention on mining safety a year after the incident.

Taking It to the Streets

Once rare in this former dictatorship, public protests have become a fixture in the political landscape. Starting during the term of Bachelet, Chilean students – nicknamed *pinguinos* (penguins) for their uniforms – began to protest the dismal quality of state schooling en masse. Violence marred some protests, yet they eventually succeeded in propelling the government to implement improvements in primary and secondary education.

Inequity has driven the issue: on a national test, private-school fourth-graders were outperforming their public-school counterparts by 50%. Less than half of Chilean students attend the underfunded public schools, while those who can afford private education gain significant advantages. The Bachelet administration promised state grants and a new quality agency for monitoring education. Under the administration of Sebastián Piñera, the issue refocused on expensive higher

While trapped underground, the 33 miners requested wine and cigarettes to help cope with the stress. But their NASA doctor sent nicotine patches instead.

For a gripping account of the survival of the 33 Chilean miners trapped for 69 days in the San José mine, read Hector Tobar's *Deep Down Dark*.

HISTORY THE RESCUE OF LOS 33

2010	**2011**	**2011**	**2011**
The world is captivated by the saga of 33 Chilean miners trapped for 69 days 700m underground near Copiapó – the longest entrapment in history.	In an attempt to solve Chile's greatest unsolved mystery, the remains of ex-president Salvador Allende are exhumed to investigate whether his death had in fact been suicide.	A devastating military plane crash off Isla Robinson Crusoe kills 21, including a Chilean TV icon and nonprofit leaders inaugurating the island for tourism post-tsunami.	After student protests demanding better education reach a fever pitch, their 23-year-old university-student leader Camila Vallejo dialogues with the government and becomes an international icon.

education. When the Piñera government failed to respond, protesters broke out into Michael Jackson's *Thriller* and paraded as zombies outside the presidential palace. The Chilean Winter became the largest public protest in decades.

In Februrary of 2012, citizen protests in Puerto Aisén and Coyhaique shut down much of the Patagonian province for nearly a month. Joined by unions, protesters from the Social Movement for the Aysén Region organized blockades and shut down roads, turning the biggest tourism month into a no-show. The issues included the region's lack of quality health care, education and infrastructure, in addition to the much higher costs of living in the neglected provinces.

Along with public appeals, large protests also had a heavy hand in the government's 2014 canceling of the US$3.2 billion HidroAysén dam projects. The largest energy project ever proposed in Chile, it planned five major dams on two Patagonian rivers with a heavy impact on surrounding communities and parks.

Mapuche unrest has been another constant. Land disputes with forestry companies and individuals resulted in fatal arson attacks between 2011 and the present. Relations with the state were already poor since police killings of Mapuche youth in 2005 and 2008, which had sparked massive demonstrations and vandalism. Tensions continue between the state and the Mapuche indigenous community, who today number around one million.

> When the world economic crisis hit in 2008, Chile stepped up to the plate and offered loans to the United States, a role reversal which played well for then-president Bachelet.

Brave New World

In the first decade of the millennium Chile rose as an economic star – boosted by record prices for its key export, copper. When the world economic crisis hit, Chile remained in good standing. It was the first Latin country to enter into a free trade agreement with the US, though now its main trading partner is China. As hard as Chile tries to diversify, copper still accounts for a whopping 60% of exports. Yet, with diminishing demand for copper in China, the once-bulletproof Chilean peso is finally slipping in value.

Chile closed out 2013 by electing Michelle Bachelet once again to the presidency. Lacking an absolute majority in the November elections, she surged ahead of conservative Evelyn Matthei at the December 15 runoff, though voter turnout was notably low. It was the first presidential election in Chile in which voting was no longer mandatory. The elections also brought young reform candidates to congress like Camila Vallejo and Giorgio Jackson, the former undergraduate leaders of the student protests.

Navigating its way through financial highs and domestic snags, Chile may have to reset its north to find its way through mounting social, ecological and economic issues; it's complicated, but par for the course of progress.

> September 11 is of as much significance to Chileans as North Americans. The date of the 1973 coup, it's commemorated with a major avenue in Santiago.

2013	2013	2014	2015
Progressives hail the belated inauguration of the tallest building on the continent, the 64-story Gran Torre Santiago. Delays had plagued the project after the 2008 world financial crisis.	With a December 15 runoff election, former president Michelle Bachelet is elected, bringing the left back into power. The first election with voting no longer mandatory, turnout was low.	A Chilean court ordered US$7.5 million to be paid to 30 former political prisoners and victims of torture held on remote Isla Dawson for two years during the dictatorship.	The remains of poet Pablo Neruda are exhumed a second time to examine if poisoning played a role in his death, with results still pending.

Life in Chile

On this supposed island between the Andes and the sea, isolation may have nurtured Chilenos for decades but globalization has arrived. The social media and internet are radically recalibrating the values, tastes and social norms of this once ultra-conservative society. Yet change is uneasy. There is still a provincial side to Chile – witness the sacred backyard barbecue and Sundays reserved for family, all generations included. At a cultural crossroads, Chile leaves the visitor with much to enjoy, debate and process.

The National Psyche

Centuries with little outside exposure, accompanied by an especially influential Roman Catholic Church, fostered a high degree of cultural conformity and conservatism in Chile. If anything, this isolation was compounded during the Pinochet years of repression and censorship. Perhaps for this reason outsiders often comment on how Chileans appear more restrained than other Latin American nationalities: they seem a less verbal, more heads-down and hard working people.

But the national psyche is now at its most fluid, as Chile undergoes radical social change. The Catholic Church itself has become more progressive. Society is opening up, introducing liberal laws and challenging conservative values. Nowhere is this trend more evident than with the urban youth.

In the past, Chileans were known for compliance and passive political attitudes, but read today's news and you'll see unrest simmers. Social change comes at the behest of Generations Y and Z – the first to grow up without the censorship, curfew or restrictions of the dictatorship. As a result, they are far more questioning and less discouraged by theoretical consequences. Authorities may perceive it as a threat, but Chile's youth has stood up for what's theirs in a way their predecessors would not have. The momentum has also influenced the provinces, namely Magallanes and Aisén, to protest higher costs and general neglect by the central government.

Yet, above all, this is a harmony-loving society. The most lasting impression you'll take away of Chileans is undoubtedly their renowned hospitality, helpfulness, genuine curiosity and heartfelt eagerness to make travelers feel at home.

For an inside scoop on Mapuche culture and issues, check out the four-language Mapuche international site (www.mapuche-nation.org), created with foreign collaboration.

Lifestyle

Travelers crossing over from Peru or Bolivia may wonder where the stereotypical 'South America' went. Superficially, Chilean lifestyle has many similarities to Europe. Dress can be conservative, leaning toward business formal; the exception being teens. And while most Chileans are proud of their traditional heritage, there's a palpable lack of investment in it.

The average Chilean focuses energy on family, home and work. Children are not encouraged to grow up too quickly, and families spend a great deal of time together. Independence isn't nearly as valued as family unity and togetherness. Regardless, single motherhood is not uncommon. Still a very traditional society, it is one of a handful where abortion is still illegal, though the current Bachelet administration is working towards its legalization.

DOS AND DON'TS

➡ Keep your behavior circumspect around indigenous peoples, especially in the altiplano and in the Mapuche centers of the south.

➡ Upon greeting and leaving, cheek kisses are exchanged between men and women and between women. Both parties gently touch cheek to cheek and send the kiss to the air. Men exchange handshakes.

➡ For Chileans, their dictatorship past is old news. Discussions should start with a focus on more contemporary issues.

➡ Chileans often reserve strong opinions out of politeness. Quickly asserting an opinion is frowned upon.

The legalization of divorce a decade ago helped remove the stigma of failed partnerships and created a backlog of cases in the courts. While not aggressively antigay, Chile had long denied public support for alternate lifestyles. Yet with the approval of civil unions for homosexual couples (as well as heterosexual unmarrieds) in January, 2015, Chile is taking a big step forward. Generally, the famous Latin American *machismo* (chauvinism) is subtle in Chile and there's a great deal of respect for women. However, this doesn't mean that it's exactly liberal. In Chile, traditional roles still rule and close friendships are usually formed along the lines of gender.

Chileans have a strong work ethic, and often work six days a week, but are always eager for a good *carrete* (party). Military service is voluntary, though the right to compulsory recruitment is retained. More women are joining the military and serving as police officers.

A yawning gulf separates the highest and lowest incomes in Chile, resulting in a dramatic gulf in living standards and an exaggerated class consciousness. Lifestyles are lavish for Santiago's *cuicos* (upper-class yuppies), with swish apartment blocks and a couple of maids, while at the other end of the scale people live in precarious homes without running water. That said, poverty has been halved in recent decades, while housing and social programs have eased the burden on Chile's poorest.

A lack of ethnic and religious diversity in Chile makes racism less of an issue, although Mapuche still face prejudice and marginalization, and class barriers remain formidable.

Population

While the vast majority of the population is of Spanish ancestry mixed with indigenous groups, several moderate waves of immigrants have also settled here – particularly British, Irish, French, Italians, Croatians (especially in Magallanes and Tierra del Fuego) and Palestinians. Germans also began immigrating in 1848 and left their stamp on the Lakes District. Today Chile's immigrant population is climbing, led by Peruvians and Argentines, but including increasing numbers of Europeans, Asians and North Americans.

The northern Andes is home to around 69,200 indigenous Aymara and Atacameño peoples. Almost 10 times that amount (around 620,000 people) are Mapuche, mainly from La Araucanía. Their name stems from the words *mapu* (land) and *che* (people). About 3800 Rapa Nui, of Polynesian ancestry, live on Easter Island.

About 75% of Chile's population occupies just 20% of its total area, in the main agricultural region of Middle Chile. This region includes Gran Santiago (the capital and its suburbs), where over a third of the country's estimated 17 million people reside. More than 85% of Chileans live in cities. In Patagonia, the person-per-square-kilometer ratio in Aisén is just 1:1 – in the Región Metropolitana that ratio is closer to 400:1.

Chilean Wine by Grant Phelps

Many happy factors make Chile a winemakers' paradise with few pests and an ideal climate. The major grape-growing regions thrive under a dry growing season, which has allowed Chilean producers to turn increasingly to organic and biodynamic viticulture. Add to this moderate summer temperatures, sunshine over 250 days per year, new winemaking technology, and low costs in labor and land, and it is not surprising that Chilean wine is taking the world by storm. Wine touring presents wonderful options for travelers to explore.

Grant Phelps is the chief winemaker at Viña Casas del Bosque.

A Tale of Boom & Bust

As in many parts of the New World it was Christianity that originally brought the grapevine to Chile. The first-recorded plantings in the country were made in 1548 by the Catholic priest Francisco de Carabantes, who brought a selection of vines from Spain. These *pais* grapes, similar to California's mission grapes, were sturdy but lacking finesse, best for table wine.

Quality wine production only began during the last half of the 19th century with the introduction of noble French vines such as Cabernet Sauvignon and Merlot. Technical know-how soon followed with the sudden arrival of French winemakers, desperate for work after phylloxera had left so many of Europe's vineyards decimated.

By 1877 winegrowing had become the country's most prosperous agricultural activity, and Chilean wineries were already exporting to Europe. In the following 20 years production doubled and by 1900 Chile had 400 sq km of vineyards producing some 275 million liters. At this point, Chile's annual wine consumption had reached a historical high of 100L per capita, sending alcoholism spiraling. To combat this, the government introduced an aggressive alcohol tax in 1902, which was followed by a second law in 1938 prohibiting the planting of new vineyards, leading to more than 30 years of stagnation.

THE BIG SPILL

On February 27, 2010, the wine-growing Maule Region was the epicenter of an 8.8 earthquake that shook Chile's wine industry. At 3:34am, the country awoke to chaos. In three minutes, cracks zippered Hwy 5, houses collapsed and bridges fell. Even though modern constructions in Chile were designed to withstand earthquakes, the more historic winery buildings (primarily constructed of adobe) along with the tanks and stacks of barrels weren't. Walls crumbled, tanks split their seams and tens of thousands of oak casks simultaneously hit the ground. In total, up to 200 million liters (40% of stored wine), worth an estimated US$250 million, was lost. With just days remaining until the start of harvest, Chile's winery workers toiled 24 hours a day to patch up the holes in their tanks and old rivalries were forgotten as neighbors bent over backwards to help each other make it through harvest in one piece. Remarkably in spite of all the adversity 2010 turned out to be a landmark vintage.

In 1974, under Pinochet's free-market reforms, new vineyards were finally permitted. However, this sudden freedom resulted in a planting boom. Overproduction marked the early '80s, causing an eventual collapse of wine prices. By 1986 almost half of the country's vineyards had been uprooted and many of the most famous wineries were on the verge of bankruptcy.

Chile's fortunes turned, however, with the arrival of foreign companies such as Miguel Torres of Spain and Baron Rothschild of Bordeaux. These companies brought not only technical expertise but also modern winemaking equipment – notably temperature-controlled stainless-steel tanks and imported oak barrels. The result was a rapid improvement in wine quality. Seeing the potential to exploit new export markets, traditional Chilean producers soon followed suit. By the mid-1990s good fortune was once again smiling on Chile and exports were booming. Between 2000 and 2010 grape plantations increased more than 80%. Chile exports over 70% of its total production in what has become a $1.7 billion industry. Chilean wine is exported to a total of 150 different countries and reaches 1.5 billion consumers each year, making it the world's fifth biggest exporter.

> Chile happens to be the only country in the world free of the two most destructive grapevine pests – downy mildew and the infamous root louse phylloxera.

Chilean Specialties

In spite of recent fascination with lesser-known grape varieties, Chile's number-one red grape continues to be Cabernet Sauvignon. The two best areas for Cab production are undeniably the Maipo and Colchagua Valleys, and most wines under CH$10,000 from these areas will generally be solid value. Chile's darling grape variety is definitely Carmenere. A little-known grape originally from the Bordeaux region of France, Carmenere largely disappeared in the 19th century due to its tendency to ripen poorly in Bordeaux's uneven climate. It was widely planted in Chile in the late 18th century where it was for a long time mistaken for Merlot. It was not until 1994 that Carmenere was 'rediscovered' in Chile and since then it has proven itself to be capable of producing some exceptional wines here.

> Although Chile initially made its name internationally with cheap, drinkable reds, it is becoming recognized for superpremium wines increasingly grown on low-yielding hillside vineyards.

While hotter-climate styles of Syrah made inroads in world markets for well over a decade, it's the freshness and natural acidity of Syrah's cool-climate exponents that grab headlines. For Chilean Pinot Noir, nowhere does it better than the cool-climate regions of Casablanca and San Antonio.

Although Chile is best known for its reds, it also produces some exceptional white wines, especially Sauvignon Blanc and Chardonnay from the cooler coastal valleys of Casablanca and San Antonio along with the Limari region.

New Trends

The supermarket wine revolution led one UK journalist to famously compare dependable and drinkable Chilean wine to a Volvo. Yet it has made an about-face in the last five years, as winemakers have reinvented their

---

GET YOUR GRAPE ON: ENOTOURISM

Enotourism offers some of the most fun you can have in Chile. What better way to familiarize yourself with the local vintages than to chill at an elegant restaurant nestled among the vines? Of Chile's 260 wineries, around 70 are now open to the public. For their proximity to Santiago, two of the best areas to visit are the Casablanca and Maipo Valleys, both within an hour of the capital. In Casablanca visit Casas del Bosque (p107), Bodegas Re, Loma Larga and Matetic (p107). In the Maipo Valley, Concha y Toro (p81), Haras de Pirque, Perez Cruz and De Martino (p81) are firm favorites. Further afield, the Colchagua Valley makes a great weekend getaway. Home to Montes (p112), Lapostolle (p112), Viu Manent (p112) and a dozen other wineries open to the public, the best time to visit is during the annual harvest festival held in the main square mid-March.

OUR BEST PICKS UNDER US$10

Want to enjoy good juice on a budget? *Ningún problema* – here are our recommendations:

Sparkling Viña Mar Brut

Sauvignon Blanc Casas del Bosque Reserva

Chardonnay Veramonte Reserva

Riesling Cousiño Macul Isidora

Rosé Emiliana Adobe Reserva

Pinot Noir Santa Carolina Estrella de Oro

Syrah Leyda Reserva

Carmenere Tarapacá Gran Reserva

Cabernet Sauvignon Casa Silva Doña Dominga

product and polished its image abroad. The main push rescues Chile's past, with a focus on the more southerly valleys and long-neglected grape varieties, often from century-old vineyards.

The common *país* variety, once relegated mainly to nondescript jug wines, almost disappeared as its plantings plummeted between 2006 and 2012. Sensing its imminent extinction, leading producer Míguel Torres brought the variety back from the brink. The result was the revelatory sparkling Santa Digna Estelado, now consistently rated as one of Chile's best, together with a lighter-bodied Beaujolais-style red called Reserva del Pueblo. While the Cinsault variety was a slower starter, it has now eclipsed *país* in the reinvention game. Even the big players like Concha y Toro have recently released very good examples. In Santiago's top wine bars, Cinsault is now a hot pick.

Another old variety making a comeback is Carignan. Formed in 2011 by 12 visionary producers, the Vigno movement has given Maule's old vine Carignan vineyards a new lease on life. Governed by a series of strict, self-imposed rules, wines displaying the VIGNO (pronounced 'veenio') logo must be produced from dry-farmed vineyards at least 35 years old producing 65% Carignan. For a good introduction to the Vigno wines, try the outstanding bottlings of Garcia-Schwaderer, Valdivieso, Morandé and Odjfell.

Some 80% of Chile's annual output comes from just the big three: Concha y Toro, San Pedro and Santa Rita. Conspicuously absent have been smaller scale, boutique winemakers. This changed with the formation of the *movimiento de viñateros independientes* (MOVI) collective several years ago. While production levels are still small, wines from this 20-member group can be found in most serious wine bars in Chile. Go-to producers are Polkura, Garcia-Schwaderer, Garage Wine Co, Gillmore and Flaherty.

Chilean wine promises a strong future in organics. Few countries are in a better position to implement organic viticulture on a national level. Chile is already home to the world's biggest organic winery, Viñedos Organicos Emiliana (or VOE), producing a solid range of good value wines. Lapostolle and Matetic have gone one step further by becoming fully biodynamic.

Particularly popular among new, young wine consumers, sales of sparkling wine more than doubled between 2012 and 2014. It's a suitable accompaniment to Chile's top-quality seafood. For splurging on oysters, nothing beats a fine *blanc de noir* (white sparkling made from Pinot Noir). Currently 20 wineries produce top-quality fizz. The best offerings are invariably the drier versions labelled 'Brut' or 'Extra Brut'. Undurraga Titillum, Morandé Brut Nature and Miguel Torres Cordillera are good places to start.

For a primer on Chilean wine, check out www.winesofchile.org. Get in on the garage wine movement at www.movi.cl.

Literature & Cinema

While poetry has long been the golden nugget of this narrow country, Chilean cinema is gaining world recognition. In the last generation, the military dictatorship prompted an artistic exodus and censorship, but modern Chile has rebounded with a fresh and sometimes daring emphasis on the arts.

Literature & Poetry

Sex, drugs, and poetry recitation drive *Los Detectives Salvajes* (The Savage Detectives), late literary bad boy Roberto Bolaño's greatest novel. Like him, the main character is a Chilean poet exiled in Mexico and Spain.

Twentieth-century Chile has produced many of Latin America's most celebrated writers. The most acclaimed are poets Pablo Neruda and Gabriela Mistral, both Nobel Prize winners.

Mistral (born Lucila Godoy Alcayaga; 1889–1957) was a shy young rural schoolmistress from Elqui Valley who won great acclaim for her compassionate, reflective and mystical poetry. She became South America's first Nobel Prize winner for literature in 1945. Langston Hughes' *Selected Poems of Gabriela Mistral* provides an introduction.

Nicanor Parra (b 1914) drew Nobel Prize attention for his hugely influential and colloquial 'antipoetry.' *De Hojas de Parra* (From the Pages of Parra) and *Poemas y antipoemas* (Poems and Antipoems) are his best known. Bohemian Jorge Teillier (1935–96) wrote poetry of teenage angst and solitude.

Fragile social facades were explored by José Donoso (1924–96). His celebrated novel *Curfew* offers a portrait of life under the dictatorship through the eyes of a returned exile, while *Coronación* (Coronation), made into a hit film, follows the fall of a dynasty.

Chile's most famous contemporary literary export is Isabel Allende (b 1942), niece of late president Salvador Allende. She wove 'magical realism' into best-selling stories with Chilean historic references, such as *House of the Spirits, Of Love and Shadows, Eva Luna, Daughter of Fortune, Portrait in Sepia* and *Maya's Notebook. My Invented Country* (2004) gives insight into perceptions of Chile and Allende herself. She was granted the US Presidential Medal of Freedom in 2014.

US resident Ariel Dorfman (b 1942) is another huge literary presence, with plays *La Negra Ester* (Black Ester) and *Death and the Maiden.* The latter is set after the fall of a South American dictator, and is also an acclaimed movie.

Novelist Antonio Skármeta (b 1940) became famous for *Ardiente Paciencia* (Burning Patience), inspired by Neruda and adapted into the award-winning film *Il Postino* (The Postman).

Luis Sepúlveda (b 1949) is one of Chile's most prolific writers, with such books as *Nombre de Torero* (The Name of the Bullfighter), a tough noir set in Germany and Chile; and the excellent short-story collection *Patagonia Express.* For a lighter romp through Chile, Roberto Ampuero (b 1953) writes mystery novels, such as *El Alemán de Atacama* (The German of Atacama), whose main character is a Valparaíso-based Cuban detective.

Justly considered one of the greats in Latin American literature, the work of Roberto Bolaño (1955–2005) is enjoying a renaissance. The posthumous publication of his encyclopedic *2666* has sealed his cult-hero status, but it's worth checking out other works. Born in Santiago, he spent most of his adult life in exile in Mexico and Spain.

POET-POLITICIAN PABLO NERUDA

The combative, sentimental, surreal and provocative poetry of Pablo Neruda (1904–73) tells much about the soul of Chile while his own life story has played an intimate part in its history.

Born in a provincial town as Neftalí Ricardo Reyes Basoalto, Neruda devised his famous alias fearing that his blue-collar family would mock his ambition. The leftist poet led a flamboyant life, building gloriously outlandish homes in Santiago, Valparaíso and Isla Negra. His most famous house, La Chascona, was named after his third wife Matilde Urrutia's perpetually tangled shock of hair.

Awarded a diplomatic post after early literary success, he gained international celebrity wearing his political opinions on his sleeve. He helped political refugees flee after the Spanish Civil War and officially joined the Communist Party once back in Chile, where he was elected senator. After helping Gabriel González Videla secure the presidency in 1946, he had to escape over the Andes into exile when the president outlawed the Communist Party.

All the while Neruda wrote poems. A presidential candidate in 1969, he pulled out of the race in support of Salvador Allende. While serving as Allende's ambassador to France, he received a Nobel Prize, becoming only the third Latin American writer to win the award.

Shortly afterward he returned to Chile with failing health. Pressure was mounting on Allende's presidency. Mere days after the 1973 coup, Neruda died of cancer and a broken heart. His will left everything to the Chilean people through a foundation. The Pinochet regime set about sacking and vandalizing his homes. Later his widow lovingly restored them, and they are now open to the public.

Neruda's work includes *Heights of Macchu Picchu, Canto General* and *Passions and Impressions,* available in translation.

Bestselling author Marcela Serrano (b 1951) tackles women's issues in books such as *Antigua Vida Mia* (My Life Before: A Novel) and others. Homosexuality and other taboo subjects are treated with top-notch shock value by Pedro Lemebel (b 1950), author of novel *Tengo Miedo Torero* (My Tender Matador). Younger writers rejecting the 'magical realism' of Latin literature include Alberto Fuguet (b 1964), whose *Sobredosis* (Overdose) and *Mala Onda* (Bad Vibes) have earned acclaim and scowls. Among other contemporary talents, look for the erotic narratives of Andrea Maturana, novelist Carlos Franz, Marcelo Mellado, Gonzalo Contreras and Claudia Apablaza.

Chile: A Traveler's Literary Companion (2003), edited by Katherine Silver, is an appetite-whetting whiz through Chile's rich literary tradition, with snippets from the work of many top writers, including Neruda, Dorfman, Donoso and Rivera Letelier.

Cinema

Before the 1973 coup Chilean cinema was among the most experimental in Latin America and it is now returning to reclaim some status. Alejandro Jodorowsky's kooky *El Topo* (The Mole; 1971) is an underground cult classic that mixed genres long before Tarantino.

There was little film production in Chile during the Pinochet years, but exiled directors kept shooting. Miguel Littín's *Alsino y el Condor* (Alsino and the Condor; 1983) was nominated for an Academy Award. Exiled documentary-maker Patricio Guzmán has often made the military dictatorship his subject matter. The prolific Paris-based Raúl Ruiz is another exile. His English-language movies include the psychological thriller *Shattered Image* (1998).

Post-dictatorship, Chile's weakened film industry was understandably preoccupied with the after-effects of the former regime. Ricardo Larrain's *La Frontera* (The Borderland; 1991) explored internal exile, and Gonzalo Justiniano's *Amnesia* (1994) used the story of a Chilean soldier forced to shoot prisoners to challenge Chileans not to forget past atrocities.

Then the mood lightened somewhat. The most successful Chilean movie to date, Cristian Galaz's *El Chacotero Sentimental* (The Sentimental Teaser; 1999) won 18 national and international awards for the true

ANDRÉS WOOD

Chile's hottest filmmaker, Andrés Wood, may have studied in New York, but his subject matter is purely Chileno, from *Fiebre de Locos* (Loco Fever), the story of a Patagonian fishing village, to the acclaimed *Machuca* and Sundance Jury Prize–winner *Violeta Se Fue a Los Cielos* (Violeta; 2012), about artist-musician Violeta Parra. He fills us in on Chilean cinema.

You tell stories from a microperspective that also reflects a globalized Chile... Do you think that perspective is missing in Chilean cinema? It's very difficult to generalize...but we are more interested in what foreigners think of us, and gaining approval in their eyes. It's a country with a kind of identity crisis, caused by different factors, but with insecurity in our own thoughts and feelings.

Chilean cinema is having a lot of international success. Is this a good moment? The younger generations are more profoundly connected to the world, making barriers more and more invisible. The problem is that often we find ourselves creating works to explain who we are to the world rather than being mirrors that can allow us to think, argue and self-reflect. This gap needs to close for us to better connect with our audiences.

Are there certain characteristics that define Chilean cinema? We don't have a solid body of work but that's fine by me. Chilean film is pretty heterogeneous in aesthetics and subject matter.

story of a frank radio host whose listeners reveal their love entanglements. Silvio Caiozzi, among Chile's most respected veteran directors, adapted a José Donoso novel to make *Coronación* (Coronation; 2000), about the fall of a family dynasty. Comedy *Taxi Para Tres* (Taxi for Three; 2001), by Orlando Lubbert, follows bandits in their heisted taxi. Pablo Larraín's *Tony Manero* (2008) sends up a disco-obsessed murderer.

The film industry has worked through Chile's traumatic past in a kind of celluloid therapy, while gaining international success. A period drama about the referendum on the Pinochet presidency, *No* (2013), directed by Pablo Larraín and starring Gael García Bernal, was the first Chilean film nominated for an Oscar for Best Foreign Film. *Machuca* (2004), directed by Andrés Wood, shows two boys' lives during the coup. *Sub Terra* (2003) dramatizes mining exploitation. *Mi Mejor Enemigo* (My Best Enemy; 2004), a collaboration with Argentina and Spain, is set in Patagonia during the Beagle conflict (a 1978 territorial dispute between Argentina and Chile over three islands in the Beagle Channel).

It's not all war, torture and politics, though. The new breed of globally influenced teen flicks originated with *Promedio Rojo* (loosely translated as Flunking Grades; 2005) from director Nicolás López. *Crystal Fairy and the Magic Cactus* (2013) brought comedic actor Michael Cera to Chile to play an arrogant tourist on a quest to trip on San Pedro cactus. Director Matías Bize's *La Vida de los Pesces* (The Life of Fish; 2010) and *En La Cama* (In Bed; 2005) both gained attention abroad. Another filmmaker to watch for is Alicia Scherson, director of *Il Futuro* (The Future; 2013), a moody Bolaño adaptation that was well-received at Sundance.

Emerging tendencies include examining the rich theme of class conflict and using more female protagonists to tell Chilean stories. Darling of the Sundance Film Festival, *La Nana* (2009) tells the story of a maid whose personal life is too deeply entwined with her charges. On its heels, *Gloria* (2013) was another favorite of international film festivals.

Fabulous scenery makes Chile a dream location for foreign movies too; contemporary films to have been shot here include *The Motorcycle Diaries* (2004) and the Bond movie *Quantum of Solace* (2008). The documentary-style film *180° South* (2010) uses a surfer's quest to explore Patagonia to highlight environmental issues, with gorgeous scenery footage. Upcoming film *The 33* puts Antonio Banderas in the role of the ringleader in the film version of the real-life Chilean mining drama.

The Natural World

With even Santiago skyscrapers dwarfed by the high Andean backdrop, nature can't help but prevail in visitors' impressions of Chile. Geography students could cover almost their entire syllabus in this slinky country: some 4300km long and 200km wide, Chile is bookended by the Pacific Ocean and the Andes. Stunning in variety, it features the driest desert in the world, temperate rainforest and an ice-capped south, linked by 50 active volcanoes and woven together by rivers, lakes and farmland. In recent years, mining, salmon farming and hydroelectric proposals have put many parts of this once-pristine environment under imminent threat.

The Land

Chile's rugged spine, the Andes, began forming about 60 million years ago. While southern Chile was engulfed by glaciers, northern Chile was submerged below the ocean: hence today the barren north is plastered with pastel salt flats and the south is scored by deep glacially carved lakes, curvaceous moraine hills and awesome glacial valleys.

Still young in geological terms, the Chilean Andes repeatedly top 6000m and thrust as high as 6893m at Ojos del Salado, the second-highest peak in South America and the world's highest active volcano.

Much like a totem pole, Chile can be split into horizontal chunks. Straddling the Tropic of Capricorn, the Norte Grande (Big North) is dominated by the Atacama Desert, the driest in the world with areas where rainfall has never been recorded. The climate is moderated by the cool Humboldt Current, which parallels the coast. High humidity conjures up a thick blanket of fog known as *camanchaca*, which condenses on coastal ranges. Coastal cities here hoard scant water from river valleys, subterranean sources and distant stream diversions. The canyons of the precordillera (foothills) lead eastward to the altiplano (high plains) and to high, snowy mountain passes. Further south, Norte Chico (Little North) sees the desert give way to scrub and pockets of forest. Green river valleys that streak from east to west allow for agriculture.

South of the Río Aconcagua begins the fertile heartland of Middle Chile, carpeted with vineyards and agriculture. It is also home to the capital, Santiago (with at least a third of the country's population), vital ports and the bulk of industry.

Descending south another rung, the Lakes District undulates with green pastureland, temperate rainforest and foothill lakes dominated by snowcapped volcanoes. The region is drenched by high rainfall, most of which dumps between May and September, but no month is excluded. The warm but strong easterly winds here are known as *puelches*. Winters feature some snow, making border crossings difficult.

The country's largest island, Isla Grande de Chiloé, hangs off the continent here, exposed to Pacific winds and storms. The smaller islands on its eastern flank make up the archipelago, but there's no escaping the rain: up to 150 days per year.

The Aisén region features fjords, raging rivers, impenetrable forests and high peaks. The Andes here jog west to meet the Pacific and the

Did you know that Chile contains approximately 10% of all the world's active volcanoes?

vast Campo de Hielo Norte (Northern Ice Field), where 19 major glaciers coalesce, nourished by heavy rain and snow. To the east, mountainous rainforest gives way to barren Patagonia steppe. South America's deepest lake, the enormous Lago General Carrera, is shared with Argentina.

The Campo de Hielo Sur (Southern Ice Field) walls off access between the Carretera Austral and sprawling Magallanes and Tierra del Fuego. Weather here is exceedingly changeable and winds are brutal. At the foot of the continent, pearly blue glaciers, crinkled fjords, vast ice fields and mountains jumble together before reaching the Magellan Strait and Tierra del Fuego. The barren eastern pampas stretches through northern Tierra del Fuego, abruptly halting by the Cordillera Darwin.

In Inka times there were millions of vicuña that ranged throughout the Andes. Today in Chile, there are only 25,000.

Wildlife

A bonus to Chile's glorious scenery is its fascinating wildlife. Bounded by ocean, desert and mountain, the country is home to a unique environment that developed much on its own, creating a number of endemic species.

Animals

Chile's domestic camelids and their slimmer wild cousins inhabit the northern altiplano. Equally unusual are creatures such as the ñandú (ostrichlike rhea), found in the northern altiplano and southern steppe, and the plump viscacha (a wild relative of the chinchilla) that hides amid the rocks at high altitude.

Though rarely seen, puma still prowl widely through the Andes. Pudú, rare and diminutive deer, hide out in thick forests throughout the south. Even more rare is the huemul deer, an endangered species endemic to Patagonia.

Chile's long coastline features many marine mammals, including colonies of sea lions and sea otters, as well as fur seals in the south. Playful dolphin pods and whales can be glimpsed, while seafood platters demonstrate the abundance of fish and shellfish.

Birdwatchers will be well satisfied. The northern altiplano features interesting birdlife from Andean gulls to giant coots. Large nesting colonies of flamingos speckle highland lakes pink, from the far north down

ANDEAN CAMELIDS

For millennia, Andean peoples have relied on the New World camels – the wild guanaco and vicuña, and the domesticated llama and alpaca – for food and fiber.

The delicate guanaco, a slim creature with stick-thin legs and a long, elegant neck, can be found in the far north and south, at elevations from sea level up to 4000m or more. It is most highly concentrated in the plains of Patagonia, including Parque Nacional Torres del Paine. It is less common and flightier in the north, where you're most likely to get photos of guanaco behinds as they hightail it to a safe distance.

The leggy vicuña is the smallest camelid, with a swan neck and minuscule head. It lives only above 4000m in the puna and altiplano, from south-central Peru to northwestern Argentina. Its fine golden wool was once the exclusive property of Inka kings, but after the Spanish invasion it was hunted mercilessly. In Parque Nacional Lauca and surrounds, conservation programs have brought vicuña back from barely a thousand in 1973 to over 25,000 today.

Many highland communities in northern Chile still depend on domestic llamas and alpacas for their livelihood. The taller, rangier and hardier llama is a pack animal whose relatively coarse wool serves for blankets, ropes and other household goods, and its meat makes good *charqui* (jerky). It can survive – even thrive – on poor, dry pastures.

The slightly smaller but far shaggier alpaca is not a pack animal. It requires well-watered grasslands to produce the fine wool sold at markets in the north.

IN DEFENSE OF THE BIG GUYS

The largest animal in the world came perilously close to extinction just a few decades ago. So it was with great excitement in 2003 that what seems to be a blue whale 'nursery' was discovered in sheltered fjords just southeast of Chiloé in the Golfo de Corcovado. More than 100 whales gathered here to feed, including 11 mothers with their young.

In 2008 Chile banned whale hunting off the entire length of its coast. Then in early 2014, the Chilean government created the 120,000-hectare marine sanctuary of Área Marina Costera Protegida de Tic Toc, to help recover declining populations of marine wildlife. For conservation information, try the **Whale and Dolphin Conservation Society** (www.wdcs.org).

Whale-watching is increasingly popular in Patagonia. A variety of species can be spotted, including fin, humpback, killer and sperm whales. Current hubs for Patagonian whale-watching trips include the coastal village of Raúl Marín Balmaceda, and in Argentina Puerto Madryn.

to Torres del Paine. The three species here include the rare James variety (*parina chica,* in Spanish). Colonies of endangered Humboldt and Magellanic penguins scattered along Chile's long coastline are another crowd-pleaser seen at Parque Nacional Pingüino de Humboldt, off the northwestern coast of Chiloé and near Punta Arenas. Recently, a colony of king penguins was discovered on Tierra del Fuego.

The legendary Andean condor circles on high mountain updrafts throughout Chile. The ibis, with its loud knocking call, is commonly seen in pastures. The queltehue, with black, white and gray markings, has a loud call used to protect its ground nests – people claim they are better than having a guard dog.

Plants

Chile has a wealth of interesting and unique plant life. While few plants can eke out an existence in its northern desert, those that manage it do so by extraordinary means. More than 20 different types of cacti and succulents survive on moisture absorbed from the ocean fog. One of the most impressive varieties is the endangered candelabra cactus, which reaches heights of up to 5m.

The high altiplano is characterized by patchy grassland, spiky scrub stands of queñoa and ground-hugging species like the lime-green llareta, a dense cushiony shrub. The native tamarugo tree once covered large areas of Chile's northern desert; it digs roots down as far as 15m to find water.

The desert's biggest surprise comes in years of sudden rainfall in Norte Chico. Delicate wildflowers break through the barren desert crust in a glorious phenomenon called the *desierto florido,* which showcases rare and endemic species.

From Norte Chico through most of Middle Chile, the native flora consists mostly of shrubs, the glossy leaves of which conserve water during the long dry season. However, pockets of southern beech (the *Nothofagus* species) cling to the coastal range nourished by the thick ocean fog. Few stands of the grand old endemic Chilean palm exist today; those that remain are best viewed in Parque Nacional La Campana.

Southern Chile boasts one of the largest temperate rainforests in the world. Its northern reaches are classified as Valdivian rainforest, a maze of evergreens, hugged by vines, whose roots are lost under impenetrable thickets of bamboo-like plants. Further south, the Magellanic rainforest has less diversity but hosts several important species. Equally breathtaking is the araucaria forest, home to the araucaria – a grand old pine that

When heading into the wild, grab a great field guide like *Birds of Patagonia, Tierra del Fuego & Antarctic Peninsula* (2003) and *Flora Patagonia* (2008), formerly published by Fantástico Sur.

THE DISAPPEARING LAKE

In April 2008, Lago Cachet 2 lost its 200 million cu meter of water in just a matter of hours, releasing water downstream to the Baker, Chile's highest-volume river and generating a downstream wave that rolled on out to the Pacific. In nature, strange things happen. But following this mysterious one, the event repeated a total of seven times in two years.

According to *Nature* magazine, the cause is climate change. Called a glacial-lake outburst flood (GLOF), it results from the thinning and receding of nearby Patagonian glaciers, weakening the natural dam made by the glaciers. After the lake drains, it fills again with glacial melt. It's a constant threat to those who live on the banks of the Río Colonia, though with assistance from NASA and a German university, monitoring systems are now in place.

can age up to 1000 years. The English name became 'monkey puzzle,' since its forbidding foliage and jigsaw-like bark would surely stump a monkey.

Meanwhile in the southern lakes region, the alerce is one of the longest-living trees in the world, growing for up to 4000 years. You can admire them in Parque Nacional Alerce Andino and Parque Pumalín.

On Chiloé, in the Lakes District and Aisén, the rhubarb-like nalca is the world's largest herbaceous plant, with enormous leaves that grow from a single stalk; the juicy stalk of younger plants is edible in November.

The Archipiélago Juan Fernández is a major storehouse of biological diversity: of the 140 native plant species found on the islands, 101 are endemic.

Environmental Issues

With industry booming, Chile is facing a spate of environmental issues. Along with Mexico City and Sao Paolo, Santiago is one of the Americas' most polluted cities. The smog blanket is at times so severe that people sport surgical face masks, schools suspend sports activities and the elderly are advised to stay indoors. The city has no-drive days for private cars and is looking to add bike lanes and extend subway lines. In 2014, Chile became the first South American country to fine polluters for carbon emissions with the Green Act.

Chile's forests continue to lose ground to plantations of fast-growing exotics, such as eucalyptus and Monterey pine. Caught in a tug-of-war between their economic and ecological value, native tree species have also declined precipitously due to logging. The alerce is protected by laws that prohibit its export and the felling of live trees. But loggers and traffickers of the wood continue undaunted, finding ways around the laws or ignoring them.

You can catch up with the latest conservation headlines through English-language news portal the *Santiago Times*, www.santiago times.cl, by selecting its Environment header.

Canadian beavers, first introduced for their fur, have caused extensive environmental damage across Tierra del Fuego, and now are heading to the mainland continent. A plague of introduced mink has also forced the government to take action in southern Chile.

Water and air pollution caused by the mining industry is a longtime concern. Some mining towns have suffered such severe contamination that they have been relocated. Part of the problem is that the industry also demands huge energy and water supplies, and mining locations can interfere with water basins, contaminating the supply and destroying farming.

A series of controversial dams proposed by HidroAysén on Río Baker and Río Pascua, among other Patagonian rivers, ignited massive public protests. In July, 2014, the government reversed its approval for these projects, effectively canceling them. Other waterways, most notably the pristine Río Puelo, remain under threat.

Another issue is the intensive use of agricultural chemicals and pesticides to promote Chile's flourishing fruit exports, which during the southern summer furnish the northern hemisphere with fresh produce. In 2011, the Chilean government approved the registration of genetically modified seeds, opening the door for the controversial multinational Monsanto to shape the future of Chilean agriculture. Likewise, industrial waste is a huge problem.

The continued expansion of southern Chile's salmon farms is polluting water, devastating underwater ecology and depleting other fish stocks. A 2007 *New York Times* report revealing widespread virus outbreaks in Chilean salmon and questioning aquaculture practices rocked the industry and inspired tighter government controls and monitoring. Yet production has rebounded, with Chile the world's second-largest producer of salmon. A study published by Oxford University Press in 2014 notes that the use of antibiotics has created antibiotic-resistant bacteria in fish and polluted fish-farming environments in Chile.

Forest fires continue to threaten many of Chile's wild areas and parks, most notably a devastating 2011 Torres del Paine blaze ignited accidentally by an illegal camper. New public wildfire awareness campaigns hope to compensate for the country's lack of funding for professional firefighting.

Easter Island (Rapa Nui) is under mounting pressure from increasing visitor numbers. Limited natural resources mean that the island must depend on the distant mainland for all supplies and fuel. In 2014, the government set aside US$165 million to improve infrastructure, adding sewage treatment and a new airport.

The growing hole in the ozone layer over Antarctica has become such an issue that medical authorities recommend wearing protective clothing and heavy sunblock to avoid cancer-causing ultraviolet radiation, especially in Patagonia.

Global warming is also having a significant impact on Chile. Nowhere is it more apparent than with the melting of glaciers. Scientists have documented many glaciers doubling their thinning rates in recent years while the northern and southern ice fields continue to retreat. In particular, the Northern Patagonian Ice Field is contributing to rising ocean levels at a rate one-quarter higher than formerly believed. Reports say that glaciers are thinning more rapidly than can be explained by warmer air temperatures and decreased precipitation. The change also stands to impact on plant and animal life, water levels in lakes and rivers, and overall sustainability.

> Spanish-language picture book *Patagonia Chile ¡Sin Represas!* (2007), edited by Chilean environmentalist Juan Pablo Orrego, uses before and after images to illustrate the impact of proposed hydroelectric projects in Patagonia.

Environmental Organizations

Ancient Forest International (AFI; ☎707-923-4475; www.ancientforests. org) US-based organization with close links to Chilean forest-conservation groups.

Codeff (Comité Pro Defensa de la Fauna y Flora; ☎02-777-2534; www.codeff.cl; Ernesto Reyes 035, Providencia, Santiago; 🖵) Campaigns to protect the country's flora and fauna, especially endangered species. Trips, seminars and work projects are organized for volunteers.

Greenpeace Chile (☎02-634-2120; www.greenpeace.cl; Agromedo 50, Centro, Santiago) Focuses on forest conservation, ocean ecology and dealing with toxic waste.

Patagonia Sin Represas (Patagonia Without Dams; www.patagoniasin represas.cl) A coalition of Chilean environmental groups supporting the anti-dam movement in Patagonia.

Terram (☎02-269-4499; www.terram.cl; Bustamente 24, Providencia, Santiago) One of the biggest-hitting pressure groups at the moment.

WWF (☎063-244-590; www.wwf.cl; Carlos Andtwander 624, Valdivia, Casa 4) Involved with the preservation of the temperate rainforests around Valdivia, conservation in southern Patagonia and protection of the native wildlife.

National Parks

Twenty percent of Chile is preserved in over 100 national parks, national monuments and nature reserves. Among Chile's top international attractions, the parks receive around two million visitors yearly, almost doubling visitation in the last decade. But while scene-stealing parks such as Torres del Paine are annually inundated, the majority of Chile's protected areas remain underutilized and wild. Hikers have their pick of trails, and solitude is easily found, especially outside the summer high season of January and February.

Chile's protected areas comprise three different categories: *parques nacionales* (national parks); *reservas nacionales* (national reserves), which are open to limited economic exploitation; and *monumentos naturales* (natural monuments), which are smaller but strictly protected areas or features.

National parks and reserves are administered by Conaf (p445), the National Forestry Corporation. Different from a National Parks Service, the main focus of Conaf is managing Chile's forests and their development. Because of this distinction, tourism is not often a primary concern of the organization. In recent years, the management of huts and services within parks has been given to private concessionaires. Advocates are lobbying for a National Parks Service to be created, but for the time being, the status quo remains.

In Santiago, visit Conaf's central **information office** (☑02-663-0000; Av Bulnes 265, Centro; ☺9:30am-5:30pm Mon-Fri) for basic maps and brochures. Increasingly, in-park amenities like *refugios* (rustic shelters), campgrounds and restaurants are being run by private concessionaires.

CHILE'S NATIONAL PARKS

PROTECTED AREA	FEATURES	HIGHLIGHTS	BEST TIME TO VISIT
Parque Nacional Archipiélago Juan Fernández (p142)	remote archipelago, ecological treasure trove of endemic plants	hiking, boat trips, diving, flora	Dec-Mar
Parque Nacional Bernardo O'Higgins (p353)	remote ice fields, glaciers, waterfalls; cormorants, condors	boat trips	Dec-Mar
Parque Nacional Bosques de Fray Jorge (p203)	cloud forest in dry desert, coastline	hiking, flora	year-round
Parque Nacional Chiloé (p298)	coastal dunes, lagoons & folklore-rich forest; rich birdlife, pudú, sea lions	hiking, wildlife watching, kayaking, horse trekking	Dec-Mar
Parque Nacional Conguillío (p230)	mountainous araucaria forests, lakes, canyons, active volcano	hiking, climbing, skiing, boating, skiing	Jun-Oct

CHILE'S NATIONAL PARKS (CONTINUED)

PROTECTED AREA	FEATURES	HIGHLIGHTS	BEST TIME TO VISIT
Parque Nacional Huerquehue (p246)	forest, lakes, waterfalls & outstanding views	hiking	Dec-Mar
Parque Nacional La Campana (p108)	coastal cordillera: oak forests & Chilean palms	hiking, flora	Nov-Feb
Parque Nacional Laguna del Laja (p135)	Andean foothills, waterfalls, lakes, rare trees; condors	hiking	Dec-Mar
Parque Nacional Laguna San Rafael (p322)	glaciers reach the sea at this stunning ice field	boat trips, flights, hiking, climbing	Sep-Mar
Parque Nacional Lauca (p192)	altiplano volcanoes, lakes, steppe; abundant birdlife & vicuñas	hiking, wildlife watching, traditional villages, hot springs	year-round
Parque Nacional Llanos de Challe (p214)	coastal plains; 'flowering desert' occurs after heavy rains; guanaco	flora & fauna	Jul-Sep in rainy years
Parque Nacional Nahuelbuta (p136)	high coastal range of araucaria forests, wildflowers; pumas, pudú, rare woodpeckers	hiking	Nov-Apr
Parque Nacional Nevado Tres Cruces (p217)	volcano Ojos del Salado; flamingos, vicuñas, guanacos	climbing, hiking, wildlife	Dec-Feb
Parque Nacional Pan de Azúcar (p220)	coastal desert; penguins, otters, sea lions, guanacos & cacti	boat trips, wildlife, swimming, hiking	year-round
Parque Nacional Patagonia	restored steppe & high alpine terrain; guanaco, flamingo, puma	hiking, wildlife watching	Dec-Mar
Parque Nacional Puyehue (p257)	volcanic dunes, lava rivers, forest	hiking, skiing, hot springs, biking, lake canoeing	hiking Dec-Mar, skiing Jun-Oct
Parque Nacional Rapa Nui (p406)	isolated Polynesian island with enigmatic archaeological treasures	archaeology, diving, hiking, horseback riding	year-round
Parque Nacional Torres del Paine (p353)	Chile's showpiece park of spectacular peaks, forest, glaciers; guanacos, condors, ñandú, flamingos	trekking, wildlife watching, climbing, glacier trekking, kayaking, horseback riding	Dec-Mar
Parque Nacional Vicente Pérez Rosales (p268)	Chile's oldest national park, crowded with lakes & volcanoes	hiking, climbing, skiing, boat trips, rafting, kayaking, canyoning, skiing	Jun-Oct
Parque Nacional Villarrica (p243)	smoking volcanic cone overlooking lakes & resorts	trekking, climbing, skiing	hiking Dec-Mar, skiing Jun-Oct
Parque Nacional Volcán Isluga (p177)	remote altiplano, volcanoes, geysers, unique pastoral culture; rich birdlife	villages, hiking, birdwatching, hot springs	year-round

TORRES IN FLAMES

On December 27, 2011, a forest fire in Torres del Paine consumed 42,000 acres. A camper was charged with the fire, fined US$10,000 and agreed to plant 50,000 trees. New wildfire awareness campaigns are educating the public, and the Nueva Ley del Bosque (New Forest Law) has stricter regulations. This translates into visitors to Torres del Paine signing an agreement to observe the park's stated rules, which are now vigorously enforced.

Conaf is chronically underfunded and many parks are inadequately protected, which makes issues like forest fires a particularly serious concern. However, other government-financed projects are showing a commitment to ecotourism, including the mega-long Sendero de Chile, which links 8000km of trails from Chile's top to bottom.

Available from Conaf, a Parks Pass covers all national parks with the exception of Torres del Paine and Parque Nacional Rapa Nui. One year is CH$10,000 per individual and CH$30,000 per family.

Private Protected Areas

Chilean law permits private nature reserves: *áreas de protección turística* (tourist protection areas) and *santuarios de la naturaleza* (nature sanctuaries). But private parks began making Chilean headlines when American conservationists Kris and Douglas Tompkins started creating parks throughout Patagonia. Their first was Parque Pumalín, followed by Corcovado National Park and Yendegaia National Park in Tierra del Fuego, donated in 2014. Kris Tompkins' ambitious Futuro Parque Nacional Patagonia is open for visitors. These parks have ignited a great debate about land ownership and use, but they have also inspired others, including former President Sebastián Piñera, who created Chiloé's Parque Tantauco.

Chile has around 133 private parks, totaling almost 4000 sq km. Codeff (p439) maintains a database of properties that have joined together to create Red de Areas Protegidas Privadas (RAPP; Network of Private Protected Areas).

Survival Guide

Directory A–Z

Accommodations

Chile has accommodations to suit every budget. Listings are organized in order of our preference considering value for cost. All prices listed are high-season rates for rooms that include breakfast and a private bathroom, unless otherwise specified. Room rates may be the same for single or double occupancy. Yet there may be a price difference between a double with two beds and one matrimonial bed (often with the shared bed more expensive). Wi-fi is common.

In tourist destinations, prices may double during the height of high season (late December through February), and extra high rates are charged at Christmas, New Year and Easter week. If you want to ask about discounts or cheaper rooms, do so at the reservation phase. Bar-gaining for better accommodation rates once you have arrived is not common and frowned upon.

At many midrange and top-end hotels, payment in US dollars (either cash or credit) legally sidesteps the crippling 19% IVA (*impuesto de valor agregado*, value-added tax). If there is any question as to whether IVA is included in the rates, clarify before paying. A hotel may not offer the discount without your prodding. In theory, the discount is strictly for those paying in dollars or with a credit card.

If trying to reserve a room, note that small lodgings in Chile are not always responsive to emails. To get it done quicker, call.

Cabins

Excellent value for small groups or families, Chile's *cabañas* are common in resort towns and national-park areas, and are integrated into some campgrounds. Most come with a private bathroom and fully equipped kitchen (these come without free breakfast). Resort areas cram *cabañas* into small lots, so if you're looking for privacy, check on the details when booking.

Camping

Chile has a developed camping culture, though it's more of a sleepless, boozy singalong atmosphere than a back-to-nature escape. Most organized campgrounds are family-oriented with large sites, full bathrooms and laundry, fire pits, a restaurant or snack bar and a grill for the essential *asado* (barbecue). Many are costly as they charge a five-person minimum. Try requesting per person rates. Remote areas have free camping, often without potable water or sanitary facilities.

Wild camping may be possible, though police are cracking down on it in the north. In rural areas, ask landowners if you can stay. Never light a fire without permission and use an established fire ring. Camping equipment is widely available, but international brands have a significant markup.

Santiago's **Sernatur** (www.chile.travel/en.html) has a free pamphlet listing campsites throughout Chile. Another website with listings is solocampings.com.

Guesthouses & Rural Homestays

For more local culture, stay at a *casa de familia* (guesthouse). Particularly in the south, where tourism is less formal, it's common for families and rural farms to open up their homes. Guests do not always have kitchen privileges, but usually can pay fair prices for abundant meals or laundry service. Tourist offices maintain lists of such accommodations.

Organized networks are most notably in Chiloé and Lago Ranco, around Pucón and in Patagonia. For Patagonia, check out Coyhaique's **Casa del Turismo Rural** (Map p318; ☏cell 7954-4794; www.casaturismorural.cl; Plaza de Armas; ☉10:30am-7:30pm Mon-Fri, 2-6pm Sat). For countrywide options, visit **Turismo Rural** (www.turismoruralchile.cl) or inquire at tourist offices.

Hospedajes

Both *hospedajes* and *residenciales* (budget options) offer homey, simple accommodations, usually with foam-mattress beds, hard pillows, clean sheets and blankets. Bathrooms and shower facilities are often shared, but a few will have rooms with a private bathroom. You may have to ask staff to turn on the *calefón* (hot-water heater) before taking a shower. Breakfast is usually coffee and rolls.

Hostels

Dorm-style lodgings usually set aside a few more expensive doubles for couples who want a social atmosphere but greater creature comforts. Look for pamphlets for **Backpackers Chile** (www.backpackerschile.com), which has many European-run listings and good standards. Most places don't insist on a Hostelling International (HI) card, but charge a bit more for nonmembers. The local affiliate of HI is **Asociación Chilena de Albergues Turísticos Juveniles** (☏022-577-1200; www.hostelling.cl; Hernando de Aguirre 201, Oficina 602, Providencia, Santiago). One-year membership cards are available at the head office for CH$14,000.

Hotels

From one-star austerity to five-star luxury, hotels provide a room with private bathroom, a telephone and cable or satellite TV. Breakfast is always served, even if basic, and often included.

Reservations are necessary if you'll be arriving at an awkward hour, during the summer high season or over a holiday weekend.

In South America the term 'motel' is a euphemism for a 'love hotel,' some with by-the-hour rates.

Refugios

Within some national parks, **Conaf** (Corporación Nacional Forestal; www.conaf.cl) maintains *refugios* (rustic shelters) for hikers and trekkers. Many lack upkeep due to Conaf's limited budget. There is a growing trend, already in place in Torres del Paine, for private concessions to manage *refugios* and park restaurants. Private reserves sometimes have *refugios* for hut-to-hut trekking.

Rental Accommodations

For long-term rentals in Santiago, check listings in Sunday's **El Mercurio** (www.elmercurio.cl), **Santiago Craigslist** (http://santiago.en.craigslist.org) or the weekly classified listing **El Rastro** (www.elrastro.cl). In vacation areas such as Viña del Mar, La Serena, Villarrica or Puerto Varas, people line main roads in summer to offer housing. You can also check tourist offices, bulletin boards outside grocery stores, or local papers.

Addresses

Names of streets, plazas and other features are often unwieldy, and usually appear abbreviated on maps. So Avenida Libertador General Bernardo O'Higgins might appear on a map as Avenida

B O'Higgins, just O'Higgins or even by a colloquial alternative (Alameda). The common address *costanera* denotes a coastal road.

Some addresses include the expression *local* (locale) followed by a number. *Local* means it's one of several offices at the same street address. Street numbers may begin with a zero, eg Bosque Norte 084. This confusing practice usually happens when an older street is extended in the opposite direction, beyond the original number 1.

The abbreviation 's/n' following a street address stands for *sin número* (without number) and indicates that the address has no specific street number.

Customs Regulations

Check **Chilean customs** (www.aduana.cl) for what and how much you can take in and out of the country.

There are no restrictions on import and export of local and foreign currency. Duty-free allowances include purchases of up to US$500.

Inspections are usually routine, although some travelers have had more thorough examinations. Travelers leaving the duty-free Regións I and XII are subject to internal customs inspections.

When entering the country, check your bags for food. There are heavy fines for fruit, dairy, spices, nuts, meat and organic products. SAG (Servicio Agrícola-Ganadero; Agriculture and Livestock Service) checks bags and levies fines to prevent the spread of diseases and pests that might threaten Chile's fruit exports.

X-ray machines are used at major international border crossings, such as Los Libertadores (the crossing from Mendoza, Argentina) and Pajaritos (the crossing from Bariloche, Argentina).

Electricity

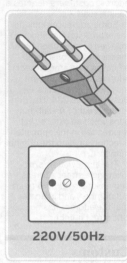

220V/50Hz

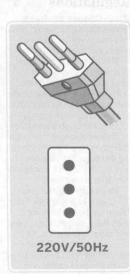

220V/50Hz

Embassies & Consulates

Argentinian Consulate – Antofagasta (☎055-222-0440; Blanco Encalada 1933)

Argentinian Consulate – Puerto Montt (☎065-228-2878; www.cpmon.cancilleria.gov.ar/; Pedro Montt 160, 6th fl; ⊗9am-2pm Mon-Fri)

Argentinian Consulate – Punta Arenas (☎061-226-1912; Av 21 de Mayo 1878)

Argentinian Embassy (☎022-582-2606; http://csigo.cancilleria.gov.ar/; Vicuña Mackenna 41, Santiago)

Australian Embassy (☎022-550-3500; www.chile.embassy.gov.au; Goyenechea 3621, 12th fl, Las Condes, Santiago) Australian Embassy in Santiago handles services for Chile, Colombia, Ecuador and Venezuela.

Bolivian Consulate – Antofagasta (☎055-225-9008; Washington 2675)

Bolivian Consulate – Arica (☎058-223-1030; www.consuladobolivia.cl; Lynch 298)

Bolivian Consulate – Calama (☎055-234-1976; www.consuladobolivia.cl; Latorre 1395)

Bolivian Consulate – Iquique (☎057-242-1777; Gorostiaga 215, Dept E)

Bolivian Embassy (☎022-232-8180; cgbolivia@manque-hue.net; Av Santa María 2796, Santiago)

Brazilian Embassy – Santiago (☎022-698-2486; www.embajadadebrasil.cl; Ovalle 1665)

Canadian Embassy (☎022-362-9660; enqserv@dfait-maeci.gc.ca; Tajamar 481, 12th fl, Santiago)

French Embassy (☎022-470-8000; www.france.cl; Av Condell 65, Santiago)

German Consulate (☎058-223-1657; Arturo Prat 391, 10th fl, Oficina 101, Arica)

German Embassy (☎022-463-2500; www.embajadade alemania.cl; Las Hualtatas 5677, Vitacura, Santiago)

Peruvian Consulate – Arica (☎058-223-1020; 18 de Septiembre 1554)

Peruvian Consulate – Iquique (☎057-241-1466; Zegers 570, 2nd fl)

Peruvian Embassy (☎022-235-4600; conpersantiago@adsl.tie.cl; Padre Mariano 10, Oficina 309, Providencia, Santiago)

Spanish Consulate (☎061-224-3566; José Menéndez 910, Punta Arenas)

UK Consulate – Punta Arenas (☎061-224-4727; Cataratas del Niagara 01325)

UK Consulate – Valparaíso (☎032-221-3063; Blanco 1199, 5th fl; ⊗9am-1pm Mon-Fri)

UK Embassy (☎022-370-4100; www.gov.uk/government/world/chile; Av El Bosque Norte 0125, 3rd fl, Las Condes, Santiago)

US Embassy (☎022-232-2600; santiago.usembassy.gov; Av Andrés Bello 2800, Las Condes, Santiago)

Food

Restaurant listings are organized according to author preference, considering value for cost.

All restaurants are non-smoking, unless there is a separate, enclosed area designated for smokers.

Those interested in food tours and a comprehensive Chilean food blog in English should check out **Foody Chile** (www.foodychile.com).

Meals

In general, Chilean food is hearty and traditional. Soups, meat and potatoes, and wonderful casseroles, such as *pastel de choclo* (maize casserole) and *chupe de jaiva* (crab casserole), are staples.

Most coastal towns have a *mercado de mariscos* (seafood market) where you can buy fresh fish or eat at small kitchens. If you like spice, seek out the Mapuche *merkén* (spice-smoked chili powder) or *ají Chileno*, an OK and moderately hot sauce sometimes found in restaurants.

Breakfast usually consists of white rolls with butter and jam, tea and instant coffee. Whole bean coffee is referred to as *café en grano*, available at some cafes and lodgings.

Set meals served at lunchtime, known as *menú del día*, are a good deal. They include a starter or dessert and main dish.

At home, people often eat light in the evening, with a tea time of bread, tea, cheese and ham. Known as *onces* (elevenses), afternoon tea is popular in the south, where German influence adds küchen (sweet, German-style cakes).

Drinks

Wine may have center stage, but there is plenty more to try. Pisco, a grape brandy, is Chile's national alcohol, grown in the dry soil of the north. Pisco sours are a popular start to cocktail hours, and consist of pisco, sugar and fresh *limon de pica*. Students prefer piscolas, mixing the alcohol with Coke or other soft drinks.

Draft beer is known as *schop*. Microbrews and regional artisan brewing have become popular, particularly in the south where German influence remains. Try brews made by Szot, Kross and Spoh.

Gay & Lesbian Travelers

Chile is a very conservative, Catholic-minded country yet strides in tolerance are being made. In 2015, Chile legalized same-sex civil unions. Santiago has an active gay scene, which concentrates in Barrio Bellavista. **Movil H** (Movement for the Integration and Liberation of Homosexuals; www.movilh.cl) advocates for gay rights. **Guia Gay Chile** (www.guiagay.cl) lists gay nightlife throughout Chile.

Health

Travelers who follow basic, common-sense precautions should have few problems traveling in Chile. Chile requires no special vaccines, but travelers should be up to date with routine shots. In temperate South America, mosquito-borne illnesses are generally not a problem, while most infections are related to the consumption of contaminated food and beverages.

Availability & Cost of Health Care

These modern facilities in Santiago offer 24-hour walk-in service for urgent problems, as well as specialty care (by appointment) and in-patient services: **Clínica Las Condes** (☎022-210-4000; www.clinicalascondes.cl; Lo Fontecilla 441, Las Condes) and **Clínica Alemana** (☎022-212-9700; http://portal.alemana.cl; Av Vitacura 5951, Santiago). For a list of additional physicians, dentists and laboratories in Santiago, go to the website of the **US Embassy** (http://chile.usembassy.gov).

Medical care in Santiago and other cities is generally good, but it may be difficult to find assistance in remote areas. Most doctors and hospitals expect payment in cash, regardless of whether you have travel health insurance. You can find a list of medical evacuation and travel insurance companies on the website of the **US State Department** (http://travel.state.gov).

Most pharmacies are well stocked and have trained pharmacists. Medication quality is comparable to other industrialized countries. Drugs that require a prescription elsewhere may be available over the counter here. If you're taking medication, have its generic (scientific) name handy for refills.

Medical care on Easter Island and in towns of Northern Patagonia is extremely limited. Rural *postas* (clinics) are rarely well stocked with medicine and are usually attended by paramedics only. Serious medical problems require evacuation to a major city.

Infectious Diseases & Environmental Hazards

BARTONELLOSIS (OROYA FEVER)

This is carried by sand flies in the arid river valleys on the western slopes of the Andes, between altitudes of 800m and 3000m. The chief symptoms are fever and severe body pains. Complications may include marked anemia, enlargement of the liver and spleen, and sometimes death. The drug of choice is chloramphenicol, though doxycycline is also effective.

HANTA VIRUS

A rapidly progressing, life-threatening infection acquired through exposure to the excretion of wild rodents. An outbreak was reported from rural areas in the southern and central parts of Chile in late 2010. Sporadic cases have been reported since that time. The disease occurs in those who live in close association with rodents.

It is unlikely to affect most travelers, though

those staying in forest areas may be at risk. Backpackers should never camp in an abandoned *refugio*, where there may be a risk of exposure to infected excretion. Pitching a tent is the safer option.

If backpacking in an area with hanta virus, campers can get more information from ranger stations.

ALTITUDE SICKNESS

Altitude sickness may develop in those who ascend rapidly to altitudes greater than 2500m. Symptoms may include headaches, nausea, vomiting, dizziness, malaise, insomnia and loss of appetite. Severe cases may be complicated by fluid in the lungs (high-altitude pulmonary edema) or swelling of the brain (high-altitude cerebral edema).

The best treatment for altitude sickness is descent. If you are exhibiting symptoms, do not ascend. If symptoms are severe or persistent, descend immediately.

When traveling to high altitudes, it's also important to avoid overexertion, eat light meals and abstain from alcohol. Some high-altitude areas have a clinic where oxygen is available.

CHILEAN RECLUSE SPIDERS

Found throughout the country, the Chilean recluse spider is not aggressive. Its venom is very dangerous: reactions can include lesions, renal failure and even death.

Chilean recluse spiders are 8mm to 30mm long (including legs) and are identified by their brown color, violin-like markings and unusual six eyes (most spiders have eight). If bitten, put ice on the bite and get immediate medical attention.

WATER

The tap water in Chile's cities is generally safe but has a high mineral content that can cause stomach upsets; bottled water is a good idea for delicate stomachs and in the north.

Vigorous boiling for one minute is the most effective means of water purification. At altitudes greater than 2000m, boil for three minutes. You can also disinfect water with iodine pills, a water filter or Steripen.

Internet Access

Most regions have excellent internet connections; it is typical for hotels, hostels and coffee shops to have wi-fi. Family guesthouses, particularly outside urban areas, lag behind in this area, though free public wi-fi is available in some communities on the plaza. Internet cafe rates range from CH$500 to CH$1200 per hour, with very high rates only in remote areas.

Legal Matters

Chile's *carabineros* (police) have a reputation for being professional and polite. Penalties for common offenses are similar to those given in much of Europe and North America. Chile has a zero-tolerance policy toward drinking and driving, so avoid alcohol if you plan to drive.

Drug possession, use or trafficking – including soft drugs such as cannabis – is treated very seriously and results in severe fines and imprisonment.

Police can demand identification at any time, so carry your passport. Throughout the country, the toll-free emergency telephone number for the police is ☎133.

Chileans often refer to police as *pacos*, a disrespectful (though not obscene) term that should *never* be used to a police officer's face.

Members of the military take themselves seriously, so avoid photographing military installations.

If you are involved in any automobile accident, your license (usually your international permit) will be confiscated until the case is resolved, although local officials will usually issue a temporary driving permit within a few days. A blood-alcohol test is obligatory. After this, you will be taken to the station to make a statement and then, under most circumstances, released. Ordinarily you cannot leave Chile until the matter is resolved; consult your consulate, insurance carrier and a lawyer at home.

Don't *ever* make the error of attempting to bribe the police, whose reputation for institutional integrity is high.

Maps

In Santiago, the **Instituto Geográfico Militar** (☎022-460-6800; www.igm.cl; Dieciocho 369, Centro; ☺8:30am-1pm & 2-5pm Mon-Fri), just south of the Alameda, produces excellent maps, also sold online. The IGM's 1:50,000 topographic series is valuable for trekkers, although the maps are out of date and those of sensitive border areas (where most national parks are) may not be available.

JLM Mapas publishes maps for all of the major regions and trekking areas at scales ranging from 1:50,000 to 1:500,000. The maps are widely distributed, easy to use and provide decent information, but they don't claim to be perfectly accurate.

In most major Chilean cities the **Automóvil Club de Chile** (Acchi; www.automovilclub.cl) has an office that sells highway maps, although not all of them are equally well stocked.

Santiago maps are available on **Map City** (www.mapcity.cl). Drivers might find Copec maps by **Compass** (www.mapascompass.cl) useful, available in Copec gas stations. Some local government websites have interactive maps that allow you to search for a street address in major cities.

Money

The Chilean unit of currency is the peso (CH$). Bank notes come in denominations of 500, 1000, 2000, 5000, 10,000 and 20,000 pesos. Coin values are one, five, 10, 50, 100 and 500 pesos, although one-peso coins are fast disappearing, and even fives and tens are uncommon. Carry small bills with you. It can be difficult to change large bills in rural areas; try gas stations and liquor stores by asking, '¿Tiene suelto?'.

Exchange rates are usually best in Santiago. Chile's currency has been pretty stable in recent years. The value of the dollar seems to decline during peak tourist season and shoot back up again come March. Paying a bill with US cash is sometimes acceptable, especially at tour agencies (check their exchange rate carefully). Many top-end hotels publish rates in US dollars with a lower exchange rate than the daily one. It's best to pay all transactions in pesos.

Money wire-transferred should arrive in a few days; Chilean banks can give you money in US dollars on request. Western Union offices can be found throughout Chile, usually adjacent to the post office.

ATMs

Chile's many ATM machines, known as *redbanc,* are the easiest and most convenient way to access funds. Both ATMs and your bank will likely charge a small fee for each transaction. Most have instructions in Spanish and English. Choose the option *tarjeta extranjera* (foreign card) before starting the transaction. You *cannot* rely on ATMs in Pisco Elqui, Bahía Inglesa or in small Patagonian towns. Throughout Patagonia, many small villages only have one bank, Banco del Estado, whose ATMs only sometimes accept MasterCard affiliates.

Those crossing overland from El Chaltén in Argentina to Villa O'Higgins should bring plenty of Chilean pesos, as the nearest reliable banks are in Coyhaique.

Note that ATMs now charge up to CH$4000 per transaction. Some foreign banks will reimburse these fees; it's worth checking in advance. Also, withdrawals are limited to a sum of CH$200,000.

Cash

Some banks and *casas de cambio* (exchange houses) will exchange cash, usually US dollars only. Check the latter for commissions and poor rates. More costly purchases, such as tours and hotel bills, can sometimes be paid in US cash.

Credit Cards

Plastic (especially Visa and MasterCard) is welcome in most established businesses; however, many businesses will charge up to 6% extra to cover the charge they have to pay for the transaction. Credit cards can also be useful to show 'sufficient funds' before entering another South American country.

Tipping

It's customary to tip 10% of the bill in restaurants (the bill may include it under 'servicio'). Taxi drivers do not require tips, although you may round off the fare.

Opening Hours

We list high-season hours in the book. In many provincial cities and towns, restaurants and services are closed on Sunday and tourist offices close in low season.

Banks	9am-2pm weekdays, sometimes 10am-1pm Sat
Government offices & businesses	9am-6pm on weekdays
Museums	often close on Mon
Restaurants	noon-11pm, many close 4-7pm
Shops	10am-8pm, some close 1-3pm

Public Holidays

National holidays, when government offices and businesses are closed, are listed below. There is pressure to reduce these or to eliminate so-called sandwich holidays, which many Chileans take between an actual holiday and the weekend, by moving some to the nearest Monday.

Año Nuevo (New Year) January 1

Semana Santa (Easter Week) March or April

Día del Trabajo (Labor Day) May 1

Glorias Navales Commemorating the naval Battle of Iquique; May 21

Corpus Christi May/June; dates vary

Día de San Pedro y San Pablo (St Peter and St Paul's Day) June 29

Asunción de la Virgen (Assumption) August 15

Día de Unidad Nacional (Day of National Unity) First Monday of September

Día de la Independencia Nacional (National Independence Day) September 18

Día del Ejército (Armed Forces Day) September 19

Día de la Raza (Columbus Day) October 12

Todo los Santos (All Saints' Day) November 1

Inmaculada Concepción (Immaculate Conception) December 8

Navidad (Christmas Day) December 25

Safe Travel

Compared with other South American countries, Chile is remarkably safe. Petty thievery is a problem in larger cities and bus terminals and at beach resorts in summertime, so always keep a close eye on all belongings. Photographing military installations is strictly prohibited.

GOVERNMENT TRAVEL ADVICE

The following government websites offer travel advisories and information on current hot spots.

Australian Government (www.smartraveller.gov.au)

Canadian Government (www.travel.gc.ca)

German Foreign Office (www.auswaertiges-amt.de)

Japan Ministry of Foreign Affairs (www.mofa.go.jp)

Netherlands Ministry of Foreign Affairs (www.government.nl)

New Zealand Government (www.safetravel.govt.nz)

UK Foreign & Commonwealth Office (www.fco.gov.uk/en/travel-and-living-abroad)

US State Department (http://travel.state.gov)

Dogs & Bugs

Chile's stray canines are a growing problem. Scabies can be common in street dogs; don't pet those that have bad skin problems, it's highly contagious. If driving, be prepared for dogs barking and running after the bumper.

Summertime in the south brings about the pesty *tábano*, a large biting horsefly that is more an annoyance than a health risk. Bring along insect repellent and wear light-colored clothing.

Natural Hazards

Earthquakes are a fact of life for most Chileans. Local construction often does not meet seismic safety standards; adobe buildings tend to be especially vulnerable. The unpredictability of quakes means there is little that a traveler can do to prepare.

Active volcanoes are less likely to threaten safety, since they usually give some warning. Nevertheless, unexpected eruptions in recent years have the country monitoring volcanoes more closely than ever.

Many of Chile's finest beaches have dangerous offshore rip currents, so ask before diving in and make sure someone on shore knows your whereabouts. Many beaches post signs that say *apto para bañar* (swimming OK) and *no apto para bañar* (swimming not OK) or *peligroso* (dangerous).

In the winter, the smog in Santiago can become a health risk. The city declares 'pre-emergency' or 'emergency' states when the level of smog is dangerously high and takes measures to limit emissions. Children, senior citizens and people with respiratory problems should avoid trips to downtown Santiago at these times.

Personal Security & Theft

Crime is more concentrated in the dense urban areas, though picks up in tourist destinations in summer. Those staying in cabins should close and lock windows before heading out, particularly in popular resort towns. At the beach, be alert for pickpockets and avoid leaving valuables around while you go for a swim. Never leave an unattended car unlocked and keep all valuables in the trunk.

Don't fall for distractions, such as a tap on the shoulder, spitting or getting something spilled on you; these 'accidents' are often part of a team effort to relieve you of some valuables. Be mindful of your belongings and avoid conspicuous displays of expensive jewelry.

Stay clear of political protests, particularly in the capital; they have a tendency to attract violent clashes.

Baggage insurance is a good idea. Do not leave valuables such as cash or cameras in your room. Some travelers bring their own lock. Upmarket hotels often have secure strongboxes in each room.

Shopping

Chile is one of the few countries in the world where the semiprecious stone lapis lazuli is found. It is a deep navy-blue color and makes sophisticated jewelry that can be bought in most Chilean jewelers and a few *ferias* (artisans' markets). However, this unique stone can empty your wallet in a flash: expect a pair of good-quality earrings to cost around CH$20,000. Check the quality of the setting and silver used – they are often only silver plated and very soft.

Craft markets can be found throughout the country. In the north, artisans put shaggy llama and alpaca wool to good use by making thick jumpers, scarves and other garments to take the bite off the frigid highland nights. Many of these goods are similar to those in Bolivia and Peru. You'll also see

crafts made with cactus wood, and painstakingly crafted leather goods in Norte Chico.

In Chiloé and Patagonia, hand-knit woolens such as bulky fishermen's sweaters and blankets are reasonably priced and useful in winter. In the Araucanía, look for jewelry based on Mapuche designs, which are unique to Chile. They also produce quality weavings and basketry. In the Lakes District and Patagonia, artisans carve wooden plates and bowls out of the (sustainable) hardwood *raulí*.

Wine lovers will not want for Chilean wines to choose from: stick to the boutique wineries with wines that you can't find in your own country, or pick up bottles of the powerful grape-brandy pisco, which is difficult to find outside Chile. Other artisanal edibles include *miel de ulmo*, a very aromatic and tasty honey special to Patagonia, and *mermelada de murtilla*, a jam made of a tart red berry. As long as such goods are still sealed, there shouldn't be a problem getting them through international customs.

Many cities have good antiques markets, most notably Santiago's Mercado Franklin and Valparaíso's Plaza O'Higgins. Flea markets are commonly known as *ferias persas* (Persian fairs).

For a preview, check out the website of **Fundación Artesanías de Chile** (Chilean Craft Foundation; www. artesaniasdechile.cl) to see a selection of local *artesanías*.

Bargaining

Crafts markets are the only acceptable venue for bargaining. Transport and accommodations rates are generally fixed and prominently displayed. Chileans can be offended by aggressive haggling as it's not part of the culture.

Telephone

Throughout Chile there are call centers with private cabins and reasonable interna-

CALLING ARGENTINE CELL PHONES

When dialing an Argentine cell phone from another country, dial your international exit code, then 54, then 9, then the area code without the 0, then the number – leaving out the 15 (which most Argentine cell phone numbers start with).

tional rates, although these are rapidly being replaced by internet cafes with Skype. Remote tour operators and lodges have satellite phones with a Santiago prefix.

Calling from cell phones or land lines requires different prefixes. The book lists phone numbers as called by cell phones, given the prevalence of travelers who buy local SIM cards.

Cell Phones

Cell-phone numbers have eight digits. If calling from a land line or Skype, add the two-digit prefix 09. Throughout this book, cell numbers are listed without prefix. If calling cell to landline, use the landline's three-digit area code (included in listings here).

Cell phones sell for as little as CH$12,000 and can be charged up by prepaid phone cards. Cell phones have a 'caller pays' format. Calls between cell and landlines are expensive and quickly eat up prepaid card amounts.

Do your homework if you want to bring your own cell phone: you'll need a SIM-unlocked GSM-compatible phone that operates on a frequency of 850MHz or 1900MHz (commonly used in the US). If you have such a phone, you can buy a new SIM card from a Chilean operator such as Entel or Movistar. Then purchase phone credit from the same carrier in kiosks, pharmacies or supermarket check-outs. In Patagonia, Entel has much better coverage than other companies.

There's reception in most inhabited areas, with the poorest reception in the middle of the Atacama Desert and parts of Patagonia.

Phone Codes

Chile's country code is ☑56. All telephone numbers in Santiago and the Metropolitan Region have seven digits; all other telephone numbers have six digits except for certain toll-free and emergency numbers. The toll-free number for the police is ☑133, ambulance is ☑131. You'll reach directory assistance at ☑103.

Long-distance calls are based on a carrier system: to place a call, precede the number with the telephone company's code: **Entel** (☑123), for example. To make a collect call, dial ☑182 to get an operator.

Toilets

Pipes and sewer systems in older buildings are quite fragile: used toilet paper should be discarded in wastebaskets. Cheaper accommodations and public toilets rarely provide toilet paper, so carry your own wherever you go. Better restaurants and cafes are good alternatives to public toilets, which are often dirty.

Tourist Information

Every regional capital and some other cities have a local representative of **Sernatur** (☑022-731-8310; www.chile.travel/en.html), the national tourist service. Offices vary in usefulness – some have astonishingly knowledgeable multilingual staff, but others have little hands-on knowledge of the destinations that they cover.

Many municipalities also have their own tourist office, usually on the main plaza or at the bus terminal. In some areas, these offices may be open during the summer only.

If you plan on hiking, buy good topo maps of the area you plan to visit from an outdoor store, as parks rarely have detailed maps of their own for visitors.

Some official international representatives for Chilean tourism can be found abroad. Consulates in major cities may have a tourist representative, but more accessible and comprehensive information can be found through specialized travel agencies and on the internet.

Chile has a few general travel agencies that work with affiliates around the world. **Chilean Travel Service** (CTS; ☑02-251-0400; www.ctsturismo.cl; Antonio Bellet 77, Providencia) has well-informed multilingual staff and can organize accommodations and tours all over Chile through your local travel agency.

Travelers with Disabilities

Travel within Chile is still a robust challenge for those with disabilities, though patient planning can open a lot of doors. Even top-end hotels and resorts cannot be relied upon to have ramps or rooms adapted for those with impaired mobility; an estimated 10% of hotels in Santiago cater to wheelchairs. Lifts are more common in large hotels and the law now requires new public buildings to provide disabled access.

Santiago's **Metro** (www.metrosantiago.cl; ◷6:30am-11pm Mon-Sat, 8am-11pm Sun) is in the process of making subway lines more accessible. Public bus company **Transantiago** (☑800-730-073; www.transantiago.cl) has access ramps and spaces for wheelchairs on new

buses. Some street lights have noise-indicated crossings for the blind. Those in wheelchairs will find Chile's narrow and poorly maintained sidewalks awkward to negotiate. Crossing streets is also tricky, but most Chilean drivers are remarkably courteous toward pedestrians – especially those with obvious handicaps.

American organization **Accessible Journeys** (☑in USA 800-846-4537; www.disabilitytravel.com) organizes independent travel to Chile for people with disabilities.

National parks are often discounted and sometimes free for disabled visitors – check ahead with **Conaf** (Corporación Nacional Forestal; www.conaf.cl). Cruises or ferries such as Navimag sometimes offer free upgrades to disabled travelers, and some of the ski resorts near Santiago have outrigger poles for disabled skiers.

Visas

Nationals of the US, Canada, Australia and the EU do not need a visa to visit Chile. Passports are obligatory and are essential for cashing traveler's checks, checking into hotels and other routine activities.

The Chilean government collects a US$117/132/23 'reciprocity' fee from arriving Australian/Canadian/Mexican citizens in response to these governments imposing a similar fee on Chilean citizens applying for visas. The fee for US residents has been lifted. This cash or credit card payment applies only to tourists arriving by air in Santiago and is valid for the life of the passport.

Always carry your passport: Chile's police can demand identification at any moment, and many hotels require you to show it upon check-in.

If your passport is lost or stolen, notify the police, ask them for a police statement, and notify your consulate as soon as possible.

Tourist Cards

On arrival, you'll be handed a 90-day tourist card. Don't lose it! If you do, go to the **Policía Internacional** (☎02-737-1292; Borgoño 1052, Santiago; ⊗8:30am-5pm Mon-Fri) or the nearest police station. You will be asked for it upon leaving the country.

It's possible to renew a tourist card for 90 more days at the **Departamento de Extranjería** (Map p50; ☎02-550-2484; www.extranjeria.gob.cl; Agustinas 1235, Santiago; ⊗9am-2pm Mon-Fri). Bring photocopies of your passport and tourist card. You can also visit the Departamento de Extranjería in a regional capital. Many visitors prefer a quick dash across the Argentine border and back.

Volunteering

Experienced outdoor guides may be able to exchange labor for accommodations during the busy high season, if you can stick out the entire season. Language schools often place students in volunteer work as well. At Parque Nacional Torres del Paine, volunteers can help with trail maintenance, biological studies or an animal census. Spanish-language skills are always a plus.

AMA Torres del Paine (www.amatorresdelpaine.org) Located in the national park, works with a limited number of volunteers.

Experiment Chile (www.experiment.cl) Organizes 14-week language-learning/volunteer programs.

Global Community Project (www.globalcommunityproject.blogspot.com) US-based outfit that takes student-exchange volunteers with advance notice.

Go Voluntouring (www.govoluntouring.com) International organization that consolidates listings from various NGOs, such as Earthwatch, in addition to social and teaching programs.

Un Techo Para Chile (www.untechoparachile.cl) Nonprofit organization that builds homes for low-income families throughout the country.

WWOOF Chile (Worldwide Opportunities on Organic Farms; ☎cell 9129-5033; http://www.wwoofchile.cl) Volunteers (wwoofers) live and learn on organic properties.

Work

It's increasingly difficult to obtain residence and work permits for Chile. Consequently, many foreigners do not bother to do so, but the most reputable employers will insist on the proper visa. If you need one, go to the **Departamento de Extranjería** (Map p50; ☎02-550-2484; www.extranjeria.gob.cl; Agustinas 1235, Santiago; ⊗9am-2pm Mon-Fri).

In Santiago, many youth hostels offer work, an offer usually stated on their websites. **Contact Chile** (www.contactchile.cl) lists internship opportunities online; they are mainly in the service sector. It is not unusual for visiting travelers to work as English-language instructors in Santiago and other cities. In general, pay is hourly and full-time employment is hard to come by without a commitment to stay for some time.

Transportation

GETTING THERE & AWAY

Flights, cars and tours can be booked online at lonelyplanet.com/bookings.

Entering the Country

Entry is generally straightforward as long as your passport is valid for at least six months beyond your arrival date.

Onward Tickets

Chile requires travelers to have a return or onward ticket. You may be asked to provide evidence at the flight counter in your departure country. The solution is to either purchase a refundable return air ticket or get the cheapest possible onward bus ticket from a bus company that offers online sales and print your receipt.

Air

Chile has direct connections with North America, the UK, Europe, Australia and New Zealand, in addition to its neighboring countries. International flights within South America are fairly expensive unless purchased as part of intercontinental travel. There are bargain round-trip fares between Buenos Aires or Lima and Santiago.

Airports

Most long-distance flights to Chile arrive at Santiago, landing at **Aeropuerto Internacional Arturo Merino Benítez** (www.aeropuertosantiago.cl) in the suburb of Pudahuel. Flights from neighboring countries may reach regional airports such as Arica, Iquique and Punta Arenas.

Tickets
INTERCONTINENTAL (RTW) TICKETS

Most intercontinental airlines traveling to Chile also offer round-the-world (RTW) tickets in conjunction with the airlines they have alliances with. Other companies, such as **Airtreks** (☑North America 415-977-7100, toll-free 877-247-8735; www.airtreks.com), offer more flexible, customized RTW tickets that don't tie you into airline affiliates. Similar

'Circle Pacific' fares allow you to take excursions between Australasia and Chile, often with a stop at Easter Island. Check the fine print for restrictions. Agencies selling RTW tickets include the following:

Flight Centre (www.flight-centre.com)

STA (www.statravel.com)

Australia & New Zealand

Lan and Qantas share a flight from Sydney to Santiago, stopping in Auckland. **Lan** (☑1800 126 038; www.lan.com) also has an office in Australia.

Canada

Air Canada flies to Santiago from Toronto, or connect via US cities with other airlines.

Continental Europe

There are regular direct flights from Madrid to Santiago with Lan and Iberia. Several airlines have flights from major European cities via Argentina or Brazil, including Lufthansa. Flights with American carriers with connections via the USA are competitively priced.

French Polynesia

Lan flies once a week to and from Papeete in Tahiti, stopping at Easter Island.

South America

Many airlines fly daily between Santiago and Buenos Aires, Argentina, for a stand-

---

ARRIVAL FEES

A one-time reciprocity fee is charged to *arriving* Australians (US$117), Canadians (US$132) and Mexicans (US$23), valid for the life of the passport. A Chilean departure tax for international flights is included in airfares.

CLIMATE CHANGE & TRAVEL

Every form of transport that relies on carbon-based fuel generates CO_2, the main cause of human-induced climate change. Modern travel is dependent on airplanes, which might use less fuel per mile per person than most cars but travel much greater distances. The altitude at which aircraft emit gases (including CO_2) and particles also contributes to their climate change impact. Many websites offer 'carbon calculators' that allow people to estimate the carbon emissions generated by their journey and, for those who wish to do so, to offset the impact of the greenhouse gases emitted with contributions to portfolios of climate-friendly initiatives throughout the world. Lonely Planet offsets the carbon footprint of all staff and author travel.

ard fare of about US$275 round-trip. However, European airlines that pick up and discharge most of their passengers in Buenos Aires sometimes try to fill empty seats by selling cheap round-trips between the Argentine and Chilean capitals.

There are reasonable Lan flights from Santiago to Mendoza (round-trip US$210, twice daily) and to Córdoba (round-trip US$250, twice daily).

Lan and Taca have numerous daily flights from Lima, Peru, to Santiago for about US$550 (round-trip), and many discount fares pop up on this route. From Lima, Lan also goes direct to Easter Island. Lan also flies from Lima to the southern city of Tacna, only 50km from the Chilean border city of Arica (round-trip US$300). Lan flies daily from Santiago to La Paz, Bolivia (round-trip US$400), with a stop in northern Chile.

Taca and Avianca link Santiago daily with Bogotá, Colombia (round-trip US$750), sometimes with another South American stop. Lan flies to Montevideo, the Uruguayan capital (round-trip US$450). Gol and TAM fly to Brazilian and Paraguayan destinations.

Recommended agencies:

ASATEJ (Al Mundo; ☎0810-777-2728; www.asatej.com) In Argentina.

Student Travel Bureau (☎011-3038-1551; www.stb.com.br) In Brazil.

UK & Ireland

At the time of writing there were no direct flights between London and Santiago. Connections from the UK go through Madrid, Buenos Aires and the US. Prices average between £760 and £900, depending on the time of year. **Journey Latin America** (☎020-8747-3108; www.journeylatinamerica.co.uk) is a reputable agency.

USA

From the USA, the principal gateways to South America are Miami, New York, Los Angeles, Atlanta and Dallas. For those who plan to travel in the Atacama Desert, one time-saving alternative to landing in Santiago is to fly to Lima, Peru, and on to the Peruvian border city of Tacna, or to Arica (in northern Chile).

Exito (www.exitotravel.com) is recommended for online bookings.

Land

Border Crossings

Chile's northern border touches Peru and Bolivia, while its vast eastern boundary hugs Argentina. Of the numerous border crossings with Argentina, only a few are served by public transportation. Most international buses depart from Terminal de Buses in Santiago.

Bus

Common destinations are served by the following bus companies, all located in the **Terminal de Buses Santiago** (www.terminaldebusessantiago.cl).

ARGENTINA

Andesmar (☎0810-122-1122; www.andesmar.com) Mendoza.

Buses Ahumada (☎022-696-9337; www.busesahumada.cl) Buenos Aires.

Cata (☎022-779-3660; www.catainternacional.com) Mendoza.

Crucero del Norte (☎022-776-2416; www.crucerodelnorte.com.ar) Also goes to Brazil and Paraguay.

El Rápido (☎022-779-0316; www.elrapidoint.com.ar) Also goes to Uruguay.

Via Bariloche (www.viabariloche.com.ar) Bariloche from Chilean Lakes District.

BRAZIL

Chilebus Internacional (☎022-776-5557)

Pluma (☎022-779-6054; www.pluma.com.br)

PERU

Ormeño (☎022-779-3443; www.grupo-ormeno.com.pe) Also goes to Ecuador and Argentina.

Tas-Choapa (☎022-776-7307; www.taschoapa.cl) Lima; also goes to Argentina.

Car & Motorcycle

There is paperwork and possibly additional charges to take a hired car out of Chile; ask the rental agency to talk you through it.

From Argentina

Unless you're crossing in Chile's extreme south there's no way to avoid the Andes. Public transportation is offered on only a few of the crossings to Argentina, and many passes close in winter.

NORTHERN ROUTES

Calama to Jujuy and Salta A popular year-round route over the Andes via San Pedro de Atacama, Ruta 27 goes over the Paso de Jama. It has a regular bus service (with advance booking advisable). Slightly further south, on Ruta 23, motorists will find the 4079m Paso de Lago Sico a rougher but passable summer alternative. Chilean customs are at San Pedro de Atacama.

Iquique to Oruro A few scattered bus services run along a paved road from Iquique past the Parque Nacional Volcán Isluga to the Paso Colchane; catch a truck or bus on to Oruro from here (on an unpaved road).

Copiapó to Catamarca and La Rioja There is no public transportation over the 4726m Paso de San Francisco; it's a dirt road that requires high clearance, but rewards with spectacular scenery – including the luminous Laguna Verde.

La Serena to San Juan Dynamited by the Argentine military during the Beagle Channel dispute of 1978–79, the 4779m Paso del Agua Negra is a beautiful route, but the road is unpaved beyond Guanta and buses eschew it. It is a good bicycle route and tours run to hot springs that are on the Argentine side.

MIDDLE CHILE

Santiago or Valparaíso to Mendoza and Buenos Aires A dozen or more bus companies service this beautiful and vital lifeline to Argentina, along Ruta 60 through the Los Libertadores tunnel. Winter snow sometimes closes the route, but rarely for long.

Talca to Malargüe and San Rafael There's no public transportation along Ruta 115 to cross the 2553m Paso Pehuenche,

southeast of Talca. Another crossing from Curicó over the 2502m Paso Vergara is being developed but is still hard to access.

SOUTHERN MAINLAND ROUTES

Several scenic crossings squeeze through to Argentina from Temuco south to Puerto Montt, some involving bus-boat shuttles that are popular in summer (book ahead).

Temuco to Zapala and Neuquén A good road crosses over the 1884m Paso de Pino Hachado, directly east of Temuco along the upper Río Biobío. A secondary unpaved route just south of here is the 1298m Paso de Icalma, with occasional bus traffic in summer.

Temuco to San Martín de los Andes The most popular route from Temuco passes Lago Villarrica, Pucón and Curarrehue en route to the Paso de Mamuil Malal (known to Argentines as Paso Tromen). On the Argentine side, the road skirts the northern slopes of Volcán Lanín. There is a regular summer bus service, but the pass may close in winter.

Valdivia to San Martín de los Andes This mix-and-match route starts with a bus from Valdivia to Panguipulli, Choshuenco and Puerto Fuy, followed by a ferry across Lago Pirihueico to the village of Pirihueico. From Pirihueico a local bus goes to Argentine customs at 659m Paso Huahum, where travelers can catch a bus to San Martín.

Osorno to Bariloche via Paso Cardenal Samoré This crossing, commonly known as Pajaritos, is the quickest land route in the southern Lakes District, passing through Parque Nacional Puyehue on the Chilean side and Parque Nacional Nahuel Huapi on the Argentine side. It has a frequent bus service all year.

Puerto Varas to Bariloche Very popular in summer but open all year, this bus-ferry combination via Parque Nacional Vicente Pérez Rosales starts in Puerto Varas. A ferry goes from Petrohué, at the western end of Lago

Todos Los Santos, to Peulla, and a bus crosses 1022m Paso de Pérez Rosales to Argentine immigration at Puerto Frías. After crossing Lago Frías by launch, there's a short bus hop to Puerto Blest on Lago Nahuel Huapi and another ferry to Puerto Pañuelo (Llao Llao). From Llao Llao there is a frequent bus service to Bariloche.

SOUTHERN PATAGONIAN ROUTES

Puerto Ramírez to Esquel There are two options here. From Villa Santa Lucía on the Carretera Austral, a good lateral road forks at Puerto Ramírez. The north fork goes to Futaleufú, where a bridge crosses the river to the Argentine side with colectivos to Esquel. The south fork goes to Palena and Argentine customs at Carrenleufú, with less-frequent buses to Trevelin and Esquel. The more efficient crossing is Futaleufú.

Coyhaique to Comodoro Rivadavia There are several buses per week, often heavily booked, from Coyhaique to Comodoro Rivadavia via Río Mayo. For private vehicles, there is an alternative route from Balmaceda to Perito Moreno via the 502m Paso Huemules.

Chile Chico to Los Antiguos From Puerto Ibáñez take the ferry to Chile Chico on the southern shore of Lago Carrera and a shuttle bus to Los Antiguos, which has connections to Atlantic coastal towns and Ruta 40. There is bus service to Chile Chico from Cruce el Maitén at the southwestern end of Lago General Carrera.

Cochrane to Bajo Caracoles Linking Valle Chacabuco (Parque Nacional Patagonia), 647m Paso Roballos links Cochrane with a flyspeck outpost in Argentina's Santa Cruz province.

Puerto Natales to Río Turbio and El Calafate Frequent year-round buses connect Puerto Natales to Río Gallegos and El Calafate via Río Turbio. Buses from Puerto Natales go direct to El Calafate, the gateway to Parque Nacional Los Glaciares, via Paso Río Don Guillermo.

Punta Arenas to Río Gallegos

Many buses travel between Punta Arenas and Río Gallegos. It's a five- to eight-hour trip because of slow customs checks and a rough segment of Argentine Ruta Nacional (RN) 3.

Punta Arenas to Tierra del Fuego

From Punta Arenas a 2½-hour ferry trip or a 10-minute flight takes you to Porvenir, on Chilean Tierra del Fuego, but there are currently no buses that continue to the Argentine side. The best option is direct buses from Punta Arenas to Ushuaia via Primera Angostura, with shorter and more frequent ferry service.

Puerto Williams to Ushuaia

Year-round passenger boat service from Puerto Williams, on Isla Navarino (reached by plane or boat from Punta Arenas), to the Argentine city of Ushuaia is weather dependent.

From Bolivia

Between Bolivia and Chile a paved highway runs from Arica to La Paz. The route from Iquique to Colchane is also paved – although the road beyond to Oruro is not. There are buses on both routes, but more on the former.

It's possible to travel from Uyuni, Bolivia, to San Pedro de Atacama via the Portezuelo del Cajón on organized jeep trips.

From Peru

Tacna to Arica is the only overland crossing, with a choice of bus, colectivo or taxi, with train service currently on hiatus.

GETTING AROUND

Traveling Chile from head to tail is easy, with a constant procession of flights and buses connecting cities up and down the country. What is less convenient is the service east to west, and south of Puerto Montt, where the country turns into a labyrinth of fjords, glaciers and mountains. However, routes are improving.

Air

Time-saving flights have become more affordable in Chile and are sometimes cheaper than a comfortable long-distance bus. Consider flying from Arica to Santiago in a few short hours, compared to a crippling 28 hours via bus. Other than slow ferries, flights are often the only way to reach isolated southern regions in a timely manner. Round-trip fares are often cheaper.

Airlines in Chile

Chile has two principal domestic airlines. Regional airlines and air taxis connect isolated regions in the south and the Juan Fernández archipelago. Most Chilean cities are near domestic airports with commercial air service. Santiago's **Aeropuerto Internacional Arturo Merino Benítez** (www.aeropuertosantiago.cl) has a separate domestic terminal; Santiago also has smaller airfields for air-taxi services to the Juan Fernández archipelago. Tickets include departure tax.

Lan (☑600-526-2000; www.lan.com) Centro (Paseo Huérfanos 926-B, Centro, Santiago); Las Condes (Av El Bosque Norte 0194, Las Condes, Santiago); Providencia (Providencia 2006, Providencia, Santiago) The dominant carrier of South America, with the most extensive system of connecting cities, including flights to Easter Island.

Sky Airline (☑600-600-2828; www.skyairline.cl; Huérfanos 815, Santiago) Can be cheaper.

Air Passes

The best rates with Lan are found on its Chilean website, accessed only in-country, where weekly specials give cut-rate deals with as much as 40% off, especially on well-traveled routes such as Puerto Montt to Punta Arenas. Booking ahead and buying round-trips save money.

LanPass offers miles on the One World alliance, with partners such as American Airlines, British Airways, Iberia and Qantas.

DESTINATION	COST (ROUND-TRIP, CH$)
Antofagasta	105,000
Arica	160,000
Calama	100,000
Concepción	80,000
Copiapó	85,000
Coyhaique	120,000
Iquique	115,000
La Serena	60,000
Puerto Montt	75,000
Punta Arenas	165,000
Temuco	90,000

Bicycle

To pedal your way through Chile, a bici todo terreno (mountain bike) or touring bike with beefy tires is essential. The climate can be a real challenge: from Temuco south, be prepared for rain; from Santiago north, especially in the vast expanses of the Atacama Desert, water sources are infrequent and towns are separated by long distances. In some areas wind is a serious factor; north to south is generally easier than south to north, with some readers reporting strong headwinds going south in summer. Chilean motorists are usually courteous, but on narrow two-lane highways without shoulders, cars can be a real hazsard.

Car ferries in Patagonia often charge a bicycle fee. Outside the Carretera Austral, most towns have bike-repair shops. Buses will usually take bikes, though airlines may charge extra; check with yours.

Hire

Most of Chile's more touristy towns rent bikes, although their quality may vary. There are relatively few bike-rental shops, but *hospedajes* (budget accommodations) and tour agencies often have a few handy. Expect to pay between CH$8000 and CH$12,000 per day. A quality mountain bike with front suspension and decent brakes can cost CH$18,000 per day or more, but you're only likely to find them in outdoor activity destinations such as the Lakes District and San Pedro de Atacama.

It's common to leave some form of deposit or guarantee: an ID will often suffice.

Purchase

Bikes are not especially cheap in Chile. A decent mountain bike with suspension sells for CH$150,000 and up. If you're looking to sell your wheels at the end of your trip, try approaching tour agencies that rent bikes.

Boat

Chile's preposterously long coastline is strung with a necklace of ports and harbors, but opportunities for travelers to get about by boat are concentrated in the south.

Navigating southern Chile's jigsaw-puzzle coast by ferry is about more than just getting from A to B – it's an essential part of the travel experience. From Puerto Montt south, Chilean Patagonia and Tierra del Fuego are accessed by ferries traveling the intricate maze of islands and fjords with spectacular coastal scenery.

Note that the end of the high season also marks limited ferry service.

Navimag's ferry service that runs from Puerto Montt to Puerto Natales is one of the continent's great travel experiences. The following information lists only the principal passenger-ferry services. Also on offer are a few exclusive tour operators that run their own cruises.

Common routes include the following:

Castro to Laguna San Rafael Navimag cruises *Mare Australis* to the stunning Laguna San Rafael.

Chiloé to Chaitén Transmarchilay, Naviera Austral and Navimag run between Quellón, on Chiloé, and Chaitén in summer. There are also summer services from Castro to Chaitén.

Hornopirén to Caleta Gonzalo In summer, Naviera Austral ferries take the Ruta Bi-Modal, two ferries linked by a short land stretch in the middle, to Parque Pumalín's Caleta Gonzalo, about 60km north of Chaitén.

La Arena to Puelche Ferries shuttle back and forth across the gap, about 45km southeast of Puerto Montt, to connect two northerly segments of the Carretera Austral.

Mainland to Chiloé Regular ferries plug the gap between Pargua and Chacao, at the northern tip of Chiloé.

Puerto Ibáñez to Chile Chico Sotramin operates automobile/passenger ferries across Lago General Carrera, south of Coyhaique. There are shuttles from Chile Chico to the Argentine town of Los Antiguos.

Puerto Montt to Chaitén Naviera Austral runs car-passenger ferries from Puerto Montt to Chaitén.

Puerto Montt to Laguna San Rafael Expensive cruises with Catamaranes del Sur and Cruceros Skorpios go direct to take a twirl about Laguna San Rafael.

Puerto Montt to Puerto Chacabuco Navimag goes from Puerto Montt to Puerto Chacabuco; buses continue on to Coyhaique and Parque Nacional Laguna San Rafael.

Puerto Montt to Puerto Natales Navimag departs Puerto Montt weekly, taking about four days to puddle-jump to Puerto Natales. Erratic Patagonian weather can play havoc with schedules.

Puerto Williams to Ushuaia This most necessary connection still has no public ferry but does have regular private motorboat service.

Punta Arenas to Tierra del Fuego Transbordador Austral Broom runs ferries from Punta Arenas' ferry terminal Tres Puentes to Porvenir; from Punta Delgada, east of Punta Arenas, to Bahía Azul; and from Tres Puentes to Puerto Williams, on Isla Navarino.

Naviera Austral (☑065-227-0430; www.navieraustral. cl; Angelmó 2187, Puerto Montt)

Naviera Sotramin (☑067-223-7958; http://sotramin. cl; Baquedano 1198, Coyhaique; passenger/automobile CH$2100/18,650)

Navimag (☑022-442-3120; www.navimag.cl; Av El Bosque Norte 0440, Piso 11, Santiago; ⊙9am-6:30pm Mon-Fri; ⓂTobalaba) Book ahead for ferry tickets in Chilean Patagonia.

Transbordador Austral Broom (☑061-221-8100; www.tabsa.cl; Av Bulnes 05075, Punta Arenas)

Transmarchilay (☑065-227-0700; www.transmarchilay.cl; Angelmó 2187, Puerto Montt)

Bus

Long-distance buses in Chile have an enviable reputation for punctuality, efficiency and comfort, although prices and classes vary significantly between companies. Most Chilean cities have a central bus terminal, but in some cities the companies have separate offices. The bus stations are well organized with destinations, schedules and fares prominently displayed.

Major highways and some others are paved (except for large parts of the Carretera Austral), but secondary roads may be gravel or dirt. Long-distance buses generally have toilet facilities and often serve coffee, tea and even meals on board; if not, they make regular stops. By European or North American standards, fares are inexpensive.

On Chile's back roads transportation is slower and *micros* (often minibuses) are less frequent, older and more basic.

The nerve center of the country, Santiago, has four main bus terminals serving northern, central and southern destinations.

Chile's biggest bus company is **Tur Bus** (☎600-660-6600; www.turbus.cl), with an all-embracing network of services around the country. It is known for being extremely punctual. Discounts are given for tickets purchased online (later retrieve your ticket at the counter).

Its main competitor is **Pullman** (☎600-320-3200; www.pullman.cl), which also has extensive routes throughout the country.

Specifically aimed at backpackers, **Pachamama by Bus** (☎022-688-8018; www.pachamamabybus.com; Agustinas 2113, Barrio Brasil, Santiago) is a hop-on hop-off service with two long routes exploring the north and south respectively. It's not cheap (for example, it costs CH$119,000 for a seven-day pass in the south), but it takes you straight to many out-of-the-way national parks and other attractions not accessible by public transport. It also offers pick-up and dropoff at your chosen hostel, and camping equipment at isolated overnight stops.

Argentina's **Chaltén Travel** (www.chaltentravel.com) provides transportation between El Calafate and Torres del Paine and on Argentina's Ruta 40.

Classes

An array of bewildering names denotes the different levels of comfort on long-distance buses. For a classic experience, *clásico* or *pullman* has around 46 ordinary seats that barely recline and poor bathrooms. The next step up is *executivo* and then comes *semi-cama*, both usually around 38 seats, providing extra leg room and calf rests. *Semi-cama* has plusher seats that recline more fully and buses are sometimes double-decker. *Salón cama* sleepers seat 24 passengers, with seats that almost fully recline. Super-exclusive infrequent *premium* services enjoy seats that fold down flat. Note that movie quality does not improve with comfort level. On overnighters breakfast is usually included but you can save a few bucks by not ordering dinner and bringing takeout.

Normally departing at night, *salón cama* and *premium* bus services cost upwards of 50% more than ordinary buses, but you'll be thankful on long-haul trips. Regular buses are also comfortable, especially in comparison to neighboring Peru and Bolivia. Smoking is prohibited.

Costs

Fares vary dramatically among companies and classes, so shop around. *Ofertas* (promotions) outside the high summer season can reduce normal fares by half and student fares by 25%.

Reservations

Except during the holiday season (Christmas, January, February, Easter and mid-September's patriotic holidays) or on Fridays and Sundays, it is rarely necessary to book more than a few hours in advance. On very long trips, like Arica to Santiago, or rural routes with limited services (along the Carretera Austral, for instance), advance booking is a good idea.

Car & Motorcycle

Having your own wheels is often necessary to get to remote national parks and off the beaten track, especially in the Atacama Desert and along the Carretera Austral. Security problems are minor, but always lock your vehicle and leave valuables out of sight. Because of smog problems, Santiago and the surrounding region have frequent restrictions.

The maps in the annual Copec guides are a good source of recent changes, particularly with regard to newly paved roads.

Automobile Associations

The **Automóvil Club de Chile** (Acchi; ☎600-464-4040; www.automovilclub.cl; Andrés Bello 1863, Santiago) has offices in most major Chilean cities, provides useful information, sells highway maps and rents cars. It also

SAMPLE BUS COSTS & TRIP TIMES

DESTINATION	COST (CH$)	DURATION (HR)
Asunción, Paraguay	76,000	45
Buenos Aires, Argentina	72,000	22
Córdoba, Argentina	45,000	17
Lima, Peru	95,000	48
Mendoza, Argentina	31,000	7
Montevideo, Uruguay	65,000	32
Rio de Janeiro, Brazil	104,000	72
São Paulo, Brazil	94,000	55

offers member services and grants discounts to members of its foreign counterparts, such as the American Automobile Association (AAA) in the USA or the Automobile Association (AA) in the UK. Membership includes free towing and other roadside services within 25km of an Automóvil Club office.

Bring Your Own Vehicle

It's possible to ship an overseas vehicle to Chile but costs are high. Check your local phone directory under Automobile Transporters. When shipping, do not leave anything of value in the vehicle.

Permits for temporarily imported tourist vehicles may be extended beyond the initial 90-day period, but it can be easier to cross the border into Argentina and return with new paperwork.

For shipping a car from Chile back to your home country, try the consolidator **Ultramar** (☑022-630-1000; www.ultramar.cl).

Driver's License

Bring along an International Driving Permit (IDP) as well as the license from your home country. Some rental-car agencies don't require an IDP.

Fuel & Spare Parts

The price of *bencina* (gasoline) starts from about CH$910 per liter, depending on the grade, while *gas-oil* (diesel fuel) costs less.

Even the smallest of hamlets always seem to have at least one competent and resourceful mechanic.

Hire

Major international rental agencies like **Hertz** (☑022-360-8600; www.hertz.cl), **Avis** (☑600-368-2000; www.avis.cl) and **Budget** (☑600-441-0000; www.budget.cl) have offices in Santiago, as well as in major cities and tourist areas.

Wicked Campers (☑022-697-0527; http://wickedsouthamerica.com) rents bare-bones camper vans. To rent you must have a valid international driver's license, be at least 25 years of age (though some younger readers have had success) and possess a major credit card (MasterCard or Visa) or a large cash deposit. Travelers from the USA, Canada, Germany and Australia are not required to have an international driver's license to rent a car.

Even at smaller agencies, rental charges are high, with the smallest vehicles going for about CH$24,000 per day with 150km to 200km of unlimited mileage included. Add the cost of any extra insurance, gas and the crippling 19% IVA (*impuesto de valor agregado;* value-added tax), and it becomes very pricey. Try for weekend or weekly rates with unlimited mileage.

One-way rentals are difficult to arrange, especially with nonchain agencies, and may come with a substantial dropoff charge. Some smaller agencies will, however, usually arrange paperwork for taking cars into Argentina, provided the car is returned to the original office. There may be a substantial charge for taking a car into Argentina and extra insurance must be acquired.

When traveling in remote areas, where fuel may not be readily available, carry extra fuel. Rental agencies often provide a spare *bidón* (fuel container) for this purpose.

Insurance

All vehicles must carry *seguro obligatorio* (minimum insurance). Additional liability insurance is highly desirable. Rental agencies offer the necessary insurance. Check your policy for limitations. Traveling on a dirt road is usually OK and may be necessary, but off-roading is prohibited. Major credit cards

sometimes include car-rental insurance coverage.

To visit Argentina, special insurance is required. Try any insurance agency; the cost is about CH$20,000 for one week.

Parking

Many towns charge for street parking (from CH$200 per half-hour). Street attendants leave a slip of paper under your windshield wiper with the time of arrival and charge departing drivers. Usually parking is free on the weekends – though attendants may still be there; payment is voluntary.

Purchase

For a trip of several months, purchasing a car merits consideration. You must change the vehicle's title within 30 days or risk a hefty fine; you can do this through any notary by requesting a *compraventa* for about CH$8000. You'll need a RUT (Rol Unico Tributario) tax identification number, available through **Impuestos Internos** (www.sii.cl), the Chilean tax office; issuance takes about 10 days. Chilean cars may not be sold abroad.

Note that while inexpensive vehicles are for sale in the duty-free zones of Regiónes I and XII (Tarapacá and Magallanes), only legal permanent residents of those regions may take a vehicle outside of those regions, for a maximum of 90 days per calendar year.

Road Conditions

The Panamericana has quality roads and periodic toll booths (*peajes*). There are two types: tolls you pay to use a distance of the highway (CH$500 to CH$2500), and the tolls you pay to get off the highway to access a lateral to a town or city (CH$600). You'll find a list of tolls (in Spanish) on www.turistel.cl.

Many roads in the south are in the process of being paved. Distance markers are placed every 5km along the Panamericana and the Carretera Austral. Often people give directions using these as landmarks.

Road Hazards

Stray dogs wander around on the roads – even highways – with alarming regularity, and visitors from European and North American countries are frequently disconcerted by how pedestrians use the motorway as a sidewalk.

Road Rules

Chilean drivers are restrained in comparison to South American neighbors and especially courteous to pedestrians. However, city drivers have a reputation for jumping red lights and failing to signal. Speed limits are enforced with CH$35,000 fines.

Chile has implemented a zero-tolerance policy toward drinking and driving. Even if you have had just one drink, it's over the legal limit. Penalties range from fines and license suspension to jail time.

In Santiago, *restricción vehicular* (vehicular restrictions) apply according to smog levels. The system works according to the last digits on a vehicle's license plates: the chosen numbers are announced in the news on the day before those vehicles will be subject to restrictions. Violators are subject to fines; for current restrictions, see www.uoct.cl (in Spanish).

Hitchhiking

Thumbing a ride is common practice in Chile, and this is one of the safest countries in Latin America to do it. That said, hitchhiking is never entirely safe, and Lonely Planet does not recommend it.

In summer, Chilean vehicles are often packed with families on vacation, and a wait for a lift can be long. Few drivers stop for groups and even fewer appreciate aggressive tactics. In Patagonia, where distances are great and vehicles few, hitchhikers should expect long waits. It's also a good idea to carry some snack food and plenty of water, especially in the desert north.

Local Transportation

Bus

Chilean bus routes are numerous and fares run cheap (around CH$500 for a short trip). Since many identically numbered buses serve slightly different routes, check the placards indicating their final destination. On boarding, state your destination and the driver will tell you the fare and give you a ticket.

Santiago's bus system **Transantiago** (☑800-730-073; www.transantiago.cl) has automatic fare machines. You can map your route online.

Colectivo

Handy *taxi colectivos* resemble taxis but run on fixed routes much like buses: a roof sign or placard in the window indicates the destination. They are fast, comfortable and not a great deal more expensive than buses (usually CH$500 to CH$1000 within a city).

Commuter Rail

Both Santiago and Valparaíso have commuter rail networks. Santiago's modern *metrotren* line runs from San Fernando through Rancagua, capital of Región VI, to Estación Central, on the Alameda in Santiago. Valparaíso's rail connects Viña del Mar and Valparaíso.

Metro

Santiago's superefficient subway is the metro. Try to avoid peak hours, which can get very crowded.

Taxi

Most Chilean cabs are metered. In Santiago it costs CH$300 to *bajar la bandera* (lower the flag), plus CH$130 per 200m. Taxi placards indicate authorized fares.

Tours

Altué Active Travel (☑022-235-1519; www.altue. com) One of Chile's pioneer adventure-tourism agencies; it covers almost any outdoor activity but specialties include sea kayaking and cultural trips in Chiloé.

Azimut 360 (☑022-235-1519; www.azimut360.com) Offers volcano climbing, mountain biking and sightseeing in the northern altiplano, as well as multiactivity trips in Patagonia.

Cruceros Australis (☑022-442-3115; www.australis. com) Runs large luxury cruises between Punta Arenas and Ushuaia. Itineraries range from three days to one week.

Cruceros Skorpios (☑065-227-5646; www.skorpios.cl; Av Angelmó 1660; d incl meals & alcohol from US$4000; ⊙8:30am-12:30pm & 2:30-6:30pm Mon-Fri) A legitimate cruise that calls itself 'semi-elegant.' Its most popular trip sails the *MV Skorpios II* to Laguna San Rafael with departures on Saturday from Puerto Montt from September to April. The five-day round-trip cruise stops at its exclusive hot-springs resort, Quitralco, and the Chiloé archipelago.

Geoturismo Patagonia (☑067-258-3173; www.geoturismopatagonia.cl) Reputable specialists in the Carretera Austral with good insider knowledge.

Opentravel (☑in Puerto Montt 065-226-0524; www.opentravel.cl) Offers off-the-beaten-path trekking and horseback-riding to remote areas in northern Patagonia and across the Andes to Argentina.

Pared Sur (☎022-207-3525; www.paredsur.cl) Active vacations and mountain-biking trips, with a wide variety of challenges throughout Chile.

Santiago Adventures (☎022-244-2750; www.santiagoadventures.com) Savvy English-speaking tour guides lead personalized tours covering Santiago's food and wine, day trips to the coast and throughout Chile.

Trails of Chile (☎065-233-0737; www.trailsofchile.cl) Specializes in top-shelf, professional tours and adventure travel with excellent service.

Train

Chile's railroads blossomed in the late 19th century, but now most tracks lie neglected or abandoned. There is service throughout Middle Chile, however, and a *metrotren* service goes from Santiago as far as San Fernando. For details and prices check the website of **Empresa de Ferrocarriles del Estado** (☎600-585-5000; www.efe.cl).

It's difficult but not impossible to travel by freight train from Baquedano (on the Panamericana northeast of Antofagasta) to the border town of Socompa, and on to Salta, in Argentina.

Language

Spanish pronunciation is easy, as most sounds have equivalents in English. Read our pronunciation guides as if they were English, and you'll be understood. Note that kh is a throaty sound (like the 'ch' in the Scottish *loch*), v and b are like a soft English 'v' (between a 'v' and a 'b'), and r is strongly rolled. The stressed syllables are indicated with an acute accent in written Spanish (eg *días*) and with italics in our pronunciation guides.

The polite form is used in this chapter; where both polite and informal options are given, they are indicated by the abbreviations 'pol' and 'inf'. Where necessary, both masculine and feminine forms of words are included, separated by a slash and with the masculine form first, eg *perdido/a* (m/f).

BASICS

Hello.	*Hola.*	o·la
Goodbye.	*Adiós.*	a·*dyos*
How are you?	*¿Qué tal?*	ke tal
Fine, thanks.	*Bien, gracias.*	byen *gra*·syas
Excuse me.	*Perdón.*	per·*don*
Sorry.	*Lo siento.*	lo *syen*·to
Please.	*Por favor.*	por fa·*vor*
Thank you.	*Gracias.*	*gra*·syas
You're welcome.	*De nada.*	de *na*·da
Yes./No.	*Sí./ No.*	see/ no

WANT MORE?

For in-depth language information and handy phrases, check out Lonely Planet's *Latin American Spanish Phrasebook*. You'll find it at **shop. lonelyplanet.com**, or you can buy Lonely Planet's iPhone phrasebooks at the Apple App Store.

I don't understand.

| *Yo no entiendo.* | yo no en·*tyen*·do |

My name is ...

| *Me llamo ...* | me *ya*·mo ... |

What's your name?

| *¿Cómo se llama Usted?* | ko·mo se *ya*·ma oo·*ste* (pol) |
| *¿Cómo te llamas?* | ko·mo te *ya*·mas (inf) |

Do you speak English?

| *¿Habla inglés?* | a·bla een·*gles* (pol) |
| *¿Hablas inglés?* | a·blas een·*gles* (inf) |

ACCOMMODATIONS

I'd like a single/double room.

| *Quisiera una habitación individual/doble.* | kee·*sye*·ra oo·na a·bee·ta·*syon* een·dee·vee·*dwal/do*·ble |

How much is it per night/person?

| *¿Cuánto cuesta por noche/persona?* | kwan·to *kwes*·ta por no·che/per·so·na |

Does it include breakfast?

| *¿Incluye el desayuno?* | een·*kloo*·ye el de·sa·*yoo*·no |

air-con	*aire acondicionado*	ai·re a·kon·dee·syo·*na*·do
bathroom	*baño*	ba·nyo
bed	*cama*	ka·ma
cabin	*cabaña*	ka·ba·nya
campsite	*terreno de cámping*	te·re·no de kam·peeng
guesthouse	*pensión/ hospedaje*	pen·*syon/* os·pe·da·khe
hotel	*hotel/hostal*	o·tel/os·tal
inn	*hostería*	os·te·ree·ya
youth hostel	*albergue juvenil*	al·ber·ge khoo·ve·*neel*
window	*ventana*	ven·ta·na

RAPA NUI LANGUAGE

Although the Rapa Nui of Easter Island speak Spanish, among themselves many of them use the island's indigenous language (also called Rapa Nui). Due to the island's isolation, the Rapa Nui language developed relatively untouched but retains similarities to other Polynesian languages, such as Hawaiian, Tahitian and Maori. These days the language increasingly bears the influence of English and Spanish. The hieroglyph-like Rongorongo script, developed by the Islanders after the Spanish first arrived in 1770 and in use until the 1860s, is believed to have been the earliest written form of Rapa Nui. The written Rapa Nui used today was developed in the 19th century by missionaries, who transliterated the sounds of the language into the Roman alphabet. Sadly, while most understand Rapa Nui, few of the younger Islanders speak it fluently, though work is being done to keep this endangered language, and the culture it carries, alive.

Rapa Nui pronunciation is fairly straightforward, with short and long vowels pronounced as they would be in Spanish or Italian. There are only ten consonants, plus a glottal stop ('), which is pronounced like the pause in the word 'uh-oh.' Any attempt at a few basic Rapa Nui greetings and phrases will be greatly appreciated by the locals, whatever your level of mastery. For more extensive Rapa Nui coverage, pick up a copy of Lonely Planet's South Pacific Phrasebook. To learn more, and to read about efforts to preserve the local culture, check out the Easter Island Foundation website www. islandheritage.org.

Hello.	'Iorana.	My name's ...	To'oku ingoa ko ...
Goodbye.	'Iorana.	What?	Aha?
How are you?	Pehē koe/kōrua? (sg/pl)	Which?	Hē aha?
Fine.	Rivariva.	Who?	Ko āi?
Thank you.	Maururu.	How much is this?	'Ehia moni o te me'e nei?
What's your name?	Ko āi to'ou ingoa?	To your health!	Manuia paka-paka.

DIRECTIONS

Where's ...?
¿Dónde está ...?   don·de es·ta ...

What's the address?
¿Cuál es la dirección?   kwal es la dee·rek·syon

Could you please write it down?
¿Puede escribirlo,   pwe·de es·kree·beer·lo
por favor?   por fa·vor

Can you show me (on the map)?
¿Me lo puede indicar   me lo pwe·de een·dee·kar
(en el mapa)?   (en el ma·pa)

at the corner	en la esquina	en la es·kee·na
at the traffic lights	en el semáforo	en el se·ma·fo·ro
behind ...	detrás de ...	de·tras de ...
far	lejos	le·khos
in front of ...	enfrente de ...	en·fren·te de ...
left	izquierda	ees·kyer·da
near	cerca	ser·ka
next to ...	al lado de ...	al la·do de ...
opposite ...	frente a ...	fren·te a ...
right	derecha	de·re·cha
straight ahead	todo recto	to·do rek·to

EATING & DRINKING

Can I see the menu, please?
¿Puedo ver el menú,   pwe·do ver el me·noo
por favor?   por fa·vor

What would you recommend?
¿Qué recomienda?   ke re·ko·myen·da

Do you have vegetarian food?
¿Tienen comida   tye·nen ko·mee·da
vegetariana?   ve·khe·ta·rya·na

I don't eat (red meat).
No como (carne roja).   no ko·mo (kar·ne ro·kha)

That was delicious!
¡Estaba buenísimo!   es·ta·ba bwe·nee·see·mo

Cheers!
¡Salud!   sa·loo

The bill, please.
La cuenta, por favor.   la kwen·ta por fa·vor

I'd like a table for ...	Quisiera una mesa para ...	kee·sye·ra oo·na me·sa pa·ra ...
(eight) o'clock	las (ocho)	las (o·cho)
(two) people	(dos) personas	(dos) per·so·nas

breakfast	*desayuno*	de·sa·*yoo*·no
lunch	*comida*	ko·*mee*·da
dinner	*cena*	*se*·na
restaurant	*restaurante*	res·tow·*ran*·te

EMERGENCIES

Help!	*¡Socorro!*	so·*ko*·ro
Go away!	*¡Vete!*	*ve*·te

Call ...!	*¡Llame a ...!*	*ya*·me a ...
a doctor	*un médico*	oon *me*·dee·ko
the police	*la policía*	la po·lee·*see*·a

I'm lost.
Estoy perdido/a. es·*toy* per·*dee*·do/a (m/f)

I'm ill.
Estoy enfermo/a. es·*toy* en·*fer*·mo/a (m/f)

It hurts here.
Me duele aquí. me *dwe*·le a·*kee*

I'm allergic to (antibiotics).
Soy alérgico/a a soy a·*ler*·khee·ko/a a
(los antibióticos). (los an·tee·*byo*·tee·kos) (m/f)

Where are the toilets?
¿Dónde están los don·de es·*tan* los
baños? *ba*·nyos

SHOPPING & SERVICES

I'd like to buy ...
Quisiera comprar ... kee·*sye*·ra kom·*prar* ...

I'm just looking.
Sólo estoy mirando. *so*·lo es·*toy* mee·*ran*·do

Can I look at it?
¿Puedo verlo? *pwe*·do *ver*·lo

I don't like it.
No me gusta. no me *goos*·ta

How much is it?
¿Cuánto cuesta? *kwan*·to *kwes*·ta

That's too expensive.
Es muy caro. es mooy *ka*·ro

Can you lower the price?
¿Podría bajar un po·*dree*·a ba·*khar* oon
poco el precio? *po*·ko el *pre*·syo

There's a mistake in the bill.
Hay un error ai oon e·*ror*
en la cuenta. en la *kwen*·ta

ATM	*cajero*	ka·*khe*·ro
	automático	ow·to·*ma*·tee·ko
internet cafe	*cibercafé*	see·ber·ka·*fe*
market	*mercado*	mer·*ka*·do
post office	*correos*	ko·*re*·os
tourist office	*oficina*	o·fee·*see*·na
	de turismo	de too·*rees*·mo

TIME & DATES

What time is it? *¿Qué hora es?* ke o·ra es

It's (10) o'clock. *Son (las diez).* son (las dyes)

It's half past *Es (la una)* es (la oo·na)
(one). *y media.* ee me·dya

morning	*mañana*	ma·*nya*·na
afternoon	*tarde*	*tar*·de
evening	*noche*	*no*·che
yesterday	*ayer*	a·*yer*
today	*hoy*	oy
tomorrow	*mañana*	ma·*nya*·na

Monday	*lunes*	*loo*·nes
Tuesday	*martes*	*mar*·tes
Wednesday	*miércoles*	*myer*·ko·les
Thursday	*jueves*	*khwe*·ves
Friday	*viernes*	*vyer*·nes
Saturday	*sábado*	*sa*·ba·do
Sunday	*domingo*	do·*meen*·go

TRANSPORTATION

boat	*barco*	*bar*·ko
bus	*autobús*	ow·to·*boos*
(small) bus	*micro*	*mee*·kro
plane	*avión*	a·*vyon*
shared taxi	*colectivo*	ko·lek·*tee*·vo
train	*tren*	tren
first	*primero*	pree·*me*·ro
last	*último*	*ool*·tee·mo
next	*próximo*	*prok*·see·mo

A ... ticket, *Un billete* oon bee·*ye*·te
please. *de ..., por favor.* de ... por fa·*vor*

1st-class	*primera*	pree·*me*·ra
	clase	*kla*·se
2nd-class	*segunda*	se·*goon*·da
	clase	*kla*·se
one-way	*ida*	*ee*·da
return	*ida y*	*ee*·da ee
	vuelta	*vwel*·ta

SIGNS

Abierto	Open
Cerrado	Closed
Entrada	Entrance
Hombres/Varones	Men
Mujeres/Damas	Women
Prohibido	Prohibited
Salida	Exit
Servicios/Baños	Toilets

I want to go to ...
Quisiera ir a ...   kee·sye·ra eer a ...

Does it stop at ...?
¿Para en ...?   pa·ra en ...

What stop is this?
¿Cuál es esta parada?   kwal es es·ta pa·ra·da

What time does it arrive/leave?
¿A qué hora llega/   a ke o·ra ye·ga/
sale?   sa·le

Please tell me when we get to ...
¿Puede avisarme   pwe·de a·vee·sar·me
cuando lleguemos   kwan·do ye·ge·mos
a ...?   a ...

I want to get off here.
Quiero bajarme aquí.   kye·ro ba·khar·me a·kee

airport	aeropuerto	a·e·ro·pwer·to
aisle seat	asiento de pasillo	a·syen·to de pa·see·yo
bus stop	parada de autobuses	pa·ra·da de ow·to·boo·ses
cancelled	cancelado	kan·se·la·do
delayed	retrasado	re·tra·sa·do
platform	plataforma	pla·ta·for·ma
ticket office	taquilla	ta·kee·ya
timetable	horario	o·ra·ryo
train station	estación de trenes	es·ta·syon de tre·nes
window seat	asiento junto a la ventana	a·syen·to khoon·to a la ven·ta·na

I'd like to hire a ...	Quisiera alquilar ...	kee·sye·ra al·kee·lar ...
4WD	un todo-terreno	oon to·do-te·re·no
bicycle	una bicicleta	oo·na bee·see·kle·ta
car	un coche	oon ko·che
motorcycle	una moto	oo·na mo·to
child seat	asiento de seguridad para niños	a·syen·to de se·goo·ree·da pa·ra nee·nyos

QUESTION WORDS

How?	¿Cómo?	ko·mo
What?	¿Qué?	ke
When?	¿Cuándo?	kwan·do
Where?	¿Dónde?	don·de
Who?	¿Quién?	kyen
Why?	¿Por qué?	por ke

NUMBERS

1	uno	oo·no
2	dos	dos
3	tres	tres
4	cuatro	kwa·tro
5	cinco	seen·ko
6	seis	seys
7	siete	sye·te
8	ocho	o·cho
9	nueve	nwe·ve
10	diez	dyes
20	veinte	veyn·te
30	treinta	treyn·ta
40	cuarenta	kwa·ren·ta
50	cincuenta	seen·kwen·ta
60	sesenta	se·sen·ta
70	setenta	se·ten·ta
80	ochenta	o·chen·ta
90	noventa	no·ven·ta
100	cien	syen
1000	mil	meel

diesel	petróleo	pet·ro·le·o
helmet	casco	kas·ko
hitchhike	hacer botella	a·ser bo·te·ya
mechanic	mecánico	me·ka·nee·ko
petrol/gas	bencina/ gasolina	ben·see·na ga·so·lee·na
service station	gasolinera	ga·so·lee·ne·ra
truck	camion	ka·myon

Is this the road to ...?
¿Se va a ... por   se va a ... por
esta carretera?   es·ta ka·re·te·ra

(How long) Can I park here?
¿(Cuánto tiempo)   (kwan·to tyem·po)
Puedo aparcar aquí?   pwe·do a·par·kar a·kee

The car has broken down (at ...).
El coche se ha averiado   el ko·che se a a·ve·rya·do
(en ...).   (en ...)

I had an accident.
He tenido un   e te·nee·do oon
accidente.   ak·see·den·te

I've run out of petrol.
Me he quedado sin   me e ke·da·do seen
gasolina.   ga·so·lee·na

I have a flat tyre.
Tengo un pinchazo.   ten·go oon peen·cha·so

GLOSSARY

RN indicates that a term is Rapa Nui (Easter Island) usage.

ahu (RN) – stone platform for *moai* (statues)

alameda – avenue/ boulevard lined with trees

albergue juvenil – youth hostel

alpaca – wool-bearing domestic camelid, related to llama

altiplano – Andean high plains

anexo – telephone extension

apunamiento – altitude sickness

arroyo – watercourse

asado – barbecue

ascensor – funicular (cable car)

Ayllu – indigenous community of Norte Grande

Aymara – indigenous inhabitants of Andean *altiplano* of Peru, Bolivia and northern Chile

bahía – bay

balneario – bathing resort or beach

barrio – neighborhood

bencina – petrol or gasoline

bencina blanca – white gas for camping stoves

bidón – spare fuel container

bodega – cellar or storage area for wine

bofedal – swampy alluvial pasture in altiplano

cabañas – cabins

cacique – Indian chieftain

calefón – hot-water heater

caleta – small cove

callampas – shantytowns, literally 'mushrooms'

cama – bed; also sleeper-class seat

camanchaca – ocean fog along coastal desert

camarote – sleeper class on ship, or bunk bed

carabineros – police

caracoles – winding roads; literally 'snails'

carretera – highway

casa de cambio – money exchange

casa de familia – modest family accommodations

cerro – hill

chachacoma – native Andean plant; said to relieve altitude sickness

Chilote – inhabitant of Chiloé; sometimes connotes 'bumpkin'

ciervo – deer

ciudad – city

cocinerías – greasy-spoon cafes/kitchens

Codelco – Corporación del Cobre, state-owned enterprise overseeing copper mining

colectivo – shared taxi, also called *taxi colectivo*

comparsa – group of musicians or dancers

comuna – local governmental unit

congregación – colonial-era concentration of diverse native populations in a town; see also *reducción*

cordillera – chain of mountains

costanera – coastal road; also along river or lakeshore

criollo – colonial term for American-born Spaniard

desierto florido – rare and ephemeral desert wildflower display in Norte Chico

DINA – National Intelligence Directorate; feared agency created after 1973 coup to oversee police and military intelligence

empanada – a turnover with a sweet or savory filling

encomienda – colonial labor system in which indigenous communities worked for Spanish *encomenderos*

esquí en marcha – cross-country skiing

estancia – extensive cattle- or sheep-grazing establishment with resident labor force

estero – estuary

feria – artisans' market

fuerte – fort

fundo – *hacienda;* smaller irrigated unit in central heartland

garúa – coastal desert fog

geoglyph – large pre-Columbian figures or designs on desert hillsides

golfo – gulf

golpe de estado – coup d'état

guanaco – wild camelid related to llama; also police water cannon

hacienda – large rural landholding, with dependent resident labor force

hare paenga (RN) – elliptical (boat-shaped) house

hospedaje – budget accommodations, usually family home with shared bathroom

hostal – hotel, hostel

hostería – inn or guesthouse that serves meals

huaso – horseman, a kind of Chilean gaucho or cowboy

IGM – Instituto Geográfico Militar; mapping organization

intendencia – Spanish colonial administrative unit

invierno boliviano – 'Bolivian winter'; summer rainy season in Chilean *altiplano*

isla – island

islote – small island, islet

istmo – isthmus

IVA – *impuesto de valor agregado,* value-added tax (VAT)

küchen – sweet, German-style cakes

lago – lake

laguna – lagoon

latifundio – large landholding, such as *fundo*, hacienda or *estancia*

lista de correos – poste restante

llareta – dense shrub in Chilean *altiplano* with deceptive, cushion-like appearance

local – part of address indicating office number where there are several in the same building

lomas – coastal desert hills

maori (RN) – learned men, reportedly able to read Rongo-Rongo tablets

Mapuche – indigenous inhabitants of the area south of Río Biobío

marisquería – seafood restaurant

matrimonial – double bed

matua (RN) – ancestor, father; associated with leader of first Polynesian immigrants

media pensión – half board in hotel

mestizo – person of mixed Indian and Spanish descent

micro – small bus

minga – reciprocal Mapuche Indian labor system

mirador – lookout point

moai (RN) – large anthropomorphic statues

moai kavakava (RN) – carved wooden 'statues of ribs'

motu (RN) – small offshore islet

municipalidad – city hall

museo – museum

ñandú – rhea; large flightless bird similar to ostrich

nevado – snowcapped mountain peak

oferta – promotional fare, often seasonal, for plane or bus travel

onces – 'elevenses'; Chilean afternoon tea

palafitos – rows of houses built on stilts over water in Chiloé

pampa – vast desert expanse

parada – bus stop

parrillada – a mix of grilled meats

peatonal – pedestrian mall

peña folklórica – folk music and cultural club

pensión – family home offering short-term accommodations

pensión completa – full board in hotel

picada – informal family restaurant

pingüinera – penguin colony

playa – beach

Porteño – native or resident of Valparaíso

portezuelo – mountain pass

posta – clinic or first-aid station

precordillera – foothills

propina – tip

puente – bridge

puerto – port

pukao (RN) – topknot on head of a *moai*

pukará – pre-Columbian hilltop fortress

puna – Andean highlands, usually above 3000m

punta – point

quebrada – ravine

quinoa – native Andean grain grown in northern *precordillera*

Rapa Nui – Polynesian name for Easter Island

reducción – colonial-era concentration of indigenous peoples in towns for purposes of political control or religious instruction

refugio – rustic shelter in national park or remote area

residencial – budget accommodations

rhea – flightless bird similar to ostrich; *ñandú* in Spanish

río – river

rodeo – annual cattle roundup on *estancia* or hacienda

Rongo-Rongo (RN) – indecipherable script on wooden tablets

ruka – traditional thatched Mapuche house

ruta – route, highway

salar – salt lake, salt marsh or salt pan

salón de cama – bus with reclining seats

salón de té – literally 'teahouse,' but more up-scale cafe

Santiaguino – native or resident of Santiago

seno – sound, fjord

sierra – mountain range

s/n – 'sin número'; street address without number

soroche – altitude sickness

tábano – horsefly

tabla – shared plate of appetizers

tejuelas – shingles, typical of Chiloé architecture

teleférico – gondola cable car

termas – hot springs

toqui – Mapuche chief

torres – towers

totora (RN) – type of reed used for making rafts

ventisquero – glacier

vicuña – wild relative of llama, found at high altitudes in the north

villa – village, small town

viscacha – wild Andean relative of chinchilla

volcán – volcano

Yaghans – indigenous inhabitants of Tierra del Fuego archipelago

zona franca – duty-free zone

Behind the Scenes

SEND US YOUR FEEDBACK

We love to hear from travelers – your comments keep us on our toes and help make our books better. Our well-traveled team reads every word on what you loved or loathed about this book. Although we cannot reply individually to your submissions, we always guarantee that your feedback goes straight to the appropriate authors, in time for the next edition. Each person who sends us information is thanked in the next edition – the most useful submissions are rewarded with a selection of digital PDF chapters.

Visit **lonelyplanet.com/contact** to submit your updates and suggestions or to ask for help. Our award-winning website also features inspirational travel stories, news and discussions.

Note: We may edit, reproduce and incorporate your comments in Lonely Planet products such as guidebooks, websites and digital products, so let us know if you don't want your comments reproduced or your name acknowledged. For a copy of our privacy policy visit lonelyplanet.com/privacy.

OUR READERS

Many thanks to the travelers who used the last edition and wrote to us with helpful hints, useful advice and interesting anecdotes:

Abi Mcanally, Alain Vada, Alex Anderson, Alexandra Boissonneault, Amy Skewes-Cox, Angelica Aguilar, Anna Steinert, Anne Sorensen, Armando Nogueira, Audun Lem, Barry Weiss, Brian Fagan, Bryan Booth, Carol Janney, Christopher Cheung, David Lacy, Dirk Verhulst, Eduardo Vial, Eve Masi, Gabriela Saez, Gilles Caouette, Han Wong, Helen Stanley, Houda Lazrak, Ines Ruestenberg, Joan Reid, Johan Engman, Jonathan Freeman, Juan Zuazo, Judith Baker, Juliette Giannesini, Kathrin Birner, Liz Rushton, Louis-Francois Delannoy, Manuela Holfert, Mark Miller, Martin Grancay, Martin Hellwagner, Martin Vest Nielsen, Michael Stolar, Michelle Washington, Miriam Price, Mirjam Hiller, Murray Jones, Naomi Joswiak, Naomi Sharp, Noelle Ehrenkaufer, Oskar Op de Beke, Patrick Cafferty, Pierre Naviaux, Piet Hageman, Remco Wulms, Rich Lang, Ron McDowell, Ron Witton, Roxanne Cote, Sabine Doorman, Sean Casey, Steve Sample, Susannah Glynn, Tobias Rönnertz, Tom Kowalczyk, Wendy Horton, Wendy Pickering, Wendy Salvo

AUTHOR THANKS

Carolyn McCarthy

Big thanks to copilot Estefania, hosts Angela and Jim Donini, Susanne in Natales for the lunchbox, Eliana in La Junta for car help, and Trauko for shepherding this planet like no one else. Gratitude also goes to the crew in Coyhaique, Mery and Mauricio, Nicolas Lapenna, Carolina Morgado, Andres, Philip Cary, Ruth and the amazing ladies of Puerto Williams. In the last edition, I thanked the Subarito for not breaking on the Carretera Austral. Looks like I spoke too soon.

Greg Benchwick

Gracias to my coordinating author Carolyn McCarthy and destination editor MaSovaida Morgan. Your vision made working on this book a pleasure. Beautiful Natalia was a great help finding my way through the hills of Valparaíso. And the biggest and bravest of thanks to Brian Kluepfel, who traveled with me through the *schopperias* of Arica and Iquique on my fateful first journey to this long, lean land.

Jean-Bernard Carillet

Heaps of thanks to the editorial and cartography teams at Lonely Planet for their great job. Coordinating author Carolyn deserves a *grand merci* for her support and hospitality – I won't forget my lovely retreat at her home, and the great company of Richard, *moniteur de kayak extraordinaire* (and the wine was great, too!). On Easter Island, special thanks to Sebastian, Lionel, Antoine, Henri and Michel.

Kevin Raub

Thanks to my wife, Adriana Schmidt Raub, who once again put up with my missing Christmas, my birthday and New Year's Eve! Also to MaSovaida Morgan, and my partners-in-crime, Carolyn McCarthy, Lucas Vidgen, JB Carillet and Greg Benchwick. On the road, Richard Carrier, Alfonso Spoliansky, Britt and Sandra Lewis, Fernando Claude and Amory Uslar, Mirella Montaña, Juan Pablo Mansilla, Karin Terrsy, Cyril Christensen, Tracy Katelman, Claudio Ansorena, Sarina Hinte, Vincent Baudin, Ben Miray, Raffaele di Blasé, Rodrigo Condezza, Sirce Santibañez and Mariela Del Pillar.

Lucas Vidgen

Thanks first and foremost to the Chileans for having such an excellent country to travel and work in – *ire bacán, compadres!* Thanks also to Vicky Toledo for excellence in everything, Patrizia, Flavio and Gerardo in Putre, Marco Iglesias in Vicuña, Doménica in Caldera and all the travelers who wrote in or offered tips on the road. And last but far from least: to Teresa and Sofia, for being there, and being there when I got back.

ACKNOWLEDGMENTS

Climate map data adapted from Peel MC, Finlayson BL & McMahon TA (2007) 'Updated World Map of the Köppen-Geiger Climate Classification', *Hydrology and Earth System Sciences*, 11, 163344.

Cover photograph: Parque Nacional Torres del Paine, Michele Falzone/AWL.

THIS BOOK

This 10th edition of Lonely Planet's *Chile & Easter Island* guidebook was researched and written by Carolyn McCarthy, Greg Benchwick, Jean-Bernard Carillet, Kevin Raub and Lucas Vidgen. The previous edition was written by Carolyn McCarthy, Jean-Bernard Carillet, Bridget Gleeson, Anja Mutić and Kevin Raub. This guidebook was produced by the following:

Destination Editor MaSovaida Morgan

Product Editors Carolyn Boicos, Tracy Whitmey

Senior Cartographers Mark Griffiths, Alison Lyall

Book Designer Clara Monitto

Assisting Editors Andrea Dobbin, Anne Mulvaney, Christopher Pitts, Ross Taylor, Simon Williamson

Cover Researcher Naomi Parker

Thanks to Imogen Bannister, Kate Mathews, Claire Naylor, Karyn Noble, Martine Power, Jessica Rose, Wibowo Rusli, Ellie Simpson, Tony Wheeler

Index

Map Legend

Sights

- Beach
- Bird Sanctuary
- Buddhist
- Castle/Palace
- Christian
- Confucian
- Hindu
- Islamic
- Jain
- Jewish
- Monument
- Museum/Gallery/Historic Building
- Ruin
- Shinto
- Sikh
- Taoist
- Winery/Vineyard
- Zoo/Wildlife Sanctuary
- Other Sight

Activities, Courses & Tours

- Bodysurfing
- Diving
- Canoeing/Kayaking
- Course/Tour
- Sento Hot Baths/Onsen
- Skiing
- Snorkeling
- Surfing
- Swimming/Pool
- Walking
- Windsurfing
- Other Activity

Sleeping

- Sleeping
- Camping

Eating

- Eating

Drinking & Nightlife

- Drinking & Nightlife
- Cafe

Entertainment

- Entertainment

Shopping

- Shopping

Information

- Bank
- Embassy/Consulate
- Hospital/Medical
- Internet
- Police
- Post Office
- Telephone
- Toilet
- Tourist Information
- Other Information

Geographic

- Beach
- Gate
- Hut/Shelter
- Lighthouse
- Lookout
- Mountain/Volcano
- Oasis
- Park
- Pass
- Picnic Area
- Waterfall

Population

- Capital (National)
- Capital (State/Province)
- City/Large Town
- Town/Village

Transport

- Airport
- Border crossing
- Bus
- Cable car/Funicular
- Cycling
- Ferry
- Metro station
- Monorail
- Parking
- Petrol station
- Subway/Subte station
- Taxi
- Train station/Railway
- Tram
- Underground station
- Other Transport

Note: Not all symbols displayed above appear on the maps in this book

Routes

- Tollway
- Freeway
- Primary
- Secondary
- Tertiary
- Lane
- Unsealed road
- Road under construction
- Plaza/Mall
- Steps
- Tunnel
- Pedestrian overpass
- Walking Tour
- Walking Tour detour
- Path/Walking Trail

Boundaries

- International
- State/Province
- Disputed
- Regional/Suburb
- Marine Park
- Cliff
- Wall

Hydrography

- River, Creek
- Intermittent River
- Canal
- Water
- Dry/Salt/Intermittent Lake
- Reef

Areas

- Airport/Runway
- Beach/Desert
- Cemetery (Christian)
- Cemetery (Other)
- Glacier
- Mudflat
- Park/Forest
- Sight (Building)
- Sportsground
- Swamp/Mangrove

Kevin Raub

Sur Chico, Chiloé Kevin grew up in Atlanta and started his career as a music journalist in New York, working for *Men's Journal* and *Rolling Stone* magazines. He ditched the rock 'n' roll lifestyle for travel writing and moved to Brazil. On this, his third run through Sur Chico and Chiloé, he discovered – through meticulous trial and error – that Chilean craft beer has finally arrived! If there are any holes in his chapters, blame the beer! This is Kevin's 33rd Lonely Planet guide. Follow him on Twitter (@RaubOnTheRoad).

Lucas Vidgen

Norte Grande, Norte Chico Lucas first gaped at northern Chile's wide open skies and gorgeous coastline back in 2003, and since then has made it a point of getting back whenever he can. He now lives in Guatemala and rambles around Latin America for Lonely Planet, covering destinations from Mexico to Argentine Patagonia. In his brief forays at home he publishes – and occasionally works on – Quetzaltenango's leading culture and nightlife magazine, *XelaWho*.

Contributing Author

Grant Phelps trained in the art of winemaking in his native New Zealand and embarked on a 10-year career as a 'flying winemaker,' working harvests in seven different countries before experiencing a wine-fueled epiphany in Chile. He is currently chief winemaker for Viña Casas del Bosque, in the Casablanca Valley. He wrote the Chilean Wine chapter.

OUR STORY

A beat-up old car, a few dollars in the pocket and a sense of adventure. In 1972 that's all Tony and Maureen Wheeler needed for the trip of a lifetime – across Europe and Asia overland to Australia. It took several months, and at the end – broke but inspired – they sat at their kitchen table writing and stapling together their first travel guide, *Across Asia on the Cheap*. Within a week they'd sold 1500 copies. Lonely Planet was born.

Today, Lonely Planet has offices in Franklin, London, Melbourne, Oakland, Beijing and Delhi, with more than 600 staff and writers. We share Tony's belief that 'a great guidebook should do three things: inform, educate and amuse'.

OUR WRITERS

Carolyn McCarthy

Coordinating Author, Northern Patagonia, Southern Patagonia, Tierra del Fuego For Carolyn, a trip to Patagonia is always a reminder of what's good in the world. For this trip she boarded eight ferries, explored Punta Arenas with snow flurries, punctured a tire and broke down on the Carretera Austral, crowdsourced car repairs, met hitchhikers and backpacked through Reserva Nacional Jeinimeni and Parque Nacional Patagonia. Her writing specializes in Latin America and the US West. She has contributed to over 30 titles for Lonely Planet, including *Panama, Trekking in the Patagonian Andes, Argentina, Peru, Colorado, Southwest USA* and national parks guides. She has also written for *Outside, BBC Magazine, National Geographic* and other publications. For more information, see www.carolynmccarthy.pressfolios.com or follow her on Instagram @masmerquen and Twitter @roamingMcC. Carolyn also wrote the Plan Your Trip, Understand Chile and Survival Guide sections.

Greg Benchwick

Santiago, Middle Chile Greg first came to Chile in 2000 on a diesel-charged holiday from his job as a reporter at *The Bolivian Times*. Since that first trip, Greg has returned to Chile on a regular basis. For this edition, he finally got a chance to head south of Santiago and explore the vineyards, surf breaks and Andean hikes of Middle Chile. Greg has written speeches for the United Nations, interviewed Grammy Award winners and created dozens of videos and web features for lonelyplanet.com. He is an expert on sustainable travel, international development, food, wine and having a good time.

Read more about Greg at:
www.lonelyplanet.com/members/gbenchwick

Jean-Bernard Carillet

Easter Island (Rapa Nui) Journalist and photographer Jean-Bernard is a fan of Polynesian history and culture. He's made many trips to the Polynesian Triangle, including five to Easter Island. On this gig, he searched for the best-value accommodations and restaurants, and the most spectacular hike, and spent time on the field with local archaeologists. His favorite experiences included walking around Península Poike and descending into the dead volcano Rano Kau with a local expert. Jean-Bernard has contributed to many Lonely Planet titles and writes for travel magazines.

OVER PAGE MORE WRITERS

Published by Lonely Planet Publications Pty Ltd
ABN 36 005 607 983
10th edition – Oct 2015
ISBN 978 1 74220 780 3
© Lonely Planet 2015   Photographs © as indicated 2015
10 9 8 7 6 5 4 3 2 1
Printed in China

Although the authors and Lonely Planet have taken all reasonable care in preparing this book, we make no warranty about the accuracy or completeness of its content and, to the maximum extent permitted, disclaim all liability arising from its use.